Global Practices in Inclusive Education Curriculum and Policy

Medwin Dikwanyane Sepadi
University of Limpopo, South Africa

Phineas Phuti Makweya
Independent Police Investigative Directorate, South Africa

Published in the United States of America by
IGI Global
701 E. Chocolate Avenue
Hershey PA, USA 17033
Tel: 717-533-8845
Fax: 717-533-8661
E-mail: cust@igi-global.com
Web site: https://www.igi-global.com

Copyright © 2025 by IGI Global. All rights reserved. No part of this publication may be reproduced, stored or distributed in any form or by any means, electronic or mechanical, including photocopying, without written permission from the publisher.
Product or company names used in this set are for identification purposes only. Inclusion of the names of the products or companies does not indicate a claim of ownership by IGI Global of the trademark or registered trademark.

Library of Congress Cataloging-in-Publication Data

CIP PENDING

ISBN13: 979-8-3693-4058-5
Isbn13Softcover: 979-8-3693-5142-0
EISBN13: 979-8-3693-4059-2

Vice President of Editorial: Melissa Wagner
Managing Editor of Acquisitions: Mikaela Felty
Managing Editor of Book Development: Jocelynn Hessler
Production Manager: Mike Brehm
Cover Design: Phillip Shickler

British Cataloguing in Publication Data
A Cataloguing in Publication record for this book is available from the British Library.

All work contributed to this book is new, previously-unpublished material.
The views expressed in this book are those of the authors, but not necessarily of the publisher.

Table of Contents

Foreword xxi

Preface xxiii

Acknowledgment xxxii

Statement About the Book xxxiii

Chapter 1
Conceptualizing and Evolution of Inclusive Education: A Global and National Exploration 1
    Medwin Dikwanyane Sepadi, University of Limpopo, South Africa

Chapter 2
Teacher Empathy in Schools: Inclusivity and Sustainable Education in a Global South Context 25
    Francis R. Ackah-Jnr, Griffith University, Australia
    John K. Appiah, University of Cape Coast, Ghana
    Awudu Salaam Mohammed, University of Cape Coast, Ghana

Chapter 3
Teacher Training and Support for Assistive Technology in Inclusive Education: A Global Perspective 53
    Deepak Kumar Sahoo, Biju Patnaik University of Technology, Rourkela, India
    Shashank Mittal, O.P. Jindal Global University, India
    Ajay Chandel, Lovely Professional University, India
    Neeti Goyal, University of Petroleum and Energy Studies, India
    Xuan-Hoa Nghiem, Vietnam National University, Vietnam

Chapter 4
The Crucial Role of Empathy in Fostering Inclusive Learning Environments ... 77
    Phineas Phuti Makweya, Independent Police Investigative Directorate, South Africa
    Medwin Sepadi, University of Limpopo, South Africa

Chapter 5
Practitioner Insights on Policy-Driven Shifts in College-Based Education:
Navigating Transformation 91
    *G. Rathnakar, Department of Mechanical Engineering, JSS Science and
        Technology University, Mysuru, India*
    *Lalchhantluangi Pachuau, Department of Management, Pachhunga
        University College, Aizawl, India*
    *T. Geetha, Department of English, Kongu Engineering College, Erode,
        India*
    *M. Prabhuswamy, Department of Education, JSS Institute of Education,
        India*
    *S. Praveenkumar, Centre for Tourism and Hotel Management, Madurai
        Kamaraj University, India*

Chapter 6
Nurturing Inclusive Schools Through the Isibindi Ezikoleni Child and Youth
Care Work Programme 121
    *Zeni Thumbadoo, National Association of Child Care Workers, South
        Africa*
    Theresa Wilson, Independent Researcher, South Africa
    *Nicia de Nobrega, National Association of Child Care Workers, South
        Africa*
    *Donald Nghonyama, National Association of Child Care Workers, South
        Africa*

Chapter 7
Navigating Inclusion in the Industry 4.0 Horizon: Crafting a Pedagogical
Future 163
    *Pallavi Sakhahari Dhamak, Shri Vile Parle Kelavani Mandal Narsee
        Monjee Institute of Management Studies, Mukesh Patel School of
        Technology Management and Engineering, Mumbai, India*
    *Padmanabha Aital, Shri Vile Parle Kelavani Mandal Narsee Monjee
        Institute of Management Studies, Mukesh Patel School of
        Technology Management and Engineering, Mumbai, India*
    *Anand Daftardar, Shri Vile Parle Kelavani Mandal Narsee Monjee
        Institute of Management Studies, Mukesh Patel School of
        Technology Management and Engineering, Mumbai, India*

Chapter 8
Pedagogical Contents Developments and Specialized Training for Teaching
Careers 187
    Ratan Sarkar, Department of Teachers' Training, Prabhat Kumar
        College, Vidyasagar University, India
    Dhara Vinod Parmar, Department of Design and Merchandising, Parul
        Institute of Design, Parul University, India
    Nishant Bhuvanesh Trivedi, Department of Animation and VFX, Parul
        Institute of Design, Parul University, India
    S. Prabakaran, Department of English, Kongu Engineering College,
        India
    Saurabh Chandra, School of Law, Bennett University, India
    Sampath Boopathi, Department of Mechanical Engineering,
        Muthayammal Engineering College, India

Chapter 9
Is the Curriculum Assessment Policy Statement (CAPS) Advancing Diversity
and Social Justice in Rural Communities? The Plight of the LGBTQIA+
Community 217
    Medwin Dikwanyane Sepadi, University of Limpopo, South Africa

Chapter 10
Integrating Universal Design in Education Policy Through Technological
Solutions: Breaking Barriers.. 231
    Ashish Kumar Parashar, Department of Civil Engineering, School
        of Studies Engineering and Technology, Guru Ghasidas
        Vishwavidyalaya, India
    Sudheera Mannepalli, Department of Pharmaceutical Engineering, B.V.
        Raju Institute of Technology, India
    V. Manimegalai, Department of Management Studies, Nandha
        Engineering College (Autonomous), India
    B. Priyadharishini, Department of English, Kongu Engineering College,
        India
    S. Muruganandham, Department of Mathematics, Erode Arts and
        Science College, India

Chapter 11
Inclusive Education and Lifelong Learning: Beyond School Walls 261
    Phineas Phuti Makweya, Independent Police Investigative Directorate,
        South Africa
    Medwin Dikwanyane Sepadi, University of Limpopo, South Africa

Chapter 12
Implementing Flip-Flop Classroom Models With the National Education Policy (NEP) in India 281
> Ashish Kumar Parashar, Department of Civil Engineering, School of Studies Engineering and Technology, Guru Ghasidas Vishwavidyalaya, India
> Asesh Kumar Tripathy, Department of Computer Science and Engineering, Koneru Lakshmaiah Education Foundation, India
> Rippandeep Kaur, University Institute of Teachers Training and Research, Chandigarh University, India
> Manasi Vyankatesh Ghamande, Department of Engineering and Applied Science College, Vishwakarma Institute of Information Technology, India
> A. Robby Sebastian Clement, Department of Humanities and Sciences/English, Sri Sairam Engineering College, India

Chapter 13
Flipped Classroom Methods for Enhanced Student Engagement and Knowledge Developments in Indian Higher Education 313
> M. Karthikeyan, Department of Business Administration, School of Management, Vel Tech Rangarajan Dr. Sagunthala R&D Institute of Science and Technology, India
> Balpreet Singh Madan, Department of Art and Design, School of Design, Architecture, and Planning, Sharda University, India
> Vepada Suchitra, Department of Mathematics, Godavari Institute of Engineering and Technology, India
> E. M. Sri Amirtha Varshini, Department of English, Kongu Engineering College, India
> Ratan Sarkar, Department of Teachers' Training, Prabhat Kumar College, Vidyasagar University, India
> S. Boopathi, Mechanical Engineering, Muthyammal Engineering College, India

Chapter 14
Differentiated Instruction as a Strategy to Support Progressed Learners Within Inclusive Classrooms 343
> Makobo Lydia Mogale, University of the Free State, South Africa

Chapter 15
Critical Thinking in Higher Education Through Innovative Strategies: Out-of-the-Box Thinking 365
    B. Shanthi, Department of Chemistry, Easwari Engineering College, India
    C. Ravichandran, Department of Chemistry, Easwari Engineering College, India
    V. Manimegalai, Department of Management Studies, Nandha Engineering College (Autonomous), India
    Ashish Kumar Parashar, Department of Civil Engineering, School of Studies Engineering and Technology, Guru Ghasidas Vishwavidyalaya, India
    Hari B. S., Department of Mechanical Engineering, Kongu Engineering College, India

Chapter 16
Critical Junctures in the Implementation of Inclusive Education in South Africa 399
    Jabulani Ngcobo, Department of Basic Education, South Africa

Chapter 17
Assessing Challenges and Opportunities for Females' Engagement in STEM: Exploring the Integration of SDG-4 in Nigeria 437
    Uchenna Kingsley Okeke, University of Johannesburg, South Africa
    Sam Ramaila, University of Johannesburg, South Africa

Compilation of References 465

About the Contributors 519

Index 525

Detailed Table of Contents

Foreword xxi

Preface xxiii

Acknowledgment xxxii

Statement About the Book xxxiii

Chapter 1
Conceptualizing and Evolution of Inclusive Education: A Global and
National Exploration 1
    Medwin Dikwanyane Sepadi, University of Limpopo, South Africa

Inclusive education has emerged as a transformative approach that asserts the right of all students to access quality education, irrespective of their diverse backgrounds and needs. This chapter offers a comprehensive analysis of the conceptualization and evolution of inclusive education, tracing its development from global to national contexts. Through an exploration of historicaland social factors, it provides a framework for understanding the key principles underlying inclusive education and their practical implications. Drawing on various scholarly perspectives and international declarations, the chapter emphasizes inclusive education as both a human rights imperative and a strategy for achieving social justice in education systems. Additionally, it examines the challenges and opportunities associated with the implementation of inclusive practices, particularly in settings where resource limitations and pedagogical constraints exist. this chapter contributes to ongoing debates on how best to ensure equitable access to quality education for all learners.

Chapter 2
Teacher Empathy in Schools: Inclusivity and Sustainable Education in a
Global South Context... 25
    Francis R. Ackah-Jnr, Griffith University, Australia
    John K. Appiah, University of Cape Coast, Ghana
    Awudu Salaam Mohammed, University of Cape Coast, Ghana

International best practice, policy directive and buy-in underpin the adoption of a more transformative and inclusive approach to education. However, socio-cultural, economic, and political forces in the global South, coupled with resistive school practices and discrimination often lead to the exclusion of learners. Informed by learner diversities and the lingering effects of COVID-19, the chapter argues for empathy in inclusive education. The effective embedment of empathy at the heart of school practice pedagogically, physically, socially, and emotionally can leverage inclusivity for all learners. Empathy, the capacity to share a person's feelings and emotions, is also the foundation of what makes schools securing and supporting, teachers intentional and responsive, families caring and kind, and societies accepting and resourcing. This chapter essentialises empathy, inclusivity and sustainable education, teacher inclusive roles and empathic practices. Implications are offered on supporting teachers and improving their preparation to promote empathic inclusive education.

Chapter 3
Teacher Training and Support for Assistive Technology in Inclusive
Education: A Global Perspective 53
    Deepak Kumar Sahoo, Biju Patnaik University of Technology, Rourkela,
        India
    Shashank Mittal, O.P. Jindal Global University, India
    Ajay Chandel, Lovely Professional University, India
    Neeti Goyal, University of Petroleum and Energy Studies, India
    Xuan-Hoa Nghiem, Vietnam National University, Vietnam

This paper explores the integration of assistive technology (AT) in inclusive education, focusing on teacher training and support systems. It examines the role of AT in enhancing learning experiences for students with diverse needs and identifies global perspectives on effective training programs. The paper addresses challenges such as technological barriers, financial constraints, and the need for comprehensive professional development. It highlights successful case studies, discusses policy and advocacy efforts, and explores future innovations in AT. By providing a thorough analysis of these elements, the paper aims to offer insights into creating more inclusive educational environments through strategic AT implementation and support.

Chapter 4
The Crucial Role of Empathy in Fostering Inclusive Learning Environments ... 77
> *Phineas Phuti Makweya, Independent Police Investigative Directorate, South Africa*
> *Medwin Sepadi, University of Limpopo, South Africa*

Empathy is a fundamental trait crucial for fostering inclusive learning environments, enhancing student-teacher relationships, and promoting understanding among students and educators. Recent studies emphasize its significance in education, showing its positive impact on collaboration and appreciation for diversity (Davis et al., 2016). Empathy enables educators to tailor teaching strategies to meet diverse student needs, creating a more inclusive classroom atmosphere (Jennings & Greenberg, 2009). Moreover, empathy contributes to a supportive work environment for educators, enhancing collaboration and professional development (Katz, Blumler & Gurevitch, 2015). By prioritizing empathy, schools can cultivate a more compassionate and understanding educational community where everyone feels valued and respected, thus significantly contributing to the field of inclusive education.

Chapter 5
Practitioner Insights on Policy-Driven Shifts in College-Based Education: Navigating Transformation 91
> *G. Rathnakar, Department of Mechanical Engineering, JSS Science and Technology University, Mysuru, India*
> *Lalchhantluangi Pachuau, Department of Management, Pachhunga University College, Aizawl, India*
> *T. Geetha, Department of English, Kongu Engineering College, Erode, India*
> *M. Prabhuswamy, Department of Education, JSS Institute of Education, India*
> *S. Praveenkumar, Centre for Tourism and Hotel Management, Madurai Kamaraj University, India*

Examining legislative directives and institutional shifts, this chapter delves into the ever-changing terrain of higher education. Offering insights into possibilities, difficulties, and tactics, it examines how policy-driven changes affect educators, administrators, and students. Reforming curricula, evaluating techniques, financing arrangements, and technology integration are all covered in the examination. The conflict between regulations and academic freedom, the need of leadership in smooth transitions, and the effects on students' educational experiences are some of the major issues. In order to sustain educational quality and relevance while adapting to changing policy environments, stakeholders must work together

Chapter 6
Nurturing Inclusive Schools Through the Isibindi Ezikoleni Child and Youth Care Work Programme 121
    Zeni Thumbadoo, National Association of Child Care Workers, South Africa
    Theresa Wilson, Independent Researcher, South Africa
    Nicia de Nobrega, National Association of Child Care Workers, South Africa
    Donald Nghonyama, National Association of Child Care Workers, South Africa

This chapter offers a comprehensive overview of the Isibindi Ezikoleni Programme, an innovative child and youth care practice model designed to enhance inclusive education in South African schools. This model strategically embeds child and youth care workers in the school setting to address the emotional, social, and educational needs of vulnerable and at-risk learners. By doing so, it aims to create a nurturing and inclusive environment for every learner to flourish and succeed. Adopting a practice-based perspective, this chapter examines how the programme contributes to mitigating barriers to education and cultivating environments conducive to the success of all learners. Through a detailed examination of its design, implementation, and impacts, this chapter provides case examples and results to illustrate the programme's role in enhancing inclusivity in South Africa's educational system.

Chapter 7
Navigating Inclusion in the Industry 4.0 Horizon: Crafting a Pedagogical Future 163
> *Pallavi Sakhahari Dhamak, Shri Vile Parle Kelavani Mandal Narsee Monjee Institute of Management Studies, Mukesh Patel School of Technology Management and Engineering, Mumbai, India*
> *Padmanabha Aital, Shri Vile Parle Kelavani Mandal Narsee Monjee Institute of Management Studies, Mukesh Patel School of Technology Management and Engineering, Mumbai, India*
> *Anand Daftardar, Shri Vile Parle Kelavani Mandal Narsee Monjee Institute of Management Studies, Mukesh Patel School of Technology Management and Engineering, Mumbai, India*

This study investigates the integration of Industry 4.0 technologies in education, focusing on their usage across different educational levels and their impact on learning. Through a comprehensive literature review of articles from Scopus, ScienceDirect, and Web of Science databases, 51 articles were quantitatively analysed and 23 articles were qualitatively examined. Findings highlight the increasing use of augmented reality, virtual reality, the Internet of Things, and simulations, particularly in higher education, to enhance student engagement, promote active participation, and replicate real-world scenarios. Despite their benefits, these technologies are underutilised and mostly confined to manufacturing-related courses. The study underscores the potential of Industry 4.0 technologies to advance Education 4.0 across all educational levels, advocating for their broader implementation to create dynamic and effective learning environments.

Chapter 8
Pedagogical Contents Developments and Specialized Training for Teaching
Careers 187
> *Ratan Sarkar, Department of Teachers' Training, Prabhat Kumar*
>   *College, Vidyasagar University, India*
> *Dhara Vinod Parmar, Department of Design and Merchandising, Parul*
>   *Institute of Design, Parul University, India*
> *Nishant Bhuvanesh Trivedi, Department of Animation and VFX, Parul*
>   *Institute of Design, Parul University, India*
> *S. Prabakaran, Department of English, Kongu Engineering College,*
>   *India*
> *Saurabh Chandra, School of Law, Bennett University, India*
> *Sampath Boopathi, Department of Mechanical Engineering,*
>   *Muthayammal Engineering College, India*

The current chapter deals with issues of pedagogical content knowledge (PCK) and additional preparation required for teaching careers in the 21st century. In this chapter, it is discussed how instruction, curricula, and educational technology can be aligned together to maximize teacher effectiveness. The chapter is grounded on the following twin necessity aspects: one, helping teachers develop all skills to handle differences in learning; and two, the inclusion of differentiated instruction, inclusive education, and subject matter pedagogy. Discussion on the need to preserve continuing professional development with the focus that the individual should be flexible in class in respect to constantly emerging classroom dynamics as well as modern demands of education will be considered. Conversations on reflective teaching and the use of various assessment techniques for learning outcomes shall also be discussed.

Chapter 9
Is the Curriculum Assessment Policy Statement (CAPS) Advancing Diversity
and Social Justice in Rural Communities? The Plight of the LGBTQIA+
Community 217
> *Medwin Dikwanyane Sepadi, University of Limpopo, South Africa*

This chapter critically examines the Curriculum Assessment Policy Statement (CAPS) in South Africa and its role in advancing diversity and social justice, particularly focusing on the LGBTQIA+ community in rural areas. Despite CAPS's foundational principles emphasizing human rights, inclusivity, environmental and social justice, the chapter highlights a significant disconnect between these principles and the lived experiences of LGBTQIA+ individuals in rural South Africa. The chapter begins by outlining the key principles of CAPS and its commitment to fostering understanding and respect for diversity, including issues related to race, gender, language, and disability

Chapter 10
Integrating Universal Design in Education Policy Through Technological Solutions: Breaking Barriers... 231
    Ashish Kumar Parashar, Department of Civil Engineering, School of Studies Engineering and Technology, Guru Ghasidas Vishwavidyalaya, India
    Sudheera Mannepalli, Department of Pharmaceutical Engineering, B.V. Raju Institute of Technology, India
    V. Manimegalai, Department of Management Studies, Nandha Engineering College (Autonomous), India
    B. Priyadharishini, Department of English, Kongu Engineering College, India
    S. Muruganandham, Department of Mathematics, Erode Arts and Science College, India

The need to adopt universal design principles has been described to build inclusive learning environments in a technologically varied world. It is highlighting the importance of accessibility, adaptability, and inclusion while establishing educational policy. Through case studies and best practices, the chapter studies how technology might enhance educational opportunities, particularly for children with disabilities. Effective Universal Design implementations, the consequences for policy, and how to incorporate the ideas of Universal Design into financial priorities, teacher preparation programs, and educational standards are also discussed. Universal Design could affect financial priorities, teacher preparation programs, and educational standards, as illustrated in this chapter. The new technologies, providing a framework for using technology strategically, are discussed to promote cross-sector collaboration and advance universal design.

Chapter 11
Inclusive Education and Lifelong Learning: Beyond School Walls 261
Phineas Phuti Makweya, Independent Police Investigative Directorate, South Africa
Medwin Dikwanyane Sepadi, University of Limpopo, South Africa

This chapter explores how inclusive education principles extend beyond traditional schooling, enriching lifelong learning experiences and outcomes. It emphasizes learning as a continuous, lifelong process, applicable across all stages of life and contexts. Embracing inclusive education throughout lifelong learning offers several key benefits. Firstly, it creates a more equitable and accessible learning environment for people of all ages and backgrounds, enriching the learning experience for everyone involved (UNESCO, 2019; Ainscow, 2020). Secondly, it fosters a culture of respect and understanding among learners by acknowledging and accommodating individual differences. Lastly, inclusive lifelong learning promotes the development of essential skills, such as critical thinking and collaboration, preparing individuals to navigate challenges and contribute to society (Rouse, 2017). This chapter contributes to the field by highlighting the importance of inclusive lifelong learning in fostering equity and skills development, ultimately shaping a more inclusive and prosperous future.

Chapter 12
Implementing Flip-Flop Classroom Models With the National Education Policy (NEP) in India 281
    Ashish Kumar Parashar, Department of Civil Engineering, School of Studies Engineering and Technology, Guru Ghasidas Vishwavidyalaya, India
    Asesh Kumar Tripathy, Department of Computer Science and Engineering, Koneru Lakshmaiah Education Foundation, India
    Rippandeep Kaur, University Institute of Teachers Training and Research, Chandigarh University, India
    Manasi Vyankatesh Ghamande, Department of Engineering and Applied Science College, Vishwakarma Institute of Information Technology, India
    A. Robby Sebastian Clement, Department of Humanities and Sciences/ English, Sri Sairam Engineering College, India

This study looks at how Flip-Flop Classroom Models are being used in India as part of the National Education Policy (NEP), which places a strong emphasis on technology integration, active learning, and student-centered learning. In line with the NEP's tenets, the Flip-Flop Classroom Model replaces traditional teacher-led learning with an interactive, collaborative approach. In order to encourage active learning and peer engagement, the study addresses the theoretical underpinnings, curriculum creation methodologies, and classroom upgrades. It also covers how to link curriculum creation with worldwide best practices and include NEP ideas into the process. The report also discusses the potential and difficulties associated with bringing Flip-Flop Classroom Models to every state in the union and makes suggestions for transforming Indian education.

Chapter 13
Flipped Classroom Methods for Enhanced Student Engagement and
Knowledge Developments in Indian Higher Education 313
    M. Karthikeyan, Department of Business Administration, School of
        Management, Vel Tech Rangarajan Dr. Sagunthala R&D Institute of
        Science and Technology, India
    Balpreet Singh Madan, Department of Art and Design, School of
        Design, Architecture, and Planning, Sharda University, India
    Vepada Suchitra, Department of Mathematics, Godavari Institute of
        Engineering and Technology, India
    E. M. Sri Amirtha Varshini, Department of English, Kongu Engineering
        College, India
    Ratan Sarkar, Department of Teachers' Training, Prabhat Kumar
        College, Vidyasagar University, India
    S. Boopathi, Mechanical Engineering, Muthyammal Engineering
        College, India

In Indian higher education, flipped classrooms provide a viable alternative to conventional pedagogical methods, boosting student engagement and knowledge growth. While in-class time is devoted to interactive exercises, group problem-solving, and peer debates, pre-class activities such as video lectures and readings allow students to complete them independently before class sessions. However, obstacles including inadequate infrastructure, reluctance from teachers, and worries over grading and evaluation make it difficult to put them into practice. To address these obstacles, a multifaceted strategy including faculty development, technology assistance, and institutional policy reforms is required.

Chapter 14
Differentiated Instruction as a Strategy to Support Progressed Learners
Within Inclusive Classrooms 343
    Makobo Lydia Mogale, University of the Free State, South Africa

Differentiated Instruction is an integral part of learning to accommodate learner diversity and varying background knowledge rather than using "one-size-fits-all" teaching approach. This inevitable pedagogical approach gained lots of attention due to its flexible, equitable and intelligent way to approach teaching. This chapter provides insight on using Differentiated Instruction as strategy to support progressed learners. Learner progression policy in South Africa was promulgated to redress continuous retention which often leads to school dropout and foregrounds extended learning opportunities to bridge content gap. This policy was introduced in the Further and Education training Phase secondary (Grade 10 - 12) in 2013 for learners not to spend more than four years in a phase. When learners are progressed, their academic success depends on curriculum support to bridge content gap. The chapter delves deeper into inclusive pedagogical practice tailored for various progression reason.

Chapter 15
Critical Thinking in Higher Education Through Innovative Strategies: Out-of-the-Box Thinking 365
    B. Shanthi, Department of Chemistry, Easwari Engineering College, India
    C. Ravichandran, Department of Chemistry, Easwari Engineering College, India
    V. Manimegalai, Department of Management Studies, Nandha Engineering College (Autonomous), India
    Ashish Kumar Parashar, Department of Civil Engineering, School of Studies Engineering and Technology, Guru Ghasidas Vishwavidyalaya, India
    Hari B. S., Department of Mechanical Engineering, Kongu Engineering College, India

This chapter discusses the innovative strategies used by higher education institutions to promote critical thinking. It places a strong emphasis on making use of cutting-edge technology, reconsidering traditional teaching strategies, and promoting interdisciplinary collaboration. Global virtual classrooms, gamification, immersive learning environments, and real-world problem-solving projects are important fields. With competency-based testing and customized learning paths, students are given the tools they need to take control of their education. Diversity and inclusion widen perspectives and enhance the learning environment. Strategic partnerships with business and community stakeholders provide chances for practical learning and career readiness.

Chapter 16
Critical Junctures in the Implementation of Inclusive Education in South Africa 399
Jabulani Ngcobo, Department of Basic Education, South Africa

The implementation of inclusive education in South Africa has undergone significant transformation since 2001. This chapter explores the critical junctures that have shaped the implementation of inclusive education in South Africa. In this regard, the chapter examines the key moments where policy changes, programmatic interventions, legal developments, and societal shifts may have influenced the country's approach to implementing inclusive education. The chapter argues that the critical junctures, evidenced by the country's history of education, policy and legislative changes, strategic programmatic interventions, court cases and legal challenges, have shaped the trajectory of implementing inclusive education in South Africa. Finally, the chapter argues that South Africa can advance inclusive practices and ensure equitable access to education for all learners by taking advantage of the strategic windows of opportunity created by critical junctures.

Chapter 17
Assessing Challenges and Opportunities for Females' Engagement in STEM:
Exploring the Integration of SDG-4 in Nigeria 437
    Uchenna Kingsley Okeke, University of Johannesburg, South Africa
    Sam Ramaila, University of Johannesburg, South Africa

This chapter explores the integration of Sustainable Development Goal 4 (SDG 4) in Nigeria, specifically focusing on the challenges and opportunities for females' involvement in Science, Technology, Engineering, and Mathematics (STEM). Recognizing the pivotal role of gender equality in achieving SDG 4's objectives of inclusive and equitable quality education, the chapter examines the barriers hindering females' participation in STEM and identifies potential avenues for enhancement. Through a comprehensive analysis of institutional, socio-cultural, and educational factors, the chapter elucidates the complexities surrounding females' engagement in STEM in the Nigerian context. Furthermore, it explores strategies to promote females' enrollment and retention in STEM education and careers. By shedding light on both challenges and opportunities, this chapter contributes to the discourse on gender equality and educational development in Nigeria and offers insights for policymakers, educators, and stakeholders striving to advance females' participation in STEM fields in alignment with SDG 4

Compilation of References 465

About the Contributors 519

Index 525

Foreword

Inclusive education stands as one of the most pressing and transformative movements in the educational landscape today. It represents a commitment to equity, ensuring that every learner, regardless of their abilities, background, or identity, has access to quality education. As we navigate an increasingly diverse and interconnected world, inclusive education not only addresses the needs of marginalized communities but also fosters environments where all students can thrive.

Global Practices in Inclusive Education Curriculum and Policy serves as both a testament to the strides made in this field and a call to action for educators, policymakers, and researchers. The editors have masterfully curated a collection of chapters that span continents and disciplines, providing a rich and varied exploration of the policies, strategies, and innovations driving inclusive education globally. From the philosophical foundations of inclusion to the practical challenges of implementation, this book offers an in-depth look at how educators around the world are working to create inclusive learning environments.

What sets this volume apart is its global perspective. While many discussions on inclusive education are centered on specific national contexts, the chapters in this book bring together voices and experiences from around the world, with a particular emphasis on the Global South. In doing so, it highlights not only the universal principles of inclusive education but also the unique challenges and opportunities faced by different regions. Whether addressing issues of teacher training, empathy in education, the integration of technology, or policy shifts, this book provides a comprehensive overview of the state of inclusive education today.

As we stand on the cusp of a new era in education—one shaped by rapid technological advancements, shifting social dynamics, and the ongoing pursuit of social justice this book is a timely and essential resource. It reminds us that inclusive education is not a destination but a journey, one that requires continuous reflection, collaboration, and innovation.

I am confident that *Global Practices in Inclusive Education Curriculum and Policy* will inspire educators and policymakers alike, encouraging them to reflect on their practices and policies and to strive toward more inclusive and equitable educational systems. The insights and experiences shared within these pages are not only informative but also transformative, offering a vision for a future where education truly serves the needs of all learners.

It is with great enthusiasm that I commend this important work to you. May it serve as a guiding light in our collective efforts to create inclusive, empathetic, and equitable learning environments across the globe.

Mathibela Pm
University of Pretoria, South Africa

Preface

As the Editors of *Global Practices in Inclusive Education Curriculum and Policy*, we are honored to present a comprehensive exploration of the strides made in fostering inclusive education worldwide. Inclusive education is not just a framework; it is a commitment to ensuring that every student regardless of ability, background, or identity has access to equitable learning opportunities. This volume aims to highlight both the successes and ongoing challenges in creating inclusive school environments that respond to the diverse needs of all learners.

The chapters in this book provide insights from various global perspectives, documenting how inclusive education is being shaped through curriculum development, policy advancements, and practical implementation. We hope this book serves as a valuable resource for academics, policymakers, and practitioners in fields such as education, social work, psychology, educational law, policy development, and special needs education. The goal is to equip them with the knowledge and tools necessary to create learning environments that are truly inclusive and supportive of every student's growth and potential.

By sharing global best practices, we seek to inspire continued progress in inclusive education, benefitting not only educators and institutions but, most importantly, the students themselves. We are confident that the insights and experiences shared within these pages will help shape the future of inclusive education and contribute to a world where education is truly for all.

ORGANIZATION OF THE BOOK

Chapter 1: Conceptualizing and Evolution of Inclusive Education: A Global and National Exploration

This chapter traces the historical and philosophical development of inclusive education as a cornerstone of equitable educational access. By exploring the global and national dimensions of this evolution, the authors highlight the multifaceted debates surrounding the concept of inclusive education, particularly in relation to marginalized communities, students with disabilities, and those from diverse cultural and linguistic backgrounds. The chapter emphasizes the shifting definitions and interpretations of inclusivity over time, setting a foundation for a deeper understanding of how inclusive education can be actualized in practice.

Chapter 2: Teacher Empathy in Schools: Inclusivity and Sustainable Education in a Global South Context

Empathy is central to fostering inclusivity in education, particularly in the Global South, where socio-cultural, political, and economic barriers often exclude learners. This chapter highlights the significance of embedding empathy in school practices to enhance inclusivity and sustainable education. With the lingering effects of COVID-19, the authors emphasize that empathy-driven pedagogies are essential to creating supportive learning environments. This chapter also explores the role of teachers as inclusive leaders, offering strategies to cultivate empathic practices that respond to the diverse needs of students.

Chapter 3: Teacher Training and Support for Assistive Technology in Inclusive Education: A Global Perspective

This chapter examines the integration of assistive technology (AT) in inclusive education, focusing on global strategies for teacher training and support. The authors analyze the challenges of implementing AT, such as technological limitations and financial constraints, while highlighting successful case studies of AT-enhanced learning environments. By delving into global policy and advocacy efforts, the chapter provides a roadmap for creating more inclusive educational settings through effective teacher training and strategic AT adoption.

Chapter 4: The Crucial Role of Empathy in Fostering Inclusive Learning Environments

Empathy is a vital element in creating inclusive learning environments, strengthening student-teacher relationships, and fostering a culture of understanding. This chapter emphasizes how empathy enhances teaching strategies by catering to the diverse needs of students, while also promoting collaboration among educators. The authors argue that empathy not only contributes to student well-being but also improves educators' professional development, resulting in a more inclusive and compassionate educational community.

Chapter 5: Practitioner Insights on Policy-Driven Shifts in College-based Education: Navigating Transformation

This chapter provides an in-depth analysis of how policy-driven changes impact higher education institutions. The authors discuss how legislative directives influence curriculum reforms, evaluation methods, and technology integration. The chapter highlights the tension between academic freedom and regulatory compliance and underscores the importance of leadership in navigating these transformations. By focusing on collaboration between educators, administrators, and students, the chapter offers insights into sustaining educational quality amidst evolving policy landscapes.

Chapter 6: Nurturing Inclusive Schools through the Isibindi Ezikoleni Child and Youth Care Work Program

This chapter explores the Isibindi Ezikoleni Programme in South Africa, which integrates child and youth care workers into schools to support vulnerable learners. By addressing emotional, social, and educational needs, the program creates a nurturing and inclusive learning environment. The authors provide case examples to demonstrate how this model mitigates barriers to education and enhances inclusivity in South African schools. The chapter highlights the program's success in fostering a supportive and inclusive educational culture.

Chapter 7: Navigating Inclusion in the Industry 4.0 Horizon: Crafting a Pedagogical Future

Focusing on the integration of Industry 4.0 technologies in education, this chapter investigates how tools like augmented reality, virtual reality, and the Internet of Things can enhance student engagement. Despite their potential, the authors highlight that these technologies are underutilized, particularly outside of manufacturing courses. The chapter advocates for broader implementation of Industry 4.0 technologies to create dynamic, real-world learning environments that advance the goals of Education 4.0 across various educational levels.

Chapter 8: Pedagogical Content Developments and Specialized Training for Teaching Careers

This chapter addresses the importance of developing pedagogical content knowledge (PCK) and specialized training for teachers in the 21st century. The authors discuss the integration of differentiated instruction, inclusive education, and subject matter pedagogy to equip teachers with the necessary skills to manage diverse classrooms. Emphasizing the need for continuous professional development, the chapter highlights strategies for reflective teaching and innovative assessment techniques that can enhance learning outcomes in modern educational environments.

Chapter 9: Is the Curriculum Assessment Policy Statement (CAPS) Advancing Diversity and Social Justice in Rural Communities?: The Plight of the LGBTQIA+ Community

This chapter critically evaluates South Africa's Curriculum Assessment Policy Statement (CAPS) in promoting diversity and social justice, with a specific focus on the LGBTQIA+ community in rural areas. The authors explore the disconnect between CAPS's inclusive principles and the lived experiences of marginalized individuals. The chapter calls for a reassessment of CAPS's implementation to better support diversity and social justice, particularly in underrepresented and rural communities.

Chapter 10: Integrating Universal Design in Education Policy through Technological Solutions: Breaking Barriers

This chapter explores how universal design principles can be integrated into education policy to create inclusive learning environments. The authors emphasize the importance of accessibility and adaptability in policy-making, using case studies to illustrate how technology can enhance educational opportunities for students with disabilities. The chapter discusses the implications of universal design for teacher preparation, financial priorities, and educational standards, advocating for cross-sector collaboration to promote inclusion.

Chapter 11: Inclusive Education and Lifelong Learning: Beyond School Walls

This chapter extends the principles of inclusive education beyond traditional school settings, emphasizing the role of lifelong learning in creating equitable learning environments. The authors argue that inclusive education benefits learners of all ages by fostering a culture of respect and understanding. The chapter highlights how inclusive lifelong learning promotes essential skills, such as critical thinking and collaboration, preparing individuals to navigate societal challenges and contribute to a more inclusive future.

Chapter 12: Implementing Flip-Flop Classroom Models with the National Education Policy (NEP) in India

This chapter explores the adoption of Flip-Flop Classroom Models in India under the National Education Policy (NEP). The authors highlight how this interactive, student-centered approach replaces traditional teacher-led instruction. The chapter discusses curriculum development, active learning strategies, and peer engagement while addressing the challenges and opportunities of implementing this model across India. Recommendations are offered for enhancing education through the effective integration of the NEP's principles.

Chapter 13: Flipped Classroom Methods for Enhanced Student Engagement and Knowledge Developments in Indian Higher Education

This chapter investigates the use of flipped classroom methods in Indian higher education, showcasing how this approach enhances student engagement and learning outcomes. By shifting traditional in-class lectures to pre-class activities, students are empowered to take ownership of their learning. However, the authors note the challenges of implementing flipped classrooms, such as infrastructure limitations and teacher resistance, and offer solutions for overcoming these barriers through faculty development and policy reforms.

Chapter 14: Differentiated Instruction as a Strategy to Support Progressed Learners within Inclusive Classrooms

This chapter focuses on the role of differentiated instruction in supporting progressed learners in inclusive classrooms. The authors explore South Africa's learner progression policy, which aims to prevent dropouts by offering extended learning opportunities. The chapter highlights how differentiated instruction addresses diverse learning needs and helps bridge content gaps for students who have been progressed, offering practical strategies for fostering inclusive educational practices.

Chapter 15: Critical Thinking in Higher Education through Innovative Strategies: Out-of-Box Thinking

This chapter explores innovative strategies for promoting critical thinking in higher education, emphasizing the use of cutting-edge technology, interdisciplinary collaboration, and experiential learning. The authors discuss global virtual classrooms, gamification, and real-world problem-solving projects as key tools for fostering critical thinking. The chapter highlights the importance of diversity and inclusion in enhancing the learning experience and preparing students for career success in a rapidly evolving global landscape.

Chapter 16: Critical Junctures in the Implementation of Inclusive Education in South Africa

This chapter examines the key moments, or "critical junctures," that have shaped the implementation of inclusive education in South Africa. The authors analyze the impact of policy changes, legal challenges, and programmatic interventions on the country's educational landscape. By exploring these pivotal moments, the chapter provides insights into how South Africa can continue to advance inclusive education and ensure equitable access for all learners.

Chapter 17: Assessing Challenges and Opportunities for Females' Engagement in STEM: Exploring the Integration of SDG-4 in Nigeria

This chapter explores the integration of Sustainable Development Goal 4 (SDG 4) in Nigeria, with a focus on increasing female participation in Science, Technology, Engineering, and Mathematics (STEM). The authors examine the challenges and opportunities faced by women in STEM, including socio-cultural barriers and policy gaps. By highlighting strategies for promoting gender equality in STEM education, the chapter contributes to the ongoing efforts to achieve SDG 4 in Nigeria.

Research Justification

The imperative for inclusive education has never been more urgent. In the 21st century, educational systems around the world are tasked with meeting the diverse needs of all learners, regardless of their abilities, backgrounds, or circumstances. Inclusive education is not simply a pedagogical framework; it is a human right, enshrined in international commitments such as the United Nations Convention on the Rights of Persons with Disabilities (CRPD) and Sustainable Development Goal 4 (SDG 4), which advocates for inclusive, equitable, and quality education for all. However, despite these global commitments, the implementation of inclusive education remains uneven, with significant disparities between policy and practice, especially in low- and middle-income countries.

This book, Global Practices in Inclusive Education Curriculum and Policy, is justified by several pressing factors. First, there is a growing body of research that recognizes the transformative potential of inclusive education in fostering social justice, reducing inequality, and promoting sustainable development. However, gaps in both theoretical understanding and practical application persist, particularly in contexts where socio-economic, cultural, and political barriers undermine the realization of inclusive education. Existing research often focuses on high-income countries, leaving a critical void in understanding how inclusive practices can be effectively adapted and implemented in the Global South, where challenges such as poverty, limited resources, and systemic marginalization are prevalent. This volume addresses this critical gap by offering a comprehensive, global perspective that includes both high-resource and low-resource environments, with a particular focus on the Global South.

Second, the evolving nature of educational systems in the face of technological advancements, shifting socio-political landscapes, and the global repercussions of crises such as the COVID-19 pandemic, necessitate a re-examination of what it means to be inclusive in education. Technological innovations, such as assistive technologies, Industry 4.0 tools (e.g., artificial intelligence, augmented and virtual reality), and universal design for learning (UDL) have the potential to revolutionize inclusive practices, yet their integration into mainstream education remains inconsistent and under-researched. This book rigorously explores how these emerging technologies can be harnessed to overcome barriers to inclusion, and highlights the importance of teacher training, policy reform, and leadership in facilitating these changes.

Third, despite policy commitments to inclusivity, the realities on the ground often reveal significant gaps in implementation, especially when it comes to marginalized groups such as students with disabilities, girls, and LGBTQIA+ individuals, particularly in rural or underserved communities. For example, the evaluation of South Africa's Curriculum Assessment Policy Statement (CAPS) and its effectiveness in advancing diversity and social justice for the LGBTQIA+ community in rural areas, as explored in this volume, demonstrates the ongoing challenges that inclusive policies face. This book provides a critical examination of how policies, while well-intentioned, can often fall short in addressing the nuanced and intersectional needs of marginalized learners, offering practical recommendations for closing the implementation gap.

Moreover, inclusive education goes beyond formal schooling; it extends into lifelong learning, preparing individuals to navigate a rapidly changing world. As global economies shift towards knowledge-based industries and as workplaces increasingly demand critical thinking, adaptability, and collaboration, the role of education in fostering these skills is paramount. This book rigorously examines the intersection of inclusive education and lifelong learning, providing a framework for understanding how inclusive practices can be extended beyond traditional school settings to ensure that education is a continuous and adaptive process, accessible to learners at all stages of life.

Additionally, this volume contributes to the ongoing scholarly conversation on the role of empathy in education, particularly in fostering inclusive and equitable learning environments. Empathy is often undervalued in discussions of educational reform, yet it is central to building relationships between educators and students, particularly in contexts where students face significant social, emotional, or cognitive challenges. Chapters in this book, such as those examining the role of teacher empathy in the Global South, provide evidence-based strategies for embedding empathy into pedagogy, thus creating more supportive and inclusive educational spaces.

The research presented in this volume also provides a critical analysis of the policy-driven shifts impacting inclusive education. By drawing on diverse case studies, this book highlights the tensions between policy imperatives and the practical realities of educational institutions. For instance, policy reforms aimed at increasing access to education often clash with the need to maintain educational quality and adapt curricula to the needs of diverse learners. This tension is further complicated by the regulatory pressures faced by educational institutions, as well as by the rapid pace of technological and social change. The book offers insights into how institutions can navigate these challenges, drawing on leadership strategies that promote collaboration between educators, policymakers, and communities.

Finally, this volume is timely given the global movement towards more inclusive and equitable education systems. As nations grapple with the legacies of colonialism, systemic inequality, and exclusion, this book offers a roadmap for creating educational environments that are not only inclusive but also transformative. By engaging with diverse perspectives from teacher training in assistive technologies to the integration of universal design principles this book provides actionable strategies for advancing inclusive education in varied global contexts.

In conclusion, the justification for this research is rooted in the urgent need to bridge the gap between policy and practice in inclusive education, particularly in the Global South. The comprehensive exploration of global best practices, coupled with a critical examination of the challenges and opportunities in implementing inclusive education, makes this volume a valuable resource for academics, policymakers, and practitioners alike. As we move into a future defined by rapid technological change and shifting social paradigms, the insights provided in this book will be crucial in shaping inclusive educational systems that promote equity, social justice, and lifelong learning for all.

IN CONCLUSION

In conclusion, this edited volume stands as a comprehensive exploration of inclusive education, not only tracing its evolution and global conceptualization but also delving into its intricate relationship with empathy, technology, policy, and lifelong learning. As editors, we have curated a collection of chapters that address both the theoretical foundations and practical implementations of inclusive education, underscoring its importance in fostering equitable learning environments for all. The contributions from a diverse range of scholars and practitioners offer valuable insights into the challenges and opportunities of inclusive education across different global contexts, with a particular focus on the Global South, where socio-cultural, economic, and political dynamics continue to shape educational realities.

Each chapter in this book adds to the conversation on how we can transform educational systems to be more inclusive, empathetic, and responsive to the diverse needs of learners. Whether through the integration of assistive technologies, empathy-driven teaching practices, or policy-driven shifts in education, the authors provide evidence-based strategies and recommendations for advancing inclusivity. As we move toward a future defined by rapid technological change, globalization, and shifting social paradigms, the need for inclusive education has never been more pressing.

We hope that this volume will serve as a critical resource for educators, policymakers, and researchers who are committed to promoting inclusion in education. By fostering deeper understanding and collaboration, we can ensure that education remains a powerful tool for social justice, equity, and human development in the 21st century.

Acknowledgment

We would like to express our deepest gratitude to everyone who contributed to the development of this book, Global Practices in Inclusive Education Curriculum and Policy. This work would not have been possible without the invaluable support, dedication, and collaboration of many individuals and organizations.

First and foremost, we are deeply thankful to the contributing authors whose expertise, insights, and commitment to inclusive education have enriched this volume. Your thoughtful chapters reflect the global challenges and innovations in inclusive education, offering valuable knowledge to practitioners, academics, and policymakers.

We extend our heartfelt thanks to our families and loved ones for their patience, encouragement, and unwavering support throughout this journey. Their belief in the importance of this project kept us motivated and inspired.

We are also immensely grateful to the various institutions and organizations that supported our work, whether through providing resources, research opportunities, or platforms for academic exchange. A special thank you goes to our reviewers, whose insightful feedback helped shape this book into a comprehensive resource for inclusive education.

Lastly, we acknowledge the students, teachers, and communities who have been our motivation in promoting inclusive education. Their experiences and perseverance serve as a reminder of why this work matters and the positive impact it can have on creating equitable learning environments for all.

With heartfelt appreciation,

The Editors of Global Practices in Inclusive Education Curriculum and Policy

Dr Sepadi MD & Dr Makweya P

Statement About the Book

Global Practices in Inclusive Education Curriculum and Policy is a comprehensive exploration of the evolving landscape of inclusive education, with a particular focus on global perspectives and practical implementation. This volume brings together the insights of scholars, educators, and policymakers from diverse regions, offering a rich analysis of how inclusive education is being shaped by policy reforms, curriculum development, and innovative pedagogical practices.

At its core, this book addresses the critical need for educational systems that are both equitable and inclusive. It highlights the importance of ensuring that all students—regardless of ability, cultural background, or socio-economic status—have access to meaningful learning opportunities. From empathy-driven teaching approaches to the integration of assistive technologies, the chapters explore a wide range of strategies for creating learning environments that are responsive to the needs of all learners.

One of the key aspects of this book is its emphasis on the Global South, providing valuable insights into how socio-cultural, economic, and political dynamics influence inclusive education in regions often underrepresented in global discussions. It also examines how policies and programs across different countries can serve as models for others, offering practical guidance on bridging the gap between inclusive education theory and practice.

The significance of Global Practices in Inclusive Education Curriculum and Policy extends beyond theoretical discussions; it has direct implications for the field of Inclusive Education. The book underscores the importance of inclusive practices for learners with diverse educational needs and barriers, emphasizing the role of empathy, differentiated instruction, and the use of universal design principles in creating supportive learning environments. It also addresses broader issues such as teacher training, lifelong learning, and policy reform, providing a holistic view of how inclusive education can be achieved across various educational contexts.

By offering a global perspective on the challenges and successes of inclusive education, this volume serves as a vital resource for educators, researchers, policymakers, and advocates. It aims to inspire continued efforts to make education more inclusive, ensuring that all students are empowered to reach their full potential.

The implications of Global Practices in Inclusive Education Curriculum and Policy for the field of Inclusive Education are profound and far-reaching. This book addresses the critical role inclusive education plays in reshaping how we approach and support learners with diverse needs, particularly those with disabilities. Its global scope, combined with practical insights and policy recommendations, offers several key contributions to the field:

Empathy and Inclusive Pedagogy: The book emphasizes empathy as a foundational element in creating inclusive learning environments. For inclusive education, this underscores the importance of building emotional and supportive connections between teachers and students with disabilities. By integrating empathy-driven strategies into classrooms, educators can foster environments that enhance student engagement and emotional well-being.

Assistive Technologies and Inclusive Needs: A crucial aspect of inclusive education covered in this book is the integration of assistive technologies. These tools can significantly improve access to learning for students with disabilities. The book examines global examples of how assistive technologies are being implemented, providing models for inclusive education professionals to enhance the participation and success of learners with inclusive needs.

Differentiated Instruction: The book discusses differentiated instruction as a key strategy for supporting diverse learners, einclusively in inclusive education. This approach ensures that curriculum and teaching methods are tailored to meet the unique needs of students with disabilities, allowing for more personalized and effective learning experiences.

Policy-Driven Reforms in Inclusive Education: Many chapters focus on the role of policy in driving inclusive education reforms. This has direct relevance to inclusive education, where policies often determine the level of resources, support, and access available to learners with disabilities. The book advocates for policies that promote equity and inclusion, serving as a guide for policymakers and educational leaders striving to improve inclusive education systems.

Universal Design for Learning (UDL): The book highlights the importance of Universal Design for Learning (UDL) principles in ensuring accessible education for all students, including those with disabilities. UDL offers a flexible framework for curriculum development, supporting students by removing barriers to learning and accommodating a wide range of abilities and learning styles. This is essential for inclusive education professionals who seek to create inclusive and adaptive learning environments.

Global Perspectives and Case Studies: By offering insights from diverse countries and contexts, particularly in the Global South, the book expands the understanding of inclusive education's challenges and successes globally. These perspectives provide inclusive education professionals with innovative ideas and strategies that can be adapted and applied in their own contexts, helping to enrich the field with new approaches to inclusivity.

In essence, Global Practices in Inclusive Education Curriculum and Policy enriches the field of Inclusive Education by offering practical strategies, policy insights, and innovative frameworks that can enhance the learning experiences of students with disabilities. It provides a roadmap for educators and policymakers to create more inclusive and supportive educational environments where all learners, regardless of their abilities, can succeed.

Chapter 1
Conceptualizing and Evolution of Inclusive Education:
A Global and National Exploration

Medwin Dikwanyane Sepadi
University of Limpopo, South Africa

ABSTRACT

Inclusive education has emerged as a transformative approach that asserts the right of all students to access quality education, irrespective of their diverse backgrounds and needs. This chapter offers a comprehensive analysis of the conceptualization and evolution of inclusive education, tracing its development from global to national contexts. Through an exploration of historical and social factors, it provides a framework for understanding the key principles underlying inclusive education and their practical implications. Drawing on various scholarly perspectives and international declarations, the chapter emphasizes inclusive education as both a human rights imperative and a strategy for achieving social justice in education systems. Additionally, it examines the challenges and opportunities associated with the implementation of inclusive practices, particularly in settings where resource limitations and pedagogical constraints exist. this chapter contributes to ongoing debates on how best to ensure equitable access to quality education for all learners.

DOI: 10.4018/979-8-3693-4058-5.ch001

INTRODUCTION

Inclusive education has become a cornerstone of educational reform worldwide, representing a shift from exclusionary practices to systems that embrace diversity and equity in education. Defined broadly, inclusive education seeks to ensure that all students, irrespective of their abilities, backgrounds, or personal circumstances, have access to quality education in mainstream settings (UNESCO, 2020). This transformative approach is grounded in the principles of social justice and human rights, aligning with global efforts to dismantle barriers that perpetuate marginalization and exclusion in education (Ainscow, 2022).

The conceptualization of inclusive education, however, remains fluid and multifaceted, shaped by diverse political, social, and economic factors. While the global discourse on inclusive education continues to evolve, challenges persist in translating these ideals into practical, sustainable solutions within national and local contexts (Slee, 2023). The term itself is often subject to varying interpretations, leading to ambiguities in its application across different educational systems (Florian & Spratt, 2022). Consequently, there is a growing need for a deeper understanding of how inclusive education is conceptualized and implemented, particularly in relation to policy, pedagogy, and teacher preparation.

This chapter aims to provide a comprehensive analysis of the conceptualization and evolution of inclusive education from a global to a national perspective, with a particular focus on South Africa. It traces the historical trajectory of inclusive education, examining key international frameworks and national policies that have shaped its development. In doing so, the chapter seeks to offer clarity on the theoretical underpinnings of inclusive education and explore strategies for its effective implementation in diverse educational settings. By analyzing both the philosophical foundations and practical challenges of inclusive education, this chapter contributes to ongoing debates about how best to create equitable and inclusive educational environments for all students (Loreman, 2022).

Tracing the Historical Development of Inclusive Education, with Relevant Sources Integrated:

Historical Development of Inclusive Education

The evolution of inclusive education is deeply rooted in global movements advocating for the rights of marginalized groups, particularly those with disabilities. Its development can be traced through several key international declarations, policies, and social movements that have shifted educational systems from segregation towards inclusion.

The foundations of inclusive education were laid in the aftermath of World War II, with the 1948 Universal Declaration of Human Rights, which affirmed the right to education for all children. This declaration marked the first global recognition that education should be accessible to everyone, without discrimination based on ability, race, or background (UN, 1948). This principle was reinforced in the Convention on the Rights of the Child (1989), which emphasized the right of children with disabilities to be included in mainstream education, rather than segregated into special schools (UN, 1989).

During the 1990s, the concept of inclusive education gained further traction with the World Declaration on Education for All (1990) and the landmark Salamanca Statement (1994). The Salamanca Statement, adopted by over 90 countries, asserted that regular schools with inclusive orientations are "the most effective means of combating discriminatory attitudes, creating welcoming communities, and achieving education for all" (UNESCO, 1994). This was a pivotal moment in the global push for inclusion, as it formally recognized the need for educational systems to adapt to the diverse needs of all learners, regardless of disability.

In the 2000s, the focus shifted toward policy implementation. The Dakar Framework for Action (2000), under the Education for All (EFA) initiative, called for inclusive education to be at the heart of educational policies worldwide. It reinforced the need to address the educational needs of marginalized groups, ensuring that no child is excluded from quality education (UNESCO, 2000). This period also saw the introduction of the UN Convention on the Rights of Persons with Disabilities (2006), which explicitly mandated inclusive education as a human right and called for the removal of barriers to participation in mainstream education (UN, 2006).

In recent decades, inclusive education has continued to evolve, with an increasing emphasis on the practical challenges of implementation. The focus has shifted from merely integrating students with disabilities into mainstream schools to creating genuinely inclusive environments that cater to a wide range of learners, including those from different socioeconomic backgrounds, linguistic minorities, and other marginalized groups (Ainscow, 2022). However, despite international frameworks, many countries continue to struggle with the practical aspects of inclusion, especially in under-resourced regions where teachers may lack the necessary training and support (Florian & Spratt, 2022).

In South Africa, inclusive education has followed a similar trajectory. Post-apartheid reforms in education, such as Education White Paper 6 (2001), aimed to redress historical inequalities by promoting an inclusive education system. This policy framework emphasized the need for all schools to accommodate learners with diverse needs, supported by targeted interventions to remove barriers to learning

(Department of Education, 2001). However, despite progressive policies, the practical implementation of inclusive education in South Africa remains uneven, with many learners still facing exclusion due to systemic issues such as teacher preparedness, resource constraints, and inadequate infrastructure (Romm, Nel & Tlale, 2013)

Figure 1. The historical development of inclusive education. It highlights key milestones such as the 1948 Universal Declaration of Human Rights, the 1989 Convention on the Rights of the Child, the 1994 Salamanca Statement, the 2000 Dakar Framework for Action, and the 2006 Convention on the Rights of Persons with Disabilities. This timeline visually maps the progression of inclusive education policies over time

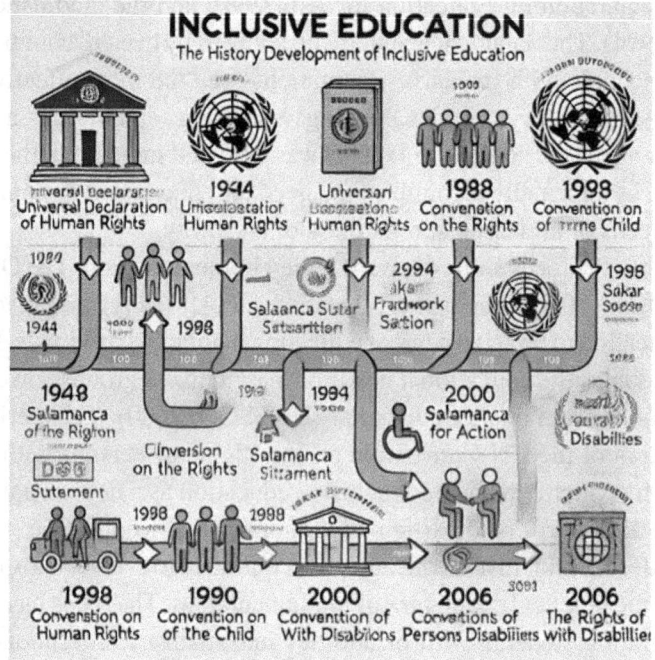

Conceptualisation of Inclusive Education

The concept of inclusive education has evolved significantly over the past decades, yet it remains a contested and multifaceted term. At its core, inclusive education refers to the process of ensuring that all students, irrespective of their abilities, socio-economic status, or cultural background, have access to quality education within mainstream settings (Ainscow, 2022). However, the absence of a universally agreed-upon definition complicates the interpretation and implementation of inclusive education policies across different contexts (Florian & Spratt, 2022).

According to UNESCO (2020), inclusive education is the most effective means of addressing discriminatory attitudes and practices that lead to the exclusion of students with disabilities or those from marginalized backgrounds. This view is reinforced by the belief that regular schools must be equipped to accommodate all children, thereby promoting equity and fostering social cohesion (UNESCO, 2020). The emphasis is on reforming educational systems to meet the diverse needs of all learners through child-centered pedagogy, differentiated instruction, and the removal of barriers to participation (Slee, 2023).

Philosophical approaches to inclusive education are varied, ranging from those that conceptualize inclusion as a fundamental human right to those that emphasize the practical removal of obstacles that prevent access to education. Loreman (2022) highlights that inclusive education is often framed as a movement for social justice, where the goal is to create an equitable learning environment for all students. This aligns with the human rights-based perspective, which asserts that access to education is not only a right but also a critical factor in ensuring the holistic development of individuals (UN, 2022).

The European Agency for Special Needs and Inclusive Education (2021) views inclusive education as essential for the creation of an equitable society, reinforcing the idea that inclusion is not merely about integrating students with disabilities into mainstream classrooms but about transforming the education system to cater to the diverse needs of all students. This broader perspective necessitates a shift away from traditional, deficit-based models of education that view certain learners as needing "special" support, towards a model that views diversity as an asset in the learning environment (Florian & Beaton, 2021).

In the South African context, inclusive education is framed by Education White Paper 6 (2001), which defines it as the process of restructuring schools and teaching methodologies to accommodate all learners. This policy emphasizes the need for systemic change and targeted interventions to ensure that all students, particularly those who have been historically marginalized, have access to quality education (Department of Education, 2001). Despite these efforts, South Africa continues to face challenges in the implementation of inclusive education, with issues such as teacher preparedness, resource limitations, and societal attitudes posing significant barriers (Romm, Nel & Tlale, 2022).

Recent scholarship suggests that inclusive education must also address the intersectionality of students' experiences, recognizing that factors such as race, gender, and socio-economic status can compound barriers to education (Slee, 2023; Ainscow, 2022). As such, inclusive education should not only focus on disability but also on the broader goal of dismantling all forms of exclusion and marginalization within the education system. This requires a critical rethinking of pedagogical practices, school cultures, and policies to create truly inclusive environments (Florian & Spratt, 2022).

Table 1. Variety of ways in which inclusive education is understood and applied, emphasizing that while there is broad agreement on its importance, the methods for achieving it differ depending on philosophical, practical, and policy perspectives

Source/Framework	Conceptual Focus	Key Features	Example of Application
UNESCO (2020)	Human rights and social justice	Inclusive education as a means to combat discriminatory attitudes and ensure education for all.	Mainstream schools are required to accommodate all learners, regardless of ability or background.
European Agency for Special Needs (2021)	Social equity and systemic transformation	Inclusive education as a mechanism for creating a fair and just society, not limited to disability.	Promotes educational reforms that focus on equity, participation, and the elimination of segregation in schools.
Loreman (2022)	Holistic development and diversity	Education is a fundamental right, with a focus on the diversity of learners' needs as assets to the system.	Classroom practices that embrace differentiated instruction, inclusive pedagogy, and collaborative learning.
Slee (2023)	Removal of exclusionary practices	Emphasizes the dismantling of systemic barriers and practices that marginalize learners.	Calls for rethinking the division between "regular" and "special" schools, advocating for schools that remove barriers.
Florian & Beaton (2021)	Inclusive pedagogy and practical implementation	Focuses on classroom-level practices and the development of inclusive teaching methods.	Teachers are encouraged to adopt flexible pedagogies that meet diverse learning needs without labeling students.
South Africa's White Paper 6 (2001)	Policy-driven inclusive education	Provides a structural approach to inclusive education through policy and systemic reform.	Calls for the restructuring of schools and curricula to ensure equitable access for all students, especially in under-resourced areas.

THE EVOLUTION OF INCLUSIVE EDUCATION

Inclusive education has undergone a significant transformation globally, moving from the margins of educational discourse to becoming a central component of policies aimed at ensuring equitable access to quality education for all learners. This evolution reflects a growing commitment to addressing exclusionary practices and promoting diversity within education systems worldwide. The historical progression of inclusive education, while globally recognized, has been shaped by continental and regional factors that have influenced how different nations approach and implement inclusive policies.

Global Context

The global movement towards inclusive education can be traced back to key human rights frameworks established in the mid-20th century. The Universal Declaration of Human Rights (1948) affirmed that education is a fundamental right for all individuals, marking the beginning of international efforts to ensure that all children, regardless of their circumstances, have access to quality education (UN, 1948). The Convention on the Rights of the Child (1989) expanded on this, emphasizing that children with disabilities must be included in mainstream education systems (United Nations, 1989). These early milestones laid the foundation for the global push towards inclusive education in subsequent decades.

A pivotal moment came with the Salamanca Statement (1994), which called for inclusive education to be the cornerstone of national education policies globally. The statement, endorsed by over 90 governments, argued that regular schools with inclusive orientations are the most effective means to combat exclusion and promote social cohesion (UNESCO, 1994). This declaration was followed by the Dakar Framework for Action (2000), which reaffirmed the global commitment to inclusive education as part of the broader goal of achieving Education for All (UNESCO, 2000). The United Nations Convention on the Rights of Persons with Disabilities (2006) further emphasized the need for inclusive education as a human right, calling on governments to remove all barriers to participation in mainstream education (UN, 2006).

More recently, UNESCO's Global Education Monitoring Report (2020) reinforced the importance of inclusive education as a global standard, pointing out that despite international commitments, exclusionary practices still persist, particularly for children with disabilities, girls, and children from marginalized communities (UNESCO, 2020).

Continental Aspects

Across different continents, the conceptualization and implementation of inclusive education have been shaped by unique historical, social, and economic factors. In Europe, the focus on inclusive education has been driven by broader social justice movements, leading to the development of comprehensive policies aimed at ensuring that all students, regardless of their abilities or backgrounds, are included in mainstream education. The European Agency for Special Needs and Inclusive Education (2021) has played a significant role in promoting inclusive education as an essential component of equitable and socially just societies, arguing that inclusion is not limited to disability but should encompass all forms of diversity, including race, gender, and socio-economic status (European Agency, 2021).

In North America, inclusive education has evolved through a legal framework, with landmark legislation such as the Individuals with Disabilities Education Act (IDEA) in the United States, which mandates that students with disabilities must be provided with a free and appropriate public education in the least restrictive environment (Turnbull et al., 2022). This legal mandate has significantly shaped how inclusive education is implemented across the United States and has influenced policies in Canada as well.

In Asia, countries such as Japan and South Korea have adopted inclusive education policies, but these have often been limited by cultural attitudes towards disability and special education. In recent years, however, there has been a shift towards more inclusive models, driven by international pressures and local advocacy movements (Yamaguchi, 2021).

In Africa, the evolution of inclusive education has been shaped by the continent's colonial history, economic constraints, and socio-political challenges. The adoption of inclusive education policies across many African countries has been slow, often constrained by limited resources, infrastructural deficits, and the challenge of meeting the basic educational needs of all children. However, continental frameworks such as the African Union's Continental Education Strategy for Africa (2016-2025) have recognized the importance of inclusive education as a critical goal for the continent's development. This strategy emphasizes the need to address all forms of exclusion in education, including those based on disability, gender, and socio-economic status (African Union, 2016).

Regional Context

In the African region, there has been a growing recognition of the importance of inclusive education as a tool for fostering social cohesion and addressing the educational disparities caused by colonial legacies. Countries such as Kenya and Rwanda have made significant strides in policy formulation aimed at promoting inclusive education, but challenges in implementation remain due to a lack of infrastructure, teacher training, and funding (Riechi, 2022). In West Africa, nations like Ghana have similarly integrated inclusive education into their national education strategies, but they face obstacles in terms of resource allocation and societal attitudes towards disability and difference (Anamuah-Mensah et al., 2023).

In Southern Africa, the evolution of inclusive education has been influenced by the socio-political changes brought about by the end of apartheid. South Africa, in particular, has taken significant steps towards creating an inclusive education system that addresses the inequalities and exclusions created by its apartheid past.

South Africa: A National Context

In South Africa, inclusive education emerged as a key component of post-apartheid educational reforms. The White Paper on Education and Training (1995) and Education White Paper 6 (2001) laid the foundation for the establishment of an inclusive education system aimed at redressing the educational inequalities entrenched by apartheid (Department of Education, 2001). These policies defined inclusive education as the process of restructuring schools and teaching methodologies to accommodate learners with diverse learning needs, including those with disabilities.

Education White Paper 6 (2001) focused on creating "full-service schools" that could support learners with disabilities within mainstream educational environments. The policy emphasized systemic transformation, advocating for a child-centered approach to teaching and learning that would cater to the diverse needs of all learners (Department of Education, 2001). The South African government's commitment to inclusive education is aligned with global initiatives, particularly those outlined in the Salamanca Statement and the UN Convention on the Rights of Persons with Disabilities.

However, despite progressive policies, the implementation of inclusive education in South Africa has been hindered by a range of challenges. These include resource limitations, insufficient teacher training, and societal attitudes towards disability, which continue to affect the full realization of inclusive practices (Romm, Nel & Tlale, 2022). Moreover, many rural schools face infrastructural challenges, which further complicate efforts to implement inclusive education (Florian & Spratt, 2022).

Recent initiatives have aimed to address these challenges by enhancing teacher training programs, increasing government funding, and promoting advocacy campaigns that seek to shift societal attitudes towards inclusion. These efforts reflect the ongoing evolution of inclusive education in South Africa, as the country continues to grapple with the legacy of apartheid while striving to create an equitable education system for all learners (Slee, 2023).

Successes of Inclusive Education

Inclusive education initiatives have made significant strides globally, from international frameworks to national policies, enhancing access to education for diverse learners. The period from 2020 to 2024 has seen particular successes in advancing inclusive education across different levels, with a focus on addressing exclusion, enhancing teacher training, and transforming schools into equitable learning environments. This section highlights key achievements in inclusive education across global, continental, regional, and local contexts, with contemporary examples.

Global Successes (2020-2024)

At the global level, the continued implementation of the United Nations Convention on the Rights of Persons with Disabilities (CRPD) and the push to meet the Sustainable Development Goals (SDGs) have driven forward inclusive education efforts. SDG 4, which aims to ensure inclusive and equitable quality education for all by 2030, has seen significant progress, with inclusive education being prioritized in many international agendas.

One of the most notable global successes has been the Global Education Monitoring Report (2020), which reinforced the need for inclusive education systems as part of the international commitment to "leave no one behind." In particular, it highlighted the importance of inclusive approaches to countering inequalities in education exacerbated by the COVID-19 pandemic, especially for children with disabilities and those from marginalized communities (UNESCO, 2020). Following this, UNESCO's 2023 report emphasized the integration of digital technologies to support inclusive education, citing success in countries like India and Chile, where digital learning has been used to bring education to remote and underrepresented communities during the pandemic (UNESCO, 2023).

In Italy, where inclusive education has long been a priority, recent evaluations in 2021 showed continued success in maintaining fully inclusive classrooms, even during the COVID-19 crisis. The use of individualized educational plans and ongoing support for teachers ensured that students with disabilities were not left behind despite the challenges posed by the shift to remote learning (D'Alessio, 2021).

Continental Successes

Across continents, inclusive education has seen varied but significant successes in recent years. In Europe, the European Agency for Special Needs and Inclusive Education has spearheaded initiatives to support countries in implementing inclusive policies. In 2021, the European Commission launched the Union of Equality:

Strategy for the Rights of Persons with Disabilities 2021-2030, which prioritized inclusive education as a central goal (European Commission, 2021). Countries like Finland have been leaders in the practical implementation of inclusive education, with recent reports showing that their flexible, equity-focused education system continues to offer strong support for diverse learners, resulting in one of the most inclusive education systems globally (Sahlberg, 2022).

In Africa, the Continental Education Strategy for Africa (CESA 2016-2025) continued to play a key role in advocating for inclusive education across the continent. In Ghana, the Inclusive Education Policy has made substantial progress by 2023, with an increase in the enrollment of children with disabilities in mainstream schools. Teacher training has been a central component of Ghana's success, with government initiatives focusing on equipping teachers with the skills to handle diverse learners (Anamuah-Mensah et al., 2023).

In Asia, countries like Japan have made notable strides in inclusive education. Following the adoption of new policies in 2021, Japan saw a significant increase in the integration of students with disabilities into regular classrooms. The use of assistive technologies and continuous professional development for teachers were key factors in these successes (Yamaguchi, 2021).

Regional Successes

At the regional level, East Africa has seen positive developments in inclusive education initiatives, particularly in Kenya and Rwanda. Kenya's Sector Policy for Learners and Trainees with Disabilities (2018) was evaluated in 2022, showing that increased government funding and international support had led to improvements in the accessibility of education for learners with disabilities, particularly in urban areas. This success is evident in the increasing number of schools adopting inclusive practices, thanks to partnerships between the government and non-governmental organizations (Mutisya & Kanaga, 2022).

In Latin America, Brazil has continued to strengthen its inclusive education system despite challenges posed by the pandemic. The National Policy on Special Education from the Perspective of Inclusive Education was further evaluated in 2021, revealing that over 90% of students with disabilities are now integrated into mainstream schools, supported by special education resource centers and teacher aides. Brazil's model of combining inclusive policies with dedicated support services has been highlighted as a regional success (Alves, 2021).

Local Successes

In South Africa, the implementation of inclusive education initiatives has progressed, especially since the government's renewed focus on strengthening the Education White Paper 6 policies during the 2020-2024 period. Local initiatives, supported by national policies such as the Screening, Identification, Assessment, and Support (SIAS) Policy, have enabled better identification and support for learners with disabilities.

One of the standout local successes has been the work of the Inclusive Education South Africa (IESA) organization, which has led several community-based projects focused on improving teacher capacity and raising awareness about inclusive education in schools. In 2022, IESA launched a digital learning initiative aimed at training teachers remotely, which has enabled educators in under-resourced areas to access continuous professional development in inclusive practices (IESA, 2022).

In provinces like Gauteng and the Western Cape, there has been a significant increase in the number of full-service schools catering to diverse learning needs. By 2023, full-service schools reported increased enrollment of students with disabilities, thanks to improved teacher training, better resource allocation, and ongoing community involvement (Romm, Nel & Tlale, 2022). These local successes demonstrate South Africa's ongoing commitment to creating an inclusive education system that caters to the needs of all learners, despite the challenges posed by historical inequalities and resource limitations.

Inclusive education initiatives have achieved significant successes globally, continentally, regionally, and locally from 2020 to 2024. These achievements highlight the importance of inclusive policies, teacher training, the use of assistive technologies, and community involvement in ensuring equitable access to education for all learners. Countries such as Italy, Finland, Ghana, Japan, Brazil, and South Africa provide powerful examples of how inclusive education can be successfully implemented, offering valuable lessons for other nations striving to make their education systems more inclusive.

Discussion

Contentious Aspects of Inclusive Education: Critiques and Potential Solutions

While inclusive education is widely regarded as a progressive and necessary approach to achieving educational equity, it remains a complex and contested concept. Several contentious aspects have emerged as countries and educational systems attempt to define, implement, and sustain inclusive education practices. These challenges include definitional ambiguity, resource constraints, teacher preparedness, societal attitudes, and systemic barriers. In this section, we discuss these contentious aspects, offer critiques, and propose potential solutions for improving the understanding and implementation of inclusive education.

Definitional Ambiguity

One of the most significant contentious aspects of inclusive education is its lack of a clear, universally accepted definition. Inclusive education is conceptualized differently across countries, cultures, and educational systems, leading to variations in how it is understood and applied. Some scholars argue that the term is too broad, encompassing everything from disability inclusion to the integration of students from diverse ethnic, linguistic, and socioeconomic backgrounds (Florian & Beaton, 2021).

Critique: This broadness can dilute the focus of inclusive education and create inconsistencies in implementation. Teachers, policymakers, and school administrators may interpret inclusive education in ways that are convenient or limited by their local contexts, leading to uneven application across schools and regions (Loreman, 2022).

Potential Solution: To address this issue, there is a need for more context-specific frameworks that provide clarity while maintaining the core principles of inclusion. National policies can establish clear guidelines that define inclusive education according to local needs while adhering to international standards such as the *Convention on the Rights of Persons with Disabilities* (UN, 2006). Collaborative efforts between governments, educational institutions, and international bodies like UNESCO could help create a global framework with adaptable guidelines to address local variations.

Resource Constraints

Resource limitations, including inadequate funding, insufficient infrastructure, and lack of teaching materials, remain a significant barrier to the successful implementation of inclusive education, particularly in low- and middle-income countries. In many cases, schools lack the resources to accommodate diverse learners, especially those with disabilities who may require specialized equipment or learning aids (Ainscow, 2022).

Critique: Resource scarcity leads to a situation where inclusive education policies are often aspirational rather than practical. Without adequate funding and infrastructure, schools struggle to create learning environments that are truly inclusive. As a result, students with disabilities or learning difficulties may remain marginalized even in so-called inclusive schools (Romm, Nel & Tlale, 2022).

Potential Solution: Governments and international donors must prioritize funding for inclusive education to ensure the necessary resources are available. Innovative solutions such as partnerships with private sectors, non-governmental organizations (NGOs), and tech companies can provide access to assistive technologies and adaptive learning materials. Additionally, allocating resources to build full-service schools that cater to diverse learners can help ensure that inclusive education is not just a policy on paper but a reality in practice.

Teacher Preparedness and Professional Development

Another critical issue in inclusive education is the lack of teacher preparedness. Many teachers feel inadequately trained to handle the complexities of inclusive classrooms, which often involve managing a wide range of learning needs, from students with disabilities to those from varied cultural or linguistic backgrounds (Forlin & Chambers, 2022).

Critique: Teachers frequently report feeling overwhelmed by the demands of inclusive education, citing a lack of professional development and support. This leads to frustration and inconsistent practices in classrooms, where some students may receive the attention they need while others do not. In many cases, teachers resort to exclusionary practices, such as referring students to special schools or segregating them within the classroom, undermining the goal of inclusion (Loreman, 2022).

Potential Solution: To address this, teacher education programs need to include robust training in inclusive pedagogy. Continuous professional development opportunities should be made available for in-service teachers, focusing on differentiated instruction, classroom management, and the use of assistive technologies. Schools can also foster a culture of collaboration, where teachers can share best practices and learn from one another. Additionally, governments should provide funding for additional support staff, such as classroom assistants or special education teachers, to alleviate the burden on mainstream teachers.

Societal Attitudes and Cultural Resistance

Societal attitudes towards disability, diversity, and difference continue to present challenges to the full realization of inclusive education. In many societies, stigma and discrimination against individuals with disabilities or from marginalized communities persist, affecting how inclusive education is perceived and implemented.

Cultural norms that prioritize academic performance or traditional teaching methods may also clash with inclusive practices (Slee, 2023).

Critique: Societal attitudes can significantly hinder the success of inclusive education. When inclusion is not valued at a societal level, it becomes more difficult to foster inclusive practices within schools. Teachers may feel unsupported in their efforts, and families of children with disabilities may be reluctant to enroll their children in mainstream schools due to fear of bullying or inadequate care (Yamaguchi, 2021).

Potential Solution: Awareness campaigns and community engagement initiatives are crucial in changing societal perceptions of inclusive education. Governments and NGOs can collaborate to promote the benefits of inclusive education, emphasizing how it contributes to a more equitable society. Schools can involve families in the inclusion process, creating strong home-school partnerships that reinforce the value of diversity. Additionally, fostering inclusive school cultures through student leadership programs and peer support systems can help reduce stigma and promote positive attitudes toward diversity.

Systemic and Structural Barriers

Systemic barriers, including rigid curricula, inflexible assessment systems, and exclusionary school policies, also pose significant challenges to the successful implementation of inclusive education. In many educational systems, standardized testing and narrow definitions of academic success exclude students who do not fit the traditional mold of learning, such as those with intellectual disabilities or different learning styles (Florian & Spratt, 2022).

Critique: These systemic barriers perpetuate the exclusion of certain learners, reinforcing the idea that only certain students can achieve success in mainstream schools. This contradicts the core principles of inclusive education, which call for a flexible and responsive education system that meets the needs of all learners (Ainscow, 2022).

Potential Solution: Educational systems must adopt more flexible curricula and assessment methods that accommodate diverse learning styles and abilities. Schools can implement alternative forms of assessment, such as portfolio-based evaluations, which allow students to demonstrate their learning in various ways. Furthermore, policies should be revised to ensure that schools are held accountable for creating inclusive environments, with regular audits to monitor progress and identify areas for improvement.

The contentious aspects of inclusive education highlight the challenges of turning a global ideal into practical, everyday reality. However, these challenges also offer opportunities for growth and innovation. By addressing definitional ambiguities, improving resource allocation, enhancing teacher preparedness, shifting societal attitudes, and removing systemic barriers, inclusive education can become more effective and sustainable. As countries and communities continue to navigate these challenges, the goal of ensuring equitable, inclusive education for all remains within reach, provided that these critiques are met with thoughtful, coordinated solutions.

Future Directions for Inclusive Education

As inclusive education continues to evolve, it is essential to address existing challenges while envisioning a more equitable and inclusive future. This section presents suggested future directions for inclusive education, highlighting key initiatives and reforms at the global, continental, regional, and local levels.

Global Future Directions

Globally, the primary future direction for inclusive education will be the alignment with the Sustainable Development Goals (SDGs), particularly SDG 4, which aims to ensure inclusive and equitable quality education by 2030. While significant progress has been made, the international community must intensify efforts to address disparities in access to inclusive education, especially for students with disabilities and those from marginalized backgrounds.

Global Cooperation and Knowledge Sharing: A key future direction will be fostering stronger international cooperation to share best practices, innovations, and research. Global bodies like UNESCO, the United Nations, and the World Bank can enhance their role by facilitating global platforms where countries can exchange knowledge on inclusive practices, policies, and technologies. This would ensure that nations with fewer resources can benefit from global advancements in inclusive education.

Technological Integration: The global community must invest in digital infrastructure to support inclusive education, especially in light of the COVID-19 pandemic, which has accelerated the adoption of remote learning. Technologies such as assistive learning tools, artificial intelligence (AI), and inclusive digital platforms will be critical in ensuring all students can access education, regardless of physical or geographical barriers (UNESCO, 2023).

Global Standards for Inclusive Education: Establishing universal standards and metrics for inclusive education can provide clearer guidelines and accountability. These standards could help ensure that countries not only adopt inclusive policies but also implement them effectively. International benchmarks could monitor progress in areas such as teacher training, infrastructure, and curriculum adaptation (Florian & Beaton, 2021).

Continental Future Directions

Across continents, the future of inclusive education will be shaped by the unique socio-economic and political contexts of each region. However, certain common themes are likely to emerge.

Africa: Strengthening Policy Implementation and Teacher Capacity: As outlined in the Continental Education Strategy for Africa (CESA 2016-2025), the future of inclusive education on the African continent depends heavily on strengthening policy implementation. While many African nations have adopted inclusive education policies, the real challenge lies in turning these policies into actionable frameworks. This will require substantial investment in teacher training, resource allocation, and infrastructure development (African Union, 2016). African governments must prioritize inclusive education in their national budgets and engage in capacity-building efforts to equip teachers with the skills to manage diverse classrooms (Anamuah-Mensah et al., 2023).

Europe: Inclusive Curricula and Diverse Assessment Models: In Europe, where inclusive education is more advanced, the future will involve refining inclusive curricula and adopting diverse assessment models. There will be an increasing push towards creating curricula that reflect and respect the diversity of learners, not only focusing on students with disabilities but also addressing issues of cultural and linguistic diversity (European Commission, 2021). Assessment models that go beyond standardized testing and embrace alternative methods such as portfolio-based evaluations or collaborative projects will also be crucial in ensuring that all students can demonstrate their learning achievements (Sahlberg, 2022).

Asia: Breaking Cultural Barriers and Expanding Access: In Asia, a critical future direction will be overcoming cultural barriers that view disability as a taboo or disadvantage. Countries such as Japan and South Korea are already making strides in this area by introducing public awareness campaigns and creating more inclusive policies (Yamaguchi, 2021). Expanding access to inclusive education will also involve bridging the gap between urban and rural areas, where resource availability and societal attitudes may differ. Greater integration of assistive technologies and digital tools will be essential in reaching remote communities and fostering inclusion across diverse regions.

Regional Future Directions

At the regional level, future directions will involve adapting global and continental initiatives to the specific needs of regions while addressing local challenges such as resource allocation, cultural resistance, and infrastructural disparities.

East Africa: Expanding Inclusive School Networks: In regions like East Africa, expanding the network of inclusive schools will be a critical step forward. Countries such as Kenya and Rwanda have made progress by establishing model inclusive schools, but scaling these efforts will require government investment and international support. Future policies should focus on creating more inclusive schools, particularly in rural and underserved areas, ensuring that all children have access to the resources and support they need (Mutisya & Kanaga, 2022).

Latin America: Integrating Inclusive Practices with Social Justice: In Latin America, the future of inclusive education will involve integrating inclusive practices with broader social justice goals. In countries like Brazil, inclusive education has been linked to addressing systemic inequalities rooted in race, gender, and socio-economic status. Future initiatives will need to continue focusing on reducing disparities by aligning inclusive education with national equity agendas, ensuring that the most vulnerable populations are prioritized in education reforms (Alves, 2021).

Local Future Directions: South Africa

At the local level, countries like South Africa will need to focus on addressing gaps in policy implementation and enhancing community involvement in inclusive education.

Scaling Full-Service Schools: In South Africa, one of the key future directions is to expand the network of "full-service schools," which cater to learners with diverse needs. By 2024, South Africa aims to have significantly increased the number of such schools, ensuring that they are adequately resourced and staffed. This expansion will be essential in addressing the exclusion of children with disabilities from mainstream education (Department of Education, 2022).

Improving Teacher Training and Support Systems: South Africa's future direction in inclusive education must also prioritize improving teacher training and professional development. The integration of inclusive practices into teacher education programs will ensure that all teachers are equipped to handle diverse classrooms. Continuous in-service training will also be critical in keeping teachers up-to-date with the latest pedagogical strategies and technologies (Romm, Nel & Tlale, 2022).

Community Engagement and Advocacy: Future initiatives must involve greater community engagement and advocacy for inclusive education. South Africa's success in inclusive education will depend not only on government policies but also on the active participation of parents, caregivers, and local communities. Future directions should focus on raising awareness about the benefits of inclusive education and dismantling societal stigma towards learners with disabilities (IESA, 2022).

The future of inclusive education will depend on a multi-level approach that spans global, continental, regional, and local contexts. While significant progress has been made, the challenges that remain will require innovative solutions, policy reforms, and continuous collaboration between governments, international organizations, and local communities. By focusing on technology integration, teacher capacity-building, resource allocation, and societal awareness, inclusive education can continue to move toward a future where all learners, regardless of their backgrounds or abilities, have equal opportunities to succeed.

RECOMMENDATIONS

Clarify the Definition of Inclusive Education

Global Level: There should be a clearer, globally recognized framework for inclusive education that defines its scope, particularly in relation to diverse learner needs (disability, socio-economic status, language, and cultural background). While maintaining flexibility, this framework should help countries adapt inclusive education models to their local contexts without diluting the core principles of equity and inclusion.

National Level: Governments should ensure that national policies on inclusive education provide clear definitions and guidelines to avoid varied interpretations, ensuring that all stakeholders, educators, administrators, and communities are aligned in their understanding of inclusion.

Invest in Teacher Training and Professional Development

Continental and Regional Levels: Future policies must emphasize capacity-building for teachers. Governments and educational authorities should prioritize the integration of inclusive pedagogy in teacher education programs. Continuous professional development opportunities, including specialized training in managing diverse classrooms, should be available to all educators.

Local Level: Schools should establish mentorship and peer-support systems where experienced teachers can assist their colleagues in adopting inclusive teaching practices.

Increase Resource Allocation for Inclusive Education

Global and National Levels: Governments and international organizations should prioritize funding for inclusive education. Adequate resources are essential to ensure schools can meet the needs of all learners, particularly those with disabilities. This includes improving infrastructure, providing assistive technologies, and employing additional support staff such as teaching assistants and special education professionals.

Regional Level: Regional cooperation among neighboring countries should focus on sharing resources, particularly in low-income areas where schools face significant infrastructural challenges.

Develop Inclusive Curricula and Assessment Models

National and Continental Levels: Education systems should develop curricula that are inclusive and culturally responsive. Assessment methods must be adapted to measure diverse learners' progress, moving beyond standardized testing to embrace more flexible and holistic evaluation techniques such as portfolio assessments, projects, and experiential learning.

Local Level: Schools should implement differentiated instruction to meet individual learner needs and ensure that diverse students can succeed in an inclusive classroom environment.

Enhance Community Engagement and Advocacy

Local Level: Parents and community members should be actively involved in the implementation of inclusive education. Schools must work to raise awareness about the benefits of inclusive education and dismantle societal stigmas against learners with disabilities and those from marginalized communities.

National Level: Governments should launch advocacy campaigns to promote inclusive education, highlighting the social, academic, and economic benefits of creating inclusive learning environments.

Leverage Technology for Inclusive Education

Global and National Levels: As demonstrated by the rapid adoption of technology during the COVID-19 pandemic, digital tools and assistive technologies can significantly enhance inclusive education. Governments and international organizations should invest in digital infrastructure, ensuring equitable access to technology for students in both urban and rural areas.

Regional and Local Levels: Schools and communities should integrate technology in everyday learning, using it to support students with diverse learning needs through personalized learning apps, digital assistive devices, and remote learning platforms.

Address Societal Attitudes and Cultural Barriers

Regional and Local Levels: To foster inclusive education, it is essential to change societal attitudes toward disability, difference, and diversity. Educational institutions, governments, and civil society organizations must engage in consistent advocacy to promote the value of inclusion. This can be achieved through awareness campaigns, teacher training on cultural sensitivity, and integrating diversity into school curricula.

Strengthen Monitoring and Accountability Mechanisms

National Level: Countries should develop robust mechanisms for monitoring the implementation of inclusive education policies. Regular audits and assessments should be conducted to evaluate the effectiveness of policies, resource allocation, and teacher preparedness. Governments must hold schools accountable for meeting inclusive education standards and ensure that all students receive equitable educational opportunities.

CONCLUSION

Inclusive education has emerged as a transformative approach that seeks to provide equitable access to quality education for all learners, regardless of their backgrounds, abilities, or socio-economic status. This chapter has traced the historical evolution of inclusive education, from global initiatives such as the Universal Declaration of Human Rights and the Salamanca Statement, to regional and national efforts, particularly in South Africa. Through this analysis, it is evident that inclusive education is not just a pedagogical framework but a fundamental human rights issue aligned with global efforts to achieve social justice and equality.

Despite the widespread adoption of inclusive education policies, its implementation remains complex and fraught with challenges. Definitional ambiguities, inadequate resources, teacher preparedness, and societal attitudes continue to hinder the full realization of inclusive practices in many contexts. However, several successes have been noted globally, continentally, regionally, and locally, from Italy's well-established inclusive schooling model to South Africa's efforts to expand full-service schools. These examples demonstrate that, when effectively implemented, inclusive education can provide meaningful opportunities for all learners to participate in and benefit from mainstream education.

This chapter also critically examined the contentious aspects of inclusive education, offering critiques and potential solutions. Key issues such as teacher training, resource constraints, and systemic barriers were discussed, with recommendations for improving both the understanding and implementation of inclusive education at all levels. The importance of community engagement, advocacy, and technological integration was highlighted as essential for fostering more inclusive educational environments.

Looking ahead, the future of inclusive education requires a concerted effort from international organizations, governments, educators, and communities. Global frameworks like the Sustainable Development Goals (SDGs) provide a clear roadmap, but success will depend on context-specific policies that address local realities. A key priority must be ensuring that all schools are adequately resourced and that teachers are equipped with the skills needed to manage diverse classrooms. Additionally, societal attitudes must shift to embrace the value of diversity, with inclusive education seen not as an obligation but as an opportunity to enrich learning environments for all.

Ultimately, the journey toward fully inclusive education is ongoing. While significant progress has been made, particularly in policy development, the gap between policy and practice remains a critical area for improvement. By focusing on practical solutions such as increased funding, teacher capacity building, and technological innovation, stakeholders at all levels can work together to create education systems that truly leave no learner behind.

REFERENCES

African Union. (2016). *Continental Education Strategy for Africa 2016-2025*. African Union.

Ainscow, M. (2022). *Inclusive education: Rethinking the task of creating equity in schools*. Routledge.

Alves, F. (2021). Inclusive education in Brazil: Progress and challenges post-pandemic. *International Journal of Inclusive Education*, 26(3), 305–320.

Anamuah-Mensah, J., Adjei, A., & Agyemang, K. (2023). Inclusive education in Ghana: Progress and challenges. *Journal of African Education*, 10(1), 12–34.

D'Alessio, S. (2021). Inclusive education in Italy: A comprehensive approach to equity and participation. *European Journal of Special Education Research*, 9(1), 45–63.

Department of Education. (2001). *Education White Paper 6: Special Needs Education: Building an Inclusive Education and Training System*. Pretoria: Government Printers.

European Agency for Special Needs and Inclusive Education. (2021). *Inclusive education in action: Lessons from practice*. European Agency.

European Commission. (2021). *Union of Equality: Strategy for the Rights of Persons with Disabilities 2021-2030*. European Commission.

Florian, L., & Beaton, M. (2021). *Inclusive pedagogy in action: A framework for teaching and learning*. Cambridge University Press.

Florian, L., & Spratt, J. (2022). *The complexity of inclusion: Understanding and addressing inclusive education practices*. Cambridge University Press.

Inclusive Education South Africa (IESA). (2022). *Annual Report 2022*. IESA.

Loreman, T. (2022). *Inclusive Education: Supporting Diversity in the Classroom* (3rd ed.). SAGE Publications.

Mutisya, P. M., & Kanaga, M. (2022). Inclusive education in Kenya: Policy, practice, and progress. *East African Journal of Education Research*, 4(2), 78–92.

Romm, N., Nel, M., & Tlale, L. (2013). Inclusive education in South Africa: Progress and challenges. *International Journal of Inclusive Education*, 17(4), 435–452.

Romm, N., Nel, M., & Tlale, L. (2022). Challenges in implementing inclusive education in South Africa: A critical analysis. *International Journal of Inclusive Education*, 25(6), 543–560.

Sahlberg, P. (2022). *Finnish lessons 3.0: What can the world learn from educational change in Finland?* Teachers College Press.

Slee, R. (2023). *Inclusive schooling: Reframing the discourse on exclusion and integration.* Routledge.

Turnbull, H. R., Turnbull, A. P., Wehmeyer, M. L., & Shogren, K. A. (2022). Individuals with Disabilities Education Act (IDEA) and its impact on inclusive education in the United States. *The Journal of Special Education*, 56(4), 250–268.

UNESCO. (1994). *The Salamanca Statement and Framework for Action on Special Needs Education.* UNESCO.

UNESCO. (2000). *Dakar Framework for Action: Education for All: Meeting our Collective Commitments.* UNESCO.

UNESCO. (2020). *Global Education Monitoring Report 2020: Inclusion and education: All means all.* UNESCO Publishing.

UNESCO. (2023). *Global Education Monitoring Report 2023: Technology and inclusion in education.* UNESCO Publishing.

United Nations (UN). (1948). *Universal Declaration of Human Rights.* United Nations.

United Nations (UN). (1989). *Convention on the Rights of the Child.* United Nations.

United Nations (UN). (2006). *Convention on the Rights of Persons with Disabilities.* United Nations.

United Nations (UN). (2022). *Convention on the Rights of Persons with Disabilities and its Optional Protocol.* United Nations.

Yamaguchi, Y. (2021). Inclusive education reforms in Japan: An analysis of policy changes and implementation challenges. *Asian Education Review*, 14(3), 123–145.

Chapter 2
Teacher Empathy in Schools:
Inclusivity and Sustainable Education in a Global South Context

Francis R. Ackah-Jnr
https://orcid.org/0000-0002-2261-4092
Griffith University, Australia

John K. Appiah
https://orcid.org/0000-0001-7717-8614
University of Cape Coast, Ghana

Awudu Salaam Mohammed
https://orcid.org/0000-0002-8915-4393
University of Cape Coast, Ghana

ABSTRACT

International best practice, policy directive and buy-in underpin the adoption of a more transformative and inclusive approach to education. However, socio-cultural, economic, and political forces in the global South, coupled with resistive school practices and discrimination often lead to the exclusion of learners. Informed by learner diversities and the lingering effects of COVID-19, the chapter argues for empathy in inclusive education. The effective embedment of empathy at the heart of school practice pedagogically, physically, socially, and emotionally can leverage inclusivity for all learners. Empathy, the capacity to share a person's feelings and emotions, is also the foundation of what makes schools securing and supporting, teachers intentional and responsive, families caring and kind, and societies accept-

ing and resourcing. This chapter essentialises empathy, inclusivity and sustainable education, teacher inclusive roles and empathic practices. Implications are offered on supporting teachers and improving their preparation to promote empathic inclusive education.

INTRODUCTION

This chapter draws attention to deploying empathy at the heart of school practice to promote inclusivity for all learners and sustainable education. Education is a powerful tool and a cornerstone for development (Ackah-Jnr, 2016). It shapes society and the extent to which schools that are inclusive or exclusive and welcoming or restrictive impact on the education and lives of children. The relevance of education—socially, psychologically, politically, economically, morally, or otherwise—is much more evident in how people feel a sense of belonging and urge to play, learn, or work together. While education is an invaluable human right for all children, *just* being in school is not an automatic assurance of learning, or a guarantee to receive appropriate education. Undeniably, many children are out of school; others do not have access; others are dissatisfied with education; and others still do not engage in any form of education. The benefits of education and schooling are widely recognized; however, these are incommensurate in the global South, including in Ghana, with a high concentration of children with some vulnerable to disability, disadvantage, and risk that fuel minimization, disempowerment, and alienation in schools and society (Ackah-Jnr, 2020a).

To expand and maximize learning experiences, social interactions and educative communities for all learners, global countries are enacting inclusive education as a blueprint policy, practice, and provision. Inclusive education refers to a process of actions that embraces diversity and builds a sense of belonging and appreciates the value and potential of every learner (UNESCO, 2021) and creates connections and motivation in schools (Ackah-Jnr, 2022). Successful inclusive education can ensure the provision of quality education, improve learners' outcomes, and promote long-term social inclusion (Kefallinou et al., 2020). For this to happen, effective teachers (Ackah-Jnr & Udah, 2021; Donath et al., 2023) with knowledge and skills to meet expectations (Salifu et al., 2024) of inclusive education are needed. These teachers also require positive qualities such as empathy, caring and passion, and they recognize the importance of being teachers for all students (McLeskey et al., 2017). Key studies (Bohns & Flynn, 2021; Gates & Curwood, 2023; Makoelle, 2019; Sousa & Tomlinson, 2018) identify teacher empathy to be valuable. Empathy is central to student learning, teaching, and socialization, and considered the foundation of what makes a school caring and secure, a teacher responsive and intentional, and a community welcoming and accepting. Ingraining empathy in inclusive practice can open more windows of hope, possibilities, and motivation for learners.

If schools and education futures are to be truly inclusive, fair, and sustaining, then empathy and inclusive education cannot be separated. Empathy, the ability to understand and share a person's feelings and emotions from their view, is crucial to inclusive classrooms. UNESCO (2022) indicated that empathy makes teaching and learning more inclusive, motivating, and empowering for not only students, but also teachers themselves. Empathy can foster healthy environments and affectionate interactions among students and teachers. Based on empathy's value, schools should operationalize learning contexts that are securing, enabling, and supporting all learners. Teacher empathy is not only a prerequisite for inclusive education but also a powerful lever for promoting understanding, compassion, and belonging (Makoelle, 2019).

Amid the socio-cultural, economic, and political influences in the global South, including Ghana, that were deepened by the COVID-19 pandemic, inclusivity, founded on empathy, becomes essential in promoting sustainable education. Ghana is selected as a case to foreground the need for empathy in teacher practice as it attempts to promote inclusivity in education and social contexts and negotiates its development pathways. To the best of our knowledge, little research exists on the recognition and need to embed empathy in inclusive education in Ghana. The authors believe empathy and empathic teachers are instrumental in enabling inclusive practice. The chapter essentializes mainly empathy, teacher inclusive roles and ways of embedding empathy at the heart of inclusivity. As background, the chapter reviews the socio-cultural and economic contexts of the global South that shape inclusive education. It delves into the definition, interplay and relevancy of inclusivity and sustainable education. The chapter ends with how to support teachers to promote empathic inclusive education within a diverse, changing school environment and society.

BACKGROUND

As the move to inclusivity in education intensifies and finds traction internationally and in Ghana, much premium is being placed on what policy, research and practice can create better and effective schools that optimizes participation and engagement experiences and success for all learners, including those with diverse abilities and needs. Strong commitment to inclusive education, beginning in early childhood, is conceived to be significant in attenuating early inequities and disadvantages and advancing young learners' growth, development, and functioning. Inclusion promises equitable and quality education and human and social capital development for nation building. Inclusivity is important to all learners, schools, teachers, and societies and integral to promoting sustainable growth, development, and education globally.

Increasing efforts are geared towards enactment and transformation of inclusive practice to attain the expectations of inclusive education. To promote inclusive education, the leadership of headteachers or principals, evident in creating collaboration opportunities for teachers, resourcing teachers and schools and strengthening parent-school partnerships that ensure improvement of learning for all students, especially for those disabilities and needs, matters (Ackah-Jnr, 2018, 2022). As the chief decision-makers in leading inclusively, teachers need effective preparation and an understanding of pedagogies, skills, and capacities (Ackah-Jnr, 2020b; Appiah, 2022; Donath et al., 2023). However, intersecting contextual factors such as negative societal, school and teacher attitudes, and inadequate teacher preparation and resources inhibit effective inclusive education (Ackah-Jnr, 2018, 2022; Mohammed & Hlalele, 2023; Opoku et al, 2019). Inclusivity is considered a burdensome task (Ackah-Jnr & Udah, 2021). However, attitudes and qualities such as passion and empathy (McLeskey et al., 2017) are key in enhancing teacher professionalism and practice of inclusion (Ackah-Jnr & Udah, 2021).

While inclusivity is a globalized ideology, and its expectations and goals are focused on enabling, enriching, and sustaining education, the context in which it occurs matters. The practice context essentially offers insights into internal and external factors acting as enablers or inhibitors to inclusive education. Inclusive practice is thus not insulated from cross-national, cross-cultural, and cross-border influences. The context shapes not only policies, resources, and knowledge around inclusive education but how teachers, particularly, receive and translate policy ideas to lead implementation. In this chapter, the global South, specifically Ghana, somewhat geographically and economically distinctive from the global North, but epistemologically and dialogically interactive and interdependent, is identified as a useful context to understand inclusive practice and map how centering empathy in teacher practice can foster inclusivity.

The current education context in the global South and in Ghana comprises an increasing number of students with vulnerabilities, disabilities, and marginalities that impact learning, acceptance and belonging. Due to such conditions, teachers' inclusive roles and qualities—empathic and sensitive—are imperative in enabling inclusive teaching and learning. Research shows that empathic and sensitive teachers (McLeskey et al., 2017) are more likely to demonstrate prosocial behaviors and responses towards others; understand and value their own emotions and feelings; and respect the feelings of others, which are positive attitudes. Because classrooms are platforms to establish useful and progressive connections and foster a sense of belonging, recognition, and community, teachers with high levels of empathy are needed for inclusive education. Essentially schools with appropriate conditions can develop thriving, supporting, and sustaining inclusive learning and social communities for learners. Studies in Spain (Navarro-Mateu et al., 2019) and Ghana (Gyimah et al., 2010; Mohammed & Hlalele, 2023; Opoku & Ackah-Jnr, 2023; Opoku et al., 2019) find positive teacher attitudes and beliefs beneficial in leading inclusive education.

Despite wide acknowledging of empathy's benefit and role in schools, research on its value and practice in inclusive school contexts is nascent in Ghana. No research has investigated empathy and teacher empathic practices as levers for inclusivity. Empathy's role in inclusive education is not clearly articulated and theorized. For inclusion to be meaningful, it must be inherently and pragmatically empathic. With such thinking teachers and schools can operate with the idea that they should understand the struggles, strengths, and success of their students; they should build hope and meet students' aspirations and changing needs. Ghana's teachers are the primary decision-makers, pedagogical leaders and partners that create supporting administrative and educative practices to guarantee that learners may improve their learning abilities and attain satisfying in schools, regardless of teachers' own capacity, skills and limitations and viewpoints (Ackah-Jnr, 2016; Appiah, 2022). As such, strategically deploying appropriate pedagogical practices embedded with empathy in teaching and learning to foster inclusivity is significant. This chapter contributes insights on how effective integration of empathy in school and teacher practice—pedagogical, curricula, class management, and others—can lever inclusive education. The issue is analyzed with a focus on Ghana that has ratified all-UN backed declarations and policies informing inclusive and sustainable education.

The Global South, Inclusivity and Empathy

This section further discusses the Global South, focusing on Ghana, and the context shaping inclusive education uptake and why 'consciously' recognizing and embedding empathy in teacher practice could increase inclusive practice outcomes. The global South, as a cursory terminology, comprises a diverse collection of countries primarily and geographically found in Africa, Asia, Latin America, and the Caribbean. It is one of a family of terms, including "Underdeveloped", "Third World" and "Periphery," that denote regions outside Europe and North America, mostly low-income and often politically, socially, or culturally marginalized. In other words, countries of the global South are those considered developing due to low or middling levels of development. Other commonalities evident among most of these nations include socio-economic weakness, self-determination conflicts, and colonial legacies. As a term, global South is used to discuss systemic inequalities stemming from the 'colonial encounter,' the continuing reverberations of (mostly) European colonialism and imperialism, and the potential of alternative sources of power and knowledge (Haug et al., 2021). Despite abounding in rich natural resources and cultural legacy, the global South still has structural difficulties that impede effective education and development. It is also beset with cycles of poverty and marginalization. Essentially but more specifically, in the global South, colonial and imported knowledge and ideologies and socio-cultural historicity's impact the education system, policy and practice. The resultant effect being that in some of these countries including Ghana, children have limited engagement in schools; there is inadequate teaching and learning resources, including textbooks and unsuitable infrastructure and physical environments that affect teaching and learning, emotional wellbeing and functioning of students. Educationally, these conditions make inclusivity to be challenging despite the good intentions, resource investment, and program initiatives.

In global South contexts, learners, especially those with special educational needs and disabilities, experience inequities, exclusion, marginalization, segregation and discrimination (Ackah-Jnr, 2020a; Kefallinou et al., 2020). According to UNICEF (2021), about 53% of school children in the global South fail to reach reading proficiency by age 10 although school attendance is increasing. Other learners suffer the consequences of disempowerment, diminishment, and intentional exclusion in education (Ackah-Jnr & Udah, 2021; Ainscow, 2020) that also affect their future job prospects, social participation and inclusion, and life. Up to 65% of children with disabilities and needs in Ghana are out of school. According to UNICEF (2021), out of the global estimate of 240 million children, ages 0–17 years, living with a disability, 28.9 million children are found in Eastern and Southern Africa. Compared with children without disabilities and obvious needs, children with disabilities are 49% more likely to have never been to school; 51% more likely to feel unhappy; and 41% more likely to feel discriminated against.

Ghana, a nation in West Africa, embodies many of the difficulties and challenges faced by countries in the global South. While Ghana's economy is among the fastest growing in the region (until COVID-19 pandemic) and a symbol of democracy and political stability, the country faces widespread poverty and inequality and poor access to essential human and social services, including quality education and healthcare. While metropolitan areas face unemployment, power fluctuations, informal settlements, and environmental deterioration, the rural areas frequently lack access to basic infrastructure, healthcare, and decent education. It is also a post-colonial and multiethnic country with a strong collectivistic culture where people cherish communal interactions and support. As a low-middle income country, Ghana has crafted policies and legislation to advance inclusive education (Ackah-Jnr, 2016; MoE, 2015). To accelerate quality education for diverse learners, the Inclusive Education Policy requires teachers to adopt universal design for learning and child friendly practices (MoE, 2015). The National Teachers' Standards (MoE,

2017) and National Teacher Education Curriculum Framework (MoE, 2018) also demand teachers promote learner-focused instruction: differentiate according to the needs of vulnerable groups such as those with disability and use culturally relevant approaches and strategies in teaching and learning. These pedagogic requirements encourage teachers to support learners but are, however, silent on effectively embedding empathy as an inclusive pedagogy to enhance inclusivity and student learning (Finkelstein et al., 2021).

With the dramatic changes in the world and education subsystem, following COVID-19, students' emotional wellbeing, emotional capital, sociability, and belonging were impacted. Across the education divide, many students experienced stress, anxiety, emotional burden, isolation, and loneliness and exclusion (Ackah et al, 2021). For learners with disabilities and other learning needs in the global South and Ghana especially, the effect was high. In a post-COVID-19 world of education and society, it is imperative new pedagogies and ideas, embedding teacher empathy, are deployed to better student learning, wellbeing, and inclusion. The disruptions of COVID-19, global South contexts and new education views, offer strong reasons to 'intentionally' embed empathy in school and teacher practice to create thriving and conducive learning spaces for all. This is because for inclusion to be meaningful, it must be empathic and humanizing. With such thinking teachers and schools can operate with the idea that they should understand their students, build hopeful bridges, and intently support their aspirations. Therefore, meaningful integration of empathy in school and teacher practice is needed to support student learning and socialization and lever enhanced inclusivity and sustainable education for all learners. Thus, the authors find that empathy is helpful and pivotal in education as it opposes exclusion practices and negative attitudes, including marginalization, objectification and dehumanization of learners.

INCLUSIVITY AND SUSTAINABLE EDUCATION

In a rapidly changing world, education plays a significant role in shaping the lives and futures of learners and societies. To address the challenges of the 21st century, world countries are prioritizing inclusivity and sustainable education as transformative approaches to leverage student learning and teaching and future contributions. This section defines inclusivity and sustainable education and the interplay between them as they support the creation of a more inclusive, just, equitable and sustainable future for all.

Inclusivity, also inclusive education, is a bursting flame in education that seeks to transform school and systemic practice. Its main goal is to eliminate inequalities and inequities in education and devise effective ways to reach all learners (Mitchell,

2017). While disagreements exist about the definition and form of inclusive education, notions of it have shifted from a sole focus on disability to broad notions of diversity. Due to ethno-sociocultural differences, marginalities, vulnerabilities, and differing abilities in learners, inclusivity is now enacted as a policy of guaranteeing all learners equitable and sustained access to varied opportunities and resources in education and society. While inclusive education remains contested (Ackah-Jnr, 2020a; Kefallinou et al., 2020), it involves intentional effort to nurture and expand learning and social experiences for all. Inclusivity in education aims to address contextual and systemic barriers that especially prevent disadvantaged and other marginalized students from receiving quality education.

Humanizing education processes for all learners is an important goal of inclusive education. While it is often critiqued to be an ineffective practice, its desirability in education systems and schools is linked to the human rights imperative, social argument (social cohesion and reducing ill-effects of exclusion), ethical-moral arguments, and economic justification (Ackah-Jnr, 2020a). Its successful practice requires teachers with professional knowledge about inclusive education, skills to address the diverse needs in classrooms, and positive beliefs towards inclusive practice (Donath et al., 2023). This makes teachers indispensable in the inclusive education space. Effective inclusive practice also requires active parental and community engagement (Ackah-Jnr, 2022; Kefallinou et al., 2020).

Inclusivity lies at the core of Sustainable Development Goal 4 (SDG4). In accelerating Agenda 2030 (UNESCO, 2021) attainment, countries are expanding education and participation opportunities for learners of different abilities, backgrounds, needs and cultures to receive an engaging education. Through inclusivity learners can build capacity, resilience and motivation for lifelong learning and work. It aims to empower learners to realize their potential and contribute meaningfully and positively to self and society (Ackah-Jnr, 2018; Ackah-Jnr & Danso, 2019). Therefore, creating receptive learning and social contexts and cultures, supportive of the changing needs, knowledge, and skill levels of learners is important.

Considering the effects of marginalization, discrimination, and exclusion, inclusion becomes a practical approach to promote sustainable education and a moral duty for all learners. Ensuring everyone has an equal opportunity to engage in, benefit or gain from the educational, economic, social, and political process—regardless of ability and background—is what it means to be inclusive. Through inclusive education countries, including Ghana can develop an education system that leaves no one behind, harness the potential of varied learners and people, and promote social cohesion. Inclusivity thus engenders attainment of sustainable education and development (UN, 2016).

Sustainable education, also education for sustainable development (ESD) is defined as the type of education that offers people the tools needed to create equal and sustainable societies. It is a comprehensive approach, comprising formal and informal education that equips students to understand and tackle complex global issues, such as environmental degradation, poverty, inequality, and climate change. ESD is a lifelong learning process and an integral part of quality education. It enhances the cognitive, socio-emotional, and behavioral dimensions of learning and encompasses learning content and outcomes, pedagogy and the learning environment itself (UNESCO, 2017, 2023). Sustainable education, according to UNESCO (2017), empowers learners to take informed decisions and responsible actions for environmental integrity, economic viability, and a just society for present and future generations. Essentially, ESD focuses on five key areas: (a) Advancing policy; (b) Transforming learning environments; (c) Building capacities of educators; (d) Empowering and mobilizing youth; and (e) Accelerating local level action (UNESCO, 2023).

From the foregoing, there is an interplay between inclusivity and sustainable education. They are inextricably related, having similar aims, ethos, and guiding principles. In today's world of fast-paced technological change and advancement, sustainable education creates opportunities for lifelong learning, empowers people, and advances inclusive development. On the one hand, inclusive education as a valued policy and practice guarantees that all students, regardless of background and ability have equal access to high-quality education and opportunities for lifelong learning, which are core to sustainable education and development. Inclusive education resonates positively with widely agreed values of creating sustainable futures by emphasizing the value of each individual, embracing education for all, and promoting sustainable wellbeing in communities. In its broadest sense, inclusive education represents universal values of social justice and incorporates the idea of constantly evolving democracy. Sustainable development is embedded in the ethos of inclusive education and fosters inclusion by guaranteeing that every student has equal access to education and opportunities to engage in sustainable development efforts. To realize the goal of sustainable education, inclusion must ensure education systems and schools and learning environments and classrooms are open, just, caring, sensitive and supportive of the diverse needs, abilities, and viewpoints of all students. The realization of inclusivity in schools and societies precipitates sustainable education, as captured in the sustainable development goals, especially Goal 4. Thus, while benefiting individual learners and societies, inclusivity contributes to creating a more sustainable and equitable world.

TEACHERS' ROLE IN INCLUSIVE TEACHING, LEARNING AND POLICY

There are varied expectations for inclusive education policy and practice. Teachers play significant roles in enabling inclusive teaching and learning. It follows that inclusivity cannot happen without teachers undertaking meaningful roles. Studies have linked teachers' role to the sustainability of inclusive education (Ackah-Jnr, 2018; Donath et al., 2023). The inclusive teaching and policy roles of teachers help to create promising experiences for learners. As the chief implementers of education policies, teachers primarily learn, understand, and translate inclusive policy ideas into practice to make inclusive education possible. By making sense of inclusive policies, teachers enact practices to support students. However, the policy-practice divide (Mavropoulou et al., 2021) often muddies the meaning teachers have of inclusive education.

While inclusive education is challenging and often resisted in schools (Ackah-Jnr & Udah, 2021), teachers perform valued roles and responsibilities to make it succeed. These roles include promoting self-reliance, employing suitable teaching, and learning methods, recognizing cultural diversity, and supervising and disciplining children (Klibthong & Agbenyega 2020). Ackah-Jnr (2020b, p.93) found that "the teacher should be learning". Teachers therefore engaged in formal and informal professional development activities to enhance their readiness, efficacy, and competence to lead practice. The learning, self-improvement and agentic activities of teachers enable them to act as pedagogical leaders and offer rich, stimulating environments to support children's learning and holistic development (Appiah, 2022; Klibthong & Agbenyega 2020). Donath et al. (2023) identified that teachers are expected to improve student behavior, achievement, and attitudes, and this is possible if teachers acquire new skills in professional development and successfully apply them in classrooms. This makes teachers' learning invaluable in inclusive education.

As schools and classrooms are increasingly becoming more modernized, diverse, and complex, the pedagogies and pedagogical choices of teachers should enhance students' participation and engagement in all the learning and curricula experiences. For teachers to play meaningfully and effectively their educative, leadership and pedagogical roles, the repertoire of capacity they possess, use, or need cannot be devoid of empathy. This makes empathy and empathic practices to be instrumental in the inclusive education ecosystem. Through the role of teachers, they also enhance the life-changing and transforming impact of teaching and learning on all learners and harness the capacity for education to foster inclusive, caring, and connected societies and communities.

Showing respect and appreciating different learning needs forms a crucial part of the inclusive roles of teachers. Sousa and Tomlinson (2018) reflected on how positive mindset enriches teachers' roles, behaviors, and inclusive practices and classrooms. A teacher with a positive mindset:

- makes the classroom safe.
- creates a positive learning environment.
- addresses the social-emotional needs of students.
- reinforces students' areas of competence.
- has a 'growth' mindset.

Other essential inclusive roles of teachers include:

1. **Enablers and facilitators of teaching and learning**: Teachers create a nurturing learning environment and adapt instruction and pedagogies to meet diverse student needs and abilities (Ackah-Jnr, 2016; Loreman, 2017; Williams, 2012). As facilitators, teachers guide learners through a process of knowledge construction and foster collaborative learning environments and self-directed learning (Williams, 2012).

2. **Pedagogical and innovative leaders**: Teachers adopt multiple inclusive pedagogical and organizational practices (Ackah-Jnr, 2016; Loreman, 2017) and introduce innovations (Donath et al., 2023) to foster student-centered, interactive, and collaborative learning and positive behavior.

3. **Assessors, organizers, and planners of learning experience:** Teachers organize and assess student learning, develop individualized plans, monitor progress, and use appropriate methods to support students to demonstrate evidence of knowledge and learning (Loreman, 2017).

4. **Collaborators and communicators:** Teachers work with parents, professionals, and peers to support student learning and well-being (Loreman, 2017) and secure resources for inclusion (Ackah-Jnr, 2022).

5. **Advocates, promoters, and supporters**: Teachers advocate, promote, and support the rights and needs of all students, and provide emotional support and promote their inclusion. Teachers demonstrate positive attitudes and take responsibility to teach all learners to ensure they attain success.

Clearly, teachers play multiple and integrative roles in schools, and the efficacy of such roles in inclusive education is not devoid of empathy and empathic practices.

CONCEPTUALISING AND ESSENTIALISING EMPATHY IN INCLUSIVISITY

The attainment of the goals of inclusivity may be impossible without caring, securing, and supporting environments. Physically, socially, and pedagogically, such environments also need to be accessible, appropriate, and suitable (Ackah-Jnr & Danso, 2019) to encourage student learning, engagement, comfortability, and motivation. Schools and teachers thus have a promise to regulate practices and attitudes that cause exclusion. Because schools are melting and distilling points that educate, socialize, and unify society, they should be receptive to learners. Given this, centering empathy in schools is a necessity.

Historically, the term empathy, coined in the early 20th century, literally means "feeling-in". Etymologically, its Greek derivative word means "physical affection or sharing a feeling". Empathy, as a concept, is used in many disciplines such as psychology, health care, education, and social work. As an inherent human capacity, it is what makes us human and to have feeling, affection, and concern for others. Essentially empathy is other-focused rather than self-focused and has various definitions in research.

Empathy is a multifaceted construct that refers to the ability to express concern and take another person's perspective through emotion, imagination, and experience. As a central element of teachers' socio-emotional competence enhancing teaching and learning effectiveness (Aldrup et al., 2022), empathy can be a powerful tool in establishing positive behaviors and relationships that benefit learners, individuals, schools, and society. In inclusive education empathy signifies what fosters understanding, celebrating, and working with difference and diversity. It is a remarkable capability that makes humans see and connect their hearts, heads, and hands to understand, relate and help others.

Eisenberg et al. (2014) noted that empathy involves individuals' capability to appreciate and share others' negative and positive emotions. According to Makoelle (2019), empathy, the capacity to share and understand the state of mind and emotions of another person, is a requisite for inclusive classrooms. Riess (2017) defined empathy as a complex capability enabling individuals to understand and feel the emotional states of others, resulting in compassionate and caring behavior. It is seen as a factor that draws individuals to helping and teaching professions and plays a key role in understanding the nuances of others' experiences and feelings in education, social and health settings. Empathy predicts an individual's willingness to help others (Bohns & Flynn, 2021). The Merriam-Webster Dictionary (n.d.) defines empathy as the action of understanding, being aware of, being sensitive to, and vicariously experiencing the feelings, thoughts, and experience of another. Berkovich (2020) identified four key conceptualizations of empathy:

1. **Empathy as a trait**: inherent or highly stable ability applied universally across all situations.
2. **Empathy as a state**: a fluid ability contingently activated in certain situations or with specific individuals
3. **Empathy as communication**: a conversational interaction involving the transfer of verbal and non-verbal messages of responsiveness.
4. **Empathy as a relationship**: ongoing, inclusive, open bond with deep commitment to other's wellbeing.

Yaseen and Foster (2019) see empathy as a process of relating to another in a mode that facilitates the creative elaboration of mutual understanding and recognition. From these definitions, empathy is about understanding, feeling, acting, and communicating with an other-focused perspective on their condition that instigates helping behaviors. It is key to creating safe, caring, inclusive learning environments.

In research, empathy is seen as a multidimensional concept, comprising mainly two distinctive elements—cognitive and affective (emotional). Cognitive empathy is the intellectual ability to understand another person's emotions and perspective, whereas affective empathy refers to capability to perceive or being affected by and sharing another's feelings or emotions (Makoelle, 2019; Meyers et al., 2019; Yaseen & Foster, 2019). Cognitive and emotional empathy complement each other, enabling individuals to develop empathic behavior and thus relate and communicate with understanding, acceptance and valuing of others.

Other researchers indicate empathy comprises a-threefold elements. Researchers (Meyers et al., 2019; Yaseen & Foster, 2019) noted empathy involves cognitive, affective, and behavioral components. The emotional component allows perception and sharing of another person's inner feelings; the cognitive component allows understanding another's feelings; and the behavioral component includes a range of pro-social actions (e.g., verbal and non-verbal response, active listening, and validation). De Waal (2008) also identified three components: emotional contagion, sympathetic concern, and empathic perspective-taking. Emotional contagion involves a low-level process where an individual is affected by another's emotional or arousal state. Sympathetic concern is the appraisal of and an attempt to understand another's condition motivated by a desire to relieve their distress. As the high-level mechanism, empathic perspective-taking occurs when an individual can model the point of view of another.

While empathy is key to establishing caring, helping relationships and behaviors, it is often used interchangeably with terms like sympathy, compassion, and kindness. In essence, sympathy, compassion, and kindness involve caring or helping response to the emotional state of another person; however, they are distinct. Sympathy is a feeling of sincere concern for someone who is experiencing something difficult or painful. It is seen as a reaction and denotes a feeling of pity or sorrow for another's misfortune or the plight of others. Considered a broader term, compassion means recognizing someone's emotions and wanting to help them. It involves an active motivation to alleviate the suffering of another person. It is characterized by an inherent desire to take purposeful and deeper action to help another person, as it evokes a sense of sympathy, concern, or pity (may not require an inclination to help) for what others are experiencing. Compassion has five key elements: recognizing the suffering of others; understanding that suffering is a universal experience of humans; understanding and empathizing with the emotional experiences of other people; tolerating distressing and uncomfortable feelings or emotions that may arise; and feeling motivated to take action to help alleviate the suffering of others (Gu et al., 2017; Strauss et al., 2016). On the one hand, while kindness is related to empathy, and involves care and concern for others, it mainly connotes conscious intentions and actions to benefit another person. It is about being generous, considerate, and thoughtful towards others. Kindness can thus be conceived as empathy, sympathy, or compassion in action.

From the foregoing definitions, empathy is vital in education, particularly inclusive education. The value of empathy in cultivating and advancing good learning experiences in education settings has been recognized in recent years. Inherent in the SDG declaration, the new ideology is that of stimulating good health and wellbeing, quality education, safe learning, and teaching environment, and ensuring holistic inclusive education for all learners, which could be impossible without empathic practices. According to Aldrup et al. (2022), empathy appears to be a promising determinant for explaining high-quality teacher-student interactions, especially emotional support for students and positive student development. Teachers recognize the utility of empathy in student learning, engagement, and relationship development (Aldrup et al., 2002; Gates & Curwood, 2023; Makoelle, 2019; Meyers et al., 2019; Zhang, 2022). Zhang (2022) indicated that teachers' empathy can reduce stress levels which tends to positively affect learners' engagement level in inclusive schools. Thus, a relationship exists between teacher empathy and learner engagement in schools. In the article, *the Science of Empathy*, the author noted that empathy plays *a critical interpersonal and societal role, enabling sharing of experiences, needs, and desires between individuals and providing an emotional bridge that promotes pro-social behavior (Riess, 2017, p.74).*

As a hardwired human competence, empathy enables us to perceive the emotions of others, resonate with them emotionally, cognitively and behaviorally, take in the perspective of others, and distinguish between our own and others' emotions. This means teacher empathy in inclusive settings can help in forming cognitive and socioemotional connections with students: understanding learners and creating authentic and lasting relationships that enhance their learning and enrich socializing environments. As Bohns and Flynn (2021) noted, highly empathic people are more attuned to the emotional drivers of others' prosocial behavior—an intrinsic desire to help and the discomfort of refusing a help request. Empathy thus can be a positive mediator to reduce gaps in teacher-student relationships and communication.

The importance of teacher empathy extends beyond greater engagement and participation in school curriculum and activities. Inclusive education demands teachers enact appropriate pedagogies and practices to support student learning and teaching (Mohammed & Hlalele, 2023) and that schools create effective supportive cultures and practices (Opoku-Nkoom & Ackah-Jnr, 2023). This requires adapting inclusive pedagogies, including teaching philosophies, beliefs, attitudes, and methodologies to meet the individual and collective needs of every student (Makoelle, 2019). Attaining these goals demands that teachers also have capacity and leadership to pursue curriculum, teaching, and service delivery to ensure inclusion.

TEACHER EMPATHY AS LEVER FOR INCLUSIVITY

Inclusivity in education requires conscious efforts, purposeful facilitation, and directed action. It does not necessarily happen in school and social settings in vacuum and without effective and intentional teachers. As noted, teachers are instrumental in leading inclusion efforts. Research shows empathetic teachers can create caring and supportive experiences for learners. Effectively embedding empathy in inclusive practice leverages creative, equitable and quality teaching. Teacher empathy thus becomes a potent tool in pursuing inclusive education, influencing classroom climate, and enhancing students' sense of belonging, security and community. Every learner may feel valued, heard, and included in welcoming and reassuring classrooms when they have empathetic teachers who not only understand them but are responsive to their diverse needs. This is because empathic teachers understand students' personal and social situations, feel care and concern in response to students' emotions, and to respond compassionately without losing the focus on student learning (Meyers et al., 2019). Through empathic practices, teachers and schools can increase in knowledge about the conditions of learners and support them appropriately. This makes teacher empathy a potent lever for inclusivity. How can teachers embed empathy in inclusive practices?

Practical Approaches

This section examines how teachers can deploy empathy in school practice to create pedagogically and physically accessible, appropriate, and suitable environments to aid student learning, engagement, and attainment outcomes (Ackah-Jnr &

Danso, 2019). However, teacher empathy requires 'great' effort and must prioritise student learning (Meyers et al., 2019). Essentially, empathy should be an integral part of the role of inclusive teaching and not an add-on. Some key practical approaches are discussed:

1. **Cultivating Self-Awareness, Deepening Values:** The process of embedding empathy in inclusive practice must begin with developing self-awareness. Teachers must examine their prejudices, experiences, and views since these might affect how they perceive and engage all students. Teachers can grow more empathetic towards learners with varied experiences and backgrounds by being aware of their own feelings, viewpoints, and cultures. Reflective activities that promote self-awareness include writing, mindfulness training, and conversations with colleagues and students. Teachers should center values of respect, concern for others, community, and social harmony, as foundations for empathic practice. They need to promote social-emotional learning.

2. **Active Listening, Positive Validation:** Actively listening and observing verbal and nonverbal cues, and valuing the emotions and experiences of students are positive empathic practices that teachers must engage in. By fostering secure and encouraging environments where children feel free, confident, and motivated to express themselves, teachers develop rapport and show empathy with their charges. Providing learners with undivided attention, summarizing their ideas and emotions, and answering their questions with passion and understanding are components of active listening. By actively listening and being present, this facilitates a sense of connection and belonging for learners, particularly those who feel excluded or alienated in schools.

3. **Encouraging Inclusive Language:** Language is a powerful architecture in learning and social settings and for building community. Teachers' inclusive language promotes empathic practices. By using inclusive language, teachers can support all learners, regardless of abilities. Ackah-Jnr et al. (2020) noted deploying inclusive language as a pedagogical and motivational tool in classrooms fosters inclusion, belonging and valuing of learners. Pedagogically, inclusive language recognizes individual differences. Motivationally, teachers use inclusive language to offer constructive feedback to learners, communicate instructions clearly, provide genuine expectations and hope for all learners (Ackah-Jnr et al., 2020). Inclusive language helps teachers understand the worries or emotions of learners and devise ways to help them. By using inclusive language, teachers encourage active listening and validate learners' concerns, and contribute to creating school environments where students and teachers socialize respectfully and appropriately.

4. **Developing Cultural Competence and Sensitivity:** Teaching with empathy requires cultural competency as it helps teachers recognize and value the identities and cultures of learners. By including culturally relevant information and views in

the curriculum, teachers can educate themselves about the cultural norms, values, and traditions of the communities in which their learners live. Teachers may show empathy by providing an inclusive environment when every student feels seen, heard, and valued by recognizing and respecting the diversity of learners. Teachers need to be sensitive to variations in learners.

5. **Building Supportive Cultures, Promoting Positive Relationships:** Building solid, genuine, and lasting relationships with learners and encouraging reciprocal respect, trust, and understanding are top priorities for empathetic teachers. Teachers must set and communicate clear expectations for students, and encourage a sense of community, care, connection, and collaboration among them. Although it requires time and work, developing relationships is crucial to fostering safe and welcoming spaces for students to speak up and express themselves. Teachers may foster strong connections with their students by being interested in their lives, offering support and encouragement, and being receptive to their wants and worries.

6. **Flexibility and Differentiation:** Teachers with empathy understand that every student is different and may have varying requirements, preferences, and skills when it comes to learning. They modify lessons to fit the learning styles, needs and abilities of their learners by embracing flexibility and differentiation in their teaching methods (Sousa & Tomlinson, 2018). This might involve giving challenging students more assistance or scaffolding, offering enrichment chances to advanced learners, or offering alternate learning activities. Teachers can employ a multi-tiered system of supports to meet social and emotional learning and positive behavioral support. Empathetic educators should show dedication to diversity and guarantee that every student can achieve and succeed by attending to their specific needs.

7. **Empowering Student Voice, Giving Autonomy:** Empathic teachers give learners an active voice in inclusive classes by encouraging them to express their opinions and beliefs or make choices. Incorporating student-led conversations, collaborative projects, and reflective exercises in learning experiences helps create opportunities for student voice and autonomy. Teachers should provide platforms for student self-expression and participation in learning to foster agency and ownership. Enabling student voice and independence fosters inclusive and respectful environments. In class, teachers should encourage students to discuss characters' feelings and motivations in books to develop perspective-taking abilities.

8. **Advocacy and Social Justice Education**: Teachers with empathy stand up for their kids, fighting for social justice and a more inclusive and equal society. They should incorporate critical conversations about privilege, power, and injustice into their curricula and teach social justice education. Teachers encourage students to become agents of change in their communities by addressing prejudice and injustice. This helps pupils develop empathy towards others. Empathetic teachers provide

pupils with the tools to confront structural injustices and strive towards a more equitable and inclusive society.

Clearly, while fostering empathy in school practice provides a socio-emotional bridge between teachers and students, its impact could be superficial without reinforcement and complementation of empathic practices from students, parents, and society. Promoting empathy must be a shared and recurring practice and responsibility of all actors in the inclusive education ecosystem. Therefore, in moving in the direction of creating more inclusive schools and a compassionate world, there is a need to enhance our collective capacities and duties to empathize as well. This is what Engelhardt (2023) identified as collective empathy and shared leadership.

SUPPORTING TEACHERS, IMPROVING THEIR PREPARATION AND PRACTICE

Advancing positive teaching and learning experiences for all students must also be contingent on teachers being competent and empathic. Improving teachers' preparation and practice is thus important in promoting inclusive education. The issue is how teachers can lead inclusive practice to leverage caring, nurturing, and supporting environments for learners. This section examines some key ways of supporting teachers and enhancing their practice capacity and motivations for inclusive education.

1. Investing in Professional Development

Providing teachers with ongoing professional development opportunities and support could ensure effective implementation of inclusive policies and practices (Ackah-Jnr, 2020b; Darling-Hammond, 2017; Donath et al., 2023; Salifu et al., 2024) and ensure teachers stay abreast of research findings, pedagogical ideas, and instructional techniques. Professional development formats, including school-based and online courses, conferences, seminars, and peer learning networks are useful. Schools and other educational institutions should offer teachers continuous professional development to keep them motivated and interested in their work. Ackah-Jnr et al. (2020) identified professional development programs that equip teachers with knowledge and skills of inclusive language use are important. Essentially and as Donath et al. (2023) found, long-term training and professional development programs with high practical relevance and active learning opportunities facilitate transfer of inclusive knowledge, skills, and beliefs to schools.

2. Providing Mentorship and Coaching

Mentoring and coaching programs are invaluable and provide direction to teachers, especially those new to teaching or experiencing issues and difficulties with their work. Skilled teachers and educators can act as coaches or mentors to offer tailored guidance and support to teachers. Such mentorship programs can assist novice teachers in acclimating to classroom challenges, creating efficient lesson plans, gaining self-confidence, and receiving clarifications on policy and practice issues. Schools can support teachers' professional development and retention by assigning them to mentors with a wealth of expertise. Coaching for inclusion should also focus on enhancing teachers' attitudes and beliefs about inclusive practices.

3. Fostering Collaboration, Communication and Collegiality

Fostering innovative cultures and continual improvement in inclusive schools could enhance opportunities for teachers to learn, collaborate and receive collegial support. Teachers need the chance to exchange ideas on best practices, work together on curriculum design, and solve problems through cross-disciplinary partnerships, professional learning teams, and collaborative learning communities. They need collegial platforms where they can freely communicate and network to share ideas about new pedagogies. Schools may address policy issues, strengthen teaching methods, and improve student learning outcomes and cultivate a collaborative culture by using the pooled experience, expertise, and creativity of their staff.

4. Emphasizing Reflective and Innovative Practice

Promoting continuous development and enhancement of teachers' pedagogic and instructional practices requires motivating them to participate in reflective and innovative practice. Such reflective practice could involve examining teaching methods critically, determining strengths and potential areas for enhancement, and modifying approaches in response to suggestion, positive criticism, and introspection. Schools may foster professional development and a culture of continuous improvement by encouraging teachers to reflect on teaching experiences, instructional decisions, and interactions with students. Importantly, teachers also need to try out new pedagogies, implement evidence-based practices, use technology and digital tools, and be creative and take risk to increase their practice capacity. Being reflective and innovative means teachers are open-minded, flexible, resourceful, collaborative, and agentic to advance teaching and learning.

5. Providing Ongoing Support and Resources

To effectively meet the diverse needs of their students and negotiate the complexity of inclusive teaching, teachers need accessible tools and continual assistance. Education systems and schools could support in ways such as via access to technology, teaching resources, and qualified personnel, including counsellors, instructional coaches, and inclusive education experts. Giving teachers the chance to collaborate, observe their peers, and get feedback may also inspire and motivate them in their work.

6. Prioritizing Well-Being and Work-Life Balance or Emotionality

Promoting work-life balance and supporting teachers' well-being or emotionality is key to prevent burnout, preserve job satisfaction, and increase retention and positive work environment in schools. By developing a pleasant school climate, encouraging community feeling and belonging, and offering tools and assistance for stress management and work-life balance, schools could enhance the well-being, health, and motivation and performance of teachers. Teachers may feel appreciated and encouraged in their professions if they have access to ongoing and timely professional development and health programs and flexible work schedules. The advent of COVID-19 also signals a great need to foster empathy and understanding among teachers. Essentially education systems and schools must address teachers' biopsychosocial needs.

7. Advocating for Policy Changes and Incentives

Sustaining systemic issues in teaching and guaranteeing teachers have adequate and timely resources and support they require to thrive requires local and national policy reforms and changes. Advocating for more school funding, reduced administrative work, reduced class sizes, and better incentives for teacher retention and professional development are important ways to help teachers to improve their practice. Governments, policymakers, and politicians should 'consciously' support measures encouraging the creation of inclusive learning environments by addressing disparities and inequalities within the educational system.

CONCLUSION

While education is a vital foundation of human life and a right for all, without transforming practices and reimagining teachers' capacity, its benefits may be elusive for many children. The authors reiterate that the fact that children are in schools does not guarantee learning and meaningful engagement; many children face recurring intimidations and pressures occasioned by teachers' pedagogies, unsuitable learning environments and unsupportive school cultures. Hence, many learners are excluded in classrooms by default or intentionally. Given this, practices, behaviors, and environments that are appropriate and empathic should characterize the teaching and learning ecosystem. Empathic inclusive education is needed and thrives when teachers, schools and society project care, compassion and understanding, and pursue quality learning environments for all students. Deploying empathy at the center of teacher and school practice pedagogically, physically, socially, and emotionally or educationally leverages inclusivity. Due to the socio-cultural, economic, and political contexts of the global South, including Ghana, the movement to a more transformative education approach in education systems and schools is challenging. In the wake of COVID-19 and before, and with the evolving diversities in schools, the chapter reawakens attention to the role of empathy in inclusive education. In this regard, pursuing empathic inclusive education, particularly in Ghana, is a practical approach to sustainable development, social advancement and social inclusion, and a moral obligation. Fostering empathy in inclusivity can unlock better futures for all learners and help accomplish the broader goals of sustainable education.

Markedly, empathy can advance diversity by creating welcoming learning experiences. Therefore, schools that establish healthy environments where everyone feels respected, understood, and equipped to thrive foster empathy. Empathy can help all children to be responsible, compassionate global citizens who comprehend and confront the complex issues affecting the world. Because empathy improves interpersonal connections and societal cohesiveness, deliberately embedding empathy in school practice may help create a more equal, compassionate, and inclusive education system. As such, teachers need to employ practical approaches to create teaching and learning climates by fostering self-awareness, active listening, inclusive language, developing cultural competence, fostering positive relationships, embracing flexibility and differentiation, amplifying students' voices, and speaking out for social justice.

Fostering inclusive quality instruction that promotes high student learning outcomes requires supporting teachers and enhancing their preparation. Doing so would inspire their motivation, efficacy beliefs and willingness to teach all children in schools. Providing tailored learning opportunities can enhance the knowledge and skills repertoire of teachers. Schools and educational institutions can foster a culture of continuous improvement in teaching by investing in relevant professional learning programs, offering mentorship and coaching, promoting collaboration, communication, and collegiality, emphasizing reflective and innovative practice, providing ongoing support and resources, prioritizing well-being and work-life balance, and advocating policy changes. By deliberately supporting teachers and enhancing their practice to be encrusted with empathy could promote inclusive and nurturing learning environments for all students. Empathy and empathic practices should not only be a silver lining in schools, but an integrative and telepathic tool in inclusivity. This is most especially important in a post-COVID education world where many learners in the global South, including in Ghana, are still battling with the effects of the pandemic. Ensuring empathic inclusive education would give better meaning to the widespread consensus on the importance of education for all (EFA).

REFERENCES

Ackah-Jnr, F. R. (2016). *Implementation of inclusive early childhood education policy and change in Ghana: Four case sites of practice.* Unpublished Doctor of Philosophy Thesis. Griffith University, Australia.

Ackah-Jnr, F. R. (2018). System and school-level resources for transforming and optimising inclusive education in early childhood settings: What Ghana can learn. *European Journal of Education Studies*, 5(6), 203–220.

Ackah-Jnr, F. R. (2020a). Inclusive education, a best practice, policy and provision in education systems and schools: The rationale and critique. *European Journal of Education Studies*, 6(10), 171–183.

Ackah-Jnr, F. R. (2020b). The teacher should be learning: In-service professional development and learning of teachers implementing inclusive education in early childhood education settings. *International Journal of Whole Schooling*, 16(2), 93–121.

Ackah-Jnr, F. R. (2022). Enabling inclusive education: The leadership ecosystem in an early childhood-school-community context. *International Journal of Leadership in Education*, •••, 1–19. DOI: 10.1080/13603124.2022.2108508

Ackah-Jnr, F. R., Appiah, J., & Kwao, A. (2020). Inclusive language as a pedagogical and motivational tool in early childhood settings: Some observations. *Open Journal of Social Sciences*, 8(9), 176–184. DOI: 10.4236/jss.2020.89012

Ackah-Jnr, F. R., Appiah, J., Udah, H., Abedi, E., Yaro, K., Addo-Kissiedu, K., Agyei, I. K., & Opoku-Nkoom, I. (2022). COVID-19 pandemic experiences: Cross-border voices of international graduate students in Australia and America. *International Journal of Learning. Teaching and Educational Research*, 21(4), 97–113.

Ackah-Jnr, F. R., & Danso, J. B. (2019). Examining the physical environment of Ghanaian inclusive schools: How accessible, suitable and appropriate is such environment for inclusive education? *International Journal of Inclusive Education*, 23(2), 188–208. DOI: 10.1080/13603116.2018.1427808

Ackah-Jnr, F. R., & Udah, H. (2021). Implementing inclusive education in early childhood settings: The interplay and impact of exclusion, teacher qualities and professional development in Ghana. *Journal of Educational Research & Practice*, 11(1), 112–125. DOI: 10.5590/JERAP.2021.11.1.08

Ainscow, M. (2020). Inclusion and equity in education: Making sense of global challenges. *Prospects*, 49(3-4), 123–134. DOI: 10.1007/s11125-020-09506-w

Appiah, J. K. (2022). *Enacting pedagogical leadership in early childhood education settings in Ghana. A cross case study of three schools*. Unpublished Doctoral Dissertation. Auburn University, Alabama.

Berkovich, I. (2020). Conceptualisations of empathy in K-12 teaching: A review of empirical research. *Educational Review*, 72(5), 547–566. DOI: 10.1080/00131911.2018.1530196

Bohns, V., & Flynn, F. (2021). Empathy and expectations of others' willingness to help. *Personality and Individual Differences*, 168, 110368. DOI: 10.1016/j.paid.2020.110368

Darling-Hammond, L. (2017). Teacher professional development: A review of the literature. *Journal of Teacher Education*, 68(4), 339–354.

De Waal, F. B. M. (2008). Putting the altruism back into altruism: The evolution of empathy. *Annual Review of Psychology*, 59(1), 279–300. DOI: 10.1146/annurev.psych.59.103006.093625 PMID: 17550343

Donath, J. L., Lüke, T., Graf, E., Tran, U. S., & Götz, T. (2023). Does professional development effectively support the implementation of inclusive education? A Meta-Analysis. *Educational Psychology Review*, 35(30), 30. Advance online publication. DOI: 10.1007/s10648-023-09752-2

Eisenberg, N., Spinrad, T. L., & Taylor, Z. E. (2014). *The handbook of virtue ethics*. Routledge.

Engelhardt, C. F. (2023). *Building and sustaining trust during the COVID-19 pandemic: Lessons in P-12 educational leadership*. Unpublished Doctoral Thesis, State University of New York, Albany.

Finkelstein, S., Sharma, U., & Furlonger, B. (2021). The inclusive practices of classroom teachers: A scoping review and thematic analysis. *International Journal of Inclusive Education*, 25(6), 735–762. DOI: 10.1080/13603116.2019.1572232

Gates, E., & Curwood, J. E. (2023). A world beyond self: Empathy and pedagogy during times of global crisis. *Australian Journal of Language and Literacy*, 46(2), 195–209. DOI: 10.1007/s44020-023-00038-2

Gu, J., Cavanagh, K., Baer, R., & Strauss, C. (2017). An empirical examination of the factor structure of compassion. *PLoS One*, 12(2), e0172471. DOI: 10.1371/journal.pone.0172471 PMID: 28212391

Gyimah, E. K., Ackah-Jnr, F. R., & Yarquah, J. A. (2010). Determinants of differing teacher attitudes towards inclusive education practice. *Ghana Journal of Education: Issues and Practice*, 2(1), 84–97.

Hattie, J. (2013). *Visible learning: A synthesis of over 800 meta-analyses relating to achievement*. Routledge.

Haug, S., Braveboy-Wagner, J., & Maihold, G. (2021). The 'Global South' in the study of world politics: Examining a meta category. *Third World Quarterly*, 42(9), 1923–1944. DOI: 10.1080/01436597.2021.1948831

Kefallinou, A., Symeonidou, S., & Meijer, C. J. W. (2020). Understanding the value of inclusive education and its implementation: A review of the literature. *Prospects*, 49(3-4), 135–152. DOI: 10.1007/s11125-020-09500-2

Loreman, T. (2017). *Pedagogy for inclusive education*. Oxford Research Encyclopedia of Education., DOI: 10.1093/acrefore/9780190264093.013.148

Makoelle, T. M. (2019). Teacher empathy: a prerequisite for an inclusive classroom. In Peters, M. A. (Ed.), *Encyclopedia of Teacher Education* (pp. 1–6). Springer Nature Singapore Pte Ltd. DOI: 10.1007/978-981-13-1179-6_43-1

Mavropoulou, S., Mann, G., & Carrington, S. (2021). The divide between inclusive education policy and practice in Australia and the way forward. *Journal of Policy and Practice in Intellectual Disabilities*, 18(1), 44–52. DOI: 10.1111/jppi.12373

McLeskey, J., Rosenberg, M. S., & Westing, D. L. (2017). *Inclusion: Effective practices for all students* (3rd ed.). Pearson.

Meyers, S., Rowell, K., Wells, M., & Smith, B. C. (2019). Teacher empathy: A model of empathy for teaching for student success. *College Teaching*, 67(3), 160–168. DOI: 10.1080/87567555.2019.1579699

Ministry of Education. (2017). *National teachers' standards for Ghana guidelines*. MoE. https://ntc.gov.gh/wp-content/uploads/2021/12/NTS.pdf

Ministry of Education. (2018). *National pre-tertiary education curriculum framework (NPECF)*. MoE. https://nacca.gov.gh/wp-content/uploads/2019/04/National-Pre-tertiary-Education-Curriculum-Framework-final.pdf

Ministry of Education. (2020). *Education sector performance report*. Ghana Ministry of Education.

Ministry of Education [MoE]. (2015). *Inclusive education policy*. Government of Ghana. https://www.sapghana.com/data/documents/Inclusive-Education-Policy-official-document.pdf

Mitchell, D. (2017). *Diversities in education: Effective ways to reach all learners*. Routledge.

Mohammed, A. S., & Hlalele, D. (2023). Shaping teachers' enactment of inclusion through understanding in Ghana: A sense-making perspective. *Education 3-13*, 1–15. Doi:DOI: 10.1080/03004279.2023.2206838

Navarro-Mateu, D., Franco-Ochoa, J., Valero-Moreno, S., & Prado-Gascó, V. (2019). To be or not to be an inclusive teacher: Are empathy and social dominance relevant factors to positive attitudes towards inclusive education? *PLoS One*, 14(12), e0225993. DOI: 10.1371/journal.pone.0225993 PMID: 31821354

Opoku, M. P., Rayner, C. S., Pedersen, S. J., & Cuskelly, M. (2021). Mapping the evidence-based research on Ghana's inclusive education to policy and practices: A scoping review. *International Journal of Inclusive Education*, 25(10), 1157–1173. DOI: 10.1080/13603116.2019.1600055

Riess, H. (2017). The science of empathy. *Journal of Patient Experience*, 4(2), 74–77. DOI: 10.1177/2374373517699267 PMID: 28725865

Salifu, I., Agyekum, B., & Nketia, D. (2024). Teacher professional development (TPD) in Ghana: Constraints and solutions. *Professional Development in Education*, 1–18. Advance online publication. DOI: 10.1080/19415257.2024.2351947

Sousa, D. A., & Tomlinson, C. A. (2018). *Differentiation and the brain: How neuroscience supports the learner-friendly classroom* (2nd ed.). Solution Tree Press., https://files.ascd.org/staticfiles/ascd/pdf/site ASCD/publications/books/ Differentiation-and-the-Brain-2nd-ed-Sample-Chapters.pdf

Strauss, C., Taylor, B. L., Gu, J., Kuyken, W., Baer, R., Jones, F., & Cavanagh, K. (2016). What is compassion and how can we measure it? A review of definitions and measures. *Clinical Psychology Review*, 31(47), 15–27. DOI: 10.1016/j.cpr.2016.05.004 PMID: 27267346

UNESCO. (2017). Education for sustainable development goals: Learning objectives. UNESCO. https://unesdoc.unesco.org/ark:/48223/pf0000247444

UNESCO. (2022). Learning for empathy: A teacher exchange and support project. UNESCO. https://unesdoc.unesco.org/ark:/48223/pf0000384004

UNESCO. (2023). What you need to know about education for sustainable development. UNESCO. https://www.unesco.org/en/education-sustainable-development/ need-know

UNICEF. (2021). *Seen, counted, included: Using data to shed light on the well-being of children with disabilities*. UNICEF.

Williams, J. C. (2012). Teachers as Facilitators. In O'Grady, G., Yew, E., Goh, K., & Schmidt, H. (Eds.), *One-Day, One-Problem*. Springer., DOI: 10.1007/978-981-4021-75-3_11

Zhang, Z. (2022). Toward the role of teacher empathy in students' engagement in English language classes. *Frontiers in Psychology*, 13, 880935. DOI: 10.3389/fpsyg.2022.880935 PMID: 35719575

ADDITIONAL READING

Batchelder, L., Brosnan, M., & Ashwin, C. (2017). The development and validation of the empathy components questionnaire (ECQ). *PLoS One*, 12(1), e0169185. DOI: 10.1371/journal.pone.0169185 PMID: 28076406

Mercer, S., & Reynolds, W. J. (2002). Empathy and quality of care. *The British Journal of General Practice*, 52, 9–12. PMID: 12389763

O'Grady, G. A. (2020). *Pedagogy, empathy, and praxis*. Palgrave., DOI: 10.1007/978-3-030-39526-1

Yaseen, Z. S., & Foster, A. E. (2019). What Is empathy? In Foster, A. E., & Yaseen, Z. S. (Eds.), *Teaching Empathy in Healthcare* (pp. 3–16). Springer., DOI: 10.1007/978-3-030-29876-0_1

KEY TERMS AND DEFINITIONS

Diversities: This refers to the state of being diverse. In inclusive education diversities broadly describe a range of learners with different backgrounds, abilities, and needs, including those with disabilities, the gifted and migrants or refugees.

Empathy: Th capacity to understand, share, feel and respond to the emotions of other people.

Global South: This often refers to less developed or developing countries of the world in Africa, Latin America, Oceania and parts of Asia and the Middle East.

Inclusivity: The practice and policy of ensuring equitable access, resources, and quality education for diverse learners, including those excluded, marginalized, disadvantaged, or have disabilities.

Inclusive Education: Policy and practice aimed at enhancing accessible, inclusive, equitable and quality education for diverse learners and groups, including those with disability and needs.

Sustainable Education: An education that promotes personal and societal transformation, fostering sustainable and lifelong learning.

Teacher Empathy: The extent to which a teacher works to deeply understand students' personal and social situations, to feel care and concern in response to students' emotions, and to respond compassionately without losing the focus on student teaching and learning.

Teacher roles: The inclusive education responsibilities and practices teachers undertake to promote student teaching and learning and meet policy implementation expectations and goals.

Chapter 3
Teacher Training and Support for Assistive Technology in Inclusive Education:
A Global Perspective

Deepak Kumar Sahoo
https://orcid.org/0009-0004-5703-8701
Biju Patnaik University of Technology, Rourkela, India

Shashank Mittal
O.P. Jindal Global University, India

Ajay Chandel
https://orcid.org/0000-0002-4585-6406
Lovely Professional University, India

Neeti Goyal
https://orcid.org/0000-0003-0007-4213
University of Petroleum and Energy Studies, India

Xuan-Hoa Nghiem
https://orcid.org/0000-0003-2292-0257
Vietnam National University, Vietnam

ABSTRACT

This paper explores the integration of assistive technology (AT) in inclusive education, focusing on teacher training and support systems. It examines the role of AT

DOI: 10.4018/979-8-3693-4058-5.ch003

Copyright © 2025, IGI Global. Copying or distributing in print or electronic forms without written permission of IGI Global is prohibited.

in enhancing learning experiences for students with diverse needs and identifies global perspectives on effective training programs. The paper addresses challenges such as technological barriers, financial constraints, and the need for comprehensive professional development. It highlights successful case studies, discusses policy and advocacy efforts, and explores future innovations in AT. By providing a thorough analysis of these elements, the paper aims to offer insights into creating more inclusive educational environments through strategic AT implementation and support.

INTRODUCTION

Inclusive education is the provision of learning opportunities to students who have different individual needs or abilities. The heart of this mission is finding an effective way to integrate assistive technology, important in supporting learners' diversity. Assistive technology refers to equipment, software, and tools that can be used to assist students in participating, learning, and communicating; it assists students in case of disability or special needs. By addressing specific challenges and barriers, AT can engage these students further in the process of education, offering every learner the potential for success (Avramidis & Kalyva, 2007).

However, the successful implementation of AT in an inclusive education setting largely depends upon the preparedness and proficiency of the educators. For these reasons, teachers ought to be trained and equipped with knowledge and skills that would allow them to select, implement, and put into practice AT devices (Zhou et al., 2012). Essentially, this calls for a stronger development of comprehensive, multilevel training for teachers, with a focus on the technical attributes of the assistive technology devices and also on effective pedagogical techniques for integrating them.

The assistive technology teacher-training landscape is huge and dynamic, reflecting the variance in development level and resources across regions and countries. Whereas a number of countries have built robust frameworks and support systems in trainings—which are beacons of best practice—in others, access to technology, money, and opportunities for professional development are challenges. It is from these global perspectives that best-practice strategies will rise to fill the gaps identified in teacher preparation (Akpan & Beard, 2014).

This chapter attempts to bring out multidimensional features of training in and support for assistive technology in teachers for inclusive education based on a global perspective. It reviews the role of AT in improving educational outcomes for students with different needs, provides an overview of pre-service and in-service teacher training programs and support structures across the world, along with an analysis of the challenges and barriers educators are facing in these different contexts (Reddy et al., 2021). The chapter uses case studies and best practices to convey insights and recommendations on improving the training and support of teachers in a bid to have them create a more inclusive and equitable educational environment.

The Potential of Assistive Technologies in Enabling Inclusive Learning

Assistive technology is a keystone to inclusive education and becomes the main tool in students with diverse learning needs and abilities. AT basically stands for a number of devices, software systems, and tools aimed at enhancing or maintaining functional capacities of students with disabilities. It includes simple tools such as pencil grips and adapted keyboards, as well as complex solutions represented by speech recognition software or individual learning platforms (Budnyk & Kotyk, 2020).

AT in an inclusive setting has various dimensions, some of which point toward the issues in the learning experience. For example, AT allows access by giving students who have a physical or sensory disability tools to interact with educational materials and be a part of classroom activities. Text-to-speech software, for example, could facilitate a student struggling to read due to either low vision or trouble processing written text by changing the written text into audible speech, thus much more accessing the curriculum (Siu & Morash, 2014).

Moreover, AT supports cognitive and learning needs through the provision of customized solutions to accommodate individual strengths and challenges. Tools like interactive apps and educational software can provide opportunities for personalized learning, permitting students to progress based on personal pace and receive targeted support (Goldhaber, 2021). This adaptability is especially useful for the case of students with learning disabilities or those who need extra reinforcement to master key concepts.

It also plays a very major role in enabling communication and social interaction. Augmentative and alternative communication devices, such as speech-generating devices and communication boards, provide a medium through which students with speech or language impairments can express and involve themselves in conversations. This goes a long way in developing not only the skill of effective communication but also in engaging and involving them in the classroom setup (Kamei-Hannan et a., 2012; Siu & Morash, 2014).

Integrated AT in inclusive education works toward the actualization of a fair learning environment. Barriers that would have acted against a student's participation and accomplishments are dealt with in a manner that gives every pupil an opportunity to succeed, no matter what challenges such a student may be facing. Effective use of AT does not only work toward the academic success of a student but also helps in building self-confidence and independence (Kamei-Hannan et a., 2012).

Despite its enormous benefits, the successful implementation of AT does require much consideration and planning. Educators must be properly trained in the selection and utilization of proper technologies that will best match the needs of the students. Continuing support and professional growth are also very important to make the teachers competent enough to adopt changing technologies and integrate them into the classroom effectively (Budnyk & Kotyk, 2020; Reddy et al., 2021).

In other words, assistive technology plays a transformative role in making it possible to achieve inclusive education by enhancing accessible support and fostering diverse learning needs and communication. Its effect comes out clearly in academics and helps in the inclusion and full support of the learners in class (Reddy et al., 2021).

Global Perspectives on Teacher Education in the Use of Assistive Technology

In effect, training in assistive technology is the component that defines the practices of inclusive education being implemented in the different educational contexts. The form that teachers take for training on how to use assistive technology varies across the world; it reflects variations in education policy and available educational and technological resources.

True training programs targeting teachers' preparation with the necessary skills for integrating AT into their classrooms occur in many high-income countries. For example, countries like the United States of America and the United Kingdom have rolled out comprehensive frameworks that contain courses on special needs targeted at AT, workshops, and professional development activities focusing on AT (Surajudeen, 2022). Quite a number of these programs are oriented to the hands-on approach, whereby a lot of technologies can be tried out by hands by the teacher and learn how their use can be modified to suit the needs of particular students. Besides this, support staff like teams of technology specialists and assistive technology consultants are usually available in these countries to extend necessary assistance and advice to teachers from time to time.

In many low- to middle-income countries, however, the availability and standards of AT training programs are seriously hampered by low levels of financing, technological infrastructures, and skilled personnel. In these regions, the area of teacher training in general is extremely problematic due to meager access to current technologies and opportunities for professional development. Consequently, AT is still poorly used even though it is highly helpful for disabled students. On a positive aspect of this falls, in some of the areas improvement in accessing training and resources occurs as a result of international partnership and projects taking place (Soon, 2023).

Many other countries have some proactive schemes for teacher education by building technology-enabled and collaborative networks. These are flexible and cost-effective ways of reaching educators in different geographical locations. For instance, online courses and virtual workshops can make available to teachers, regardless of the physical location of a teacher, very rich resources and training modules that will help in effectively using AT devices in their (Zhou et al., 2011; Soon, 2023). Besides, professional learning communities and networks provide knowledge and support sharing among teachers, which greatly helps in the effective utilization of AT in their classrooms.

This is an element of transcendental importance—that is, the incorporation of AT training in pre-service teacher education programs in the preparation of teachers for the future. Indeed, many countries have already started to involve AT training in their curricula for teacher preparation so as to ensure new teachers are equipped with proper knowledge and skills on how to use these tools at the commencement of their professional careers (Zhou et al., 2011). Such a proactive approach can serve to lay a base for effective assistive technology use and to create an increasingly inclusive educational environment right from the beginning.

In general, worldwide views on assistive technology training preparation for teachers show a mixed scene that is composed of remarkably uneven resources, support, and innovation on AT. Different regions have well-established training programs and support mechanisms. On the other hand, many of them have to work in their unique ways to overcome serious challenges that make them fall short, which in turn is a huge obstacle towards the successful implementation process (Zhou et al., 2011; Soon, 2023). This therefore calls for the need to have increased training opportunities, access to technology, and support for educators in these different contexts. Sharing good practices and coming up with targeted interventions will definitely help the global education community toward a more inclusive and fair approach to AT training and its implementation.

Curriculum and Content for Teacher Training

This is the point where the content and curriculum of assistive technology teacher training programs are meant to place the necessary knowledge and skill base into the educator, which is necessary for effective and meaningful assimilation within the inclusive classroom. An effectively designed training program ought to have prepared the teachers not only with the comprehension of the technical aspects of the various assistive technologies but also with the application of tools in a pedagogically sound manner (Özdemir, 2017).

Curriculum and Content for Teacher Training

Effective AT training programs typically focus on the development of several core competencies, including the following: understanding of the vast array of assistive technologies that can be used; mastering operational use of the technologies; and integrating their use into instructional practices (Koch, 2017). Assistive technology types include devices and materials used in communicating; reading devices such as screen readers; adaptive keyboards and other input devices; and software applications that enable a person to perform tasks involved in learning. In this respect, relevant and practical training curriculum will account for precisely how these tools work and the specific application in a learning environment.

Designing Training Programs and Resources

A good training program will account for program content that is relevant to a practicing teacher yet practical for applicability. The training modules will be built around content such as;

- **Introduction to Assistive Technology:** Different forms of AT, its purpose, and potential benefits of integrating with students that find it cumbersome to learn or are challenged by one disability or another.
- **Practice Sessions:** The teachers will undergo practice sessions with AT devices and software for practice on using these devices and how to troubleshoot/fix them in case of any problem.
- **Pedagogical Resources:** Available strategies for vigorously integrating AT devices and software in lesson plans and instructional strategies for realizing better student learning outcomes among all learners.
- **Real-life Case Studies and Best Practice:** Sharing real-life experiences/case studies of successful implementations of ATs in different school districts /educational setting.

Another issue is that the resources for training must be available as well as easy to use. This may come in the form of multimedia resources that include videos, interactive simulations, and online tutorials, due to the fact that people have different learning styles (Bruce et al., 1991). The resources will allow teachers to always learn and develop even after training has been conducted.

Integration into Pre-Service and In-Service Education

This can be made possible by incorporating the AT training into pre-service and in-service education to ensure that every teacher is well-prepared in the use of these tools. For pre-service teachers, this training can be embedded into teacher preparation programs in order for the teachers entering a teaching profession to get a foundational understanding of assistive technologies and their application in an inclusive classroom set up. This proactive approach helps in building the awareness and competencies right from the beginning of the teaching careers (Mouza et al., 2017).

For in-service teachers, there is a need for continuous professional development. The training programs should provide a way that the educators will refresh their knowledge and upgrade their skills on the introduction of new technologies and techniques. This would be attained through the use of workshops, seminars, and online courses that would provide current information and hands-on strategies for the classroom application of AT.

Collaborative Approaches to Training

The other critical constituent of good AT training is collaboration. This can be achieved by involving different specialists such as assistive technology consultants and special education experts who can provide different perspectives and further help in the use of these tools. Collaborative training may also include parents, students, and other relevant stakeholders. This means that all the needs of the participants are covered and that there is a mutual understanding regarding the purpose of AT in education (Pourdavood & Song, 2021).

Assessment and Evaluation: Finally, the effectiveness of the AT training programs needs assessment on continuous improvement factors. These might include ways and means such as feedback surveys from the trainees, checking the competence developed among the teachers to implement the AT strategies, and monitoring the impact of AT on student learning outcomes. Continuous assessment identifies areas for improvement and also ensures that training programs remain relevant and effective.

Stated differently, teacher training curriculum and content on assistive technology should comprehensively provide room for practical and flexible recommendations that advance in the field (Caner & Aydın, 2021). A focus on the definitional core competency, underpinned by hands-on experience, immersed in both pre- and in-service settings, and fostered by a collaborative approach, may provide teacher trainees with a more stringent and focused way to deal with evidenced, effective AT to address varied needs in an inclusive learning environment.

Support Systems and Resources for Teachers

Successful implementation of assistive technology in inclusive education should be based on school support mechanisms and available resources; it will help guide teachers in maneuvering and acquiring assistive technology tools (Yadav et al., 2022). Proper support structures would guarantee that facilitators receive the help, direction, and resources necessary to use AT productively and, through it, improve their teaching methods.

Institutional Support Structures

This reveals that it is central for institutions to avail the required apparatus and support to teachers. To a significant level, schools and similar places of learning can promote this by providing specific structures of support that can comprise:

- **AT Coordinators:** AT specialists can avail direct support to the educator, assist in the implementation and selection of AT, and provide training and trouble-shooting support.
- **Technical Support Teams:** Installation, maintenance, troubleshooting, and other technical concerns for AT devices and software could be handled by a team of IT experts to have the tools work effectively and be available as and when needed (Özdemir, 2017).
- **Resource Centers:** Many institutions could create resource centers or technology labs with multiple assistive devices and technologies in one place. This could provide shared access to a variety of assistive technology for purposes of training, prototyping, and troubleshooting (Siu & Morash, 2014).

Online Resources and Communities of Practice

Besides the institutional support, a large proportion of it is supported through online means too through resources and communities of practice. The online platforms can provide much information and help, such as:

- **Web-based Education Sites and Portals:** There are websites on assistive technology, which provide tutorials, reviews, and user guides. Such materials may be useful for teachers to be aware of different tools or strategies to suitably apply.
- **Professional Networks and Forums:** Web-based forums and social media groups can be accessed in order to interface/connect with other educators regarding shared experiences and to seek advice on their use. Such networks

might be used collaboratively in order to brainstorm and troubleshoot solutions (Koch, 2017).
- **Webinars and Other Online Training:** Web-based seminars and trainings may provide ongoing professional development opportunities that make it easier to stay current with the available AT advances and best practices.

Collaboration Among Educator, Specialist, and Family

Successful implementation of ATs in education requires collaborative activities. Teachers have to work tooth and nail with various stakeholders to handle and incorporate AT supports into the classroom:

- **Special Education Specialists:** Consistency between the special education teacher and other specialists can provide a teacher with an inside view of the needs of certain students and corresponding AT solutions. Such specialists can advise in the adaptation of AT tools to meet individual requirements (Özdemir, 2017).
- **Families and Caregivers**: Interaction with families of students will provide information as to the needs and preferences of the student. Families may also be helpful in providing services and support services to be used in the student's household that reinforce the skills the student is learning at school.
- **AT Vendors and Consultants:** The relationships a teacher has with both equipment vendors and other consultants, when it comes to AT, can provide tremendous amounts of professional advice and support. The professionals who may help are the ones who will be able to demonstrate equipment, train on the use of equipment, or make recommendations specific to the educational situation (Siu & Morash, 2014).

Professional Development and Training Opportunities

Professional development is the process of lifelong learning to keep in touch with new upcoming technologies and best practices. Some of the common support systems are as follows:

- **Continuous Workshops and Training Sessions:** Frequent and timely access to workshops by organizations, as well as in-school workshops. The content should relate to the latest AT provisions and how to make strategies with hands-on experience as to how to integrate AT into student learning.
- **Certification Programs**: Such programs could pave the way for teachers to receive formal recognition regarding their skills and knowledge in assistive

technology. Certification may mean that these programs—running simultaneously with the primary training and assessment—would have advanced, innovative techniques developed through which the educators could become efficient in the application of AT (Zhou et al., 2011).
- **Peer Learning and Mentorship:** Opportunities for peer learning and mentorship enhance the exchange of knowledge and support among educators. This should be inclusive of mentorship provided by more experienced teachers who would have mastered the technology of AT, involving the opportunity to mentor other teachers and practically advise them (Soon, 2023).

Funding and Resource Allocation

Adequate funding is needed to support the teachers for a resource and support. Schools and educational institutions should make sure to:

- **Budget Allocation for AT:** A budget that is set aside for buying, repairing, and modernizing assistive technologies ensure that schools would have the most up for all of them.
- **Grants and Funding Opportunities:** A search for grants and funding opportunities from governmental agencies, non-profit organizations, and private sectors likely provides alternative funding chances that supplement institutional resources for implementing AT (Bruce et al., 1991).

In other words, effective support systems and resources are very important for teachers if the assistive technology must be successfully integrated within the sphere of inclusive education. Institutional support structures, online resources, collaboration with specialists and families, on-the-job training, and sufficient finance are some of the elements that help create an environment in which the teacher is prepared to use AT effectively (Siu & Morash, 2014). In implementing AT effectively and assisting teachers to deliver quality inclusive education, attention must be paid to these areas by educational institutions.

Case Studies in Successful Training Programs

Notably, such case studies on workable training programs offer vital insights into the ways in which AT can be integrated effectively into teacher training and professional development. These case studies are an example of innovative approaches, effective strategies, and lessons learned from different parts of the world in diverse educational contexts (Smith & Jones, 1999). These case studies will, therefore, go a long way in informing educators and policymakers on how to implement and refine AT training programs in support of inclusive education.

A case in point is Finland, where the integration of AT in teacher education has been realized alongside the school system's focus on inclusive learning. The Finnish teacher preparation program consists of four core components. Preparation, of course, includes AT training. Their approach has hands-on experience with different AT tools as a big feature and collaborative projects where a student teacher is supposed to design and implement AT-based instructional strategies (Bruce et al., 1991). The richness of this program does not lie in the giving out of technical skills but further goes to instil in the candidate the pedagogical application of the assistive technology. The Finnish model testifies to the benefits of the infusion of AT training into pre-service education as an experiment or pilot project. It embodies a workable and scalable framework for other countries.

For instance, the State of California conducts a very effective in-service training program for teachers through its Assistive Technology Training Network (ATTN). It coordinates workshops, online training courses, and web-based seminars that could supply the needs for training in device selection, implementation strategies, and troubleshooting. ATTs focus on professional development on an ongoing basis, thereby ensuring that teachers are apprised of the latest progression in the field of AT and how to go about current and future changes in making provisions for the needs of the students. Such flexibility in the delivery of AT services and a regularly involved AT specialist are among the hallmarks of the program (Smith & Jones, 1999).

Another strong example is that of Kenya, where the organization "Tech for Schools" developed an innovative kind of training program to increase the use of augmented AT in rural and underserved areas. Recognizing that resource settings are likely to be poor in such areas, the program makes use of community-based training facilitated by mobile technology to access educators situated in remote areas. This model involves local "tech champions" trained extensively to train others in the clusters in which they reside Bruce et al., 1991). This model was considered successful, thus indicating that technology-driven training model may overcome the constraint posed by geography and availability of resources and, in the process make AT available to teachers in any learning domain.

The Australian model, "Assistive Technology for All," focuses on the integration of AT into the professional learning communities. This program promotes, through the periodic meetings of educators, an online forum, and peer-led AT workshops, the sharing of practices. There is an effort toward collective learning and support to create a network among educators, often exchanging knowledge and resources (Özdemir, 2017). Evaluation of the success of the program comes in two main areas: the teachers' confidence and competence to make more effective use of AT and the effect such practice has on the engagement and learning experiences of the student.

In the UK, through a comprehensive training model of the "Inclusive Education Technology Initiative," both initial and ongoing support for teachers has been completed to encompass face-to-face workshops, online modules, and one-to-one coaching. This also includes feedback mechanisms designed to help the content and delivery of training continually. This multi-prong strategy is made effective; hence, it suits different learning styles and gives teachers practical tools and strategies to actually use in practice as they implement AT in their classrooms (Avramidis & Kalyva, 2007).

Such examples from case studies show a variety of effectiveness strategies in AT training that tailor programs according to the respective regions' needs and contexts. Other key ingredients that made them successful include experiential training, continuous professional development, a community-based approach, and collaborative learning. The cases will be applied to help educators and policy makers identify best practices from the field and adopt working strategies to improve AT training programs in their own contexts (Akpan & Beard, 2014).

Case studies from effective training programs, in several ways, provide guidance on how assistive technology can be implemented successfully into an education system. The following cases can be elaborated from training programs that are guiding ways to effectively use AT to bring more inclusive and just educational setups.

Challenges and Barriers

Through inclusive teaching and assistive technology, there is great potential in benefits realized. However, there are also obstacles and effective practice challenges because the implementation of AT is not so much context-specific as it is dictated by technological challenges (Zhou et al., 2012).

Technological Challenges

In many regions, more so in low- and middle-income countries, much of the technology and Internet connectivity is found to be unreliable; this, in essence, does not provide the teachers with technologies whose strengths are reliable. And where they exist, other problems associated with the presence of technology, such as outdated equipment, poor technical support, and compatibility problems with software, only compound the situation. This will make sure that the technology in the schools is there and working (Reddy et al., 2021).

Financial Limitations

This is another constraint to all-embracing use of AT. These are the acquisition cost of AT devices and software for AT. Generally, AT devices and software would have a prescription that is too costly especially for schools with miser budgets. Additionally, most times the funds attributed to such professional development and training programs have not been enough, and these teachers find themselves without the right resources to implement AT in their classrooms (Specht et al., 2007).
. The above financial barriers require strategic allocation of resources, explore funding procedures, and develop possible cost-effective solutions to avail AT for the classroom.

Lack of Training and Professional Development

Adequate training and professional development answered the questions of proper implementation and usage of AT. Other barriers include inadequate training provided for educators in how to use AT tools, which might lead to low use or misuse. The training programs may be less catered for the different approaches to using these tools, have a limitation in practical and hand-on experiences, or be less presented in including the specific needs in different educational settings (Castro et al., 2024). Thus, it is crucial that professional development for teachers is designed and implemented in a comprehensive and sustained manner to properly train them in the use of AT.

Cultural and Systemic Barriers

Cultural and systemic barriers can also exert an influence on the integration of AT in inclusive education. Cultural beliefs have it that the pursuit of some technological devices helps in retaining knowledge in long-term memory, thus causing reluctance or resistance to technology not benefiting the application. General schooling practices and policies are not supportive or may be less innovative to adapt to new practices (Ansari, 2023). Overcoming the very barriers to the realization of the benefits of AT calls for an awareness approach, policy advocacy, and innovation cultures and institutionalized inclusion in educational institutions.

Accessibility and Usability Issues

Accessibility and usability issues are attributed to the effectiveness of AT tools. Any AT not designed around the different needs of a student is set up for failure. For instance, the assistive technology devices or software that cannot be user-friendly or adjustable may not be well used by students with varying forms of disabilities/ those with multiple disabilities. This thus underscores the need to develop AT tools with access and usability features that can be used by all students to enable them to reach their full potentials (Olowe, 2024).

Resistance to Change

Resistance to change may be a major factor in effective implementation of AT. Generally, resistance to new technologies may basically emanate from ineffectiveness that actualized the possible increase in workload and fear of the unknown among educators, administrators, and other stakeholders (Kamei-Hannan et a., 2012). This resistance may be alleviated by showing clear benefits from AT, assurances and acts of being there to provide support hence leaving no one to also suffer the resistance and involving all the stakeholders in planning and implementation stages.

Inadequate Support Systems

It would be challenging for a teacher to use AT without the guidance of specialized AT coordinators, technical support, or a peer network to guide the teacher effectively. Therefore, establishing robust support systems within institutions and providing access to personnel and resources that are specialized in AT play a crucial role in supporting teachers in order to integrate AT effectively (Surajudeen, 2022).

In short, the successful implementation of assistive technology in education for all is a challenging, wide-scoped task. The challenges and barriers identified include technological constraints, financial limitations, inadequate training, cultural and systemic issues, problems in accessibility, resistance to change, and weak support systems (Surajudeen, 2022; Soon, 2023). This will need a holistic perspective, which takes into account the issues of infrastructure, funding, training, and creating an environment for using AT. Addressing these barriers would mean that educational institutions could provide more effective support for teachers and students toward making education more proper and inclusive for all.

Policies and Advocacy

Policy and 'successful' advocacy is one of the principal key towards effective AT integration in an all-inclusive educational set-up. Meaning, major makers of educational policies and advocates for justifiable change can facilitate the removing of barriers, promoting the uptake of AT, and learning tools that are supportable for all learners.

Development of Supportive Policies

This forms the basis for the successful integration of AT, with the development of supportive policies at national, regional, and the local level. Policies at different levels should provide clear objectives regarding the use of AT in education, taking into account the accessibility norms, fund allocations, and strategies for implementation (Kamei-Hannan et a., 2012). For instance, national education policies should establish requirements for AT implementation in the classroom. They should also offer directional guidelines on appropriate AT use and ensure that there are resource allocations to these guidelines. A good policy should spark system change and provide a forum through which AT can be channelled into educational practice.

Funding and Resource Allocation

At the same time, ideas from government and private sources for funding AT resources are solicited. These include procurements, maintenance, and new development. These may be in the form of advocacy for budgetary allocations that prioritize AT and seeking grant and partnership opportunities from technology companies and non-profit organizations. By guaranteeing that financial resources are channelled towards AT, policymakers and proponents can start responding to the chasm or vacuum between the availability of technology and its peddled use in classrooms (Siu & Morash, 2014; Alborno, 2017).

Training and Professional Development Mandates

Policy also needs to be stipulated that requires training on AT, be incorporated into teacher education courses and professional development. The intent of this will be to make educators knowledgeable and equipped with necessary skills that will make them well supposedly handle AT. For instance, teacher preparation programs should be mandated by policies to require specific coursework on assistive technology and incentive for teachers to participate in workshops and certification programs of professional development (Reddy et al., 2021; Goldhaber, 2021). Then AT training can be considered as included in the standard of professionalism and can overtime build capacity within educational systems for empowering teachers in supporting diverse learners.

Accessibility and Inclusion Standards

The development of policy would also consider setting out clear standards in terms of access and inclusions. Policies should address the design and application of AT to ensure that it serves to meet the various needs of students. The goal is to establish guidelines on how to produce educational material that is accessible, promote universal design concepts, and ensure that the AT tools may conform to many disabilities (Zhou et al., 2011; Özdemir, 2017). By setting very high standards in regard to access, the policymakers can ensure that all students benefit from assistive technology.

Advocacy for inclusive practices

Advocacy is important for sensitizing the various stakeholders on the importance of AT and practices that call for mainstreaming in the area of education. Advocacy groups, including educators and parents, can join the crusade through public sensitization on the advantages of AT by, for example, demonstrating success stories to show the impact (Bruce et al., 1991; Koch, 2017). Through this, they can agitate for the including of AT-friendly policies within the educational agendas drafted at the highest policy-making levels. Campaigns in public awareness, lobbying, and full attendance on educational forums popularize the campaigns for AT and really stir the policy makers into real action on this.

Collaborations with Stakeholders

Effective policies and advocacy are only possible through stakeholders' collaboration such as the government departments, colleges, technology providers, and organizations. Advocates can collaborate with all the stakeholders in work to align the policies with the needs of the students and teachers by dialoguing the stakeholders (Siu & Morash, 2014; Budnyk & Kotyk, 2020). This can help identity the gaps in policies and work towards developing innovative solutions in integrating AT into the educational systems.

Monitoring and Evaluation

Monitoring and evaluation of the policy and advocacy measures should be affected. Assessment of the effectiveness of AT policies and programs identifies loopholes in the system in order to improve them and ensures efficiency of resource use. The strategies for evaluation may include tracking the implementation in schools, assessment made by teachers, students' feedback, and impact on the educational outcomes (Zhou et al., 2012; Akpan & Beard, 2014). By continuously evaluating and refining policies, stakeholders can ensure that AT initiatives remain effective and responsive to evolving needs.

Promoting Equity and Access

Lastly, policies and an advocacy drive should target equity and AT access across diverse educational settings. This includes the closing of access gaps to technology between both the urban and rural settings—you know how that goes—and between high- and low-income schools so that some crucial effort is made toward equal opportunities for all students (Avramidis & Kalyva, 2007).

In short, policy and advocacy should focus on developing the integration of assistive technology in inclusive education. Create an enabling policy that is supportive, addresses funding provision, and training mandates in ensuring standards in accessibility and advocates for inclusive practices by collaboration with stakeholders in monitoring effectiveness by policymakers and advocates, and then it will provide an environment where AT supports all students to enhance their educational experiences (Zhou et al., 2012; Akpan & Beard, 2014). These innovations will go a long way in enhancing educational systems, making them more inclusive and equitable. This will ensure that every student has what is required to reach their potential.

Future Directions and Innovations

As assistive technology continues to develop, future directions and innovativeness are in support of its contribution to better inclusive education for its users. Emerging technologies and novel approaches are poised to revolutionize the design, use, and application of assistive technology within classrooms, paving a way for supporting diverse learners and addressing the traditional challenges encountered by these ever-changing environments.

Advancements in Technology

Innovations such as artificial intelligence (AI), machine learning, and augmented reality (AR) will soon bring a revolutionary change to AT in being more adaptive and personalized. AI-powered tools for real-time feedback and intervention are given to enhance support, guided by the individual student's patterns (Reddy et al., 2021; Goldhaber, 2021). For example, applications of AI provide personalized learning and are able to pinpoint areas in which a student requires more support, adapting instructional content accordingly. What is even more crucial, AR can create immersive learning environments, taking care of different learning styles and disabilities, thus making it engaging and friendly.

Increased Integration with Mainstream Technologies

Integrating assistive technologies with mainstream technologies is one of the most appealing and promising directions. Now when smartphones, tablets, and laptops are so popular, implementing the main features of AT within mainstream devices will contribute both to improved accessibility and a more moderate price (Siu & Morash, 2014; Alborno, 2017). For instance, operating systems and applications that have default accessibility features can serve as an entryway for assistive tools with supportive features for students with disabilities, without becoming stand-alone devices themselves. It can also foster more inclusion design practices, where AT is considered from the outset in developing new technologies.

Personalized Learning and Customization

Advances in data analytics and adaptive technologies enable development of highly customized learning experiences, tailor-fit to every student's unique needs. Custom solutions in AT may be configured in learning style, preference, and progress, to offer tailored support that maximizes educational outcomes. This not only increases the effectiveness of the AT but also ensures that the students receive the specific support required for a successful learning journey.

Enhanced Collaboration and Communication Tools

The future AT innovations will enhance the present collaboration and communication tools. The coming up technologies of real-time language translation, advanced speech recognition, and collaboration platforms will assist in smoothing the communication between students, teachers, and peers. For example, real-time translation tools easily overcome language barriers, and students who speak several languages have interaction and collaboration on an equal footing (Akpan & Beard, 2014). Enhanced speech recognition can facilitate an improved output for students who have communication difficulties. When coupled with future innovations, they can be applied to fostering a more collaborative learning environment.

Universal Design Emphasis

The increasingly development of AT now considers the factors of universal design toward composing an inclusive and very accessible environment for all the learners. Prospective innovations are likely to accentuate universal design principles that make sure assistive technology is not only beneficial to students with disabilities but is also usable with all learners (Zhou et al., 2012; Akpan & Beard, 2014). By considering the use of AT conceived for universal accessibility, the developer can create tools that will foster greater inclusivity and require fewer types of specialized accommodations.

Rise of Open Source and Shared Development

Open source and shared development models are more and more influencing the AT field. These models promote combined integration and sharing of ideas, resources, and innovations among developers, educators, and researchers. Using open-source platforms, the educational community can tap and add meaningfully to a great variety of broad-ranging AT solutions in a manner that capitalizes on innovation and minimizes significant expenses related to perpetual redevelopment. Collaborative development also fosters the development of more learner-responsive tools because it draws on inputs from a broad range of stakeholders (Bruce et al., 1991; Koch, 2017).

Ensuring Data Privacy and Security

Systems addressing issues related to data privacy and security are the most critical now that this technology is becoming more and more advanced and becomes data-driven. Safety of student data is most critical and has to be considered first in all new developments regarding AT, and assurance of the privacy of student data has to prevail (Siu & Morash, 2014; Alborno, 2017). Innovations in levels of data encryption, secure storage of data, and privacy protocols are bound to be developed that will help protect some very sensitive information and build trust in AT solutions.

Global Collaboration and Equity

Lastly, AT in the field of education requires the development of global partners and efforts regarding equality. These worldwide alliances and joint research initiatives can help stimulate innovation and the creation of solutions that will meet global challenges and—above all—ensure AT contributes to the benefit of learning in diverse contexts. Through such global convenings, the global education community could act in unison to share expertise and resources toward common goals for achieving equitable and inclusive educational settings (Bruce et al., 1991; Koch, 2017).

Conclusion The future of the technology of inclusive education looks very promising, and there have been numerous changes and innovations. As influencing factors, the future of AT shows emerging technologies, increased integration with mainstream tools, personalized learning approaches, enhanced collaboration, universal design, open-source development, data privacy, and global collaboration. These innovations have continued to grow, offering the potential for ever more effective AT that can further support more inclusive and equitable educational practice.

CONCLUSION

The integration of assistive technology in inclusive education is that vital transformation to nurturing the creation of equitable, hence accessible learning environments for every student. The inclusion of students in learning processes in institutions from the grass root level up to higher education continues to take a positive trajectory, accordingly, establishing the fact that AT has come a milestone in filling the loopholes towards individualized learning among students. Yet at the same time, the successful establishment of AT itself introduces problems and provides unique solutions.

We have discussed the critical elements of effective AT integration, which includes the role of AT, global perspectives of teacher training, curriculum-content for training programs, support systems and resources, challenges and barriers, policy and advocacy, and future directions. Harnessing the full potential of AT interventions in education will require complex approaches that include enabling technological developments, policies, comprehensive training packages, and collaboration.

Notably, in finding the maximum potential of AT in the systems of education, there is the need to incorporate a full approach toward its implementation. The education systems need to be strategic and include policy makers, practitioners, technology developers, and support personnel working in harmony in the integration of useful AT tools onto the act of teaching. This would only be possible once the technology is there and supportive infrastructures are in place, with a regular professional development regimen for the educators and good support systems.

Issues and obstacles that have been raised in AT should be resolved to improve its effectiveness and accessibility. Technological, financial, and systemic barriers should be resolved through adequate policies, financial supply, and enhanced training provision. By being active on the resolution of issues, the educational institutions can bypass the barriers AT faces to make sure that all students benefit from such supportive technologies.

Policies and advocacy may play very important roles in driving systemic change and making sure that AT will be part of educational frameworks. The role of policies giving clear guidelines and providing funds to implement AT may work well, but not unless the policies are championed through policy influences and advocates by stakeholders. Future Prospects and Innovations

Looking forward, the future of AT in inclusive education is promising. Innovations of technology, personalized learning approaches, and the development of collaboration tools will change the way AT is provided in the classroom. Such innovation will bring tailored, effective support in the education of all students. Also, the focus on universal design globally will make educational environments able to be at benefit to all.

As we move forward, it is very critical for educators, policymakers, researchers, and technology developers to collaborate in driving the advancement of AT in education. The need to continue to invest in research and development up to the implementation level to address the current challenges and explore the new frontiers is evident. This prompts us to collaborate in such a manner that AT is to evolve to answer the needs of the growing diverse student population, and they are able to attain quality education in an equitable manner.

Therefore, it is a dynamic and continuous process that the incorporation of assistive technology into inclusive education holds in changing learning experiences for students with diverse needs. By making the committed attempt toward challenges and putting effective policies into place that will realize future innovations, we may have a more inclusive educational landscape wherein every student is afforded an ample opportunity to succeed. Continued refinement of AT is a landmark towards achieving learning equity and ensuring that every learner can get what they need for learning.

REFERENCES

Akpan, J., & Beard, L. (2014). Assistive technology and mathematics education. *Universal Journal of Educational Research*, 2(3), 219–222. DOI: 10.13189/ujer.2014.020303

Alborno, N. (2017). The 'yes ... but' dilemma: Implementing inclusive education in emirati primary schools. *British Journal of Special Education*, 44(1), 26–45. DOI: 10.1111/1467-8578.12157

Alborno, N. (2017). The 'yes ... but' dilemma: Implementing inclusive education in emirati primary schools. *British Journal of Special Education*, 44(1), 26–45. DOI: 10.1111/1467-8578.12157

Ansari, W. (2023). Effective use of assistive technology for inclusive education in developing countries.. https://doi.org/DOI: 10.14293/PR2199.000268.v1

Avramidis, E., & Kalyva, E. (2007). The influence of teaching experience and professional development on greek teachers' attitudes towards inclusion. *European Journal of Special Needs Education*, 22(4), 367–389. DOI: 10.1080/08856250701649989

Bruce, M., Podemski, R., & Anderson, C. (1991). Developing a global perspective: Strategies for teacher education programs. *Journal of Teacher Education*, 42(1), 21–27. DOI: 10.1177/002248719104200104

Budnyk, O., & Kotyk, M. (2020). Use of information and communication technologies in the inclusive process of educational institutions. *Journal of Vasyl Stefanyk Precarpathian National University*, 7(1), 15–23. DOI: 10.15330/jpnu.7.1.15-23

Caner, M., & Aydın, S. (2021). Self efficacy beliefs of pre-service teachers on technology integration. *Turkish Online Journal of Distance Education*, •••, 79–94. DOI: 10.17718/tojde.961820

Castro, J. V., & Carrillo Cruz, C. E. (2024). Dynamic efl teaching practices for students with visual impairment. *Revista Boletín Redipe*, 13(4), 109–121. DOI: 10.36260/rbr.v13i4.2114

Goldhaber, A. B. (2021). Impact of ict integration on quality of education among secondary schools in usa. *Journal of Education*, 4(6), 53–61. DOI: 10.53819/81018102t5015

Kamei-Hannan, C., Howe, J., Herrera, R., & Erin, J. (2012). Perceptions of teachers of students with visual impairments regarding assistive technology: A follow-up study to a university course. *Journal of Visual Impairment & Blindness*, 106(10), 666–678. DOI: 10.1177/0145482X1210601011

Koch, K. (2017). Stay in the box! embedded assistive technology improves access for students with disabilities. *Education Sciences*, 7(4), 82. DOI: 10.3390/educsci7040082

Mouza, C., Huí, Y., Pan, Y., Ozden, S., & Pollock, L. (2017). Resetting educational technology coursework for pre-service teachers: A computational thinking approach to the development of technological pedagogical content knowledge (tpack). *Australasian Journal of Educational Technology*, 33(3). Advance online publication. DOI: 10.14742/ajet.3521

Olowe, M., & Olowe, N. E. (2024). Counselling approaches and educational support for business education in students with visual and hearing impairments: Enhancing accessibility and learning outcomes. *British Journal of Multidisciplinary and Advanced Studies*, 5(2), 24–38. DOI: 10.37745/bjmas.2022.0466

Özdemir, S. (2017). Basic technology competencies, attitude towards computer assisted education and usage of technologies in turkish lesson: A correlation. *International Education Studies*, 10(4), 160. DOI: 10.5539/ies.v10n4p160

Pourdavood, R., & Song, X. (2021). Engaging pre-service and in-service teachers in online mathematics teaching and learning: Problems and possibilities. *International Journal of Learning Teaching and Educational Research*, 20(11), 96–114. DOI: 10.26803/ijlter.20.11.6

Reddy, P., Reddy, E., Chand, V., Paea, S., & Prasad, A. (2021). Assistive technologies: Saviour of mathematics in higher education. *Frontiers in Applied Mathematics and Statistics*, 6, 619725. Advance online publication. DOI: 10.3389/fams.2020.619725

Siu, Y., & Morash, V. (2014). Teachers of students with visual impairments and their use of assistive technology: Measuring the proficiency of teachers and their identification with a community of practice. *Journal of Visual Impairment & Blindness*, 108(5), 384–398. DOI: 10.1177/0145482X1410800504

Siu, Y., & Morash, V. S. (2014). Teachers of students with visual impairments and their use of assistive technology: Measuring the proficiency of teachers and their identification with a community of practice. Journal of Visual Impairment &Amp. *Journal of Visual Impairment & Blindness*, 108(5), 384–398. DOI: 10.1177/0145482X1410800504

Smith, S., & Jones, E. (1999). Technology infusion: Preparing teachers for transition services through web-based cases. *Career Development for Exceptional Individuals*, 22(2), 251–266. DOI: 10.1177/088572889902200207

Soon, V. Vestly Kong Liang Soon. (2023). A study of attitudes, skills, and barriers among the special education hearing impairment teachers in the use of assistive technology in teaching. *Journal of Advanced Research in Applied Sciences and Engineering Technology*, 35(1), 121–128. DOI: 10.37934/araset.34.3.121128

Specht, J., Howell, G., & Young, G. (2007). Students with special education needs in canada and their use off assistive technology during the transition to secondary school. *Childhood Education*, 83(6), 385–389. DOI: 10.1080/00094056.2007.10522956

Surajudeen, T., Ibironke, E. S., & Aladesusi, G. A. (2022). Special education teachers' readiness and self-efficacy in utilization of assistive technologies for instruction in secondary school. *Indonesian Journal of Community and Special Needs Education*, 3(1), 33–42. DOI: 10.17509/ijcsne.v3i1.44643

Yadav, A., Israel, M., Bouck, E., Cobo, A., & Samuels, J. (2022). Achieving csforall: preparing special education pre-service teachers to bring computing to students with disabilities.. https://doi.org/DOI: 10.1145/3478431.3499333

Zhou, L., Parker, A., Smith, D., & Griffin-Shirley, N. (2011). Assistive technology for students with visual impairments: Challenges and needs in teachers' preparation programs and practice. *Journal of Visual Impairment & Blindness*, 105(4), 197–210. DOI: 10.1177/0145482X1110500402

Chapter 4
The Crucial Role of Empathy in Fostering Inclusive Learning Environments

Phineas Phuti Makweya
Independent Police Investigative Directorate, South Africa

Medwin Sepadi
University of Limpopo, South Africa

ABSTRACT

Empathy is a fundamental trait crucial for fostering inclusive learning environments, enhancing student-teacher relationships, and promoting understanding among students and educators. Recent studies emphasize its significance in education, showing its positive impact on collaboration and appreciation for diversity (Davis et al., 2016). Empathy enables educators to tailor teaching strategies to meet diverse student needs, creating a more inclusive classroom atmosphere (Jennings & Greenberg, 2009). Moreover, empathy contributes to a supportive work environment for educators, enhancing collaboration and professional development (Katz, Blumler & Gurevitch, 2015). By prioritizing empathy, schools can cultivate a more compassionate and understanding educational community where everyone feels valued and respected, thus significantly contributing to the field of inclusive education.

DOI: 10.4018/979-8-3693-4058-5.ch004

INTRODUCTION

Empathy is a powerful force in education, shaping the way students learn, teachers teach, and schools function. This chapter explores the crucial role of empathy in fostering inclusive learning environments. It delves into the impact of empathy on student-teacher relationships, classroom dynamics, and overall school culture. Through a review of recent studies and policy frameworks, this chapter highlights the significance of empathy in promoting understanding, respect, and acceptance among students and educators. By examining the ways in which empathy can be cultivated and integrated into educational practices, this chapter aims to provide insights into creating more inclusive and supportive learning environments for all.

Policy Strategies for Promoting Inclusive Practices

In South Africa, policy strategies for promoting inclusive practices that support students' emotional well-being are crucial components of the country's commitment to inclusive education. These strategies are outlined in various documents and frameworks, aiming to create an inclusive and supportive learning environment for all students. One key strategy is the provision of professional development for teachers, aimed at equipping them with the necessary knowledge and skills to effectively support diverse learners.

The South African Council for Educators (SACE) plays a significant role in this regard, having developed guidelines for teacher professional development in inclusive education. These guidelines highlight the importance of ongoing training and support for teachers to enhance their understanding of inclusive practices (SACE, 2017). SACE emphasizes the need for teachers to be equipped with the skills to identify and address barriers to learning, including those related to students' emotional well-being. By enhancing teachers' understanding and skills, the guidelines aim to improve the overall quality of education for all students, particularly those with diverse needs.

Furthermore, the Department of Basic Education in South Africa recognizes the importance of professional development in inclusive education. The department's policies and frameworks emphasize the need for continuous professional development for teachers to ensure that they are able to implement inclusive practices effectively (Department of Basic Education, 2014). By investing in teacher professional development, South Africa aims to create an inclusive education system that supports the emotional well-being and academic success of all students.

In South Africa, curriculum adaptations are a crucial strategy outlined in policy frameworks to promote inclusive practices and support students' emotional well-being. The Curriculum Assessment Policy Statements (CAPS) provide comprehensive guidance on adapting the curriculum to accommodate diverse learners, including those with disabilities (Department of Basic Education, 2011). These adaptations may involve providing alternative assessment methods, modifying learning materials, and employing inclusive teaching strategies that cater to various learning styles and abilities. By incorporating these adaptations, educators can create a more inclusive learning environment that meets the needs of all learners.

Additionally, school-based mental health services are prioritized in South African policy frameworks as a vital means of supporting students' emotional well-being. The Integrated School Health Policy (ISHP) underscores the importance of providing mental health services within schools to address the emotional needs of learners (Department of Health, 2012). These services may include counseling, psychoeducation, and referral to external mental health professionals for more specialized support. By offering these services on-site, schools can ensure timely and accessible support for students experiencing emotional difficulties, promoting their overall well-being and academic success.

Moreover, the National Policy on Screening, Identification, Assessment, and Support (SIAS) in South Africa underscores the critical importance of early identification and comprehensive support for learners facing barriers to learning, including mental health challenges. The policy recognizes that timely intervention is key to addressing these barriers effectively and promoting the well-being and academic success of all learners (Department of Basic Education, 2014).

SIAS advocates for a multi-disciplinary approach to supporting learners with diverse needs, which involves collaboration among various professionals, including teachers, school psychologists, social workers, and other relevant stakeholders (Department of Basic Education, 2014). This collaborative effort ensures that learners receive holistic support that addresses their academic, emotional and social needs. By leveraging the expertise of different professionals, schools can develop tailored intervention plans that cater to the unique needs of each learner, thereby enhancing their overall well-being and educational outcomes.

In summary, the National Policy on Screening, Identification, Assessment, and Support (SIAS) plays a pivotal role in promoting inclusive education and supporting learners with barriers to learning, including mental health challenges. By emphasizing early identification and adopting a multi-disciplinary approach to support, the policy aims to create inclusive and nurturing learning environments where all learners can thrive.

In essence, South African policy strategies for promoting inclusive practices that support students' emotional well-being include providing professional development for teachers, curriculum adaptations, and school-based mental health services. These strategies are aimed at creating a supportive and inclusive environment where all learners can thrive academically and emotionally.

The Importance of Empathy in Student-Teacher Relationships

Empathy is not just a soft skill; it's a crucial tool in creating an inclusive and supportive learning environment. When teachers empathize with their students, they gain insight into their feelings, perspectives and experiences, which helps them tailor their teaching to meet individual needs (Bergin & Bergin, 2009). This understanding fosters a sense of trust and mutual respect between students and teachers, laying the foundation for positive student-teacher relationships (Jennings & Greenberg, 2009).

Inclusive education is about recognizing and valuing the diversity of all students, including their unique backgrounds, abilities and learning styles. Empathy plays a central role in this process, as it allows teachers to empathize with students' challenges and create a supportive environment where all students feel respected and included (Rimm-Kaufman & Hulleman, 2020).

Moreover, empathy enhances communication in the classroom, leading to more meaningful interactions between students and teachers. When teachers empathize with their students, they are better able to communicate their expectations and provide constructive feedback in a way that is supportive and encouraging (Davis et al., 2016). This open and empathetic communication fosters a positive classroom environment where students feel comfortable expressing themselves and engaging in learning activities.

Empathy also promotes a sense of belonging among students, which is essential for their emotional well-being. Research shows that when students feel that their teachers understand and care about them, they are more likely to feel connected to their school community and have a positive attitude towards learning (Bergin & Bergin, 2009). Moreover, empathy in student-teacher relationships fosters a sense of trust and mutual respect. Students are more likely to engage in classroom activities and discussions when they feel that their teacher understands and cares about their well-being (Davis et al., 2016). This positive relationship can have a profound impact on students' academic success and overall well-being.

Empathy is a powerful tool that enables teachers to connect with their students on a deeper level, leading to better communication and a greater understanding of students' needs and perspectives (Rimm-Kaufman & Hulleman, 2020). When teachers empathize with their students, they are able to see the world through their eyes, which allows them to tailor their teaching approaches to meet the diverse needs of their students (Jennings & Greenberg, 2009). This personalized approach not only enhances student engagement but also leads to improved learning outcomes. This positive relationship can have a profound impact on students' academic success and overall well-being. Research has shown that students who feel a strong connection with their teachers are more motivated to learn and achieve academically (Bergin & Bergin, 2009).

Furthermore, empathy plays a crucial role in creating a positive classroom climate where students feel safe, valued and respected. When teachers demonstrate empathy towards their students, they create a supportive learning environment that encourages collaboration and mutual respect among students (Rimm-Kaufman & Hulleman, 2020). This inclusive classroom environment not only benefits students academically but also helps develop their social and emotional skills, which are essential for success in school and beyond (Jennings & Greenberg, 2009).

Therefore, empathy is a fundamental component of positive student-teacher relationships and has a significant impact on student engagement, learning outcomes, and overall well-being. By fostering empathy in the classroom, teachers can create a supportive and inclusive learning environment that promotes academic success and personal growth.

Fostering Empathy Among Students

Fostering empathy among students is essential for creating a compassionate and inclusive learning environment. One effective strategy for promoting empathy is through social-emotional learning (SEL) programs. SEL programs provide students with the skills to understand and manage their emotions, empathize with others and establish positive relationships (Durlak et al., 2011). By incorporating SEL into the curriculum, schools can help students develop empathy and interpersonal skills that are crucial for success in school and beyond.

SEL programs typically include activities and lessons that help students recognize and understand their own emotions, as well as the emotions of others. For example, students may learn to identify facial expressions and body language cues that indicate how someone is feeling. They may also learn strategies for managing their own emotions, such as deep breathing or positive self-talk (Greenberg et al., 2017). By teaching students these skills, SEL programs lay the foundation for empathetic behavior towards others.

Another strategy for promoting empathy among students is through perspective-taking activities. These activities encourage students to see things from different points of view, helping them develop a deeper understanding of others' feelings and experiences (Eisenberg et al., 2015). For example, teachers can use literature or real-life scenarios to prompt discussions about empathy and perspective-taking, encouraging students to consider how others might feel in certain situations.

Research has shown that fostering empathy among students has numerous benefits, both academically and socially. Students who are empathetic towards their peers are more likely to engage in prosocial behaviors, such as helping, sharing and cooperating (Eisenberg et al., 2015). This not only creates a more positive and inclusive learning environment but also contributes to improved academic outcomes.

Furthermore, research has also consistently demonstrated the positive impact of fostering empathy among students, particularly in terms of collaboration and appreciation for diversity. When students empathize with their peers, they are more inclined to work together cooperatively and resolve conflicts peacefully (Hoffman, 2000). This cooperative behavior not only improves the overall classroom atmosphere but also enhances the learning experience for all students involved. Subsequently, by understanding and empathizing with others' experiences and perspectives, students are better equipped to appreciate the rich diversity within their classroom (Jones, 2013). This appreciation fosters a sense of inclusivity and respect, creating a learning environment where all students feel valued and accepted.

Empathy also contributes to the development of essential life skills, such as effective communication and problem-solving. Students who are empathetic are more likely to listen actively to others' viewpoints and consider alternative perspectives, leading to more thoughtful and inclusive discussions (Davis et al., 2016). This not only enriches the learning experience but also prepares students for future interactions in diverse and multicultural settings.

Therefore, fostering empathy among students has far-reaching benefits for both individuals and the broader learning community. By promoting collaboration, appreciation for diversity, and essential life skills, schools can create a more inclusive and supportive learning environment that prepares students for success in an increasingly diverse world. Also, incorporating SEL programs and perspective-taking activities into the curriculum, teachers can help students develop the empathy and interpersonal skills needed to succeed academically and socially.

Empathy and Inclusive Classroom Atmosphere

Empathy is a fundamental element in fostering an inclusive classroom environment, promoting understanding, respect, and acceptance among students. When students practice empathy, they develop a deeper appreciation for the diverse backgrounds, experiences, and perspectives that exist within the classroom (Davis et al., 2016). This heightened understanding serves to break down barriers and cultivate connections between students, leading to a more cohesive and inclusive learning community.

Moreover, empathy has been linked to a reduction in prejudice and an increase in inclusivity among students. Research indicates that when students empathize with others, they are less likely to harbor negative stereotypes or discriminatory attitudes toward individuals from different social or cultural backgrounds (Batson et al., 2002). Instead, empathy encourages students to look beyond surface-level differences and acknowledge the shared humanity that unites them with others.

Additionally, fostering empathy in the classroom has been associated with positive outcomes in terms of social behavior and academic achievement. Students who exhibit empathy are more likely to engage in prosocial behaviors, such as helping and cooperating with their peers (Eisenberg et al., 2015). Furthermore, empathy has been linked to improved communication skills and conflict resolution abilities, which are essential for creating a harmonious and inclusive classroom environment (Jennings & Greenberg, 2009).

As emphasised, empathy not only fosters understanding and respect but also contributes to increased tolerance and acceptance of diversity within the classroom. By encouraging students to consider the feelings and perspectives of others, empathy promotes a sense of fairness and justice, which are essential components of an inclusive learning environment (Sprecher & Fehr, 2005). Students who develop empathy are more likely to speak out against discrimination and advocate for the rights of marginalized groups, thus contributing to a more equitable and inclusive classroom atmosphere.

Moreover, research suggests that empathy can have a positive impact on student behavior and academic achievement. Students who exhibit empathy are more likely to engage in prosocial behaviors, such as helping and cooperating with their peers (Eisenberg et al., 2015). This behavior not only strengthens social bonds within the classroom but also contributes to a more positive and inclusive learning environment.

Further to that, empathy has been linked to improved conflict resolution skills among students. When students are able to empathize with others, they are better equipped to understand differing perspectives and find mutually beneficial solutions to conflicts (Jennings & Greenberg, 2009). This ability to empathize and resolve conflicts peacefully is essential for maintaining a harmonious and inclusive classroom atmosphere.

Therefore, empathy plays a crucial role in creating a more inclusive classroom environment by fostering tolerance, acceptance, and positive social behaviors among students. By promoting empathy, educators can help create a learning environment where all students feel valued, respected, and included.

Empathy and Tailored Teaching Strategies

Empathy is not just a personal trait but also a professional skill that educators can develop to enhance their teaching effectiveness. By understanding and empathizing with students' perspectives, teachers can tailor their instruction to meet the diverse needs of their students. According to Davis et al. (2016), teachers who exhibit empathy are better able to create a supportive and inclusive classroom environment where students feel valued and respected.

One way in which empathy influences teaching strategies is through differentiated instruction. Differentiated instruction involves adapting teaching methods, materials and assessments to accommodate the unique learning styles and abilities of each student (Tomlinson, 2017). When teachers empathize with their students, they are more likely to recognize the individual strengths and challenges of each student, allowing them to adjust their instruction accordingly.

Furthermore, research suggests that empathetic teaching strategies can have a positive impact on student motivation and engagement. When teachers demonstrate empathy towards their students, they create a sense of belonging and connectedness in the classroom, which is essential for student well-being and academic success (Rimm-Kaufman & Hulleman, 2020). Students who feel valued and understood by their teachers are more likely to be motivated to participate in class and engage in their learning.

Empathy in teaching goes beyond understanding academic challenges; it also involves recognizing and responding to students' emotional needs. An empathetic teacher can provide a safe and supportive environment for students to express their emotions and seek help when needed (Brackett et al., 2019). By being attuned to students' emotions, teachers can offer appropriate support and encouragement, helping students develop resilience and coping skills.

Moreover, research suggests that empathetic teachers are better able to create a positive classroom climate, characterized by respect, kindness and inclusivity (Durlak et al., 2011). This positive climate can have a profound impact on student well-being and academic achievement. Students who feel safe and supported are more likely to take risks in their learning and engage in classroom activities.

Furthermore, empathetic teaching strategies can help reduce instances of bullying and conflict in the classroom. When students see their teacher modeling empathy and understanding, they are more likely to emulate these behaviors towards their peers (Sprecher & Fehr, 2005). This can create a more harmonious and respectful classroom environment where students feel empowered to stand up against bullying and support each other.

In essence, empathy is a foundational skill for effective teaching. By cultivating empathy in their teaching practices, educators can create a supportive and inclusive classroom environment where all students feel valued, respected, and motivated to learn. Empathy enables educators to understand students' perspectives and tailor teaching strategies to meet diverse student needs effectively. By incorporating empathetic teaching strategies into their practice, educators can create a supportive and inclusive learning environment where all students feel valued, respected, and capable of achieving success.

Empathy in Professional Development for Educators

Empathy in professional development for educators is not just about individual growth; it's also a significant contributor to the advancement of inclusive education practices. Educators who possess empathetic skills are better equipped to understand and address the diverse needs of their students, leading to more inclusive classroom environments (Jennings & Greenberg, 2009).

One way empathy contributes to inclusive education is by fostering a deeper understanding of students' backgrounds, experiences, and challenges. Through professional development opportunities that emphasize empathy, educators can develop a greater awareness of the diverse cultural, social, and emotional factors that influence student learning (Hargreaves, 2000). This understanding enables educators to create learning environments that are responsive to the needs of all students, regardless of their backgrounds or abilities.

Furthermore, empathy in professional development encourages educators to reflect on their own biases and assumptions, leading to more inclusive teaching practices (Banks, 2015). Educators who are empathetic are more likely to recognize and challenge stereotypes and discriminatory attitudes, creating safer and more welcoming spaces for all students (Howard, 2018).

Moreover, when educators demonstrate empathy towards their colleagues, it creates a culture of collaboration and support within schools (Carrington et al., 2008). Collaborative professional development activities that emphasize empathy allow educators to share insights, resources, and strategies for supporting diverse learners, ultimately contributing to more inclusive educational practices.

Therefore, empathy in professional development for educators is a vital component of promoting inclusive education. By cultivating empathy among educators, schools can create learning environments that celebrate diversity, promote equity, and ensure that all students have the opportunity to thrive.

Cultivating Empathy in Schools

Cultivating empathy in schools is essential for creating a more compassionate and inclusive learning environment. One strategy for cultivating empathy is to incorporate social-emotional learning (SEL) into the school curriculum. SEL programs provide students with the skills to understand and manage their emotions, empathize with others, and establish positive relationships (Durlak et al., 2011). By integrating SEL into the curriculum, schools can help students develop empathy and interpersonal skills that are crucial for success in school and beyond.

Another strategy for cultivating empathy is to create opportunities for students to engage in service-learning projects. Service-learning projects allow students to apply academic knowledge and skills to address real-world issues in their communities (Eyler & Giles, 1999). These projects encourage students to develop a deeper understanding of others' experiences and perspectives, fostering empathy and compassion.

Moreover, schools can cultivate empathy by promoting a culture of kindness and respect. This can be achieved through the implementation of anti-bullying programs and initiatives that promote positive behavior (Espelage & Swearer, 2010). By fostering a culture of kindness, schools can create a more understanding and respectful learning environment where empathy is valued.

Therefore, cultivating empathy in schools is essential for creating a more compassionate and inclusive learning environment. By incorporating SEL into the curriculum, providing opportunities for service-learning, and promoting a culture of kindness, schools can help students develop the empathy and interpersonal skills needed to thrive in an increasingly diverse world.

CONCLUSION

In conclusion, empathy is not just a soft skill but a fundamental tool in creating inclusive learning environments. By fostering empathy among students, educators, and school communities, we can create a more compassionate, understanding, and respectful educational environment. Through professional development, curriculum adaptations, and a focus on mental health, schools can integrate empathy into their policies and practices to promote inclusive education. By recognizing the importance of empathy in education, we can work towards creating a future where all students feel valued, respected, and included in the learning process.

REFERENCES

Banks, J. A. (2015). *Cultural Diversity and Education: Foundations, Curriculum, and Teaching* (6th ed.). Routledge. DOI: 10.4324/9781315622255

Bergin, C., & Bergin, D. (2009). Attachment in the classroom. *Educational Psychology Review*, 21(2), 141–170. DOI: 10.1007/s10648-009-9104-0

Brackett, M. A., Rivers, S. E., & Salovey, P. (2011). Emotional intelligence: Implications for personal, social, academic, and workplace success. *Social and Personality Psychology Compass*, 5(1), 88–103. DOI: 10.1111/j.1751-9004.2010.00334.x

Carrington, B., Tymms, P., & Merrell, C. (2008). Role Models, School Improvement and the 'Net Generation'? New Evidence from Primary Schools in England. *British Educational Research Journal*, 34(3), 315–329. DOI: 10.1080/01411920701532202

Davis, D., Davis, J., & Hunt, A. (2016). The Impact of Empathy on Leadership Effectiveness in Higher Education. *The International Journal of Educational Leadership Preparation*, 11(1), 1–14.

Davis, M. H. (2016). *Empathy: A social psychological approach*. Routledge.

Davis, M. H., & Hunt, J. (2016). Empathy in the context of philosophy. In Decety, J. (Ed.), *Empathy: From Bench to Bedside* (pp. 71–81). MIT Press.

Department of Basic Education. (2011). *Curriculum Assessment Policy Statements*. CAPS.

Department of Basic Education. (2014). *National Policy on Screening, Identification, Assessment, and Support*. SIAS.

Department of Basic Education. (2014). *Policy framework on professional development for teachers in inclusive education*.

Department of Health. (2012). *Integrated School Health Policy*.

Durlak, J. A., Weissberg, R. P., Dymnicki, A. B., Taylor, R. D., & Schellinger, K. B. (2011). The impact of enhancing students' social and emotional learning: A meta-analysis of school-based universal interventions. *Child Development*, 82(1), 405–432. DOI: 10.1111/j.1467-8624.2010.01564.x PMID: 21291449

Eisenberg, N., Spinrad, T. L., & Knafo-Noam, A. (2015). Prosocial development. In Lamb, M. E., & Lerner, R. M. (Eds.), *Handbook of child psychology and developmental science* (7th ed., Vol. 3, pp. 610–656). Wiley. DOI: 10.1002/9781118963418.childpsy315

Eisenberg, N., Spinrad, T. L., & Morris, A. S. (2015). Prosocial development. In Lamb, M. E. (Ed.), *Handbook of child psychology and developmental science* (Vol. 3, pp. 610–656). Wiley. DOI: 10.1002/9781118963418.childpsy315

Espelage, D. L., & Swearer, S. M. (2010). *Bullying in American Schools: A Social-Ecological Perspective on Prevention and Intervention.* Routledge. DOI: 10.4324/9780203842898

Eyler, J., & Giles, D. E. (1999). *Where's the Learning in Service-Learning?* Jossey-Bass.

Greenberg, M. T., Weissberg, R. P., O'Brien, M. U., Zins, J. E., Fredericks, L., Resnik, H., & Elias, M. J. (2017). Enhancing school-based prevention and youth development through coordinated social, emotional, and academic learning. *The American Psychologist*, 58(6-7), 466–474. DOI: 10.1037/0003-066X.58.6-7.466 PMID: 12971193

Hargreaves, A. (2000). Mixed Emotions: Teachers' Perceptions of Their Interactions with Students. *Teaching and Teacher Education*, 16(8), 811–826. DOI: 10.1016/S0742-051X(00)00028-7

Hoffman, M. L. (2000). *Empathy and moral development: Implications for caring and justice.* Cambridge University Press. DOI: 10.1017/CBO9780511805851

Howard, T. C. (2018). *Why Race and Culture Matter in Schools: Closing the Achievement Gap in America's Classrooms.* Teachers College Press.

Jennings, P. A., & Greenberg, M. T. (2009). The Prosocial Classroom: Teacher Social and Emotional Competence in Relation to Student and Classroom Outcomes. *Review of Educational Research*, 79(1), 491–525. DOI: 10.3102/0034654308325693

Jones, S. M. (2013). Social and emotional learning: A critical appraisal. *Teachers College Record*, 115(8), 2114–2143.

Katz, D., Blumler, J. G., & Gurevitch, M. (2015). Uses and Gratifications Research. *Public Opinion Quarterly*, 38(4), 509–523. DOI: 10.1086/268109

Rimm-Kaufman, S. E., & Hulleman, C. S. (2020). Social and emotional learning: A framework for promoting mental health and reducing risk behavior in children and youth. In Weist, M. D., Lever, N. A., Bradshaw, C. P., & Owens, J. S. (Eds.), *Handbook of School Mental Health* (2nd ed., pp. 19–34). Springer.

Rimm-Kaufman, S. E., & Hulleman, C. S. (2020). *Social and emotional learning in the classroom: Promoting academic excellence and supporting social and emotional development.* Guilford Publications.

South African Council for Educators (SACE). (2017). *Guidelines for teacher professional development in inclusive education.*

Sprecher, S., & Fehr, B. (2005). Compassionate love for close others and humanity. *Journal of Social and Personal Relationships*, 22(5), 629–651. DOI: 10.1177/0265407505056439

Tomlinson, C. A. (2017). *How to differentiate instruction in academically diverse classrooms?* ASCD.

Chapter 5
Practitioner Insights on Policy-Driven Shifts in College-Based Education:
Navigating Transformation

G. Rathnakar
 https://orcid.org/0000-0003-3649-3372
Department of Mechanical Engineering, JSS Science and Technology University, Mysuru, India

Lalchhantluangi Pachuau
Department of Management, Pachhunga University College, Aizawl, India

T. Geetha
Department of English, Kongu Engineering College, Erode, India

M. Prabhuswamy
 https://orcid.org/0000-0002-8235-021X
Department of Education, JSS Institute of Education, India

S. Praveenkumar
Centre for Tourism and Hotel Management, Madurai Kamaraj University, India

ABSTRACT

Examining legislative directives and institutional shifts, this chapter delves into the ever-changing terrain of higher education. Offering insights into possibilities, difficulties, and tactics, it examines how policy-driven changes affect educators, administrators, and students. Reforming curricula, evaluating techniques, financing arrangements, and technology integration are all covered in the examination. The

DOI: 10.4018/979-8-3693-4058-5.ch005

Copyright © 2025, IGI Global. Copying or distributing in print or electronic forms without written permission of IGI Global is prohibited.

conflict between regulations and academic freedom, the need of leadership in smooth transitions, and the effects on students' educational experiences are some of the major issues. In order to sustain educational quality and relevance while adapting to changing policy environments, stakeholders must work together

INTRODUCTION

The winds of policy directions and institutional alterations have a tremendous impact on the constantly changing environment of higher education. This chapter highlights the possibilities, problems, and tactics that educators, administrators, and students face as a result of policy-driven changes that impact curriculum, assessment, financing, and technology integration (Webb & McQuaid, 2020). It examines how legislative efforts, particularly those pertaining to curriculum reform and assessment approaches, are transforming college-based education. It emphasizes the requirement of implementing challenges and meeting social demands, with a focus on outcomes-based assessments. The chapter also looks at how teachers strike a compromise between following the law and using fair methods, as well as how these changes affect financing sources (Alkhateeb et al., 2022).

We look at the difficulties administrators and teachers have when attempting to balance innovation with fair access when implementing technology in the classroom. It focuses on the viewpoints of those who are most directly impacted by these policy changes, such as educators who must adjust to new mandates, administrators who must manage the difficulties of implementing policies, and students who encounter both beneficial and detrimental effects of policy-driven changes on their academic journeys. The chapter also sheds light on the difficulties in implementing policies and how changes in policy affect the experiences of learners (Dinu & Chian, 2023). It becomes clear that effective leadership plays a crucial part in successful transitions. Leading academic departments through these transitions is their role. Examined are communication tactics, decision-making procedures, and the difficulties leaders have in coordinating the interests of many stakeholders. This results in a thorough grasp of the leadership environment in the face of changes brought about by policy (Spencer & Lucas, 2021).

The chapter highlights how crucial it is for stakeholders—including teachers, administrators, and students—to work together in order to sustain educational quality and adjust to changing legislative environments. It emphasizes how institutions must work together and engage the community in order to build a resilient learning environment. The chapter addresses the conflict between governmental mandates and academic autonomy while offering useful insights and a comprehensive knowledge of the complex terrain of policy-driven changes in college-based education (Jurasaite-O'Keefe, 2021).

The effect, difficulties, prospects, and tactical reactions to policy directives and institutional alterations are examined in relation to the dynamic changes in higher education. It draws attention to the intricate relationship that exists between policy mandates and academic autonomy since stakeholders who defend their traditional liberties frequently oppose policies (Agrawal et al., 2023; Boopathi, 2023; Durairaj et al., 2023). This demonstrates how difficult it is for educational leaders and decision-makers to negotiate the complexity of a higher education system that is always changing. In order to manage complexity in businesses, leadership is essential. It creates innovation, promotes adaptation, and assures policy compliance. Leaders steer organizations through times of transition by providing visionary direction and fostering cooperative involvement, so optimizing development prospects (Das et al., 2024; Sharma et al., 2024). This research looks at how financing arrangements, curricular modifications, assessment techniques, and technology integration are affected by policy changes. In order to improve educational efficacy and relevance, it emphasizes the necessity for educators and administrators to critically evaluate these areas in order to discover alignment and disputes.

It highlights the significance of inclusion, equity, and student-centeredness in higher education while talking about how legislative changes affect students' learning experiences. It highlights how important it is for stakeholders to work together to manage changing policy environments. Institutions may utilize collective expertise and resources to adapt, innovate, and succeed in a constantly changing educational environment by promoting conversation, cooperation, and shared ownership. This thorough handbook provides practical ideas for educational quality, equity, and sustainability in the twenty-first century and beyond. It helps readers comprehend and navigate higher education policy and institutional transition.

Background

The higher education landscape of today is characterized by dynamic developments that are driven by a range of causes, the main one being legislative mandates. Higher education institutions are faced with a changing mandate to adapt and align themselves with the requirements of the present and future against the backdrop of societal and technological changes (Faruq, 2022).

Throughout history, policies have intervened in higher education to address social requirements, employment demands, and global competitiveness. The focus on creating competent graduates has prompted a reevaluation of traditional curriculum, assessment procedures, and technological integration as economies shift to knowledge-based models. The discussion includes the historical development of higher education policies, an analysis of the foundations of contemporary policy dynamics, and the interaction of local and global factors. The need of comprehending and adjusting to these developments is underscored by the fact that institutions are responsive to national regulatory frameworks, global trends, student mobility, qualification recognition, and joint research activities (Morse, 2020).

The chapter examines how technology is becoming more and more integrated into education, emphasizing how this has affected institutional operations and the sharing of information. It draws attention to the advantages and disadvantages of digital resources, online education, and data-driven decision-making in policy talks. The background and context section lays the groundwork for an in-depth investigation of changes in college-based education brought about by policy (Ericsson, 2021).

Objectives of the Chapter

In order to guide the investigation, analysis, and presentation of practitioner views, the chapter offers a thorough grasp of developments in college-based education that are driven by policy.

- Examine important policy directives affecting higher education and conduct a critical investigation of them, paying particular attention to finance arrangements, curriculum changes, assessment techniques, and technology integration.
- Gain a sophisticated grasp of how policy-driven changes affect different stakeholders within the higher education ecosystem by delving into the experiences and perspectives of educators, administrators, and students.
- Methodically identify and talk about the difficulties practitioners have adjusting to policy demands and the possibilities these changes present. Examining implementation barriers and the tactics used to get over them is part of this.
- Examine how academic leadership functions during policy-driven changes, paying particular attention to communication tactics, decision-making procedures, and the difficulties leaders have in striking a balance between the interests of many stakeholders.
- Emphasize the value of educators, administrators, and students working together to adapt to changing policy environments. Examine effective models of inter-institutional cooperation, community participation, and collaboration.

In order to provide educators, administrators, policymakers, and researchers a better grasp of the potential and problems in this changing field, the chapter attempts to present insightful analyses of how policies have changed college-based education.

THE EVOLVING LANDSCAPE OF HIGHER EDUCATION

This section examines worldwide trends that have an impact on institutions of higher learning, emphasizing the profound change brought about by sociological, technical, and economic reasons (Bozier et al., 2020).

Globalization and Internationalization: The pursuit of higher education is becoming more and more international. Organizations are collaborating internationally, providing collaborative programs, and promoting cross-cultural exchange. Traditional beliefs about higher education are changing as a result of the mobility of professors, students, and ideas across national boundaries, resulting in a more diversified and linked learning environment.

Technology Integration: The delivery and accessibility of education have been completely transformed by the use of technology. Digital resources, interactive technology, and online learning platforms have become essential elements of higher education. This section looks at how educational institutions are using technology to increase accessibility, improve teaching strategies, and offer individualized learning opportunities.

Shifts in Pedagogy: Learning strategies that are more experiential and student-centered are replacing traditional educational techniques. Collaborative learning spaces, project-based evaluations, and active learning are becoming more and more popular. This change reflects a rising understanding of the need of giving students practical skills applicable to the current workforce in addition to academic knowledge.

Focus on Lifelong Learning: The idea that education is a one-time event is giving way to the idea of lifelong learning. Upskilling and continual skill development are becoming more and more important due to the quick changes in the labor market and significant improvements in technology. This section looks at how universities are responding to this paradigm change by providing flexible certification programs and learning paths.

Diversity, Equity, and Inclusion: The creation of diverse and inclusive learning environments is receiving more attention. Important elements of this trend include initiatives to encourage diversity among teachers and staff, integrate varied viewpoints into courses, and address gaps in access to education. This section examines the efforts being made by institutions to provide more fair learning opportunities.

Rethinking Assessment Practices: The aims of higher education are changing, and assessment techniques are changing to reflect this. Innovative assessment techniques are either replacing or supplementing traditional tests. These techniques examine not just information retention but also critical thinking, problem-solving, and the practical application of abilities.

In order for educators, administrators, and policymakers to effectively manage the possibilities and complexity of the changing environment, it is imperative that they comprehend the interplay between legislative mandates and developing trends in higher education, as this review makes clear.

Historical Context of Policy Influences

Over time, laws regarding higher education have changed in response to social demands, changes in the economy, and changes in educational philosophy. In order to promote social mobility, they increased access to higher education. The G.I. Bill changed the face of higher education by giving returning warriors access to previously unheard-of levels of study following World War II. Policies emphasizing diversity and inclusion in the 1960s and 1970s gave rise to affirmative action programs (Libby, 2021).

Market-oriented policies that prioritized competition, efficiency, and responsibility began to take shape in the 1980s. Globally, policy pertaining to higher education have been shaped by neoliberal ideals that prioritize results, performance measures, and cost-effectiveness. The cyclical nature of policy trends and shifting policy goals as each age adapts to the possibilities and difficulties of its own are reflected in this historical movement.

Current State of Policy Dynamics

Today's higher education policies address issues including access, cost, quality assurance, and technology and are shaped by institutional, national, and international influences. Globally, there is an emphasis on uniformity and reciprocal acknowledgement of credentials, with programs such as the European Union's Bologna Process fostering linked higher education. At the national level, nations strike a balance between regulation and autonomy, attending to economic needs, matching labor demands with educational requirements, and promoting innovation and research (Baumfeld Andre et al., 2020).

The purpose of institutional policies in higher education is to provide accountability and openness by means of financing systems, accreditation procedures, and evaluation frameworks. The uniformity of these principles and the recognition of different objectives and settings, however, are at odds. In order to prepare for a more thorough examination of the policy directives affecting college-based education, efforts are undertaken to strike a balance between innovation and preserving educational quality (Rastogi et al., 2021).

POLICY DIRECTIVES SHAPING HIGHER EDUCATION

This section looks at important policy measures that have shaped the objectives, makeup, and priorities of educational institutions. These initiatives range from international accords to national mandates. These rules are essential to the advancement of society and have a significant influence on how higher education is shaped (Bi et al., 2020).

Examination of Policy Initiatives:

Higher education's aims and direction are significantly influenced by national and international policy efforts. For instance, the goal of European programs like the Bologna Process is to standardize and unify the higher education systems of all participating nations. In a similar vein, national strategies can prioritize improving research and innovation, increasing educational access, or addressing concerns of inclusion and equity. Investigating these projects entails learning about their stated goals, implementation processes, and driving forces. It also necessitates a careful examination of the ways in which these policies overlap and occasionally differ, resulting in a complicated web of impacts that organizations must manage (Chakraborti et al., 2020).

Impact on Curriculum Reforms

Curriculum modifications are one of the areas where policy directives have the most noticeable and immediate consequences. Policies frequently need modifications to educational programs' content, delivery, and structure in order to better meet the requirements of the changing society and the demands of the market. This section examines the ways in which changes in policy impact the structure and content of curriculum. Curriculum changes might include adding interdisciplinary methods, stressing the development of skills in addition to theoretical knowledge, or upgrading course material to reflect newly developing fields. Policies might also support curriculum integration of technology, global viewpoints, and real-world applications to guarantee graduates are equipped to face the challenges of a world that is changing quickly (Bi et al., 2020; Chakraborti et al., 2020).

This research examines the opportunities and difficulties educators have when putting new policies into practice, with a particular emphasis on striking a careful balance between adhering to mandates and upholding fundamental principles. It offers a greater comprehension of how universities react to directives from outside sources while giving students meaningful, interesting, and life-changing educational experiences.

Implications for Assessment Methodologies

Higher education policy directives have a major impact on curriculum revisions, assessment techniques, and student learning assessments. These factors affect student performance, learning outcomes, and the efficacy of education as a whole (Harris et al., 2021).

Alignment with Learning Outcomes: The significance of distinct and quantifiable learning outcomes is frequently emphasized in policy directives. As a result, evaluation techniques have changed to better match these results. Tools and procedures for assessment are created to gauge students' comprehension of the material as well as their capacity for knowledge application, critical thought, and skill demonstration. To provide a more thorough assessment of student accomplishment, policies mandate the development of precise assessment criteria that are closely connected to the desired learning goals.

Emphasis on Formative Assessment: Along with the shift to a more outcomes-focused methodology, formative assessment is receiving greater attention. Policies acknowledge the need of continuous, iterative assessment procedures that give students immediate feedback so they may monitor their development and close any gaps in their knowledge. This change promotes a culture of continuous improvement by encouraging teachers to incorporate continuous evaluation techniques including discussions, quizzes, and project milestones into the teaching and learning process.

Diversity of Assessment Methods: Policy directions support a variety of assessment techniques in order to fully capture the spectrum of student competences and abilities. Project-based evaluations, presentations, group work, and hands-on demonstrations are used in addition to traditional exams. Policies acknowledge that a range of assessment techniques can yield a more comprehensive picture of a student's skills and more accurately reflect the complexity of learning experiences.

Incorporation of Technology: Assessment techniques are directly impacted by the use of technology into educational practices. Digital tools for feedback and grading, computer-based testing, and online exams are becoming more common. Policies frequently support the application of technology to improve the flexibility, fairness, and efficiency of evaluations. But this shift has its own set of difficulties, such as security concerns, accessibility issues, and the requirement for technology competence.

Focus on Authentic Assessment: Because of legislative impacts, authentic assessment—which emulates activities and problems found in the actual world—is becoming more and more popular. Policies stress the inclusion of evaluations that mimic professional environments and acknowledge the significance of educating students for the demands of their future employment. Case studies, simulations, or industry-specific projects that call on students to use what they've learned in real-world situations are examples of this (Chakraborti et al., 2020).

Higher education assessment practices are changing due to policy-driven shifts, which are encouraging diverse, outcomes-focused, and technologically advanced approaches. These modifications have an influence on the quality of educational outcomes, the experience of students, and the efficiency of higher education in preparing students for the complexity of the modern world. They also provide institutions and instructors with additional difficulties, such as accommodating the various requirements of students, guaranteeing equity, and organizing the logistics of technology-driven evaluations. Policies need to adapt to these real-world difficulties (Wang et al., 2020).

Figure 1. Changes in funding structures - policy directives

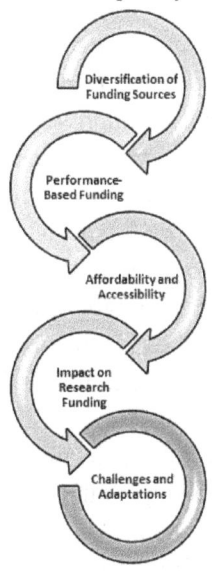

Changes in Funding Structures

Higher education institutions' financial environments are greatly impacted by policy directives, which frequently result in modifications to funding arrangements that better match overarching objectives and priorities. This section looks at how these changes in legislation impact accessibility, institutional sustainability, and overall quality of education (Bi et al., 2020). The policy directives have led to changes in funding structures as shown in Figure 1.

Diversification of financing Sources: The diversification of financing sources is a noteworthy trend that has emerged in response to governmental mandates. The conventional dependence on public funds is frequently augmented by grants for research, private investments, and charity. By encouraging institutions to have a more diverse financial portfolio, policies help to promote financial resilience and lessen reliance on any one source of income.

Performance-Based financing: A lot of legislative initiatives use financing models that tie financial distributions to measures of institutional performance. Measures of student performance, graduation rates, and research production may fall under this category. By providing incentives for excellence in areas that are in line with policy goals, performance-based financing seeks to promote efficiency and accountability in the distribution of resources across institutions.

Affordability and Accessibility: Policy directives frequently tackle issues pertaining to the accessibility and cost of postsecondary education. Initiatives to lower tuition, offer financial assistance, or improve accessibility for underrepresented groups may be supported via funding arrangements. Policies aim to improve equity and inclusivity in higher education by exerting influence on funding distribution.

Impact on Research Funding: The financial environment for research at higher education institutions is also shaped by policies. The prioritization of innovation, scientific progress, and social benefit might result in modifications to the financial mechanisms that facilitate research endeavors. Policies may promote business and academic cooperation, creating a climate that is favorable to significant research projects.

Challenges and Adaptations: Although financing structure modifications seek to solve a number of issues and bring institutions into line with policy objectives, they are not without problems of their own. During transitions, institutions could experience financial uncertainty. Policy-driven changes can also occasionally lead to inequities across institutions with different levels of adaptability. Strategic planning and resource management are necessary to strike a balance between upholding financial sustainability and fulfilling policy goals.

Role of Technological Integration

The financial environment of higher education institutions is greatly impacted by policy directives, which frequently result in modifications to financing systems that better reflect overarching objectives and priorities. This section looks at how institutional viability, accessibility, and overall quality of education are impacted by these policy-driven changes (Faruq, 2022; Jurasaite-O'Keefe, 2021).

Enhanced Teaching and Learning: Technology is a driving force behind creative educational approaches that support policy objectives. Personalized and interactive learning experiences may be facilitated by virtual classrooms, multimedia materials, and online learning platforms. Laws may support the use of these technologies in the classroom in order to improve student performance and reach more people.

Administrative Efficiency and Data-Driven Decision-Making: Policies frequently stress the need of data-driven decision-making and administrative efficiency. Simplified administrative procedures, such as resource allocation and enrollment management, are made possible by technological integration. Data analytics technologies assist organizations connect their goals with policy guidelines and show responsibility by supporting evidence-based decision-making.

Access and Flexibility: Technology can improve educational access, which is a major goal of many governmental efforts. Learners have more freedom because to digital tools, online courses, and remote learning initiatives. Policies may incentivize educational institutions to use technology to connect with marginalized communities, removing obstacles to education related to geography.

Challenges of Integration: Even while it seems promising, integrating technology raises issues with training, infrastructure, and digital fairness. To guarantee that all students can benefit from technology and that teachers are properly prepared to teach in the rapidly changing digital environment, policies must address these issues.

developments in finance arrangements and technology integration are two aspects of policy-driven developments in higher education that affect accessibility, affordability, and educational opportunities. Strategic planning, flexibility, and dedication to the objectives of higher education policies—which reflect priorities and shape institutional experiences—are necessary for effectively navigating these changes.

STAKEHOLDERS IN HIGHER EDUCATION TRANSFORMATION

The views of educators, administrators, and students about the transformation of higher education are examined in this part. Their experiences, difficulties, and solutions are highlighted, offering important insights into the complex nature of this shift (Cheng et al., 2022). The figure 2 depicts the various stakeholders involved in the transformation of higher education.

Figure 2. Stakeholders in higher education transformation

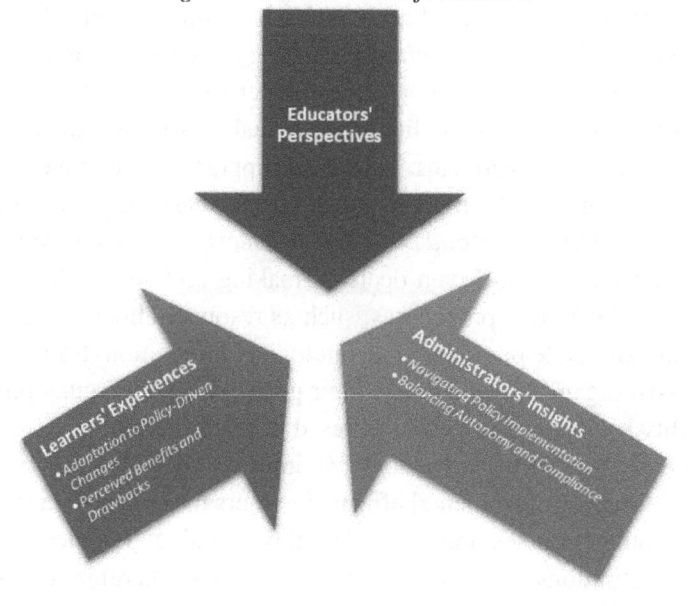

Educators' Perspectives

Teachers have difficulties while trying to match their methods of instruction with changing policies. These difficulties include the necessity for ongoing professional development, resistance to change, and the need to strike a balance between traditional and cutting-edge methods. Educators use growth mindsets, collaborative professional development, and the formation of practice communities to exchange best practices and experiences in order to overcome these obstacles. This method enhances instructional efficacy while assisting instructors in navigating the intricate web of changing rules.

Administrators' Insights

Navigating Policy Implementation: Within the organization, administrators are essential in converting policy instructions into workable programs. Understanding the nuances of the policy environment, successfully interacting with many stakeholders, and developing frameworks for successful execution are all necessary for navigating policy implementation. The institution's mission and objectives must be taken into consideration when administrators interpret policies.

Balancing Autonomy and Compliance: Striking a fine balance between preserving institutional autonomy and guaranteeing conformity with external rules is one of the fundamental issues facing administrators. This entails developing institutional policies that respect the institution's own character and goal while complying with more general requirements. Achieving this equilibrium requires open communication and cooperative decision-making procedures.

Learners' Experiences

Adaptation to Policy-Driven Changes: Changes generated by policy directly affect learners, who are the main benefactors of higher education. It might be difficult to adjust to new curriculum, evaluation techniques, and technology integration. It could be necessary for students to change the way they study, adopt digital resources, and participate in various forms of evaluation. The degree of flexibility varies depending on things like comfort level with technology and previous educational experiences.

Perceived Benefits and Drawbacks: Changes induced by policy are typically seen by learners as having both advantages and disadvantages. Benefits might include more learning freedom, exposure to a variety of teaching techniques, and education that is in line with business demands. Potential drawbacks may include difficulties adjusting to new technology, worries about the impartiality of assessments, or alterations to regular learning schedules. The viewpoints of students offer insightful commentary that helps politicians and educators improve and maximize the application of policies (Giesenbauer & Müller-Christ, 2020).

A collaborative and flexible strategy that takes into account the interwoven views, difficulties, and methods of educators, administrators, and students is necessary for the successful transformation of higher education. By comprehending their viewpoints, we may create more useful rules and procedures that raise the standard and applicability of higher education (Benavides et al., 2020).

Figure 3. Leadership in navigating policy-driven transitions

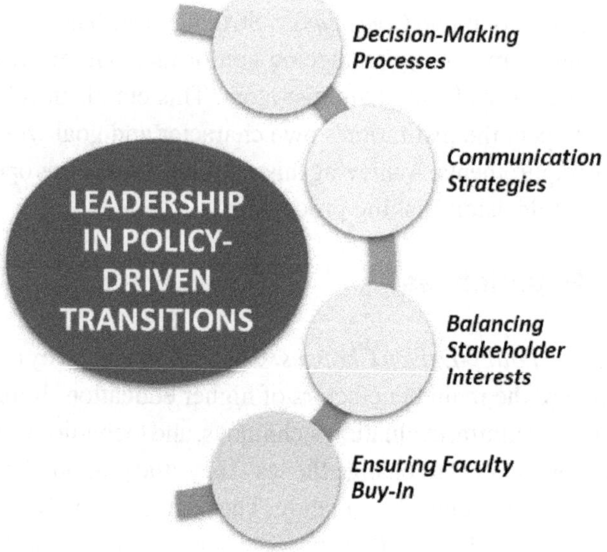

LEADERSHIP IN NAVIGATING POLICY-DRIVEN TRANSITIONS

The Role of Academic Leadership

Leading higher education institutions through the complicated transition brought about by governmental mandates is academic leadership. This section delves into the many responsibilities of academic leaders, emphasizing their approaches to decision-making and communication. Academic leaders, who design institutional transformation, must strike a careful balance between following governmental directives and maintaining the distinctive character of their institutions (Cheng et al., 2022; Giesenbauer & Müller-Christ, 2020). The figure 3 illustrates the role of leadership in navigating policy-driven transitions.

Decision-Making Processes

Strategic Alignment with Policies: Aligning institutional plans with mandates from external policies is the responsibility of academic leaders. Ensuring that institutional actions align with wider educational agendas necessitates a careful examination of policy goals and objectives. Strategic planning meetings, which frequently incorporate feedback from several stakeholders, serve as essential platforms for making decisions that are in line with policy requirements.

Incorporating Diverse Perspectives: Diverse viewpoints must be taken into account when making decisions on the restructuring of higher education. Academic leaders interact with administrators, teachers, and other stakeholders in order to obtain feedback and insights. In addition to ensuring a more thorough grasp of the opportunities and difficulties, this collaborative approach also helps people who will be impacted by the decisions feel invested in and supportive of the choices being made.

Data-Informed Decision-Making: Effective academic leadership is characterized by data-driven decision-making. Academic leaders make judgments based on information about stakeholder input, institutional performance, and student results. This evidence-based strategy improves the accuracy and efficacy of initiatives, enabling leaders to pinpoint areas that are succeeding and those that still need work to better fit with the objectives of policy.

Communication Strategies

Transparent and Inclusive Communication: Effective leadership during periods of change is mostly dependent on effective communication. In order to maintain stakeholder engagement and informedness, academic leaders place a high priority on open and inclusive communication. There are several ways to communicate the reasoning behind choices, the status of execution, and the anticipated effects on the institution: through town hall meetings, open forums, and regular updates.

Building a Shared Vision: The expression and dissemination of a common vision is one of the most important communication techniques. Academic leaders collaborate with interested parties to develop an engaging story that harmonizes policy directions with institutional objectives. This common goal serves as a compass, giving people a feeling of direction and purpose that overcomes the difficulties brought on by change.

Addressing Concerns and Feedback: The academic community frequently expresses concerns and criticism in response to transformation. Academic leaders use techniques to pay attention to issues raised, accept criticism, and give concise answers. Establishing platforms for open communication guarantees that the opinions of teachers, staff, and students are heard, which promotes a culture of flexibility and response.

Challenges Faced by Academic Leaders

In policy-driven reforms, academic leaders must manage resistance, balance stakeholder demands, and deal with budget limitations, among other difficulties. They also need to make decisions with flexibility and foresight due to the changing nature of policy environments. Through influencing how policies are implemented, coordinating objectives with instructions, encouraging open communication, and interacting with a range of viewpoints, they play a critical role in higher education. It is up to them to overcome obstacles, promote teamwork, and ignite a common goal in order to lead institutions toward a future that satisfies the changing demands of both society and students. Strategic problems for academic leaders in higher education include securing strong faculty support and striking a balance between the interests of many stakeholders (Mohamed Hashim et al., 2021).

Balancing Stakeholder Interests

Managing Divergent Perspectives: Managing the differing viewpoints and interests of many stakeholders is one of a leader's biggest problems. There may be competing interests and expectations amongst students, teachers, administrators, and outside partners. Finding a balance between following policy guidelines and attending to the particular demands of various groups calls for skillful negotiation and a thorough awareness of the institutional ecology (Dumulescu & Muțiu, 2021).

Addressing Resistance to Change: One of the biggest obstacles to the transformation of higher education is resistance to change. Stakeholders may be reluctant to change long-standing procedures out of concern for unknowns or disturbances. Leaders have to overcome this reluctance by outlining the advantages of the changes, explaining why they are necessary, and include stakeholders in the decision-making process. Creating a culture that welcomes innovation and change is becoming a crucial part of leadership.

Aligning Institutional Culture: Institutions are shaped by their own cultures. It can be difficult for leaders to implement transformative policies since they frequently call for changes to institutional culture. Achieving a successful alignment between policy requirements and institutional ethos requires a sophisticated strategy that acknowledges and preserves current cultural aspects while promoting a culture of adaptation and continual development.

Ensuring Faculty Buy-In

Engaging Faculty in Decision-Making: Getting faculty support is one of the most important components of a successful transition in higher education. A sense of ownership is facilitated by including academics in decision-making processes, soliciting their opinions, and valuing their experience. Faculty members are more likely to support and actively participate in the transition when they feel that their perspectives are appreciated and taken into consideration (Fernandez & Shaw, 2020).

Communicating the Value Proposition: Effectively conveying to academics the benefits of changes induced by policy is a challenge for leaders. Because they are so closely involved in the teaching process, faculty members must comprehend how changes will further the institution's goal, improve student learning, and advance their own professional growth. To win people over, leaders need to clearly state these advantages.

Providing Support and Resources: Fears of the real-world effects of proposed changes are frequently the root cause of resistance. It is imperative for leaders to guarantee that educators have the required assistance and materials to adjust to novel approaches, innovations, or course designs. Faculty buy-in may be facilitated by providing mentoring programs, professional development opportunities, and a welcoming climate for innovation.

Higher education leaders should take an active, inclusive leadership stance, establish trust by open communication, encourage teamwork, and respond to issues. Overcoming resistance may be facilitated by providing chances for professional development, acknowledging accomplishments, and establishing feedback loops. It is essential to comprehend the institutional setting, use efficient communication techniques, and engage in cooperative decision-making.

COLLABORATIVE EFFORTS IN ADAPTING TO POLICY LANDSCAPES

In order to adapt to the changing and complicated policy landscapes involving educators, administrators, and students, this section highlights the importance of collaborative action in higher education (Wamsler et al., 2020).

Importance of Collective Action:

Addressing Multifaceted Challenges: Working together is crucial to tackling the complex issues that arise from changes in policy. Students, administrators, and educators all contribute different viewpoints, specialties, and life experiences. Together, they may create comprehensive solutions that take into account all the many facets of implementing policies, from administrative to pedagogical alterations (Adade Williams et al., 2020; Wamsler et al., 2020).

Promoting Shared Responsibility: Sharing responsibility is necessary to adjust to changing policy environments. Working together encourages a group commitment to overcoming obstacles and seizing possibilities. A culture of shared responsibility develops when stakeholders realize that their contributions are essential to the institution's performance in the face of policy changes.

Harnessing Diverse Expertise: Every stakeholder group has a different area of expertise. Administrators give organizational viewpoints, educators offer instructional ideas, and students offer insightful feedback on the educational process. Working together makes it possible to combine different types of information, which promotes creativity and all-encompassing problem-solving.

Interactions Among Educators, Administrators, and Students:

Faculty-Administrator Collaboration: Adapting policies requires effective faculty-administrator collaboration. Administrators may make sure that rules are implemented in a way that is consistent with educational goals by utilizing educators' firsthand knowledge of teaching and learning methods. In turn, faculty members can acquire a more profound comprehension of the administrative factors that influence policy decisions (Fernandez & Shaw, 2020; Morse, 2020).

Student-Inclusive Decision-Making: It is essential to involve students in decision-making processes in order to develop policies that meet their needs and expectations. Because of their personal experiences in the classroom, students provide a distinct viewpoint. Students' opinions are heard when they participate in conversations regarding policy changes, which leads to more fair and student-centric policies.

Collaborative Professional Development: Initiatives for professional development are included in collaborative endeavors. Administrators and educators can work together to create and implement training programs that provide faculty members the abilities they need to handle policy changes. Professional growth is guaranteed to be in line with the institution's strategic goals and the changing requirements of the policy landscape thanks to this cooperative approach.

Fostering a Culture of Collaboration:

Open Communication Channels: Establishing transparent and open lines of communication is necessary to build collaborative endeavors. Frequent discussion venues, such town halls, student forums, and faculty meetings, help to foster the sharing of opinions and issues. In order to foster a culture where different viewpoints are accepted and constructive criticism is actively sought out and appreciated, leaders are essential.

Building Trust and Mutual Respect: Mutual respect and trust are essential for productive teamwork. Collaborative efforts are more probable when educators, administrators, and students feel that their contributions are appreciated and respected. Acknowledging accomplishments, promoting inclusion, and recognizing individual skills are all important components of creating a culture of trust.

Celebrating Successes Together: Collective celebration of cooperative work is appropriate. Acknowledging and commemorating accomplishments, whether they policy implementations, creative pedagogies, or student successes, strengthens the beneficial effects of teamwork. This celebration encourages stakeholders to keep up their joint efforts and adds to a culture of shared accomplishment.

Teachers, administrators, and students must work together in order to adapt to the changing policy landscape in higher education. By means of collective accountability, varied proficiency, and comprehensive deliberation, interested parties may effectively manage obstacles and augment an adaptable learning environment. Establishing a collaborative culture is crucial for effectively adjusting to changing policy dynamics.

BUILDING A SUPPORTIVE ECOSYSTEM

This section highlights how crucial it is for higher education institutions to collaborate with the community in order to create a supportive environment that will enable successful adaptation to shifts caused by policy (Aronson et al., 2020).

Community Engagement:

Stakeholder Involvement: Actively incorporating a variety of stakeholders in the decision-making process includes teachers, administrators, students, alumni, and local communities. Institutions may guarantee that policies are not just influenced by academic expertise but also matched with community needs and expectations by soliciting input, feedback, and cooperation from these various groups(Buckley et al., 2020).

Enhancing Institutional Relevance: Interacting with the larger community guarantees that universities stay current and adaptable. This involvement involves local companies, governmental bodies, and cultural institutions in addition to the academic community. Through comprehending community demands and establishing collaborative relationships, institutions may make a significant impact on both social advancement and economic expansion.

Fostering a Culture of Inclusivity: Participation in the community promotes an inclusive culture where all stakeholders' perspectives are respected and heard. In order to ensure that policies and educational practices are created with diversity, equality, and inclusion in mind, this inclusivity also extends to historically marginalized groups. Creating an inclusive culture is one way to make the academic environment more cooperative and helpful.

Collaboration Across Institutions:

Shared Resources and Expertise: When institutions collaborate, they exchange best practices, knowledge, and resources. Collaborative approaches acknowledge the possibility of mutual benefit rather than seeing other institutions as rivals. Joint research projects, cooperative efforts, and the sharing of technology infrastructure are examples of resource sharing. Higher education institutions' total capability and effectiveness are improved by this cooperative approach(Spigel & Vinodrai, 2021).

Cross-Institutional Research and Innovation: Institutions must frequently adopt novel approaches and fresh research paths as a result of policy-driven changes. Cross-institutional research projects and initiatives are facilitated by collaboration across institutions. This enhances the scholarly environment and helps address difficult problems that go beyond the purview of certain universities. Collaborative research endeavors may result in discoveries and progresses that are advantageous to the larger scientific community.

Networks for Knowledge Exchange: Establishing cooperative networks enables organizations to share information and perspectives. Academic leaders, faculty, and administrators have venues to exchange experiences, tactics, and lessons gained through professional associations, consortiums, and collaborations. These networks are great tools for understanding policy environments and staying up to date on new developments in higher education.

It is necessary to overcome obstacles like competitiveness, resource limitations, and conflicting agendas in order to create a healthy environment in higher education. Institutions may overcome obstacles and seize chances for constructive change by promoting diversity, pooling resources, and building cooperative networks. This strategy builds resilience and helps create a more adaptable and dynamic environment in higher education.

BALANCING POLICY MANDATES AND ACADEMIC AUTONOMY

This segment explores the difficult problem of striking a balance between academic autonomy and governmental demands in higher education, including case examples that demonstrate effective solutions and tactics for doing so.(Kallio et al., 2022). The figure 4 illustrates the process of balancing policy mandates and academic autonomy.

Figure 4. Balancing policy mandates and academic autonomy

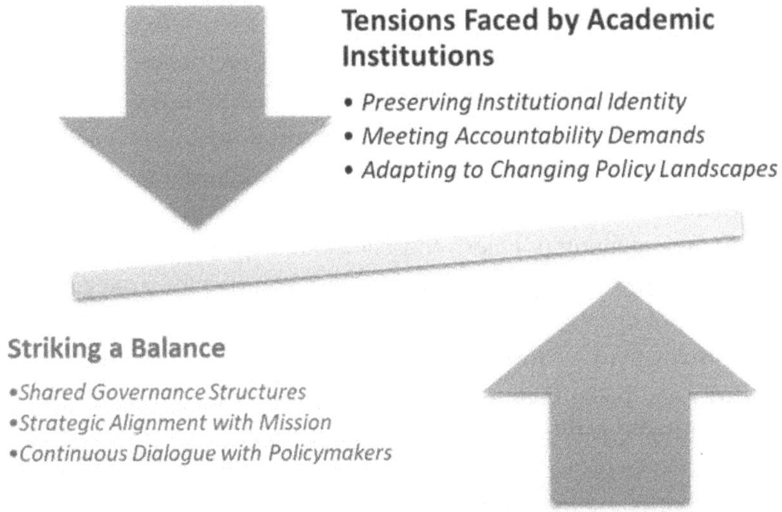

Tensions Faced by Academic Institutions
- *Preserving Institutional Identity*
- *Meeting Accountability Demands*
- *Adapting to Changing Policy Landscapes*

Striking a Balance
- *Shared Governance Structures*
- *Strategic Alignment with Mission*
- *Continuous Dialogue with Policymakers*

Tensions Faced by Academic Institutions:

Preserving Institutional Identity: Academic institutions frequently struggle to maintain their own institutional character while still complying to external legislative obligations. While policies may strive for uniformity, institutions respect their independence in defining their goals, principles, and methods of instruction. It's never easy to find a balance between protecting institutional identity and adhering to policy obligations (Hong & Hamot, 2020).

Meeting Accountability Demands: Policies usually place a strong emphasis on accountability and call for quantifiable results and performance indicators. Institutions are under pressure to operate with efficacy and efficiency as a result. Institutions may find it difficult to strike a balance between these demands and the requirement for flexibility and responsiveness to local settings, even while accountability is essential for quality assurance.

Adapting to Changing Policy Landscapes: Policy landscapes are dynamic, which brings with it uncertainty and need ongoing adaptation. Institutions have to deal with competing or quickly changing policies while navigating shifting objectives. Decision-making agility and the flexibility to modify institutional initiatives while maintaining academic program continuity and stability are necessary in this changing context.

Striking a Balance

Shared Governance Structures: Creating shared governance frameworks is a crucial tactic for striking a balance between academic autonomy and policy demands. Diverse viewpoints are taken into account when decision-making procedures involve administrators, teachers, and even students. By encouraging a feeling of ownership, shared governance enables institutions to work together to successfully traverse the challenges of implementing policies (Niesche et al., 2023).

Strategic Alignment with Mission: Institutions can strive for strategic alignment by ensuring that policy adaptations are in harmony with their overarching mission and goals. This involves a thorough examination of policy directives to identify areas of synergy and potential tension. By clearly articulating how policy changes align with institutional values, leaders can foster a sense of purpose and direction.

Continuous Dialogue with Policymakers: Establishing an ongoing dialogue with policymakers is crucial for building understanding and influencing policy directions. Institutions can actively engage with policymakers, providing feedback based on their experiences and offering insights into the practical implications of policy mandates. This dialogue can contribute to more nuanced and context-sensitive policy frameworks.

Case Studies on Successful Balancing Acts:

Harvard University - Strategic Adaptation: One prominent example of negotiating policy environments while maintaining academic autonomy is Harvard University. Harvard has carefully adjusted to these constraints while upholding its dedication to intellectual freedom and institutional autonomy, even though it is subject to a number of federal and state rules. The institution has prospered in the face of shifting regulatory environments because of its capacity to match policies with its goal (Lennert Da Silva, 2022).

University of California System - Collaborative Advocacy: A good example of cooperation in striking a balance between academic autonomy and policy obligations is the University of California System. In response to issues with state financing and changing educational policy, the campuses within the system have joined forces in advocacy campaigns. The system has impacted policy conversations and outcomes by putting up a united front and highlighting the need of academic autonomy.

Open University (UK) - Innovation Within Regulatory Frameworks: The United Kingdom's Open University has shown creativity working under legal constraints. Open University has led the way in online and remote learning while abiding by national regulations. The institution has shown that academic innovation may flourish within legal constraints by utilizing its autonomy to modify educational techniques and delivery systems.

The case examples emphasize how crucial it is to collaborate, make strategic decisions, and uphold institutional principles in order to strike a balance between legislative requirements and academic autonomy. They can provide other organizations helpful advice on how to handle complicated policy issues while preserving their own identities and purposes.

IMPLICATIONS FOR STUDENT LEARNING EXPERIENCES

This section examines how policy changes affect institutions of higher learning, with an emphasis on student involvement, educational quality, and pedagogical method adaptability to these changes (Zhai, 2022).

Quality of Education Amidst Policy Shifts:

Alignment with Policy Objectives: Changes in policy frequently need adapting instructional strategies to better meet overall goals. The standard of education may be impacted by this. Institutions must strike a compromise between upholding strict academic standards and the obligation to comply with policy. Making sure that changes driven by legislation improve rather than degrade the overall quality of the educational experience is the difficult part (Parmaxi, 2023).

Incorporating 21st-Century Skills: The development of 21st-century skills, such as critical thinking, teamwork, and flexibility, is emphasized in many policy directives. The curriculum's implications for student learning experiences include the inclusion of these competencies. Institutions may need to reconsider their approaches to instruction, offer chances for experiential learning, and create environments that help students develop the skills required by changing policy landscapes.

Student Engagement and Success:

Enhanced Student-Centric Approaches: Changes in policy frequently place more emphasis on a student-centric strategy and give individualized learning experiences priority. This means that educational institutions must improve student engagement by implementing interactive learning materials, mentorship programs, and individualized support systems. Institutions may enhance student engagement and achievement by customizing learning experiences to each person (Husaini et al., 2022).

Support for Underrepresented Groups: Institutions are required under policies centered on diversity and inclusion to offer specific assistance to minority student groups. This includes programs to address the equity gap, improve accessibility, and establish inclusive classrooms. Regardless of origin or identity, the effective implementation of such rules may have a good influence on all students' involvement and achievement.

Adapting Pedagogical Approaches:

Integration of Technology: Policy guidelines frequently promote the use of technology in the classroom. Because of this change, educators must modify their educational strategies to make use of interactive platforms, digital tools, and internet resources. Accepting technology may help students learn more collaboratively, become more engaged, and get ready for the digital demands of the modern job (Rajabalee & Santally, 2021).

Experiential and Applied Learning: Numerous policies promote chances for experiential and applied learning as a means of bridging the knowledge gap between academia and practical application. In order to integrate internships, research projects, and hands-on experiences into the curriculum, educational institutions need to modify their instructional methodologies. In addition to increasing student engagement, this experiential learning gives graduates employable skills that employers desire.

Flexibility and Personalization: Changes driven by policy frequently place an emphasis on individualized learning and flexible educational routes. This necessitates moving away from strict, one-size-fits-all methods. Teachers must modify their instructional approaches to take into account students' varying learning tempos, preferences, and styles. A more customized educational experience is made possible by competency-based evaluations, adaptable course frameworks, and personalized learning plans.

CONCLUSIONS

This chapter explains how policy directives affect higher education, emphasizing the possibilities, difficulties, and tactics faced by teachers, administrators, and students. It draws attention to how difficult it may be to navigate shifting regulatory environments, handle a variety of stakeholder interests, balance external mandates with academic institution identities, and handle transition. All of these challenges need for thoughtful solutions.

In addition to stressing the necessity for inclusive decision-making procedures, open communication, and shared governance structures, the chapter highlights the need of stakeholder participation in policy adaptation. In order to address changing policy needs and better prepare students for the future, it also emphasizes how important it is for institutions to prioritize education quality, match with policy objectives, and modify pedagogical techniques to embrace technology, experiential learning, and individualized experiences. In order to ensure that objectives and directions are aligned while preserving an institution's distinctive character, academic leadership plays a critical role in navigating policy environments. Establishing open communication, teamwork, and trust are crucial for effective leadership throughout change. Case studies of successful institutions emphasize the value of innovation and adaptation, including Harvard, the University of California System, and Open University (UK).

The chapter stresses the value of ongoing adaptation in higher education and exhorts institutions to continue being proactive, flexible, and sensitive to shifting legislative environments. It demands communication with decision-makers, interaction with a range of stakeholders, and a dedication to diversity and inclusiveness. The chapter emphasizes how these policy processes have the capacity to revolutionize the development and quality of higher education.

REFERENCES

Adade Williams, P., Sikutshwa, L., & Shackleton, S. (2020). Acknowledging indigenous and local knowledge to facilitate collaboration in landscape approaches—Lessons from a systematic review. *Land (Basel)*, 9(9), 331. DOI: 10.3390/land9090331

Agrawal, A. V., Pitchai, R., Senthamaraikannan, C., Alangudi Balaji, N., Sajithra, S., & Boopathi, S. (2023). Digital Education System During the COVID-19 Pandemic. In Bell, J., & Gifford, T. (Eds.), (pp. 104–126). Advances in Educational Technologies and Instructional Design. IGI Global., DOI: 10.4018/978-1-6684-6424-3.ch005

Alkhateeb, H., Romanowski, M. H., Sellami, A., Abu-Tineh, A. M., & Chaaban, Y. (2022). Challenges facing teacher education in Qatar: Q methodology research. *Heliyon*, 8(7), e09845. DOI: 10.1016/j.heliyon.2022.e09845 PMID: 35847612

Aronson, J., Goodwin, N., Orlando, L., Eisenberg, C., & Cross, A. T. (2020). A world of possibilities: Six restoration strategies to support the United Nation's Decade on Ecosystem Restoration. *Restoration Ecology*, 28(4), 730–736. DOI: 10.1111/rec.13170

Baumfeld Andre, E., Reynolds, R., Caubel, P., Azoulay, L., & Dreyer, N. A. (2020). Trial designs using real-world data: The changing landscape of the regulatory approval process. *Pharmacoepidemiology and Drug Safety*, 29(10), 1201–1212. DOI: 10.1002/pds.4932 PMID: 31823482

Benavides, L. M. C., Tamayo Arias, J. A., Arango Serna, M. D., Branch Bedoya, J. W., & Burgos, D. (2020). Digital transformation in higher education institutions: A systematic literature review. *Sensors (Basel)*, 20(11), 3291. DOI: 10.3390/s20113291 PMID: 32526998

Bi, J., Chowdhry, S., Wu, S., Zhang, W., Masui, K., & Mischel, P. S. (2020). Altered cellular metabolism in gliomas—An emerging landscape of actionable co-dependency targets. *Nature Reviews. Cancer*, 20(1), 57–70. DOI: 10.1038/s41568-019-0226-5 PMID: 31806884

Boopathi, S. (2023). Deep Learning Techniques Applied for Automatic Sentence Generation. In Becerra-Murillo, K., & Gámez, J. F. (Eds.), (pp. 255–273). Advances in Educational Technologies and Instructional Design. IGI Global., DOI: 10.4018/978-1-6684-3632-5.ch016

Bozier, J., Chivers, E. K., Chapman, D. G., Larcombe, A. N., Bastian, N. A., Masso-Silva, J. A., Byun, M. K., McDonald, C. F., Alexander, L. E. C., & Ween, M. P. (2020). The evolving landscape of e-cigarettes: A systematic review of recent evidence. *Chest*, 157(5), 1362–1390. DOI: 10.1016/j.chest.2019.12.042 PMID: 32006591

Buckley, R. P., Arner, D., Veidt, R., & Zetzsche, D. (2020). Building FinTech ecosystems: Regulatory sandboxes, innovation hubs and beyond. *Wash. UJL & Pol'y*, 61, 55.

Chakraborti, T., Sreedharan, S., & Kambhampati, S. (2020). The emerging landscape of explainable ai planning and decision making. *arXiv Preprint arXiv:2002.11697*.

Cheng, M., Adekola, O., Albia, J., & Cai, S. (2022). Employability in higher education: A review of key stakeholders' perspectives. *Higher Education Evaluation and Development*, 16(1), 16–31. DOI: 10.1108/HEED-03-2021-0025

Das, S., Lekhya, G., Shreya, K., Lydia Shekinah, K., Babu, K. K., & Boopathi, S. (2024). Fostering Sustainability Education Through Cross-Disciplinary Collaborations and Research Partnerships: Interdisciplinary Synergy. In Yu, P., Mulli, J., Syed, Z. A. S., & Umme, L. (Eds.), (pp. 60–88). Advances in Higher Education and Professional Development. IGI Global., DOI: 10.4018/979-8-3693-0487-7.ch003

Dinu, C. C., & Chian, M. M. (2023). Uncovering Principles for Curriculum Adaptation: A Practitioner and Researcher (Co) Reflexive Analysis. *Journal of Ethnographic and Qualitative Research*, 17(1).

Dumulescu, D., & Muţiu, A. I. (2021). Academic leadership in the time of COVID-19—Experiences and perspectives. *Frontiers in Psychology*, 12, 648344. DOI: 10.3389/fpsyg.2021.648344 PMID: 33959076

Durairaj, M., & Jayakumar, S. Monika, Karpagavalli, V. S., Maheswari, B. U., & Boopathi, S. (2023). Utilization of Digital Tools in the Indian Higher Education System During Health Crises: In C. S. V. Negrão, I. G. P. Maia, & J. A. F. Brito (Eds.), *Advances in Logistics, Operations, and Management Science* (pp. 1–21). IGI Global. DOI: 10.4018/978-1-7998-9213-7.ch001

Ericsson, N. R. (2021). Dynamic Econometrics in action: A biography of David F. Hendry. *International Finance Discussion Paper, 1311*.

Faruq, A. (2022). *A Phenomenological Examination of African American Men's Experiences in Community College* [PhD Thesis]. Walden University.

Fernandez, A. A., & Shaw, G. P. (2020). Academic leadership in a time of crisis: The Coronavirus and COVID-19. *Journal of Leadership Studies*, 14(1), 39–45. DOI: 10.1002/jls.21684

Giesenbauer, B., & Müller-Christ, G. (2020). University 4.0: Promoting the transformation of higher education institutions toward sustainable development. *Sustainability (Basel)*, 12(8), 3371. DOI: 10.3390/su12083371

Harris, S., Martin, M., & Diener, D. (2021). Circularity for circularity's sake? Scoping review of assessment methods for environmental performance in the circular economy. *Sustainable Production and Consumption*, 26, 172–186. DOI: 10.1016/j.spc.2020.09.018

Hong, H., & Hamot, G. E. (2020). Differential effects of state testing policies and school characteristics on social studies educators' gate-keeping autonomy: A multilevel model. *Theory and Research in Social Education*, 48(1), 74–100. DOI: 10.1080/00933104.2019.1655508

Husaini, D. C., Mphuthi, D. D., Chiroma, J. A., Abubakar, Y., & Adeleye, A. O. (2022). Nursing students' experiences of service-learning at community and hospital pharmacies in Belize: Pedagogical implications for nursing pharmacology. *PLoS One*, 17(11), e0276656. DOI: 10.1371/journal.pone.0276656 PMID: 36327317

Jurasaite-O'Keefe, E. (2021). *Individual, School, and National Factors Impacting Teachers' Workplace Learning: Discourses of Informal Learning in North America and Lithuania*. Routledge. DOI: 10.4324/9780367816605

Kallio, T. J., Kallio, K.-M., Huusko, M., Pyykkö, R., & Kivistö, J. (2022). Balancing between accountability and autonomy: The impact and relevance of public steering mechanisms within higher education. *Journal of Public Budgeting, Accounting & Financial Management*, 34(6), 46–68. DOI: 10.1108/JPBAFM-10-2020-0177

Lennert Da Silva, A. L. (2022). Comparing teacher autonomy in different models of educational governance. *Nordic Journal of Studies in Educational Policy*, 8(2), 103–118. DOI: 10.1080/20020317.2021.1965372

Libby, P. (2021). The changing landscape of atherosclerosis. *Nature*, 592(7855), 524–533. DOI: 10.1038/s41586-021-03392-8 PMID: 33883728

Mohamed Hashim, M. A., Tlemsani, I., & Matthews, R. (2021). Higher education strategy in digital transformation. *Education and Information Technologies*, •••, 1–25. PMID: 34539217

Morse, S. R. (2020). *A Phenomenological Study on Career Readiness among Graduates from College and Career Academy High Schools*.

Niesche, R., Eacott, S., Keddie, A., Gobby, B., MacDonald, K., Wilkinson, J., & Blackmore, J. (2023). Principals' perceptions of school autonomy and educational leadership. *Educational Management Administration & Leadership*, 51(6), 1260–1277. DOI: 10.1177/17411432211034174

Parmaxi, A. (2023). Virtual reality in language learning: A systematic review and implications for research and practice. *Interactive Learning Environments*, 31(1), 172–184. DOI: 10.1080/10494820.2020.1765392

Rajabalee, Y. B., & Santally, M. I. (2021). Learner satisfaction, engagement and performances in an online module: Implications for institutional e-learning policy. *Education and Information Technologies*, 26(3), 2623–2656. DOI: 10.1007/s10639-020-10375-1 PMID: 33199971

Rastogi, S., Sharma, V., Bharti, P. S., Rani, K., Modi, G. P., Nikolajeff, F., & Kumar, S. (2021). The evolving landscape of exosomes in neurodegenerative diseases: Exosomes characteristics and a promising role in early diagnosis. *International Journal of Molecular Sciences*, 22(1), 440. DOI: 10.3390/ijms22010440 PMID: 33406804

Sharma, D. M., Venkata Ramana, K., Jothilakshmi, R., Verma, R., Uma Maheswari, B., & Boopathi, S. (2024). Integrating Generative AI Into K-12 Curriculums and Pedagogies in India: Opportunities and Challenges. In Yu, P., Mulli, J., Syed, Z. A. S., & Umme, L. (Eds.), (pp. 133–161). Advances in Higher Education and Professional Development. IGI Global., DOI: 10.4018/979-8-3693-0487-7.ch006

Spencer, E., & Lucas, B. (2021). *Meta-Skills: Best practices in work-based learning A literature review*. University of Winchester.

Spigel, B., & Vinodrai, T. (2021). Meeting its Waterloo? Recycling in entrepreneurial ecosystems after anchor firm collapse. *Entrepreneurship and Regional Development*, 33(7–8), 599–620. DOI: 10.1080/08985626.2020.1734262

Wamsler, C., Wickenberg, B., Hanson, H., Olsson, J. A., Stålhammar, S., Björn, H., Falck, H., Gerell, D., Oskarsson, T., & Simonsson, E. (2020). Environmental and climate policy integration: Targeted strategies for overcoming barriers to nature-based solutions and climate change adaptation. *Journal of Cleaner Production*, 247, 119154. DOI: 10.1016/j.jclepro.2019.119154

Wang, L., O'Connor, D., Rinklebe, J., Ok, Y. S., Tsang, D. C., Shen, Z., & Hou, D. (2020). Biochar aging: Mechanisms, physicochemical changes, assessment, and implications for field applications. *Environmental Science & Technology*, 54(23), 14797–14814. DOI: 10.1021/acs.est.0c04033 PMID: 33138356

Webb, A., & McQuaid, R. (2020). Recruitment and workforce development challenges in low-status sectors with high labour demand–childcare work. *CIPD Applied Research Conference 2020, The Shifting Landscape of Work and Working Lives*.

Zhai, X. (2022). ChatGPT user experience: Implications for education. *Available at SSRN* 4312418.

Chapter 6
Nurturing Inclusive Schools Through the Isibindi Ezikoleni Child and Youth Care Work Programme

Zeni Thumbadoo
National Association of Child Care Workers, South Africa

Theresa Wilson
 https://orcid.org/0000-0002-5841-8448
Independent Researcher, South Africa

Nicia de Nobrega
National Association of Child Care Workers, South Africa

Donald Nghonyama
National Association of Child Care Workers, South Africa

ABSTRACT

This chapter offers a comprehensive overview of the Isibindi Ezikoleni Programme, an innovative child and youth care practice model designed to enhance inclusive education in South African schools. This model strategically embeds child and youth care workers in the school setting to address the emotional, social, and educational needs of vulnerable and at-risk learners. By doing so, it aims to create a nurturing and inclusive environment for every learner to flourish and succeed. Adopting a practice-based perspective, this chapter examines how the programme contributes

DOI: 10.4018/979-8-3693-4058-5.ch006

to mitigating barriers to education and cultivating environments conducive to the success of all learners. Through a detailed examination of its design, implementation, and impacts, this chapter provides case examples and results to illustrate the programme's role in enhancing inclusivity in South Africa's educational system.

THE SOUTH AFRICAN EDUCATION CONTEXT

South Africa has one of the highest dropout rates in the world (Hartnack, 2017) with 40% of South African learners who start school never completing Grade 12 (Zero Dropout Campaign, 2021). 1 Despite South Africa's progress in expanding access to education, its quality of education remains behind that of other upper middle-income countries. Globally, South Africa remains at the bottom in addressing learning outcomes in reading, maths, and science (Sapire et al, 2024; Schirmer et al, 2023). Literature shows that two out of 10 Grade 4 learners can read for meaning in any language, and only 37% of learners in Grade 5 have acquired the basic subject knowledge and skills in maths for their grade (DGMT, 2023). The gap in learning outcomes is especially pronounced in poorer regions, perpetuating long-standing disparities in academic success and school completion rates (Atkins & Cilliers, 2024).

While apartheid significantly contributed to the existing educational inequities through the creation of a racially segregated education system that offered black children poor-quality education in urban townships or designated 'homelands' (Khumalo, & Hodgson, 2017; Thobejane, 2013), other barriers to learning are widespread in South Africa impeding a child's ability to learn. These are broadly categorised as follows:

- Extrinsic barriers (societal/environmental) such as extreme poverty, dysfunctional family units, violence against children and high unemployment.
- Intrinsic barriers that include any specific learning barrier that children experience within themselves, such as a reading problem or cognitive impairment.
- Systemic barriers (caused by limitations in the education system) such as overcrowded classrooms, 2nd language teaching, inadequate facilities, poorly equipped teachers, and a rigid curriculum.

Key extrinsic and intrinsic barriers that contribute to poor academic achievement include learner pregnancies, substance use, child protection issues resulting from abuse and neglect, and bullying (DBE, 2014). Further, the community and home environments of many learners are characterized by high levels of community violence, substance use, child abuse and gender-based violence, all of which are detrimental to children's social, emotional, and educational development and mental well-being (NACCW, 2022; NACCW, 2024). In many communities there are also few job opportunities for young people, contributing to a lack of hope for the future, and there is an urgent need for skilled workforce development and career pathing for youth, especially women (Jamieson, 2013).

Defining Inclusive Education

Inclusion in education is about ensuring that every learner feels valued and respected and can enjoy a sense of belonging (UNESCO, 2020). This includes learners requiring extra support because of learning or physical disability, social disadvantage, cultural difference, or other barriers to learning (Inclusive Education South Africa, 2019).

Inclusive education and educational outcomes, such as reading proficiency and dropout rates, are closely connected. If a significant number of learners are unable to read upon leaving school or many do not complete their education, it raises questions about the inclusivity and effectiveness of the education system. True inclusivity requires adapting to diverse learning needs to prevent dropout, ensure all learners achieve essential literacy skills, and complete their education (UNESCO, 2020).

Overview of the Isibindi Ezikoleni Programme

Isibindi Ezikoleni (meaning 'courage in schools' in IsiZulu) is an innovative school-based child and youth care work practice model developed in 2016 by the National Association of Child Care Workers (NACCW) to meet the many and complex psychosocial needs of vulnerable children and youth. Isibindi Ezikoleni aids the retention and progression of learners in schools by providing school-based child and youth care psychosocial care and support services. Services are provided by trained and supervised child and youth care workers (CYCWs). The programme started with CYCWs in 20 schools in 2016 and has expanded to more than 400 schools in 2023.

Isibindi Ezikoleni supports the national Department of Basic Education (NDBE) to realise its aim of improving psychosocial support to learners and NACCW has entered a memorandum of understanding (MOU) with NDBE in this respect (first in 2018 and renewed in 2023) and has also entered an MOU with the KwaZulu-Natal Provincial Department of Education for the provision of psychosocial support in schools.

Objective and Focus of this Chapter

This chapter describes the Isibindi Ezikoleni programme and the integral role of the child and youth care workforce in addressing barriers to learning, including poverty, violence, abuse, pregnancy, learning difficulties and disabilities in the South African context. It is informed by a practice-based perspective, emphasizing the significance of knowledge and learning acquired by practitioners through years of programme implementation, reflection, and refinement. Practice-based knowledge is an important source of learning, but is not always captured, used, or valued by the field.2 Importantly, the chapter's authors include members of staff who are directly involved in the development and implementation of the programme, and are also CYCWs. Their contributions ensure a blend of theoretical insights with real-world experiences.

THE CONTEXT OF INCLUSIVE EDUCATION IN SOUTH AFRICA

South Africa has established a comprehensive framework of educational policies to tackle barriers to learning, aiming to enhance learner wellbeing and academic success. These policies address a wide range of needs, from inclusive education to psychosocial support and collectively strive to create a more inclusive, supportive, and effective educational system:

- Education Sector Plan for Schooling 2030: Aligned with the National Development Plan (NDP), this plan calls for strengthening the implementation of inclusive education and ensuring broader access to educational support within local schools, especially for previously disadvantaged learners.
- Psychosocial Support Strategy for Learners in the Educational System of South Africa 2015-2020 (DBE, 2016): Outlines the need for interventions beyond academic programmes to prevent and address adverse psychosocial outcomes, highlighting the importance of partnerships and networks for specialized services.
- Policy on Screening, Identification, Assessment, and Support (SIAS) (2015): Guides schools on serving as access points for public services, including health and psychosocial support, to aid learners facing barriers to education.
- Care and Support for Teaching and Learning Conceptual Framework (CSTL) (DBE & MIET, 2010): Outlines the education department's approach to overcoming barriers to learning such as poverty, prejudicial attitudes, health issues, violence, and inadequate infrastructure. Ten priority action areas for care and support are identified, ranging from nutritional and health promo-

tion to safety and curriculum support. It serves not as a new policy but as an overarching framework to coordinate and harmonize existing initiatives for vulnerable learners, under the leadership of the Department of Basic Education and provincial education departments.

- White Paper 6 (2001): Focuses on special needs education and building an inclusive education and training system. It advocates for accommodating all learners, regardless of their learning abilities or disabilities, within the mainstream education system.
- National Education Policy Act (No. 27 of 1996): Assigns responsibility to the Minister of Education and education departments for the development and implementation of education support services policies, including counselling and guidance.
- South African Schools Act (Act 84 of 1996): Mandates compulsory attendance for children aged 7 to 15 years or until completing Grade 9 and introduces measures to manage absenteeism and dropout rates.

Current debates as well as legislative obligations in education support the role of schools in facilitating the holistic development of learners as well as ensuring the achievement of educational objectives. While the NDBE has highlighted the goal of placing skilled care and support practitioners in every school to enhance the schooling experience for all learners, particularly vulnerable learners (Department of Basic Education, 2018), many schools lack caring teachers, counsellors and social service practitioners (such as social workers and CYCWs) who can offer this support, and where such resources exist, they are insufficient to address the extent of the challenges facing learners (Gray & Lombard, 2022; Reyneke, 2018; Vergottini & Weyers, 2020). Because of this, Life Orientation teachers often become the primary source of assistance for vulnerable and at-risk learners due to their accessibility within the school. However, they lack the training and the time to provide this support (Mahwai et al, 2023). Although CYCWs are not specifically mentioned in existing policy documents as part of the school-based psychosocial service workforce given the nascency of the professionalization of CYCWs in South Africa, their role is crucial (Reyneke, 2018). In schools, departments of education should consider the deployment of social service practitioners that include both social workers and CYCWs and brings in the diversity of psychosocial service workers in their pool of school-based staff.

EVOLUTION AND PRACTICE OF CHILD AND YOUTH CARE WORK IN SOUTH AFRICA

What is Child and Youth Care Work

Child and youth care work is a profession that provides protective, developmental, and therapeutic services in the lifespace of children with both 'normal' and special development needs to promote and facilitate optimum development through planned use of everyday life events and programmes to facilitate their ability to function effectively within different contexts (SACSSP, 2021). CYCWs are frontline essential social service practitioners who provide care, and protection and facilitate developmental and therapeutic interventions in the lifespace of the child and family (Thumbadoo, 2013).

Phelan (2015) describes child and youth care work as "a process of experiencing life alongside others and supporting them to use this experience to change". There is an immediacy to child and youth care work as it does not take place in a "sterilised" environment. A core element of child and youth care work is the provision of care which supports the development of young people (Krueger, 2015). In child and youth care work, CYCWs make specific use of lifespace work and lifespace counselling to support children; lifespace work involves CYCWs using everyday life events at school and home to provide the context and opportunity for development and healing as life unfolds for children; lifespace counselling involves verbal interventions conducted by CYCWs with children designed to mobilize them towards positive action in difficult circumstances. In this way, CYCWs can help learners to learn how to resolve problems as they come up, building on their skills, and helping them to be ready to address the next problem.

Gharabaghi (2019 & 2018), Garfat et al (2018), and Phelan (2015), who have written extensively on child and youth care practice, emphasize the importance of 'relational practice' in child and youth care work which is grounded in how caring and effective support transcends ordinary job duties, requiring practitioners to engage deeply and empathetically with individuals. Through these connections, practitioners effectively address the challenges and needs of those they serve, fostering development, trust, and healing. A study examining the role of CYCWs in schools highlights the importance of relationship between the CYCW and the young person to preventing school-based violence:

"If we consider relationships through a systemic lens, a relationship with a child and youth worker that helps young persons to feel that they matter (that is, they are valued by and significant to others) can be a major factor in addressing the finding that a lack of mattering is among the main contributors to school-based violence. With this in mind, we propose that both relationships and activity

programming, of all the child and youth care work areas of competency, are the most pertinent to mediating against violence" (VanderVen et al, 1999).

Development of the Child and Youth Care Profession in South Africa

The child and youth care profession in South Africa has seen substantial development over the last 50 years, marked by a rise in the number of professionals and advancements in practice. This growth has been driven by a confluence of factors.

A key influence has been the global rise of child and youth care as a recognized field, particularly noted in North America since the mid-20th century (Krueger, 2019). Concurrently, post-apartheid, in the local context underwent transformative shifts with the adoption of a developmental model of social welfare in the early 1990s. This developmental model allowed for the expansion of social service professions to include social workers, CYCWs, and community development workers (Gray and Lombard, 2022).

The National Association of Child Care Workers (NACCW), a registered non-profit organisation and the only professional association of CYCWs in South Africa, has also played a pivotal role in driving the growth of the sector through advocating for the child and youth care profession's development and recognition (Gray and Lombard, 2022). This advocacy culminated in legislative milestones, with the Children's Act (Act 38 of 2005) and the Social Service Practitioners Policy (2016) acknowledging the crucial services provided by CYCWs in both residential and community settings, focusing on children's protection, well-being, and development.

Government initiatives have also significantly contributed, particularly in recent years, by supporting the training and expansion of a predominantly young and female workforce to implement a community-based model of child and youth care – the Isibindi programme, now known as the Risiha programme implemented by the Department of Social Development (DSD). These efforts saw the extension of community-based child and youth care services to vulnerable children and families, especially in rural and historically underserved areas (Huijbregts et al, 2023; Jamieson, 2013; Thumbadoo, 2013).

The journey towards professional recognition and statutory regulation of the child and youth care profession has been long but fruitful, culminating in the establishment of the Professional Board for Child and Youth Care within the South African Council for Social Service Professions in 2005; and the gazetting of Regulations for Child and Youth Care Workers, Auxiliary Child and Youth Care Workers, and Student Child and Youth Care Workers in October 2014 (Professional Board for Child and Youth Care Work, 2021). These regulations, among other requirements, mandate the registration of all CYCWs with the South African Council of Social

Service Professions at either auxiliary or professional (degreed) levels (Department of Social Development, 2014).

The South African Council of Social Service Professions has registered 11,282 CYCWs, more than double the number registered in 2016 (SACSSP, 2021). Of these, most were registered at auxiliary level (68%) or student auxiliary level (28%), with only 1% registered at professional level and 2% at student professional level. These trends reflect the bottom-up approach to the development of the profession as well as the impact of the stimulation of demand for CYCWs at auxiliary level, primarily through the five-year roll-out of the community-based child and youth care programme by government. The low numbers of registered CYCWs at a professional level stem from both limited opportunities for higher education studies as well as the scarcity of employment opportunities in the public and private sector. Developing and the deployment of the professional level of CYCWs is critical to ensure that the workforce has skilled practitioners who can address complex problems and take on management and supervisory roles (PBCYCW, 2021).

The numbers of registered CYCWs do not reflect the total number of trained CYCWs in the country, as not all CYCWs are registered to practice. It is estimated that there are over 20,000 trained CYCWs in South Africa, many of whom are unemployed and could be available for employment in school and community-based programmes should the opportunity arise (Thumbadoo, 2021).

At a recent summit on the crisis in the child and youth care field, the need for more social service professionals, including CYCWs, at community level to address growing challenges such as bullying of children in schools was highlighted by the Minister of Social Development (SACSSP, 2021). CYCWs are seen to be an integral part of the multi-disciplinary team who can handle many of the social issues in schools, however, to fulfil this role, they need to be given the same kind of attention that police, nurses and teachers receive from government.

Child and Youth Care Scope of Practice

South African legislation defines child and youth care work broadly as "the acts performed by a child and youth care worker which focuses on children and youth within the context of the family, the community, and the lifespan of a person" (Department of Social Development, 2014).

The elements of child and youth care work practice are outlined in the scope of practice in Regulations 18 and 19 of the Regulations for CYCWs, auxiliary CYCWs and student CYCWs. These elements include, amongst others, the provision of care, the management of behaviour, the implementation of developmental programmes, the engagement in developmental assessments, the maintenance of planned environments, the support of developmental play, the advocacy for children, working in multi-disciplinary teams, and undertaking administration (Professional Board for Child and Youth Care Work, 2021). All these activities take place within the context of lifespace work which involves entering into the lifespace of, and the caring use of daily life events as they are occurring, for the therapeutic benefit of a child, youth or family (see Key Terms and Definitions).

The Regulations allow for the practice of child and youth care work at auxiliary (non-degreed) and professional (degreed) levels. In South Africa, the role played by auxiliary workers is unique to a given profession depending on the stage of development of the profession. For example, in a profession such as social work, auxiliaries assist professionals with complex tasks. However, in the child and youth care profession, CYCWs at auxiliary level work independently and perform basic child care tasks. CYCWs at a professional level can deal with complex problems and take on management and supervisory roles as envisaged in the scope of practice. A distinctive aspect of the child and youth care profession is the similarity in the scope of practice between professional and auxiliary level workers. The primary difference lies in the level of practice; the professional level demonstrates a more advanced degree of skill and application.

The context of poverty in which practice takes place impacts on all aspects of child and youth care work practice. In addition, the roles and functions are filtered through the lens of children's rights and social justice. These two elements, the context of poverty and the framework of children's rights, has influenced the practice of child and youth care work in South Africa (Allsopp, 2020).

Child and Youth Care Worker Training

At auxiliary level, CYCWs are required to have a Further Education and Training Certificate in child and youth care work which may take one to two years to complete, while a professional level CYCW requires a four-year degree. Training opportunities for CYCWs at auxiliary level are currently available at Level 4 and Level 5 of the National Qualifications Framework. The Level 5 qualification (Occupational Certificate: Child and Youth Care Worker) was introduced in late 2019. With this qualification it is anticipated that a CYCW qualified at auxiliary level will be able to apply for a degree programme.

Two universities currently offer child and youth care work degree programmes in South Africa: Durban University of Technology (DUT) and Monash, a private university. DUT also offers a Master's degree in Child and Youth Care and have admitted child and youth care work students into their PhD programme in Health Sciences (Professional Board for Child and Youth Care Work, 2021).

Child and Youth Care Practice Settings

The important role that CYCWs play in providing services in residential settings and community settings for children's protection, wellbeing and development is recognised in the Children's Act 38 of 2005 and the Social Service Practitioners Policy, 2016. As such, child and youth care work can be practiced in multiple settings including, but not limited to:

- Residential care settings e.g. secure care centres, children's' homes and places of safety;
- Community-based programmes e.g. Isibindi, Rishia, drop-in centres;
- Educational settings including mainstream schools, full-service schools, special needs schools, farm schools, hostels, and early childhood development centres;
- Health care facilities including clinics, children's hospitals and hospices; and
- Courts – family and sexual offences courts as intermediaries.

In the early stages of the child and youth care field in South Africa (in the late 1970s), CYCWs were mainly employed in residential care settings for children. Local adaptations of child and youth care work have emerged since the mid-1990's with an emphasis on community-based child and youth care work, and a particular 'African' spirit, flavour and identity within local child and youth care practice (Allsopp, 2013). In the mid-1990s, CYCWs were employed in community-based settings to support children who were orphaned due to HIV/AIDS or made vulnerable for other reasons such as child abuse or neglect. There is one mention in the literature of a child and youth care intervention in some schools in Chatsworth, Durban in 1998 (McCully, 2001), however this practice did not expand until the mid-2000's when CYCWs were placed in schools through the Isibindi Ezikoleni programme.

Community-based CYCWs increased significantly between 2013 and 2018, when the national Department of Social Development (DSD) and the NACCW, expanded Isibindi, a community-based child and youth care programme. Isibindi Ezikoleni is a 'sister' model to Isibindi as it was developed based on the learnings and expansion of the Isibindi programme developed in the early 2000's by NACCW. After almost 10 years of development, DSD undertook the national roll-out of Isibindi in partnership with NACCW. The scale-up included training and employing 10,000 community-based CYCWs. The estimated cost of this investment was R3.8 billion (444 million USD) over a five-year period (Jamieson, 2013). After the successful implementation of Isibindi, DSD took over the programme's funding and management and transitioned the programme into a prevention and early intervention community care programme called Rishia which is currently being implemented by local community-based organisations (Huijbregts et al, 2023; Thumbadoo, 2021).

The development of the different adaptations of child and youth care work has been a direct response to the transformation of the child and youth care sector since the 1990's, with its emphasis on prevention and early intervention services, and promoting the least restrictive, most empowering environments for children's care, alongside the introduction of the Children's Act (Act 38 of 2005). This transformation leveraged on social service professionals, including CYCWs, to deliver a spectrum of services tailored to children's needs. Isibindi Ezikoleni is aligned to the developmental ethos within the Children's Act's, effectively addressing the continuum of care for learners, through the following distinct yet interconnected layers of service:

- Prevention services promote learner well-being through whole-school, class and other group-based activities such as co-facilitated life orientation classes, discussions during assembly, and awareness campaigns.
- Early Intervention services target learners at risk of heightened vulnerability, offering group-based services such as structured development programmes, homework supervision, and study groups. This layer acts as a safeguard, preventing at-risk children from escalating into situations that necessitate intensive intervention.
- Full Intervention/Intensive Support Services are for learners requiring more personalized care and support. This includes learners facing significant challenges such as chronic illness, substance use, irregular school attendance, or abuse and neglect. Within this level, learner assessments and development plans are co-created, and CYCWs facilitate in-depth support through one-on-one sessions, home visits, and multi-disciplinary teamwork.

Supervision of Child and Youth Care Workers

The purpose of supervision is improved quality of service and improved outcomes for children and youth (The Alliance for Child Protection in Humanitarian Action, 2018; Child Hub Academy; Undated). In child and youth care work, the supervisory relationship serves as a model for the relationship between the CYCW and the child/youth; the supervisor should be to the worker what the worker should be to the child (Michael, 2005).

In South Africa, CYCWs must be supervised by someone from the child and youth care profession. This requirement is stipulated in the Regulations (Department of Social Development, 2014) and the Social Service Practitioners Policy (2016). Employers are expected to maintain this statutory requirement. However, many CYCWs are being supervised by other professionals who often do not understand the intricate and therapeutic tasks of child and youth care work (Professional Board for Child and Youth Care Work, 2021). This presents a challenge to the development of the profession and is to be addressed in the design and funding of child and youth care programmes.

ISIBINDI EZIKOLENI PROGRAMME: ORIGINS, AIMS, AND DEVELOPMENT

Origins of Isibindi Ezikoleni

Schools present an accessible service point ideally suited to the provision of prevention, care, and support activities for vulnerable and at-risk learners for the following reasons:

- Schools are permanent institutions and can help to maintain new organisational structures.
- Schools are central and relatively accessible and often represent the only substantial infrastructure in poor rural areas.
- South Africa has relatively high school enrolment rates up to age 15 allowing easy access to large numbers of children.
- Support within schools bring children to schools and keep children – including those above 15 years of age – in school, with long-term benefits for learners, their families, communities, and the country.
- Many children who would otherwise fall through the service gaps can be identified through schools.
- CYCWs in schools can serve as a valuable resource in the delivery of the Life Orientation curriculum.

While schools provide an ideal setting for the provision of child and youth care services, school-based child and youth care work is a relatively new concept in South Africa. It has however been successfully practiced in several countries. For example, CYCWs have been involved in a variety of ways in the Canadian educational system for the past 40 years (Denholm, 2005; Denholm, 1998).

The NACCW has been working to improve the quality of services and care for vulnerable and at-risk children and youth since 1975 through promoting the field of child and youth care and developing the skills and abilities of CYCWs so that they are able to advocate on behalf of children. In response to the needs of children and youth, the NACCW has gone beyond the traditional role of a professional association by designing and overseeing the implementation of innovative child and youth care service delivery models, with large-scale implementation, such as Isibindi. Following the success of Isibindi, the NACCW recognised the potential for child and youth care services in schools and developed Isibindi Ezikoleni in 2016 as a model of school-based child and youth care work.

The programme, initially piloted in 2016 with donor funding in a select few schools in one province, has to date been cumulatively implemented in a total of 474 schools across seven of the nine provinces (see Figure 1). This expansion was made possible through a combination of government and private donor funds, each contributing under their specific funding requirements. The programme has been implemented in the three categories South Africa's public schools: ordinary/ mainstream schools, full-service schools, and special schools. While it spans all three types, the programme is primarily implemented in mainstream schools which serve as neighbourhood schools that accommodate all children, including those with disabilities, by offering 'reasonable accommodations' for inclusivity. Full-service schools are adapted to support learners with a range of disabilities, mainly those with 'moderate' or 'low' needs, and special schools provide specialized programs for learners with 'severe' disabilities, requiring intensive support, often necessitating hostel stays due to the distance from their homes (Khumalo & Hodgson (2017).

Figure 1. Coverage of schools and child and youth care workers in Isibindi Ezikoleni model

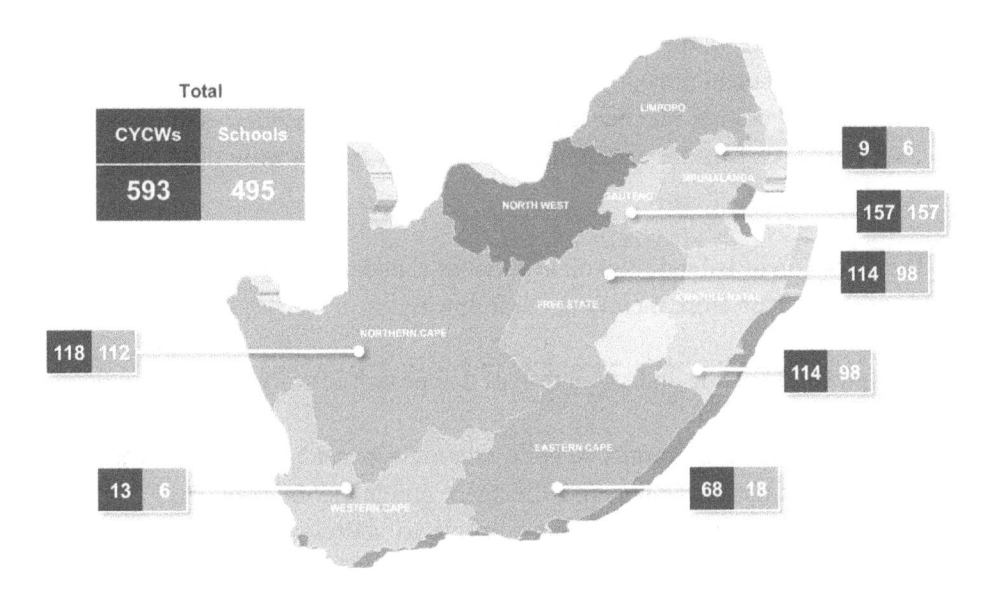

Programme Goal and Approach

The goal of Isibindi Ezikoleni is to support the retention and progression of learners in schools through improved access to psychosocial support services by a locally developed child and youth care workforce. The intention of the programme is to provide professional child and youth care services in a school setting guided by the child and youth care approach to identify and address barriers to learning and contribute to positive educational objectives.

The replication of Isibindi Ezikoleni as a school-based child and youth care service delivery model projects requires that a standardised approach be followed in all provinces, as follows:

- Isibindi Ezikoleni services must be implemented by trained CYCWs in partnership with schools and the Department of Education at provincial, district and circuit office levels.
- Isibindi Ezikoleni CYCWs must be recognized as school support staff members and included in relevant staff activities and have access to relevant information in the South African School Administration Management System (SA-SAMS) and other data management systems.
- Isibindi Ezikoleni CYCWs must work flexible hours so they can be available when children need them, including after-school, weekends and school holidays.
- Isibindi Ezikoleni CYCWs must be supervised and mentored by senior child and youth care workers.
- Isibindi Ezikoleni projects must adhere to the standardised Isibindi Ezikoleni standard operating procedures (SOPs) for the management and delivery of services (see Box 1), and standardised forms for reporting and monitoring and evaluation.

The provision of Isibindi Ezikoleni services is underpinned by key principles of child and youth care work including the following:

- Applying a holistic and strength-based approach to work with young people and families.
- Using crisis as opportunity to build relationships and to teach consequences.
- Working in the young person's life-space and in the moment.
- Conducting activities with young people to address their unmet needs i.e. intentional and purposeful.
- Working in a multi-disciplinary approach.

- Observing young people, assessing their needs, and creating developmental plans to meet their needs.

All Isibindi Ezikoleni CYCWs are expected to adhere to the professional Code of Ethics for Child and Youth Care Workers which embodies these principles. They must also be registered with the South African Council of Social Service Professionals (SACSSP) and if they behave unethically, they may be asked to appear for the Professional Board for Child and Youth Care (PBCYC) and may be fined, or possibly deregistered as a CYCW (depending on the offence).

Box 1. Isibindi Ezikoleni Service-Related Standard Operating Procedures

- Isibindi Ezikoleni Bullying Prevention and Response SOP, May 2023
- Isibindi Ezikoleni Child Protection SOP, August 2023
- Isibindi Ezikoleni Dropout SOP, September 2018
- Isibindi Ezikoleni Homework Club and Study Group SOP, February 2024
- Isibindi Ezikoleni Learner Pregnancy Prevention and Response SOP February 2024
- Isibindi Ezikoleni Safe Space Programme SOP, updated February 2024
- Isibindi Ezikoleni Service and Practice SOP, February 2024
- Isibindi Ezikoleni Suicide Prevention SOP, February 2024
- Isibindi Ezikoleni Supervision SOP, updated February 2024
- NACCW Child Safeguarding Policy (Abridged Version), February 2024

Alignment With National Goals for Educational Inclusivity

Isibindi Ezikoleni was designed to align with education policy, laws and guidelines in South Africa which provides the framework for an inclusive education system that encourages schools to address barriers to learning (see Table 1).

Of particular relevance is the DBE's CSTL Programme. Rooted in a holistic view of education, the CSTL framework integrates key theoretical perspectives, such as Bronfenbrenner's Ecological Systems Theory and Maslow's Hierarchy of Needs, emphasizing the multi-layered influences on child development and the importance of supportive relationships (DBE & MEIT, 2010). This approach synergizes well with child and youth care work, particularly evident in the Isibindi Ezikoleni programme. Furthermore, there is synergy between Bloom's Taxonomy, widely used in educational settings to structure curriculum learning objectives, assessments, and activities to encourage higher-level thinking (Anderson et al, 2001). In Isibindi Ezikoleni, CYCWs apply Bloom's Taxonomy by understanding, applying, analysing, evaluating, and creating tailored support strategies for ensuring the holistic development and wellbeing of learners.

The Isibindi Ezikoleni monitoring and evaluation (M&E) system is also aligned with NDBE's psychosocial indicators.

Table 1. Alignment of Isibindi Ezikoleni with department of education policy

Department of Basic Education Laws, Policies and Guidelines	Isibindi Ezikoleni Alignment
Care and Support for Teaching and Learning (CSTL) Framework.	Services address all the 10 CSTL priorities.
Challenging Homophobic Bullying in Schools Guidelines, 2014.	The Isibindi *Ezikoleni Bullying Prevention and Response SOP* addresses LGBTQ+ related bullying.
Guidelines on e-Safety in Schools, 2018	The *Isibindi Ezikoleni Bullying Prevention and Response SOP* addresses virtual bullying.
Integrated School Health Policy (ISHP). Department of Health and Basic Education. 2012.	Health promotion services support the implementation of the ISHP. This includes an emerging response to underage drinking through the Alcohol Harm Reduction sub-programme in Isibindi Ezikoleni.
National Education Policy of 1996	The *Isibindi Ezikoleni Bullying Prevention and Response SOP* responds to the requirement for schools to be a safe learning environment.
Policy on Learner Attendance. 2010	The *Isibindi Ezikoleni School Dropout SOP* provides for the identification of learner absenteeism and dropouts and supporting the principal to follow-up on reasons and provide the necessary support services.
Policy on the Prevention and Management of Learner Pregnancy in Schools. 2021.	The *Isibindi Ezikoleni Prevention and Management of Learner Pregnancy SOP* promotes the right of learners to basic education by ensuring they are not excluded from school because of pregnancy and childbirth, and to provide a supportive environment for them to continue and complete their basic education. It also includes the provision of complimentary Comprehensive Sexuality Education (CSE) and access to adolescent and youth friendly SRH services.
Practical Guidelines: How parents can contribute meaningfully to the success of their children in schools. 2017.	The *Isibindi Ezikoleni Homework Club and Study Group SOP* incorporates these guidelines.
Protocol for the Management and Reporting of Sexual Abuse and Harassment in Schools. 2018.	The *Isibindi Ezikoleni Child Protection SOP* procedures for reporting and responding to cases of sexual abuse are in line with the protocol provisions, including reporting incidents to the school principal.
South African Schools Act 84 of 1996,	The Isibindi *Ezikoleni Bullying Prevention and Response SOP* responds to the requirement for schools to be a safe learning environment.
Strategy on Psychosocial Support (PSS) for Learners in South African Schools. 2016.	The concept of CYCWs being placed in schools is in line with the strategy which emphasises the need for interventions in schools that extend beyond academic programmes to prevent adverse psychosocial outcomes amongst learners impacted cognitively, emotionally, and behaviourally by family and societal adversities, and help when such outcomes arise. CYCWs serve as a protective presence for learners facing challenges that adversely affect their psychosocial wellbeing and mental health. The *Isibindi Ezikoleni Suicide Prevention SOP* also responds to the need for suicide prevention services in schools.

PROGRAMME DESIGN AND IMPLEMENTATION STRATEGIES

Isibindi Ezikoleni delivers a core package of school-based services at individual, group, and whole-school levels, supported by home visits where necessary and referrals to a range of government and non-government services. A safe child-friendly physical space is created in the school to meet with children individually and provide group activities (e.g., converting an unused classroom or a Safe Park). The Isibindi Ezikoleni programme operates across four distinct levels: individual, group, class, and the entire school, as outlined in Table 2. As mentioned in the previous section, these levels incorporate prevention, early intervention and response services depending on the risk level of the learner.

Table 2. Level and target of Isibindi Ezikoleni services

Level	Target
Individual:	■ Services provided to one child at a time. These services can be short-term/once-off/crisis interventions for low to medium risk learners or longer-term case management services for high-risk learners. ■ High risk learners are learners identified as needing intensive support including those who have previously dropped out, not attending school regularly, involved in substance use, pregnant or young mothers. CYCWs provide case management services informed by an individual development plan (IDP) with home visits as needed.
Group:	■ Services provided to groups of learners, usually small groups between 5-20 learners. Although the numbers may vary, the key distinction between group and classroom level services is that group services bring together learners from different classes together and comprises usually smaller numbers compared to the total number of learners in classes. ■ Group services are for learners identified as at lesser risk than high risk learners but nevertheless at some clear risk – for example, progressed learners, those with chronic illness. These learners would be targeted for early intervention in the form of group interventions such as structured development programmes, homework clubs and study groups. Learners needing intensive support would also be directed to these interventions alongside the individual interventions. They may also receive short term life-space counselling or life-space crisis interventions.
Class:	■ Services provided to all learners in a specific class at a time. Class sizes will depend on the school. Class activities include co-facilitation of life orientation classes, talks on various psychosocial issues, homework supervision, and meetings with class parents.
Whole-school:	■ Services provided to large numbers of learners, usually almost all school learners, at one time or over a specified period in the day. Whole-school activities include gate and corridor monitoring to identify learners who may be vulnerable or at risk, talks in assembly, career expos, various psychosocial-support campaigns, holiday programmes, commemoration of national holidays, and meetings with parents. These activities would also reach learners who are receiving individual services and group services.

The programme design and examples of services provided is illustrated in Figure 2.

Figure 2. The Isibindi Ezikoleni model

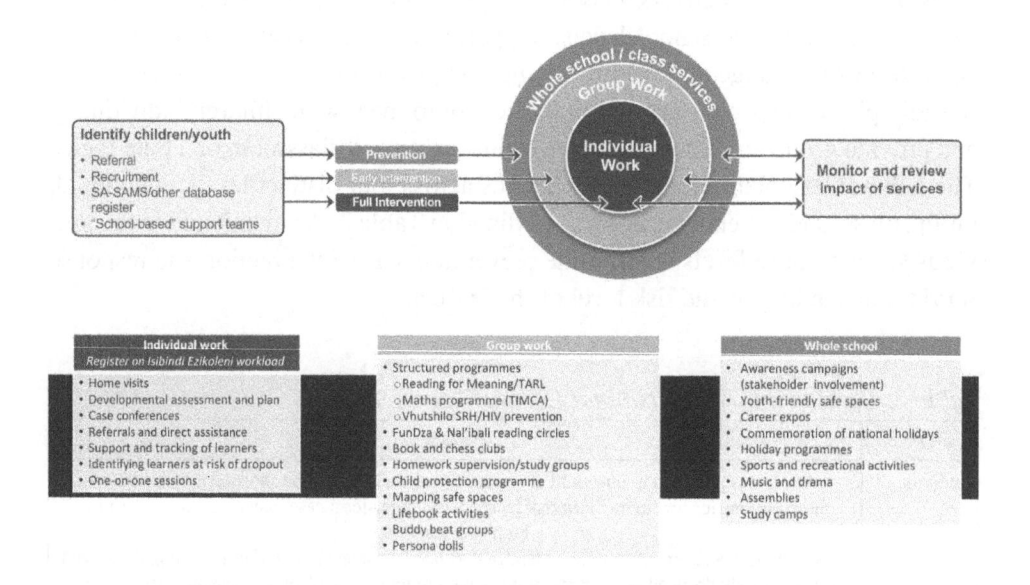

The flexible yet structured approach of the programme enables addressing critical areas including academic support, child protection, psychosocial support, learner pregnancy, bullying prevention, and strategies to prevent and respond to school dropouts. Programme services have evolved in response to learners' needs identified through programme research and mapping exercises (NACCW, 2024; NACCW, 2022; Wilson, 2022).

Academic support services may include tailored interventions such as Teaching at the Right Level (TaRL) (see Box 2) and homework supervision groups. Child protection efforts encompass individual case management, therapeutic group programmes, and whole-school awareness initiatives. Responses to learner pregnancy involve comprehensive support and education on sexual and reproductive health, while bullying prevention includes both individual counselling and whole-school education efforts. Psychosocial support is a cornerstone of CYCW activities, offering daily interventions and referrals as needed. Suicide prevention and sexual reproductive health services vary depending on donor requirements and capacity but aim to include both targeted group discussions and wider educational efforts. Substance use prevention and response also form an essential part of the programme, with CYCWs facilitating referrals to support services and conducting awareness-raising activities.

Box 2. Teaching at the Right Level (TaRL) – example of a structured academic support programme

Teaching at the Right Level (TaRL) is an evidence-based strategy developed by Pratham in India during the early 2000s, now implemented in several African countries, including South Africa. This approach tailors instruction to children's learning abilities, focusing on essential reading and math skills, and groups students by learning level rather than age or grade. It aims for accelerated learning, providing an alternative for students lacking basic literacy and numeracy skills by Grade 4. The NACCW collaborated with a donor to integrate the TaRL approach into their Reading for Meaning (R4M) programme at Isibindi Ezikoleni sites, starting with a pilot in two KwaZulu-Natal primary schools in 2022 and expanding to 10 schools across Free State, KwaZulu-Natal, and Northern Cape. CYCWs dedicate 65% of their time to TaRL, managing two groups yearly with a total of 80 learners, and receive specialized 10-day training before implementation. This programme has shown encouraging outcomes for Grade 3 to 5 learners, significantly improving their numeracy skills as evidenced in a KwaZulu-Natal pilot.

At the heart of Isibindi Ezikoleni is the identification, engagement, and provision of services and support to learners at risk of dropping out of school, usually indicated by frequent absenteeism. Emphasis is also placed on reintegrating learners who have dropped out of school. Depending on the reason for absenteeism, CYCWs can implement a variety of interventions to respond to the needs of learners guided by their individual assessment and development plan. Table 3 provides examples of the types of interventions provided to learners.

Table 3. Interventions to respond to absenteeism

Reason for absenteeism	Intervention (informed by Individual Assessment and Developmental Plan)
Pregnant learners may be embarrassed to attend school when their pregnancy starts to show or struggling with the psychosocial issues around their pregnancy.	■ Family group conferences to address family issues around the pregnancy and family support for the pregnant learner. ■ Referral to available local NGO services for pregnant learners/young mothers. ■ Referral to clinics for contraceptives and sexual and reproductive health information. ■ Referral to social worker. ■ Include learner in available Isibindi Ezikoleni SDPs on sexual and reproductive health. ■ Buddy Beat groups with other pregnant learners to create a support system.
Young mothers often find it difficult to balance their schooling career with being a mother. In some cases, young mothers are unable to secure care facilitates for their children while at school.	■ Family group conferences to address childcare arrangements and family support to the young mother. ■ Creation of timetables to help balance being a learner and a mother. ■ Referral to clinics for contraceptives and sexual and reproductive health information. ■ Referral to available local NGO services for pregnant learners/young mothers. ■ Referral to available Isibindi Ezikoleni SDPs on sexual and reproductive health. ■ Referrals for child support grants. ■ Buddy Beat groups with other young mothers to create a support system.
Survivors of sexual, physical, and emotional abuse often experience emotional trauma that affects their school attendance.	■ Lifespace counselling ■ Reporting to a child protection authority ■ Referral for therapeutic support ■ Assistance in court cases ■ Referral to Isibindi Ezikoleni Safe Spaces Programme for therapeutic interventions.
Older learners (Learners older than their grade cohort) often lose interest in attending school as they feel mocked by their peers and are intimidated by the schoolwork. Older learners are often progressed learners.	■ Creation of timetables to create routine study habits. ■ Buddy Beat groups with other older learners to create a support system for the learner. ■ Referral to Isibindi Ezikoleni academic support SDPs e.g. TaRL (primary school learners). ■ Referral to external reading clubs to provide academic support to the learner. ■ Referral to Isibindi Ezikoleni homework clubs and study groups. ■ Referrals to skill centres/Technical and Vocational Education and Training (TVET) Colleges for other education options.

continued on following page

Table 3. Continued

Reason for absenteeism	Intervention (informed by Individual Assessment and Developmental Plan)
Learners addicted to alcohol or drugs	■ Referral to available local substance abuse NGOs e.g. South African National Council on Alcoholism and Drug Dependence (SANCA) ■ Referral to Department of Social Development social worker (where NGO programmes not available). ■ Referral to Isibindi Ezikoleni substance abuse structured development programme e.g. Alcohol Harm Reduction (ARH) (*where available*).
Bullying	■ Use of a restorative justice approach where learners who bully others are provided with support while also taking responsibility for their behaviour. ■ Lifespace counselling for learners who are bullied and are engaged in bullying behaviour. ■ Behaviour management support by including learners in other activities e.g. study groups, buddy beat groups and others. ■ Class and whole-school discussions on bullying prevention.
Suicidal ideation	■ Referral for therapeutic services (counsellor, psychologist, social worker). ■ Lifespace counselling and work with the family to support learner. ■ Inclusion in other programmes, e.g. peer support groups. ■ Prevention initiatives in school through group-based activities to raise awareness on suicide prevention and the assistance available.

Tailored Approach to Programme Implementation

Isibindi Ezikoleni has been implemented in slightly different ways in schools in different provinces, depending on the unique contexts of schools and their surrounding communities, provincial education departments and funder requirements.

To tailor Isibindi Ezikoleni interventions for each school, the Isibindi Ezikoleni Mentor works with the CYCW/s, school principal or another delegated teacher to complete a school assessment at the start of the implementation period and annually thereafter. The assessment includes a mapping exercise with a group of learners to gather their insights. This exercise recognises the importance of child participation in the programme, emphasising the value of understanding and integrating the perspectives of young people into the planning and implementation processes. Box 3 provides more details on the mapping methodology.

The school assessment helps in understanding and addressing the distinct needs of each school, allowing for the development of tailored plans with targets to effectively tackle these challenges. It also ensures that all Isibindi Ezikoleni services, whether individual, group, or school-wide, are guided by a comprehensive needs assessment and thoughtful planning process.

Box 3. Children's Mapping

> Children's mapping is an engaging method that allows children to visually express their locations, experiences, memories, or emotions through drawing or painting, focusing on the significance of place. This activity can be both structured and unstructured, offering varying levels of guidance. In the Isibindi Ezikoleni programme, children's mapping has used to delve into children's physical, social, and emotional realms. This process facilitates their active participation in mapping of experienced and shaping services while ensuring a safe space for discussing sensitive topics (Thumbadoo et al, 2023; NACCW 2024). Mapping activities serve as both a participatory tool and a therapeutic method within child care work practice, enabling the exploration of factors influencing children's lives and facilitating the expression of issues and trauma through art (Thumbadoo, R., 2023).

Stakeholder Partnerships

Isibindi Ezikoleni represents a collaborative effort between schools, government departments, and local stakeholders to provide comprehensive support to vulnerable learners, enabling them to overcome challenges and achieve their full potential in education and beyond. Isibindi Ezikoleni CYCWs are school support staff members who are included in relevant staff activities and have access to relevant information on learners. Services such as home visits, child protection follow up, accessing resources from government stakeholders or material support to learners requires CYCWs to work with or report to the School Based Support Team (SBST) coordinator and/or School Management Team (SMT) member. Working with the SMT/SBST facilitates referrals from educators to the CYCWs, as well to provide feedback on any changes in learners' behaviour and academic performance. Parents/caregivers are also an important internal stakeholder. External stakeholders include the departments of education at provincial, district and circuit levels, departments of health, social development and police, designated child protection organisations, NGOs, community-based organisations, faith-based organisations, the private sector, and funders.

The programme is implemented as a partnership between NACCW, schools and the provincial Departments of Education. In most cases, schools serve as 'implementing partners' and are responsible for employing the CYCWs (through the School Governing Bodies) and paying their salaries with funds received via NACCW or the Department of Education. NACCW provides the training, supervision for the CYCWs and overall project management and monitoring and evaluation.

CYCWs work in collaboration with educators to implement the programme, especially the Life Orientation teacher and the SBST, to ensure a coordinated approach. Working with the SBST facilitates referrals from educators to the CYCWs, as well as feedback on any changes in the learners' behaviour and academic performance. The CYCWs can also provide guidance to the educators on how to deal with behavioural and other issues among the learners in their class in a way that focuses on building strength and resilience rather than punishment and humiliation.

Developmental Approach to Monitoring and Evaluation

Isibindi Ezikoleni employs a developmental monitoring and evaluation (M&E) approach. This is a flexible and adaptive process designed to support the ongoing development and refinement of a programme that is responsive to context in real time. Unlike traditional M&E frameworks that often focus on predetermined outcomes and rigid methodologies, a developmental approach emphasizes learning and adaptation based on emerging data and insights (Gamble, 2008; McDonald, 2016). By integrating developmental M&E, Isibindi Ezikoleni ensures that its activities remain relevant, effective, and aligned with the evolving needs of learners and schools This approach facilitates an ongoing learning process for programme implementers, enabling the identification of best practices, areas for improvement, and the optimal allocation of resources to maximize impact for learners.

This developmental approach to M&E contributed to the development and ongoing refinement of data collection tools, reporting and SOPs for the management and delivery of Isibindi Ezikoleni services, including different interventions, superivison, and M&E requirements.

LOCALLY RECRUITED, TRAINED AND SUPERVISED CHILD AND YOUTH CARE WORKFORCE

Recruitment

Isibindi Ezikoleni adopts a targeted strategy for recruiting CYCWs, specifically focusing on local youth aged 20 to 35 from the same communities where the schools are located. This approach not only contributes to mitigating youth unemployment in areas with scarce opportunities but also ensures the retention of skills within these communities by offering meaningful employment. By drawing CYCWs from the communities they serve, the programme ensures that these professionals are well-acquainted with the local context, understand its unique challenges, and can leverage their personal knowledge to tailor the programme effectively. Furthermore, this strategy facilitates the transfer of acquired knowledge and skills beyond the school environment, enriching the CYCWs' homes and broader social lives, thereby reinforcing the community's overall capacity for support and development.

Isibindi Ezikoleni is supported by a diverse funding model. This includes government funding, including the Presidential Youth Employment - Basic Education Employment Initiative (PYE - BEEI) 3 and the Health and Welfare Sector Education and Training Authority (HWSETA), as well as donations from local and international donors. Within the PYEI-BEEI framework, youth are appointed to various educational support roles such as Teaching Assistants, Education Assistants, Learner Support Agents, and General School Assistants. CYCWs are included among these roles, highlighting the initiative's recognition of their integral role in providing comprehensive support to learners. This approach is a key part of the PYEI's strategy to combat youth unemployment in South Africa, generating employment opportunities within public sectors and placing a strong emphasis on skills development.

All recruited CYCWs are screened and cleared (or are in the process of being cleared) against the Department of Social Development Child Protection Register. All CYCWs, including those in training, are registered with the South African Council of Social Service Professionals and must adhere to a professional code of conduct and ethics in their work.

Training

If the recruited staff do not already have a child and youth care qualification, they are trained in an auxiliary child and youth care qualification offered by the NACCW and other registered child care training service providers. On-going in-service training opportunities are provided by the mentor and other project staff in all aspects of the Isibindi Ezikoleni programme.

Job Descriptions and Workloads

Isibindi Ezikoleni CYCW job descriptions require them to provide the following services:

- Working together with teachers to identify vulnerable and at-risk learners and enrolling these young people on their workloads. Conducting assessments and developing Individual Development Plans (IDPs) for learners, using assessment forms completed by teachers in schools where DBE's Screening, Identification, Assessment and Support (SIAS) approach is being implemented. CYCWs are expected to manage caseloads of 20-25 high-risk learners yearly, aiming to extend their reach to 50 learners by addressing and closing cases as progress is made.

- Management/support of the learner including home visits, when and where needed.
- Case management and case conferencing within a school-based multi-disciplinary team. This includes child protection case management and other forms of case management depending on the needs of the learner.
- Provision of structured developmental programmes with groups of vulnerable and at-risk young people including life skills programmes, sexual and reproductive health programmes, and substance use programmes.
- Provision of other forms of structured support to groups of vulnerable and at-risk young people including peer support groups, HIV & AIDS prevention programmes, and academic support e.g. homework supervision, reading clubs and structured academic support programmes such as Teaching at the Right Level – TaRL.
- Advocacy and referrals of young people for social grants, education fee waivers and subsidies and other social protection as well as health services.
- School-based holiday programmes, providing a range of structured recreational and developmental activities.
- Whole-school preventive interventions such as input in assemblies and campaigns of particular topics.

CYCW workloads include managing a caseload of high-risk learners, providing short term/crisis interventions to medium/low risk individual learners, and implementing a range of group and whole school prevention and early intervention activities. The planning of these activities and allocation of time per activity and setting of targets requires some flexibility depending on funder requirements, the number of learners and CYCWs in the school. The project mentor is responsible for providing individual and group supervision to CYCWs to assist them to plan their activities, allocate their time effectively, and deliver quality services. All the Isibindi Ezikoleni service SOPs provide guidance on the type and frequency of services to be provided at individual, group, class and whole-school levels.

Isibindi Ezikoleni CYCWs are expected work flexible hours so that they are available when children need them most e.g. early morning before going to school and late afternoon when they come home from school and on weekends. These flexible working hours are provided for in the Basic Conditions of Employment Act and other laws. Depending on the needs of the learners in the school and their families, the CYCW may need to be available for one- or two-hours before school starts. CYCWs may also need to work in the early evening to engage with the learner's caregivers. CYCWs who work in hostels may also work in the evening or on weekends if the parent/caregiver is not available during school hours. Human resource tools, including work plans, diaries, timesheets, and appraisals, are instrumental in assisting Isibindi Ezikoleni CYCWs manage their workloads. Mentors also guide CYCWs to maintain a healthy balance between their work duties and their personal and family care and commitments.

Supervision

Supervision is provided by NACCW mentors who are qualified and experienced CYCWs. One mentor is responsible for the mentorship and supervision of 10 – 12 CYCWs. Mentors have been found to exemplify the relational nature of child and youth care work, emphasizing practices such as role modelling and collaboration with CYCWs (De Nobrega et al, 2023). The roles and responsibilities of mentors include the following:

- Supporting CYCWs to apply child and youth care theory from their training into practice. Mentors act as co-facilitators in the orientation and training of the CYCWs.
- Supervising the day-to-day work of CYCWs to ensure they implement and follow-up on tasks.
- Providing case consultation/case management support especially for high-risk, complex cases, ensuring that these cases ensuring the learners receive the assistance they need.
- Fulfilling programme administration and monitoring and evaluation (M&E) requirements.
- Maintaining stakeholder relations including liaising with relevant partners/ stakeholders, building relationships with school staff and providing regular updates to the School Management Team (SMT).
- Conducting Routine Data Quality Assessments (RDQAs) and school assessments.

Career Development

The programme structure provides internal opportunities for career development and internal promotions are encouraged as this contributes to local leadership development. The programme also creates a platform for CYCWs to pursue other workforce opportunities independently of NACCW/Isibindi Ezikoleni. These career paths that would require further education and training and include child and youth care work (degree); social work; psychology (educational, clinical); occupational therapy; and teaching.

OVERCOMING EDUCATIONAL BARRIERS: RESULTS OF THE ISIBINDI EZIKOLENI PROGRAMME

To date, over 40 research and evaluation studies have been conducted on NACCW's work, both internally and externally. Of these, seven are focused on the Isibindi Ezikoleni programme, while the others address various aspects of child and youth care work in communities.

A study of Isibindi Ezikoleni in one district (Reyneke, 2023) found that CYCWs engaged in a range of semi-professional tasks that were crucial in aiding learners to deal with their everyday challenges. Tasks included offering psychosocial support, leading awareness initiatives, facilitating group discussions, and organizing educational activities. CYCWs were also found to often serve as stand-in parental figures and mentors for particularly vulnerable children.

Hartnack's (2018) assessment of the Isibindi Ezikoleni pilot project in KwaZulu-Natal revealed several key insights and impacts after a year of implementation. The model was found to represent a cost-effective and impactful approach to tackling school dropout and disengagement through focused, multidisciplinary teams at the school level. The incorporation of CYCWs was found to have significantly bolstered the effectiveness of Learner Support Agents, particularly in providing psychosocial support, counselling, and family and community interventions. The project also showed promising outcomes in enhancing the functioning of SBSTs.

Isibindi Ezikoleni's success stories, as outlined by Budlender and Wilson (2019), highlight its adaptability and the crucial role CYCWs play in addressing the needs of learners at risk of dropout. These success stories underscore the programme's ability to tailor interventions to the specific needs of learners and the unique contexts of schools. Key results include:

- Consistent reports by schools of reductions in absenteeism, truancy bullying, incorrect/untidy uniforms – attributed to CYCWs gate monitoring, corridor monitoring and psycho-social support interventions, particularly with individual learners identified as 'troublemakers', having a positive ripple effect on behaviour of other learners throughout the school.
- Young people found CYCWs to be approachable and trustworthy, could talk to them about anything, and go to them for care and support – this was especially evident in informal contacts in corridors, break time etc. and in the

stream of young people going to the CYCW's office (where they had a dedicated office).
- Isolated children found companionship and friends through participating in reading and peer support groups.
- Home visits helped identify and address barriers to learning which the school was unaware of e.g. extreme poverty, no parental supervision, family bereavements.
- Crisis/emergency interventions addressed child protection and health needs of young people.

The existing evidence in evaluations of the programme, anecdotal evidence and practice examples collected from implementation offers significant insights into the benefit of the programme. These stories and examples demonstrate the programme's positive effects on learners' well-being and educational outcomes. Based on internal monitoring and evaluation reports from the NACCW on Isibindi Ezikoleni, since its initiation in schools in 2016, there has been a positive contribution to learner wellbeing outcomes. The reach of the programme since 2016 is presented in Box 4 with further results provided for the matric support component of the programme in Box 5.

Box 4. Overall results of the programme

Since 2016, Isibindi Ezikoleni has reached over 20,000 high-risk learners and reached more than 100,000 low to medium-risk learners through whole-school, class, and group activities in 474 schools. Close to half of all learners enrolled in the programme are referred by educators:
- CYCWs helped re-integrate over 200 learners back to school.
- CYCWs identified close to 1,000 child survivors of abuse and neglect with CYCWs often the first point of disclosure for learners.
- CYCWs supported over 1,000 pregnant teenagers/young mothers/fathers in the programme.
- Schools showed positive matric – final school year – results for learners that have been in the programme (close to 90% pass rate in 2023).
- Services provided to learners are 110,000 individual lifespace counselling sessions, 100,000 group sessions, 50,000 homework sessions, 40,000 structured development programmes, 35,000 home visits, and close to 3,000 learners have been referred and supported with social services, health services, and services to other organisations.

Box 5. Academic improvements

The NACCW's report on the Isibindi matric results in 2023 (National Association of Child Care Workers, 2024a), show that 367 Isibindi Ezikoleni beneficiaries took their matric examinations, with 315 achieving a pass, translating to an 85.8% pass rate. This surpasses the national average of 82.9% with 73 students earning distinctions despite facing challenging circumstances. The CYCWs played a crucial role in providing educational and psychosocial support, including reintegrating learners who had dropped out, assisting with homework, facilitating study groups, and ensuring access to study materials. They also motivated learners and helped them navigate post-matriculation opportunities, in addition to mobilizing resources like solar lamps for night study, uniforms, and stationery. The improved pass rate reflects the collective effort and determination of the learners, school staff, families, friends, and CYCWs involved in the Isibindi Ezikoleni programme. Insights from analysing the matric results have highlighted the need for targeted support for learners facing greater challenges, such as those older than their grade cohort or dealing with teenage pregnancy. It is important to note that the success of these learners could be the result of their own perseverance, the dedication of school staff, and the comprehensive support from CYCWs, among others. Without empirical evidence, it is not possible to credit the Isibindi Ezikoleni programme solely for these outcomes.

The observed outcomes are also derived from Isibindi Ezikoleni stories of change, and below are results from the programme implemented in the Gauteng province in collaboration with the Matthew Goniwe School of Leadership and Governance in 2019 (see Table 4).

Table 4. Isibindi Ezikoleni programme observed outcomes

Level	Observed outcome
Learner Level results	■ Increased school attendance by learners who were attending school irregularly or who had dropped out of school and assisted to be re-admitted back to school. ■ Improved knowledge of learners on key topics impacting them. This was achieved through activities on Sexual and Reproductive Health (SRH), HIV/AIDS, substance abuse, child protection, teenage pregnancy and other topics facilitated by CYCWs. ■ Improved school performance through homework supervision, reading clubs and study groups. ■ Improved parenting and school attendance by young mothers. These mothers were supported to attend school and learn to better care for their children through Early Childhood Development (ECD) support by CYCWs. ■ Improved behaviour management. This was addressed for learners who are in conflict with the school regulations such as with learners who are bullying others. CYCWs have supported them using a 'restorative justice' approach.
Family level results	■ Improved family strengthening during family work. CYCWs visited the homes of particularly vulnerable learners and supported the family during these visits. ■ At a parental level, there have been cases of change in the home environments, caregiver attitudes of 'problem' learners. ■ Improved access to social assistance. CYCWs assisted learners and their families to access social grants, either in cases where it was not present or where a family member has misused it. ■ Improved access to social and other services. There have been successful referrals and linkages with social service professionals and other practitioners. For instance, during child protection cases and other cases in need of multidisciplinary teamwork.
School level results	■ Improved 'school culture'. There have been shifts in the 'school vibe/tone' towards a better working environment and at-risk learners are supported and nurtured. ■ Improved shifts in school staff working with learners. Steps have been made in creating a shift in the attitude of school leadership and teachers towards at-risk and 'problem' learners – towards a more vigilant, supportive and nurturing environment for them. ■ There is evidence that the project has spin-offs for the school in the form of leveraging additional resources, greater parent/community buy-in and support, greater linkages, recognition and support from external role-players and education departments.

To conclude this section, the following case vignettes provide further illustrations of some of the anecdotal impacts of the programme.

Learner pregnancy support: A 16-year-old pregnant learner lived with her unemployed single mother. The only source of income was the learners child support grant. The learner felt overwhelmed, stressed, and was struggling with her schoolwork. She was at the point of failing her grade. The CYCW arranged a family meeting and provided psychosocial support to the learner and her mother. The CYCW also provided educational support to the learner through homework support and developing a study timetable. When the learner went to the clinic, the CYCW ensured that she got the schoolwork that she missed out on. The CYCW also linked the learner with health staff who assisted her in acquiring more information on her pregnancy. The CYCW also advised the mother to start a vegetable garden at home. The learner is now coping better at school and feels more empowered to manage her pregnancy.

Schoolwork support: The CYCW helped a 7-year-old learner in grade 3 who consistently struggled to complete his schoolwork, following a referral from his teacher. After discussing the learner's challenges with his parents and exploring ways to assist him, the CYCW included him in her after-school homework supervision and reading groups. She continued to monitor his progress, and after a meeting with the class teacher, it was clear that the teacher was satisfied with the learner's improvement. By the term's end, the learner's parents were pleased to learn that he had successfully passed the grade.

Child protection support: The CYCW identified a teenage learner who frequently arrived late to school due to living alone with her often ill baby. The learner hadn't seen her mother in two years, lived off her child's social welfare, grant, and relied on neighbours for food. The CYCW located her mother in the Eastern Cape, who was unaware of her grandchild. After discussing the importance of her support, the CYCW and a local social worker intervened, providing the learner with food, and arranging for her to live with her aunt for better care. This support helped her attend school regularly with a clean uniform and improve her focus on her schoolwork. The learner and her mother are now reconnecting, with her mother keeping in regular contact.

Matric support: A learner was referred to the CYCW because he was doing his matric but was told he could not write his exams because he did not have a South African identity document (ID). The CYCW contacted his family and found out that his mother had used his father's surname instead of her surname on the birth certificate, therefore a family member from the father's side was required to assist for the learner to get his ID. The CYCW arranged to meet with the learner's father and accompanied the learner to the Department of Home Affairs. Through the assistance of the CYCW, the learner was able to get an ID and register for his exams. The learner wrote the exam and passed grade 12.

Substance abuse support: A CYCW provided lifespace counselling to a 12-year-old boy after he was reported to her for fighting during a class session. During the discussion, the child confessed that he was smoking cigarettes and 'dagga' (marijuana). A meeting with his grandmother and the principal was arranged and his grandmother reported that he would sometimes break windows at home when he was high. The CYCW referred the case to the community social worker and is exploring options for rehabilitation programmes.

Bullying support: A 14-year-old learner was referred to the CYCW because other learners were mocking her as she came from a very poor family and did not have a proper school uniform. The CYCW and her teacher did a home visit and spoke to her parents about how to address the matter, and the CYCWs assisted them to secure a new uniform. The CYCW had an anti-bullying session with her class, and the learners who had been bullying her came forward and asked for her forgiveness.

Drop-out support: A CYCW identified a 16-year-old teenage mother who had dropped out of Grade 7 to take care of her 4-month-old child. The CYCW met with the family and arranged for the learners' mother to take care of the child so that she could go back to school. The learner is now attending school regularly and the CYCW meets with her regularly to provide life space counselling and motivate her to complete her studies.

Suicide prevention support: A learner approached the CYCW with a letter her friend had written threatening to kill herself. The CYCW immediately went to find the girl in the school and referred her to a social worker for counselling. The CYCW has encouraged the girl to come see her every day at school so that they can talk about how she is feeling and her situation at home.

LESSONS LEARNT

The implementation of Isibindi Ezikoleni occurs within a challenging environment, compounded by both systemic issues in the public education system and the unique characteristics of each school, including size, resources, location, teacher-to-learner ratios, operational hours, and cultural aspects. The extent of a CYCW's role and activities is often determined by the principal and other staff, as well as the school's size. These factors can hinder the uniform application of Isibindi Ezikoleni's standard service package across schools. Moreover, the complexity is further increased by varying requirements, expectations, and realities across different provincial Departments of Education and distinct requirements from funders (Budlender & Wilson, 2019). However, through these challenges, valuable lessons have been learned, which are crucial for the programme's evolution and the broader application of the Isibindi model.

Advocacy and development through the professional association: The NACCW plays a key role in advocating for and driving the development and recognition of the school-based child and youth care workforce, supporting their integration into the school environment. The NACCW has been pivotal in navigating the diverse expectations of government departments and funders and developing a practice-based framework for the standardised integration of CYCWs in schools.

The critical role of professional supervision: Professional supervision for CYCWs is essential, providing the guidance and oversight necessary to adapt and effectively implement the programme within challenging contexts. A fundamental requirement of child and youth care supervision is to create a supportive environment that mirrors the care CYCWs are expected to provide to learners and ensuring that services provided are implemented according to established standards.

Addressing national challenges through workforce expansion: Expanding the child and youth care workforce addresses major national challenges such as inequality, poverty, and unemployment, making it a top political priority. This expansion can create local 'decent' jobs with a clear career path and at the same time support vulnerable learners to obtain an education and complete their schooling. This requires both ministerial support and a clear policy framework for securing financial resources and providing a foundation for the expansion of CYCWs into schools, ensuring every child has access to necessary care and support services for their well-being and academic success.

Participatory approach for tailored services: Encountering the unique needs of each school environment taught the value of a participatory approach. Involving school and community stakeholders, as well as children through mapping exercises, in planning ensures that the services provided by CYCWs are well-aligned with the specific requirements of learners and respect local cultural contexts.

Importance of local recruitment and structured career paths: The approach of locally recruiting and training CYCWs ensures that workers services are delivered by individuals familiar with and committed to their communities. It also keeps skills and incomes in communities. In addition, establishing a structured career path for CYCWs allows for their ongoing professional development and ability to serve learners effectively.

Developmental monitoring and evaluation for continuous improvement: Adopting a developmental approach to monitoring and evaluation has allowed for ongoing reflection and adaptation of the model, ensuring the programme meets its objectives effectively. It has led to the development of practice-based standard operating procedures, guiding a standardized implementation of the programme across different schools and provinces. This ensures consistency and quality of service delivery, addressing the unique challenges and opportunities within each context.

These lessons highlight the multifaceted approach needed to successfully integrate CYCWs into the South African school system, addressing both the challenges and opportunities presented by Isibindi Ezikoleni.

FUTURE DIRECTIONS AND POLICY RECOMMENDATIONS

Considering the future of school-based child and youth care, the focus is on enhancing the programme's effectiveness, expanding its reach, and increasing its positive influence on learners' lives. This will involve examining and refining policies, practices, and research priorities as outlined in this section.

Sustainability through strategic engagement and policy integration: Guaranteeing the programme's continued success requires education departments to recognise the significant contributions of CYCWs as support staff in schools. This process includes strategic communication with the education ministry and departments and forming MOUs with provincial departments. These agreements aim to formally recognize and support the integration of school-based child and youth care services. Part of this strategic approach involves securing funding for CYCW positions to transition their current roles into permanent posts within the school system, thus ensuring their sustainability. In addition, maintaining compliance with child and youth care regulations is essential, requiring that school based CYCWs receive professional supervision. Identifying and establishing mechanisms for the provision and financing of this supervision must also be addressed in the strategic engagement.

Enhancing programme leadership: Developing leadership capabilities within the child and youth care workforce is essential for the sustainability of the programme. By strategically investing in the professional development of current staff, such as Project Coordinators and mentors, this empowerment would enable them to effectively champion and steer the programme at school, district, provincial, and national levels.

Expansion to diverse educational settings: The programme, currently active in ordinary/mainstream schools, could extend to special needs schools, public boarding schools, and farm schools. These settings often include residential support roles, such as house mothers, which could be filled by trained CYCWs. Adapting the programme to these environments would require specialized service SOPs, building on the existing foundational ones.

Development of a costed business case: A detailed business case is essential to advocate for CYCW employment by education departments, potentially requiring amendments to legislation, policies, and budgeting processes. This case would outline the financial aspects of the programme across various sites, recommending CYCW-to-learner ratios and identifying opportunities for cost savings. The goal is to broaden the funding base and strengthen financial sustainability.

Future Research Needs: To advance the field of school-based child and youth care work, several research areas have been identified:

- An independent evaluation of the Isibindi Ezikoleni model is also necessary to provide impartial evidence of its effectiveness and identify opportunities for its refinement.
- A deeper exploration into the practices and outcomes of school-based child and youth care work is required, with a particular focus on academic achievement, psychosocial wellbeing, and broader outcomes. Such research, ideally spearheaded by child and youth care practitioners in partnership with social scientists, is critical for shaping relevant policies and improving services related to child and youth care in educational contexts, thereby enriching the overall framework of support for students within schools (Reyneke, 2023; Ponsamy, 2021).
- Further exploration the role of CYCWs in supporting schools to 'reasonably accommodate' children with disabilities in ordinary/mainstream schools, and their role in full service and special needs schools.
- Research into the models for delivering and financing CYCW supervision—potentially by the NACCW or equally qualified professionals—is essential for upholding legal standards and enhancing the quality of child support.
- Assessing the implementation and effectiveness of the Teaching at the Right Level (TaRL) initiative, led by CYCWs, in improving reading skills among primary school learners.

These strategic directions have the potential to not only sustain but also to enhance the Isibindi Ezikoleni programme's capacity to make a profound difference in the lives of learners in South Africa's schools and their academic success.

CONCLUSION

The Isibindi Ezikoleni programme, funded from various sources, has operated in 474 schools countrywide, reaching over 100,000 vulnerable learners. Overall, the positive feedback from school stakeholders and results in school attendance, and reductions in bullying and substance use attest to the significant impact of the Isibindi Ezikoleni programme. The contributions of CYCWs have not only improved learners' personal circumstances but have also relieved school staff by addressing complex learner challenges. While the presence of an Isibindi Ezikoleni CYCW can have a positive influence on overall school culture, and some principals say that absenteeism rates have dropped since introducing the programme, some caution is needed in attributing all positive changes to the Isibindi Ezikoleni programme, especially if there are other initiatives taking place in the school to improve the quality of teaching and learning.

The programme emerges as a promising approach to addressing learners' unmet developmental needs, fostering holistic development, and ensuring successful educational progression. It has the potential to transform the lives of many more vulnerable learners among South Africa's 12 million public school learners. Furthermore, the programme demonstrates adaptability to local needs through the deployment of a child-centred and regulated child and youth care workforce.

Isibindi Ezikoleni has enabled NACCW and the national and provincial Departments of Education to explore the possibilities and limitations of providing school-based child and youth care work services in different school settings and contexts, emphasizing psychosocial interventions that are not only welfare oriented but are strategically implemented to enhance learners' educational achievements. Overall, Isibindi Ezikoleni CYCWs are viewed as an important workforce in supporting schools to provide care and support services to learners. The programme showcases the potential of integrating structured child and youth care practice in schools to cultivate inclusive educational environments with the overall objective of achieving educational outcomes. Research, programme data and anecdotal evidence points to the role that CYCWs, when integrated into the educational system with defined functions and proper oversight, can play in advancing an inclusive educational experience for all learners. However, the scope of CYCWs does not extend to rectifying the systemic challenges facing South Africa's education system including inequalities in resource distribution, quality of teaching, and infrastructure. These issues require comprehensive interventions at a national level, beyond the direct influence and capacity of the programme.

The integration of CYCWs into schools capitalizes on an already established, regulated workforce in South Africa, highlighting the necessity of promoting and maximizing this resource. The vision extends beyond simply replicating the Isibindi Ezikoleni programme to embedding CYCWs within the school system to enhance inclusive practices and educational attainment. This requires developing a generic school-based child and youth care scope of practice, including specialized training and professional supervision, to ensure the effective application of child and youth care practices in this new setting.

REFERENCES

Allsopp, J. M. (2013). An enquiry into the factors that have contributed to the growth of the field of child and youth care work in South Africa [Unpublished master's thesis]. University of South Africa, Pretoria, South Africa.

Allsopp, J. M. (2020). Child and Youth Care Work in the South African Context: Towards a Model for Education and Practice [Unpublished doctoral dissertation]. Durban University of Technology, South Africa.

Anderson, L. W., Krathwohl, D. R., Airasian, P. W., Cruikshank, K. A., Mayer, R. E., Pintrich, P. R., Raths, J., & Wittrock, M. C. (2001). *A taxonomy for learning, teaching, and assessing: A revision of Bloom's taxonomy of educational objectives, abridged edition*. Pearson.

Atkins, E. R., & Cilliers, J. (2024). Education. ISS African Futures. https://futures.issafrica.org/thematic/06-education/#cite-this-research

Budlender, D., & Wilson, T. (2019). Isibindi Ezikoleni: Reflections on the model. Unpublished manuscript, National Association of Child Care Workers (NACCW).

Child Hub Academy. (Undated). Practicing Supervision in Child Protection Settings. Online Training Course. Centre of Excellence for Looked After Children in Scotland (CELCIS), University of Strathclyde.

De Nobrega, N., Shezi, N., Mlambo, N., Nkwane, E., Thabede, S., Nxumalo, G., Lunga, A., Buthelezi, S., Louw, I., Radebe, A., Mazibuko, J., Ntintili, K., & Thumbadoo, Z. (2023). The role of mentorship in relational child and youth care management: Stories from child and youth care mentors in South Africa. Relational Child & Youth Care Practice, 36(1), 60 – 78. ISSN 2410-2954.

Denholm, C. (2005). Challenges and Questions facing the Development of Child and Youth Care work in Canadian Educational Settings. CYC-Net. https://cyc-net.org/CYC-Online/cycol-0805-denholm.html

Denholm, C. J. (1989). Child and youth care in school settings: Maximizing support and minimizing friction. *Journal of Child and Youth Care Work*, 5, 54–61.

Department Basic Education Republic of South Africa. (2018). *Keynote address by the Minister of Basic Education Mrs*. Angie Motshekga. Department Basic Education Republic of South Africa.

Department of Basic Education, (2023). Presentation to the Portfolio Committee on Basic Education on Progress in the Implementation of Inclusive Education.

Department of Basic Education (DBE) and MIET Africa. (2010). *The Action Step: National Model Conceptual Framework for Care and Support for Teaching and Learning. MIET Africa. Durban Department of Basic Education South Africa. (2014). A message to schools on identifying and supporting learners who are vulnerable.* Department of Basic Education South Africa.

Department of Social Development. (2014). Regulations for child and youth care workers, auxiliary child and youth care workers, and student child and youth care workers. Government Gazette, (No. R. 838), 31 October 2014.

Department of Social Development. Republic of South Africa. (2019). National child care and protection policy: Working together to advance the rights of all children to care and protection. Department of Social Development, Republic of South Africa. https://www.gov.za/sites/default/files/gcis_document/202102/national-child-care-and-protection-policy.pdf

DGMT. (2023). Escaping the inequality trap. Five year strategy: 2023 – 2027.

Gamble, J. (2008). *A Developmental Evaluation Primer*. The J.W. McConnell Family Foundation.

Garfat, T., Freeman, J., Gharabaghi, K., & Fulcher, L. (2018). Characteristics of a relational child and youth care approach revisited. *CYC-Online*, (10), 7–45.

Gharabaghi, K. (2018). Professionalization through doing. CYC-Net, (243), 32-35. https://cyc-net.org/cyc-online/may2019.pdf

Gharabaghi, K. (2019). Re-Launching Child and Youth Care Practice. CYC-Online, (September 2019), 9-15. https://www.cyc-net.org/cyc-online/sep2019.pdf

Gray, M., & Lombard, A. (2022). Progress of the social service professions in South Africa's developmental social welfare system: Social work, and child and youth care work. International Journal of Social Welfare, 1– 13. DOI: 10.1111/ijsw.12562

Hartnack, A. (2019). Zero Dropout Schools Initiative – 2018 final qualitative evaluation report. Unpublished report.

Huijbregts, M., Spadafora, T., & Patel, L. (2023). Cash plus programmes for children and families in eastern and southern Africa: Examples from practice and lessons learnt. In *Handbook on Social Protection and Social Development in the Global South* (pp. 382–399). Edward Elgar Publishing. DOI: 10.4337/9781800378421.00038

Inclusive Education South Africa. (2019). *IESA EU Factsheet: What is inclusive education?* Inclusive Education South Africa.

Jamieson, L. (2013). *Child and youth care workers in South Africa: A technical brief.* AIDSTAR-Two Project, Management Sciences for Health.

Khumalo, S., & Hodgson, T. F. (2017). The right to basic education for learners with disabilities. In Basic Education Rights Handbook – Education Rights in South Africa (Chapter 5). https://section27.org.za/wp-content/uploads/2017/02/Chapter-5.pdf

Krueger, M. (2019). Central themes in child and youth care. CYC-Net. https://www.cyc-net.org/cyc-online/cycol-0100-krueger.html

Mahwai, L. P., & Ross, E. (2023). Life orientation teachers' experiences of providing psychosocial support to high school learners in the Johannesburg West district. *South African Journal of Education*, 43(4), 2199. Advance online publication. DOI: 10.15700//saje.v43n4a2199

McCully, C. (2001) Child and youth care work in the school environment. CYC-Net. https://cyc-net.org/cyc-online/cycol-0101-schools.html

McDonald, H. (2016). *Developmental evaluation: A tool to support innovation. 2016.* New Zealand Council for Educational Research., DOI: 10.18296/em.0012

Michael, J. (2005). Life-space supervision in child and youth care practice. In Garfat, T., & Gannon, B. (Eds.), *Aspects of Child and youth care practice in the South African context*. Pretext.

National Association of Child Care Workers. (2022). Output 1: Analysis of the programme and local needs and opportunities in the Lesedi and Letsatsi Solar Park Trust catchment areas. Unpublished research report, November 2022.

National Association of Child Care Workers. (2024). Experiences of learning barriers in education: Reflections of learners in Gauteng schools in the Isibindi Ezikoleni Programme. Unpublished research report, February 2024.

National Association of Child Care Workers. (2024). Isibindi Ezikoleni matric results: class of 2023

Phelan, P. (2015). *The Long and Short of it Child and Youth Care*. CYC-Net Press.

Ponsamy, J. (2021). An exploration of the roles of child and youth care workers at schools within the Isibindi Ezikoleni programme [Master's thesis]. Durban University of Technology.

Professional Board for Child and Youth Care Work. (2021). *Concept note: The current crisis in the child and youth care work profession.* SACSSP.

Reyneke, R. (2023). Unveiling the significant contribution of child and youth care workers in South African township schools. University of the Free State. DOI: 10.2139/ssrn.4647035

Sapire, I., Tshuma, L., & Herholdt, R. (2024). Spotlight on basic education completion and foundational learning: South Africa. Global Education Monitoring Report Team. Association for the Development of Education in Africa. https://unesdoc.unesco.org/ark:/48223/pf0000389034

Schirmer, S., & Visser, R. (2023). *One: Time to Fix South Africa's Failing Education System*. Centre for Development and Enterprise.

South African Council for Social Service Professions (SACSSP). (2014). Rules relating to conduct of child and youth care workers in practising their profession (Code of Ethics). Government Gazette, (38128), 31 October 2014.

South African Council for Social Service Professions (SACSSP). (2021). *Summit on the crisis in the child and youth care sector in South Africa and its impact on the welfare of children and youth: Summary of proceedings and resolutions*. SACSSP.

The Alliance for Child Protection in Humanitarian Action. (2018). *Child Protection Case Management Supervision and Coaching Training*.

Thobejane, T. D. (2013). History of apartheid education and the problems of reconstruction in South Africa. *Sociolinguistic Studies*, 3(1), 1–12.

Thumbadoo, R. V. (2024). Children's mapping in Africa: Building on the Barbara Petchenik children's map competition. Cartouche, (100).

Thumbadoo, Z. (2013). Ways in Which Child and Youth Care Workers Support Child-Headed Households in Communities [Masters Thesis]. University of South Africa.

Thumbadoo, Z. (2021). The current crisis in the child and youth care work profession [PowerPoint presentation]. Professional Board for Child and Youth Care Work, South African Council for Social Service Professionals.

Thumbadoo, Z., Ntintili, K., Taylor, D., & Thumbadoo, R. (2023). Children mapping their realities and aspirations: An innovative methodological tool with implications for practice, programme and policy. [ICA]. *Abstracts of the International Cartographic Association*, 6, 1–1. DOI: 10.5194/ica-abs-6-257-2023

Thumbadoo, Z. S. (2020). Towards the development of a theoretical framework to guide child and youth care practice in South Africa [Doctoral dissertation]. Durban University of Technology.

UNESCO. (2020). Global education monitoring report. Inclusion in education: All means all. United Nations Educational Cultural and Scientific Organisation, France. https://unesdoc.unesco.org/ark:/48223/pf0000373718

VanderVen, K., & Torre, C. A. (1999). A dynamical systems perspective on mediating violence in schools: Emergent roles of child and youth care workers. *Child and Youth Care Forum*, 28(6), 411–436. DOI: 10.1023/A:1022843525790

Vergottini, M., & Weyers, M. (2020). The foundations and nature of South African school social work: An overview. Social Work/Maatskaplike Werk, 56(2).

Wilson, T. (2022). Report on the Baseline Research to Inform a 5-Year Strategy for NACCW's Work in Schools in the Lesedi and Letsatsi Solar Park Trust Catchment Areas.

Zero Dropout Campaign. (2021). School Dropout Gender Matters.

KEY TERMS AND DEFINITIONS

Behaviour management: Behaviour is recognised as one of the key factors affecting a young persons' prospects at school. Managing the young person's behaviour with respect and dignity enables them to gain as much self-control as possible. Routine child and youth care behaviour management techniques include proximity control, touch control and making things simpler. Other behaviour management measures include building competency and trial-and-error learning to ensure that young people have the necessary skills and are given opportunities to practice them.

Child and youth care work: The acts performed by a child and youth care worker which focuses on children and youth within the context of the family, community, and the lifespan of a person.

Life space work: Life-space work is at the centre of relational practice and represents the total physical and emotional space where young people and child and youth care workers interact. Child and youth care work is more than anything else about being with young people in their everyday experiences, in their life-space, in their here and now. Life-space work includes the following dimensions: (1) the physical dimension, which not only involves physical locations but the experience of those locations by the five senses; (2) the mental dimension, which involves thoughts, feelings, and how a young person constructs or makes sense of his or her life-space; (3) the relational dimension, which is about what young people do with and within their relationships. This dimension can have a profound impact on how the various physical locations of life-space are experienced (and constructed) by the young person; and (4) the virtual dimension, which includes "those environments in which we interact and relate to others, but where all the senses are not fully utilised. Through life-space work, CYCWs engage with children in the times and contexts in which other professionals do not. This refers, for example, to bedtime, or early morning before leaving for school, or the way to and from school. It includes times in schools, in recreational settings, in the family, on the streets, or in residential care settings. In these contexts, a specific, internationally recognised methodology for interaction is used by CYCWs. (Thumbadoo, 2021).

Working in the moment: In child and youth care every moment in the young person's life is considered highly significant and CYCWs spend a proportionately large amount of time/most of their workday with, sharing and influencing their experiences on a moment-by-moment basis. Working in the moment is based on the developmental approach, which understands development as being continuous rather than linear, and taking place through an accumulation of 'moments' all of which can make a difference to development. Development does not take place in leaps and bounds but in tiny little steps which most of the time go unnoticed. In work with children and youth the CYCW should notice these tiny steps and encourage and applaud them so that those with poor self-esteem may be encouraged to move on.

ENDNOTES

[1] School dropout has been defined as "leaving education without obtaining a minimal credential" and is described by the DGMT Zero Dropout Campaign as someone who "permanently leaves school before writing the National Senior Certificate (matric) exam or obtaining another National Qualification Framework (NQF) Level 4 qualification".

[2] Using this approach allows for a thorough exploration of the operational details of the Isibindi Ezikoleni programme, and reflections on the programme's intended and unintended consequences, drawing on insights gained from observations, conversations, direct experience, and programme monitoring data. https://prevention-collaborative.org/guide-programming/practice-based-knowledge/

[3] Since its inception in December 2020, the PYEI-BEEI has undergone several phases, and by early 2023 the initiative had created more than 850,000 job opportunities. Presidential Youth Employment Initiative: Basic Education Employment Initiative https://www.education.gov.za/Programmes/BEEI.aspx. Basic Education commences phase IV employment initiative: https://www.gov.za/news/media-statements/basic-education-commences-phase-iv-employment-initiative-31-jan-2023#:~:text=Basic%20education%20sector%20to%20officially,on%20Wednesday%2C%201%20February%202023.

Chapter 7
Navigating Inclusion in the Industry 4.0 Horizon:
Crafting a Pedagogical Future

Pallavi Sakhahari Dhamak
https://orcid.org/0009-0001-3229-4512
Shri Vile Parle Kelavani Mandal Narsee Monjee Institute of Management Studies, Mukesh Patel School of Technology Management and Engineering, Mumbai, India

Padmanabha Aital
Shri Vile Parle Kelavani Mandal Narsee Monjee Institute of Management Studies, Mukesh Patel School of Technology Management and Engineering, Mumbai, India

Anand Daftardar
Shri Vile Parle Kelavani Mandal Narsee Monjee Institute of Management Studies, Mukesh Patel School of Technology Management and Engineering, Mumbai, India

ABSTRACT

This study investigates the integration of Industry 4.0 technologies in education, focusing on their usage across different educational levels and their impact on learning. Through a comprehensive literature review of articles from Scopus, ScienceDirect, and Web of Science databases, 51 articles were quantitatively analysed and 23 articles were qualitatively examined. Findings highlight the increasing use of augmented reality, virtual reality, the Internet of Things, and simulations, particularly in higher education, to enhance student engagement, promote active participation, and replicate real-world scenarios. Despite their benefits, these technologies are underutilised and mostly confined to manufacturing-related courses. The study

DOI: 10.4018/979-8-3693-4058-5.ch007

underscores the potential of Industry 4.0 technologies to advance Education 4.0 across all educational levels, advocating for their broader implementation to create dynamic and effective learning environments.

1. INTRODUCTION

Since the formulation of the term "Industry 4.0," which was first introduced in Germany in 2011, all sectors of society have been required to make adjustments by adopting a greater amount of digital technology to support their operations *(Abulibdeh et al., 2024;Aditi et al., 2024)*. The phrase "Industry 4.0" refers to the employment of new materials, automation, and digital technology in the construction sector. It is an evolution of the construction industry that is driven by advancements in technology, especially in the areas of artificial intelligence, robotics, big data analytics and the internet of things (IoT). Bur recently the COVID-19 pandemic has worsened the situation of all sectors *(Alshboul et al., 2024;Ayyildiz & Erdogan, 2024)*. Even education was no different. The educational system has consistently adjusted to the requirements and principles of the industries of each era. Within the context of the current economic climate, we are also in the era of Education 4.0, which is characterised by the student taking an active part in the process of their own learning while the instructor serves as a tutor. Students learn at their own pace, following their own schedule and requirements. Furthermore, the time allocated for problem-solving either alone or in cooperation with peers is extended, even outside the classroom setting. *Baratta et al., 2024* establish a connection between Education 4.0 and Industry 4.0, stating that the core education sector is influenced by cognitive and cloud technologies, Internet of Things (IoT), computing, cyber-physical systems (CPS), and other factors introduced by Industry 4.0 as shown in Figure 1. *Calciolari et al., 2024* suggest that using digital technologies in Education 4.0 enhances learning outcomes by thoroughly examining the intersection of digital technologies and education. It has been established through research that the Fourth Industrial Revolution (Industry 4.0) has brought about new requirements for professional education.

Figure 1. Word cloud of Education 4.0

In the landscape of Education 4.0, where higher education institutions are embracing Industry 4.0 technologies to revolutionize learning, a word cloud emerges, painting a vivid picture of the transformative elements at play *(Cavalieri et al., 2024;Huang et al., 2024)*. At its core lies the integration of innovative communication technologies, including artificial intelligence, augmented reality, and virtual reality, fostering immersive and personalized learning experiences. These technologies are integrated into digital transformation, allowing for smart classrooms with IoT devices, robotics, and cyber-physical systems. Big data analytics and cloud computing support the educational system by enabling data-driven decision-making and the development of flexible learning environments *(Kumar et al., 2024;Masudin et al., 2024)*. Online education platforms, blended learning methods, and mobile learning applications address various learning requirements, while social media and gamification techniques boost involvement and cooperation. Blockchain ensures the integrity and security of educational records, while wearable technology and 3D printing open new frontiers in experiential learning. Continuous innovation, coupled with a commitment to digital literacy and lifelong learning, defines the ethos of Education 4.0, shaping the future of higher education with a dynamic and interconnected ecosystem that empowers learners and educators alike *(G. Narkhede et al., 2023;G. B. Narkhede et al., 2024)*. Industry 4.0 includes smart manufacturing, self-organization, adaptability, and cyber-physical systems to human requirements. Implementing Industry 4.0 is a key focus for global economies. The goal is to establish intelligent factories equipped with autonomous systems, including self-monitoring capabilities and self-configuration *(Ozuna & Steinhoff, 2024;Pacheco et al., 2024)*. New industrial techniques, using human-machine cooperation, will achieve unprecedented levels of efficiency and production. Technologies including

Robotics, Virtual Reality (VR), Mobile and Wearable devices, Additive Manufacturing, IoT, Augmented Reality (AR), 3-D Printing, Simulation, Blockchain, Big Data, Industrial Security, Artificial Intelligence, Systems Integration, Cloud Computing and are used to achieve these levels *(Pasi, Dongare, et al., 2022,2023)*. Moreover, the modern economy necessitates workers to possess new talents. *Pasi et al., n.d., 2019, 2020b, 2020a* discusses the developing abilities associated with Industry 4.0 and their significance for organisations. The technical worker has to have knowledge of the equipment, processes, and applicable technologies and the technical skill overall. Authors emphasise that operators, like production/Site engineers, Managers and executives, need to cultivate methodological traits like creativity, decision-making, problem-solving, and analytical and research abilities. Engineers and CEOs must possess social and personal abilities. Examples include communication, leadership (social), collaboration, autonomy, responsibility (personal) and adaptability *(Pasi, Mahajan, et al., 2022a, 2022b, 2023)*. Figure 2 illustrates the relationship between competence categories and their significance for each function. Education 4.0 arises from the need to revamp the educational system to align with new technologies and cater to the demands of the industry by fostering skill development. Education 4.0 represents a paradigm shift in educational practices, guided by nine core principles that underscore its transformative potential in shaping the future of learning *(Pistolesi et al., 2024; Riggs et al., 2024)*. The principles are fundamental pillars that form the basis of Education 4.0, encompassing essential beliefs focused on creating inclusive, dynamic, and learner-centered educational experiences. Education 4.0's first principle focuses on unrestricted learning, moving away from traditional classroom teaching to embrace flexible and widespread learning options. According to *Spaltini et al. (2024)* and *Spreitzenbarth et al. (2024)*, students may interact with educational materials and resources at their own speed and convenience in the age of digital connection and technical breakthroughs, overcoming limitations related to time and location. This idea emphasises how education should be distributed fairly, giving everyone equal access to educational opportunities regardless of where they live or what their personal circumstances are. Personalised learning, the second tenet of Education 4.0, adjusts instruction to the unique requirements and skills of every student while taking into account their varied learning styles and learning profiles. By using technology and data analytics, instructors may customise learning opportunities to align with individual student skills, interests, and learning styles. This tailored approach increases student motivation and engagement, which in turn leads to a deeper comprehension and retention of the content and, eventually, more meaningful and successful learning outcomes *(Telukdarie et al., 2024; Wang et al., 2024)*. The third tenet of Education 4.0 emphasises the significance of giving students the autonomy to choose the materials and instruments that best suit them, enabling them to take charge of their educational process. With a range of resources and tools that match their interests and learning objectives, students may now tailor their educational experiences. In order to provide students, the freedom and adaptability they need to thrive in a knowledge-driven, dynamic economy, this concept highlights the need of teaching them lifelong learning and self-directed learning abilities. The fourth tenet of Education 4.0, "Project/Problem/Outcome/Work-based learning," promotes contextualised, hands-on learning that closes the knowledge gap between theory and practice. Teachers may help students develop critical thinking, problem-solving, and collaborative skills—all of which are necessary for success in today's workforce—by immersing them in real-world projects, challenges, and results. In order to help students grasp ideas and principles more fully, this principle highlights the need of practical learning experiences that let them apply their theoretical knowledge to actual circumstances. The significance of hands-on learning opportunities, such internships and collaborations, in augmenting students' career preparedness and job-securing capacity is underscored by the sixth principle of Education 4.0. This is accomplished by giving kids exposure to the actual world and chances for hands-on learning *(G. Narkhede et al., 2023;G. B. Narkhede et al., 2024)*. Teachers may help students make the transition from academic learning to professional practice by encouraging partnerships with industry stakeholders and providing internships and apprenticeships. This method gives pupils the abilities and practical knowledge they need to succeed in their chosen industries. The significance of giving students real-world learning experiences that equip them for success in a fast-changing global economy is highlighted by this idea. The sixth Education 4.0 concept emphasises how data analytics powers evidence-based choices and instructional design *(Pistolesi et al., 2024;Riggs et al., 2024)*. This idea is all about using data interpretation to find patterns and trends. Educators may tailor instructional tactics to match the unique learning demands of each student by using data analytics to analyse the learning trajectories of their students and pinpoint their areas of strength and weakness. This concept highlights how crucial it is to use data to inform instructional strategies in order to enhance learning outcomes and maximise the efficacy of education. A practical and outcome-oriented evaluation method that gauges students' capacity to apply their knowledge and abilities in real-world situations is recommended by Education 4.0's sixth principle *(Spaltini et al. (2024)*. Teachers should switch from using old standardised testing techniques to genuine assessments that mimic real-life circumstances and obstacles in order to better gauge pupils' readiness for the demands of the contemporary labour market. In order to support deep learning and the development of critical abilities, this concept emphasises the need of matching assessment techniques with the demands of the modern workplace. Adaptability, customisation, data-driven decision-making, and experiential learning are all included into the educational vision embodied by the concepts of Education 4.0.

Adopting these ideas may help educators build inclusive, dynamic learning environments that equip students to succeed in a world becoming more linked and complicated by the day. Education 4.0 is pointing us in the direction of a future in which all students in the digital age have access to, and get an enriching, empowering, and equitable educational experience *(Cavalieri et al., 2024;Huang et al., 2024)*.

Figure 2. Industry 4.0 competencies and their importance for performing roles in the company

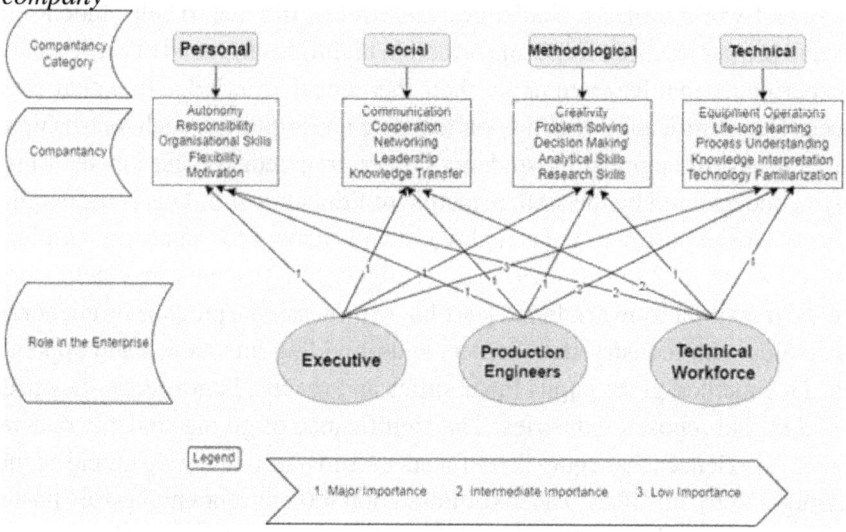

Education has evolved throughout time and is now closely connected with Industry 4.0 technologies in the contemporary period known as Education 4.0. *Calciolari et al., 2024* conducted a metareview of 73 systematic literature reviews that fully examined the integration of different technologies in education. While previous eras of education, namely Education 1.0, 2.0, and 3.0, marked different stages of evolution, Education 4.0 stands out for its emphasis on placing the student at the centre of the learning process, facilitated by advanced Industry 4.0 technologies. The journey of education through these eras can be correlated with the advancements in industrial revolutions, with Education 1.0 coinciding with the First Industrial Revolution, Education 2.0 and 3.0 corresponding to subsequent industrial developments, and Education 4.0 aligning with the emergence of Industry 4.0 in the early 21st century. However, the exact timelines for these educational phases are subject to debate among scholars.

The study aims led to the development of the following research questions:

1. What are the uses of Industry 4.0 technologies in education and how do they improve learning outcomes?
2. At what educational level are they used?

Spreitzenbarth et al., 2024 provide a historical perspective by linking each educational era to the corresponding industrial revolution. Education 1.0, characterized by authoritarian teaching methods with the teacher as the central authority figure and passive learning by students, emerged alongside the First Industrial Revolution in the late 18th and early 19th centuries. Subsequent industrial revolutions led to the development of Education 2.0 and 3.0, with Education 2.0 emphasizing student initiative and Education 3.0 further enhancing interactive learning methods. The advent of the internet, particularly Web 2.0, played a significant role in shaping Education 2.0, fostering collaborative and participatory learning experiences. Web 3.0, currently in development, is anticipated to further revolutionize education by integrating emerging technologies and enhancing personalized learning experiences. A significant change in educational approaches is brought about by the move to Education 4.0, which is defined by student-centered learning that makes use of Industry 4.0 technologies. Augmented reality (AR), virtual reality (VR), and mobile apps are examples of Industry 4.0 technologies which if integrated might greatly improve learning results *(Spreitzenbarth et al. 2024)*, Through the use of various technologies, educators may construct dynamic and immersive learning environments that foster critical thinking, creativity, leadership, collaboration, and initiative among students. Furthermore, by accommodating different learning styles and preferences, these technologies provide opportunities for personalised learning experiences. Research by et Aditi al. (2024) emphasises how critical it is to assess how Industry 4.0 technology is being used in education at all levels. It is crucial to comprehend the levels of learning at which these technologies are used in order to integrate them into instructional practices in an efficient manner. Education 4.0's theoretical framework emphasises how crucial it is to use contemporary technology to advance creative approaches to learning and revolutionise conventional teaching techniques. The main components of Education 4.0 are outlined by Alshboul et al. (2024), who also describe the duties and obligations of families, administrators, teachers, and students throughout the educational ecosystem. Teachers are essential in teaching science and technology, and students participate in educational activities and strive to meet their engineering skills and management objectives. Administrators oversee infrastructure maintenance and facilitate the use of technology in teaching environments *(Pasi, Mahajan, et al., 2022a, 2022b, 2023)*. Families provide financial resources to assist with the creation of "cyberspaces," or learning settings enhanced by technology. This all-encompassing approach to education places a strong emphasis on growth, creativity, and teamwork, fostering a vibrant learning environment that supports the acquisition of modern skills. A variety of techniques for instruction and pedagogical techniques are used in education 4.0, such as project-based learning, hybrid learning, flipped classrooms, STEAM (Science, Technology, Engineering, Arts, and Mathematics) education, and cultural maker projects. Online and offline components are combined in hybrid learning to provide flexibility and convenient access to learning. Project-based learning emphasises real-world applications and the development of problem-solving techniques, which stimulates critical thinking and creativity. By providing educational information online and using class time for interactive discussions and activities, flipped classrooms subvert conventional teaching approaches. Multidisciplinary ideas are integrated into STEAM education to encourage creativity and innovation in a variety of sectors. Through practical experiences and group projects, culture maker programmes seek to promote an innovative and creative culture. Globally, there is a disparity in the adoption of Education 4.0. Wealthy countries have made considerable strides in incorporating Industry 4.0 technology into their educational procedures, whereas less developed nations are still moving from previous educational phases. It is imperative to acknowledge that the incorporation of contemporary technology ought to supplement conventional teaching approaches, rather than supplant them. Even though Education 4.0 places a strong emphasis on interactive pedagogies and student-centered learning, there are still situations in which conventional teaching methods are still appropriate *(Kumar et al., 2024;Masudin et al., 2024)*.

Furthermore, the advanced capabilities and adaptability provided by contemporary technology allow for personalised learning experiences that accommodate a wide range of student requirements and preferences. The incorporation of Industry 4.0 technology into education signifies a significant change towards student-centered learning and creative teaching methods. Education 4.0 prioritises the use of immersive technology and interactive learning settings to foster collaboration, creativity, and critical thinking. Gaining a comprehensive understanding of the underlying principles and real-world consequences of Education 4.0 is essential for educators, policymakers, and stakeholders to successfully navigate the changing field of education in the 21st century. Additional investigation is required to examine the many uses of Industry 4.0 technologies in different educational settings and levels, while also providing fair access and equal opportunity for all learners *(Abulibdeh et al., 2024;Aditi et al., 2024)*. Table 1 shows evaluation of eras of education.

Table 1. Evolution of eras of education

Education 4.0	Monitor and observer of learning	Technology based dynamic and three-dimensional material	Creative, skilful, innovative and dynamic activities are performed, classroom is boundary less	Independent, active, innovative and self-directed learning style	E-learning is totally based on new innovative technological tools	In the globally networked human body
Education 3.0	Facilitator of collaborative knowledge	Different resources are used such as e books, and educational web series	Open, Collaborative, Flexible and Creative activities beyond the classroom	Active, enthusiastic, string and confidence	E-learning driven from the point of view of personal independent learning environment	Everywhere in a creative society
Education 2.0	Guide and source of knowledge	Copyright and free education material for students	Collaborative Learning Activities but in classroom	Passive to active	E-learning and collaboration was there by involving other universities	In specific building or online
Education 1.0	Authoritarian and source of knowledge	Traditional books and copyright handouts	Traditional paragraphs, test assignments and sometimes groups within classroom	Largely Passive	E-learning was enabled only through electronic management within an Institute	Specific Building
Characteristics	Primary role of teacher/ professor	Source of content	Classroom activities	Students' behaviour	Technology	Location of schools

2. METHODOLOGY

A systematic literature review (SLR) was performed using the PRISMA methodology specifically designed for Industry 4.0 technologies Systematic Reviews and Meta-Analyses. The objective was to thoroughly identify, evaluate, and analyse relevant papers concerning the incorporation of Industry 4.0 technologies in education, and their influence on learning outcomes in various educational settings. The technique, as shown in Table 2, had four distinct phases: identification, screening, eligibility, and inclusion. Based on the frameworks presented by *Wang et al. in 2024*, the screening procedure involved using different search keywords related to Industry 4.0 technologies. This approach covered the time period from 2011, when the idea was introduced, until August 2023. The search was performed on renowned databases such as Scopus (Elsevier), Web of Science (Clarivate Analytics), and Science Direct (Elsevier).

The research prioritised original articles to focus on identifying applications of Industry 4.0 technologies in educational contexts, analysing their effectiveness in enhancing learning experiences, and determining the educational levels where these technologies are mostly used. Initially, 260 documents were found in the search results, however many of them were duplicates. Using Mendeley software version 1803, duplicate works were carefully removed, leaving a refined set of 51 publications for further research. The screening method meticulously evaluated titles and abstracts to exclude papers not directly related to the study's focus on Industry 4.0 technologies in education. Publications related to the management of educational institutions were added from a previous search since some of them incorporated Industry 4.0 technology for managerial and educational uses, which matched the main focus of the research.

The analysis that followed included both quantitative and qualitative methods, starting with a quantitative assessment using the SciMat programme. During this phase, pertinent information was extracted from the chosen articles, such as main themes, principal authors, technology integrations, and other relevant elements. A qualitative analysis was conducted on the most relevant papers to meet the precise inquiries indicated in the study's introduction. The study aimed to offer insights into the various implications of Industry 4.0 technologies on educational practices and learning outcomes by synthesising information from chosen articles.

Figure 3. Integration flowchart for practical activities in institution

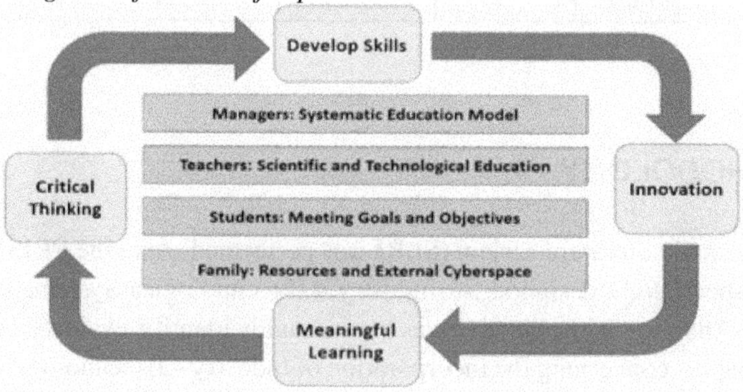

The methodological approaches used in this systematic literature review were carefully devised to ensure thoroughness and precision in discovering, analysing, and synthesising relevant material on the integration of Industry 4.0 technologies in education as shown in Figure 3. The study aims to contribute to the discussion on the transformative potential of Industry 4.0 technologies in education by following recognised protocols and using advanced analytical techniques.

3. RESULTS AND DISCUSSIONS

The SciMat programme was crucial in analysing the keywords in papers and grouping them into specific time periods from 2011 to 2023. The historical categorization offered useful insights into the development and direction of conversations about Industry 4.0 technology in education. Between 2011 and 2013, the phrase "e-learning" suggested early conversations about remote learning methods, even before Industry 4.0 technologies were formally mentioned. Yet, "Education 4.0" started to become more prominent in the years following, especially between 2016 and 2017. This phase involved incorporating Industry 4.0 principles, like smart factory concepts, into educational frameworks, with a main emphasis on industrial processes rather than a whole educational approach. The article emphasised the necessity of adjusting disciplines and curricula in higher education to match the significant influence of new technologies on companies, as discussed in "Requirements for Education and Qualification of People in Industry 4.0." In 2018 and 2019, Industry 4.0 technologies began to gain significance in educational settings. Machine learning has become a useful tool for problem-solving and critical thinking, while games and simulations are being incorporated into university courses, especially for college students, showing their use in higher education. Virtual reality (VR) has become increasingly popular, especially in virtual laboratories and engineering instruction, being used in advanced levels of schools and higher education institutions. Simulation has proven to be crucial in engineering education, particularly regarding industrial concepts like automated production systems and optimization. This emphasises how important simulation is when it comes to higher learning. During this time, "Education 4.0" had a rebirth, highlighting its link to industry-related ideas like self-governing robots, cyber-physical production systems, vocational training, and educational institutions. Moreover, its advantageous connections with other Industry 4.0 technologies, such as big data and cloud computing, as shown in Figure 4, highlight how easily it may be included into educational frameworks. Industry 4.0 technologies developed in diversity and affordability in 2020 and 2021, catering to a wider range of educational backgrounds. Early childhood education has made use of simulation and games, proving the importance they are in fostering cornerstone learning experiences. Mobile learning is important in health-related fields including health education and healthcare, showing its relevance in higher education, however it has little relevance in engineering education. Augmented reality and cloud computing were associated with understanding factory principles and automation, demonstrating its relevance in educational institutions across several fields. Furthermore, the revival of "Education 4.0" in this period confirmed its interdependent connection with Industry 4.0, particularly focusing on education related to industrial procedures. Robots being integrated with the Internet of Things (IoT) showcase the use of Industry 4.0 technology in educational settings at different levels.

The SciMat programme enabled a detailed investigation of Industry 4.0 technologies in education. Augmented reality (AR) was the most commonly mentioned technology in nine papers, followed by simulation in five publications. IoT, big data, VR, CPS, cloud computing, and blockchain were highlighted in three documents, emphasising their importance in educational settings. One publication discussed artificial intelligence, machine learning, and autonomous robotics, highlighting their early but potential use in teaching. Table 1 provides a detailed analysis of the different uses and frequencies of Industry 4.0 technologies in educational environments, setting the stage for future investigations and evaluations.

The data produced by the SciMat programme, along with the analytical insights from the authors, formed a strong basis for addressing the main questions in the study. By tracing the trajectory of discussions surrounding Industry 4.0 technologies in education over time and elucidating their diverse applications and impacts across different educational levels, the study aimed to contribute to a nuanced understanding of the evolving intersection between technology and education in the 21st century. Table 2 shows methodological steps based on the PRISMA protocol.

Table 2. Methodological steps based on the PRISMA protocol

Identification Database:	The Scopus, Science Direct, and Web of Science databases were selected for their high renown in the field of science and technology.
Keywords:	Terms related to Education and Industry 4.0 technologies were used.
The keywords were associated according to the following list:	Query: "Education 4.0"("Internet of Things", "IOT"," IIOT") Query: "Education 4.0" AND "Machine Learning") Query: "Education 4.0" AND ("Virtual Reality", VR, "Augmented Reality", AR) Query: "Education 4.0" AND ("Big Data Analytics") Query: "Education 4.0" AND ("Cloud Computing") Query: "Education 4.0" AND ("3D Printing", "Additive Manufacturing",) Query: "Education 4.0" AND ("Simulation", "Digital Twin", "Virtual Environment") Query: "Education 4.0" AND ("Autonomous Robots", "Collaborative Robots") Query: "Education 4.0" AND ("Cybersecurity", "Cyber Security", "Blockchain") Query: "Education 4.0" AND ("CPS", "Cyber Physical System", "Cyber-Physical System") Query: "Education 4.0" AND ("Integrated Systems") Query: "Education 4.0" AND ("AI", Artificial Intelligence", "Neural Network")
Years Publication/Language:	The selection criteria were developed based on the timeframe from 2011 to August 2023.
Language:	English language texts only
Screening	Examine deceitfulness. The Mendeley software version 1803 was utilised to detect any duplication among the chosen articles. Selection of articles based on reading titles, abstracts, and keywords according to the theme.
Eligibility	Evaluate the feasibility of obtaining the whole texts of the articles for quantitative analysis using SciMAT software.
Inclusion	Articles pertaining to the topic from several journal databases Regarding additional previously identified articles

Articles featuring the technology discussed in the preceding paragraph were chosen for reading. 23 papers were identified since they had several technologies in their keywords. Table 3 was created to summarise how the industry 4.0 technologies mentioned in the works contribute to learning. Most study emphasises that technology not only enhance learning but also cultivate soft skills in students, including communication, creativity, teamwork, and problem-solving abilities. This finding is also present in the meta-analysis conducted by *Masudin et al., 2024*. These are crucial skills required for Industry 4.0, as outlined by *Cavalieri et al., 2024*. Skills like personnel management and consumer interaction may be honed via the use of virtual reality technology. It enables students to experience uncomfortable circumstances without the real-life consequences that may result from a failure to communicate effectively, such as losing a significant customer or a key team member. Two studies suggest that certain technology may help decrease costs. Examined the use of Augmented Reality (AR) and Cloud.

Figure 4. PRISMA protocol for article selection

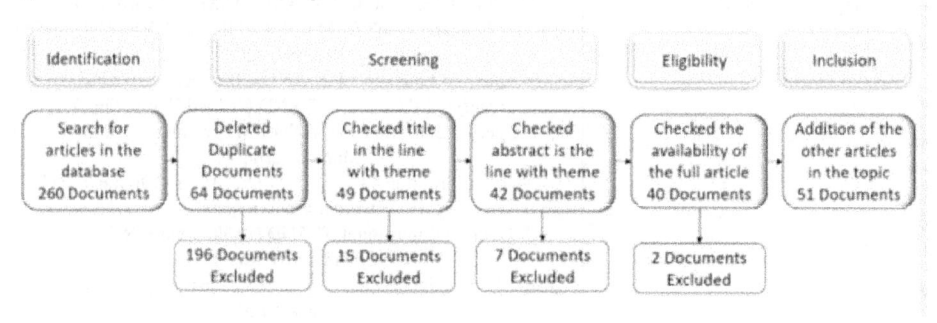

Identification	Screening			Eligibility	Inclusion
Search for articles in the database 260 Documents	Deleted Duplicate Documents 64 Documents	Checked title in the line with theme 49 Documents	Checked abstract is the line with theme 42 Documents	Checked the availability of the full article 40 Documents	Addition of the other articles in the topic 51 Documents
	196 Documents Excluded	15 Documents Excluded	7 Documents Excluded	2 Documents Excluded	

Computing in collaborative creation inside the Learning institutes environment. These two technologies facilitate cost-efficient product creation by minimising expenses on other resources. Simulation and Cyber-Physical Systems (CPSs) help avoid costly errors and problems. Research indicates that utilising simulation and augmented reality in the industry can result in cost savings by allowing for study without changing the product or physical process. Industry 4.0 technologies like VR and AR are highly advantageous for visualising materials and improving immersion in the learning process. The article "Augmented reality to promote guided discovery learning for STEM (Science Technology Engineering management) learning" is utilised in chemistry education. Incorporating augmented reality into chemistry education: A means to achieve the industrial revolution 4.0 Discuss how the comprehension of atomic models, structures, and material qualities has improved via the use of Augmented Reality (AR). Similar scenarios occur in both physical and remote labs, where tests are conducted. more comprehensible with the use of such technology. For disciplines that are not prominent in students' everyday lives, these materials serve as an outstanding support tool. Previous experiments may be explained using augmented reality on mobile phones and tablets. VR glasses allow you to see the three-dimensional structure of an atom, a feat not achievable on a flat surface like paper. This technology enhances learning and is crucial for boosting student involvement, particularly given that an individual's attention span typically lasts a maximum of 20 minutes. Demonstrated that using various resources, such as hands-on experience with Robotics and the Internet of Things (IoT), enhances student satisfaction and motivation to learn. Technologies familiar to students, such cell phones, are seen to better capture their attention. Furthermore, less common materials like VR and AR pique curiosity and, as a result, enhance students' attention. Amid the COVID-19 epidemic, it was recognised the significance of flexible learning, where students have to study remotely and at different times, covering material often taught in person. Three works were notable for providing materials that enable schooling in any location. Emphasise the use of mobile devices. Smartphones, which are almost like an extension of ourselves in our times, have great potential to be used as educational tools. Active approaches are used in education, aligning with the criteria of Education 4.0 as described by *Pistolesi et al., 2024*. Problem/ Project/Outcome/ Work Based Learning is used in the research conducted by *Riggs et al., 2024* and *Telukdarie et al., 2024*. Maker Culture is evident in several instances.

Table 3(a). Relationship between Industry 4.0 technologies and Education 4.0

Cyber physical System	X			
Blockchain	X			X
Big data	X			
Digital Twin	X		X	
Internet of Things	X			
Simulation	X	X		X
Augmented Reality and Virtual Reality	X	X	X	
Industry 4.0 technologies * Education 4.0	Soft skills Development	Cost Reduction	Greater Impression in the content	Greater Interpersonal immersion

Table 3(b). Relationship between Industry 4.0 technologies and Education 4.0

X		X		
				X
			X	X
	X	X		
X				X
X	X	X		
X	X		X	X
Greater Student Engagement	Risk Reduction	Not limited to time and space	Real work scenario simulation	Knowledge of technologies

Where students take charge of managing and programming their own learning process. All these features and resources are crucial for enhancing student engagement. Mobile devices, of practical student learning, particularly in Learning Factories. *Baratta et al., 2024* used the concepts outlined by *Ayyildiz & Erdogan, 2024* to establish hauntological practices in Mobile Devices, simulation, and virtual reality allow for learning that is not constrained by time or location. Numerous studies underscore the integration of diverse technologies into the learning process, reflecting a multifaceted approach to educational innovation. *Verner et al. (2021)* demonstrate this pattern by combining robotics with the Internet of Things (IoT) to improve learning experiences using a robot with dual capabilities. Block et al. (2018) and Zarte and Pechmann (2020) use computerised patient simulators (CPSs) and simulation approaches in Learning Institutes to replicate real-life situations in educational environments using sophisticated technologies. *Mourtzis et al. (2018)* enhance this model by incorporating Big Data and Augmented Reality (AR) into simulation-based learning settings, enhancing the educational experience. Various educational curricula have been created to provide students with the necessary information and abilities to meet the increasing need for competent professionals in technology-driven businesses. *Catal and Tekinerdogan (2019)* developed educational curricula focused on prominent Industry 4.0 technologies like IoT, Big Data, Additive Manufacturing, AR, Cloud Computing, CPSs, and Cybersecurity. The need for these new technologies to be fully integrated into educational frameworks was stressed. In response to the changing needs of the digital workforce, *Ellahi et al. (2019)* unveiled a new curriculum intended specifically for Higher Education that integrates topics like Big Data, Internet of Things, Cloud Computing, Artificial Intelligence, and Augmented Reality. As seen in *Figure 5*, the curriculum emphasises the significance of equipping students with the transdisciplinary expertise and abilities necessary for success in Industry 4.0.

Figure 5. Cluster of Education 4.0

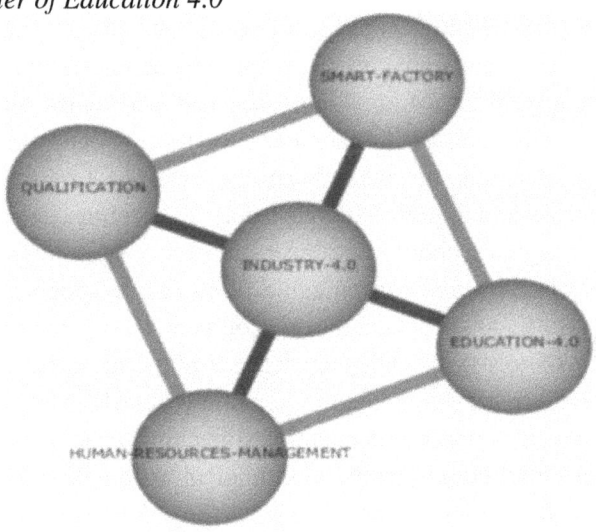

3.1. Education 4.0 and E-learning

The benefits that come with integrating Industry 4.0 technology into education closely match the benefits that come with e-learning and distant learning methods. These advantages include lower risks, more cost-effectiveness, and the ability to provide time- and location-independent, flexible learning opportunities. These technological developments have completely changed the way that education is taught, giving students unparalleled access to resources and information, no matter where they live. While e-learning systems are a valuable way of disseminating information, they often fail to recognise the value of building soft skills and cultivating interpersonal interactions, which are better developed in face-to-face learning situations. This difference draws attention to the intricacies present in contemporary educational frameworks, which call for a cautious balancing act between incorporating technology and preserving human-centered learning opportunities. There are obstacles in the way of the widespread adoption of Industry 4.0 technologies, especially in non-academic contexts where many people find the cost of adopting these technologies to be unreasonably expensive. These technologies, albeit widely available, pose difficulties because of their complexity, which results in a steep learning curve that exacerbates already-existing inequities in technical expertise and access. Additionally, the learning environment and student behavior—two important variables impacting engagement and information retention—have an impact on how successful learning experiences are. These challenges are made worse by a lack of resources, which are further exacerbated by a lack of physical infrastructure, poor internet connection, and limited access to technological gadgets. Even while e-learning and education 4.0 are similar, they vary greatly, making them appropriate for multiple circumstances and settings. The goal of Education 4.0 is to create a holistic learning environment that is marked by engaging and immersive experiences for learning by incorporating Industry 4.0 technologies into educational systems. To satisfy the changing needs of a connected and digitally linked society, e-learning systems, on the other hand, mainly use digital technology to distribute information remotely. Although e-learning is very flexible and convenient, it often fails to support all components of learning, including social contact, the development of collaborative abilities, and the enhancement of soft skills. The convergence of e-learning and Education 4.0 highlights the revolutionary potential of technology in influencing the direction of education. Teachers may improve conventional teaching techniques by using Industry 4.0 technology to include creative pedagogical tactics that meet the different interests and learning requirements of their students. Understanding the intricate interactions that exist between teaching philosophies, technological developments, and sociocultural variables is necessary for effective technology integration in the classroom. It is critical to provide equal access to technology and bridging the digital divide top priority while implementing educational reforms in order to guarantee that every student may succeed in the digital age. Technologies related to Industry 4.0 have the potential to completely transform schooling. Nonetheless, in order to correct current disparities and guarantee equitable access to educational opportunities, their integration must be handled thoughtfully and inclusively. The e-learning and Education 4.0 approaches complement each other in maximising the potential of technology in the classroom. Every strategy has unique benefits and associated difficulties. Teachers can develop dynamic, inclusive learning environments that provide students with the skills they need to flourish in an increasingly digital and linked world by using the benefits of both modalities.

4. CONCLUSIONS

When Industry 4.0 technologies are examined in the context of Education 4.0, a world full of possibilities for creative teaching methods is revealed. This inquiry yields many possibilities. By using ideas from many publications, it becomes clear why incorporating Industry 4.0 innovations into learning settings is beneficial. Principal benefits include heightened involvement with information, decreased expenses, and minimised hazards. Furthermore, these innovative technologies serve as catalysts for the development of critical skills that will be needed in the workforce in the future, such creativity and problem-solving aptitude. Technology expertise is often learned by students via specialised courses or programmes. Robotics programmes, for instance, provide students hands-on involvement and immersive learning experiences that equip them with practical knowledge and skills. Three key instruments that greatly improve learning are virtual reality (VR), augmented reality (AR), and simulation. These technologies provide immersive and interactive learning environments that go beyond conventional teaching techniques. Big data and cloud computing have been integrated to enhance the learning process by giving teachers and students easy access to materials and teamwork tools as well as sophisticated data analytics capabilities. Although these developments are mostly used in higher education, they have the ability to change educational practices both theoretically and practically. They may be applied to educational production facilities as well as traditional classrooms. Although Industry 4.0 technology has been successfully incorporated into courses in higher education, there is still room for improvement when it comes to applying these advancements to education in early childhood and elementary school. In order to promote a culture of lifelong learning and technological literacy from an early age, future research will concentrate on investigating the use of Industry 4.0 technologies in early childhood and primary education. Acknowledging the intrinsic worth of these settings, these endeavours aim to improve learning results and maintain student involvement, especially for individuals who may find conventional teaching approaches unsuitable for their preferred modes of learning. Teachers can develop a generation of digitally savvy people with the abilities and competences required to succeed in the digital age by using Industry 4.0 technology. With the help of these technologies, learning environments that are dynamic and appealing to a wide range of student requirements and preferences may be created. The integration of Industry 4.0 technology into Education 4.0 represents a significant departure from traditional educational methods and opens up previously unheard-of opportunities for innovation and change. Teachers have the chance to set the path for a time when learning is dynamic, engaging, and inclusive in addition to being accessible and inclusive. Teaching and learning experiences may be greatly improved by using novel strategies and realising their full potential. In order to guarantee that people of all ages and backgrounds completely benefit from Industry 4.0 technology as we move in educational innovation, it is imperative that we take into account the specific requirements and situations of learners.

REFERENCES

Abulibdeh, A., Zaidan, E., & Abulibdeh, R. (2024). Navigating the confluence of artificial intelligence and education for sustainable development in the era of industry 4.0: Challenges, opportunities, and ethical dimensions. *Journal of Cleaner Production*, 437, 140527. Advance online publication. DOI: 10.1016/j.jclepro.2023.140527

Aditi, G., Govindan, K., & Jha, P. C. (2024). Modelling of barriers in implementing sustainable manufacturer-supplier collaboration and coping strategies. *Journal of Cleaner Production*, 434, 139635. Advance online publication. DOI: 10.1016/j.jclepro.2023.139635

Alshboul, O., Al Mamlook, R. E., Shehadeh, A., & Munir, T. (2024). Empirical exploration of predictive maintenance in concrete manufacturing: Harnessing machine learning for enhanced equipment reliability in construction project management. *Computers & Industrial Engineering*, 190, 110046. Advance online publication. DOI: 10.1016/j.cie.2024.110046

Ayyildiz, E., & Erdogan, M. (2024). Addressing the challenges of using autonomous robots for last-mile delivery. *Computers & Industrial Engineering*, 190, 110096. Advance online publication. DOI: 10.1016/j.cie.2024.110096

Bag, S., Sabbir Rahman, M., Ghai, S., Kumar Srivastava, S., Kumar Singh, R., & Mishra, R. (2024). Unveiling the impact of carbon-neutral policies on vital resources in Industry 4.0 driven smart manufacturing: A data-driven investigation. *Computers & Industrial Engineering*, 187, 109798. Advance online publication. DOI: 10.1016/j.cie.2023.109798

Baratta, A., Cimino, A., Longo, F., & Nicoletti, L. (2024). Digital twin for human-robot collaboration enhancement in manufacturing systems: Literature review and direction for future developments. *Computers & Industrial Engineering*, 187, 109764. Advance online publication. DOI: 10.1016/j.cie.2023.109764

Calciolari, S., Cesarini, M., & Ruberti, M. (2024). Sustainability disclosure in the pharmaceutical and chemical industries: Results from bibliometric analysis and AI-based comparison of financial reports. *Journal of Cleaner Production*, 447, 141511. Advance online publication. DOI: 10.1016/j.jclepro.2024.141511

Cavalieri, A., Reis, J., & Amorim, M. (2024). Socioenvironmental assessment and application process for IOT: A comprehensive approach. *Journal of Cleaner Production*, 436, 140348. Advance online publication. DOI: 10.1016/j.jclepro.2023.140348

Huang, R., Shen, Z., & Yao, X. (2024). How does industrial intelligence affect total-factor energy productivity? Evidence from China's manufacturing industry. *Computers & Industrial Engineering*, 188, 109901. Advance online publication. DOI: 10.1016/j.cie.2024.109901

Kumar, D., Soni, G., Jabeen, F., Kumar Tiwari, N., Sariyer, G., & Ramtiyal, B. (2024). A hybrid Bayesian approach for assessment of industry 4.0 technologies towards achieving decarbonization in manufacturing industry. *Computers & Industrial Engineering*, 190, 110057. Advance online publication. DOI: 10.1016/j.cie.2024.110057

Masudin, I., Tsamarah, N., Restuputri, D. P., Trireksani, T., & Djajadikerta, H. G. (2024). The impact of safety climate on human-technology interaction and sustainable development: Evidence from Indonesian oil and gas industry. *Journal of Cleaner Production*, 434, 140211. Advance online publication. DOI: 10.1016/j.jclepro.2023.140211

Narkhede, G., Pasi, B., Rajhans, N., & Kulkarni, A. (2023). Industry 5.0 and the future of sustainable manufacturing: A systematic literature review. In *Business Strategy and Development* (Vol. 6, Issue 4, pp. 704–723). John Wiley and Sons Inc. DOI: 10.1002/bsd2.272

Narkhede, G. B., Pasi, B. N., Rajhans, N., & Kulkarni, A. (2024). Industry 5.0 and sustainable manufacturing: A systematic literature review. *Benchmarking*. Advance online publication. DOI: 10.1108/BIJ-03-2023-0196

Ozuna, E., & Steinhoff, L. (2024). "Look me in the eye, customer": How do face-to-face interactions in peer-to-peer sharing economy services affect customers' misbehavior concealment intentions? *Journal of Business Research*, 177, 114582. DOI: 10.1016/j.jbusres.2024.114582

Pacheco, D. A. de J., Rampasso, I. S., Michels, G. S., Ali, S. M., & Hunt, J. D. (2024). From linear to circular economy: The role of BS 8001:2017 for green transition in small business in developing economies. *Journal of Cleaner Production*, 439, 140787. Advance online publication. DOI: 10.1016/j.jclepro.2024.140787

Pasi, B. N., Dongare, P. V., & Rawat, S. J. (2022). Prioritization of risks associated with the implementation of project-based learning concept in engineering institutions. *Higher Education. Skills and Work-Based Learning*, 12(6), 1070–1083. DOI: 10.1108/HESWBL-05-2022-0117

Pasi, B. N., Dongare, P. V., Rawat, S. J., Oza, A. D., Padheriya, H., Gupta, M., Kumar, S., & Kumar, M. (2023). Design and modeling to identify a defective workpiece in manufacturing process: An industry 4.0 perspective. *International Journal on Interactive Design and Manufacturing*. Advance online publication. DOI: 10.1007/s12008-023-01544-w

Pasi, B. N., Mahajan, S. K., & Rane, S. B. (2020a). Enabling Technologies and Current Research Scenario of Industry 4.0: A Systematic Review. *Lecture Notes in Mechanical Engineering*, 265–273. DOI: 10.1007/978-981-15-4485-9_28

Pasi, B. N., Mahajan, S. K., & Rane, S. B. (2020b). The current sustainability scenario of Industry 4.0 enabling technologies in Indian manufacturing industries. *International Journal of Productivity and Performance Management*, 70(5), 1017–1048. DOI: 10.1108/IJPPM-04-2020-0196

Pasi, B. N., Mahajan, S. K., & Rane, S. B. (2022a). Development of innovation ecosystem framework for successful adoption of industry 4.0 enabling technologies in Indian manufacturing industries. *Journal of Science and Technology Policy Management*, 13(1), 154–185. DOI: 10.1108/JSTPM-10-2020-0148

Pasi, B. N., Mahajan, S. K., & Rane, S. B. (2022b). Development of innovation ecosystem framework for successful adoption of industry 4.0 enabling technologies in Indian manufacturing industries. *Journal of Science and Technology Policy Management*, 13(1), 154–185. DOI: 10.1108/JSTPM-10-2020-0148

Pasi, B. N., Mahajan, S. K., & Rane, S. B. (2023). Strategies for risk management in adopting Industry 4.0 concept in manufacturing industries. *Journal of Science and Technology Policy Management*, 14(3), 563–591. DOI: 10.1108/JSTPM-04-2021-0057

Pasi, B. N., Mahajan, S. K., & Rane, S. B. (n.d.). REDESIGNING OF SMART MANUFACTURING SYSTEM BASED ON IoT: PERSPECTIVE OF DISRUPTIVE INNOVATIONS OF INDUSTRY 4.0 PARADIGM. In www.tjprc.org*SCOPUS Indexed Journal editor@tjprc.org*. www.tjprc.org

Pasi, B. N., Shinde, V. V., & Chavan, M. R. (2019). Teacher's perception towards their role in Course Level Project-Based Learning environment. In *Journal of Engineering Education Transformations, Special Issue* (Issue 1).

Pistolesi, F., Baldassini, M., & Lazzerini, B. (2024). A human-centric system combining smartwatch and LiDAR data to assess the risk of musculoskeletal disorders and improve ergonomics of Industry 5.0 manufacturing workers. *Computers in Industry*, 155, 104042. Advance online publication. DOI: 10.1016/j.compind.2023.104042

Riggs, R., Felipe, C. M., Roldán, J. L., & Real, J. C. (2024). Information systems capabilities value creation through circular economy practices in uncertain environments: A conditional mediation model. *Journal of Business Research*, 175, 114526. Advance online publication. DOI: 10.1016/j.jbusres.2024.114526

Spaltini, M., Terzi, S., & Taisch, M. (2024). Development and implementation of a roadmapping methodology to foster twin transition at manufacturing plant level. *Computers in Industry*, 154, 104025. Advance online publication. DOI: 10.1016/j.compind.2023.104025

Spreitzenbarth, J. M., Bode, C., & Stuckenschmidt, H. (2024). Designing an AI purchasing requisition bundling generator. *Computers in Industry*, 155, 104043. Advance online publication. DOI: 10.1016/j.compind.2023.104043

Telukdarie, A., Katsumbe, T., Mahure, H., & Murulane, K. (2024). Exploring the green economy – A systems thinking modelling approach. *Journal of Cleaner Production*, 436, 140611. Advance online publication. DOI: 10.1016/j.jclepro.2024.140611

Wang, Y., Shi, J., & Qu, G. (2024). Research on collaborative innovation cooperation strategies of manufacturing digital ecosystem from the perspective of multiple stakeholders. *Computers & Industrial Engineering*, 190, 110003. Advance online publication. DOI: 10.1016/j.cie.2024.110003

Chapter 8
Pedagogical Contents Developments and Specialized Training for Teaching Careers

Ratan Sarkar
Department of Teachers' Training, Prabhat Kumar College, Vidyasagar University, India

Dhara Vinod Parmar
Department of Design and Merchandising, Parul Institute of Design, Parul University, India

Nishant Bhuvanesh Trivedi
Department of Animation and VFX, Parul Institute of Design, Parul University, India

S. Prabakaran
Department of English, Kongu Engineering College, India

Saurabh Chandra
https://orcid.org/0000-0003-4172-9968
School of Law, Bennett University, India

Sampath Boopathi
https://orcid.org/0000-0002-2065-6539
Department of Mechanical Engineering, Muthayammal Engineering College, India

ABSTRACT

The current chapter deals with issues of pedagogical content knowledge (PCK) and additional preparation required for teaching careers in the 21st century. In this chapter, it is discussed how instruction, curricula, and educational technology can be aligned together to maximize teacher effectiveness. The chapter is grounded on the following twin necessity aspects: one, helping teachers develop all skills to handle differences in learning; and two, the inclusion of differentiated instruction,

DOI: 10.4018/979-8-3693-4058-5.ch008

inclusive education, and subject matter pedagogy. Discussion on the need to preserve continuing professional development with the focus that the individual should be flexible in class in respect to constantly emerging classroom dynamics as well as modern demands of education will be considered. Conversations on reflective teaching and the use of various assessment techniques for learning outcomes shall also be discussed.

INTRODUCTION

Rapid technological development, shifting social needs, and increased understanding of how students learn. Against this backdrop, PCK and professional preparation for careers in teaching have never been as important. Pedagogical content knowledge refers to the integration of knowledge content with the capacity to successfully use that knowledge to teach in a classroom environment. It deals with understanding how students learn in a particular discipline and the best pedagogical practices to support that learning. Specialized training equips teachers for teaching in heterogeneous and contemporary learning environments. Together, PCK and specialized preparation define most programs of teacher preparation-to ensure that content experts, educators in this case, do not only possess a potentially great wealth of knowledge in their subject area but can also translate that into meaningful and accessible learning experiences for all students (Vilppu et al., 2019).

The last several years witnessed a turning tide towards more student-centered approaches to learning as fundamental considerations in the teaching profession. From the more traditional models of teaching where information was dispensed directly from the teacher, today's more collaborative and interactive pedagogies have now pushed its way through to modern teaching styles. A teacher is now supposed to facilitate students' learning actively instead of just imparting information. It means there is a need for educators to acquire new skills about classroom management, instructional design, and the handling of technology in their classrooms. This made teacher training specialized, including all features of teaching, so educators could cater to the diversity of learner needs (Shwartz & Dori, 2020).

Another trend that marks teaching careers is the integration of technology in learning. The utilizations of digital tools and online resources for education purposes, together with technology-driven learning platforms, have dramatically transformed the face of classrooms and altered the very manner in which information is presented and received. Teachers need to be both equipped in more conventional pedagogic techniques and have the knowledge of how to utilize technology in support of student learning. Professional development programs more and more take focus on digital literacy, so the professional teacher would be able to learn both the tool and the strategies for incorporating technology in a productive and meaningful way. Examples include virtual tools for teamwork, lesson planning for combined or online classes, and data analytics for tracking student learning. The teachers need to be prepared to bridge the digital divide so that all students can equally access learning material and resources irrespective of socio-economic situations (Ballantyne & Retell, 2020).

Teaching to the learning need of learners is differentiated instruction, which is tailoring teaching to the need of learners of different kinds-all hallmarks of this day and age. The classes today are more diverse than in any other time, with students of diverse cultural, linguistic, and socioeconomic backgrounds, and of diverse learning abilities or difficulties. In such diversity, the educator is called upon to be very flexible, using a multiplicity of teaching strategies to achieve what is needed for students' different learning styles and paces. Specialized training for differentiated instruction is designed to provide a framework from which teachers can design flexible curricula, create inclusive learning environments, and assess in ways that accurately reflect each student's progress. Such teaching may involve working with students with special needs that will enable the teacher to provide support toward learners who have physical, emotional, or cognitive challenges (Raduan & Na, 2020).

Related to this is an increasing trend in the implementation of inclusive education, deemed ineludible and increasingly indispensable for ensuring opportunities for all students to learn equitably. In essence, inclusion ensures all students, with whatever abilities and backgrounds they may have, have the opportunity to fully engage in the learning process. Doing so not only benefits these students but also produces a classroom atmosphere where diversity is celebrated and understanding among all students enhanced. For example, inclusive education training enables teachers to adapt their teaching methods and classroom environment to the capabilities and needs of every learner. For instance, through the use of assistive technologies, adapting Curriculum materials or negotiating individualized learning plans with special education professionals (Ismail & Jarrah, 2019).

The technical and instructional competencies that are being required out of modern teaching would nowadays also play a very essential role in keeping and improving teacher competencies through CPD. They should consider themselves as lifelong learners, one who needs to update knowledge and professional skills in keeping with constant changes in trends, policies, and technologies of education. Professional development programs offer teachers opportunities to practice critically, share experience among peers, and sometimes further pursue degrees or certifications. These programs usually feature very specific topics, such as leadership, curriculum development, and new teaching methods(Ödalen et al., 2019). These enable educators to further specialize in a certain area and continue their professional growth. Perhaps one of the significant areas of professional development includes reflective teaching; that is, facilitating the critical thinking of teachers regarding their teaching methods and getting them to make adjustments for the betterment of student outcomes.

The techniques applied in formulating assessment and evaluation strategies have also advanced with time, keeping in step with developments in pedagogical approaches. Formative assessment, which provides ongoing feedback to the learners, has become a vital part of current schooling in which teachers can monitor the learning process of the students and adapt their instructions to meet the needs of the students within real-time. With professional education in conducting assessments, teachers are geared up to design valid, reliable, and student learning-objectivealigned assessments (Glutsch & König, 2019). Also, teachers are prepared to apply data-driven insights to support change in instructional practice; thus, assessment is not only a tool to measure student performance but also a stepping stone toward improvement in learning.

Teacher education at the end of the day is seeing the gap between theory and practice close slowly. The focus of teacher preparation programs has been on experiential learning, providing aspiring teachers with the chance to put their conceptual understanding into play in real classrooms. This on-the-job experience is priceless to help the new teacher gain confidence, hone her teaching methods, and understand student behavior and learning more profoundly. Modern programs in training most involve mentorship, peer collaboration, and internship, thus making it possible for teachers to have a supportive learning environment as they journey from theory to practice(Varadharajan et al., 2020).

Hence, the development of pedagogical content knowledge and professional training for careers in teaching is the broader directions happening in education. The demands on teachers are expanding because classrooms are becoming increasingly diverse and technology enabled and student centered. Professional training, inclusion, differentiation, and lifelong learning form the fundamental components of modern teaching education. With a focus on comprehensive teacher development, in both subject matter expertise and instructional skill building, teacher preparation programs are in a very critical position to determine the future direction of education, which, in turn, constitutes success for students(Berger & Lê Van, 2019).

SPECIALIZED TRAINING IN TEACHER EDUCATION

Teaching has never been tougher than it is today. The present educator must make efforts to understand the different classrooms they teach; incorporate sophisticated, high technology tools into instruction; and employ research-based methods of teaching instruction. Specialized training in teacher education is critical for equipping teachers with acquiring competencies, knowledge, and flexibility to address changing demands. Training beyond basic instructional practices focuses on specific pedagogical strategies, differentiated instruction, inclusive education practices, and subject-specific content. This training extends beyond the building of instructional competencies for teachers to preparing them for an environment that fosters the learning and social development of diverse students(S. W. Lee, 2019).

The Importance of Specialized Training in Modern Teaching

The importance of specialized training in modern teaching cannot be overstated. Modern classrooms are diverse in every sense: culturally, linguistically, and in terms of students' learning needs. Teachers must be able to take on such challenges head-on, using innovative and research-based methods of teaching their students. Specialized preparation will benefit a teacher because it makes the teacher prepare to understand the needs of students who are challenged or may not have a command of a majority of the language spoken in their surroundings, or those whose socioeconomic status is different. Thus, through such training, teachers will develop ways of instructional strategies that allow for equity and inclusion; an element that is now crucial in current education policy.

Besides, technological innovation is rather fast and significantly transforming the face of education. Blended learning, online classrooms, and data analytics in assessing student performance call for serious knowledge in educational technology knowledge since this is applied in class. This training equips the teachers with skills on how to use the tools for effective levels of student engagement as well as augmenting the several outcomes related to learning.

Teacher efficacy and retention in class is improved only through specialized training. While findings reveal prepared teachers experience fewer instances of burnout and will continue in teaching at higher rates than their less prepared counterparts, teacher preparation programs can serve two purposes toward the ends of educator satisfaction and student success by offering focused instruction in the areas of classroom management, subject-specific instructional strategies, and formative assessment to teach.

Focus Areas of Teacher Training Programs

Specialized training in teacher education focuses on a wide range of areas. These areas specialize in developing well-rounded educators who can address the complexity of modern teaching. Some of the primary focus areas include:

a) Pedagogical Content Knowledge (PCK): This is the heart of good teaching. Therefore, a teacher must be knowledgeable in his subject matter and at the same time recognize ways to communicate this knowledge to learners in clear, effective manners. Pre-service training aims to prepare education practitioners to fill the gap between content knowledge and teaching skill, thereby ensuring that educators adapt the teaching approach to suit the needs of the learning students.

b) Classroom management; arguably, the most difficult aspect of teaching, especially with diversified and inclusive classes. This kind of training will help the teacher learn how to set up a positive classroom, as well as ideas for managing some of the behavioral challenges that arise, create respect and cooperation among the students.

c) An important component of inclusive education is the growing emphasis on preparing teachers to train students with diverse needs, including working with students with disabilities. The training involves teaching educators how to approach instruction modification, assistive technology application, and individualized learning planning to ensure equal access to educational opportunities for all.

d) Differentiated Instruction: Today's class comes with a varied level of prior knowledge, preferred ways of learning, and differing abilities. Specialized training in differentiated instruction is given so the teacher can arm them with techniques to incorporate the lessons in such a way that it meets the differences. Thereby, flexible learning activities are designed, and different assessment tools are used by the teacher, and then personalized feedback is offered to the students.

e) The use of digital tools in learning and teaching has made educational technology a very essential area that needs specialized training. It requires teachers to master the application of educational software, manage digital platforms, and use analytics data to track students' performance. Training here will keep abreast educators with changing technological advancements and how they can be used in teaching to enhance their pupils' learning outcomes.

f) Assessment Techniques: Formative and summative assessment helps ensure the actual student learning in relation to instructional goals. Well-prepared teachers are empowered to build aligned assessment, then make decisions based on data from assessments used more than just grading, but to improve strategies.

Theorists: Bridging Theory and Practice in Teacher Education

One of the greatest challenges for teacher education is bridging the gap between theory and practice. In this respect, training is important as it ensures experiential learning through the actual application of knowledge gained by future teachers in real classroom settings. Application or practical-based training equips new teachers with teaching skills and honours instructional practice rooted in real classroom experience(Loughran, 2019).

The most popular way to bridge theory and practice is through student teaching internships. Student educators gain practical experience through these internships by teaching in actual classrooms alongside the experienced instructors. This setting enables them to learn about how to plan and manage lessons, and assess students. The student teachers receive evaluations from their mentors after the internship, usually with feedback about how they can reflect on their teaching approaches and change them if necessary.

Mentorship programs are therefore very important, as they ensure that newly qualified teachers can make theoretically acquired knowledge operational. In this program, newly qualified teachers work with established teachers who guide and support them as they undertake the challenges facing a classroom. Mentorship helps new teachers acquire professional skills and increase their confidence through constructive feedback and collaboration in improving instructional techniques.

Professional learning communities have emerged as perhaps the most highly valued bridge between theory and practice. PLCs involve bringing together teachers that share concerns, best practices, and collaboration regarding instructional strategies. These communities are considered 'a culture of continuous learning and improvement, keeping teachers fresh with new research and new pedagogical innovations, while only applying them to their classroom-based practice'.

In a nutshell, intensive training in teacher education is required to make the teacher more adept in the skills, knowledge, and flexibility levels and better equipped to function well today within a very complex and highly demanding educational environment. One can ensure that teachers are well prepared regarding all the needs of their students through support areas like pedagogical content knowledge, classroom management, inclusive education, differentiated instruction, and technology integration. Such programs ensure that teachers not only know their subject matter but are also effective teachers by the experiential learning opportunities, mentoring, and professional collaboration that help to bridge the gap between theory and practice.

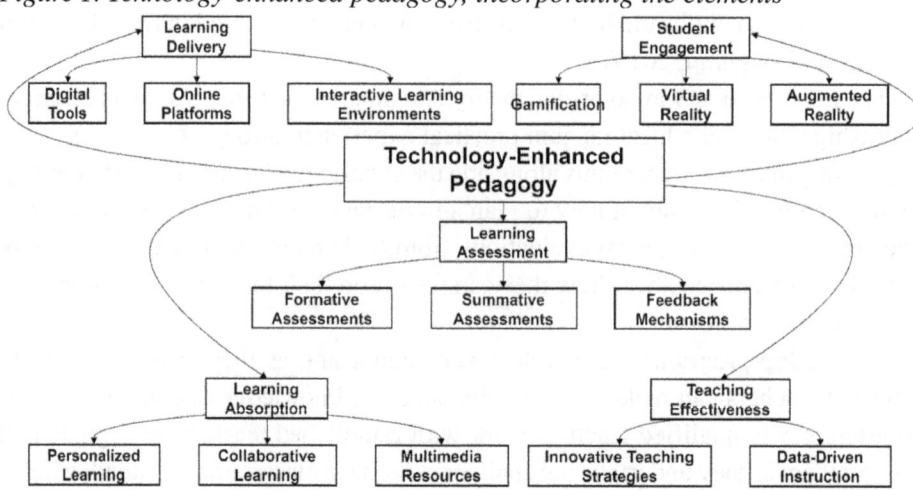

Figure 1. Tchnology-enhanced pedagogy, incorporating the elements

TECHNOLOGY-ENHANCED PEDAGOGY

Technology has transformed the way learning is delivered, absorbed, and assessed in today's contemporary educational landscape. Technology-enhanced pedagogy describes the ways through which digital tools, platforms, and resources can be used to make teaching more effective and increase the engagement of students. Using educational technology in the classroom allows teachers to render learning more interactive and personalized. However, the challenge is how to distribute these resources in an equitable way to not widen the digital divide and get teachers ready in a way that enhances access to technology for learners(Tierney, 2020).

The Digitization of the Learning Environment

These include interactive whiteboards and learning management systems, among others. All these have dramatically transformed the delivery and experience of education. Technology has, more than ever, become a very integral component of the modern learning environment. This enables teachers to make lessons much more engaging through more content, such as video, animations, and interactive simulations that provide a good understanding of abstract ideas.

Flipped classrooms are also becoming more common today, where students learn lecture material online in advance of the class but focus during class on discussion and application. This model gives the student control over his or her own learning pace and also helps teachers to use their classroom time more effectively, engaging in higher-order thinking such as problem-solving, collaboration, and critical analysis. Assessments of student performance have also been altered in significant ways by teachers. Kahoot, Google Forms, or Edmodo can provide real-time quizzes, polls, and feedback on how well students understand the material. In comparison to paper-based tests, these assessments are now more dynamic and less intrusive, making it easier for teachers to quickly check for comprehension and prepare accordingly to teach their students.

Additionally, digital resources support collaborative learning; students can work on projects, no matter where the person sits. Such cloud-based platforms as Google Workspace or Microsoft Teams allow co-authorship of assignments, sharing resources, and even live discussions with peers, contributing to teamwork and giving training in the right kind of literacy that will be necessary for a 21st-century workplace. Another area of realization in the curriculum is gamification. Game-like elements are utilized, such as badges, points, and leaderboards, can motivate the learning of more substantial students. Classcraft or Minecraft Education Edition are the tools that allow more connectivity, entertainment, and interaction towards learning to further engage students among younger learners.

Application of Educational Technology for Better Learning

To benefit from the inclusion of technology in pedagogy, the educators should go beyond simple substitution, such as replacing traditional methods with digital tools. Instead, they should look into using educational technology to augment learning more than they are doing, putting things in a digital format that simply replicates current practice(Nixon et al., 2019).

Some of the most vital forms through which educational technology can be channeled is through personalized learning. Today, technology has the potential to create an adaptive system that will adapt according to the student's learning style, preference, and pace. Pathways presented on sites such as Khan Academy or DreamBox change the content depending on how one responds and what proficiency levels demonstrate. This creates the ability for a student to require extra time to master the concept to move at his pace; meanwhile, the advanced student is challenged with a more robust set of material. Data-driven instruction is another powerful tool for using educational technology. Analytics tools embedded in learning platforms can help teachers to track how students are progressing, identify gaps in students' understanding, and make appropriate changes in instructional strategies. This instant feedback allows for swift intervention so that support is available if the student suffers a setback.

Blended learning is a flexible model that combines face-to-face teaching with online elements. This hybrid model is the best to benefit from the dynamics of classic classroom teaching and at the same time the efficiency and scalability of all the available online resources. For example, schools can apply Moodle, Canvas, or any other learning management system to deliver assignments, resources, and assessments online but maintain traditional in-person interaction for deeper discussions and activities that benefit from physical presence. Educational technology also promotes the development of 21st-century skills such as critical thinking, collaboration, creativity, and digital literacy. It makes students think critically about digital information, collaborates with each other through virtual means, and comes up with creative solutions in settings of project-based learning environments. The skills provide the student with a prepared background to result in the growing trend of a progressively digital and interconnected world.

However, effectiveness in using technology also comes hand in hand with adequate preparation from the educator's side. Professional development in terms of digital pedagogy guides teachers, not just comfort with the use of digital tools but the effective integration of their use. Continuing education helps update teachers on new technologies and how to implement them in teaching goals.

Guaranteeing Equitable Access: Crossing the Digital Divide

While so much potential exists in educational technology to make learning more effective, the main challenge remains the digital divide. This means the gap created by access to technology between some students and others. Digital divides are brought about for reasons of socioeconomic status, a particular geographic location, or lack of infrastructure such as high-speed internet(Tierney, 2020).

Just like any other country, pupils from poor backgrounds or rural households fail to access gadgets, internet, or support systems to improve technology-mediated learning. COVID-19 simply made such inequalities manifest when the schools were forced to close and deliver classes online; most students, in turn, were ill-prepared to follow virtual learning systems. This matter requires a collaborative effort at all levels to be addressed. Government level policies related to funding are necessary, such as equipping schools with high-speed internet and computers for the students in disadvantageous locations. Most schools already follow 1:1 device implementation, where each student is offered a tablet or a laptop; these should be expanded and assisted with resourceful means.

herefore, schools and school districts must partner with community organizations, libraries, as well as firms that manufacture technology to facilitate the availability of free internet, lending of devices, and training for students and their parents on the proper use of the tools. Another aspect of equal access is digital literacy. Providing students with the device and internet access is no longer sufficient; students and their families should learn how to employ these tools effectively. An institutionalized digital literacy program for schools should therefore be a manner where students will be adequately trained beyond the basic technologies as far as responsible use of the internet, online safety, and critical thinking when handling digital content is concerned. Besides, special attention would have to be given to students with disabilities, who would also require some form of assistive technology in order to fully interact with the digital learning interfaces. The institutions should ensure that these digital tools introduced are accessible and integrated so that all students, irrespective of their ability to fully participate in the learning experience.

In conclusion, technology-enhanced pedagogy is one of the powerful tools offered to transform education-a chance for more personalized, collaborative, and evidence-driven learning. However, the full benefits can only be achieved by training educators on how better to include the digital tools and efforts toward balancing out the digital divide in such a manner that the advantages offered through technology reach all students.

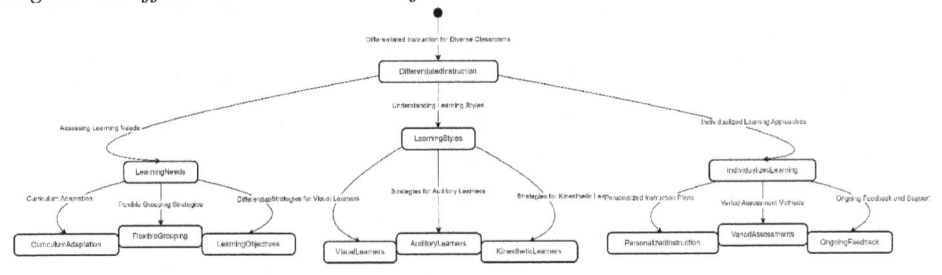

DIFFERENTIATED INSTRUCTION FOR DIVERSE CLASSROOMS

Teaching to meet the different needs, learning styles, and abilities of students inside the classroom, differentiated instruction is undoubtedly tailored for and brings about individualized learning in all contemporary lessons. As classes become more heterogeneous than ever in today's diverse cultural, academic level, and learning preference educational landscape, it will be necessary to identify the differences in order to use differentiated instruction strategies that will allow an inclusive learning environment and maximize the potential of every student(Nixon et al., 2019). Figure 2 depicts differentiated instruction for diverse classrooms.

Figure 2. Differentiated instruction for diverse classrooms

Learner Diversity

Learner diversity needs to be appreciated for differentiated instruction to take effect. Students come into the classroom with unique experiences, strengths, challenges, and perspectives. Consider factors of diversity that concern socio-economic background, language proficiency, cognitive abilities, and learning preferences. For example, some are excellent in verbal communication but are weak in terms of mathematical concepts, while others may have it the other way around.

Cultural and linguistic backgrounds also have much to play in learning. ELLs might require support because of the language in which they learn, but that doesn't necessarily mean that they're not meant to participate in or learn from curriculum content. Teachers need to be aware of the differential experiences so that they can make a classroom environment more inclusive in terms of respecting and valuing each student's background.

To make learner diversity accessible, educators can use surveys, formative assessments, and observations as tools for assessment. This will help the teacher to collect information on students' learning preferences, strengths, and areas needing support; thus, appropriate instruction for differentiated teaching will become possible in their classes. Such knowledge is necessary for designing a lesson plan that can be used to engage and learn with everyone.

Differential Instruction Strategies

There are varied ways a teacher goes about applying differentiated instruction, which is in providing for the students' needs(Fonsén & Ukkonen-Mikkola, 2019). Some strategies for differentiation include the following:

a) Flexible Grouping: Whenever students are grouped according to ability, interest, or learning type, it is possible for them to learn together afterwards. Homogeneous groups place students together with peers they can work well with, but heterogeneous groups foster diverse skills and views that also enhance understanding. Provide students with choices in their assignments and projects to encourage autonomy and motivate them. Choice boards allow students to choose tasks that are aligned with their interests or learning modality through artistic expression, writing a report, or oral presentation.

b) Tiered Assignments: Teachers provide multiple tasks of various levels of complexity so that all children work at their appropriate level of ability. For example, a mathematics teacher may create several multiple problems at increasingly higher levels of difficulty, yet all center on the same concept. Thus, students are allowed to work at their own pace. This strategy involves scaffolding the breakdown of complex difficulty in a task so that it is broken down into manageable smaller steps, where one provides support and gradually withdraws it based on increased confidence and mastery by learners so as to increase their independence.

c) The use of technology: This can be used in personalizing the learning experience with this integration technology-based instructional methods. Since this software adjusts to the ability of each learner, it provides necessary practice and feedback based on how different individuals and teams perform, hence giving scopes for analyzing the performance of the students and adapting content according to needs. The proper implementation of differentiated instruction requires adapting teaching methods. Teachers should be flexible and responsive to students' needs and adapt methods when required. These include some of the following approaches:

d) Varied instructional strategies: Blended instructional methods, namely direct instruction, inquiry-based learning, and cooperative learning, will ensure diverse learning preferences are met. Visual learners need graphic organizers and video; kinesthetic learners require hands-on activities. Personalised Learning Outcomes The use of differentiated learning outcomes will allow for the learners to move toward specific endpoints based upon their strengths and weaknesses. Co-establishment of such goals with students can motivate and better own the learning journey of students.

e) Regular Feedback: Timely and Constructive Feedback is the Secret of Students' Growth Differentiated instruction requires constant assessment and modification based on the growth they are experiencing. Regular Check-ins: Provide Ongoing Feedback In-class check-in and feedback indicate where there is a gap between students' potential, missteps, and what is in their way in reaching for it.

f) Creating a Supportive Environment: Encouraging taking of risks and resilience among students within a positive learning environment of the classroom. Here, classroom norms of collaboration, respect, and open communication help the kids to feel secure and supported while learning.

Thus, differentiated instruction is the most important one to support the diverse needs of students in today's classrooms. Understanding learner diversity, using various instructional strategies, and tailoring teaching means creating a social environment that enhances every student's learning journey. This approach not only has the potential to enhance academic outcomes but also serves to develop a respect for diversity and appreciation thereof, setting the stage for the students' success in the multicultural world.

Figure 3. Components and processes involved in creating equitable learning environments for students

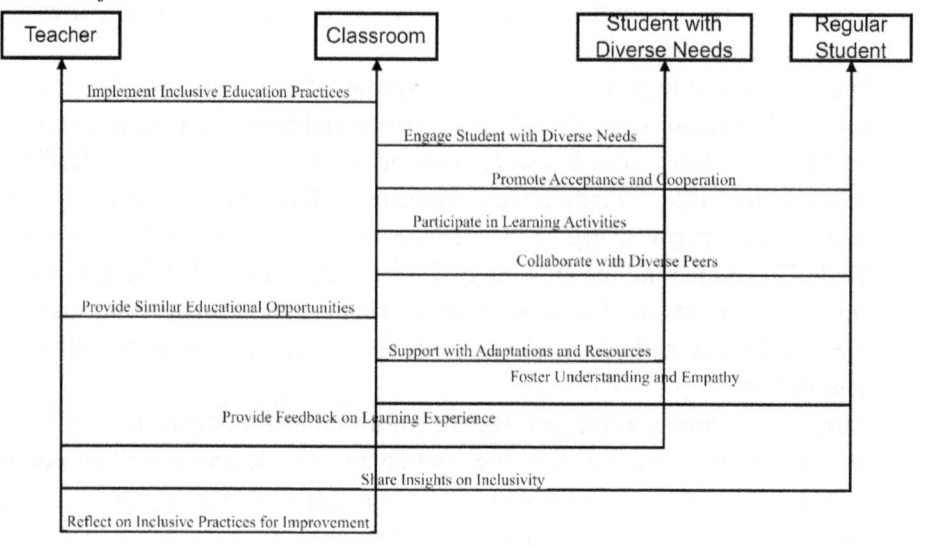

Teacher	Classroom	Student with Diverse Needs	Regular Student

Implement Inclusive Education Practices

Engage Student with Diverse Needs

Promote Acceptance and Cooperation

Participate in Learning Activities

Collaborate with Diverse Peers

Provide Similar Educational Opportunities

Support with Adaptations and Resources

Foster Understanding and Empathy

Provide Feedback on Learning Experience

Share Insights on Inclusivity

Reflect on Inclusive Practices for Improvement

INCLUSIVE EDUCATION PRACTICES

More importantly, inclusive education practices are some of the major tools for creating equitable environments where students with diverse needs learn within other regular students with varied abilities. Inclusion is more than placing diversely able students in mainstream classes; it involves actively engaging students with diverse needs in the learning process and providing them with similar educational opportunities to those without diverse abilities(Li & Flowerdew, 2020). This approach serves not only children with disabilities but also helps in teaching learners, some about acceptance, tolerance, and cooperation, amongst each other. Figure 3 illustrates the various components and processes involved in creating an equitable learning environment for students.

Importance of Inclusion in Education

Inclusion is very important in education. This is because it facilitates a feeling of belonging and community among the students. When they learn together, children pick up social skills, relationships, and appreciation of diversity. This reduces stigmas and stereotypes by those who have disabilities and creates a cultural pattern of acceptance and respect.

Inclusive education also has increased acute social outcomes. Empirical evidence shows that students of inclusive classrooms are more active, academically accomplishable and motivated than students outside the class. Diverse learners can work well academically and also make meaningful contributions in the classroom environment when appropriately supported and resourced.

Inclusive is in consonance with ideals of equity and social justice. Every child must be allowed to access quality education without reason for rejection, including children with disabilities as well as those from socio-economic backgrounds. This way, the school structure can particularly address and dismantle the systemic barriers to education among students.

Training Teachers for Inclusive Classrooms

Effective inclusive education requires that teachers be well-skilled and supported with enough education to arm them with knowledge, skills, and strategies to meet the needs of different learners. Preparing the teachers involves designing those educational arrangements in ways that incorporate all the specific components guiding the practices(Schaefer & Clandinin, 2019):

a) Understanding Diversity: To understand the nature of disabilities, the range of learning needs, and the importance of cultural competence in the classroom, teachers should be educated. This would enable teachers to understand the particular needs of different students and respond in appropriate ways. The teachers have to learn how to differentiate instruction through effective differentiated instruction. This means taking teaching methods, materials, and assessments to fitting varying styles and abilities into learning. Such training must include creating flexible grouping, tiered assignments, and scaffolding techniques.
b) Teamwork and Collaboration: Inclusion thrives on teamwork amongst teachers, support staff, and the family. Training schemes should focus on the need for collaboration with and without each other in developing an Individualized Education Program and collaboration in working with a special education professional .
c) Classroom Management Techniques: Classroom management focuses on creating a good social climate in the class by formulating the appropriate response to positive behavior as well as challenging behaviors of students.

d) Continuous Professional Development: Inclusion is an area in which continuous professional development is required; therefore, teachers must constantly update themselves on best practices, new research, and innovative strategies for inclusion.

Use of Assistive Technology with Special Needs Student

Assistive technology plays a very vital role in the support of learning needs for students who have disabilities. These can include tools and resources that increase accessibility, facilitate communication, and provide participation in the learning process. Some critical ways assistive technology supports inclusive education(Booth et al., 2021):

a) Communication Aids: For children with speech and/or language impairment, it is possible to use assistive communication aids like speech-generating devices or communication boards. They can improve the opportunities that the child has to share messages with fellow learners and instructors. Students therefore can exchange ideas in such discussions while sharing their contributions in a collaborative learning process.
b) Adaptive Learning Tools: There are software and apps specifically designed for special needs learners. These programs may offer a means of receiving text-to-speech, speech-to-text, or even the ability to customize the interface in ways which best benefit the individual learner. This can allow students to access the curriculum in a fashion that leverages their individual strengths and compensates for challenges.
c) Including multisensory approaches with assistive technology supports the reinforcement of learning. All different learning styles can be catered through visual, auditory, or tactile tools while incorporating all of these factors into lessons keeps it interesting for all.
d) Accessibility Features Most digital platforms and educational resources provide accessibility features such as adjusting the font size, contrast color, and closed captioning, in order to give full access to students.
e) Progress Monitoring. The teachers will resort to assistive technology tools for monitoring the student's progress in learning and pinpointing specific areas that would necessitate interventions. The data that result from these tools can direct an intervention or inform the instructional decision.

The only mode of inclusive education is one that creates a fair and nurturing atmosphere for learning. By promoting inclusion, providing teacher training on teaching children with special needs, and properly utilizing assistive technology, educators can create classrooms that make it possible for every student to succeed academically and socially. Indeed, by promoting inclusion, educators enable learning that benefits the whole student body because this is learning that serves as preparation for a diversified and interconnected world.

PROFESSIONAL DEVELOPMENT AND LIFELONG LEARNING

In the fast-changing world of education, professional development and lifelong learning offer the tools that educators need to develop their practice and learn about recent trends in pedagogy, as well as answer the diversified needs of students. CPD, reflective teaching practices, and programs dedicated to specialization are among the key tools for the ability of teachers to provide valuable instruction. The three topics mentioned below are all significant to educators who aim to develop themselves professionally in order to be able to offer quality instruction(Buchanan et al., 2022; van Rooij et al., 2019).

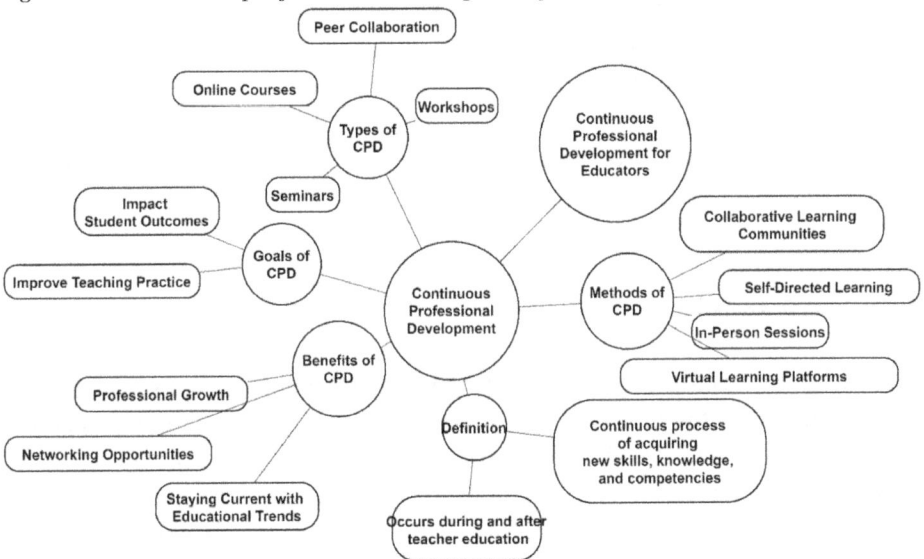

Figure 4. Continuous professional development for educators

Continuous Professional Development for Educators

Continuous Professional Development Continuous professional development refers to the continuous process of acquiring new skills, knowledge, and competencies during and after a teacher's education. CPD assumes many different forms, such as workshops, seminars, online courses, and peer collaboration, all meant to improve teaching practice and impact the overall outcomes for students. Figure 5 depicts continuous professional development for educators. Figure 5 depicts continuous pr4fessional development for educators.

One of the most significant reasons that motivate CPD is that it places teachers abreast of the latest research, trends, and innovative technologies in education studies. The ever-changing educational landscape-groaning under the weight of digital tools and innovative teaching strategies-was largely due to CPD and has enabled teachers to adapt and refine their practices to enhance student engagement and learning. In addition, CPD fosters a collaborative community of teachers. Professional learning communities experienced among the teaching fraternity allow them to share their experiences, resources, and strategies with one another, fostering a support environment which encourages growth. Since it improves the overall practices of teachers, this collaboration not only enhances individual teaching practices but also strengthens the overall community.

Apart from the value that CPD provides, most school systems realize its importance and would also provide incentives such as increased salary, promotions, or even leadership positions for professionals who are active in CPD. Investments in CPD reflect that educational institutions value constant progress and development in training for better teaching effectiveness.

Reflective Teaching as a Tool for Growth

Reflective teaching is an important practice that encourages evaluation by a teacher with respect to his or her instructional approach, interaction with learners, and general classroom effectiveness. Reflective teaching therefore provides teachers with insight into both their strengths and weaknesses so that practice can be further professionalized. Reflective teaching may occur in a variety of ways, such as journaling, peer observations, and self-assessment. Through journaling, educators are able to record experiences, thoughts, and feelings about practices, thus being able to identify patterns and areas that need more attention. Peer observations provide opportunity to the teachers to observe each other's practices, hence leading to discussions that yield new insights and approaches.

Self-assessment is another very effective technique for reflective teaching. Assessments can use frameworks to describe how the practitioner will be able to evaluate the actual practices against any set criteria. The process promotes accountability and helps the educator focus on setting clear goals toward professional growth. Moreover, reflective teaching is very supportive of the tenets of lifelong learning. In contemplating and modifying their practices based on ongoing reflective appraisal, educators are more responsive to their students. Through this kind of continuous commitment to reflection, individual teaching is enhanced, which consequently benefits student achievement.

Specialization and Advanced Certification Programs

Specialization and advanced certification programs enable teachers to delve deeper into areas in which they want to acquire expertise, such as special education, instructional technology, or curriculum development. These courses further enable teachers to gain very specialized skills and knowledge relative to their interests and the needs of their students. Some of the specializations take the form of coursework, practical experiences, and mentoring to prepare education providers for either school or district-wide leadership functions. For example, special education certification for educators covers all strategies for instruction for diverse learning needs in a student's classroom in order to create an inclusive classroom.

Advanced degree programs also create career opportunities for classroom teachers. Many school districts actively seek to hire teachers with advanced teaching credentials, because they know these professionals will be better equipped to solve the kinds of problems that are difficult in today's classrooms. Additional specialized training can also mean higher salaries and greater job satisfaction, as teachers work "on scope" with issues in which they are invested. In addition, most such programs make sure that they are integrated into the freshest conducted research as well as best practices in education, which means that educators are well-equipped with relevant, evidence-based strategies. For this very reason, specialization and advanced certification programs greatly enhance the overall quality of education through the education of very specialized and knowledgeable educators.

Professional development and lifelong learning are essential for educators in the new world of education. Continuous professional development mirrors refreshed teaching practices, specialisation programs, and fosters the skills of educators in the arena to constantly be viable and relevant. Therefore, by professional growth, an educator gets not only a better practice but also contributes to the next change for the system.

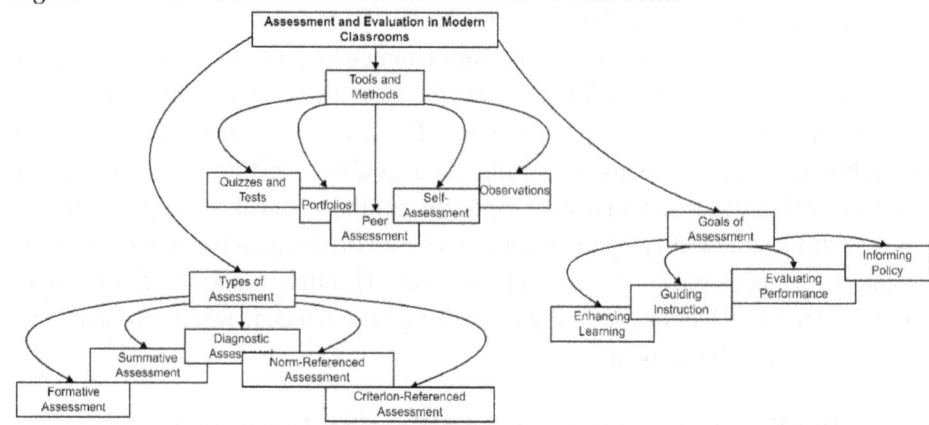

Figure 5. Assessment and evaluation in modern classrooms

ASSESSMENT AND EVALUATION IN MODERN CLASSROOMS

One of the crucial elements of this new kind of contemporary education is the emphasis that assessment and evaluation must play as part of the teaching and learning process. A shift away from the classic method of summative assessments and towards a more holistic approach in which formative assessments are given an equal or greater place reflects better knowledge of how students learn and develop. This chapter explores the changing landscape of assessment technique, data-driven instruction, and how keeping pace with learning outcomes impacts assessments (Buchanan et al., 2022; J.-A. Lee et al., 2019; van Rooij et al., 2019). Figure 5 depicts the process of assessment and evaluation in modern classrooms.

Evolution in the Assessment Methods: Formative to Summative

For a long time, summative methods of assessment form the foundation for education, ensuring that the acquired knowledge is accounted for by evaluation at the end of an instructional unit through standardized tests and final exams. Despite the fact that assessments are important in evaluating student performance, they are often not a true depiction of the student's real understanding and skills.

With this being so, educators had to embrace formative assessment in recent years since it provides monitoring of the learning processes and feedback during the learning process. Quizzes, classroom discussions, peer review, and interaction activities are deemed assessments that can aid teachers to know, at the moment, how well students understand what they are being taught. The loop of continuous feedback helps detect gaps in learning. This further informs decisions on teaching, whereby adjustments can be made for the sake of student needs.

Last but not least, formative assessments foster a growth mindset in students. It encourages risk-taking behavior as well as understanding that mistakes afford an opportunity to learn while building resilience. In so doing, this new mindset helps bring about a better attitude toward learning because they start to perceive assessments as learning opportunities rather than a measuring scale of one's ability.

Data-Driven Instruction and Its Influence on Learning

Data-driven instruction brought with it a new way to assess and evaluate student learning in the teaching practice, making it an essential procedure for educators who integrate formative assessment data when they make decisions for the improvement of teaching to maximize student learning. The process of gathering data to come up with its analysis and interpretation of trends and patterns in students' performances is what data-driven instruction is all about. Educators must understand the depth of student learning by using various sources, such as assessment outcomes, attendance records, and classroom observations. This way, teachers can differentiate instruction according to diverse student needs for success in lessons.

For instance, if data shows that a significant number of students are struggling to cope with particular content, teachers can adjust the instruction approach to offer more support and resources. Active application of data inspires educators to construct a responsive learning environment that supports success. Another strength of data-driven instruction is that it empowers students by engaging them in the assessment process. When there is a student who is made aware of what is to be learned and how much there is in terms of their learning stage, they become the owners of their education. Educators can encourage self-assessment and reflection, allowing students to set personal learning objectives and track the progress.

Alignment of Assessment with Learning Outcomes

The critical aim of effective assessments is that they align with and serve to measure learning outcomes. Rather clear learning objectives are an overview to teaching and indeed to assessing, and they help an educator determine progress made by students toward specified learning outcomes. When assessments are closely linked with learning, teachers can always tell whether students have learned all that the curriculum intended to be taught. Teachers establish the learning outcomes for each lesson or unit, such as being specific and measurable. Assessments are thus created to find out whether or not the student has acquired the desired outcome appropriately. For example, one assessment may be a project, which can give information regarding how a student can apply the knowledge in real life situations. Another will be the written test, which tests the comprehension of theoretical matters about the student.

If assessments are aligned to learning outcomes, then they can quite well ensure the transparency and fairness of an assessment. It is clear to students about the expectations of their performance and the direct relationship between their learning activities and assessment criteria. Clarity leads to motivation and engagement because it depicts relevance in the context of work conducted for them. By embracing the developing techniques of assessment, incorporating data-driven instruction, and matching assessments to learning outcomes, educators can create a rich, comprehensive assessment framework that not only measures learning but also enhances the process of it. Ultimately, through such an approach, it prepares students for success in the rapidly changing world with whom it fosters critical thinking, problem-solving skills, and lifelong learning.

PRACTICAL APPLICATIONS OF PEDAGOGICAL CONTENT KNOWLEDGE

PCK is exactly what connects content knowledge and pedagogical skills into meaningful learning environments. Educators get the information they need to make adjustments to fit students' needs and ensure deep mastery of subject matter. The chapter will explore real-world applications of PCK in teacher preparation via experiential learning, mentorship, and peer collaboration as well as best practices for applying PCK in the classroom(Agrawal et al., 2023).

Experiential Learning in Teacher Preparation

Experiential learning is an essential part of teacher preparation programs designed with PCK integrated. This is an approach that focuses on hands-on experiences so that the pupil teachers learn through living through real situations in a classroom setting. Practicum placements could be where the student teachers get to observe and interact with established educators, thus providing an experiential learner with practical application or application of theoretical knowledge in real settings(Durairaj et al., 2023).

During such practices, pre-service teachers can evolve their PCK by trying out the most appropriate methodologies to deliver instruction and then assessing what works and what doesn't work. For example, by asking a set of questions related to the students' understanding, a student teacher can assess which questions bring maximum engagement and critical thinking and reflect on which strategies have worked for them. It is an ongoing cycle enabling the development of teaching skills in the student teachers and increasing confidence within the practice.

Experiential learning also provides a sense of attachment to the subject matter. A teacher who understands content under real conditions often understands better how to pass on complex ideas on to their own students. This practical application of PCK will arm future educators with cutting-edge and relevant teaching strategies that resonate well within circles of their own students.

Mentorship as well as Peer Collaboration in Teacher Training

Mentorship and peer cooperation are the vital components of outstanding teacher preparation that supports the development of PCK. Experienced teachers become mentors to guide the novice teacher through the insanity of teaching the class. This relationship allows them the opportunity to share best practices, knowledge, and constructively critique each other to foster a supportive environment for professional growth. Mentorship makes it easy for new teachers to view their mentor teaching students, in the sense of deconstruction about how professional teachers handle various learning needs through PCK (Das et al., 2024). Feedback is sought in lesson planning, classroom management, and instructional techniques guiding novice teachers toward perfecting their practice. This kind of relationship facilitates open dialogue, which supports never-ending learning toward overcoming challenges and being able to celebrate success.

The peer collaboration of teachers also promotes sharing of PCK. Professional Learning Communities offer a space where teachers can focus on discussion regarding the instructional approaches that best impact learning and student work, as well as solve problems collaboratively. Through these approaches, teachers may advance mutual understanding of pedagogies with unique experiences. Thus, peer collaboration encourages reflective and innovative practices. Through discussions of teachers about their practices, areas of improvement could be identified and even new ideas to improve the learning environments could be explored. This community inquiry would even further develop the best practice of an individual teacher while furthering the community's vision on sound pedagogy.

Best Practices for Using PCK in the Classroom

The application of PCK in the class calls for a clear plan and thoughtful implementation. One best practice is the use of formative assessments, which are used to measure students' understanding throughout the learning process. The more diversified use of assessments-multiple quizzing, discussions, hands-on activities-measures how students learn, which enables the instructor to modify instruction. That way, all strategies implemented by the teacher shall be appropriate for the learners' needs, hence strengthening the learning process. Differentiation is another best practice that has to do with handling different types and abilities in the classroom. Teachers are able to use their PCK as they change lessons that meet the requirements of students using different instructional strategies, resources, and activities. For instance, graphic organizers may be useful for visual students while hands-on experiments may be best for kinesthetic students. This can be viewed as a way of making the teaching environment inclusive since the students are encouraged to be active through engagement and achievement (Prabhuswamy et al., 2024; Sharma et al., 2024).

Second, technology integration in the classroom can facilitate the operationalization of PCK. Such digital materials and tools support the development of an interactive learning environment that nurtures peer to peer interaction and critical thinking among the students. This is by applying online models such that complex ideas may be visualized and collaborative online platforms that will foster peer to peer interaction and feedback amongst the students. With such an integration of technology, more supportive learning for students can be better achieved through enhanced instructional practices by the teachers.

Chapter main argument is that the application of Pedagogical Content Knowledge is very important to the professionalism of teacher preparation and classroom instruction. What I have established in this paper is that through experiential learning, mentorship, peer collaboration, and implementation of best practices, educators can develop PCK so that meaningful experiences are created for their students. As teachers continue to sharpen their pedagogical skills and adapt to the evolving educational landscape, the application of PCK will remain a cornerstone of effective teaching.

FUTURE TRENDS IN TEACHING AND LEARNING

These trends are changing the face of teaching and learning in the modern ever-evolving landscape of education. Along with emergent technologies and pedagogical innovations and global perspectives on teacher education, one can reconstruct educational practices(Singh Madan et al., 2024; Vaithianathan et al., 2024).

Emerging Technologies and Pedagogical Innovations

Integrating emerging technologies in the classroom is making a revolutionary change in the way educators teach and students learn. Innovations that include AI, VR, and AR improve learning experiences through immersive and interactive environments. For example, using VR can transport students to historical sites or even scientific laboratories to experience experiential learning opportunities that enhance understanding as well as engagement. In addition, AI-based tools are personalizing learning by analyzing data on student learning to identify their strength and weakness points and apply customized instructional strategies. The technologies support adaptive learning, wherein the content of education is adapted real-time according to changing requirements of learners. Personalized learning shifts the scenario towards a much more inclusive learning environment that accommodates diverse learning styles and abilities(Kalaiselvi et al., 2024; Saravanan et al., 2024). New online and blended learning models have also changed how we view traditional paradigms of education. Such flexible modes allow access to much material and collaborative learning with other students from other parts of the world. Platforms allowing for asynchronous learning promote autonomous learning as student take charge of own time, learning at their pace.

International Perspectives on Teacher Education

In a world increasingly interconnected by modern means of communication, global teacher education perspectives influence pedagogical practices. Collaborative efforts and programs of exchange promote cross-cultural understanding and professional development among educators. Such experiences provide insights into different educational systems, methodologies, and assessment practices, enriching pedagogical approaches. Additionally, teacher education with a focus on global competencies prepares teachers to prepare students with skills they will need to be successful in a melting pot of a changing and diverse world(Prabhuswamy et al., 2024; Sharma et al., 2024; Venkatasubramanian et al., 2024). Critical thinking, teamwork, and cultural sensitivity are becoming pillars of teacher preparation programs as instructed by the shifting societal global needs. It is seen, then, that future teaching and learning were designed here in emerging technologies, pedagogical innovations, and global perspectives. By embracing these trends, learning environments are better fostered to be engaging, inclusive, and effective in preparing students for success in an increasingly diverse and fast-changing world.

CONCLUSION

In essence, what the chapter on Pedagogical Content Development and Specialized Training for Teaching Careers is out to say is that, in modern classrooms, teachers need training and equipping for their knowledge and practice. Pedagogical Content Knowledge integrated with practicality can aid teachers to create more effective, engaging, and inclusive learning experiences for students. The necessity of carrying on professional development is revealed in the discussion, with emphasis on continuous professional development, that is, mentorship and peer collaboration-ultimately essential for developing reflective practice and responsiveness to diverse learner needs. Introductions of new technologies along with pedagogical innovations transform the educational landscape; a new opportunity for embracing personalized adaptive learning experiences valued by students of different abilities and background.

Fourth, embracing global perspectives in teaching education open sources rich in preparing educationists for a world of complex interrelations. As such, the inquiry of society and forever changing about education no doubt cultivates lifelong learning amongst educators. These are the facets that would give the next-generation educator an enormously challenging approach, enabling him to inspire his students with a culture of inquiry, inclusion, and critical thinking into the foreseeable future.

REFERENCES

Agrawal, A. V., Pitchai, R., Senthamaraikannan, C., Balaji, N. A., Sajithra, S., & Boopathi, S. (2023). Digital Education System During the COVID-19 Pandemic. In *Using Assistive Technology for Inclusive Learning in K-12 Classrooms* (pp. 104–126). IGI Global. DOI: 10.4018/978-1-6684-6424-3.ch005

Ballantyne, J., & Retell, J. (2020). Teaching careers: Exploring links between well-being, burnout, self-efficacy and praxis shock. *Frontiers in Psychology*, 10, 2255. DOI: 10.3389/fpsyg.2019.02255 PMID: 32132940

Berger, J.-L., & Lê Van, K. (2019). Teacher professional identity as multidimensional: Mapping its components and examining their associations with general pedagogical beliefs. *Educational Studies*, 45(2), 163–181. DOI: 10.1080/03055698.2018.1446324

Booth, J., Coldwell, M., Müller, L.-M., Perry, E., & Zuccollo, J. (2021). Mid-career teachers: A mixed methods scoping study of professional development, career progression and retention. *Education Sciences*, 11(6), 299. DOI: 10.3390/educsci11060299

Buchanan, R., Mills, T., & Mooney, E. (2022). Working across time and space: Developing a framework for teacher leadership throughout a teaching career. In *Leadership for Professional Learning* (pp. 65–77). Routledge. DOI: 10.4324/9781003357384-5

Das, S., Lekhya, G., Shreya, K., Shekinah, K. L., Babu, K. K., & Boopathi, S. (2024). Fostering Sustainability Education Through Cross-Disciplinary Collaborations and Research Partnerships: Interdisciplinary Synergy. In *Facilitating Global Collaboration and Knowledge Sharing in Higher Education With Generative AI* (pp. 60–88). IGI Global.

Durairaj, M., Jayakumar, S., Karpagavalli, V., Maheswari, B. U., & Boopathi, S. (2023). Utilization of Digital Tools in the Indian Higher Education System During Health Crises. In *Multidisciplinary Approaches to Organizational Governance During Health Crises* (pp. 1–21). IGI Global. DOI: 10.4018/978-1-7998-9213-7.ch001

Fonsén, E., & Ukkonen-Mikkola, T. (2019). Early childhood education teachers' professional development towards pedagogical leadership. *Educational Research*, 61(2), 181–196. DOI: 10.1080/00131881.2019.1600377

Glutsch, N., & König, J. (2019). Pre-service teachers' motivations for choosing teaching as a career: Does subject interest matter? *Journal of Education for Teaching*, 45(5), 494–510. DOI: 10.1080/02607476.2019.1674560

Ismail, S. A. A., & Jarrah, A. M. (2019). Exploring Pre-Service Teachers' Perceptions of Their Pedagogical Preferences, Teaching Competence and Motivation. *International Journal of Instruction*, 12(1), 493–510. DOI: 10.29333/iji.2019.12132a

Kalaiselvi, D., Ramaratnam, M. S., Kokila, S., Sarkar, R., Anandakumar, S., & Boopathi, S. (2024). Future Developments of Higher Education on Social Psychology: Innovation and Changes. In *Advances in Human and Social Aspects of Technology* (pp. 146–169). IGI Global. DOI: 10.4018/979-8-3693-2569-8.ch008

Lee, J.-A., Kang, M. O., & Park, B. J. (2019). Factors influencing choosing teaching as a career: South Korean preservice teachers. *Asia Pacific Education Review*, 20(3), 467–488. DOI: 10.1007/s12564-019-09579-z

Lee, S. W. (2019). The impact of a pedagogy course on the teaching beliefs of inexperienced graduate teaching assistants. *CBE Life Sciences Education*, 18(1), ar5. DOI: 10.1187/cbe.18-07-0137 PMID: 30707641

Li, Y., & Flowerdew, J. (2020). Teaching English for Research Publication Purposes (ERPP): A review of language teachers' pedagogical initiatives. *English for Specific Purposes*, 59, 29–41. DOI: 10.1016/j.esp.2020.03.002

Loughran, J. (2019). Pedagogical reasoning: The foundation of the professional knowledge of teaching. *Teachers and Teaching*, 25(5), 523–535. DOI: 10.1080/13540602.2019.1633294

Nixon, R. S., Smith, L. K., & Sudweeks, R. R. (2019). Elementary teachers' science subject matter knowledge across the teacher career cycle. *Journal of Research in Science Teaching*, 56(6), 707–731. DOI: 10.1002/tea.21524

Ödalen, J., Brommesson, D., Erlingsson, G. Ó., Schaffer, J. K., & Fogelgren, M. (2019). Teaching university teachers to become better teachers: The effects of pedagogical training courses at six Swedish universities. *Higher Education Research & Development*, 38(2), 339–353. DOI: 10.1080/07294360.2018.1512955

Prabhuswamy, M., Tripathi, R., Vijayakumar, M., Thulasimani, T., Sundharesalingam, P., & Sampath, B. (2024). A Study on the Complex Nature of Higher Education Leadership: An Innovative Approach. In *Challenges of Globalization and Inclusivity in Academic Research* (pp. 202–223). IGI Global. DOI: 10.4018/979-8-3693-1371-8.ch013

Raduan, N. A., & Na, S.-I. (2020). An integrative review of the models for teacher expertise and career development. *European Journal of Teacher Education*, 43(3), 428–451. DOI: 10.1080/02619768.2020.1728740

Saravanan, S., Chandrasekar, J., Satheesh Kumar, S., Patel, P., Maria Shanthi, J., & Boopathi, S. (2024). The Impact of NBA Implementation Across Engineering Disciplines: Innovative Approaches. In *Advances in Higher Education and Professional Development* (pp. 229–252). IGI Global. DOI: 10.4018/979-8-3693-1666-5.ch010

Schaefer, L., & Clandinin, D. J. (2019). Sustaining teachers' stories to live by: Implications for teacher education. *Teachers and Teaching*, 25(1), 54–68. DOI: 10.1080/13540602.2018.1532407

Sharma, D. M., Ramana, K. V., Jothilakshmi, R., Verma, R., Maheswari, B. U., & Boopathi, S. (2024). Integrating Generative AI Into K-12 Curriculums and Pedagogies in India: Opportunities and Challenges. *Facilitating Global Collaboration and Knowledge Sharing in Higher Education With Generative AI*, 133–161.

Shwartz, G., & Dori, Y. J. (2020). Transition into Teaching: Second career teachers' professional identity. *Eurasia Journal of Mathematics, Science and Technology Education*, 16(11), em1891. DOI: 10.29333/ejmste/8502

Singh Madan, B., Najma, U., Pande Rana, D., & Kumar, P. K. J., S., S., & Boopathi, S. (2024). Empowering Leadership in Higher Education: Driving Student Performance, Faculty Development, and Institutional Progress. In *Advances in Educational Technologies and Instructional Design* (pp. 191–221). IGI Global. DOI: 10.4018/979-8-3693-0583-6.ch009

Tierney, A. (2020). The scholarship of teaching and learning and pedagogic research within the disciplines: Should it be included in the research excellence framework? *Studies in Higher Education*, 45(1), 176–186. DOI: 10.1080/03075079.2019.1574732

Vaithianathan, V., Subbulakshmi, N., Boopathi, S., & Mohanraj, M. (2024). Integrating Project-Based and Skills-Based Learning for Enhanced Student Engagement and Success: Transforming Higher Education. In *Adaptive Learning Technologies for Higher Education* (pp. 345–372). IGI Global. DOI: 10.4018/979-8-3693-3641-0.ch015

van Rooij, E. C. M., Fokkens-Bruinsma, M., & Goedhart, M. (2019). Preparing science undergraduates for a teaching career: Sources of their teacher self-efficacy. *Teacher Educator*, 54(3), 270–294. DOI: 10.1080/08878730.2019.1606374

Varadharajan, M., Buchanan, J., & Schuck, S. (2020). Navigating and negotiating: Career changers in teacher education programmes. *Asia-Pacific Journal of Teacher Education*, 48(5), 477–490. DOI: 10.1080/1359866X.2019.1669136

Venkatasubramanian, V., Chitra, M., Sudha, R., Singh, V. P., Jefferson, K., & Boopathi, S. (2024). Examining the Impacts of Course Outcome Analysis in Indian Higher Education: Enhancing Educational Quality. In *Challenges of Globalization and Inclusivity in Academic Research* (pp. 124–145). IGI Global.

Vilppu, H., Södervik, I., Postareff, L., & Murtonen, M. (2019). The effect of short online pedagogical training on university teachers' interpretations of teaching–learning situations. *Instructional Science*, 47(6), 679–709. DOI: 10.1007/s11251-019-09496-z

KEY TERMS AND DEFINITIONS

PCK: - Pedagogical Content Knowledge
CPD: - Continuous Professional Development
PLC: - Professional Learning Community
COVID: - Coronavirus Disease (specifically referring to COVID-19)
ELL: - English Language Learner
AI: - Artificial Intelligence
VR: - Virtual Reality
AR: - Augmented Reality

Chapter 9

Is the Curriculum Assessment Policy Statement (CAPS) Advancing Diversity and Social Justice in Rural Communities?
The Plight of the LGBTQIA+ Community

Medwin Dikwanyane Sepadi
University of Limpopo, South Africa

ABSTRACT

This chapter critically examines the Curriculum Assessment Policy Statement (CAPS) in South Africa and its role in advancing diversity and social justice, particularly focusing on the LGBTQIA+ community in rural areas. Despite CAPS's foundational principles emphasizing human rights, inclusivity, environmental and social justice, the chapter highlights a significant disconnect between these principles and the lived experiences of LGBTQIA+ individuals in rural South Africa. The chapter begins by outlining the key principles of CAPS and its commitment to fostering understanding and respect for diversity, including issues related to race, gender, language, and disability

DOI: 10.4018/979-8-3693-4058-5.ch009

INTRODUCTION

The Curriculum Assessment Policy Statement (CAPS) A National Curriculum and Assessment Policy Statement is a single, comprehensive, and concise policy document introduced by the Department of Basic Education for all the subjects listed in the National Curriculum Statement for Grades R – 12 in South Africa. Curriculum and Assessment Policy Statement is a guides or describes the teaching, learning, and assessment process in the South African Education System at both primary and post-primary phases of learning

CAPS gives detailed guidance for teachers on what they should teach and how to assess. in South Africa outlines the national curriculum for basic education. One of its core principles is "Human rights, inclusivity, environmental and social justice." This principle emphasizes integrating social justice, human rights, and environmental consciousness into the curriculum, fostering inclusivity and understanding of diversity.

This chapter explores the effectiveness of the CAPS curriculum in advancing diversity and social justice for the LGBTQIA+ community in rural South Africa. Despite referencing diversity in various aspects, the reality in rural communities paints a different picture. Here, LGBTQIA+ issues remain largely taboo, contributing to a high rate of violence against this community.

This chapter delves into the following:

- The CAPS curriculum and its principles of diversity and social justice.
- Challenges faced by the LGBTQIA+ community in rural South Africa.
- The current state of LGBTQIA+ representation and education within the CAPS curriculum.
- The effectiveness of current strategies (if any) in promoting LGBTQIA+ understanding in rural communities.
- Recommendations for improving the CAPS curriculum to better address the needs of the LGBTQIA+ community.

The CAPS Curriculum and its Commitment to Diversity

The CAPS curriculum acknowledges the importance of diversity and aims to foster understanding among citizens. It recognizes various dimensions of diversity, including race, language, religion, and disability. The Curriculum Assessment Policy Statement (CAPS) in South Africa is designed with a strong commitment to diversity, aiming to foster an inclusive and equitable educational environment. This section explores the various ways in which the CAPS curriculum demonstrates its dedication to diversity, ensuring that it is sensitive to and inclusive of the diverse backgrounds, experiences, and needs of learners in brief concise narration.

Inclusivity and Human Rights

The CAPS curriculum is founded on the principles of human rights, inclusivity, environmental, and social justice. These principles are integrated into the teaching and learning materials, promoting understanding and respect for diversity. This includes recognizing and valuing the diverse cultures, languages, races, genders, and abilities of learners.

Diversity Awareness

The curriculum content is developed to be sensitive to diversity issues such as poverty, inequality, race, gender, language, age, disability, and other factors. It encourages learners to understand and appreciate the diverse backgrounds of their peers, fostering an environment of acceptance and respect.

Anti-Discrimination and Anti-Bias Education

CAPS incorporates elements that address discrimination and bias, aiming to challenge stereotypes and prejudices. It seeks to educate learners about the importance of equality and the rights of all individuals, regardless of their background or identity.

Culturally Responsive Teaching

The curriculum promotes culturally responsive teaching practices, which involve using instructional strategies that are sensitive to the cultural backgrounds of learners. This approach helps to make learning more relevant and engaging for students from diverse backgrounds.

Inclusive Language and Representation

The use of inclusive language and the representation of diverse groups in teaching materials are emphasized. This includes the depiction of people from various racial, ethnic, and cultural backgrounds, as well as those with different abilities and sexual orientations, in a respectful and accurate manner.

Professional Development for Educators

The CAPS curriculum includes guidelines and resources for teacher training that focus on diversity and inclusion. This professional development aims to equip educators with the knowledge and skills to address diversity issues effectively in the classroom.

Assessment and Evaluation

The assessment policies within CAPS are designed to be fair and inclusive, taking into account the diverse needs and circumstances of learners. This includes providing accommodations for students with disabilities and ensuring that assessment tools do not discriminate against any group.

Community Engagement

The curriculum encourages schools to engage with the broader community to promote understanding and respect for diversity. This can involve partnerships with community organizations, cultural events, and initiatives that celebrate the richness of South Africa's diverse society.

However, engagement with LGBTQIA+ issues remain limited, particularly in rural areas. The Curriculum and Assessment Policy Statement serves as the blueprint for teaching and learning in South African schools, encompassing various subjects and grade levels. It outlines the content, skills, and assessment standards that educators should integrate into their teaching practices to facilitate meaningful learning experiences (Department of Basic Education, 2011). More importantly, CAPS is underpinned by a commitment to inclusivity, equity, and social justice, reflecting South Africa's journey towards a democratic and egalitarian society post-apartheid.

Diversity is a cornerstone of the CAPS curriculum, acknowledging the multifaceted identities, backgrounds, and experiences of South African learners (Francis, 2012). CAPS recognizes that diversity encompasses not only racial and ethnic differences but also factors such as socioeconomic status, language, culture, religion, gender identity, and ability (Francis, & Msibi, 2011). It emphasizes the importance of representing this diversity in educational materials, classroom discussions, and teaching methodologies to create an inclusive learning environment where all students feel valued and respected (Department of Basic Education, 2011).

CAPS promotes diversity through Inclusive Content, CAPS encourages the integration of diverse perspectives, histories, and cultural narratives across all subject areas. By incorporating content that reflects the lived experiences of various demographic groups, educators can validate students' identities and broaden their understanding of the world (Department of Basic Education, 2011).

Social justice lies at the heart of the CAPS curriculum, aiming to redress historical inequalities and empower marginalized communities through education. CAPS recognizes that access to quality education is a fundamental human right and a catalyst for social transformation. Therefore, it seeks to dismantle systemic barriers to learning and create pathways for equitable participation and achievement and foster understanding of different identities including the LGBTQ+ society (Department of Basic Education, 2011).

Challenges Faced by the LGBTQIA+ Community in Rural South Africa

Rural South Africa often holds conservative social views, with strong adherence to traditional gender roles and heteronormativity. This creates a hostile environment for the LGBTQIA+ community, leading to:

Social Stigma and Discrimination: In rural communities, adherence to traditional gender roles and heteronormative expectations is often deeply ingrained. LGBTQIA+ individuals may face ostracization, verbal abuse, or even physical violence due to their sexual orientation or gender identity (Human Rights Watch, 2019). Fear of being rejected by their families or communities may lead to isolation and psychological distress among LGBTQIA+ individuals in rural areas (Herek, 2012).

Limited Access to Support Services: Compared to urban centers, rural areas in South Africa often lack LGBTQIA+-specific support services and resources. Counseling, healthcare, and advocacy organizations may be scarce or nonexistent, leaving LGBTQIA+ individuals without essential support networks (Human Rights Watch, 2019). This lack of access exacerbates the challenges faced by rural LGBTQIA+ individuals, particularly concerning mental health and well-being (Itaborahy, 2012).

Economic Marginalization: Economic opportunities in rural areas are often limited, particularly for marginalized groups such as LGBTQIA+ individuals. Discrimination in the workplace based on sexual orientation or gender identity can lead to unemployment or underemployment (Meyer, 2017). For LGBTQIA+ youth, the prospect of leaving rural areas in search of employment and acceptance in urban centers may pose significant challenges, including financial barriers and the risk of further marginalization.

Inadequate Legal Protections: While South African law prohibits discrimination based on sexual orientation and gender identity, enforcement in rural areas may be lax or nonexistent. LGBTQIA+ individuals may be reluctant to report instances of discrimination or hate crimes due to fear of reprisal or lack of confidence in the legal system (Human Rights Watch, 2019). This lack of effective legal recourse further undermines the safety and security of LGBTQIA+ individuals in rural communities.

Cultural and Religious Resistance: Traditional cultural and religious beliefs often perpetuate negative attitudes towards LGBTQIA+ individuals in rural South Africa. These beliefs may view non-heteronormative identities as immoral or unnatural, contributing to the marginalization and exclusion of LGBTQIA+ individuals (Human Rights Watch, 2019). Breaking free from these deeply entrenched cultural norms can be challenging and may require concerted efforts to promote education and dialogue within rural communities.

The challenges faced by the LGBTQIA+ community in rural South Africa are complex and multifaceted, rooted in a combination of social, economic, cultural, and legal factors. Addressing these challenges requires a holistic approach that acknowledges the intersectionality of identities and experiences within rural communities (Msibi, 2012). Efforts to combat social stigma, improve access to support services, promote economic empowerment, strengthen legal protections, and foster dialogue on diversity and inclusion are essential steps towards creating safer and more inclusive environments for LGBTQIA+ individuals in rural South Africa (South African Government, 2022).

The Limited Representation of LGBTQIA+ Issues in the CAPS Curriculum

CAPS serves as the guiding framework for education in South Africa, aiming to provide learners with a comprehensive and inclusive educational experience. However, despite the progressive strides made in promoting diversity and social justice within the CAPS curriculum, there remains a notable gap in the representation of LGBTQIA+ issues. Limited Understanding: Students are not equipped with the knowledge and empathy needed to understand and accept LGBTQIA+ individuals (Sauntson, 2013).

The CAPS curriculum is designed to provide learners with the knowledge, skills, and values necessary to navigate an increasingly complex and interconnected world. It encompasses various subjects and grade levels, outlining the content, teaching methodologies, and assessment standards for each learning area (Department of Basic Education, 2011). While CAPS emphasizes the importance of inclusivity, diversity, and social justice, the representation of LGBTQIA+ issues within the curriculum remains minimal (Van Klinken, A. S., & Gunda, 2012).

The limited representation of LGBTQIA+ issues in the CAPS curriculum contributes to the erasure of LGBTQIA+ identities and experiences in educational settings. By failing to acknowledge the existence and validity of diverse sexual orientations and gender identities, the curriculum perpetuates a heteronormative and cisnormative worldview that marginalizes LGBTQIA+ learners (Epprecht, 2012).

Education plays a crucial role in challenging stereotypes, combating prejudice, and promoting acceptance of diversity. However, the absence of LGBTQIA+ content in the CAPS curriculum deprives learners of opportunities to engage critically with issues such as homophobia, transphobia, and gender-based discrimination (Russell & McGuire, 2008). This lack of education perpetuates ignorance and perpetuates harmful attitudes towards LGBTQIA+ individuals.

The absence of LGBTQIA+ representation in the curriculum can have detrimental effects on the well-being and academic achievement of LGBTQIA+ learners. Without access to affirming and inclusive education, LGBTQIA+ students may experience feelings of invisibility, shame, and isolation, leading to increased rates of absenteeism, mental health issues, and dropout (Kosciw et al., 2016).

South Africa is a diverse and multicultural society, where LGBTQIA+ individuals are integral members of communities across the country. The limited representation of LGBTQIA+ issues in the CAPS curriculum fails to reflect the lived realities of many learners and perpetuates a narrow understanding of human diversity (Russell & McGuire, 2008).

Perpetuation of Prejudice: Silence on LGBTQIA+ issues allow existing prejudices to continue unchallenged.

The Inadequacy of Current Strategies in Rural Communities, efforts to promote LGBTQ+ inclusion and acceptance have gained momentum globally, but significant challenges persist, particularly in rural communities. Despite progress in some areas, the strategies implemented to foster LGBTQ+ inclusion in rural settings often fall short of addressing the complex intersection of cultural, social, and economic factors.

Rural communities are often characterized by conservative social norms, limited access to resources, and close-knit social structures. These factors can contribute to heightened stigma, discrimination, and marginalization of LGBTQ+ individuals (Mogul, Ritchie, & Whitlock, 2011). Moreover, the lack of LGBTQ+-specific support services and advocacy organizations in rural areas further exacerbates the challenges faced by LGBTQ+ individuals seeking acceptance and affirmation.

Many rural communities lack access to comprehensive and inclusive information about LGBTQ+ identities and issues. Current strategies often focus on raising awareness through mainstream media campaigns or educational initiatives, but these efforts may not effectively reach rural populations (Ryan et al., 2010). Without access to accurate and culturally sensitive information, misconceptions and stereotypes about LGBTQ+ individuals persist, perpetuating stigma and prejudice.

LGBTQ+ individuals in rural communities often face significant barriers in accessing LGBTQ+-specific support services, such as counseling, healthcare, and community centers. The scarcity of resources and trained professionals in rural areas leaves LGBTQ+ individuals without essential support networks (Grossman et al., 2019). Moreover, the fear of being ostracized or outed may prevent individuals from seeking help, further isolating them from necessary support.

Traditional cultural and religious beliefs prevalent in rural communities may contribute to resistance towards LGBTQ+ inclusion efforts. Prevailing attitudes that view non-heteronormative identities as immoral or unnatural can hinder acceptance and affirmation of LGBTQ+ individuals (Dahlhamer et al., 2016). Current strategies often fail to address these deeply entrenched beliefs and may even inadvertently reinforce them through insensitive or culturally inappropriate messaging. There's a lack of clear information on how the CAPS principles of diversity and social justice translate into concrete strategies for addressing LGBTQIA+ issues in rural schools.

The inadequacy of current strategies in rural communities to promote LGBTQ+ inclusion underscores the need for more holistic and context-specific approaches. Efforts to foster LGBTQ+ acceptance and affirmation must address the complex interplay of cultural, social, economic, and legal factors that shape the experiences of LGBTQ+ individuals in rural contexts. By centering the voices and needs of LGBTQ+ individuals in rural communities and collaborating with local stakeholders, policymakers, and advocacy organizations can develop more effective strategies that create safer, more inclusive, and more supportive environments for all individuals, regardless of sexual orientation or gender identity.

CAPS Heteronormative Framework:

The limited representation of LGBTQIA+ issues in South Africa's Curriculum and Assessment Policy Statement (CAPS) has been a point of concern, given the country's progressive constitution which guarantees equality for all, irrespective of sexual orientation or gender identity. Despite these legal protections, the educational system, particularly the CAPS curriculum, has not kept pace with these ideals, often excluding or marginalizing LGBTQIA+ identities in key areas such as sex education and Life Orientation.

One of the primary issues is the heteronormative framework within the CAPS curriculum, which shapes the way relationships, families, and gender roles are taught (Francis, 2019). The curriculum tends to focus on heterosexual family structures and avoids discussing diverse sexual orientations or gender identities, reinforcing traditional gender roles and excluding the lived experiences of LGBTQIA+ learners. This erasure leads to the invisibility of these identities within the school system, contributing to feelings of isolation among LGBTQIA+ students (Msibi, 2012).

Moreover, the absence of comprehensive LGBTQIA+ education is problematic. CAPS do not explicitly cover topics such as sexual orientation, gender identity, or the struggles faced by LGBTQIA+ individuals (DePalma & Francis, 2014). As a result, students are deprived of critical knowledge about sexual and gender diversity. This lack of inclusion contributes to misinformation, ignorance, and the perpetuation of stigma and discrimination (Mavhandu-Mudzusi & Sandy, 2015). Without structured discussions on LGBTQIA+ issues, there is little space for students to learn about the diversity of identities and the importance of respect and understanding.

Sex education under CAPS also presents significant gaps. The curriculum lacks inclusive sex education for LGBTQIA+ learners, failing to address their specific health and emotional needs (Francis, 2019). There is little discussion on safe sex practices for LGBTQIA+ individuals, or mental health challenges they may face, such as bullying and exclusion due to their sexual or gender identity. By ignoring these realities, the curriculum indirectly signals that the issues facing LGBTQIA+ learners are unimportant or irrelevant, exacerbating the struggles these students face in navigating their sexual identity in a heteronormative environment.

Life Orientation (LO), which is the subject where topics related to social development and sexuality are taught, presents a missed opportunity for inclusivity. While LO has the potential to foster conversations about diversity, inclusivity, and human rights, CAPS does not provide explicit guidelines on teaching LGBTQIA+ topics (Francis & Reygan, 2016). Teachers are left to navigate these discussions on their own, often skipping them due to lack of training, personal discomfort, or societal pressure (Soudien, 2012). This leads to inconsistent teaching, where LGBTQIA+ issues are either inadequately addressed or ignored altogether, further perpetuating the silence around these identities in classrooms.

Furthermore, many teachers express discomfort or lack of preparedness when dealing with LGBTQIA+ topics (Francis, 2017). Personal beliefs, lack of professional development, and the influence of societal or cultural norms often prevent educators from effectively addressing LGBTQIA+ issues, even when they arise in the classroom (Reygan, 2019). This lack of teacher training on inclusivity creates an environment where LGBTQIA+ learners feel unsupported and misunderstood, which in turn impacts their academic performance and mental well-being (Mavhandu-Mudzusi, 2016).

The limited representation of LGBTQIA+ issues in the CAPS curriculum has far-reaching consequences for LGBTQIA+ students in South African schools. The curriculum's heteronormative focus, coupled with inadequate teacher training and lack of inclusive sex education, contributes to the marginalization of LGBTQIA+ identities in education. To ensure that all students are respected and valued, there is a critical need for CAPS to integrate comprehensive LGBTQIA+ education, along with teacher training to foster inclusive learning environments.

Current Strategies in Promoting LGBTQIA+ Understanding in Rural Communities

In rural South Africa, strategies promoting LGBTQIA+ understanding are seeing some positive impact, though they face significant hurdles. One of the main efforts is the National Intervention Strategy for the LGBTI Sector, a government-led initiative focused on public education and raising awareness about LGBTQIA+ rights. This strategy aims to counter homophobia and promote inclusivity by engaging with rural communities to shift traditional views and address societal prejudice (South African Government, 2023).

Additionally, non-governmental organizations (NGOs) are instrumental in advocating for LGBTQIA+ rights in rural areas. They provide educational workshops, support groups, and community engagement programs. These initiatives are often community-led, with NGOs working closely with local leaders and residents to foster understanding and tolerance. For example, OUT LGBT Well-being and Triangle Project have played significant roles in promoting LGBTQIA+ visibility and providing healthcare and legal support to rural populations (Polity, 2020).

In the healthcare sector, efforts are being made to improve access to LGBTQIA+-friendly care in rural settings by training healthcare workers to offer inclusive services. Research has highlighted the importance of training providers to ensure LGBTQIA+ individuals feel safe and respected when accessing health services. For example, programs have been developed to sensitize health professionals on LGBTQIA+ issues, which has shown promise in reducing healthcare-related discrimination in rural areas (Rural Health Research Gateway, 2022).

While these strategies are effective in some areas, they still face challenges such as cultural resistance, lack of resources, and ongoing stigmatization, which limit the broader success of these efforts. Sustained engagement, funding, and community-driven advocacy are crucial to ensuring long-term progress.

Recommendations for Improvement

To truly advance diversity and social justice for the LGBTQIA+ community in rural South Africa, the CAPS curriculum needs significant improvements:

- Curriculum Revision: Integrate age-appropriate content that introduces LGBTQIA+ identities and challenges heteronormative assumptions.
- Teacher Training: Provide teachers with comprehensive training on LGBTQIA+ issues, equipping them to handle the topic sensitively and effectively in the classroom.

- Community Engagement: Engage with rural communities to address cultural sensitivities and foster a more inclusive environment for LGBTQIA+ individuals.
- Safe Spaces: Create safe spaces within schools where students can explore their identities and receive support without fear of discrimination.
- Collaboration: Collaborate with LGBTQIA+ organizations to develop resources and strategies for educators in rural settings.

CONCLUSION

The CAPS curriculum holds the potential to be a powerful tool for promoting diversity and social justice. However, its current approach falls short in addressing the needs of the LGBTQIA+ community, particularly in rural areas. By implementing the recommendations outlined above, the CAPS curriculum can become a more inclusive and equitable learning environment for all students, fostering acceptance and understanding of the LGBTQIA+ community.

REFERENCES

DePalma, R., & Francis, D. A. (2014). Silence, nostalgia, violence, poverty...: What does 'culture' mean for South African sexuality educators? *Culture, Health & Sexuality*, 16(5), 547–561. DOI: 10.1080/13691058.2014.891050 PMID: 24654938

Francis, D. A. (2012). Teacher positioning on the teaching of sexual diversity in South African schools. *Culture, Health & Sexuality*, 14(6), 597–611. DOI: 10.1080/13691058.2012.674558 PMID: 22574876

Francis, D. A. (2017). Homophobia and sexuality diversity in South African schools: A review. *Journal of LGBT Youth*, 14(4), 307–323. DOI: 10.1080/19361653.2017.1326868

Francis, D. A. (2019). "You know the homophobic stuff is not in me, like us, it comes from the community": The influence of broader social attitudes on South African teachers' attitudes toward homosexuality. *Sex Education*, 19(4), 413–427.

Francis, D. A., & Msibi, T. (2011). Teaching about heterosexism: Challenging homophobia in South Africa. *Journal of LGBT Youth*, 8(2), 157–173. DOI: 10.1080/19361653.2011.553713

Francis, D. A., & Reygan, F. (2016). *Sexuality, society & pedagogy*. Bloomsbury Publishing.

GenderDynamix. GenderIdentity&Gender ExpressioninSouthAfrica: School'sManual.

Herek, G. (2012). Homosexuality and mental health. *Sexual Orientation: Science, Education, and Policy*. Retrieved from http://psychology.ucdavis.edu/rainbow/html/facts_mental_health.html#note1_text

Itaborahy, L. (2012). State-sponsored homophobia: *A world survey of laws criminalising same-sex sexual acts between consenting adults*. Retrieved from http://www.irnweb.org/en/resources/chapters/view/state-sponsored-homophobia-aworld-survey-of-laws-criminalising-same-sex-sexual-acts-between-consentingadults

Maphanga, Canny. Transgender activistAreMphela foundmurdered,boyfriendquestioned, Mavhandu-Mudzusi, A. H. (2016). Experiences of lesbian, gay, bisexual, transgender and intersex students regarding sports participation in a South African rural-based university. *S.A. Journal for Research in Sport Physical Education and Recreation*, 38(2), 111–120.

Msibi, T. (2012). "I'm used to it now": Experiences of homophobia among queer youth in South African township schools. *Gender and Education*, 24(5), 515–533. DOI: 10.1080/09540253.2011.645021

Msibi, T. (2012). 'I'm used to it now': Experiences of homophobia among queer youth in South African township schools. *Gender and Education*, 24(5), 515–533. DOI: 10.1080/09540253.2011.645021

news24. 09 January 2020. Available: https://www.news24.com/news24/southafrica/news/transgender-activist-nare-mphelafound-murdered-boyfriend-questioned-20200109

Polity. (2020). South Africa's National LGBTI Strategy. Retrieved from Polity

Reygan, F. (2019). Challenging homophobia and heteronormativity in South African schools. In *Research Handbook on Gender*. Sexuality and the Law.

Rural Health Research Gateway. (2022). *Improving Access to LGBTQIA+-Friendly Care in Rural Areas*. Retrieved from Rural Health Research Gateway.

Sauntson, H. (2013). Sexual diversity and illocutionary silencing in the English National Curriculum. *Sex Education: Sexuality, Society and Learning*, 13, 395–408. Town. 22.

South African Government. (2023). LGBTQIA+ Public Education Campaigns. Retrieved from gov.za

Van Klinken, A. S., & Gunda, M. R. (2012). Taking up the cudgels against gay rights? Trends and trajectories in African Christian theologies on homosexuality. *Journal of Homosexuality*, 59(1), 114–138. DOI: 10.1080/00918369.2012.638549 PMID: 22269050

Van Schie, K. (2012). Lesbian stands up to attackers. The Star. Retrieved from http://www.iol.co.za/the-star/lesbian-stands-up-to-attackers-1.1351609#.UJfE22c4Hbh

Van Schie, K. (2012). Lesbian stands up to attackers. *The Star*. Retrieved from http://www.iol.co.za/the-star/lesbian-stands-up-to-attackers-1.1351609#.UJfE22c4Hbh

Chapter 10
Integrating Universal Design in Education Policy Through Technological Solutions:
Breaking Barriers

Ashish Kumar Parashar
Department of Civil Engineering, School of Studies Engineering and Technology, Guru Ghasidas Vishwavidyalaya, India

Sudheera Mannepalli
Department of Pharmaceutical Engineering, B.V. Raju Institute of Technology, India

V. Manimegalai
Department of Management Studies, Nandha Engineering College (Autonomous), India

B. Priyadharishini
Department of English, Kongu Engineering College, India

S. Muruganandham
Department of Mathematics, Erode Arts and Science College, India

ABSTRACT

The need to adopt universal design principles has been described to build inclusive learning environments in a technologically varied world. It is highlighting the importance of accessibility, adaptability, and inclusion while establishing educational

DOI: 10.4018/979-8-3693-4058-5.ch010

Copyright © 2025, IGI Global. Copying or distributing in print or electronic forms without written permission of IGI Global is prohibited.

policy. Through case studies and best practices, the chapter studies how technology might enhance educational opportunities, particularly for children with disabilities. Effective Universal Design implementations, the consequences for policy, and how to incorporate the ideas of Universal Design into financial priorities, teacher preparation programs, and educational standards are also discussed. Universal Design could affect financial priorities, teacher preparation programs, and educational standards, as illustrated in this chapter. The new technologies, providing a framework for using technology strategically, are discussed to promote cross-sector collaboration and advance universal design.

INTRODUCTION

A framework known as Universal Design in Education (UDE) seeks to provide inclusive learning settings that meet the various requirements of every student. Drawing on the tenets of Universal Design, Universal Design Education (UDE) prioritizes the development of inclusive, captivating, and productive learning environments for individuals of different capacities and backgrounds. This strategy is essential in the varied educational environment of today. The idea of "universal design" in education places a strong emphasis on the use of many media for interaction, action and expression, and representation. To accommodate a range of learning styles and aptitudes, it entails delivering information and content in a variety of methods, including visual aids, audio resources, and hands-on exercises. This method guarantees that students with cognitive, auditory, or visual impairments can take part completely in the educational process(McKenzie & Dalton, 2020).

UDE encourages the use of alternative assessment techniques, such as projects, digital media, and oral presentations, to provide students a more accurate indication of their comprehension and to foster a sense of agency and ownership over their education. Conventional evaluation methods, which frequently involve written exams and essays, could not fairly represent the skills of all pupils. By focusing on students' interests and presenting suitable challenges, the many methods of engagement principle in education aims to engage and motivate pupils. Including real-world subject applications, giving students choices in their learning activities, and giving frequent feedback are all ways to improve engagement. Students' motivation is maintained and active engagement is encouraged in this dynamic and engaging learning environment(Galkiene & Monkeviciene, 2021).

In order to implement universal design in education, we must move from seeing pupils as deficiencies to appreciating their range of assets and skills. It entails anticipatory planning and design, recognizing and resolving any learning obstacles early on. In addition to helping students with impairments, this proactive approach fosters a more welcoming and encouraging learning environment. The effective implementation of Universal Design Education (UDE) is contingent upon technological breakthroughs, as students with disabilities are supported by assistive technology such as screen readers and adaptive learning platforms. Additionally, these technologies make it simple to customize digital information, increasing accessibility and flexibility in education and promoting an inclusive learning environment for all students(Zhang et al., 2024a).

A revolutionary strategy in education, universal design seeks to provide fair and welcoming learning environments for every student. Various modes of representation, action, expression, and interaction are integrated, guaranteeing that a wide range of learning requirements is met. With the help of technology developments and UDE's proactive approach, every student is guaranteed the chance to excel and realize their full potential. Adopting Universal Design principles will be essential as education institutions change. The way information is taught and gained in the current educational system is being revolutionized by technology, which is improving learning opportunities and democratizing access to make it more accessible and equal(Bradshaw, 2020).

With the use of technology in education, accessibility has greatly increased, removing geographical boundaries and granting students from underprivileged and rural places access to high-quality instruction. An international learning community is fostered via online platforms such as Massive Open Online Courses (MOOCs). With the use of assistive technology, students with visual, auditory, and motor disabilities may now fully participate in the educational process by having access to learning materials. Examples of these technologies include screen readers, speech-to-text software, and adaptable keyboards(O'Neill, 2021).

Through adaptive learning technologies, which employ data analytics to adjust material to individual student learning styles and paces, technology in education provides the personalization of learning experiences. By focusing on each person's unique strengths and shortcomings, this method increases engagement and boosts learning results. Algorithms are used by platforms such as Coursera and Khan Academy to suggest exercises and other materials depending on student performance. Technology, through interactive tools like as discussion boards, collaborative papers, and virtual classrooms, fosters critical thinking and collaborative learning. These platforms promote teamwork, idea sharing, and project collaboration among students, simulating real-world situations. Technology also gives kids access to a wide range of resources, allowing them to critically assess sources, do research, and analyze data—all of which help them develop their analytical and problem-solving abilities(O'Neill, 2021).

The use of technology in the classroom has greatly enhanced instructional strategies and given teachers access to digital resources that can be used to improve instruction and better engage students. These resources, which accommodate various learning preferences and inspire students, include gamified learning experiences, virtual laboratories, and multimedia presentations. Through online materials and courses, technology also makes it easier for educators to continue their professional development(Pinna et al., 2020).

Technology is essential to lifelong learning because it makes it possible for people to learn new things in a world that moves quickly. All ages may benefit from flexible learning options provided by e-learning platforms, smartphone apps, and digital libraries, which help people adjust to changing labor market demands and develop a workforce capable of thriving in a quickly changing technological context(Kelly et al., 2022).

The digital divide, data privacy, and insufficient teacher preparation are some of the obstacles that face the incorporation of technology in education. It is essential to guarantee fair access to technology and the internet in order to stop marginalization of underprivileged communities. Robust regulations that safeguard students' information and privacy help foster an inclusive, dynamic, and productive learning environment.

FOUNDATIONS OF UNIVERSAL DESIGN IN EDUCATION

Principles of Universal Design

The Universal Design in Education (UDE) program applies the principles of Universal Design, which have their roots in architecture, to the creation of inclusive and useful learning environments that are accessible to all people, regardless of their abilities or disabilities. All students should have equal access to educational resources and settings to ensure that no one is left out of the learning process. In order to accommodate various learning requirements and styles, this idea promotes the use of a variety of teaching techniques and resources. For learning resources to be inclusive and accessible to all students, regardless of background, subject matter, or language proficiency, they must be clear, concise, and easy to use(Rozeboom, 2021).

The essay underscores the significance of accessibility in education, encompassing children with sensory impairments, by utilizing several forms such as tactile, visual, and aural. It also highlights the necessity of creating an atmosphere that requires little physical exertion and makes sure that activities are made to be both comfortable and effective, especially for students who have physical limitations. The text also emphasizes the need for appropriate space for approach, reach, manipulation, and use, regardless of the student's body size, posture, or mobility(Rozeboom, 2021).

Historical Context and Evolution

With the intention of establishing accessible surroundings for all people, universal design in education (UD) had its start in the late 20th century, mostly in the field of architecture. Architect Ronald Mace understood that inclusive design was essential. The 1990s saw the introduction of UD concepts into education as a result of the rising awareness of the shortcomings of conventional methods and the demands of varied learners. The United States' Individuals with Disabilities Education Act (IDEA) was essential in advancing inclusive education and standing up for the rights of children with disabilities, which ultimately resulted in the integration of UD concepts into educational environments(Law et al., 2020a).

With an objective to establish inclusive, engaging, and productive learning environments for all students, regardless of individual characteristics, UDE's focus has expanded to incorporate cognitive and emotional accessibility.

Important Theories and Models

The foundation of universal design in education is made up of a number of theories and models, some of which are important and offer a framework for carrying out its ideas(Pinna et al., 2020).

- **Universal Design for Learning (UDL)**: The UDL framework, created by the Center for Applied Special Technology (CAST), directs the creation of learning objectives, evaluations, techniques, and resources. Three fundamental tenets of UDL are action and expression, representation, and different modes of involvement. This method takes into account the differences in the requirements and preferences of learners to guarantee that every student has an equal opportunity to study.
- **Differentiated Instruction**: According to this paradigm, training should be customized to each student's unique needs. Adapting the curriculum, procedures, end products, and learning environment to each student's readiness level, interests, and learning profile is known as differentiated education. This strategy is in line with UDE's flexibility concept.
- **Response to Intervention (RTI)**: RTI is a multi-tiered strategy for early detection and assistance of kids who require assistance with their behavior and/or learning. In order to increase student accomplishment and decrease behavioral issues, it incorporates evaluation and intervention into a multi-level

preventive approach. Through ensuring that each student receives the right amount of help based on their unique requirements, RTI offers a framework for implementing UDE.
- **Assistive Technology**: UDE relies heavily on the usage of assistive technologies. Learning experiences can be greatly improved by the use of equipment and tools made specifically for people with impairments. The concepts of equitable usage and visible information are supported by assistive technology, which ranges from interactive whiteboards to speech-to-text software.

In order to provide a flexible, welcoming, and encouraging learning environment that meets the requirements of a wide range of students, universal design in education integrates ideas and models. This shows a dedication to educational quality and equity.

TECHNOLOGICAL SOLUTIONS ENHANCING UNIVERSAL DESIGN

Figure 1. Technological solutions enhancing universal design

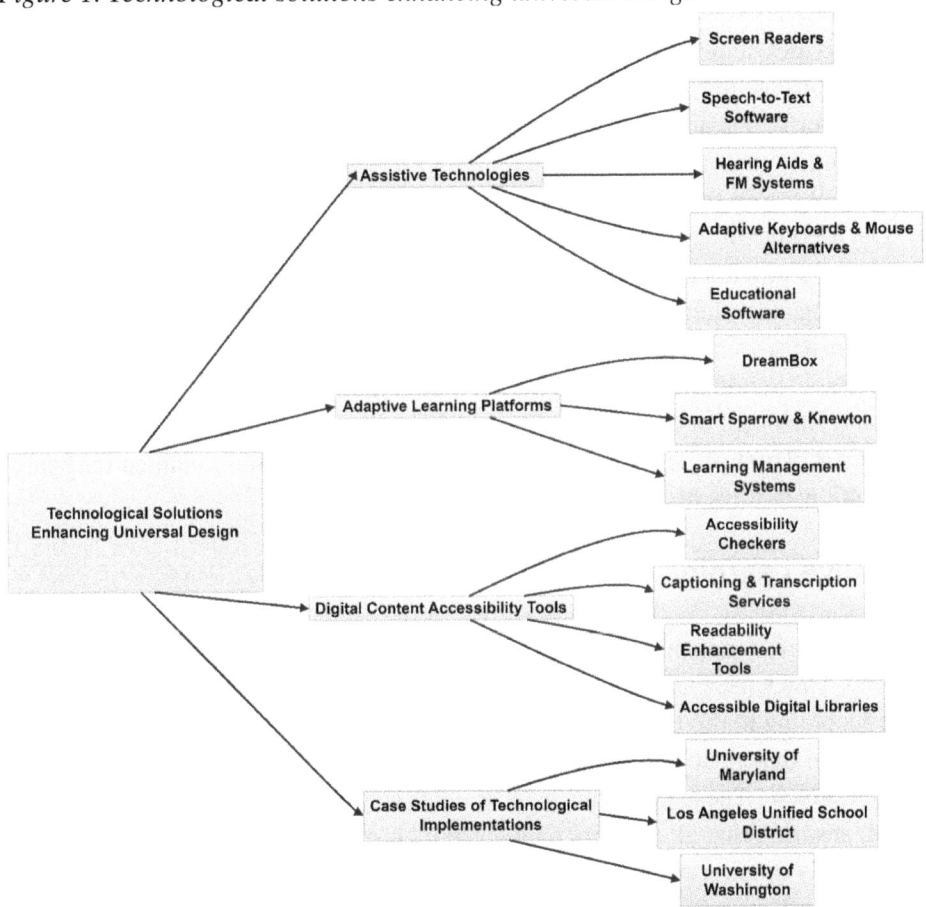

The four primary categories of technology solutions that improve Universal Design in Education are Assistive Technologies, Adaptive Learning Platforms, Digital Content Accessibility Tools, and Case Studies of technology Implementations. These categories are shown in a flowchart in Figure 1.

Assistive Technologies

In order to better implement Universal Design in Education (UDE), assistive technology (AT) are crucial for meeting the various requirements of students with disabilities. These tools make it easier to get instructional materials, take part in class activities, and succeed academically. For visually challenged students, screen readers translate text on the screen into voice or Braille so they may interact with digital information and take part in online learning settings. For those with physical or learning limitations, speech-to-text software transcribes spoken words into written text, making note-taking and writing tasks easier(Kelly et al., 2022).

Devices known as assistive technologies (AT) facilitate technological interaction for students who have hearing or movement limitations. These include FM systems and hearing aids, alternate keyboards and mice that are adaptable, and instructional software such as text-to-speech applications. By reading aloud digital material, these devices assist children who struggle with reading in developing their comprehension and fluency. For kids who struggle with speech, assistive technology (AAC) equipment like voice-generating machines and symbol-based communication boards offer alternate ways of communicating.

Adaptive Learning Platforms

Personalized education has advanced significantly with adaptive learning systems, which use data analytics and algorithms to modify course content in real-time according to the needs of each individual student. DreamBox, a mathematics application that customizes courses to fit each student's individual learning path, is one example. These platforms help students stay engaged and grow at their own speed, ensuring that all learners may reach their maximum potential. They do this by regularly monitoring performance and offering the proper amount of challenge and support(Heyer, 2021).

Adaptive learning technologies are used by Knewton and Smart Sparrow to provide engaging learning environments. They provide individualized content to improve comprehension and retention after analyzing student interactions to pinpoint learning gaps and strengths. These platforms support a variety of learning types, such as kinesthetic, auditory, and visual learners, which promotes inclusion. They guarantee that all students, including those with disabilities, have access to successful and interesting educational experiences by providing a variety of teaching methodologies.

Digital Content Accessibility Tools

In order for Universal Design Education (UDE) to guarantee that all students can access and engage with digital educational resources, digital content accessibility solutions are essential. These resources, which include accessibility checkers, examine websites and digital documents for accessibility problems—like inadequate color contrast or missing alt text—and offer suggestions for fixes. With the aid of these resources, educators may produce digital material that complies with accessibility guidelines such as the Web material Accessibility Guidelines (WCAG)(Durairaj et al., 2023).

Students with hearing impairments can access information with the use of digital content accessibility solutions like Amara and Otter.ai, which provide automatic captioning and transcription services for audio and video recordings. Through the provision of written and visual representations of spoken material, these services also aid in learning. Tools for improving readability such as Read &Write and Bee-Line Reader alter the way text is presented by changing the font size, color, and reading recommendations. With features like highlighted text and synced audio, digital libraries such as Book-share provide accessible eBooks for students with visual and learning challenges.

Case Studies of Technological Implementations

One of the best examples of how technology may be used to enhance Universal Design for Education (UDE) is the University of Maryland. Accessibility and Disability Service (ADS) at the university provides students with other AT tools such as speech-to-text software and screen readers. In order to ensure that all digital information is inclusive and accessible, the institution also includes universal design principles into the creation of its courses. This strategy encourages diversity in education and supports the varied student body(Das et al., 2024).

DreamBox has been effectively incorporated into the mathematics curriculum of the Los Angeles Unified School District (LAUSD), improving student engagement and achievement. The efficacy of adaptive learning platforms in advancing inclusive education is demonstrated by this case study. With its DO-IT Center, which offers educators tools and training on producing accessible digital content, the University of Washington is a pioneer in developing accessible online learning environments. In order to serve students with disabilities, the center also creates guidelines and tools to assist teachers in making sure their courses adhere to accessibility requirements(Agrawal et al., 2023).

The case studies highlight how assistive technologies, adaptive learning platforms, and digital content accessibility tools can create inclusive learning environments, promoting equitable access and academic success. They also show how technological solutions have a transformative effect on Universal Distance Education (UDE).

BEST PRACTICES

Successful Integration in K-12 Education

Strategic planning, professional development, and ongoing evaluation are necessary for the effective implementation of Universal Design in Education (UDE) in K–12 education, along with the inclusion of important best practices(Prabhuswamy et al., 2024; Sharma et al., 2024).

Figure 2. Steps for integration in K-12 education

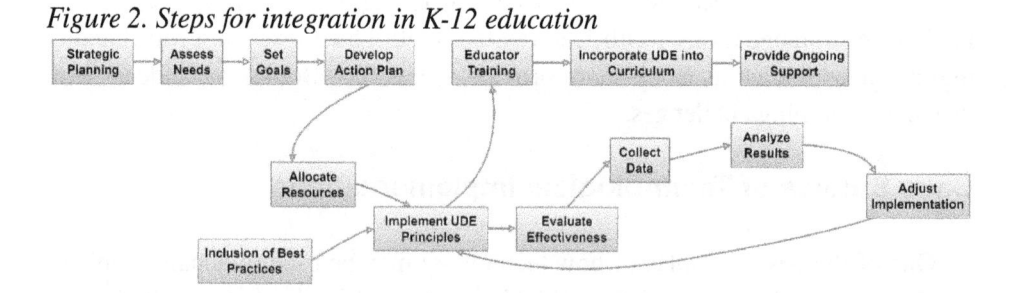

Figure 2 outlines the steps involved in successfully integrating UDE in K-12 education, from strategic planning to ongoing evaluation, with a focus on professional development and the incorporation of best practices.

a) **Teacher Training and Professional Development**: In addition to receiving sufficient training in UDE principles, educators also need to understand how to use digital content accessibility tools, assistive technology, and adaptive learning platforms. Programs for professional development should be continuous and should include seminars, practical instruction, and access to materials that facilitate the use of new technologies in the classroom.
b) **Collaborative Planning and Implementation**: Collaboration between IT experts, administrators, and educators is necessary for successful integration. To ensure that all stakeholders are included in the planning and supervision of the adoption of UDE technology, schools should form multidisciplinary teams.

c) **Pilot Programs and Scaling**: Schools can test new technologies on a limited scale before they are widely adopted by putting pilot programs into place. This method aids in identifying possible obstacles and honing tactics for wider application. Then, successful pilots may be expanded, facilitating a more seamless transition to complete integration.
d) **Student-Centered Approach**: Students' wants and choices should be the driving force for technology integration. Student input on a regular basis may help with tool selection and modification, making sure that the tools adequately serve a range of learning requirements and styles.
e) **Accessible Digital Resources**: The development and utilization of digital resources that adhere to accessibility guidelines has to be given top priority in schools. This entails offering captioned films, interactive information, and e-books that are accessible to all students, including those with impairments.

Higher Education Initiatives

Higher education institutions are adopting UDE, emphasizing inclusive learning environments with the use of new technology and best practices such as(Prabhuswamy et al., 2024; Venkatasubramanian et al., 2024):

a) **Inclusive Course Design**: UDE ideas have to be incorporated into course design from the beginning by universities. This entails developing accessible and adaptable curricula, resources, and evaluations that meet a variety of learning requirements. To do this, faculty education on accessibility guidelines and UDE principles is crucial.
b) **Technology-Enhanced Learning**: In order to provide tailored learning experiences, higher education institutions should invest in assistive technology and adaptive learning systems. Ensuring that all students can effectively engage with course content is possible with the use of tools like Learning Management Systems (LMS) that include built-in accessibility capabilities.
c) **Support Services and Resources**: Offering strong support services is essential to the adoption of UDE successfully. To support students with disabilities, universities should provide resources including accessible computer stations, assistive technology laboratories, and staff members who are committed to their work. Online portals that offer extensive accessibility materials and lessons can also enable students to make use of the technologies that are now available.
d) **Continuous Improvement and Evaluation**: Institutions of higher learning should set up systems for ongoing assessment and development of UDE procedures. This entails conducting frequent accessibility audits, gathering input

from students through surveys, and working with accessibility specialists to pinpoint areas that need improvement.
e) **Policy and Advocacy**: Universities ought to be leaders in promoting inclusive institutional and governmental policies. This entails creating and implementing regulations that require accessibility in all administrative and academic settings, encouraging an inclusive and equitable culture.

International Examples and Comparisons

The widespread use of UDE and technology-based solutions provides insightful information about best practices and demonstrates a variety of methods for using technology into education for inclusion(S. Saravanan et al., 2024).

- **Finland**: Personalized learning and inclusion are priorities in Finland, a country renowned for its cutting-edge educational system. Using resources like digital portfolios and interactive e-learning platforms, Finnish schools use technology to build flexible learning environments. Comprehensive modules on UDE and the use of assistive devices are included in Finnish teacher training programs, guaranteeing that teachers are prepared to accommodate a varied student body.
- **Australia**: Significant progress has been achieved by Australian institutions and schools in incorporating UDE concepts. The National Disability Strategy of the nation encourages inclusive education and is bolstered by programs such as the Digital Technologies Hub, which offers tools to educators for the accessible integration of technology. Australian universities, such as the University of Sydney, which is a leader in accessible practice and research, likewise prioritize developing inclusive online learning environments.
- **Japan**: In Japan, a crucial element of inclusive education is the use of technology to assist students with impairments. A variety of assistive technologies are used in schools, such as digital textbooks with integrated accessibility features and voice recognition software. Policies requiring accessible learning settings and subsidizing assistive technology development show the government's support for UDE.
- **Canada**: Canadian educational systems integrate technology to promote diversity and accessibility. Initiatives such as OCAD University's Inclusive Design Research Centre focus on creating and sharing accessible techniques and technology. Technology businesses and Canadian colleges and universities frequently work together to develop specialized solutions that cater to the various demands of their student bodies.

Analyzing global models can give educators and policymakers insights into practical approaches to combining technology with UDE, proving that inclusiveness, strategic planning, training, and ongoing development can greatly enhance student results.

POLICY IMPLICATIONS

Current Educational Policies and Frameworks

There is growing recognition of the need of inclusivity and accessibility in education, and several nations have passed laws to guarantee that students with disabilities receive the necessary accommodations and assistance. In the US, all children with disabilities are required to receive a free and suitable education under the Individuals with Disabilities Education Act (IDEA), and equal access to educational programs and activities is guaranteed under the Americans with Disabilities Act (ADA). The UK's Equality Act 2010 shields disabled individuals from discrimination, while the European Accessibility Act establishes guidelines for improving the accessibility of goods and services(A. Saravanan et al., 2022).

Universal Design for Learning (UDL), which promotes adaptable learning environments that meet a range of learning demands, serves as the foundation for the policies. For inclusive learning, UDL supports the use of a variety of representation, interaction, and expression techniques.

Gaps and Challenges in Existing Policies

Even with advancements, there are still large gaps in educational policies that prevent Universal Design in Education (UDE) from being fully implemented. The uneven implementation and enforcement of accessibility requirements in various locales and educational settings is one significant gap. While some colleges and universities have advanced significantly, others have not kept up because they lack funding, awareness, or dedication. A major obstacle is funding, as many schools find it difficult to set aside enough money for adaptive learning platforms and assistive technology, which makes it harder for them to offer inclusive learning environments.

One major issue is the dearth of thorough training provided to educators on assistive te(Venkatasubramanian et al., 2024)chnology and Universal Design for Education (UDE) principles. Even while accessibility regulations are mandated, they frequently get little support, which leaves many educators ill-prepared to put these standards into reality. Systemic obstacles, such a general lack of awareness and support for inclusive education, might cause educators, administrators, and legislators to oppose UDE adoption because they see it as an extra burden rather than a required development.

Strategies for Policy Improvement

It is possible to use strategies to improve educational frameworks and policies, which will increase their ability to support Universal Design in Education(O'Neill, 2021; Pinna et al., 2020).

Figure 3. Strategies to improve educational frameworks and policies

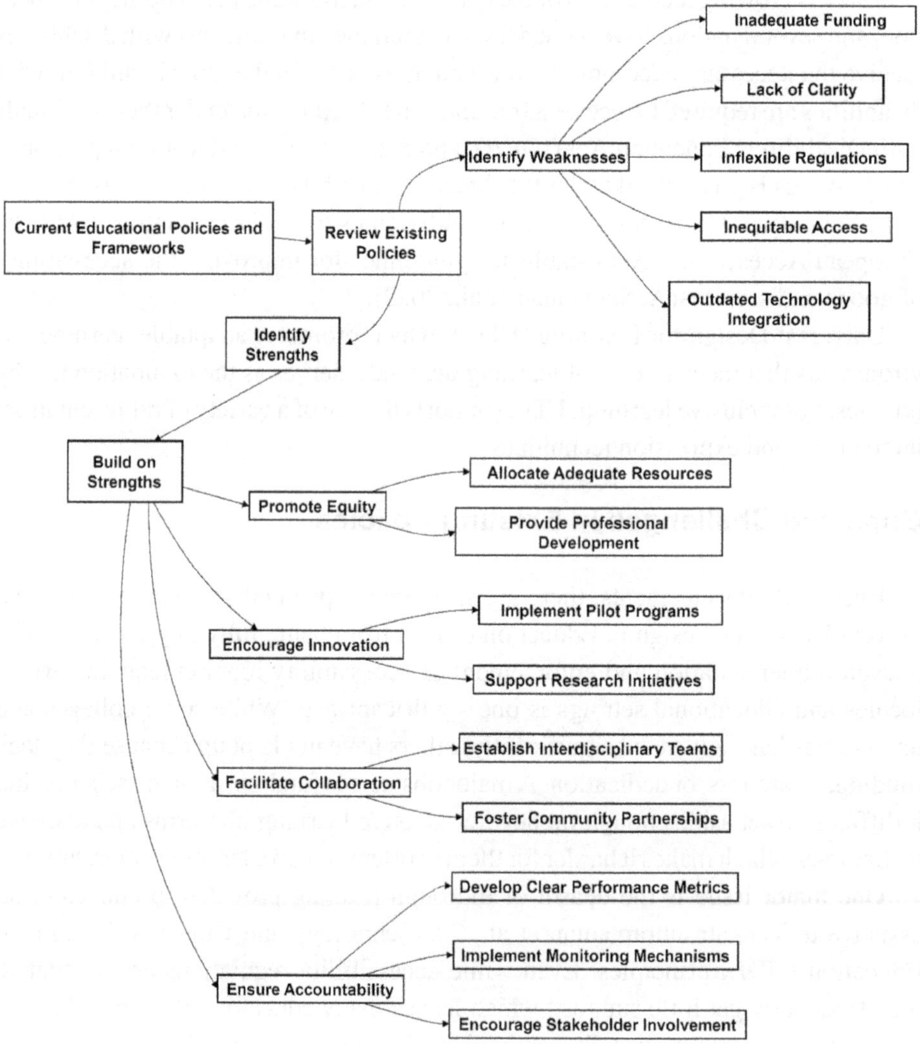

With an emphasis on issues including finance, clarity, flexibility, access, and technology integration, Figure 3 describes the procedure for evaluating the frameworks and regulations already in place for education, finding any gaps, and putting reform initiatives into action. It places a strong emphasis on enhancing strengths, advancing equity, stimulating creativity, fostering teamwork, and guaranteeing responsibility.

a) **Increased Funding and Resources**: Increased funding is needed to support governments and educational institutions in implementing UDE. This includes financing for teacher professional development, assistive technology, and flexible learning spaces. Grants and subsidies may be available to underfunded schools in order to ensure that they have the resources necessary to provide inclusive learning environments.

b) **Comprehensive Educator Training**: Policies should mandate that teachers keep up-to-date on UDE ideas and appropriate technology use during their professional development. Training programs that are integrated into teacher education curricula must to include experiential learning opportunities that are relevant and practical. Teachers will have the skills and confidence necessary to successfully implement inclusive practices as a result of this.

c) **Standardized Accessibility Guidelines**: To ensure consistency in UDE implementation, identical accessibility regulations should be enforced at all educational levels and standardized guidelines should be developed for them. For these guidelines to provide a clear framework for creating environments and resources that are accessible for education, they must be compliant with international standards, such as the Web Content Accessibility Guidelines (WCAG).

d) **Stakeholder Collaboration**: Policy should promote collaboration among educators, students, parents, technologists, and politicians. By working together, it is ensured that the needs and opinions of all parties involved are considered during the planning and execution of UDE initiatives. It may be necessary to create task forces or advisory groups to oversee and manage these projects.

e) **Awareness and Advocacy**: Raising public awareness of the benefits of UDE and the value of inclusive education is crucial. Legislators and leaders in education should support UDE by holding events, seminars, and public campaigns. By highlighting their positive outcomes, case studies and success stories might encourage a broader adoption of inclusive policies.

f) **Continuous Monitoring and Evaluation**: Establishing mechanisms for continuous monitoring and evaluation of UDE implementation can help identify areas for improvement and ensure accountability. Frequent audits, stakeholder input, and data-driven evaluations may offer insightful information about how well policies and procedures are working, which can inform future improvements.

By eliminating gaps and obstacles and establishing inclusive, egalitarian, and supportive learning environments, targeted initiatives can successfully promote the principles of Universal Design in Education and enable every student to realize their full potential.

DEVELOPING INCLUSIVE EDUCATION POLICIES

Figure 4. Developing inclusive education policies

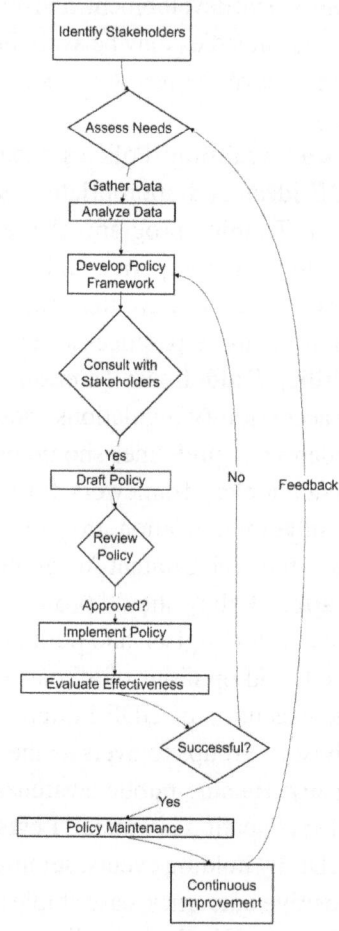

Figure 4 provides a structured approach to developing and maintaining inclusive education policies, ensuring they are responsive to the needs of all stakeholders and promote continuous improvement.

Integrating Universal Design Principles

To encourage inclusion and accessibility in learning spaces, education policy must incorporate Universal Design principles. Policies should require the application of UDE principles in instructional design, curriculum creation, and assessment procedures to guarantee that all students, with or without disabilities, have access to learning environments and resources(Galkiene & Monkeviciene, 2021; McNutt & Craddock, 2021a; Zhang et al., 2024a).

- Education legislation must to clearly mandate the use of Universal Design principles into every facet of education, ranging from designing lessons to creating physical spaces. This guarantees that UDE ceases to be an optional concern and instead becomes a basic component of educational practice.
- Curriculum Design: In keeping with the Universal Design for Learning (UDL) paradigm, policies ought to support the creation of curricula that integrate a variety of representational, interactive, and expressive mediums. This entails giving students access to a variety of assessment alternatives, providing other forms for the delivery of knowledge, and encouraging their participation through a variety of teaching techniques.
- Clear accessibility standards should be established via policies, drawing on global recommendations like the Web Content Accessibility Guidelines (WCAG). In order to guarantee that educational materials are accessible to pupils with diverse abilities, these requirements have to be applied to both digital and physical resources.

Teacher Training and Professional Development

Policies that prioritize inclusive education must provide teacher training and professional development in order to provide educators the tools they need to successfully use Universal Design principles in the classroom.

- UDE Training Programs: It should be required by policy for pre-service and in-service teacher education to include UDE training programs. UDE concepts, assistive technology, adaptive learning techniques, and designing accessible learning environments should all be included in these programs.
- Practical Workshops and Seminars: Funding and support should be made available by policies for practical workshops, seminars, and conferences centered around inclusive teaching methods and UDE. These gatherings give educators the chance to network with peers, exchange best practices, and gain knowledge from subject matter experts.

- Online Communities and Resources: Policies ought to encourage the growth of online communities and resources so that teachers may exchange materials, get information, and look for UDE-related assistance. Professional networking and continuous learning can be facilitated by social media groups, discussion forums, and online platforms.

Funding Priorities and Resource Allocation

Careful planning and budgetary distribution are necessary for inclusive education policies in order to uphold Universal Design principles and supply teachers, schools, and educational establishments with resources(Bradshaw, 2020; McNutt & Craddock, 2021a; O'Neill, 2021).

- Infrastructure for Accessibility: Funding should be set aside by policies for the creation and upkeep of accessible facilities in educational settings. This entails making investments in digital content development tools, accessible facilities, and assistive technology.
- Grants for Professional Development: Policies ought to offer financial assistance and grants to teachers so they may seek professional development in inclusive teaching methods and UDE. These awards can help with conference attendance, training program enrollment, and joint project involvement.
- fair Resource allocation: To guarantee that schools and districts serving underrepresented groups receive sufficient support for implementing UDE, policies should encourage fair resource allocation. This might be resource-sharing arrangements, grant programs, or focused financial campaigns.
- Research and Innovation Grants: Funding should be set aside by policies for innovative projects in the area of inclusive education, such as the creation of new instruments for assessment, instructional methodologies, and technology. Projects that investigate the efficacy of UDE implementation and pinpoint best practices may be funded by research grants.

Education policies that incorporate Universal Design principles, provide teacher training, and allocate resources efficiently can promote inclusive learning environments. By guaranteeing equal opportunity, these rules foster academic performance and fair educational opportunities for all children.

EMERGING TECHNOLOGIES AND FUTURE TRENDS

The personalized learning experiences, immersive surroundings, and easily available materials provided by emerging technologies such as AI, VR, and AR have the potential to completely transform inclusive education. By using these tools wisely, all kids may achieve academic, social, and emotional success(Kelly et al., 2022; Rozeboom, 2021).

Artificial Intelligence in Education

AI has the power to completely transform education by improving results, automating administrative duties, and customizing learning experiences. It can be especially helpful in inclusive education, meeting the different requirements of students with disabilities and offering customized support(Kelly et al., 2022; Rozeboom, 2021).

- Customized learning: Adaptive learning systems driven by artificial intelligence (AI) examine student data to tailor resources and learning pathways according to each learner's unique preferences, strengths, and learning styles. All students, including those with impairments, will be given the individualized attention they require to achieve.
- Assistive Technologies: With the help of artificial intelligence (AI), students with impairments may access educational information and engage in classroom activities more successfully. Examples of these technologies include speech recognition software, predictive text algorithms, and natural language processing tools. These tools can help students with a range of needs learn more effectively by offering real-time support with reading, writing, and communication assignments.
- Analytics and Intervention: Artificial intelligence algorithms are capable of sifting through vast amounts of educational data to find trends, patterns, and areas in need of improvement. AI-powered analytics can assist teachers in monitoring student progress, identifying obstacles to learning, and delivering focused interventions to assist difficult students in the context of inclusive education. This data-driven strategy makes it possible to identify children who might need more help early on and to provide timely interventions to meet their requirements.
- Language Translation and Accessibility: In order to foster inclusion in multicultural learning environments, AI-powered language translation solutions may help students from different linguistic backgrounds communicate and work together. Furthermore, AI-driven accessibility features ensure fair access to educational materials for students with disabilities by improving the

accessibility of digital information through features like audio descriptions and automated captioning.

Virtual and Augmented Reality

Technologies like augmented reality (AR) and virtual reality (VR) provide students with immersive learning experiences that improve understanding. VR and AR in inclusive education offer special chances for students with disabilities to creatively explore and engage with instructional materials(Revathi et al., 2024).

- Experiential learning: Through the use of VR and AR simulations, students may immerse themselves in learning settings that closely mimic real-world situations, bringing abstract ideas to life and enhancing their engagement. Virtual reality (VR) and augmented reality (AR) can offer inclusive learning experiences that support many sensory modalities and encourage students with disabilities to actively engage in classroom activities.
- Enhancements for Accessibility: Virtual reality and augmented reality technology may be tailored to meet the requirements of students with impairments, offering them other ways to engage and tactile input. For instance, students with visual impairments can benefit from tactile feedback and aural signals in VR settings, while students with difficulties with spatial awareness can benefit from real-time visual overlays in AR applications.
- Virtual Collaboration and Communication: Regardless of physical or geographic constraints, VR and AR platforms allow students to cooperate and communicate in virtual settings. For students with disabilities, these immersive communication technologies can help with peer relationships, group projects, and social learning experiences, creating a feeling of community and belonging in inclusive learning environments.
- Multisensory Stimulation and Exploration: Virtual reality and augmented reality may concurrently excite several senses, offering students with disabilities chances for multisensory learning. Customizable immersive environments enable students to experience instructional information in meaningful and engaging ways, according to individual sensory preferences and sensitivities.

Future Opportunities for Inclusive Education

New technologies such as AI, VR, and AR have the power to completely transform inclusive education and guarantee that every student has fair access to education(Prabhuswamy et al., 2024; Sharma et al., 2024; Venkatasubramanian et al.,

2024). A methodical strategy for utilizing cutting-edge technologies like AI, VR, and AR to improve inclusive education and guarantee equitable access to education for all students is shown in Figure 5.

Figure 5. Future opportunities for inclusive education

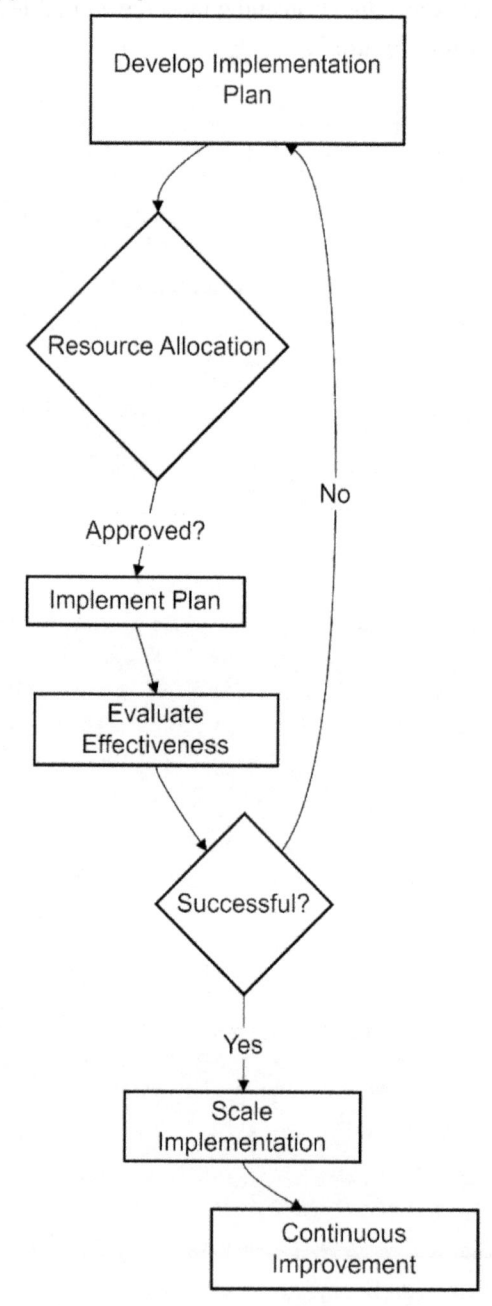

- Personalized Learning paths: As artificial intelligence (AI) continues to advance, more and more personalized learning paths that are tailored to the individual requirements, skills, and preferences of every student will be made available. Through these individualized learning opportunities, students will feel empowered to take charge of their education and realize their greatest potential.
- Immersive Learning Environments: As VR and AR technology proliferate and become more reasonably priced, it will be possible to design immersive learning environments that accommodate a variety of learning preferences and sensory modalities. Through interactive inquiry and discovery, these immersive experiences will help students retain and get a better knowledge of the material being taught.
- Educational Resources That Are Easy to Access: Students with disabilities will have better access to digital information and educational resources thanks to advancements in AI-driven accessibility solutions. Through the use of AI-powered speech recognition, text-to-speech, and language translation, educational materials will be accessible to students in their chosen language and format, removing obstacles to learning.
- Collaborative Learning Spaces: By enabling virtual cooperation and communication amongst students with different backgrounds and skill levels, VR and AR platforms will support inclusion and diversity in collaborative learning environments. Students will be able to collaborate on assignments, find solutions to issues, and exchange ideas in these virtual worlds' realistic, interactive settings.

RECOMMENDATIONS FOR POLICYMAKERS

The proposals seek to establish a more inclusive educational system that encourages every student to participate fully and reach their full potential, regardless of their circumstances, talents, or backgrounds. For this to have revolutionary potential, ongoing dedication, teamwork, and creativity are needed(Law et al., 2020b; Zhang et al., 2024b).

Policy Development and Implementation Strategies

a) Integrate Universal Design Principles: To guarantee that all students have fair access to learning opportunities, policymakers should include Universal Design principles into education legislation. This entails applying UDE concepts to

the creation of curricula, methods of instruction, and frameworks for assessments(Alquraini & Rao, 2020).
b) Flexibility and adaptation: To meet the varied requirements and preferences of learners, policies should place a high priority on flexibility and adaptation. This entails encouraging the use of adaptable teaching techniques, different approaches to evaluation, and learning paths that are tailored to the needs and skills of each unique student.
c) Inclusive Resource Allocation: To assist in the execution of inclusive education programs, policymakers should strategically allocate resources. This covers financing for efforts including stakeholders, accessibility improvements, professional development courses, and assistive technology.
d) Data-Driven Decision Making: In order to track advancement, pinpoint regions in need of development, and assess the results of inclusive education programs, policies have to support the application of data-driven decision-making techniques. In order to guide the creation and application of policies, this entails gathering and evaluating data on stakeholder input, accessibility measures, and student results.

Collaborative Approaches with Stakeholders

a) Involve Administrators and Teachers: To jointly develop inclusive education policy, legislators should work closely with administrators, teachers, and educational associations. In order to make sure that policies represent the needs and reality of the education community, this entails asking stakeholders for their opinions, views, and expertise(McNutt & Craddock, 2021b).
b) Parents and Students Should Be Empowered: Policies should enable parents and students to speak out in favor of inclusive education and take part in the decision-making process. Giving parents and students the chance to participate in committees, working groups, and policy advisory boards is one way to do this.
c) Form Partnerships with Community Organizations: To better utilize their knowledge and resources in advancing inclusive education, policymakers should establish alliances with advocacy groups, community organizations, and disability rights organizations. These collaborations can help with community outreach, awareness-raising, and capacity-building initiatives.
d) Work Together Across Government Agencies: To guarantee a coordinated approach to the creation and execution of inclusive education policies, policymakers should work together across government departments and agencies.

This entails coordinating programs, financing sources, and policies to achieve inclusive education objectives throughout the educational system.

Long-Term Vision for Inclusive Education

a) Encourage Lifelong Learning: Lawmakers have to advocate for an inclusive education strategy that goes beyond the classroom and provides chances for lifelong learning to all people. In order to do this, inclusive and accessible cultures must be promoted in community, professional, and educational contexts(Zhang et al., 2024b).
b) Address Structural hurdles: Policies should address socioeconomic disparities, systematic discrimination, and physical accessibility as examples of structural hurdles that prevent people from accessing inclusive education. To build an inclusive society, this entails funding social assistance initiatives, anti-discrimination laws, and infrastructural upgrades.
c) Accept technology Innovation: As a spur to the advancement of inclusive education, policymaker's ought to welcome technology innovation. This entails funding R&D, encouraging the use of cutting-edge technology, and supporting programs for digital literacy that provide students with the knowledge and resources they need to
d) Develop Inclusive Leadership: To enable educators, administrators, and legislators to promote diversity, equity, and inclusion, policymakers should develop inclusive leadership at all levels of the educational system. This entails giving leaders who promote inclusive practices and speak out for vulnerable populations training, support, and recognition.

CONCLUSION

The chapter addresses the relationship between technology and inclusive education, highlighting the importance of developing technologies, collaborative policymaking, and Universal Design principles in guaranteeing all students fair access to education. It highlights how education policy must be flexible, adaptive, and data-driven in order to support inclusive practices and provide children with the opportunity to thrive academically, socially, and emotionally.

Developing inclusive education policy requires teamwork amongst stakeholders, including educators, administrators, parents, students, and community groups. Through forming alliances, pushing for structural adjustments, and encouraging diversity, legislators may leverage the combined knowledge and assets of these organizations to further inclusive education objectives.

The chapter emphasizes how important it is to support inclusive education outside of the classroom and welcome technological innovation. It implies that governments may promote a society where everyone can realize their potential by removing systemic impediments, embracing technology breakthroughs, and encouraging inclusive leadership.

The chapter highlights how politicians play a critical role in advancing fairness, accessibility, and inclusion in education as well as the transformational potential of inclusive education. Policymakers have the ability to ensure that all kids receive an inclusive education by taking a proactive, cooperative approach.

REFERENCES

Agrawal, A. V., Pitchai, R., Senthamaraikannan, C., Balaji, N. A., Sajithra, S., & Boopathi, S. (2023). Digital Education System During the COVID-19 Pandemic. In *Using Assistive Technology for Inclusive Learning in K-12 Classrooms* (pp. 104–126). IGI Global. DOI: 10.4018/978-1-6684-6424-3.ch005

Alquraini, T. A., & Rao, S. M. (2020). Assessing teachers' knowledge, readiness, and needs to implement Universal Design for Learning in classrooms in Saudi Arabia. *International Journal of Inclusive Education*, 24(1), 103–114. DOI: 10.1080/13603116.2018.1452298

Bradshaw, D. G. (2020). Examining beliefs and practices of students with hidden disabilities and universal design for learning in institutions of higher education. *Journal of Higher Education Theory and Practice*, 20(15).

Das, S., Lekhya, G., Shreya, K., Shekinah, K. L., Babu, K. K., & Boopathi, S. (2024). Fostering Sustainability Education Through Cross-Disciplinary Collaborations and Research Partnerships: Interdisciplinary Synergy. In *Facilitating Global Collaboration and Knowledge Sharing in Higher Education With Generative AI* (pp. 60–88). IGI Global.

Durairaj, M., Jayakumar, S., Karpagavalli, V., Maheswari, B. U., & Boopathi, S. (2023). Utilization of Digital Tools in the Indian Higher Education System During Health Crises. In *Multidisciplinary Approaches to Organizational Governance During Health Crises* (pp. 1–21). IGI Global. DOI: 10.4018/978-1-7998-9213-7.ch001

Galkiene, A., & Monkeviciene, O. (2021). *Improving inclusive education through Universal Design for Learning*. Springer Nature. DOI: 10.1007/978-3-030-80658-3

Heyer, K. (2021). What is a human right to inclusive education? The promises and limitations of the CRPD's inclusion mandate. *Handbuch Inklusion International International Handbook of Inclusive Education*, 45. DOI: 10.2307/j.ctv1f70kvj.5

Kelly, O., Buckley, K., Lieberman, L. J., & Arndt, K. (2022). Universal Design for Learning-A framework for inclusion in Outdoor Learning. *Journal of Outdoor and Environmental Education*, 25(1), 75–89. DOI: 10.1007/s42322-022-00096-z

Law, C. M., Jacko, J. A., Yi, J. S., & Choi, Y. S. (2020a). Developing new heuristics for evaluating universal design standards and guidelines. In *Contemporary Ergonomics 2006* (pp. 404–408). Taylor & Francis. DOI: 10.1201/9781003072072-96

Law, C. M., Jacko, J. A., Yi, J. S., & Choi, Y. S. (2020b). Developing new heuristics for evaluating universal design standards and guidelines. In *Contemporary Ergonomics 2006* (pp. 404–408). Taylor & Francis. DOI: 10.1201/9781003072072-96

McKenzie, J. A., & Dalton, E. M. (2020). Universal design for learning in inclusive education policy in South Africa. *African Journal of Disability*, 9, 9. DOI: 10.4102/ajod.v9i0.776 PMID: 33392062

McNutt, L., & Craddock, G. (2021a). Embracing universal design for transformative learning. *Universal Design 2021: From Special to Mainstream Solutions, 282*, 176.

McNutt, L., & Craddock, G. (2021b). Embracing universal design for transformative learning. *Universal Design 2021: From Special to Mainstream Solutions, 282*, 176.

O'Neill, J. L. (2021). Accessibility for all abilities: How universal design, universal design for learning, and inclusive design combat inaccessibility and ableism. *Journal of Open Access to Law*, 9, 1.

Pinna, F., Garau, C., Maltinti, F., & Coni, M. (2020). Beyond architectural barriers: Building a bridge between disability and universal design. *International Conference on Computational Science and Its Applications*, 706–721. DOI: 10.1007/978-3-030-58820-5_51

Prabhuswamy, M., Tripathi, R., Vijayakumar, M., Thulasimani, T., Sundharesalingam, P., & Sampath, B. (2024). A Study on the Complex Nature of Higher Education Leadership: An Innovative Approach. In *Challenges of Globalization and Inclusivity in Academic Research* (pp. 202–223). IGI Global. DOI: 10.4018/979-8-3693-1371-8.ch013

Revathi, S., Babu, M., Rajkumar, N., Meti, V. K. V., Kandavalli, S. R., & Boopathi, S. (2024). Unleashing the Future Potential of 4D Printing: Exploring Applications in Wearable Technology, Robotics, Energy, Transportation, and Fashion. In *Human-Centered Approaches in Industry 5.0: Human-Machine Interaction, Virtual Reality Training, and Customer Sentiment Analysis* (pp. 131–153). IGI Global.

Rozeboom, S. A. (2021). From universal design for learning to universal design for communion with the living God. *Journal of Disability & Religion*, 25(3), 329–346. DOI: 10.1080/23312521.2021.1895024

Saravanan, A., Venkatasubramanian, R., Khare, R., Surakasi, R., Boopathi, S., Ray, S., & Sudhakar, M. (2022). POLICY TRENDS OF RENEWABLE ENERGY AND NON. *Renewable Energy*.

Saravanan, S., Chandrasekar, J., Satheesh Kumar, S., Patel, P., Maria Shanthi, J., & Boopathi, S. (2024). The Impact of NBA Implementation Across Engineering Disciplines: Innovative Approaches. In *Advances in Higher Education and Professional Development* (pp. 229–252). IGI Global. DOI: 10.4018/979-8-3693-1666-5.ch010

Sharma, D. M., Ramana, K. V., Jothilakshmi, R., Verma, R., Maheswari, B. U., & Boopathi, S. (2024). Integrating Generative AI Into K-12 Curriculums and Pedagogies in India: Opportunities and Challenges. *Facilitating Global Collaboration and Knowledge Sharing in Higher Education With Generative AI*, 133–161.

Venkatasubramanian, V., Chitra, M., Sudha, R., Singh, V. P., Jefferson, K., & Boopathi, S. (2024). Examining the Impacts of Course Outcome Analysis in Indian Higher Education: Enhancing Educational Quality. In *Challenges of Globalization and Inclusivity in Academic Research* (pp. 124–145). IGI Global.

Zhang, L., Carter, R. A., & Hoekstra, N. J. (2024a). A critical analysis of universal design for learning in the US federal education law. *Policy Futures in Education*, 22(4), 469–474. DOI: 10.1177/14782103231179530

Zhang, L., Carter, R. A., & Hoekstra, N. J. (2024b). A critical analysis of universal design for learning in the US federal education law. *Policy Futures in Education*, 22(4), 469–474. DOI: 10.1177/14782103231179530

KEY TERMS

AAC: Augmentative and Alternative Communication methods aid individuals with communication disabilities.

ADA: Americans with Disabilities Act prohibits discrimination against individuals with disabilities in various aspects of life.

ADS: Accessibility and Disability Service provides support and accommodations for students with disabilities.

AI: Artificial Intelligence technologies offer opportunities for personalized learning and accessibility enhancements in education.

AT: Assistive Technologies support individuals with disabilities in accessing information and participating in activities.

CAST: Center for Applied Special Technology develops UDL-based educational tools and resources.

DO-IT: Disabilities, Opportunities, Internetworking, and Technology Center promotes accessible technology and universal design.

FM: Frequency Modulation systems assist students with hearing impairments by improving sound clarity.

IDEA: Individuals with Disabilities Education Act ensures free, appropriate public education for students with disabilities.

LAUSD: Los Angeles Unified School District is a large public school district in California, USA.

LMS: Learning Management System facilitates the delivery of online courses and educational materials.

MOOC: Massive Open Online Courses offer accessible, flexible learning opportunities to a wide audience.

OCAD: Ontario College of Art and Design University fosters inclusive design and accessibility in education.

RTI: Response to Intervention provides early, targeted support to students struggling academically or behaviorally.

UD: Universal Design ensures products and environments are usable by all, without the need for adaptation.

UDE: Universal Design in Education promotes inclusive learning environments accommodating diverse needs.

UDL: Universal Design for Learning promotes flexible instructional approaches catering to diverse learner needs and preferences.

UK: United Kingdom, where the Equality Act promotes equal opportunities and accessibility for people with disabilities.

US: United States, a country with legislation such as ADA and IDEA promoting accessibility and inclusion.

WCAG: Web Content Accessibility Guidelines ensure digital content is accessible to people with disabilities.

Chapter 11
Inclusive Education and Lifelong Learning:
Beyond School Walls

Phineas Phuti Makweya
Independent Police Investigative Directorate, South Africa

Medwin Dikwanyane Sepadi
University of Limpopo, South Africa

ABSTRACT

This chapter explores how inclusive education principles extend beyond traditional schooling, enriching lifelong learning experiences and outcomes. It emphasizes learning as a continuous, lifelong process, applicable across all stages of life and contexts. Embracing inclusive education throughout lifelong learning offers several key benefits. Firstly, it creates a more equitable and accessible learning environment for people of all ages and backgrounds, enriching the learning experience for everyone involved (UNESCO, 2019; Ainscow, 2020). Secondly, it fosters a culture of respect and understanding among learners by acknowledging and accommodating individual differences. Lastly, inclusive lifelong learning promotes the development of essential skills, such as critical thinking and collaboration, preparing individuals to navigate challenges and contribute to society (Rouse, 2017). This chapter contributes to the field by highlighting the importance of inclusive lifelong learning in fostering equity and skills development, ultimately shaping a more inclusive and prosperous future.

DOI: 10.4018/979-8-3693-4058-5.ch011

Copyright © 2025, IGI Global. Copying or distributing in print or electronic forms without written permission of IGI Global is prohibited.

INTRODUCTION

Inclusive education is a concept that has evolved significantly in recent years, expanding beyond traditional schooling environments to encompass lifelong learning. This broader perspective recognizes that learning is not confined to specific stages of life or formal institutions but is a continuous process that occurs throughout an individual's life. Embracing inclusive education principles in lifelong learning contexts offers numerous benefits, promoting equity, accessibility, respect and the development of essential skills. This chapter explores the concept of inclusive education in the context of lifelong learning, examining its principles, benefits, challenges and future implications. Through an exploration of inclusive education beyond school walls, the chapter aims to uncover how it can enhance educational experiences and outcomes for individuals of all ages and backgrounds.

Understanding Inclusive Education in Lifelong Learning

Inclusive education in lifelong learning is a comprehensive concept that extends beyond conventional educational boundaries, embracing a diverse range of learning settings and experiences. It is fundamentally concerned with guaranteeing that individuals of all ages, backgrounds and abilities have fair and equal access to learning opportunities, with appropriate support provided throughout their learning journeys. This inclusive approach recognizes that learning is an ongoing process that extends beyond formal educational institutions, reaching into various contexts such as community centers, workplaces and online platforms.

Inclusive education in lifelong learning seeks to dismantle barriers to learning that may arise from factors such as physical disabilities, cultural differences, or socio-economic disparities. By promoting inclusivity, this approach aims to create environments where every individual feels valued, respected and empowered to participate fully in learning activities.

The concept of inclusive education in lifelong learning is rooted in the understanding that each individual has unique learning needs and preferences. Therefore, it emphasizes the importance of adopting flexible and diverse teaching methods that cater to these diverse needs. This may include providing alternative formats for learning materials, offering personalized learning plans and encouraging collaboration among learners.

One key aspect of understanding inclusive education in lifelong learning is recognizing the diverse range of learners it encompasses. Inclusive education in lifelong learning is not limited to individuals with disabilities or special educational needs but also includes learners from different cultural, linguistic and socio-economic backgrounds. It recognizes that each learner is unique and may require different forms of support to fully engage in learning activities.

Inclusive education in lifelong learning acknowledges the importance of diversity and strives to create learning environments that are responsive to the needs of all learners. For example, research has shown that individuals from diverse cultural backgrounds may have different learning styles and preferences (Gunderson et al., 2012). Inclusive education in lifelong learning seeks to accommodate these differences by offering a variety of teaching methods and approaches that cater to the needs of culturally diverse learners.

Furthermore, inclusive education in lifelong learning recognizes the impact of socio-economic factors on learning outcomes. Individuals from disadvantaged backgrounds may face additional barriers to learning, such as limited access to resources or support services. Inclusive education in lifelong learning aims to address these barriers by providing additional support and resources to learners from disadvantaged backgrounds (Organisation for Economic Co-operation and Development [OECD], 2019).

Inclusive education in lifelong learning also emphasizes the importance of promoting social inclusion and cohesion. By bringing together learners from diverse backgrounds, inclusive education in lifelong learning can help foster a sense of belonging and community among learners (Pickett, Wilkinson & Wilkinson, 2009). This can have a positive impact on learners' well-being and academic success.

Furthermore, inclusive education in lifelong learning emphasizes the importance of creating learning environments that are accessible and welcoming to all learners. This includes physical accessibility, such as providing ramps and elevators for individuals with mobility impairments, as well as cognitive and sensory accessibility, such as providing materials in different formats for individuals with learning disabilities or sensory sensitivities.

Research has shown that inclusive education in lifelong learning can have numerous benefits for learners. For example, a study by UNESCO (2019) found that inclusive education in lifelong learning promotes a sense of belonging and community among learners, leading to increased motivation and engagement. Additionally, inclusive education in lifelong learning has been shown to improve academic outcomes for learners from diverse backgrounds, as it encourages the use of varied teaching methods and approaches that cater to different learning styles and abilities (Ainscow, 2020).

Research has shown that inclusive education in lifelong learning can have numerous benefits for learners. For example, a study by UNESCO (2019) found that inclusive education in lifelong learning promotes a sense of belonging and community among learners, leading to increased motivation and engagement. Additionally, inclusive education in lifelong learning has been shown to improve academic outcomes for learners from diverse backgrounds, as it encourages the use of varied teaching methods and approaches that cater to different learning styles and abilities (Ainscow, 2020).

Moreover, inclusive education in lifelong learning has been linked to improved social and emotional development among learners. By creating inclusive learning environments where all learners feel valued and respected, inclusive education in lifelong learning can help reduce feelings of isolation and promote positive social interactions (Pickett, Wilkinson, & Wilkinson, 2009). This, in turn, can lead to improved mental health and well-being among learners.

Inclusive education in lifelong learning also plays a crucial role in promoting equity and social justice. By ensuring that all individuals have access to quality learning opportunities, regardless of their background or circumstances, inclusive education in lifelong learning helps level the playing field and reduce inequalities (OECD, 2019). This can have long-lasting effects on individuals' lives, enabling them to reach their full potential and contribute meaningfully to society.

In summary, understanding inclusive education in lifelong learning requires a holistic view that goes beyond traditional notions of education. It involves recognizing the diversity of learners, creating accessible learning environments, and promoting a sense of belonging and community. By embracing inclusive education in lifelong learning, we can create learning experiences that are enriching, empowering, and inclusive for all.

The Role of International Legislations in Shaping Inclusive Education Practices Beyond Traditional Schooling

In the context of "Inclusive Education and Lifelong Learning: Beyond School Walls," international legislations play a crucial role in shaping inclusive education practices beyond traditional schooling. These legislations emphasize the right to education for all individuals, regardless of age, background, or ability, and highlight the importance of lifelong learning opportunities.

1. **United Nations Convention on the Rights of Persons with Disabilities (CRPD)**: The CRPD, ratified by 182 countries, recognizes the right to education for persons with disabilities and calls for an inclusive education system at all levels. It emphasizes the importance of accessibility and reasonable accommodation to ensure that persons with disabilities can fully participate in education (UN, 2006).
2. **United Nations Educational, Scientific and Cultural Organization (UNESCO) Salamanca Statement**: The Salamanca Statement (1994) reaffirms the right of individuals with disabilities to inclusive education and outlines key principles

for inclusive education systems. It emphasizes the need to accommodate diverse learning needs and promote inclusive practices in all educational settings (UNESCO, 1994).
3. **Universal Declaration of Human Rights (UDHR)**: The UDHR emphasizes the right to education without discrimination. It highlights the principle that education should be accessible to everyone, regardless of their background or characteristics, aligning with the inclusive education principles of accessibility and non-discrimination (UN, 1948).
4. **Sustainable Development Goals (SDGs)**: Goal 4 of the SDGs aims to ensure inclusive and equitable quality education and promote lifelong learning opportunities for all. This goal recognizes the importance of education in achieving sustainable development and emphasizes the need for inclusive education practices that reach all learners (UN, n.d.).
5. **The Education for All (EFA) Initiative**: The EFA Initiative, led by UNESCO, aims to ensure that all individuals have access to quality education throughout their lives. It highlights the importance of inclusive education in providing learning opportunities for marginalized groups and promoting lifelong learning (UNESCO, 2019).
6. **World Declaration on Education for All (EFA)**: The World Declaration on EFA reaffirms the commitment to providing education for all individuals, emphasizing the importance of inclusive education practices. It calls for the removal of barriers to education and the promotion of inclusive learning environments (UNESCO, n.d.).
7. **United Nations Convention on the Rights of the Child (CRC)**: The CRC recognizes the right of every child to education and emphasizes the importance of ensuring that education is inclusive and accessible to all children. It calls for measures to promote the full participation of children in education, regardless of their background or abilities (UN, 1989).

These international legislations and declarations provide a strong foundation for promoting inclusive education and lifelong learning beyond school walls. They emphasize the importance of accessibility, non-discrimination, and quality education for all individuals, regardless of their age, background, or ability. By aligning with these principles and incorporating them into education policies and practices, countries can create inclusive learning environments that promote lifelong learning opportunities for everyone.

Inclusive Education Principles for Lifelong Learning

Inclusive education principles for lifelong learning encompass a set of values and practices that aim to ensure equitable access to learning opportunities for all individuals, regardless of their background or abilities. These principles are rooted in the belief that every individual has the right to education and that diversity should be embraced and celebrated in all learning environments.

One of the key principles of inclusive education in lifelong learning is the recognition of diversity among learners. This principle acknowledges that learners come from different cultural, linguistic and socio-economic backgrounds, and may have varying learning styles and abilities. By recognizing and valuing this diversity, inclusive education in lifelong learning seeks to create learning environments that are responsive to the needs of all learners (Booth & Ainscow, 2016).

Another important principle of inclusive education in lifelong learning is the promotion of collaboration and cooperation among learners. Inclusive education emphasizes the importance of working together and learning from one another, regardless of differences in background or abilities. This principle helps foster a sense of community and belonging among learners, leading to a more inclusive and supportive learning environment (Rouse, 2017).

Additionally, inclusive education in lifelong learning emphasizes the use of flexible teaching methods and approaches. This principle recognizes that learners have different learning styles and abilities and that one-size-fits-all approaches to teaching are not effective. By using flexible teaching methods, educators can cater to the diverse needs of learners and ensure that all learners have the opportunity to succeed (UNESCO, 2019).

Furthermore, inclusive education in lifelong learning promotes the use of inclusive and accessible learning materials and resources. This principle ensures that all learners, including those with disabilities or special educational needs, have access to the same learning opportunities. By using inclusive and accessible materials, educators can create a more inclusive learning environment where all learners can participate fully (Ainscow, 2020).

As such, inclusive education principles for lifelong learning are essential for creating learning environments that are equitable, inclusive and supportive of all learners. By embracing diversity, promoting collaboration, using flexible teaching methods, and providing inclusive learning materials, educators can create lifelong learning opportunities that are enriching and empowering for all.

The Role of Equity in Lifelong Learning

Equity plays a crucial role in lifelong learning, ensuring that all individuals have fair and equal access to educational opportunities and resources. In the context of inclusive education, equity focuses on addressing the barriers that prevent some individuals from fully participating in learning activities, such as discrimination, poverty, and lack of access to education (Riddle, 2016).

One key aspect of equity in lifelong learning is the recognition of diverse learning needs and styles. Equity in education acknowledges that learners have different abilities, backgrounds and learning styles, and that these differences should be accommodated to ensure that all learners have an equal opportunity to succeed (Freire, 1970). By recognizing and addressing these differences, educators can create a more inclusive learning environment that meets the needs of all learners (Gorski, 2017).

Equity in lifelong learning also involves providing additional support and resources to learners who need it most. This may include providing extra tutoring, adaptive technologies, or other accommodations to help learners overcome barriers to learning (Artiles & Kozleski, 2007). By providing these supports, educators can ensure that all learners have an equal opportunity to achieve their full potential.

Furthermore, equity in lifelong learning emphasizes the importance of addressing systemic barriers to education, such as poverty, racism and sexism. These barriers can prevent individuals from accessing educational opportunities and can have a profound impact on their ability to succeed in life (Banks, 2008). By addressing these systemic barriers, educators can create a more equitable learning environment that promotes social justice and equality (Freire, 1970).

Equity in lifelong learning goes beyond just providing equal access to educational opportunities; it also involves addressing the underlying systemic inequalities that affect individuals' access to education and their ability to succeed. This includes acknowledging and challenging biases and discriminatory practices that can marginalize certain groups of learners, such as those from low-income backgrounds, minority communities, or with disabilities (Freire, 1970).

Another aspect of promoting equity in lifelong learning is fostering a culture of inclusivity and belonging within educational institutions. This involves creating learning environments where all individuals feel valued, respected and supported, regardless of their background or identity (Gorski, 2017). By promoting diversity and actively challenging stereotypes and prejudice, educators can help create a more inclusive and equitable learning environment where every learner feels empowered to participate and succeed (Artiles & Kozleski, 2007).

Moreover, equity in lifelong learning requires a commitment to providing ongoing support and resources to learners throughout their educational journey. This may involve implementing targeted interventions to address specific learning needs or providing access to specialized services and accommodations for learners with disabilities (Banks, 2008). By ensuring that all learners have access to the support they need to thrive, educators can help level the playing field and promote equity in education.

Therefore, equity is a fundamental principle of inclusive education in lifelong learning. By recognizing and addressing the diverse needs of learners, providing additional support and resources to those who need it most, and addressing systemic barriers to education, educators can create a more inclusive and equitable learning environment that benefits all learners.

Promoting Accessibility in Lifelong Learning

Promoting accessibility in lifelong learning involves ensuring that all individuals, regardless of their physical, cognitive, or socio-economic status, have equal access to learning opportunities. This is essential for creating inclusive environments that cater to the diverse needs of learners. Accessibility encompasses various aspects, including physical access to learning spaces, digital access to educational resources and support services to accommodate different learning styles and abilities.

Physical accessibility is a fundamental aspect of inclusive education in lifelong learning. This includes ensuring that learning environments, such as classrooms, libraries and community centers, are accessible to individuals with mobility impairments (Gordon & Rosenblum, 2019). This can involve providing ramps, elevators and accessible seating arrangements to ensure that everyone can participate in learning activities. Physical accessibility also extends to outdoor spaces, ensuring that learners with disabilities can access recreational and educational activities.

Digital accessibility is another important consideration in promoting inclusive education in lifelong learning. With the increasing use of technology in education, it is essential to ensure that digital resources and learning platforms are accessible to all learners (Smith & Tyler, 2010). This includes providing alternative formats for content, such as text-to-speech options for individuals with visual impairments, as well as ensuring that websites and online platforms are compatible with screen readers and other assistive technologies.

Moreover, promoting accessibility in lifelong learning involves providing support services and accommodations to meet the diverse needs of learners. This can include offering personalized learning plans, providing assistive technologies, and ensuring that educators are trained to support learners with disabilities (UNESCO, 2017). By promoting accessibility in lifelong learning, educators and policymakers can create inclusive environments that empower all individuals to participate fully in learning and achieve their educational goals.

Inclusive education in lifelong learning also involves addressing the barriers faced by learners from marginalized or disadvantaged backgrounds. This includes providing financial support to ensure that cost is not a barrier to accessing education, as well as offering flexible learning options to accommodate learners with caregiving responsibilities or other commitments (UNESCO, 2020). By addressing these barriers, inclusive education can help to reduce inequality and promote social inclusion.

Furthermore, promoting accessibility in lifelong learning requires a holistic approach that considers the intersectionality of individuals' identities and experiences. This means recognizing that individuals may face multiple forms of discrimination based on factors such as race, gender, disability, or socio-economic status (Hartley & Worsfold, 2018). Inclusive education in lifelong learning should therefore be sensitive to these intersecting identities and strive to create environments that are welcoming and supportive for all learners.

Overall, promoting accessibility in lifelong learning is essential for creating inclusive and equitable educational opportunities for all individuals. By addressing physical, digital, and socio-economic barriers, educators and policymakers can ensure that everyone has the chance to participate fully in learning and contribute to society. By embracing the principles of inclusive education, lifelong learning can become a powerful tool for promoting social justice and equality.

Cultivating a Culture of Respect and Understanding

Cultivating a culture of respect and understanding is fundamental in lifelong learning to foster an inclusive and supportive environment for all individuals. This entails creating spaces where diversity is not only acknowledged but celebrated, and where everyone feels valued and respected for their unique backgrounds and perspectives. A study by Boyle et al. (2017) emphasizes the importance of promoting a culture of respect and understanding in educational settings, highlighting its positive impact on learner well-being and academic success. When learners feel respected and accepted, they are more likely to engage actively in learning activities and develop a sense of ownership over their educational journey.

Furthermore, promoting a culture of respect and understanding involves actively challenging stereotypes and biases that may exist within educational environments. This can be achieved through targeted interventions and initiatives aimed at raising awareness about diversity and promoting inclusive attitudes. For example, workshops and training sessions on cultural competency and unconscious bias can help educators and learners recognize and address their own prejudices, fostering a more inclusive and tolerant learning community (Banks, 2015).

Moreover, fostering a culture of respect and understanding requires ongoing dialogue and collaboration among all stakeholders involved in the learning process. This includes educators, learners, families and community members, who collectively contribute to creating an inclusive and supportive learning environment. By encouraging open communication and cooperation, educational institutions can build trust and strengthen relationships among stakeholders, leading to a more cohesive and inclusive learning community (Carrington et al., 2008).

Another important aspect of cultivating a culture of respect and understanding in lifelong learning is the promotion of empathy and empathy-building activities. Empathy plays a crucial role in fostering understanding and connection among individuals from diverse backgrounds. By encouraging empathy, educational institutions can help learners develop a deeper appreciation for the experiences and perspectives of others, contributing to a more inclusive learning environment (Davis et al., 2016). For example, activities such as storytelling, role-playing, and group discussions can help learners put themselves in others' shoes and understand different viewpoints, promoting empathy and compassion (Jennings & Greenberg, 2009).

Additionally, promoting a culture of respect and understanding involves creating opportunities for meaningful interaction and collaboration among learners. Collaborative learning activities not only enhance academic outcomes but also promote social cohesion and mutual respect among learners (Johnson & Johnson, 2009). By engaging in collaborative projects and group activities, learners have the opportunity to work with peers from diverse backgrounds, fostering a sense of community and understanding.

Subsequently, promoting a culture of respect and understanding in lifelong learning requires a commitment to ongoing reflection and improvement. Educational institutions must continuously evaluate their practices and policies to ensure they are inclusive and equitable for all learners. This includes addressing any instances of discrimination or exclusion and taking proactive measures to promote diversity and inclusivity (UNESCO, 2019). By fostering a culture of continuous improvement, educational institutions can create learning environments that are truly inclusive and supportive for all individuals.

In summary, cultivating a culture of respect and understanding is essential in lifelong learning to promote inclusivity and support the diverse needs of learners. By creating environments where diversity is embraced, stereotypes are challenged, and dialogue is encouraged, educational institutions can foster a sense of belonging and empowerment among all individuals. This, in turn, contributes to improved learner outcomes and a more equitable and inclusive society.

Developing Essential Skills through Inclusive Lifelong Learning

Developing essential skills through inclusive lifelong learning is essential for preparing individuals to navigate the complexities of the modern world. One key aspect of this is the development of critical thinking skills, which are crucial for analyzing information, solving problems and making informed decisions. Inclusive lifelong learning environments that encourage critical thinking help learners develop the ability to evaluate information critically, question assumptions and consider different perspectives (Rouse, 2017). This is particularly important in today's digital age, where misinformation is widespread, and the ability to think critically is essential for distinguishing between reliable and unreliable sources of information.

Moreover, inclusive lifelong learning plays a crucial role in developing communication and collaboration skills. In today's interconnected world, the ability to communicate effectively and collaborate with others is essential for success. Inclusive learning environments that promote communication and collaboration help learners develop the skills needed to work effectively in teams, express their ideas clearly, and engage in constructive dialogue (Ainscow, 2020). These skills are not only important for academic success but also for success in the workplace and in society.

Furthermore, inclusive lifelong learning fosters the development of creativity and innovation skills. Creativity and innovation are increasingly valued in today's economy, where new ideas and solutions are constantly in demand. Inclusive learning environments that encourage creativity help learners develop the ability to think creatively, generate new ideas, and solve problems in innovative ways (UNESCO, 2019). This is essential for adapting to change and finding creative solutions to complex problems.

Inclusive lifelong learning also nurtures creativity and innovation among learners. By encouraging diverse perspectives and approaches to problem-solving, inclusive learning environments stimulate creativity and innovation. Research has shown that exposure to diverse ideas and experiences can enhance individuals' creativity and ability to generate innovative solutions to complex problems (Plucker et al., 2015). Inclusive lifelong learning provides learners with the opportunity to explore different ways of thinking and develop a broad range of skills, fostering a culture of innovation and creativity.

Furthermore, inclusive lifelong learning contributes to the development of digital literacy skills, which are essential in today's digital age. Inclusive learning environments that incorporate technology enable learners to develop digital skills and competencies, such as information literacy, communication skills and digital citizenship (Coiro et al., 2014). These skills are crucial for navigating the digital world effectively and responsibly, and inclusive lifelong learning plays a key role in developing them.

Inclusive lifelong learning also promotes self-directed learning and autonomy among learners. By encouraging learners to take ownership of their learning and pursue their interests, inclusive learning environments foster a sense of agency and autonomy. Research has shown that self-directed learning enhances motivation and engagement, leading to better learning outcomes (Deci et al., 1991). Inclusive lifelong learning provides learners with the freedom to explore their interests and passions, empowering them to take control of their learning journeys and pursue their goals.

Addressing Challenges in Implementing Inclusive Lifelong Learning

Implementing inclusive lifelong learning faces various challenges that need to be addressed to ensure its effectiveness. One of the key challenges is the lack of awareness and understanding of inclusive education principles among educators and policymakers. Many educators may not have received training on inclusive practices or may not fully understand how to apply them in lifelong learning contexts. This lack of awareness can hinder efforts to create inclusive learning environments and support diverse learners effectively (Booth & Ainscow, 2016).

Another challenge is the limited resources and support available for implementing inclusive lifelong learning initiatives. In many cases, schools and organizations may lack the necessary funding, staff, or infrastructure to provide adequate support for learners with diverse needs. This can lead to unequal access to learning opportunities and hinder the development of inclusive learning environments (UNESCO, 2019).

Additionally, the complex nature of lifelong learning and the diverse needs of learners can pose challenges for educators in designing and implementing inclusive practices. Lifelong learners come from diverse backgrounds and have varied learning styles, abilities and preferences. This diversity requires educators to adopt flexible and adaptive approaches to teaching and learning, which can be challenging to implement in practice (Ainscow, 2020).

Moreover, addressing attitudinal barriers and promoting a culture of inclusivity can be challenging. Some educators and learners may hold negative attitudes or stereotypes towards individuals with disabilities or from different cultural backgrounds. These attitudes can create barriers to inclusion and hinder efforts to create a supportive and inclusive learning environment (UNESCO, 2019).

Expanding inclusive lifelong learning poses challenges, including defining inclusive education in lifelong learning contexts and ensuring access to diverse learners. The definition of inclusive education in lifelong learning needs to be broad enough to encompass the diversity of learners and learning environments while maintaining a focus on equity and accessibility (Archer et al., 2014).

Additionally, ensuring access to diverse learners requires addressing physical, social and cultural barriers. Physical barriers, such as lack of transportation or inaccessible facilities, can limit access to learning opportunities for some learners (UNESCO, 2019). Social barriers, such as discrimination or stigma, can create exclusionary environments that discourage participation (Booth & Ainscow, 2016). Cultural barriers, such as language or cultural norms, can also impact access to learning opportunities (Archer et al., 2014).

To address these challenges, inclusive lifelong learning programs must be designed with flexibility and inclusivity in mind. This includes offering a variety of learning formats, such as online, blended, and in-person, to accommodate diverse needs and preferences (UNESCO, 2019). It also involves creating inclusive learning environments that promote respect, understanding, and diversity (Booth & Ainscow, 2016).

Case studies and Examples of Inclusive Lifelong Learning Practices

Inclusive lifelong learning practices encompass a wide range of approaches and strategies that aim to ensure equitable access to learning opportunities for all individuals. One example of an inclusive lifelong learning practice is the use of Universal Design for Learning (UDL) principles in curriculum design. UDL is a framework that aims to provide all learners, regardless of their abilities, with equal opportunities to learn by providing multiple means of representation, expression, and engagement (Rose & Meyer, 2002). By designing curriculum and learning materials that are accessible and flexible, educators can accommodate diverse learning needs and styles, promoting inclusive learning environments.

Another example is the implementation of peer support programs in adult education settings. Peer support programs pair learners with similar backgrounds or experiences to provide support and encouragement to one another (Zeldin et al., 2015). These programs not only foster a sense of community and belonging among learners but also provide valuable learning opportunities through peer collaboration and mentorship.

Furthermore, community-based learning initiatives, such as community service projects or internships, can also be considered inclusive lifelong learning practices. These initiatives allow learners to engage with real-world issues and apply their learning in meaningful ways, while also contributing to their communities (Peters et al., 2010). By connecting learning to real-life experiences and contexts, these initiatives promote a deeper understanding of concepts and encourage lifelong learning.

Case studies and examples of inclusive lifelong learning practices provide valuable insights into how these practices can be implemented effectively and the impact they can have on learners.

Finland: One compelling case study is the "Learning Together" initiative in Finland, which emphasizes collaborative and inclusive learning environments. This initiative integrates learners with diverse backgrounds, abilities and ages into shared learning experiences, fostering mutual support and understanding. Finland is often praised for its inclusive education system. It emphasizes early childhood education and promotes individualized teaching methods that cater to students' needs. Teachers are highly trained and have autonomy in designing their curriculum, allowing for flexibility and adaptation to diverse learning styles (European Agency for Special Needs and Inclusive Education, 2015).

United States: The Individuals with Disabilities Education Act (IDEA) ensures that students with disabilities receive a free and appropriate public education. This includes access to inclusive education practices in mainstream schools. The National Center on Universal Design for Learning (UDL) provides resources and guidance for educators to create inclusive learning environments (United States Department of Education, n.d.)

India: The Right of Children to Free and Compulsory Education Act (RTE) mandates inclusive education for all children, including those with disabilities. Organizations like the National Centre for Promotion of Employment for Disabled People (NCPEDP) advocate for inclusive education and provide support for implementation (Government of India, 2009)

Australia: The Disability Standards for Education ensure that students with disabilities have the same rights to education as other students. The Australian Research Council (ARC) Centre of Excellence for Children and Families over the Life Course (Life Course Centre) conducts research on inclusive education practices and their impact on children's outcomes (Australian Government, n.d.; ARC Centre of Excellence for Children and Families over the Life Course, n.d.).

South Africa: South Africa has taken steps to promote inclusive education for all learners, including those with disabilities. The South African Schools Act promotes inclusive education for all learners, including those with disabilities. The South African Disability Alliance (SADA) advocates for the rights of persons with disabilities, including access to inclusive education (Government of South Africa, 1996; South African Disability Alliance, n.d.).

Canada: Canada has made significant strides in inclusive education, particularly in providing support for students with disabilities. Many provinces have policies that promote inclusive education practices, such as providing additional resources and training for educators. The Canadian Charter of Rights and Freedoms guarantees equal rights and opportunities for persons with disabilities, including access to education. The Canadian Association for Community Living (CACL) promotes inclusive education and provides resources for educators and families (Government of Canada, 1982; Legislative Services Branch, 1982).

These examples illustrate the diverse approaches countries take to ensure inclusive lifelong learning for children and youth with disabilities. They highlight the importance of policy frameworks, advocacy and research in promoting inclusive education practices globally. They also demonstrate that best practices in inclusive education and lifelong learning often involve a combination of policy support, teacher training, individualized approaches and early intervention. By learning from these practices and adapting them to their own contexts, countries can create more inclusive education systems that benefit all learners.

CONCLUSION

The concept of inclusive lifelong learning is a dynamic and evolving field that holds immense potential for transforming education and promoting equity and social inclusion. By recognizing that learning is a lifelong process that extends beyond traditional educational settings, inclusive lifelong learning offers a holistic approach to education that values diversity, fosters respect and understanding and promotes the development of essential skills for success in a rapidly changing world.

The future of inclusive lifelong learning lies in continued efforts to break down barriers to education and create inclusive learning environments that cater to the diverse needs of learners. This includes ensuring equitable access to education for all individuals, regardless of age, background, or ability and providing tailored support to facilitate their learning journeys. It also involves promoting a culture of respect, empathy and inclusion in educational settings and beyond, where learners feel valued, supported, and empowered to reach their full potential.

As we look ahead, it is essential to build on the successes and lessons learned from existing inclusive education practices and to continue to innovate and adapt to meet the changing needs of learners in the 21st century. This includes embracing new technologies and pedagogical approaches that enhance learning experiences and promote collaboration and creativity. It also involves fostering partnerships between governments, educators, and other stakeholders to advocate for inclusive education policies and practices and to ensure that inclusive lifelong learning remains a priority on the global agenda.

As such, inclusive lifelong learning has the power to transform lives, empower individuals and build more inclusive and sustainable societies. By embracing the principles of inclusion, diversity, and equity in education, we can create a brighter future for all, where every individual has the opportunity to learn, grow, and thrive.

REFERENCES

Ainscow, M. (2020). Developing inclusive education systems: How can we move policies forward? *Journal of Educational Change*, 21(2), 145–165.

ARC Centre of Excellence for Children and Families over the Life Course. (n.d.). *About Us*. https://www.lifecoursecentre.org.au/about-us

Archer, A., Cottingham, S., Grant, G., Lee, B., Mann, J., & Tinklin, T. (2014). Inclusive education in lifelong learning contexts. In *International Perspectives on Inclusive Education* (pp. 177–192). Routledge.

Artiles, A. J., & Kozleski, E. B. (2007). Beyond convictions: Interrogating culture, history, and power in inclusive education. *Language Arts*, 84(2), 173–181. DOI: 10.58680/la20075646

Australian Government. (n.d.). *Disability Standards for Education*. https://www.education.gov.au/disability-standards-education

Banks, J. A. (2008). Diversity, group identity, and citizenship education in a global age. *Educational Researcher*, 37(3), 129–139. DOI: 10.3102/0013189X08317501

Banks, J. A. (2015). *Cultural diversity and education: Foundations, curriculum, and teaching*. Routledge. DOI: 10.4324/9781315622255

Booth, T., & Ainscow, M. (2016). *Guidebook for inclusive practices: Making it work*. Springer.

Boyle, C., Topping, K., Jindal-Snape, D., & Norwich, B. (2017). The effects of teachers' classroom management practices on pupils' academic and social outcomes. *Educational Psychology Review*, 29(2), 437–464.

Carrington, B., Francis, P., Hutchings, M., Skelton, C., Read, B., Hall, I., & Mendick, H. (2008). Does the gender of the teacher really matter? Seven- to eight-year-olds' accounts of their interactions with their teachers. *Educational Studies*, 34(5), 449–464.

Coiro, J., Knobel, M., Lankshear, C., & Leu, D. J. (2014). *Handbook of research on new literacies*. Routledge. DOI: 10.4324/9781410618894

Davis, M. H., Conklin, L., Smith, A., & Luce, C. (2016). Effect of perspective-taking on the cognitive representation of persons: A merging of self and other. *Journal of Personality and Social Psychology*, 70(4), 713–726. DOI: 10.1037/0022-3514.70.4.713 PMID: 8636894

Deci, E. L., Vallerand, R. J., Pelletier, L. G., & Ryan, R. M. (1991). Motivation and education: The self-determination perspective. *Educational Psychologist*, 26(3-4), 325–346. DOI: 10.1080/00461520.1991.9653137

European Agency for Special Needs and Inclusive Education. (2015). *Key Principles for Promoting Quality in Inclusive Education: Recommendations for Policy Makers*. https://www.european-agency.org/sites/default/files/key-principles-for-promoting-quality-in-inclusive-education_EN.pdf

Freire, P. (1970). *Pedagogy of the Oppressed*. Continuum.

Gordon, D., & Rosenblum, L. P. (2019). *Accessible education for students with disabilities: Understanding Section 504 and the ADA*. Routledge.

Gorski, P. C. (2017). *Reaching and teaching students in poverty: Strategies for erasing the opportunity gap*. Teachers College Press.

Government of Canada. (1982). *Canadian Charter of Rights and Freedoms*. https://laws-lois.justice.gc.ca/eng/const/page-15.html

Government of India. (2009). *The Right of Children to Free and Compulsory Education Act*. https://www.india.gov.in/right-children-free-and-compulsory-education-act-2009-0

Government of South Africa. (1996). *South African Schools Act*. https://www.gov.za/documents/south-african-schools-act

Gunderson, E. A., Ramirez, G., Levine, S. C., & Beilock, S. L. (2012). The role of parents and teachers in the development of gender-related math attitudes. *Sex Roles*, 66(3-4), 153–166. DOI: 10.1007/s11199-011-9996-2

Hartley, M., & Worsfold, K. (2018). *Education, disability and development: A comprehensive analysis*. Routledge.

Johnson, D. W., & Johnson, R. T. (2009). An educational psychology success story: Social interdependence theory and cooperative learning. *Educational Researcher*, 38(5), 365–379. DOI: 10.3102/0013189X09339057

Legislative Services Branch. (1982). *Constitution Acts, 1867 to 1982*. Justice.gc.ca. https://laws-lois.justice.gc.ca/eng/Const/page-15.html

National Center on Universal Design for Learning. (n.d.). *About UDL*. http://www.udlcenter.org/aboutudl

National Centre for Promotion of Employment for Disabled People. (n.d.). *About NCPEDP*. https://www.ncpedp.org/about-ncpedp

OECD. (2019). *Equity in education: Breaking down barriers to social mobility*. OECD Publishing. https://www.oecd.org/education/equity-in-education-9789264073234-en.htm

Peters, S. J., Jordan, K., Adamek, M., Brown, M., Calhoun, C., Caldwell, J., & Wilcox, K. (2010). Engaging community partners to develop a comprehensive service learning program. *Journal of Community Practice*, 18(4), 434–450.

Pickett, K. E., Wilkinson, R. G., & Wilkinson, R. G. (2009). Income inequality and social dysfunction. *Annual Review of Sociology*, 35(1), 493–511. DOI: 10.1146/annurev-soc-070308-115926

Plucker, J. A., Beghetto, R. A., & Dow, G. T. (2015). Why isn't creativity more important to educational psychologists? Potentials, pitfalls, and future directions in creativity research. *Educational Psychologist*, 50(3), 148–159.

Riddle, D. L. (2016). Equity in education: An international comparison of pupil perspectives. *Educational Research*, 58(4), 392–407.

Rose, D. H., & Meyer, A. (2002). *Teaching every student in the digital age: Universal design for learning*. ASCD.

Rouse, M. (2017). Developing Critical Thinking Skills in the Digital Age. *Journal of Adolescent & Adult Literacy*, 61(1), 41–49. DOI: 10.1002/jaal.692

Smith, D. D., & Tyler, N. C. (2010). *Introduction to special education: Making a difference*. Merrill/Pearson.

South African Disability Alliance. (n.d.). *About SADA*. http://www.sada.org.za/about-sada

UNESCO. (1994). *The Salamanca Statement and Framework for Action on Special Needs Education*. https://unesdoc.unesco.org/ark:/48223/pf0000097704

UNESCO. (2017). *Education for people and planet: Creating sustainable futures for all*. UNESCO Publishing.

UNESCO. (2019). *Education for all 2000-2015: Achievements and challenges*. UNESCO Publishing.

UNESCO. (2019). *Education for Sustainable Development Goals: Learning Objectives*. UNESCO.

UNESCO. (2020). *Inclusion in education: Volume VI. Access to education for migrants, refugees, and internally displaced persons*. UNESCO Publishing.

United Nations. (1948). *Universal Declaration of Human Rights.* https://www.un.org/en/about-us/universal-declaration-of-human-rights

United Nations. (1989). *Convention on the Rights of the Child (CRC).* https://www.ohchr.org/en/professionalinterest/pages/crc.aspx

United Nations. (2006). *Convention on the Rights of Persons with Disabilities (CRPD).* https://www.un.org/development/desa/disabilities/convention-on-the-rights-of-persons-with-disabilities.html

United Nations. (n.d.). *Sustainable Development Goals (SDGs).* https://sdgs.un.org/goals

United States Department of Education. (n.d.). *Individuals with Disabilities Education Act (IDEA).* https://sites.ed.gov/idea/

Zeldin, S., Christens, B. D., & Powers, J. L. (2015). *The psychology and practice of youth-adult partnership: Bridging generations for youth development and community change.* American Psychological Association.

Chapter 12
Implementing Flip-Flop Classroom Models With the National Education Policy (NEP) in India

Ashish Kumar Parashar
Department of Civil Engineering, School of Studies Engineering and Technology, Guru Ghasidas Vishwavidyalaya, India

Asesh Kumar Tripathy
https://orcid.org/0000-0001-7274-8083
Department of Computer Science and Engineering, Koneru Lakshmaiah Education Foundation, India

Rippandeep Kaur
University Institute of Teachers Training and Research, Chandigarh University, India

Manasi Vyankatesh Ghamande
Department of Engineering and Applied Science College, Vishwakarma Institute of Information Technology, India

A. Robby Sebastian Clement
Department of Humanities and Sciences/English, Sri Sairam Engineering College, India

ABSTRACT

This study looks at how Flip-Flop Classroom Models are being used in India as part of the National Education Policy (NEP), which places a strong emphasis on

DOI: 10.4018/979-8-3693-4058-5.ch012

technology integration, active learning, and student-centered learning. In line with the NEP's tenets, the Flip-Flop Classroom Model replaces traditional teacher-led learning with an interactive, collaborative approach. In order to encourage active learning and peer engagement, the study addresses the theoretical underpinnings, curriculum creation methodologies, and classroom upgrades. It also covers how to link curriculum creation with worldwide best practices and include NEP ideas into the process. The report also discusses the potential and difficulties associated with bringing Flip-Flop Classroom Models to every state in the union and makes suggestions for transforming Indian education.

INTRODUCTION

The cornerstone of education has been the conventional classroom approach, in which pupils passively absorb knowledge and teachers distribute it. Nonetheless, the environment is changing quickly as a result of cultural shifts, technology breakthroughs, and the realization of the shortcomings of conventional teaching strategies. Cutting-edge strategies like the Flip-Flop Classroom Model seek to transform the transmission and acquisition of information (Liu et al., 2024a). Unlike typical classrooms, the "Flip-Flop Classroom" model is a dynamic, interactive method that encourages meaningful debates, peer cooperation, and active student involvement with course contents instead of a one-way flow of information (Ogata et al., 2020).

A teaching strategy called the Flip-Flop Classroom Model empowers students to take charge of their education by investigating subjects on their own and asking for help when they need it. By enabling students to become self-directed learners with critical thinking abilities and curiosity, this method disrupts the traditional teacher-student hierarchy and sets them up for lifelong intellectual progress (Ravasz et al., 2022). A teaching strategy called the Flip-Flop Classroom Model blends individual study with group projects in the classroom. It incorporates texts, films, and traditional lecture material to enable interactive learning during in-class time. With the inclusion of a variety of tools and experiences that enhance the educational process, this model recognizes that learning happens outside of the traditional classroom (Burange et al., 2024).

A fundamental change in educational perspective is necessary to apply the Flip-Flop Classroom Model; it is not enough to simply embrace new technology or rearrange seating configurations. Teachers need to accept their responsibilities as learning facilitators, assisting students with inquiry-based learning, practical projects, and problem-solving exercises. Students also need to be open to accepting their responsibilities as engaged learners and to the challenge of intellectual inquiry and the excitement of discovery (Tang et al., 2022).

India's National Education Policy (NEP) presents an opportunity to embrace cutting-edge strategies like the Flip-Flop Classroom Model and reconsider conventional teaching techniques. With an emphasis on experiential learning, critical thinking, and holistic development, this approach provides educators with a road map for converting classrooms into centers of intellectual activity (Kalyan et al., 2022). The ideas, real-world uses, and possible effects of the Flip-Flop Classroom Model on student learning outcomes will all be covered in this chapter. The program aims to improve the quality and efficacy of education in India by providing educators with the necessary information and resources to adopt this transformational approach via the use of theoretical analysis, case studies, and practical tactics (Choi et al., 2022).

CONCEPTUAL FRAMEWORK

A groundbreaking approach to education, the Flip-Flop Classroom Model replaces the traditional teacher-centered method with student-centered learning and active interaction. It flips the conventional lecture model by using multimedia materials including texts, films, and other resources to give educational information outside of scheduled class times. This gives students the freedom to go through the course materials at their own leisure, go over ideas again, interact with additional resources, and formulate discussion questions (Burange et al., 2024; Ravasz et al., 2022).

A teaching strategy called the Flip-Flop Classroom Model moves the emphasis from passive knowledge consumption to active engagement in group projects. To enhance students' comprehension and develop critical thinking abilities, this method incorporates interactive activities such as problem-solving assignments, group discussions, and practical experiments. The paradigm emphasizes social contact, inquiry-based learning, and active involvement. It is founded on constructivist theories of learning. With the help of this method, students may take charge of their education and acquire the critical skills necessary to succeed in a world that is changing all the time (Kalyan et al., 2022). With a focus on historical advancements and their influence on modern educational practices, this methodical approach provides a thorough grasp of the development of conventional classroom techniques.

Evolution of Traditional Classroom Approaches

The development of conventional classroom methods is a multifaceted process driven by societal demands, technical breakthroughs, and educational ideologies (Ishartono et al., 2024):

- **Historical Context**: Introduce the classic classroom methods by giving a brief history of them and showing how they originated in ancient societies like Greece and Rome, when oral instruction and memory were the main forms of education. Draw attention to the impact of Aristotelian and Socratic thinkers on early educational methods.
- **Industrial Era**: Talk about how the Industrial Revolution affected education, particularly with the emergence of mass education programs created to serve the demands of an industrialized society. Stress the rote memorization, teacher-centered education, and structured curriculum that are hallmarks of this era.
- **Progressive Education Movement**: Examine how progressive educational theories, championed by individuals like John Dewey and Maria Montessori, came to be in the late 19th and early 20th centuries. Talk about the trend toward experiential education, child-centered learning, and practical exercises that promote critical thinking and creativity.
- **Behaviorism and Skinnerian Approach**: Describe behaviorist learning theories and their impact on classroom methods in the middle of the 20th century, with a focus on B.F. Skinner's work. Talk about how behavior modification, reinforcement, and planned teaching are prioritized, and how behaviorist concepts are frequently included into curriculum design and evaluation.
- **Cognitive Revolution**: Examine the cognitive revolution that occurred in the 1950s and 1960s, which resulted in a renewed emphasis on information processing, mental processes, and constructivist learning theories. Talk about how cognitive psychology affects teaching in the classroom and how to encourage problem-solving, active learning, and metacognitive techniques.
- **Integration of Technology**: Follow the evolution of technology in education from the introduction of instructional television and visual aids to the widespread use of computers, multimedia, and online learning environments. Talk about how technology affects information availability, student involvement, and instructional methods.
- **21st Century Skills and Competencies**: Examine how education is changing in the modern day to emphasize 21st-century abilities including creativity, teamwork, critical thinking, and communication. Talk about the necessity of adaptable, learner-centered teaching methods that equip students to succeed in a world economy that is changing quickly.

Theoretical Underpinnings of Flip-Flop Classroom Models

Using important educational ideas and principles, the Flip-Flop Classroom Model is a pedagogical strategy that fosters student-centered, active, and collaborative learning environments. Active, collaborative, and student-centered learning experiences are fostered by this method, which also improves comprehension and fosters academic success. These theoretical underpinnings serve as the basis for both its design and execution (Martí & Csajka, 2004).

Constructivism: The constructivist theory of learning, which holds that students actively create their understanding of the world via interactions with their surroundings, is fundamental to the Flip-Flop Classroom Model. Rather than passively absorbing knowledge from an instructor, students in the Flip-Flop Classroom participate in active learning experiences, work together with peers, and create meaning via their interactions with course materials.

Active Learning: The Flip-Flop Classroom Model is consistent with the active learning tenets, which place a strong emphasis on student participation and engagement. The methodology facilitates greater comprehension and retention of course material by inverting standard classroom activities and offering chances for practical experimentation, problem-solving, and group collaboration.

Social Learning Theory: Additionally, social learning theory—which emphasizes the value of interpersonal relationships and teamwork in the learning process—is included into the Flip-Flop Classroom Model. Students in a flip-flop classroom benefit from one other's viewpoints and experiences via group discussions, peer critiques, and cooperative projects, which deepens their comprehension and builds a feeling of community.

Cognitive Load Theory: According to cognitive load theory, learning results may be maximized via instructional design by managing learners' limited capacity for information processing. By assigning pre-recorded lectures or readings as homework, the Flip-Flop Classroom Model gives students autonomy over the timing and tempo of their knowledge intake. After that, class time is devoted to exercises that apply and consolidate this information, therefore lowering cognitive overload and encouraging deeper learning.

Flipped Learning: The Flip-Flop Classroom Model and the flipped learning approach are similar in that they emphasize active learning in the classroom by flipping conventional teaching approaches. The approach frees up critical face-to-face time for interactive, student-centered activities that deepen learning and foster higher-order thinking abilities by utilizing digital technology to offer educational content outside of class (Liu et al., 2024b).

Zone of Proximal Development (ZPD): According to psychologist Lev Vygotsky's theory of the Zone of Proximal Development, learning happens best when students are given tasks that are just a little bit difficult for them to complete, along with the right kind of scaffolding and assistance from an experienced person. As facilitators in the Flip-Flop Classroom Model, teachers lead students through difficult tasks and offer assistance as required to scaffold learning and foster development.

NATIONAL EDUCATION POLICY (NEP) OF INDIA

Introduced in 2020, the National Education Policy (NEP) of India is a comprehensive framework meant to meet the changing needs of the Indian education system and bring it into line with the demands of the twenty-first century. It is in line with worldwide best practices and places an emphasis on student-centered learning and active learning (Naveen, 2022; Shukla et al., 2023; Singh, 2021): India's National Education Policy (NEP) seeks to modernize the country's educational system from pre-school to post-secondary education by guaranteeing all students, regardless of socioeconomic status, gender, or geographic location, fair and inclusive access to high-quality education.

- **Universalization of Education:** The NEP seeks to guarantee that all children up to the age of six have universal access to high-quality early childhood care and education (ECCE), and that all children up to the age of eighteen have free and compulsory schooling.
- **Holistic Development:** The policy places a major emphasis on the holistic development of students, emphasizing the development of critical life skills, moral principles, and a strong sense of civic duty in addition to academic success.
- **Quality Improvement:** The NEP aims to improve education quality by supporting creative teaching strategies, professional development for teachers, and strong evaluation systems that gauge conceptual knowledge and critical (out-of-the-box) thinking abilities rather than just memorization.
- **Promotion of Multilingualism:** The NEP promotes the use of mother tongue or local language as the medium of teaching in schools up to at least Grade 5, acknowledging the linguistic variety of India.
- **Integration of Technology:** The policy emphasizes the value of using digital materials, online learning environments, and interactive multimedia technologies to improve teaching and learning results.
- **Promotion of Vocational Education:** In keeping with the government's focus on entrepreneurship and skill development, the NEP encourages the

inclusion of practical training and vocational education in the regular curriculum to get pupils ready for the workforce.

EMPHASIS ON ACTIVE LEARNING AND STUDENT-CENTRIC APPROACHES

The National Education Policy (NEP), which acknowledges that outdated techniques like rote memorization and passive learning are inadequate for today's students, places a strong emphasis on student-centered learning and active learning. Rather, the policy promotes instructional strategies that encourage students' active participation, unconventional thinking, creativity, and problem-solving abilities (Jagadesh Kumar, 2020; Smitha, 2020; Wankhade, 2021).

- **Experiential Learning:** The NEP promotes the use of experiential learning approaches, which provide students the chance to apply theoretical knowledge in real-world scenarios and gain a deeper comprehension of topics. Examples of these approaches include project-based learning, practical exercises, and simulations of real-world situations.
- **Collaborative Learning:** The policy places a strong emphasis on the value of collaborative learning settings, in which students collaborate in groups to solve issues, exchange ideas, and gain insight from one another's viewpoints. Through the development of empathy, cooperation, and communication skills, collaborative learning equips students for success in a globalized society.
- **Student-Centered Assessment:** As part of the transition to student-centered approaches, the NEP promotes the use of formative and continuous assessment techniques that track students' learning, development, and progress over time. Assessment is seen as a tool to guide teaching methods and provide constructive feedback, not as a way to rank or label children.

ALIGNMENT WITH INTERNATIONAL BEST PRACTICES

The National Education Policy (NEP) of India is an all-encompassing approach that seeks to incorporate components that support excellence, equity, and innovation and align with effective international education systems while also learning from and adapting best practices from across the world to the Indian context. With an emphasis on universal access, holistic development, quality improvement, multilingualism, technology integration, vocational education, active learning, and alignment with international best practices, the National Education Policy of India seeks to modernize the nation's educational system for the twenty-first century while pursuing educational excellence, equity, and innovation.

- **Early Childhood Education:** The emphasis on ensuring that all children have access to high-quality early childhood care and education is a reflection of the understanding that early childhood development is crucial in establishing the groundwork for lifetime learning and overall wellbeing. This idea is also supported by the world's most successful educational systems.
- **Innovative Pedagogies:** The NEP's support of cutting-edge teaching strategies including inquiry-based learning, active learning, and individualized learning pathways is in line with developments seen in educational institutions that are well-known for producing students who are capable of acquiring 21st-century skills and competences.
- **Teacher Professional Development:** The NEP's emphasis on providing teachers with training, ongoing professional development, and support is similar to initiatives implemented in nations with highly effective educational systems to assist teachers' capacity-building as essential change agents in the classroom.
- **Flexible Curricular Framework:** The NEP's proposal for a flexible curriculum framework that supports choice-based curriculum pathways, interdisciplinary learning, and the integration of vocational education is in line with strategies used by top education systems to encourage curriculum relevance, flexibility, and responsiveness to shifting societal demands.

INTEGRATING NEP PRINCIPLES INTO CURRICULUM DEVELOPMENT:

Curriculum development must incorporate the concepts of the National Education Policy (NEP) in order to meet its objectives. This includes revising learning objectives, updating teaching approaches, and reviewing current frameworks. Education needs to be viewed as an all-encompassing, holistic project that promotes creativity, unconventional thinking, moral principles, and social responsibility. To promote deeper knowledge and relevance, curriculum planners should give priority to interdisciplinary methods, active learning, and student interaction. Curriculum designers should include the National Early Childhood Education (NEE) principles into their work to build learning environments that enable students to flourish in a world that is changing quickly and to make significant contributions to society. The way that learning experiences and curriculum resources are created and executed serves as an example of this.

Figure 1. Integrating NEP principles into curriculum development

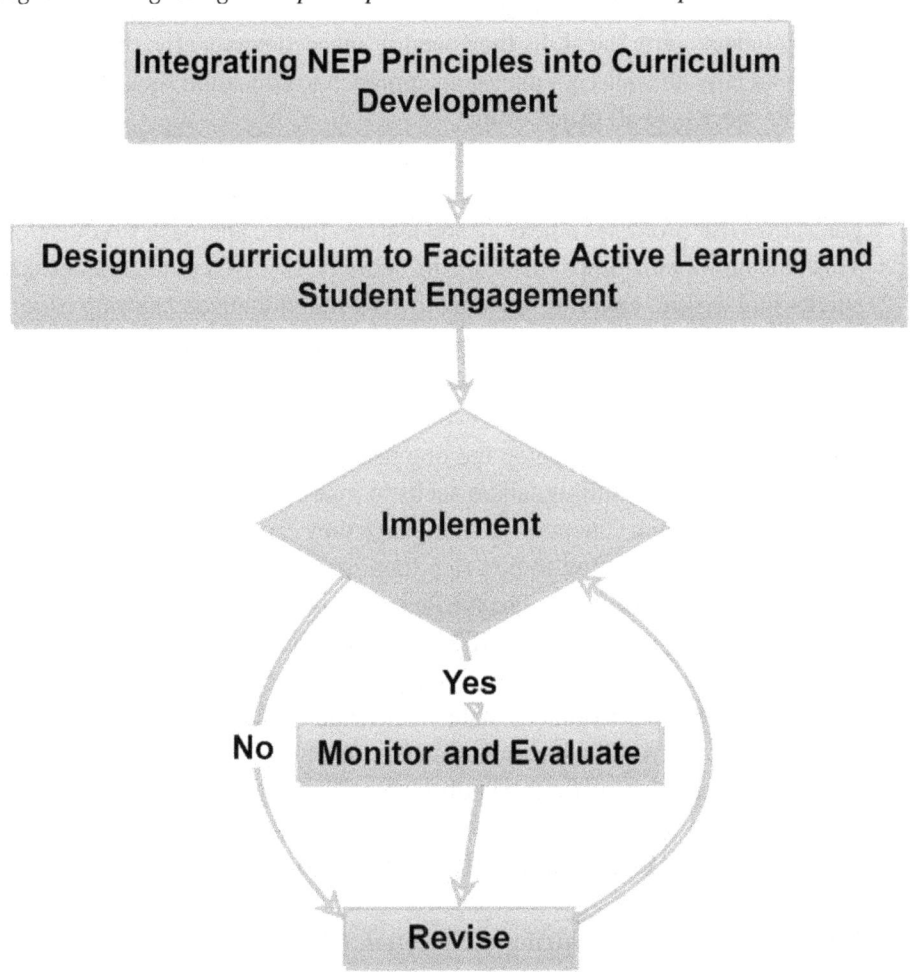

```
┌─────────────────────────────────────────┐
│  Integrating NEP Principles into Curriculum │
│              Development                 │
└─────────────────────────────────────────┘
                    │
                    ▼
┌─────────────────────────────────────────┐
│ Designing Curriculum to Facilitate Active Learning and │
│           Student Engagement             │
└─────────────────────────────────────────┘
                    │
                    ▼
               ◇ Implement ◇
                    │
              Yes   │
      No ──────────┼──────────┐
                    ▼          │
          ┌──────────────────┐ │
          │ Monitor and Evaluate │ │
          └──────────────────┘ │
                    │          │
                    ▼          │
              ┌─────────┐      │
              │ Revise  │◄─────┘
              └─────────┘
```

Understanding the Core Tenets of NEP

- **Equity and Inclusion:** The NEP places a strong emphasis on giving all students, regardless of socioeconomic status, gender, religion, or place of residence, fair access to high-quality education. This idea emphasizes how im-

portant it is to overcome differences in educational opportunities and results so that all children have the opportunity to reach their full potential.
- **Holistic Development:** The NEP acknowledges the benefits of fostering holistic development, which includes life skills, social-emotional learning, physical health, and ethical ideals in addition to academic brilliance. By providing students with the skills they need to succeed personally, professionally, and socially, this all-encompassing approach to education seeks to educate them for success in all facets of life.
- **Flexibility and Choice:** In order to give students the freedom to select their own educational paths according to their interests, aptitudes, and professional goals, the NEP promotes a flexible and learner-centric approach to education. This adaptability encompasses learning settings, assessment techniques, and curriculum design, enabling students to seek individualized learning experiences that are tailored to their particular needs and objectives.
- **Multilingualism and Cultural Diversity:** The NEP encourages the use of mother tongue or local language as the medium of teaching in schools up to at least Grade 5, acknowledging the linguistic and cultural diversity of India. This dedication to multilingualism seeks to guarantee that every student has access to a top-notch education in a language they can comprehend while also preserving and celebrating India's rich linguistic legacy.
- **Integration of Technology:** The NEP highlights the transformational potential of technology in education and promotes its integration with digital tools, online resources, and virtual learning platforms to improve teaching and learning results, in accordance with worldwide trends. This involves using technology to increase educational access, enable individualized learning, and promote creative curriculum delivery.

Mapping NEP Goals to Curriculum Objectives

- **Equitable Access:** Prioritizing the creation of inclusive learning resources and teaching techniques that address the needs and backgrounds of various learners should be a top priority for curriculum objectives. To guarantee that all students have fair access to educational opportunities, this may entail resolving language obstacles, offering assistance to students with impairments, and adding culturally relevant curriculum.
- **Holistic Development:** Academic knowledge should be included in curriculum objectives, but so should the growth of social and emotional intelligence, critical thinking, and ethical principles. In order to foster holistic development, this may entail introducing chances for reflection and self-evaluation

into the curriculum, encouraging collaborative projects, and adding experiential learning activities.
- **Personalized Learning:** The goal of curriculum objectives should be to provide students the freedom and flexibility to choose how they want to study. Offering optional courses, letting students work on individual projects, and giving assignment alternatives flexibility to suit a range of interests and learning preferences are a few ways to do this.
- **Cultural and Linguistic Diversity:** The goals of the curriculum should take into account the linguistic and cultural variety of India by include lessons that honor many dialects, customs, and viewpoints. In order to foster language competency and cultural awareness, this may entail including works of literature, artwork, and historical accounts from different parts of India in addition to offering assistance for bilingual or multilingual education.
- **Integration of Technology:** Technology integration should be embraced by curriculum objectives as a means of improving teaching and learning. This might entail giving educators the guidance and assistance they need to successfully incorporate technology into their teaching techniques, as well as introducing digital resources, multimedia presentations, and interactive simulations into the curriculum.

Designing Curriculum to Facilitate Active Learning and Student Engagement

Careful planning, thoughtful selection, and the development of meaningful learning experiences are necessary when designing a curriculum for active learning and student participation.

- **Identify Learning Objectives:** Start by outlining the curriculum's learning objectives in detail. What talents, abilities, and knowledge do you want your pupils to possess? Make sure that these goals are in line with the learning outcomes and curricular requirements.
- **Choose Active Learning Strategies:** Choose a range of active learning techniques that encourage involvement and engagement from the students. As examples, consider:

    i. Present real-world issues or challenges to students for group problem-solving in problem-based learning.
    ii. Encourage students to pose queries, look into subjects, and come to conclusions via practical investigation in inquiry-based learning.

iii. Project-based learning: Assign students to work on lengthy assignments that call for investigation, ingenuity, and critical thought.
iv. Enable students to collaborate in groups, learn from one another, and exchange ideas by providing chances for peer teaching and mentoring.

- **Integrate Technology:** Use technological resources and tools to improve hands-on learning opportunities. To engage students and support self-directed learning, this might involve utilizing interactive learning platforms, multimedia presentations, online simulations, or educational applications.
- **Provide Opportunities for Reflection:** Provide chances for students to express their ideas and insights and to reflect on their learning experiences. Journaling, debates in groups, or reflective writing projects where students assess their own learning and pinpoint areas for improvement might all be part of this.
- **Promote Student-Centered Instruction:** Give students more control and ownership over their education to reorient the emphasis from teacher-centered instruction to student-centered learning. Give children the freedom to explore interests, choose objectives, and be accountable for their own education.
- **Use Active Learning Spaces:** Establish a setting that is favorable to learning that encourages participation and teamwork. Organize the furniture in the classroom to support group projects, provide students easy access to tools and supplies, and use variable seating configurations to meet the needs of various learning styles.
- **Assess Learning Outcomes:** Create evaluations that measure students' comprehension, critical thinking abilities, and application of information in line with the aims of active learning. Think about implementing real-world evaluations, such performance activities, presentations, or portfolios, which let students show what they've learned in relevant ways.
- **Provide Ongoing Support:** Throughout the learning process, provide pupils with assistance and direction. This might entail mentoring and peer cooperation, as well as scaffolding and providing feedback on work in progress.

Active learning principles can be effectively integrated into curriculum design to create engaging, student-centered learning experiences that promote deeper understanding, critical thinking, and lifelong learning skills.

Enhancing Classroom Dynamics Through Flip-Flop Models

By encouraging active learning, student-centered strategies, and dynamic interactions, the Flip-Flop Classroom Model is revolutionizing traditional classroom dynamics in education. This paradigm shift changes how educators interact with students and support learning experiences. It departs from traditional teacher-led education and passive student engagement (Morin & Li, 1989). Fundamentally, the Flip-Flop Classroom Model promotes a more participatory and collaborative learning environment by challenging the conventional division of labor between the roles of instructor and student. The name of the model implies a reciprocal exchange of learning materials, with traditional in-class lectures being "flipped" to outside-of-class activities like readings or pre-recorded video lectures, and class time devoted to active learning and the practical application of knowledge (Agrawal et al., 2023; Durairaj et al., 2023).

This method not only encourages critical thinking, peer cooperation, and greater involvement among students, but it also gives them the power to take charge of their education. Teachers may provide students with opportunity to freely investigate topics, participate in meaningful debates, and apply what they have learned in real-world circumstances by flipping the script on the typical classroom model (Devaux, 1993; Ishartono et al., 2024).

A teaching strategy called the Flip-Flop Classroom Model makes use of technology to enhance classroom dynamics. It offers individualized training, interactive learning opportunities, and quick feedback via the use of digital tools and resources. This paradigm accommodates a wide range of learning preferences and styles. We examine the model's guiding concepts, workable implementation techniques, and possible effects on student learning outcomes. For all parties involved, it transforms education and gives students more control. The model challenges educators, decision-makers, and interested parties in education to seize its opportunities and rethink what education will look like in the future.

Transitioning From Teacher-Centric to Student-Centric Learning Environments

The paradigm of education has changed significantly from teacher-centric to student-centric learning settings, affecting classroom dynamics and pedagogy. With an emphasis on critical thinking, active participation, and customized learning opportunities, this change replaces the traditional teacher-driven method with one that is more student-centered. Figure 2 shows how learning environments are changing from being teacher-centric to being student-centric (Burange et al., 2024; Ogata et al., 2020).

Figure 2. Teacher-centric to student-centric learning environments

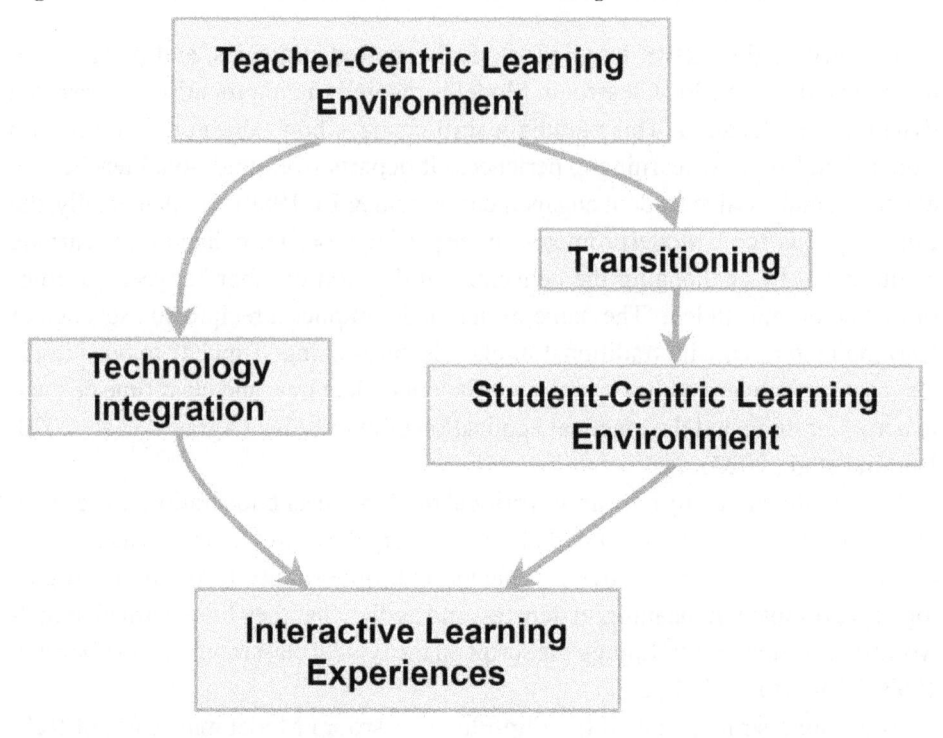

```
        ┌─────────────────────────┐
        │ Teacher-Centric Learning│
        │      Environment        │
        └─────────────────────────┘
           │                    │
           │                    ▼
           │          ┌──────────────────┐
           │          │   Transitioning  │
           │          └──────────────────┘
           │                    │
           ▼                    ▼
  ┌────────────────┐  ┌──────────────────────────┐
  │   Technology   │  │ Student-Centric Learning │
  │  Integration   │  │      Environment         │
  └────────────────┘  └──────────────────────────┘
           │                    │
           ▼                    ▼
        ┌─────────────────────────┐
        │  Interactive Learning   │
        │      Experiences        │
        └─────────────────────────┘
```

Empowering Student Agency: Students are given the freedom to take charge of their education in a setting that is focused on them. Teachers ought to provide pupils the freedom to choose how they want to study, to create objectives, and to follow interests. This might entail giving students authority over the speed and sequencing of their education, letting them choose from a variety of learning activities, or assigning project-based projects (Das et al., 2024; Sharma et al., 2024).

Facilitating Inquiry and Exploration: Learning settings that prioritize students foster curiosity, investigation, and questioning. Teachers ought to provide their pupils the chance to explore subjects, pose questions, and look for solutions via study and experimentation. Teachers may ignite students' innate drive and encourage a better comprehension of subjects by cultivating an inquiry-based culture.

Promoting Collaboration and Peer Learning: In learning settings that prioritize students, collaboration is essential. Teachers should provide chances for pupils to collaborate, exchange ideas, and gain insight from one another's viewpoints. Collaborative problem-solving exercises, group projects, and peer teaching are useful methods for fostering social-emotional learning, communication abilities, and cooperation.

Personalizing Learning Experiences: Every student is different, having their own interests, abilities, and learning styles. Recognizing this variability, student-centric learning settings aim to tailor instruction to each individual student's requirements. Teachers may customize lessons and give students focused support by utilizing formative assessment data, adaptive learning tools, and differentiated instruction.

Emphasizing Active Learning Strategies: The foundation of student-centric learning environments is active learning. Teachers should use a range of active learning techniques, such as flipped classrooms, problem-based learning, and experiential learning, to get students involved in practical exercises, critical thinking exercises, and group projects. These techniques encourage longer-term memory retention, higher-order cognitive abilities, and greater comprehension.

Creating a Supportive Learning Environment: Student welfare and socioemotional growth are given top priority in student-centric learning settings. Teachers ought to provide a welcoming and inclusive environment in the classroom where learners are encouraged to take chances, voice their opinions, and grow from their errors. Establishing a development mentality, nurturing healthy connections, and offering emotional support are all crucial components of establishing a favorable learning environment (Venkatasubramanian et al., 2024).

Fostering Reflective Practice: In settings where the focus is on the learner, reflection is a crucial component of the learning process. Teachers must to motivate pupils to think back on what they have learned, pinpoint their areas of weakness, and make plans to do better. Reflective practices that encourage metacognitive awareness and equip students to become independent learners include journaling, self-evaluation, and peer feedback.

The shift from teacher-centric to student-centric learning settings calls for adjustments to classroom procedures, pedagogy, and mentality. Teachers may build dynamic, engaging, and empowering learning environments by empowering student agency, encouraging collaboration, customizing experiences, stressing active learning practices, establishing a supportive environment, and developing reflective practice.

Leveraging Technology for Interactive Learning Experiences

Through a variety of techniques, educators may employ technology to create interactive learning environments that improve student engagement, encourage active learning, and enable deeper conceptual comprehension (Liu et al., 2024a; Tang et al., 2022):

- **Online Collaboration Tools**: Use synchronous and asynchronous communication tools like Zoom, Microsoft Teams, and Google Workspace. Students may collaborate on group projects, take part in conversations, and exchange

ideas in real time, all without having to be in the same physical area, thanks to these technologies.
- **Interactive Multimedia Content**: Include interactive multimedia components in your classes, such animations, virtual reality experiences, simulations, and films. There are many interactive materials available on websites such as Khan Academy, PhET Interactive Simulations, and TED-Ed, covering a wide range of disciplines.
- **Digital Whiteboards and Annotation Tools**: Employ tools for digital whiteboards, such as Explain Everything or Jamboard, to help with group brainstorming, concept mapping, and problem-solving. During live presentations or debates, students can mark PDFs, photos, and documents with annotation tools.
- **Interactive Quizzing and Polling Tools**: Use interactive polling and quizzing platforms like Mentimeter, Kahoot!, and Poll Everywhere to include students in formative evaluation and feedback. With the help of these resources, teachers may design polls, surveys, and quizzes to assess student comprehension and get immediate feedback.
- **Gamification and Educational Games**: To make learning more engaging and entertaining, incorporate gamification components and instructional games into your sessions. Students are encouraged to practice and grasp academic ideas through gamified learning experiences provided by Quizizz, Quizlet, and Prodigy Math Games.
- **Virtual Labs and Simulations**: Provide science, engineering, and other practical disciplines with virtual lab experiences and simulations. Students can perform experiments, study concepts, and visualize scientific phenomena in virtual lab settings provided by platforms such as Labster, Explore Learning Gizmos, and PhET Interactive Simulations.
- **Augmented Reality (AR) and Virtual Reality (VR)**: Explore AR and VR applications to create immersive learning experiences that bring abstract concepts to life. AR apps like Elements 4D and VR platforms like Google Expeditions allow students to explore virtual environments, interact with 3D models, and gain deeper insights into complex topics(Paul et al., 2024).

Flipped Classroom Approach: Use technology to distribute instructional information outside of class to adopt a flipped classroom model. This will free up in-class time for interactive exercises, group discussions, and practical learning opportunities. Educators may create and distribute interactive video courses with integrated questions using platforms such as Flipgrid, Edpuzzle, and Screencast.

In addition to enabling educators to create dynamic, engaging environments where students can actively participate, collaborate, and develop 21st-century skills, technology can also improve interactive learning experiences by enabling personalized learning, accommodating a variety of learning styles, and giving students access to resources outside of traditional classrooms.

Promoting Collaborative Learning and Peer Interaction

In order to create a dynamic classroom where students may learn from one other, build cooperation skills, and improve their grasp of course material through diverse tactics, it is imperative that collaborative learning and peer interaction be encouraged (Hosen et al., 2021; Saykili, 2019). When these tactics are used, a collaborative learning atmosphere is created in which students actively interact with the subject, pick up knowledge from their peers, and develop the communication and collaboration skills that are essential for success in the classroom.

- **Group Projects and Assignments**: Give students cooperative or group tasks that need them to solve issues, evaluate information, or make presentations. Urge students to split up assignments, take turns, and play to each other's skills in order to accomplish shared objectives.
- **Peer Teaching and Mentoring**: Give students the chance to assume the roles of mentors and instructors by letting them lead conversations, elucidating ideas to their peers, or offering criticism on their peers' work. Peer teaching helps students who receive instruction as well as the student teachers by reinforcing comprehension.
- **Collaborative Problem-Solving Activities**: Create case studies or problem-solving exercises that need students to work together and apply what they've learned to actual situations. Urge students to collaborate to identify the best answers by having discussions about various strategies and methods.
- **Structured Group Discussions**: Organize debates or group discussions on course subjects that are arranged so that students may voice their ideas, pose questions, and practice critical thinking. Establish rules for participation, promote attentive listening, and guarantee that each group member participates equally.
- **Online Collaboration Tools**: Utilize online platforms and tools for collaboration to support peer contact and virtual group projects. No matter where they are physically located, students may interact, exchange files, and work together on projects in real time using platforms like Microsoft Teams, Slack, and Google Workspace.

- **Peer Review and Feedback**: As part of the evaluation process, include peer review exercises where students give helpful criticism on each other's work. Give students instructions for courteous and productive communication, and encourage them to provide precise, actionable feedback based on predetermined criteria.
- **Think-Pair-Share**: Use the think-pair-share method, in which students consider a subject or prompt on their own first, then discuss it with a companion before presenting their views to the class. Active involvement, peer interaction, and a greater understanding of the course material are all encouraged by this approach.
- **Jigsaw Method**: Encourage student cooperation and interdependence by using the jigsaw approach. Segment the course content, give each group a separate task, and then help the groups become subject matter experts in their own segments. Next, divide the students into new groups, with one person from each of the original groups remaining to impart their knowledge to the other members of their new group.
- **Collaborative Learning Spaces**: Assign seats in the classroom so that students may collaborate and work in groups. Employ movable seating configurations, such groups of tables or desks, to promote collaboration and teamwork. Think of including areas for discussion or breakout sessions where students can congregate for group projects as examples of collaborative learning spaces.

STRATEGIES FOR IMPLEMENTATION

Successful implementation of collaborative learning strategies necessitates meticulous planning, clear communication, and intentional instructional design, with several strategies listed for successful execution (Hosen et al., 2021; Saykili, 2019; Tohara & others, 2021). Implementing these strategies fosters a supportive learning environment where students collaborate, learn from each other, and develop crucial teamwork skills for academic success and lifelong learning.

- **Clear Learning Objectives**: Start by clearly defining the goals of collaborative learning activities in the form of learning objectives. Inform students of these aims in a straightforward manner, stressing the need of cooperation, communication, and teamwork in accomplishing common objectives.
- **Structured Group Dynamics**: Establish a defined framework for group work that assigns each member of the group certain duties and responsibilities. To guarantee that every student makes a significant contribution to group activ-

ities, establish criteria for productive cooperation, such as active listening, courteous communication, and equitable involvement.
- **Explicit Instruction**: Give clear guidance on collaborative tactics and abilities, such as effective communication, handling conflict, and problem-solving methods. Give pupils the chance to develop and hone their teamwork skills by modeling these abilities through role-playing exercises or demonstrations.
- **Regular Feedback and Reflection**: Provide students with regular feedback on their group projects, emphasizing their areas of success and need for development. In order to discover areas for improvement and tactics that proved beneficial, encourage students to reflect on their experiences collaborating. To encourage responsibility and introspection, including peer and self-evaluation.
- **Flexibility and Adaptability**: When it comes to your approach to collaborative learning, be adaptive and flexible, keeping in mind that group dynamics might change over time. Keep a careful eye on group interactions and step in when necessary to resolve disputes, clear up confusion, or offer further assistance. As needed, change the makeup of the groups or the activities to keep every kid interested and challenged.
- **Integration of Technology**: Use technology to promote peer connection and cooperation by giving students access to digital communication channels, virtual meeting platforms, and online collaboration tools. Make sure that technology fosters meaningful connections and information exchange during collaborative learning, rather than taking away from it.
- **Celebration of Success**: Celebrate the victories and accomplishments that come from cooperative learning initiatives, emphasizing both individual and group efforts. To further emphasize the importance of cooperation as a key element of the learning process, showcase excellent collaborative work through presentations, exhibitions, or peer appreciation ceremonies.

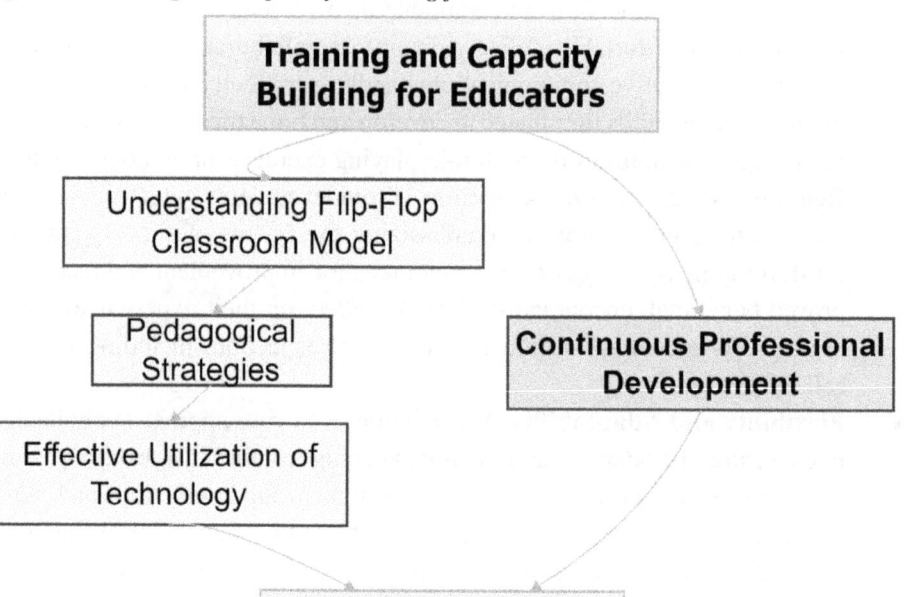

Figure 3. Training and capacity building for educators

Teachers must get extensive training and capacity development before implementing collaborative learning and peer interaction tactics. Here are some tips for approaching training, dealing with obstacles and resistance, and setting up systems for observation and assessment: The process of training and capacity building for educators is shown in Figure 3.

Training and Capacity Building for Educators

- Professional Development Workshops: Provide educators with training, seminars, or workshops that cover the fundamentals and tactics of peer interaction and collaborative learning. Provide tools and chances for practical experience so that teachers may use these tactics in the classroom.
- Peer Observations and Mentoring: Encourage the development of peer observations and mentoring connections among educators so that more seasoned instructors may serve as role models for successful cooperative learning strategies and offer guidance and assistance to their colleagues.
- Internet-Based Communities and Resources: Give educators access to professional learning forums, articles, videos, and online resources so they can

exchange ideas, learn about best practices, and work together with other educators.
- Set aside specific time for teachers to work together to prepare lessons. This will give them the chance to exchange ideas, come up with creative solutions, and create well-thought-out plans for integrating collaborative learning into their classrooms.

Overcoming Challenges and Resistance

- Managing Time Restraints: Acknowledge that putting collaborative learning techniques into practice might take more time and money. Give teachers the freedom and encouragement to try out new strategies and modify their teaching methods as needed.
- Taking Care of Comfort Zone and Mindset: Recognize that certain instructors can be reluctant to adapt or uneasy with collaborative learning strategies. Provide coaches, support, and chances for professional development to assist instructors get over their worries and gain confidence while applying new teaching practices.
- Managing Group Dynamics: Conflicts, uneven participation, and off-task conduct are some of the issues that educators may run into while trying to manage group dynamics. Give advice on how to resolve conflicts, facilitate group agreements, and set clear expectations in order to manage group interactions in an efficient manner.

Monitoring and Evaluation Mechanisms

- Formative Assessment: Use formative assessment techniques to get continuous input on how collaborative learning methodologies are being applied. Make use of self-assessment tools, student comments, and observations to track your development and pinpoint areas that need work.
- Gathering and Analyzing Data: Gather information on the involvement, engagement, and learning objectives of students in relation to cooperative learning activities. To evaluate the efficacy of instructional tactics and make data-driven decisions for improvement, analyze this data on a regular basis.
- Contemplation and Evaluation: It is recommended that educators engage in frequent reviews of their collaborative learning experiences and reflect on their work. Give educators the chance to confer with colleagues about their accomplishments, difficulties, and lessons learned. Then, utilize this input to improve and modify the implementation tactics.

- Feedback Loops: To guarantee ongoing development and alignment with corporate objectives, create feedback loops including educators, administrators, and other stakeholders. Ask for feedback from all parties involved, such as parents, community members, and students, in order to improve accountability and openness in decision-making.

Prioritizing training, increasing capacity, resolving obstacles, and including strong monitoring and evaluation methods into their teaching practices are some of the ways that educators may improve student engagement, learning results, and classroom dynamics (Ali & Abdel-Haq, 2021; Crompton et al., 2020).

CONTINUOUS IMPROVEMENT AND ADAPTATION OF FLIP-FLOP MODELS

Educators can ensure ongoing refinement and adaptation of flip-flop models in education through continuous improvement and adaptation. Figure 4 depicts the continuous improvement and adaptation of flip-flop models(Ali & Abdel-Haq, 2021; Crompton et al., 2020).

Figure 4. Continuous improvement and adaptation of flip-flop models

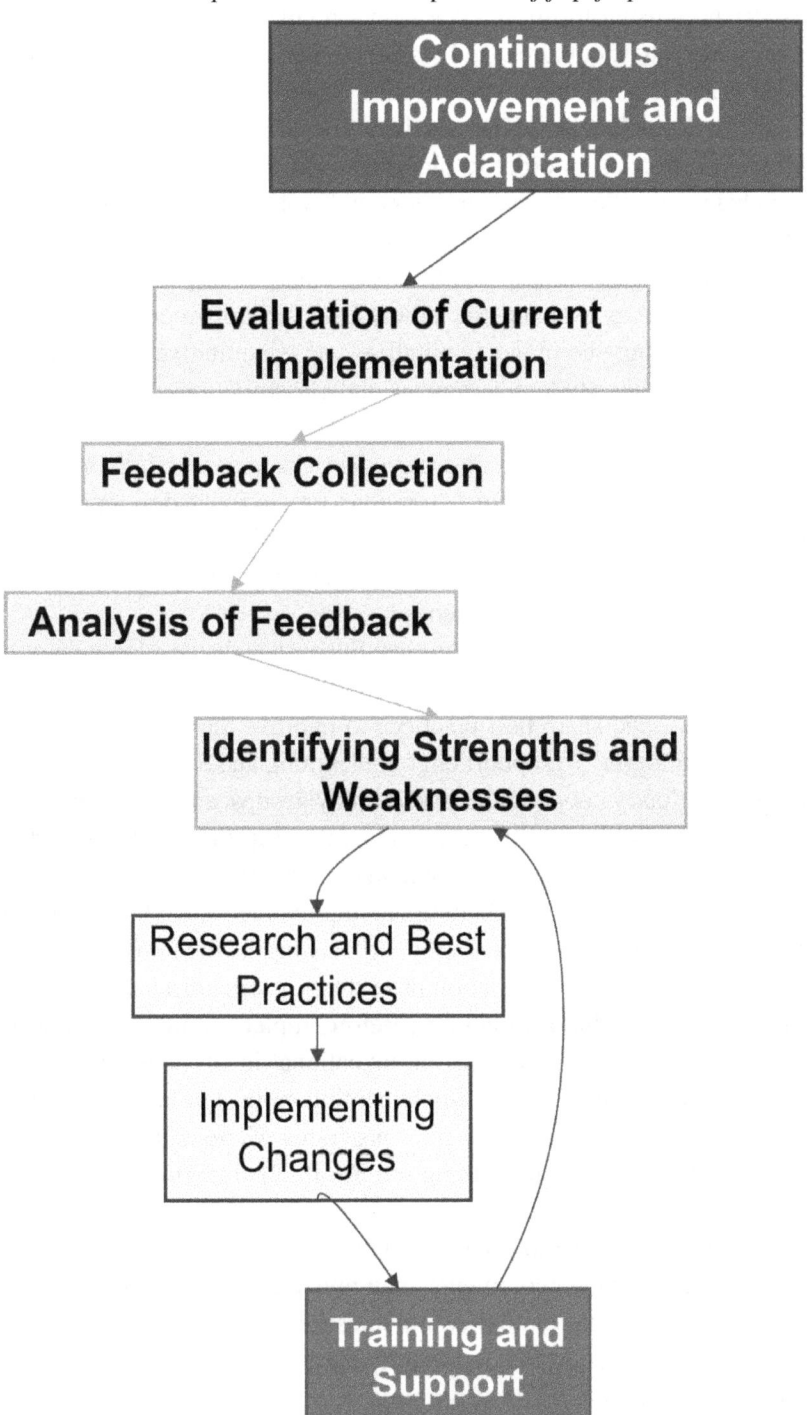

- Collect Feedback: Ask stakeholders, instructors, and students about their experiences using flip-flop models on a regular basis. Utilize focus groups, interviews, questionnaires, and classroom observations to learn more about what is and is not doing properly in the classroom.
- Consider Your Practice: Urge teachers to evaluate their own work and exercise self-reflection in order to pinpoint areas that need work. Give teachers the chance to reflect with their peers and work together to develop ways to improve the way the flip-flop approach is implemented.
- Analyzing Data: Analyze performance, engagement, and satisfaction data from students to evaluate the efficacy of flip-flop models. To help with decision-making, combine qualitative and quantitative information from sources including student comments and classroom observations, as well as assessment results and attendance records.
- Professional Development: To assist educators in successfully using flip-flop models, provide chances for continuous professional development. To address the particular requirements of flip-flop classrooms, offer training on instructional tactics, technological integration, assessment procedures, and classroom management approaches.
- Collaborative Learning Communities: Encourage the development of collaborative learning communities where educators may exchange ideas, troubleshoot issues, and share best practices to improve the implementation of the flip-flop paradigm. To support ongoing learning and development, encourage multidisciplinary cooperation, lesson study groups, and peer mentorship.
- Adaptability and Flexibility: Understand that flip-flop models could need to be modified in response to student demands and preferences, modifications to curricular requirements, technological improvements, or changes in the goals of education. Be willing to adapt your teaching methodologies, material delivery techniques, and evaluation procedures as circumstances demand.
- Pilot Programs & Innovation Labs: Before implementing novel concepts and advancements in bigger classes or educational institutions, test them out in smaller environments. Before implementing more significant changes, establish innovation laboratories or pilot programs where educators may test out novel strategies for implementing the flip-flop paradigm and obtain data on their efficacy.
- Constant Communication To tell stakeholders about changes to flip-flop models and to get their comments, maintain lines of communication open and transparent. Promote mutual communication among educators, administrators, students, parents, and community members to guarantee that all parties are included in the process of progress.

Adopting a culture of continuous improvement and adaptability can help educators maximize student learning experiences, increase the efficacy of flip-flop models, and promote creativity and excellence in the classroom.

FUTURE DIRECTIONS AND SUSTAINABILITY

The use of flip-flop models in education will likely become national in the future, with a focus on integration with educational policy, long-term sustainability, and scaling up implementation. Here's how these goals can be accomplished (Devaux, 1993; Kalyan et al., 2022; Martí & Csajka, 2004):

Scaling Up Implementation Nationwide

- Policy Support: To encourage the acceptance and expansion of flip-flop models, obtain the backing of national policymakers and educational authorities. Promote laws that provide special attention to student-centered learning strategies, technological integration, and creative teaching techniques.
- Professional Development: To increase educators' ability to successfully adopt flip-flop models across the nation, offer them thorough training and professional development opportunities. Provide training opportunities such as seminars, workshops, online courses, and peer mentorship programs to assist teachers in using innovative teaching techniques and utilizing technology to improve student learning.
- Resource Allocation: Provide funds, infrastructure, and resources to enable the widespread use of flip-flop models in classrooms across the country. Ensure that all teachers and students have access to the resources and assistance they need for a successful implementation by making investments in digital materials, professional development programs, and technological infrastructure.
- Networks of Collaboration: Create cooperative networks and alliances between government agencies, educational institutions, districts, and schools to exchange resources, best practices, and implementation insights for flip-flop models. Encourage cooperation and information sharing to hasten the uptake and expansion of cutting-edge teaching strategies.

Ensuring Long-Term Sustainability and Integration with Educational Policies

- Embedding in Curriculum Standards: Promote the inclusion of student-centered learning strategies and flip-flop models in national curricula and educational frameworks. Make sure that the curriculum standards emphasize the value of technological integration, teamwork, and active learning as essential elements of contemporary education.
- Certification and Accreditation of Teachers: Provide flip-flop model and creative teaching practice training as part of teacher certification programs and accreditation requirements. As a prerequisite for their professional development, mandate that educators exhibit mastery of both technology integration and student-centered pedagogies.
- Monitoring and Assessment: To determine the effects of flip-flop models on student learning outcomes, engagement, and satisfaction, procedures for tracking and assessing their national adoption should be established. To find opportunities for development and to guide policy decisions, use data-driven insights.
- Community Involvement: To guarantee broad support and sustainability, involve parents, students, neighbors, and other stakeholders in the implementation of flip-flop models. Encourage collaborations with nearby companies, prominent figures in the field, and neighborhood associations to give students access to more resources, possibilities for mentorship, and hands-on learning experiences.
- Research & Innovation: Fund research and innovation projects to investigate new avenues for augmenting the educational experiences of students and to continually refine flip-flop models. Encourage research projects, pilot projects, and innovation centers to provide evidence-based approaches and promote ongoing educational development.

Flip-flop models have the capacity to revolutionize education, give students more agency, and equip the next generation of learners for success in a world that is changing quickly if they are adopted nationally and incorporated with educational policy.

CONCLUSIONS

The chapter concludes that there are tremendous prospects to transform education in India through the use of Flip-Flop Classroom Models under the National Education Policy (NEP). Flip-Flop Classroom Models may accommodate the different learning requirements of students, promote collaboration and peer interaction, and provide students with the skills they need to succeed in the twenty-first century by adopting student-centered learning, active involvement, and technology integration. Flip-Flop Classroom Models have the potential to revolutionize educational practices and improve learning results across the country since they are in line with the goals and principles of the NEP. However, in order to overcome obstacles and guarantee long-term sustainability, effective execution necessitates professional development, strategic planning, and constant assistance. India can develop dynamic, inclusive, and creative learning environments that enable students, teachers, and communities to flourish in a world that is becoming more complicated and linked by utilizing the benefits of both the NEP and Flip-Flop Classroom Models.

REFERENCES

Agrawal, A. V., Pitchai, R., Senthamaraikannan, C., Balaji, N. A., Sajithra, S., & Boopathi, S. (2023). Digital Education System During the COVID-19 Pandemic. In *Using Assistive Technology for Inclusive Learning in K-12 Classrooms* (pp. 104–126). IGI Global. DOI: 10.4018/978-1-6684-6424-3.ch005

Ali, M., & Abdel-Haq, M. K. (2021). Bibliographical analysis of artificial intelligence learning in Higher Education: Is the role of the human educator and educated a thing of the past? In *Fostering Communication and Learning With Underutilized Technologies in Higher Education* (pp. 36–52). IGI Global. DOI: 10.4018/978-1-7998-4846-2.ch003

Burange, R., Agrawal, G., & Ingole, K. (2024). Design and implementation of low power D flip flop for embedded application. *AIP Conference Proceedings*, 2974(1), 020042. DOI: 10.1063/5.0182465

Choi, J., Cho, J., Choi, W. J., Lee, M., & Kim, B. (2022). A Layout Generator of Latch, Flip-Flop, and Shift Register for High-Speed Links. *2022 19th International SoC Design Conference (ISOCC)*, 19–20.

Crompton, H., Bernacki, M., & Greene, J. A. (2020). Psychological foundations of emerging technologies for teaching and learning in higher education. *Current Opinion in Psychology*, 36, 101–105. DOI: 10.1016/j.copsyc.2020.04.011 PMID: 32604064

Das, S., Lekhya, G., Shreya, K., Shekinah, K. L., Babu, K. K., & Boopathi, S. (2024). Fostering Sustainability Education Through Cross-Disciplinary Collaborations and Research Partnerships: Interdisciplinary Synergy. In *Facilitating Global Collaboration and Knowledge Sharing in Higher Education With Generative AI* (pp. 60–88). IGI Global.

Devaux, P. F. (1993). Lipid transmembrane asymmetry and flip-flop in biological membranes and in lipid bilayers: Current Opinion in Structural Biology 1993, 3: 489–494. *Current Opinion in Structural Biology*, 3(4), 489–494. DOI: 10.1016/0959-440X(93)90072-S

Durairaj, M., Jayakumar, S., Karpagavalli, V., Maheswari, B. U., & Boopathi, S. (2023). Utilization of Digital Tools in the Indian Higher Education System During Health Crises. In *Multidisciplinary Approaches to Organizational Governance During Health Crises* (pp. 1–21). IGI Global. DOI: 10.4018/978-1-7998-9213-7.ch001

Hosen, M., Ogbeibu, S., Giridharan, B., Cham, T.-H., Lim, W. M., & Paul, J. (2021). Individual motivation and social media influence on student knowledge sharing and learning performance: Evidence from an emerging economy. *Computers & Education*, 172, 104262. DOI: 10.1016/j.compedu.2021.104262

Ishartono, N., Kholid, M. N., Arlinwibowo, J., & Afiyah, A. N. (2024). Integrating STEAM into flip flop model to improve students' understanding on composition of functions during online learning. *Infinity Journal*, 13(1), 45–60. DOI: 10.22460/infinity.v13i1.p45-60

Jagadesh Kumar, M. (2020). National Education Policy: How does it Affect Higher Education in India? [). Taylor & Francis.]. *IETE Technical Review*, 37(4), 327–328. DOI: 10.1080/02564602.2020.1806491

Kalyan, B. S., Kaur, H., Pachori, K., & Singh, B. (2022). An efficient design of D flip flop in quantum-dot cellular automata (QCA) for sequential circuits. In *VLSI architecture for signal, speech, and image processing* (pp. 253–272). Apple Academic Press New York, USA.

Liu, B., Ash, J., Goel, S., Krishnamurthy, A., & Zhang, C. (2024a). Exposing attention glitches with flip-flop language modeling. *Advances in Neural Information Processing Systems*, •••, 36.

Liu, B., Ash, J., Goel, S., Krishnamurthy, A., & Zhang, C. (2024b). Exposing attention glitches with flip-flop language modeling. *Advances in Neural Information Processing Systems*, •••, 36.

Martí, J., & Csajka, F. S. (2004). Transition path sampling study of flip-flop transitions in model lipid bilayer membranes. *Physical Review. E*, 69(6), 061918. DOI: 10.1103/PhysRevE.69.061918 PMID: 15244628

Morin, L., & Li, H. (1989). Design of synchronisers: A review. *IEE Proceedings. Part E. Computers and Digital Techniques*, 136(6), 557–564. DOI: 10.1049/ip-e.1989.0076

Naveen, H. (2022). NEP, 2020: General Education Embedded with Skill and Vocational Education. *International Journal of Scientific Research in Science, Engineering and Technology*, 9(01), 65–75.

Ogata, B., Stelovsky, J., & Ogawa, M.-B. C. (2020). Flip-Flop Quizzes: A Case Study Analysis to Inform the Design of Augmented Cognition Applications. *Augmented Cognition. Human Cognition and Behavior: 14th International Conference, AC 2020, Held as Part of the 22nd HCI International Conference, HCII 2020, Copenhagen, Denmark, July 19–24, 2020. Proceedings*, 22(Part II), 106–117.

Paul, A., & Thilagham, K. KG, J.-, Reddy, P. R., Sathyamurthy, R., & Boopathi, S. (2024). Multi-criteria Optimization on Friction Stir Welding of Aluminum Composite (AA5052-H32/B4C) using Titanium Nitride Coated Tool. *Engineering Research Express*.

Ravasz, R., Hudec, A., Maljar, D., Ondica, R., & Stopjakova, V. (2022). Introduction to Teaching the Digital Electronics Design using FPGA. *2022 20th International Conference on Emerging eLearning Technologies and Applications (ICETA)*, 549–554.

Saykili, A. (2019). Higher education in the digital age: The impact of digital connective technologies. *Journal of Educational Technology and Online Learning*, 2(1), 1–15. DOI: 10.31681/jetol.516971

Sharma, D. M., Ramana, K. V., Jothilakshmi, R., Verma, R., Maheswari, B. U., & Boopathi, S. (2024). Integrating Generative AI Into K-12 Curriculums and Pedagogies in India: Opportunities and Challenges. *Facilitating Global Collaboration and Knowledge Sharing in Higher Education With Generative AI*, 133–161.

Shukla, B., Soni, K., Sujatha, R., & Hasteer, N. (2023). Roadmap to inclusive curriculum: A step towards Multidisciplinary Engineering Education for holistic development. *Journal of Engineering Education Transformations*, 36(3), 134–145. DOI: 10.16920/jeet/2023/v36i3/23105

Singh, I. (2021). Role of Modern Technology in Education: An Overview of Indian National Education Policy 2020. *Multidisciplinary Issues in Social Science Research*, 101–120.

Smitha, S. (2020). National education policy (NEP) 2020-Opportunities and challenges in teacher education. [IJM]. *International Journal of Management*, 11(11).

Tang, Y., Hare, R., & Ferguson, S. (2022). Classroom Evaluation of a Gamified Adaptive Tutoring System. *2022 IEEE Frontiers in Education Conference (FIE)*, 1–5.

Tohara, A. J. T. (2021). Exploring digital literacy strategies for students with special educational needs in the digital age. [TURCOMAT]. *Turkish Journal of Computer and Mathematics Education*, 12(9), 3345–3358.

Venkatasubramanian, V., Chitra, M., Sudha, R., Singh, V. P., Jefferson, K., & Boopathi, S. (2024). Examining the Impacts of Course Outcome Analysis in Indian Higher Education: Enhancing Educational Quality. In *Challenges of Globalization and Inclusivity in Academic Research* (pp. 124–145). IGI Global. DOI: 10.4018/979-8-3693-1371-8.ch009

Wankhade, R. S. (2021). Higher Education and NEP-2020. *International Journal of Researches in Social Science and Information Studies*, 8(1), 51–56.

KEY TERMS

AR: Augmented Reality
ECCE: Early Childhood Care and Education
ET: Educational Technology
NEP: National Education Policy
PDF: Portable Document Format
TED: Technology, Entertainment, Design (also refers to TED Talks)
VR: Virtual Reality
ZPD: Zone of Proximal Development

Chapter 13
Flipped Classroom Methods for Enhanced Student Engagement and Knowledge Developments in Indian Higher Education

M. Karthikeyan
https://orcid.org/0009-0003-9694-2560
Department of Business Administration, School of Management, Vel Tech Rangarajan Dr. Sagunthala R&D Institute of Science and Technology, India

Vepada Suchitra
Department of Mathematics, Godavari Institute of Engineering and Technology, India

E. M. Sri Amirtha Varshini
Department of English, Kongu Engineering College, India

Balpreet Singh Madan
Department of Art and Design, School of Design, Architecture, and Planning, Sharda University, India

Ratan Sarkar
Department of Teachers' Training, Prabhat Kumar College, Vidyasagar University, India

S. Boopathi
Mechanical Engineering, Muthyammal Engineering College, India

ABSTRACT

In Indian higher education, flipped classrooms provide a viable alternative to con-

DOI: 10.4018/979-8-3693-4058-5.ch013

ventional pedagogical methods, boosting student engagement and knowledge growth. While in-class time is devoted to interactive exercises, group problem-solving, and peer debates, pre-class activities such as video lectures and readings allow students to complete them independently before class sessions. However, obstacles including inadequate infrastructure, reluctance from teachers, and worries over grading and evaluation make it difficult to put them into practice. To address these obstacles, a multifaceted strategy including faculty development, technology assistance, and institutional policy reforms is required.

INTRODUCTION

The flipped classroom model represents a pedagogical approach that redefines the traditional classroom dynamic by restructuring the typical sequence of instruction. In a flipped classroom, the traditional roles of in-class lectures and homework assignments are reversed. Students engage with instructional content outside of class, typically through pre-recorded lectures, readings, or multimedia materials, prior to attending face-to-face class sessions. During class time, the focus shifts towards active learning activities, collaborative problem-solving, and application of concepts under the guidance of the instructor(Sravat & Pathranarakul, 2022).

The flipped classroom model focuses on maximizing face-to-face interaction by utilizing class time for higher-order cognitive activities like critical thinking, analysis, and synthesis. This inversion of traditional instruction emphasizes student-centered learning, self-directed study, and peer collaboration, fostering deeper engagement and understanding of course material. The model's principle of learner-centered education is central, empowering students to take ownership of their learning process and progress at their own pace. This shift towards self-regulated learning encourages essential skills like time management, self-discipline, and metacognitive awareness, crucial for lifelong learning and success in academic and professional pursuits(Sevillano-Monje et al., 2022).

The flipped classroom model encourages active learning through constructivist principles. Students are actively involved in understanding through interactions with course material, peers, and instructors. In-class activities like group discussions, problem-solving exercises, and peer teaching allow students to apply their knowledge, deepen their understanding, and receive immediate feedback. The flipped classroom model is a flexible approach that caters to diverse learning styles and needs(Bishnoi, 2020). It offers instructional content in various formats, such as videos, readings, and interactive multimedia, allowing students to engage with course material in ways that align with their individual learning styles. This model also fosters a more inclusive learning environment by eliminating barriers to access and participation, allowing students to engage with course material anytime, anywhere. This flexibility is particularly beneficial for students with diverse backgrounds, learning needs, or responsibilities outside academia, such as working professionals, caregivers, or individuals with disabilities. The flipped classroom model is a pedagogical innovation that shifts instruction sequences, promoting active learning, student engagement, and self-directed study, based on learner-centered principles and constructivist theories, fostering deeper understanding and critical thinking(Sosa Díaz et al., 2021a).

The flipped classroom model, introduced in the early 2000s, has been widely adopted in education due to technological advancements, pedagogical innovations, and changing student demographics. The model aims to enhance learning outcomes by providing alternative methods to traditional teaching methods. Digital technologies and online resources have facilitated the creation and dissemination of instructional content outside traditional classrooms(Shaw & Patra, 2022). Video-sharing platforms, learning management systems, and open educational resources have made it easier for educators to create and share pre-recorded lectures, interactive tutorials, and multimedia materials, making it accessible to students anytime, anywhere(Kannan et al., 2020).

The decline of traditional lecture-based instruction has sparked interest in alternative methods like active learning and flipped classrooms. Research indicates that passive methods, like lectures, often fail to engage students or promote deep understanding of course material. Active learning strategies, like collaborative problem-solving, peer teaching, and hands-on activities, have been proven to enhance engagement, critical thinking, and knowledge retention(Fuchs, 2021a).

The flipped classroom model in Indian higher education is justified by various factors, including(Fuchs, 2021a; Kannan et al., 2020):

a. Addressing the limitations of traditional lecture-based instruction: Like their counterparts in other parts of the world, educators in Indian higher education institutions have recognized the need to move beyond traditional lecturing and adopt more student-centered and interactive teaching approaches. The flipped classroom model offers a compelling alternative that leverages technology to deliver instructional content outside of class, freeing up valuable class time for active learning activities that promote deeper understanding and application of course concepts.

b. Enhancing student engagement and motivation: The flipped classroom model has been shown to enhance student engagement and motivation by providing opportunities for active participation, collaboration, and interaction with course material and peers. By allowing students to engage with instructional content at their own pace and revisit concepts as needed, the model accommodates diverse learning styles and preferences, leading to higher levels of student satisfaction and academic success.

c. Fostering critical thinking and problem-solving skills: The flipped classroom model promotes the development of critical thinking and problem-solving skills by engaging students in meaningful learning activities that require them to analyze, synthesize, and apply course concepts in real-world contexts. By actively participating in discussions, debates, and hands-on exercises during class time, students gain a deeper understanding of course material and develop the skills necessary to navigate complex issues and challenges in their academic and professional lives.

d. Addressing challenges related to access and equity: In a country as diverse and geographically vast as India, access to quality education can be a significant challenge, particularly for students residing in rural or remote areas with limited access to educational resources and infrastructure. The flipped classroom model has the potential to address these challenges by leveraging digital technologies to deliver instructional content online, thereby expanding access to education and reducing disparities in learning opportunities.

The flipped classroom model in Indian higher education aims to improve teaching effectiveness, student learning outcomes, and create an inclusive environment. As educators refine this model, it's crucial to evaluate its impact on student engagement, learning outcomes, and overall educational quality. Adapting and innovating based on emerging best practices and evidence-based research is essential for enhancing the learning experience.

STUDENT BEHAVIOR IN FLIPPED CLASSROOMS

Engagement Levels and Motivation

Student behavior in flipped classrooms is characterized by increased engagement levels and motivation, driven by several important factors: Thus, the flipped classroom model empowers students to take an active role in their learning process, fostering higher levels of engagement, motivation, and achievement. Figure 1 depicts the effect of flipped classrooms on engagement levels and motivation. By providing opportunities for personalized learning, immediate feedback, peer collaboration, and real-world relevance, flipped classrooms create a dynamic and stimulating learning environment that inspires students to excel academically and professionally(Lai et al., 2021).

- Active Participation: Flipped classrooms encourage active participation as students are required to engage with instructional content independently before class. This pre-class preparation primes students to come to class ready to participate in discussions, problem-solving activities, and collaborative projects.
- Personalized Learning: The flexibility of the flipped classroom model allows students to engage with course material at their own pace and according to their individual learning preferences. This personalized approach fosters a sense of ownership over learning, leading to higher levels of motivation and engagement.
- Immediate Feedback: In-class activities in flipped classrooms provide students with immediate feedback from their peers and instructors, facilitating a deeper understanding of course concepts and encouraging continuous improvement. This timely feedback loop enhances motivation by reinforcing positive learning behaviors and addressing areas of confusion or misunderstanding.
- Peer Collaboration: Flipped classrooms promote peer collaboration and interaction through group discussions, problem-solving exercises, and peer teaching opportunities. Collaborative learning experiences not only deepen understanding but also foster a sense of community and belonging among students, enhancing motivation and engagement.
- Real-world Relevance: The application-oriented nature of in-class activities in flipped classrooms allows students to see the relevance of course concepts to real-world scenarios. By connecting theoretical knowledge to practical applications, flipped classrooms motivate students by demonstrating the tangible benefits and implications of their learning.

Self-regulated Learning and Responsibility

Flipped classrooms foster self-regulated learning and responsibility, which significantly enhance academic success and personal development among students. Flipped classrooms foster self-regulated learning and responsibility, allowing students to take control of their education, set goals, and develop lifelong learning skills(Bishnoi, 2020). This supportive environment promotes autonomy, accountability, metacognitive awareness, resource management, and resilience, preparing students for success in academic and professional contexts.

- Autonomy and Accountability: In flipped classrooms, students take on greater responsibility for their learning journey. They are tasked with managing their time effectively to engage with pre-class materials, ensuring they come prepared to participate meaningfully in in-class activities. This autonomy

fosters a sense of accountability, as students understand that their success depends on their active participation and effort.
- Goal Setting and Monitoring: Self-regulated learners in flipped classrooms set clear learning goals and monitor their progress towards achieving them. They may establish targets for completing pre-class assignments, mastering specific course concepts, or improving their problem-solving skills. Regular self-assessment allows students to track their growth and identify areas for improvement, enhancing their overall learning experience.
- Metacognitive Strategies: Flipped classrooms provide opportunities for students to develop metacognitive awareness—the ability to monitor, evaluate, and regulate their learning processes. By reflecting on their learning experiences, identifying effective study strategies, and adjusting their approach as needed, students become more adept at managing their learning and optimizing their academic performance.
- Resource Management: Self-regulated learners in flipped classrooms effectively manage resources such as time, materials, and support networks to facilitate their learning. They prioritize tasks, allocate sufficient time for studying and reviewing course content, and seek assistance from peers, instructors, or online resources when needed. This proactive approach to resource management enables students to overcome challenges and achieve their academic goals.
- Adaptability and Resilience: Flipped classrooms cultivate adaptability and resilience in students, as they learn to navigate uncertainties and overcome obstacles in their learning journey. By taking ownership of their learning process and persisting in the face of difficulties, students develop the resilience needed to overcome setbacks and achieve success in their academic endeavors.

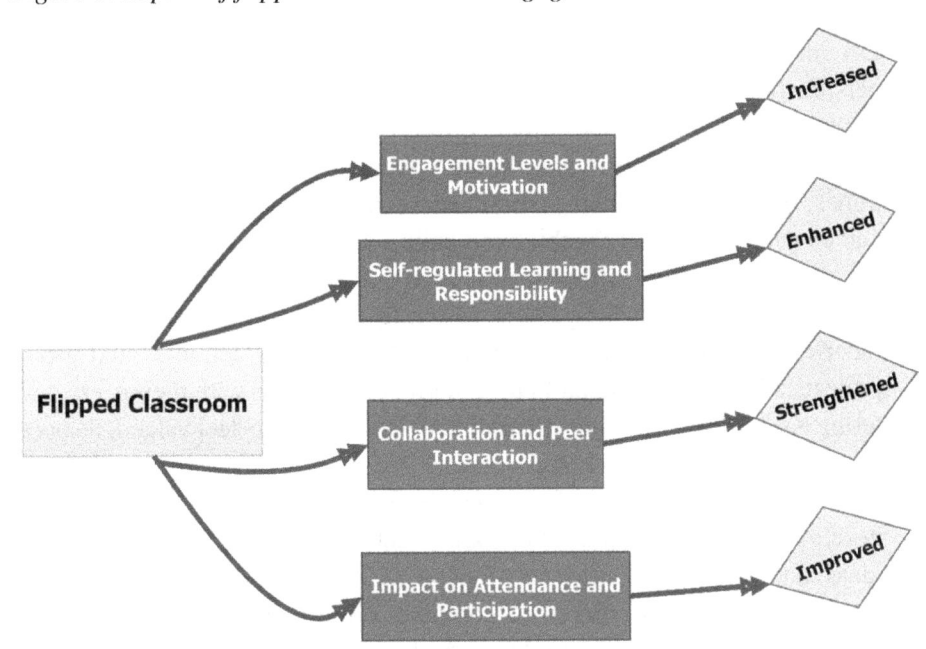

Figure 1. Impact of flipped classrooms on engagement levels and motivation

Collaboration and Peer Interaction

Flipped classrooms promote collaboration and peer interaction, enhancing student behavior, critical thinking, and social-emotional development through deeper understanding and deeper interaction(Yildiz Durak, 2022a). Flipped classrooms foster active engagement, deeper learning, and social-emotional development by promoting collaboration and peer interaction. They foster knowledge sharing, diverse perspectives, social support, and communication skills, creating a dynamic and interactive learning environment that prepares students for success in academic, professional, and social contexts.

- Peer Learning: Flipped classrooms provide ample opportunities for peer learning, as students engage in collaborative activities, discussions, and problem-solving exercises during in-class sessions. By working together with their peers, students can exchange ideas, perspectives, and insights, which can enhance their understanding of course material and promote deeper learning.
- Knowledge Sharing: Peer interaction in flipped classrooms facilitates the sharing of knowledge and expertise among students. Through group discussions, peer teaching, and collaborative projects, students have the opportunity

to draw upon their individual strengths and experiences to contribute to the learning process, enriching the collective understanding of the class.
- Diverse Perspectives: Collaboration with peers exposes students to diverse perspectives and approaches to problem-solving, which can broaden their understanding of course concepts and encourage critical thinking. By engaging with classmates from different backgrounds, cultures, and academic disciplines, students gain a more comprehensive understanding of complex issues and develop their ability to think critically and analytically.
- Social Support: Peer interaction in flipped classrooms provides students with social support and encouragement, fostering a sense of belonging and camaraderie within the learning community. Collaborative activities and group projects allow students to build meaningful connections with their peers, fostering a supportive learning environment where students feel valued, respected, and motivated to succeed.
- Communication Skills: Collaboration in flipped classrooms helps students develop essential communication skills, such as active listening, articulating ideas, and providing constructive feedback. By engaging in discussions and group work, students refine their communication abilities and learn how to effectively express their thoughts and ideas to their peers, enhancing their interpersonal and professional skills.

Impact on Attendance and Participation

The flipped classroom model significantly influences attendance and participation in higher education settings. The flipped classroom model positively impacts attendance and participation, enhancing engagement, improving learning outcomes, and creating a more inclusive environment. It motivates students to attend regularly and actively participate, thereby enhancing their academic success and satisfaction(Meyliana et al., 2021).

- *Increased Attendance:* Flipped classrooms often see an increase in attendance rates as compared to traditional lecture-based classes. Because students are required to engage with pre-class materials before coming to class, they are more likely to attend in order to participate in the collaborative activities, discussions, and problem-solving exercises that characterize in-class sessions. The active learning environment and opportunities for peer interaction also make class sessions more engaging and worthwhile for students, motivating them to attend regularly.
- *Improved Participation:* Flipped classrooms promote higher levels of participation among students during in-class activities. Because students have

already been exposed to the foundational concepts through pre-class assignments, they come to class better prepared to engage in discussions, ask questions, and contribute to group activities. This increased preparation and engagement lead to more meaningful interactions and a deeper exploration of course material, enhancing the overall learning experience for both students and instructors.
- **Enhanced Learning Outcomes:** The combination of increased attendance and improved participation in flipped classrooms often translates into enhanced learning outcomes for students. By actively engaging with course material both before and during class, students have more opportunities to reinforce their understanding, clarify concepts, and apply their knowledge in real-world contexts. The collaborative nature of in-class activities also fosters peer learning and knowledge sharing, contributing to deeper learning and retention of course content.
- **Accountability and Responsibility:** Flipped classrooms promote a sense of accountability and responsibility among students, which can further contribute to improved attendance and participation. Because students are expected to come to class prepared and ready to engage with course material, they take on greater ownership of their learning and are more likely to actively participate in class discussions and activities. This sense of accountability fosters a positive learning environment where students feel motivated to contribute and succeed.
- **Inclusive Learning Environment:** Flipped classrooms can also help create a more inclusive learning environment by accommodating diverse learning styles, preferences, and needs. The flexibility of the model allows students to engage with course material in ways that suit their individual learning styles, whether through videos, readings, or interactive online modules. This flexibility, coupled with the active learning opportunities provided during class, ensures that all students have the opportunity to participate and succeed, regardless of their background or learning abilities.

ACTIVITIES AND STRATEGIES IN FLIPPED CLASSROOMS

The flipped classroom model uses various strategies to enhance student engagement, deepen understanding, and facilitate knowledge application. These strategies involve pre-class preparation, such as watching video lectures, reading materials, or completing online modules. These activities prepare students for more advanced discussions and activities during face-to-face sessions, fostering a sense of responsibility and ownership over learning. By utilizing these activities, students are better prepared for the more complex content and more engaging learning experiences(Zou et al., 2022).

Figure 2 depicts various activities and strategies in flipped classrooms. Flipped classrooms offer interactive and collaborative learning experiences, promoting critical thinking, peer interaction, and knowledge application. Students engage in group discussions, problem-solving exercises, case studies, simulations, and hands-on activities, fostering deeper understanding. These activities allow students to apply theoretical concepts to real-world scenarios, receive immediate feedback, and develop essential skills like communication, collaboration, and critical thinking. Post-class reflections in flipped classrooms help students consolidate their learning and evaluate their understanding of course material. This can involve completing assessments, projects, or reflective journals, demonstrating mastery of key concepts, applying knowledge in new contexts, and evaluating their learning process. Post-class reflections also allow students to receive feedback, identify areas for improvement, and set future learning goals. This dynamic learning environment fosters deeper engagement, critical thinking, and knowledge application. Flipped classrooms use technology to deliver instructional content outside of class, maximizing face-to-face class time for active learning and collaboration(Silverajah et al., 2022).

Figure 2. Activities and strategies in flipped classrooms

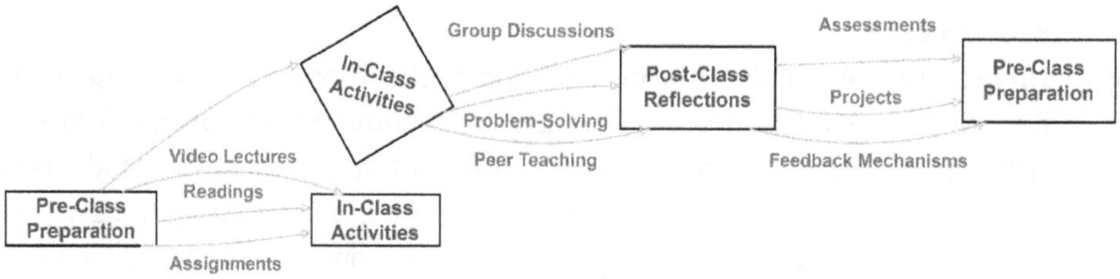

In-Class Activities: Group Discussions, Problem-Solving, and Peer Teaching

Flipped classrooms emphasize in-class activities for deeper understanding, critical thinking, and collaborative learning, focusing on group discussions, problem-solving, and peer teaching(Azizah et al., 2022). Flipped classrooms involve in-class activities like group discussions, problem-solving, and peer teaching, which promote active learning, collaborative engagement, and deeper understanding among students. These activities enhance the learning experience, prepare students for success in academic and professional contexts, by allowing them to apply their knowledge meaningfully.

- **Group Discussions**: In-class group discussions allow students to actively engage with course material, share perspectives, and explore complex topics in a collaborative setting. These discussions provide opportunities for students to articulate their thoughts, ask questions, and challenge assumptions, fostering critical thinking and deeper understanding. By exchanging ideas and insights with peers, students gain new perspectives and develop their communication and interpersonal skills.
- **Problem-Solving**: Problem-solving activities in flipped classrooms encourage students to apply their knowledge and skills to real-world scenarios, challenges, or case studies. Working collaboratively in groups, students analyze problems, identify relevant information, and develop creative solutions. Through problem-solving exercises, students learn to think critically, evaluate evidence, and make informed decisions, while also honing their teamwork and decision-making skills.
- **Peer Teaching**: Peer teaching involves students taking on the role of instructors by explaining concepts, leading discussions, or facilitating learning activities for their peers. This approach not only reinforces students' understanding of course material but also promotes active engagement and peer collaboration. By teaching others, students deepen their own understanding, develop communication skills, and gain confidence in their ability to convey complex ideas effectively.
- **Promoting Active Learning**: In-class activities in flipped classrooms are designed to promote active learning by engaging students in hands-on, participatory experiences. Rather than passively absorbing information, students actively construct knowledge through interaction, exploration, and discovery. Group discussions, problem-solving tasks, and peer teaching activities provide opportunities for students to actively engage with course content, apply their knowledge, and make meaningful connections between theory and practice.
- **Facilitating Peer Interaction**: In-class activities facilitate peer interaction, allowing students to learn from and with their peers. Through collaborative learning experiences, students benefit from diverse perspectives, collective problem-solving, and peer feedback, enriching their learning experience. Peer interaction also fosters a sense of community and belonging within the classroom, creating a supportive learning environment where students feel valued, respected, and motivated to succeed.

Post-Class Reflections: Assessments, Projects, and Feedback Mechanisms

Post-class reflections in flipped classrooms aim to consolidate learning, assess understanding, and provide feedback to students through three common activities. Post-class reflections in flipped classrooms enhance learning, assess student progress, and promote continuous improvement. Through assessments, projects, and feedback, students demonstrate their understanding, apply knowledge, and receive valuable feedback, thereby contributing to their academic success.

- **Assessments**: Post-class assessments are used to evaluate students' understanding of the material covered in both pre-class and in-class activities. These assessments can take various forms, such as quizzes, tests, essays, or problem sets, and are designed to measure students' mastery of key concepts, skills, and learning objectives. Assessments provide valuable feedback to students and instructors, helping to identify areas of strength and weakness and inform future instruction.
- **Projects**: Post-class projects are hands-on assignments that allow students to apply their knowledge and skills to real-world problems or scenarios. Projects may involve individual or group work and can take many forms, including research papers, presentations, case studies, simulations, or creative works. By engaging in project-based learning, students deepen their understanding of course material, develop critical thinking and problem-solving skills, and gain practical experience relevant to their field of study.
- **Feedback Mechanisms**: Post-class feedback mechanisms provide opportunities for students to reflect on their learning experiences and receive constructive feedback from peers and instructors. These mechanisms may include peer evaluations, self-assessments, instructor feedback, or course evaluations. By soliciting feedback from multiple sources, students gain insights into their strengths and areas for improvement, while also providing valuable input to instructors for course refinement and improvement.

KNOWLEDGE DEVELOPMENT AND LEARNING OUTCOMES

Flipped classrooms enhance knowledge development and learning outcomes by promoting active engagement and deeper understanding of content. They facilitate mastery of content through pre-class preparation and in-class activities, allowing students to familiarize themselves with key concepts. This allows for more meaningful discussions and activities during face-to-face sessions. In-class activities, such as group discussions, problem-solving tasks, and peer teaching, reinforce learning by encouraging students to apply and synthesize their knowledge in collaborative settings(Azizah et al., 2022).

Flipped classrooms foster critical thinking skills by requiring students to analyze, evaluate, and apply course material in novel contexts. Through problem-solving exercises, case studies, and collaborative projects, students learn to identify patterns and connect disparate ideas, preparing them for academic and professional challenges. Additionally, flipped classrooms emphasize the practical application of knowledge in real-world scenarios, allowing students to see the relevance of course concepts. This approach fosters a deeper appreciation for the significance of learning and motivates students to invest more in their education(Anjomshoaa et al., 2022).

Flipped classrooms foster metacognitive awareness, allowing students to monitor and regulate their learning process. Through self-directed study, reflection, and peer interaction, students develop a deeper understanding of their learning preferences and strengths. This metacognitive awareness enables students to become more effective and independent learners, adapting their strategies to meet academic and professional demands. Flipped classrooms offer a dynamic, student-centered approach to education, promoting holistic knowledge development and preparing students for success in a complex, interconnected global society. Figure 3 depicts the knowledge development and learning outcomes of a flipped classroom.

Several strategies can be employed by educators to enhance content mastery and critical thinking skills in flipped classrooms(Kang & Kim, 2021).

- *Pre-Class Engagement:* Encourage students to engage deeply with pre-class materials, such as video lectures, readings, or online modules. Provide guided questions or prompts to help students actively process the content and make connections to prior knowledge. This pre-class engagement primes students for deeper discussions and analysis during in-class activities.
- *Socratic Questioning:* Use Socratic questioning techniques during in-class discussions to stimulate critical thinking and inquiry. Encourage students to ask probing questions, challenge assumptions, and explore alternative perspectives. By engaging in rigorous dialogue and debate, students develop critical thinking skills and gain a deeper understanding of complex concepts.
- *Problem-Based Learning:* Incorporate problem-based learning (PBL) activities into flipped classroom sessions, where students work collaboratively to solve real-world problems or case studies. PBL tasks require students to apply their knowledge, analyze information, and generate creative solutions, fostering critical thinking and problem-solving skills.
- *Peer Collaboration:* Foster peer collaboration and peer teaching opportunities during in-class activities. Encourage students to work together in small

groups to discuss and solve problems, analyze case studies, or peer-review each other's work. Peer collaboration promotes critical thinking by providing diverse perspectives, fostering intellectual debate, and encouraging students to defend their ideas and conclusions.
- **Reflective Practices:** Integrate reflective practices into the learning process, where students are encouraged to reflect on their learning experiences, identify areas of strength and weakness, and set goals for improvement. Provide opportunities for students to write reflective journals, engage in self-assessment exercises, or participate in peer feedback sessions. Reflection promotes meta-cognitive awareness and helps students develop strategies for monitoring and regulating their learning process.

The goal is to enhance the practical application of knowledge in real-world scenarios(Anjomshoaa et al., 2022).

- **Authentic Assessment:** Design assessments that require students to apply their knowledge and skills to authentic, real-world tasks or situations. This could include case studies, simulations, projects, or fieldwork experiences that mirror professional contexts. Authentic assessments provide students with opportunities to demonstrate their understanding in practical contexts and develop transferable skills.
- **Project-Based Learning:** Implement project-based learning (PBL) experiences where students work collaboratively to solve complex problems, address real-world challenges, or create tangible products. PBL tasks encourage students to apply their knowledge, engage in inquiry, and work towards meaningful outcomes, fostering deeper learning and application of knowledge.
- **Community Engagement:** Foster partnerships with local organizations, businesses, or community groups to provide students with opportunities for real-world application of their learning. This could involve service-learning projects, internships, or experiential learning opportunities that allow students to apply their knowledge in authentic settings and make meaningful contributions to their communities.
- **Case Studies and Scenarios:** Use case studies, scenarios, or role-playing exercises to simulate real-world situations and challenges relevant to the course content. Encourage students to analyze information, make decisions, and propose solutions based on their understanding of course concepts. This experiential learning approach helps students develop problem-solving skills and apply theoretical knowledge in practical contexts.
- **Reflection and Feedback:** Incorporate opportunities for reflection and feedback into real-world application activities. Encourage students to reflect on

their experiences, assess their performance, and identify lessons learned. Provide constructive feedback and guidance to help students improve their skills and refine their understanding of how course concepts apply in real-world scenarios.

Flipped classroom instruction can enhance content mastery, critical thinking skills, and knowledge application in real-world scenarios, preparing students for success in academic, professional, and personal contexts.

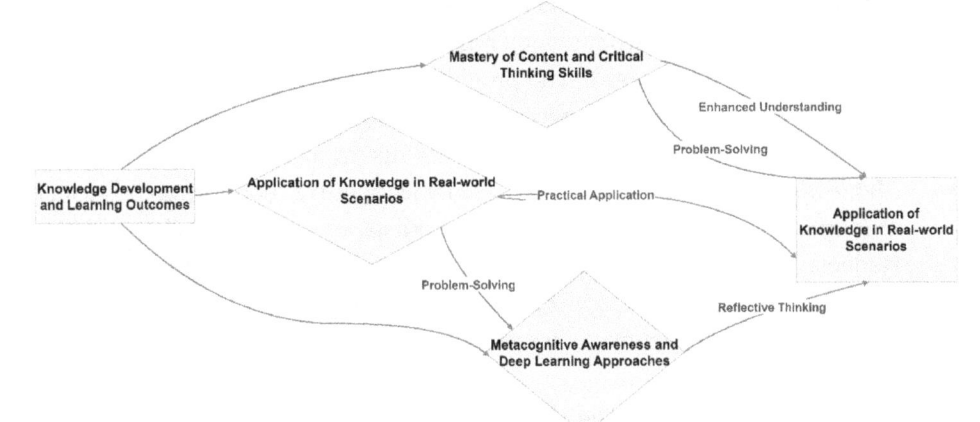

Figure 3. Knowledge development and learning outcomes of flipped class room

Metacognitive Awareness and Deep Learning Approaches

Various strategies can be employed by educators to promote metacognitive awareness and deep learning approaches in flipped classrooms(Kevser, 2021). Educators can enhance metacognitive awareness and deep learning strategies in flipped classrooms, empowering students to take ownership of their learning, develop effective study strategies, and achieve meaningful learning outcomes.

- *Explicit Instruction:* Provide explicit instruction on metacognitive strategies and deep learning approaches, such as self-regulation, goal-setting, and reflective practices. Educate students about the importance of monitoring their learning process, setting learning goals, and employing effective study strategies to promote deep understanding and retention of course material.
- *Scaffolded Learning Activities:* Design learning activities that scaffold students' metacognitive development and promote deep learning. Start with

structured activities that guide students through the process of setting learning goals, monitoring their progress, and reflecting on their learning experiences. Gradually release responsibility to students as they become more proficient in applying metacognitive strategies independently.

- *Reflection Prompts:* Integrate reflection prompts into pre-class assignments, in-class activities, and post-class assessments to encourage students to reflect on their learning process, identify challenges, and set goals for improvement. Provide guiding questions or prompts to help students articulate their thoughts, analyze their learning strategies, and identify areas for growth.
- *Peer Collaboration and Feedback:* Foster peer collaboration and peer feedback opportunities that promote metacognitive awareness and deep learning. Encourage students to work together in small groups to discuss their learning goals, share study strategies, and provide constructive feedback on each other's work. Peer collaboration allows students to gain new perspectives, receive peer support, and develop metacognitive skills through social interaction.
- *Metacognitive Monitoring Tools:* Use metacognitive monitoring tools, such as learning journals, self-assessment checklists, or progress trackers, to help students track their learning progress and evaluate their understanding of course material. Provide opportunities for students to regularly assess their own learning, set benchmarks for achievement, and adjust their learning strategies based on feedback.
- *Formative Assessment and Feedback:* Incorporate formative assessment strategies, such as quizzes, concept maps, or low-stakes assignments, to provide students with ongoing feedback on their learning progress. Use formative assessment data to identify areas where students may need additional support or intervention and provide timely feedback to guide their learning process.

BARRIERS TO IMPLEMENTING FLIPPED CLASSROOMS IN INDIAN HIGHER EDUCATION

Infrastructure Challenges: Access to Technology and Internet Connectivity

Figure 4 depicts the obstacles faced in implementing flipped classrooms in Indian higher education. Infrastructure challenges, particularly in technology and internet connectivity, are a significant obstacle to implementing flipped classrooms in Indian higher education(Fuchs, 2021b).

- **Limited Access to Technology**: Many students in Indian higher education institutions may not have access to personal computers, laptops, or other digital devices required to engage with online materials outside of class. This is especially true for students from rural or economically disadvantaged backgrounds who may lack access to technology due to financial constraints or limited availability of resources.
- **Inconsistent Internet Connectivity**: Even for students who have access to technology, inconsistent internet connectivity poses a significant challenge. In many parts of India, especially rural areas, internet infrastructure may be unreliable or inadequate, leading to slow internet speeds, frequent disruptions, or complete lack of access. This hampers students' ability to access online materials, participate in virtual discussions, or complete online assignments reliably.
- **Digital Divide**: The digital divide exacerbates the challenge of implementing flipped classrooms in Indian higher education. Disparities in access to technology and internet connectivity between urban and rural areas, as well as between socioeconomic groups, widen existing inequalities in educational opportunities. Students who lack access to technology or reliable internet connectivity may be at a disadvantage compared to their peers who have better access to digital resources.
- **Infrastructure Limitations**: Beyond student access, infrastructure limitations within educational institutions, such as inadequate computer labs, outdated technology, or insufficient bandwidth, can hinder the implementation of flipped classrooms. Educational institutions may lack the necessary infrastructure to support the technological requirements of flipped learning, making it difficult to effectively deliver online content or facilitate virtual interactions.
- **Cost Considerations**: Implementing flipped classrooms often entails investment in technology infrastructure, software platforms, and internet connectivity solutions. For many educational institutions, especially those with limited financial resources, the costs associated with upgrading infrastructure and providing access to technology may be prohibitive, further hindering the adoption of flipped learning approaches.

Policymakers, educational institutions, and stakeholders must invest in digital infrastructure, expand internet connectivity, and bridge the digital divide to address infrastructure challenges. Alternative strategies like blended learning models, which combine online and face-to-face instruction, may be more feasible in areas with infrastructure limitations. This will enable Indian higher education institutions to create inclusive, equitable learning environments.

Faculty Training and Pedagogical Support

The implementation of flipped classrooms in Indian higher education faces significant challenges due to a lack of faculty training and pedagogical support(Sosa Díaz et al., 2021b).

- **Limited Familiarity with Flipped Learning**: Many faculty members in Indian higher education institutions may be unfamiliar with the principles and practices of flipped learning. Traditional lecture-based methods are often entrenched in academic culture, and faculty may lack exposure to alternative pedagogical approaches such as flipped classrooms. This lack of familiarity can create resistance to change and reluctance to adopt new teaching methods.
- **Lack of Training Opportunities**: Faculty members may face challenges in accessing professional development opportunities and training programs focused on flipped learning. While there is a growing interest in innovative teaching practices, including flipped classrooms, in Indian higher education, the availability of formal training programs and workshops tailored to the specific needs of faculty members may be limited. This lack of training opportunities can hinder faculty members' ability to effectively design, implement, and assess flipped learning activities.
- **Pedagogical Support**: Even if faculty members are interested in implementing flipped classrooms, they may lack the necessary pedagogical support and guidance to do so successfully. Flipped learning requires careful planning, instructional design, and assessment strategies to ensure that learning objectives are met and student engagement is maximized. Without access to pedagogical support services, such as instructional designers, educational technologists, or teaching mentors, faculty members may struggle to develop and implement effective flipped learning experiences.
- **Time Constraints**: Faculty members in Indian higher education institutions often face heavy teaching loads, research commitments, and administrative responsibilities, leaving limited time for professional development and curriculum redesign. The additional time and effort required to transition from traditional teaching methods to flipped classrooms may be perceived as a barrier, particularly in the absence of adequate support and incentives.
- **Resistance to Change**: Resistance to change is a common barrier to innovation in higher education. Faculty members may be hesitant to adopt flipped learning approaches due to concerns about their own competence, student resistance, or institutional culture. Overcoming resistance to change requires

strong leadership, effective communication, and opportunities for collaboration and shared decision-making among faculty members.

Addressing the barrier of faculty training and pedagogical support requires a multifaceted approach that includes providing professional development opportunities, fostering a culture of innovation and collaboration, and investing in resources to support faculty members in their teaching endeavors. By empowering faculty members with the knowledge, skills, and support needed to implement flipped classrooms effectively, Indian higher education institutions can enhance teaching quality, student engagement, and learning outcomes.

Figure 4. Barriers to implementing flipped classrooms in Indian higher education

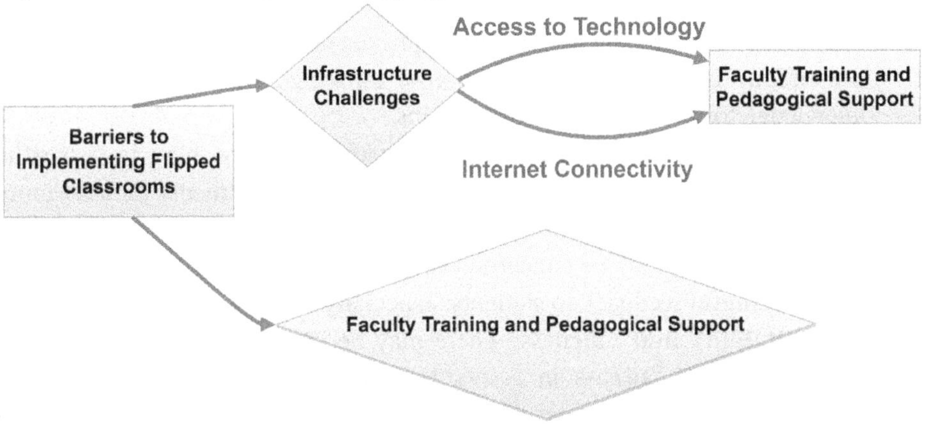

Cultural and institutional resistance, as well as assessment and grading concerns, pose additional barriers to implementing flipped classrooms in Indian higher education(Aidoo et al., 2022; Fuchs, 2021b).

Cultural and Institutional Resistance

- **Traditional Teaching Paradigms**: Indian higher education institutions often have deeply ingrained traditional teaching paradigms centered around lecture-based instruction. Flipped classrooms represent a departure from these established practices, which can face resistance from faculty members, administrators, and even students.
- **Hierarchy and Authority**: In Indian academic culture, there may be a strong emphasis on the authority of the instructor and passive roles for students. Flipped classrooms, which promote active learning and student-centered ap-

proaches, may challenge these traditional power dynamics, leading to resistance from both faculty members and students.
- **Perceptions of Technology**: There may be skepticism or apprehension towards the use of technology in education, particularly among older faculty members or those with limited experience with digital tools. Concerns about technological competence, accessibility, and reliability can contribute to resistance towards flipped learning initiatives.

Assessment and Grading Concerns

- **Alignment with Traditional Assessment Methods**: Flipped classrooms may require reevaluation and adaptation of assessment methods to align with active learning approaches and encourage deeper understanding. Traditional assessment methods, such as exams or quizzes focused on recall of facts, may not effectively measure the higher-order thinking skills and application of knowledge fostered in flipped classrooms.
- **Grading Workload**: Implementing flipped classrooms may increase the grading workload for instructors, particularly if assessments include more open-ended or project-based tasks that require individualized feedback. Faculty members may be concerned about the feasibility of providing timely and meaningful feedback to students, especially in large classes.
- **Accountability and Fairness**: There may be concerns about ensuring accountability and fairness in assessment and grading practices in flipped classrooms. Faculty members may worry about students' engagement with pre-class materials, the validity of self-paced learning activities, or the equitable distribution of workload and grading standards across diverse student populations.

To overcome cultural and institutional barriers in Indian higher education, a combination of cultural change, institutional support, and pedagogical innovation is needed, including faculty development programs, collaborative initiatives, supportive policies, authentic assessment methods, clear communication, and technology-enabled tools.

METHODS OF IMPLEMENTING FLIPPED CLASSROOMS IN INDIAN HIGHER EDUCATION

The implementation of flipped classrooms in Indian higher education necessitates strategic planning, faculty development, and technological integration, with two important methods are discussed below(Doğan et al., 2023):

Faculty Development Programs and Training Workshops:

Faculty development programs and training workshops are essential for educators to design, implement, and assess flipped classrooms effectively. They equip them with the knowledge, skills, and resources needed to transition from traditional teaching methods to flipped learning approaches(Mandasari & Wahyudin, 2021).

- **Pedagogical Training**: Faculty development programs offer pedagogical training focused on active learning strategies, instructional design principles, and student-centered approaches. Workshops may cover topics such as designing engaging pre-class materials, facilitating interactive in-class activities, and promoting effective student engagement and collaboration.
- **Technology Integration**: Faculty development programs also provide training on integrating technology tools and digital resources into flipped classroom instruction. Educators learn how to use learning management systems (LMS), online platforms, video creation tools, and other educational technologies to deliver pre-class content, facilitate communication, and assess student learning effectively.
- **Assessment Strategies**: Flipped classroom training workshops address assessment strategies aligned with active learning approaches. Faculty members learn how to design formative and summative assessments that measure student understanding, critical thinking skills, and application of knowledge. They explore alternative assessment methods such as project-based assessments, peer evaluations, and self-assessments.
- **Peer Collaboration and Support**: Faculty development programs provide opportunities for peer collaboration and support, allowing educators to share best practices, exchange ideas, and learn from each other's experiences. Collaborative workshops, peer mentoring programs, and communities of practice foster a supportive environment where faculty members can collaborate, troubleshoot challenges, and refine their flipped classroom practices.
- **Evaluation and Continuous Improvement**: Finally, faculty development programs include mechanisms for evaluating the effectiveness of flipped classroom implementation and promoting continuous improvement. Educators

receive feedback on their teaching practices, student outcomes, and course design through peer observation, student evaluations, and self-assessment processes. This feedback informs ongoing professional development efforts and contributes to the refinement of flipped classroom strategies over time.

Technological Integration: Learning Management Systems, Online Platforms:

Technological integration is crucial for the successful implementation of flipped classrooms in Indian higher education, utilizing learning management systems, online platforms, and educational technologies to enhance pre-class material delivery, facilitate communication, and support assessment and feedback processes(Chua & Islam, 2021; Collado-Valero et al., 2021).

- **Learning Management Systems (LMS)**: LMS platforms such as Moodle, Blackboard, or Canvas serve as centralized hubs for organizing course materials, delivering pre-class content, and facilitating communication between instructors and students. Educators can use LMS platforms to upload video lectures, readings, quizzes, and other resources, allowing students to access course materials anytime, anywhere.
- **Online Platforms for Content Delivery**: Online platforms such as YouTube, Khan Academy, or Coursera offer a wealth of educational resources that can supplement pre-class materials in flipped classrooms. Educators can curate or create video lectures, interactive tutorials, e-books, and other multimedia resources to engage students and enhance their understanding of course concepts.
- **Interactive Tools and Collaboration Platforms**: Educational technologies such as discussion forums, wikis, virtual whiteboards, and collaborative document editors facilitate interaction and collaboration among students in flipped classrooms. These tools enable students to engage in online discussions, collaborate on group projects, and provide peer feedback, fostering a sense of community and enhancing learning outcomes.
- **Assessment and Feedback Tools**: Technological integration supports assessment and feedback processes in flipped classrooms. Online quizzes, polls, surveys, and self-assessment tools allow educators to gauge student understanding, monitor progress, and provide timely feedback. Digital platforms also enable peer assessment, automated grading, and analytics that inform instructional decision-making and promote student engagement.
- **Accessibility and Flexibility**: Technology-enhanced flipped classrooms offer greater accessibility and flexibility for diverse learners. Digital resourc-

es can be accessed on multiple devices, including smartphones and tablets, accommodating students with varying learning preferences and schedules. Online communication tools facilitate asynchronous interactions, allowing students to engage with course materials and participate in discussions at their own pace.

Indian higher education institutions can implement flipped classrooms by investing in faculty development programs, providing technological infrastructure, and fostering a culture of innovation. This approach can enhance teaching quality, student engagement, and learning outcomes, preparing students for success in the 21st century through strategic use of educational technologies.

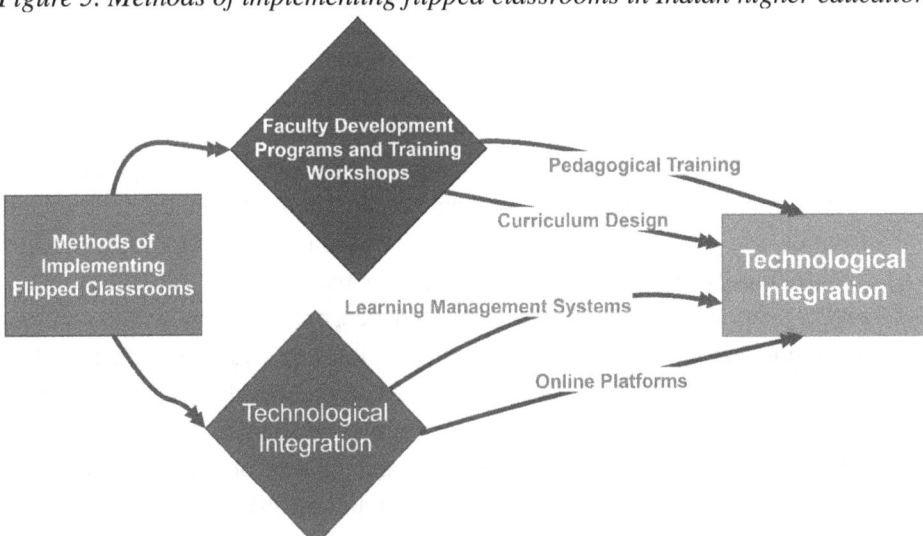

Figure 5. Methods of implementing flipped classrooms in Indian higher education

Flipped classrooms in Indian higher education require faculty training, technological integration, student support services, and robust research and evaluation mechanisms, with two key methods being discussed. Figure 5 outlines the implementation methods of flipped classrooms in Indian higher education.

Student Support Services: Academic Advising, Tutoring, and Mentoring:

Student support services are crucial for flipped classroom success and engagement. They offer academic advising, tutoring, and mentoring to help students navigate challenges and maximize learning outcomes. These services facilitate the implementation of flipped classrooms(Anjomshoaa et al., 2022; Shaw & Patra, 2022).

- **Academic Advising**: Academic advisors can help students understand the flipped classroom model, select appropriate courses, and develop personalized learning plans that align with their academic goals and learning preferences. Advisors can also provide guidance on time management, study skills, and effective use of technology to support student success in flipped classrooms.
- **Tutoring Services**: Tutoring services offer additional academic support to students who may be struggling with course content or adapting to the flipped learning environment. Tutors can provide one-on-one or small-group assistance, clarify concepts, and reinforce learning through guided practice and review sessions. Tutoring services can be particularly beneficial for students from diverse backgrounds or those with varying levels of prior knowledge.
- **Mentoring Programs**: Mentoring programs pair students with faculty mentors or peer mentors who can provide guidance, encouragement, and academic support throughout their flipped learning journey. Mentors can share their experiences with flipped classrooms, offer advice on effective study strategies, and provide feedback on student progress and performance. Mentorship relationships foster a sense of belonging and connection within the learning community, enhancing student engagement and retention.
- **Peer Support Networks**: Establishing peer support networks or study groups allows students to collaborate, share resources, and exchange ideas outside of class. Peer support networks provide opportunities for students to discuss course materials, clarify concepts, and work together on assignments or projects. Peer interactions foster a sense of camaraderie and mutual support, promoting active learning and academic success.
- **Accessibility and Inclusivity**: Student support services should be accessible and inclusive, ensuring that all students, regardless of background or ability, have equal opportunities to succeed in flipped classrooms. Institutions should provide accommodations and resources to support students with disabilities, English language learners, or other diverse learning needs. Culturally sensitive and responsive support services can help create a supportive and inclusive learning environment for all students.

Research and Evaluation: Monitoring Progress and Assessing Impact:

Research and evaluation are crucial for the successful implementation of flipped classrooms, providing evidence-based insights into their effectiveness and impact. By monitoring student progress and assessing their impact on learning outcomes, institutions can identify strengths, address challenges, and inform continuous improvement efforts(Silverajah et al., 2022; Zou et al., 2022).

- **Monitoring Student Progress**: Institutions can monitor student progress and engagement in flipped classrooms through various means, such as course analytics, learning management system (LMS) data, and student surveys. Tracking indicators such as student participation, completion rates, quiz scores, and self-assessment data allows institutions to identify patterns, trends, and areas for intervention.
- **Assessing Learning Outcomes**: Institutions should assess the impact of flipped classrooms on student learning outcomes, including knowledge acquisition, critical thinking skills, and application of knowledge. Using both formative and summative assessment measures, institutions can evaluate student performance on course assessments, projects, and assignments to determine the effectiveness of flipped learning approaches.
- **Gathering Student Feedback**: Soliciting feedback from students through surveys, focus groups, or course evaluations provides valuable insights into their experiences with flipped classrooms. Students can provide feedback on the effectiveness of pre-class materials, in-class activities, assessment methods, and overall satisfaction with the flipped learning experience. This feedback informs adjustments and improvements to flipped classroom practices based on student needs and preferences.
- **Faculty Reflection and Collaboration**: Faculty members should engage in reflection and collaboration to evaluate the impact of flipped classrooms on their teaching practices and student learning outcomes. Collaborative discussions, peer observations, and faculty development activities provide opportunities for educators to share successes, challenges, and lessons learned from implementing flipped learning approaches. By reflecting on their experiences and collaborating with colleagues, faculty members can refine their instructional strategies and enhance the effectiveness of flipped classrooms.

Indian higher education institutions can effectively implement flipped classrooms by providing comprehensive student support services and implementing robust research and evaluation mechanisms. Through ongoing assessment, feedback, and collaboration, institutions can continuously improve flipped classroom practices and meet diverse learners' needs.

FUTURE DIRECTIONS

Future directions of flipped classroom methods are influenced by education trends, technology advancements, and evolving pedagogical approaches, with potential future directions being shaped by these factors(Doğan et al., 2023; Yildiz Durak, 2022b; Zou et al., 2022).

a) **Personalized Learning Pathways**: Flipped classrooms may evolve towards more personalized learning pathways tailored to individual student needs, preferences, and learning styles. Adaptive learning technologies and data analytics can be used to customize pre-class materials, in-class activities, and assessments based on students' prior knowledge, pace of learning, and areas of interest, promoting greater engagement and mastery of content.

b) **Blended Learning Models**: Flipped classrooms may increasingly integrate with other instructional models, such as blended learning, to create hybrid learning environments that combine face-to-face instruction with online learning experiences. Blended learning models offer flexibility and scalability, allowing educators to leverage the benefits of both traditional and digital learning modalities to meet diverse learning needs and optimize learning outcomes.

c) **Interactive and Immersive Technologies**: The integration of interactive and immersive technologies, such as virtual reality (VR), augmented reality (AR), and gamification, can enhance the engagement and effectiveness of flipped classrooms. These technologies enable experiential learning, simulation-based activities, and interactive storytelling, providing students with immersive learning experiences that foster deeper understanding and retention of course material.

d) **Global Collaboration and Cross-Cultural Exchanges**: Flipped classrooms can facilitate global collaboration and cross-cultural exchanges by connecting students and educators from diverse geographical locations and cultural backgrounds. Virtual collaboration platforms, online forums, and international partnerships enable students to collaborate on projects, share perspectives, and engage in intercultural dialogue, fostering global competence and cultural understanding.

e) **Professional Development and Support for Educators**: As flipped classroom methods continue to evolve, there will be a growing need for professional development and support for educators to effectively implement flipped learning approaches. Faculty development programs, training workshops, and communi-

ties of practice can provide educators with the knowledge, skills, and resources needed to design, implement, and assess flipped classrooms successfully.
f) **Research and Evidence-Based Practices**: Future directions of flipped classrooms will be informed by ongoing research and evidence-based practices that examine the impact of flipped learning approaches on student outcomes, teaching effectiveness, and institutional practices. Research studies, case reports, and meta-analyses can provide insights into best practices, challenges, and opportunities for improvement in flipped classroom implementation.
g) **Accessibility and Inclusivity**: Ensuring accessibility and inclusivity will be a key consideration in the future development of flipped classrooms. Efforts to address digital equity, accommodate diverse learning needs, and promote inclusive instructional practices will help ensure that flipped classrooms are accessible to all students, regardless of background, ability, or learning preference.

Flipped classrooms are expected to evolve into a transformative educational approach, enhancing teaching effectiveness, student engagement, and learning outcomes in diverse educational contexts. This is achieved through innovation, collaboration, and a commitment to student-centered learning, fostering global collaboration and professional development.

CONCLUSIONS

Flipped classrooms in Indian higher education are a transformative approach that can significantly enhance student engagement, knowledge development, and learning outcomes. These classrooms shift the focus from passive information consumption to interactive and collaborative activities, enabling students to develop a deeper understanding of course material, cultivate critical thinking skills, and apply their knowledge in real-world scenarios. This chapter explores various aspects of flipped classrooms, including strategies, barriers to implementation, methods of adoption, and their impact on student behavior.

Flipped classrooms in Indian higher education face challenges such as infrastructure limitations, faculty resistance, and concerns about assessment and grading. To overcome these, a comprehensive approach is needed, including faculty development programs, technological integration, and institutional support. Effective implementation strategies include providing pedagogical training, integrating learning management systems and online platforms, and fostering collaboration and innovation. By addressing these challenges, educators can create dynamic learning environments that foster deeper engagement, critical thinking, and knowledge development, preparing students for success in a complex world.

REFERENCES

Aidoo, B., Macdonald, M. A., Vesterinen, V.-M., Pétursdóttir, S., & Gísladóttir, B. (2022). Transforming teaching with ICT using the flipped classroom approach: Dealing with COVID-19 pandemic. *Education Sciences*, 12(6), 421. DOI: 10.3390/educsci12060421

Anjomshoaa, H., Ghazizadeh Hashemi, A. H., Jasim Alsadaji, A., Jasim Mohammed, Z., & Masoudi, S. (2022). The effect of flipped classroom on student learning outcomes; An overview. *Medical Education Bulletin*, 3(2), 431–440.

Azizah, T., Fauzan, A., & Harisman, Y. (2022). "FLIPPED CLASSROOM TYPE PEER INSTRUCTION-BASED LEARNING" BASED ON A WEBSITE TO IMPROVE STUDENT'S PROBLEM SOLVING. *Infinity Journal*, 11(2), 325–348. DOI: 10.22460/infinity.v11i2.p325-348

Bishnoi, M. M. (2020). Flipped classroom and digitization: An inductive study on the learning framework for 21st century skill acquisition. *JETT*, 11(1), 30–45.

Chua, K., & Islam, M. (2021). The hybrid Project-Based Learning–Flipped Classroom: A design project module redesigned to foster learning and engagement. *International Journal of Mechanical Engineering Education*, 49(4), 289–315. DOI: 10.1177/0306419019838335

Collado-Valero, J., Rodríguez-Infante, G., Romero-González, M., Gamboa-Ternero, S., Navarro-Soria, I., & Lavigne-Cerván, R. (2021). Flipped classroom: Active methodology for sustainable learning in higher education during social distancing due to COVID-19. *Sustainability (Basel)*, 13(10), 5336. DOI: 10.3390/su13105336

Doğan, Y., Batdı, V., & Yaşar, M. D. (2023). Effectiveness of flipped classroom practices in teaching of science: A mixed research synthesis. *Research in Science & Technological Education*, 41(1), 393–421. DOI: 10.1080/02635143.2021.1909553

Fuchs, K. (2021a). Innovative teaching: A qualitative review of flipped classrooms. *International Journal of Learning. Teaching and Educational Research*, 20(3), 18–32.

Fuchs, K. (2021b). Innovative teaching: A qualitative review of flipped classrooms. *International Journal of Learning. Teaching and Educational Research*, 20(3), 18–32.

Kang, H. Y., & Kim, H. R. (2021). Impact of blended learning on learning outcomes in the public healthcare education course: A review of flipped classroom with team-based learning. *BMC Medical Education*, 21(1), 1–8. DOI: 10.1186/s12909-021-02508-y PMID: 33509176

Kannan, V., Kuromiya, H., Gouripeddi, S. P., Majumdar, R., Madathil Warriem, J., & Ogata, H. (2020). Flip & Pair–a strategy to augment a blended course with active-learning components: Effects on engagement and learning. *Smart Learning Environments*, 7(1), 1–23. DOI: 10.1186/s40561-020-00138-3

Kevser, H. (2021). The effects of the flipped classroom on deep learning strategies and engagement at the undergraduate level. *Participatory Educational Research*, 8(1), 379–394. DOI: 10.17275/per.21.22.8.1

Lai, H.-M., Hsieh, P.-J., Uden, L., & Yang, C.-H. (2021). A multilevel investigation of factors influencing university students' behavioral engagement in flipped classrooms. *Computers & Education*, 175, 104318. DOI: 10.1016/j.compedu.2021.104318

Mandasari, B., & Wahyudin, A. Y. (2021). Flipped classroom learning model: Implementation and its impact on EFL learners' satisfaction on grammar class. *Ethical Lingua: Journal of Language Teaching and Literature*, 8(1), 150–158.

Meyliana, Sablan, B., Surjandy, & Hidayanto, A. N. (2021). Flipped learning effect on classroom engagement and outcomes in university information systems class. *Education and Information Technologies*, •••, 1–19.

Sevillano-Monje, V., Martín-Gutiérrez, Á., & Hervás-Gómez, C. (2022). The flipped classroom and the development of competences: A teaching innovation experience in higher education. *Education Sciences*, 12(4), 248. DOI: 10.3390/educsci12040248

Shaw, R., & Patra, B. K. (2022). Classifying students based on cognitive state in flipped learning pedagogy. *Future Generation Computer Systems*, 126, 305–317. DOI: 10.1016/j.future.2021.08.018

Silverajah, V. G., Wong, S. L., Govindaraj, A., Khambari, M. N. M., Rahmat, R. W. B. O., & Deni, A. R. M. (2022). A systematic review of self-regulated learning in flipped classrooms: Key findings, measurement methods, and potential directions. *IEEE Access : Practical Innovations, Open Solutions*, 10, 20270–20294. DOI: 10.1109/ACCESS.2022.3143857

Sosa Díaz, M. J., Guerra Antequera, J., & Cerezo Pizarro, M. (2021a). Flipped classroom in the context of higher education: Learning, satisfaction and interaction. *Education Sciences*, 11(8), 416. DOI: 10.3390/educsci11080416

Sosa Díaz, M. J., Guerra Antequera, J., & Cerezo Pizarro, M. (2021b). Flipped classroom in the context of higher education: Learning, satisfaction and interaction. *Education Sciences*, 11(8), 416. DOI: 10.3390/educsci11080416

Sravat, N., & Pathranarakul, P. (2022). Flipped learning pedagogy: Modelling the challenges for higher education in India. *International Journal of Learning and Change*, 14(2), 221–240. DOI: 10.1504/IJLC.2022.121137

Yildiz Durak, H. (2022a). Flipped classroom model applications in computing courses: Peer-assisted groups, collaborative group and individual learning. *Computer Applications in Engineering Education*, 30(3), 803–820. DOI: 10.1002/cae.22487

Yildiz Durak, H. (2022b). Flipped classroom model applications in computing courses: Peer-assisted groups, collaborative group and individual learning. *Computer Applications in Engineering Education*, 30(3), 803–820. DOI: 10.1002/cae.22487

Zou, D., Luo, S., Xie, H., & Hwang, G.-J. (2022). A systematic review of research on flipped language classrooms: Theoretical foundations, learning activities, tools, research topics and findings. *Computer Assisted Language Learning*, 35(8), 1811–1837. DOI: 10.1080/09588221.2020.1839502

Chapter 14
Differentiated Instruction as a Strategy to Support Progressed Learners Within Inclusive Classrooms

Makobo Lydia Mogale
University of the Free State, South Africa

ABSTRACT

Differentiated Instruction is an integral part of learning to accommodate learner diversity and varying background knowledge rather than using "one-size-fits-all" teaching approach. This inevitable pedagogical approach gained lots of attention due to its flexible, equitable and intelligent way to approach teaching. This chapter provides insight on using Differentiated Instruction as strategy to support progressed learners. Learner progression policy in South Africa was promulgated to redress continuous retention which often leads to school dropout and foregrounds extended learning opportunities to bridge content gap. This policy was introduced in the Further and Education training Phase secondary (Grade 10 - 12) in 2013 for learners not to spend more than four years in a phase. When learners are progressed, their academic success depends on curriculum support to bridge content gap. The chapter delves deeper into inclusive pedagogical practice tailored for various progression reason.

DOI: 10.4018/979-8-3693-4058-5.ch014

INTRODUCTION

In today' diverse classrooms, teachers face the challenge of meeting educational needs for all learners, including those that are identified to progress to the next class without mastering competencies of the current. These learners, often referred to as progressed learners are primarily advanced due to age or social considerations rather than academic performance (Jimerson, 2006). According to Holmes (2006), this well-intentioned practice sometimes leaves significant academic gaps which delays success in classes progressed to. Differentiated instruction offers a engaging strategy to address some of the challenges through tailored instructional practices and learning experiences to accommodate the diverse needs of all learners by supporting their academic growth and availing inclusive learning environments. Differentiated Instruction is an educational approach to accommodate learner diversity and varying background knowledge rather than using a "one-size-fits-all" teaching approach (Bondie, Dahnke & Zusho, 2019; Melesse, 2019, Tomlinson, 2014). This inevitable pedagogical approach gained a lot of attention due to its flexible, equitable and intelligent way to approach teaching. Differentiation is a tailored instruction approach to meet individual needs of learners (Ginja & Chen, 2020).

According to (Roberts & Inman, 2023), differentiation is an instructional approach whereby the teacher *"matches the content (from basic to complex), the level of the cognitive (thinking) processes, the sophistication of the product, and/ or the assessment to the strengths, readiness, and interests of the student or cluster of learners"*. That is, creating supportive and responsive learning environment to grant learners opportunities to thrive. This inclusive pedagogic practice creates a learning climate where learners belong and are responsible for their own learning (Gregory & Chapman, 2013). This chapter brings insights on how differentiated instruction can be used as a strategy to support progressed learners in the context of inclusive pedagogy. Inclusive pedagogy strengthens the importance of creating equitable and accessible learning environments where all learners get opportunities to pursue with their academics (Florian & Black-Hawkins, 2011). This inclusive instructional strategy can be instrumental for teachers to meet diverse needs of progressed learners, particularly assisting them to bridge content gap eventually achieve their full potential. The chapter argues for differentiated instruction as a vital strategy to support progressed learners by examining principles and practices and its implication to progressed learners' individual needs in a diverse inclusive classroom. Furthermore, the chapter intends to provide practical strategies and insights to foster conducive learning environment that promotes equity and academic successes for all learners.

1. UNDERSTANDING PROGRESSED LEARNERS

Progressed learner is a concept used to define learners advanced to the next class without fulfilling the promotion requirements. The rationale behind this practice is to ensure that learners move with their age cohort by preventing continuous retention which may lead to decreased motivation, worse school dropout (Holmes, 2006, Mogale & Modipane, 2021). Amongst a wide range of progressed learners' characteristics, they may have foundational knowledge and skills gaps that prevent their ability to grasp complex content of the next class (Spaull, 2015). Generally, they might lack reading comprehension skills, mathematical reasoning and/or specific competencies in different subjects (Brophy, 2006). Jimerson (2006), contends that progressed learners may experience social as well as emotional exclusions if they think of themselves as being less capable than their peers. International perspectives of progressed learner is associated with social promotion and automatic promotion whereby learners are identified to advance to avoid retention. Subsequently, South African education system also progress learners to minimise retention and then support them academically to bridge content gap (Department of Basic Education, 2015). While the policy intends to keep learners in schools until they obtain grade 12 certificate, there has been challenges in the provision of relevant curriculum support for these learners' academic success. This was also seen in countries such as Finland where early intervention and continuous assessment is emphasised to ensure that identified learners receive the necessary support for their academic success (Sahlberg, 2011).

Challenges Faced by Progressed Learners

Learners identified for progression face a range of obstacles that may negatively impact their learning experiences and success. These obstacles may emerge from various factors such as academic, institutional and social and emotional challenges.

- **Academic Challenges**

Learners who have advanced frequently possess deficiencies in fundamental knowledge and abilities that are necessary for grasping increasingly complex ideas. These gaps can be found in fundamental areas like physics, arithmetic, reading, and writing and can make it more difficult for them to comprehend and interact with new information (Allington, 2013). These learners may find it difficult to keep up with the class level expected competencies which may lead to distractions and disengagements eventually falling behind over period. Amongst several academic challenges lies learners not able to read for comprehension. The implication is that language barriers make it difficult for learners to participate in classroom engagements if they can't comprehend. For instance, learners struggling to understand instruction, limited verbal communication and vocabulary acquisition.

- **Institutional challenges**

Institutional challenges may impede progressed learners' ability to advance academically. Challenges emerge from education system that may not sufficiently meet individual demands, especially that progression in South Africa is implemented for various reasons stipulated in the policy. Thus, age cohort, subjects adjustments or condone as well as some conditions such as fulfilling school attendance conditions and partaking in formal assessments (Department of basic Education, 2015). Some of the challenges progressed learners face at the institution include rigid curriculum and assessment systems (Tomlinson, 2014), lack of resources and support systems (Vaughun & Bos, 2015), Inadequate teacher training and professional development (Florina & Black-Hawkins, 2011), Overcrowded classrooms and high learner-teacher ratios (Blatchford, Bassett & Brown, 2011, Mogale & Modipne, 2021), limited access to inclusive practices and policies (Booth & Ainscow, 2011) and inconsistent implementation of intervention programs (Fuchs & Fuchs, 2006). These challenges can have compounding effect whereby learner it difficult to comprehend new information because they do not have the have the necessary background knowledge (Brophy, 2006). In order to assist progressed learners to reach their full potential, addressing institutional problems might result in more inclusive and supportive environment.

- **Social and emotional challenges**

Learners identified for progression may have social and emotional difficulties affect their motivation and willingness for full participation in classroom activities. As a result, they could feel alone Thus, they may feel alone or labelled which may lead to low self-esteem and the stress of perceiving oneself as unable to meet required academic standards (Jimmerson 2006; Holmes, 2006). Learners who experience anxiety may have problems to participate in class discussions or presentations, affecting their ability to showcase knowledge and skills.

Use this table below to identify gaps:

Table 1. Academic gaps

Academic gaps	Indicators	Examples Behaviours
1. Academic Challenges		
2. Institutional Challenges		
3. Social and emotional challenges		

Now that you identified academic gaps, how do you then address to close gaps?

The recognition of diversity in a classroom becomes critical so that teachers implement adequate and relevant support that respond to individual needs of these learners. There is a need to create conducive and supporting learning environments that foster all the learners learning successes. For example, provision of specific support for the academic fundamental skills through remedial programmes, personalised instruction and tutoring. Institutionally, some schools may not develop inclusive policies and practices that accommodates different learning needs such as progressed learners needs' with the varied reasons for progression. Subsequently, by virtue of being progressed, these learners' social and emotional being may be affected wherein they withdraw from social activities. Hence the need to identify specific challenges in order to develop inclusive intervention programmes aligned to affected learners' needs.

2. DIFFERENTIATED INSTRUCTION: AN OVERVIEW

Differentiated instruction is a teaching philosophy which focuses on the tailored instructional practices that accommodates diverse needs of learners. It acknowledges that learners differ and needs varied pathways to succeed academically (Tomilson, 2014). The differentiated instruction grants equitable learning opportunities that enable all the learners engage meaningfully in the curriculum. This flexible approach to teach involves modification of the curriculum, methods of teaching, resources and activities that cater for the diverse needs of learners (Tomlison & Imbeau, 2010) including those identified for progression. The principles of Differentiated Curriculum include but not limited to:

- **Learner- centred approach** – places learners at the centre in the learning process to emphasise autonomy and engagements. The teacher facilitates, guides learners based on their unique needs and preferences.
- **Responsive teaching:** Teachers adapt their methods and resources to learners evolving needs through continuous assessment to inform decisions to support learning paths.

- **Flexible grouping:** grouping learners according to their individual needs for learning to allow dynamic interactions and collaborations between learners which fosters peer learning.

Differentiated learning advocates for qualitative changes to instructional practices to enrich learning pathways that are relevant to each learner.

2.1. Benefits for Learners

- **Enhanced Engagement and Motivation:** By providing learning experiences that align with learners' interests and readiness levels, differentiated instruction increases student engagement and motivation. When learners find the material relevant and appropriately challenging, they are more likely to invest in their learning (Heacox, 2012).
- **Improved Academic Outcomes:** Differentiated instruction addresses individual learning gaps and promotes mastery of content, leading to improved academic performance. By offering multiple pathways to success, it helps learners build confidence and achieve their learning goals (Tomlinson & Moon, 2013).
- **Development of Critical Thinking Skills:** Differentiated instruction encourages learners to think critically and independently by exposing them to diverse perspectives and problem-solving approaches. This fosters a deeper understanding of the content and the ability to apply knowledge in various contexts (Tomlinson, 2014).
- **Social and Emotional Growth:** Differentiated instruction supports the social and emotional development of learners by creating a supportive learning environment where they feel valued and respected. It promotes positive interactions, collaboration, and a sense of belonging among learners (Subban, 2006).

2.2. Benefits for Educators

- **Increased Professional Satisfaction:** Educators who implement differentiated instruction often report higher levels of professional satisfaction. By meeting the needs of all learners, they experience a sense of accomplishment and fulfillment in their teaching practice (Tomlinson & Imbeau, 2010).
- **Improved Classroom Management:** Differentiated instruction fosters a positive classroom environment where learners are engaged and motivated. This reduces behavioral issues and disruptions, allowing teachers to focus more on instruction and less on discipline (Heacox, 2012).

- **Professional Growth and Learning:** Implementing differentiated instruction requires educators to continuously reflect on their practice and develop new strategies for addressing student needs. This ongoing professional growth enhances their teaching effectiveness and adaptability (Tomlinson & Moon, 2013).

2.3. Implementing Differentiated Instruction

Implementing differentiated instruction involves several key steps and considerations:

1. **Assessment and Diagnosis:** Teachers must assess learners' readiness levels, interests, and learning profiles to inform instructional decisions. This can be done through formal assessments, observations, and student feedback (Tomlinson, 2014).
2. **Curriculum Planning:** Teachers design flexible and responsive curriculum plans that allow for adjustments based on student needs. This involves identifying essential learning objectives and creating diverse learning activities and materials (Heacox, 2012).
3. **Instructional Strategies:** Educators use a variety of instructional strategies, such as tiered assignments, learning stations, and choice boards, to provide differentiated learning experiences. These strategies offer multiple entry points for learners to engage with the content (Subban, 2006).
4. **Collaboration and Reflection:** Teachers collaborate with colleagues, share best practices, and reflect on their teaching to continuously improve their implementation of differentiated instruction. This collaborative approach enhances professional learning and support (Tomlinson & Imbeau, 2010).

Differentiated instruction is a dynamic and responsive teaching approach that enables educators to meet the diverse needs of all learners, including progressed learners. By embracing its principles and practices, educators can create inclusive and equitable learning environments that promote student engagement, achievement, and growth.

2.4. Implementing Differentiated Instruction for Progressed Learners

Implementing differentiated instruction effectively requires a nuanced understanding of the unique needs of progressed learners. These learners, having been advanced to the next grade level without fully mastering prior content, require targeted instructional strategies that address their specific gaps while fostering engagement and growth. By adopting a differentiated approach, educators can provide progressed learners with the necessary support to succeed academically and socially within an inclusive classroom setting.

- **Assessment and Diagnosis**

The first step in implementing differentiated instruction for progressed learners is conducting thorough assessments to identify their individual needs, strengths, and areas for improvement. Ongoing assessment allows educators to tailor instruction to each student's readiness level, ensuring that all learners have access to appropriately challenging and supportive learning experiences (Tomlinson, 2014).

- **Diagnostic Assessments**

Diagnostic assessments are crucial for identifying the specific academic gaps and strengths of progressed learners. These assessments can take various forms, including standardized tests, formative assessments, and teacher observations. The goal is to gather comprehensive data on each student's current knowledge and skills (Black & Wiliam, 2009).

For instance, in mathematics, educators might use pre-tests to determine which foundational concepts a progressed learner has mastered and which areas require additional support. In literacy, teachers can assess reading comprehension and fluency to identify specific challenges that may need targeted interventions (Tomlinson & Moon, 2013).

- **Formative Assessments**

Formative assessments are ongoing and provide continuous feedback on student progress. These assessments inform instructional decisions and allow teachers to make timely adjustments to their teaching strategies (Heritage, 2010). Examples include exit tickets, quick quizzes, and informal observations during classroom activities.

By regularly monitoring the progress of progressed learners, educators can identify areas where learners are excelling or struggling, enabling them to adapt instruction to better meet individual needs (Black & Wiliam, 2009).

2.5. Strategies for Differentiation

Differentiated instruction involves adapting various aspects of teaching—content, process, and product—to align with the diverse needs of progressed learners. Here are some practical strategies for each dimension:

- **Content Differentiation**

Content differentiation involves modifying the curriculum to ensure that progressed learners can access and engage with the material. This may involve adjusting the complexity of texts, providing alternative resources, or offering supplemental materials that cater to different learning levels (Tomlinson, 2014).

Use of Varied Resources: Teachers can incorporate a range of resources, such as videos, articles, and hands-on activities, to accommodate different learning styles and preferences. For example, visual learners might benefit from diagrams and infographics, while auditory learners may prefer podcasts or recorded lectures (Heacox, 2012).

Tiered Assignments: Tiered assignments allow teachers to provide varying levels of challenge within the same lesson. By designing tasks with different levels of complexity, educators can ensure that all learners are appropriately challenged and supported (Tomlinson & Imbeau, 2010). For example, in a science lesson, learners could explore a concept through basic definitions, case studies, or advanced experiments, depending on their readiness levels.

- **Process Differentiation**

Process differentiation involves varying the ways in which learners engage with the content and develop their understanding. This can be achieved through flexible grouping, scaffolded instruction, and personalized learning experiences (Tomlinson, 2014).

Flexible Grouping: Teachers can group learners based on their readiness levels, interests, or learning profiles for specific activities. This allows for targeted instruction and peer collaboration, enabling progressed learners to receive support from both teachers and classmates (Heacox, 2012).

Scaffolded Instruction: Scaffolding provides progressed learners with the necessary support to build their understanding and skills gradually. This might include breaking tasks into smaller, manageable steps, offering guided practice, and using visual aids or graphic organizers to help learners organize their thoughts (Tomlinson & Moon, 2013).

Learning Stations: Learning stations are a versatile approach to process differentiation. learners rotate through different stations, each offering varied activities that address specific learning objectives. This approach allows progressed learners to engage with content at their own pace and explore topics in depth (Subban, 2006).

- **Product Differentiation**

Product differentiation focuses on providing diverse ways for learners to demonstrate their understanding and skills. By offering a range of assessment options, teachers can accommodate different learning styles and preferences (Tomlinson & Imbeau, 2010).

Choice Boards: Choice boards give learners the opportunity to select from various assignments or projects, allowing them to choose how they demonstrate their learning. For example, in a history class, learners might choose between writing an essay, creating a video presentation, or designing a poster to showcase their understanding of a historical event (Heacox, 2012).

Performance Tasks: Performance tasks involve applying knowledge and skills in real-world contexts. These tasks allow progressed learners to demonstrate their understanding through creative and practical applications, such as simulations, role-playing, or problem-solving scenarios (Tomlinson, 2014).

- **Classroom Management and Environment**

Creating a supportive and inclusive classroom environment is essential for the successful implementation of differentiated instruction. Teachers must establish a classroom culture that values diversity, fosters respect, and encourages collaboration (Subban, 2006).

Positive Classroom Culture: Teachers should cultivate a classroom culture where all learners feel valued and respected. This involves promoting a growth mindset, encouraging risk-taking, and celebrating diverse perspectives and contributions (Tomlinson & Imbeau, 2010).

Routines and Procedures: Clear routines and procedures help maintain an organized and efficient classroom environment. This includes establishing expectations for behavior, transitions, and collaboration, ensuring that all learners understand and adhere to classroom norms (Heacox, 2012).

Inclusive Environment: An inclusive classroom environment accommodates diverse learning needs by providing accessible materials, flexible seating arrangements, and assistive technologies. Teachers should strive to create a physical and emotional space that supports the engagement and participation of all learners (Tomlinson, 2014).

Implementing differentiated instruction for progressed learners involves a comprehensive approach that considers assessment, content, process, and product differentiation, as well as classroom management and environment. By embracing these strategies, educators can provide progressed learners with the tailored support they need to overcome academic challenges, build confidence, and achieve their full potential in an inclusive classroom setting.

3. CASE STUDIES AND EXAMPLES

Understanding the practical application of differentiated instruction for progressed learners is essential for educators seeking to implement these strategies effectively. This section presents several case studies and examples that illustrate how differentiated instruction can be tailored to support progressed learners in various educational settings.

3.1. Case Study 1: Differentiated Instruction in a Diverse Middle School Classroom

Context

Ms. Martinez, a middle school teacher in a diverse urban school, faced the challenge of supporting a group of progressed learners in her sixth-grade science class. These learners had been promoted despite struggling with foundational science concepts and literacy skills. Ms. Martinez implemented differentiated instruction to address their unique needs and foster academic growth.

Strategies Implemented

- **Diagnostic Assessments**

Ms. Martinez began by conducting diagnostic assessments to identify the specific gaps in her learners' understanding of key science concepts. She used formative assessments, such as quizzes and observations, to gain insights into each student's readiness level and learning preferences (Tomlinson, 2014).

- **Content Differentiation**
  o **Tiered Assignments:** Ms. Martinez created tiered assignments that allowed learners to explore science topics at different complexity levels. For example, while some learners worked on basic vocabulary and defi-

nitions, others engaged in hands-on experiments and research projects (Heacox, 2012).
- **Use of Varied Resources:** To accommodate diverse learning styles, Ms. Martinez incorporated videos, diagrams, and interactive simulations into her lessons. This approach ensured that all learners had access to the content in formats that matched their preferences (Tomlinson & Imbeau, 2010).

- **Process Differentiation**
  - **Flexible Grouping:** Ms. Martinez used flexible grouping to facilitate collaborative learning. She organized learners into small groups based on their readiness levels and interests, allowing them to work together on science investigations and problem-solving activities (Subban, 2006).
  - **Scaffolded Instruction:** Ms. Martinez provided scaffolded support to help learners gradually build their understanding of complex concepts. She used graphic organizers and guided practice sessions to support learners as they tackled challenging topics (Tomlinson, 2014).

- **Product Differentiation**
  - **Choice Boards:** Ms. Martinez implemented choice boards, offering learners a variety of options for demonstrating their learning. For instance, learners could choose to create a poster, write a report, or develop a multimedia presentation on a science topic of their choice (Heacox, 2012).
  - **Performance Tasks:** learners engaged in performance tasks that required them to apply their knowledge in real-world contexts. For example, they participated in a class project to design and build simple machines, allowing them to demonstrate their understanding of physics principles (Tomlinson & Imbeau, 2010).

Outcomes

Ms. Martinez observed significant improvements in her progressed learners' engagement and academic performance. By tailoring instruction to their individual needs, learners were able to grasp key science concepts, build confidence, and develop a deeper understanding of the subject matter. Additionally, inclusive classroom environment fostered positive interactions and collaboration among learners, promoting a sense of community and belonging.

3.2. Case Study 2: Implementing Differentiated Literacy Instruction in an Elementary School

Context

Mr. Johnson, fourth-grade teacher at an elementary school in a rural area, faced the challenge of supporting a group of progressed learners who struggled with reading comprehension and literacy skills. He implemented differentiated instruction to address their diverse needs and promote literacy development.

Strategies Implemented

- **Assessment and Diagnosis**

Mr. Johnson used formative assessments to assess each student's reading level, fluency, and comprehension skills. These assessments provided valuable insights into the specific areas where learners needed targeted support (Heritage, 2010).

- **Content Differentiation**
    - **Use of Varied Texts:** Mr. Johnson provided a range of reading materials, including leveled books, articles, and graphic novels, to accommodate different reading levels and interests. This approach ensured that learners could access texts that matched their abilities and preferences (Tomlinson, 2014).
    - **Tiered Reading Assignments:** Mr. Johnson designed tiered reading assignments that offered varying levels of complexity. For example, some learners focused on decoding and vocabulary development, while others engaged in more advanced comprehension and analysis tasks (Heacox, 2012).
- **Process Differentiation**
    - **Guided Reading Groups:** Mr. Johnson used guided reading groups to provide targeted instruction. learners were grouped based on their reading levels, and Mr. Johnson worked with each group to develop specific skills and strategies, such as predicting, summarizing, and making inferences (Tomlinson & Moon, 2013).
    - **Literacy Stations:** Mr. Johnson implemented literacy stations, allowing learners to rotate through different activities that focused on specific literacy skills. These stations included phonics games, writing exercises, and listening comprehension activities (Subban, 2006).
- **Product Differentiation**
    - **Creative Writing Projects:** Mr. Johnson encouraged learners to express their understanding through creative writing projects. learners

could choose to write stories, poems, or plays, allowing them to demonstrate their literacy skills in diverse and imaginative ways (Tomlinson & Imbeau, 2010).

- o **Multimedia Presentations:** To accommodate different learning styles, Mr. Johnson provided opportunities for learners to create multimedia presentations on topics of interest. This approach allowed learners to combine text, images, and audio to showcase their understanding (Heacox, 2012).

Outcomes

Mr. Johnson observed notable improvements in his progressed learners' literacy skills and overall confidence as readers and writers. By providing differentiated instruction tailored to their individual needs, learners developed stronger comprehension, fluency, and vocabulary skills. The diverse and engaging learning experiences fostered a love for reading and empowered learners to take ownership of their literacy development.

Example 1: Differentiated Math Instruction in a High School Setting

In a high school algebra class, Mr. Chen implemented differentiated instruction to support progressed learners who struggled with foundational math concepts. He used diagnostic assessments to identify specific areas of difficulty and designed tiered assignments that allowed learners to engage with algebraic concepts at different complexity levels.

Mr. Chen provided scaffolded instruction and used flexible grouping to facilitate peer collaboration and support. learners worked in small groups on problem-solving tasks, with Mr. Chen providing guidance and feedback as needed. By offering choice in how learners demonstrated their understanding, such as through written explanations, visual models, or oral presentations, Mr. Chen empowered learners to take ownership of their learning and build confidence in their math skills (Tomlinson, 2014).

Example 2: Differentiated History Instruction in a Secondary School

In a secondary school history class, Ms. Patel implemented differentiated instruction to accommodate the diverse needs of her progressed learners. She used varied resources, including primary sources, videos, and interactive simulations, to provide multiple entry points for learners to engage with historical content.

Ms. Patel used flexible grouping and learning stations to allow learners to explore historical topics from different perspectives and at their own pace. She encouraged learners to choose from a range of project options, such as creating timelines, writing essays, or developing multimedia presentations, to demonstrate their understanding of historical events (Heacox, 2012).

4. CHALLENGES AND CONSIDERATIONS

While differentiated instruction offers significant benefits for supporting progressed learners, it also presents various challenges that educators must navigate. Understanding these challenges and considerations is crucial for implementing differentiated instruction effectively and ensuring that all learners receive equitable learning opportunities.

4.1. Challenges of Differentiated Instruction

- **Time Constraints**

Challenge: Differentiated instruction requires careful planning and preparation, which can be time-consuming for educators. Developing multiple lesson plans, creating diverse learning materials, and assessing individual student progress demands significant time and effort (Tomlinson & Imbeau, 2010).

Consideration: To manage time effectively, educators can collaborate with colleagues to share resources and strategies. Utilizing digital tools and online platforms can streamline lesson planning and facilitate the organization of differentiated materials. Additionally, integrating differentiation into regular planning routines can help teachers allocate time efficiently (Gregory & Chapman, 2013).

- **Limited Resources**

Challenge: Access to diverse and appropriate resources is essential for differentiated instruction. However, limited availability of resources, such as books, technology, and manipulatives, can hinder the implementation of effective differentiation strategies (Heacox, 2012).

Consideration: Educators can leverage free online resources, open educational materials, and community partnerships to supplement their instructional materials. Collaborating with school libraries and utilizing digital libraries can provide access to a wider range of resources. Additionally, teachers can create their own materials tailored to their learners' needs (Subban, 2006).

- **Classroom Management**

Challenge: Managing a classroom with diverse learning needs can be challenging, particularly when implementing differentiated instruction. Ensuring that all learners are engaged and on task while accommodating different learning paths requires effective classroom management skills (Tomlinson, 2014).

Consideration: Establishing clear routines, expectations, and procedures can help maintain an organized and productive classroom environment. Teachers should communicate the learning goals and behavioural expectations to learners, fostering a sense of responsibility and accountability. Additionally, incorporating student voice and choice can enhance engagement and motivation (Gregory & Chapman, 2013).

- **Teacher Preparedness**

Challenge: Some educators may feel unprepared or lack confidence in implementing differentiated instruction, especially if they have limited experience or training in this approach. This can lead to reluctance or resistance to adopting differentiation strategies (Tomlinson & Imbeau, 2010).

Consideration: Professional development and ongoing training opportunities are essential for building teacher capacity and confidence in differentiated instruction. Schools can provide workshops, coaching, and collaborative learning communities to support teachers in developing their skills and knowledge. Encouraging reflection and sharing of best practices among colleagues can also foster a culture of continuous improvement (Subban, 2006).

- **Assessment and Grading**

Challenge: Differentiated instruction requires assessing and grading learners based on their individual progress and growth, rather than using a one-size-fits-all approach. This can be challenging for teachers accustomed to traditional assessment methods (Tomlinson & Moon, 2013).

Consideration: Educators can use a variety of assessment strategies, including formative assessments, performance tasks, and self-assessments, to gather evidence of student learning. Providing clear criteria and rubrics for different assignments can ensure consistency and transparency in grading. Emphasizing progress and effort, rather than just final outcomes, can support a growth-oriented approach to assessment (Heacox, 2012).

4.2. Considerations for Effective Implementation

- **Understanding Student Needs**

A deep understanding of each student's strengths, interests, and areas for growth is crucial for successful differentiation. Educators should prioritize building relationships with learners and using assessment data to inform instructional decisions. Regular communication with learners and their families can provide valuable insights into individual needs and preferences (Tomlinson, 2014).

- **Building a Supportive Learning Environment**

Creating a supportive and inclusive classroom environment is essential for differentiated instruction. Teachers should foster a culture of respect, collaboration, and mutual support among learners. Encouraging a growth mindset and emphasizing the value of diversity can enhance student motivation and engagement (Gregory & Chapman, 2013).

- **Collaborative Planning and Reflection**

Collaboration among educators is vital for the successful implementation of differentiated instruction. Teachers can work together to share resources, ideas, and strategies, as well as to reflect on their practice and make improvements. Collaborative planning time and professional learning communities can facilitate this process and promote a culture of continuous learning and innovation (Tomlinson & Imbeau, 2010).

- **Flexibility and Adaptability**

Flexibility and adaptability are key components of differentiated instruction. Teachers should be willing to adjust their plans and approaches based on student feedback and evolving needs. Embracing a growth-oriented mindset and being open to experimentation and change can lead to more effective and responsive instruction (Heacox, 2012).

- **Leveraging Technology**

Technology can be a powerful tool for supporting differentiated instruction. Digital resources, educational apps, and online platforms can provide learners with access to personalized learning experiences and resources. Educators can use technology to facilitate communication, collaboration, and assessment, enhancing the overall effectiveness of differentiation strategies (Subban, 2006).

Implementing differentiated instruction for progressed learners presents both challenges and opportunities for educators. By understanding these challenges and considering strategies for effective implementation, teachers can create inclusive and supportive learning environments that meet the diverse needs of all the learners. Through ongoing professional development, collaboration, and reflection, educators can continuously improve their practice and empower progressed learners to achieve their full potential.

4.3. Considerations for Advancing Inclusive Pedagogy

- **Professional Development and Training**

Ongoing professional development and training are essential for educators to develop the skills and knowledge needed to implement inclusive pedagogy effectively. Schools and districts should provide opportunities for teachers to engage in professional learning communities, workshops, and coaching to enhance their understanding of inclusive practices (Florian & Black-Hawkins, 2011).

- **Collaboration with Families and Communities**

Collaboration with families and communities is crucial for creating inclusive learning environments. Educators should actively engage families in the educational process, seeking their input and involvement in decision-making. Building strong partnerships with community organizations can also provide additional resources and support for learners (Bennett et al., 2018).

- **Reflection and Continuous Improvement**

Educators should engage in regular reflection and continuous improvement to enhance their practice and advance inclusive pedagogy. By reflecting on their teaching, seeking feedback from learners and colleagues, and staying informed about best practices, educators can make informed adjustments to their instructional approaches (Tomlinson, 2014).

- **Advocacy for Inclusive Policies**

Advocacy for inclusive policies and practices at the school, district, and national levels is essential for promoting equitable and inclusive education. Educators can advocate for policies that prioritize diversity, equity, and inclusion and work to eliminate systemic barriers that hinder student success (Florian, 2014).

5. CONCLUSION

These case studies and examples highlight the successful implementation of differentiated instruction for progressed learners across various educational settings. By embracing a flexible and responsive approach, educators can effectively address the unique needs of progressed learners, fostering their academic growth and development within inclusive classrooms. Through tailored instruction, ongoing assessment, and diverse learning experiences, educators can empower progressed learners to overcome challenges, build confidence, and achieve their full potential.

Inclusive pedagogy is a powerful approach to creating equitable and supportive learning environments for all learners, including progressed learners. By embracing the principles of inclusive pedagogy and implementing differentiated instruction, educators can provide meaningful and responsive learning experiences that empower learners to achieve their full potential. Through ongoing professional development, collaboration, and advocacy, educators can advance inclusive practices and create a more equitable and inclusive educational landscape.

REFERENCES

Bennett, S. V., Gunn, A. A., & Peterson, B. M. (2018). Preparing teachers for inclusive education: Key ingredients for success. *The Educational Forum*, 82(3), 301–314.

Black, P., & Wiliam, D. (2009). Developing the theory of formative assessment. *Educational Assessment, Evaluation and Accountability*, 21(1), 5–31. DOI: 10.1007/s11092-008-9068-5

Brophy, J. (2006). Grade repetition. In R. Burns & D. Livingston (Eds.), *The Concise Encyclopedia of Education*. Pergamon.

Department of Basic Education, South Africa. (2015). Policy on progression and promotion requirements. *Government Gazette*.

Florian, L. (2014). Reimagining special education: Why new approaches are needed. *The SAGE Handbook of Special Education*, 9-23.

Florian, L., & Black-Hawkins, K. (2011). Exploring inclusive pedagogy. *British Educational Research Journal*, 37(5), 813–828. DOI: 10.1080/01411926.2010.501096

Gregory, G. H., & Chapman, C. (2013). *Differentiated instructional strategies: One size doesn't fit all*. Corwin Press.

Heacox, D. (2012). *Differentiating instruction in the regular classroom: How to reach and teach all learners*. Free Spirit Publishing.

Heritage, M. (2010). *Formative assessment: Making it happen in the classroom*. Corwin Press. DOI: 10.4135/9781452219493

Holmes, C. T. (2006). Low test scores + high retention rates = more dropouts. *Kappa Delta Pi Record*, 42(2), 56–58.

Jimerson, S. R., Pletcher, S. M. W., Graydon, K., Schnurr, B. L., Nickerson, A. B., & Kundert, D. K. (2006). Beyond grade retention and social promotion: Promoting the social and academic competence of students. *Psychology in the Schools*, 43(1), 85–97. DOI: 10.1002/pits.20132

Jimerson, S. R., Pletcher, S. M. W., Graydon, K., Schnurr, B. L., Nickerson, A. B., & Kundert, D. K. (2006). Beyond grade retention and social promotion: Promoting the social and academic competence of students. *Psychology in the Schools*, 43(1), 85–97. DOI: 10.1002/pits.20132

Mogale, M. L., & Modipane, M. C. (2021). The implementation of the progression policy in secondary schools of the Limpopo province in South Africa. *South African Journal of Education*, 41(1), 1853. DOI: 10.15700/saje.v41n1a1853

Niemi, H., Toom, A., & Kallioniemi, A. (Eds.). (2012). *The miracle of education: The principles and practices of teaching and learning in Finnish schools*. Sense Publishers. DOI: 10.1007/978-94-6091-811-7

Roderick, M. (1994). Grade retention and school dropout: Investigating the association. *American Educational Research Journal*, 31(4), 729–759. DOI: 10.3102/00028312031004729

Sahlberg, P. (2011). *Finnish lessons: What can the world learn from educational change in Finland?* Teachers College Press.

Spaull, N. (2015). Schooling in South Africa: How low-quality education becomes a poverty trap. *South African Journal of Childhood Education*, 5(2), 111–131.

Subban, P. (2006). Differentiated instruction: A research basis. *International Education Journal*, 7(7), 935–947.

Tomlinson, C. A. (2014). *The differentiated classroom: Responding to the needs of all learners* (2nd ed.). ASCD.

Tomlinson, C. A., & Imbeau, M. B. (2010). *Leading and managing a differentiated classroom*. ASCD.

Tomlinson, C. A., & Moon, T. R. (2013). *Assessment and student success in a differentiated classroom*. ASCD.

Watts-Taffe, S., Laster, B. P., Broach, L., Marinak, B., McDonald Connor, C., & Walker-Dalhouse, D. (2012). Differentiated instruction: Making informed teacher decisions. *The Reading Teacher*, 66(4), 303–314. DOI: 10.1002/TRTR.01126

Chapter 15
Critical Thinking in Higher Education Through Innovative Strategies:
Out-of-the-Box Thinking

B. Shanthi
Department of Chemistry, Easwari Engineering College, India

C. Ravichandran
Department of Chemistry, Easwari Engineering College, India

V. Manimegalai
Department of Management Studies, Nandha Engineering College (Autonomous), India

Ashish Kumar Parashar
Department of Civil Engineering, School of Studies Engineering and Technology, Guru Ghasidas Vishwavidyalaya, India

Hari B. S.
Department of Mechanical Engineering, Kongu Engineering College, India

ABSTRACT

This chapter discusses the innovative strategies used by higher education institutions to promote critical thinking. It places a strong emphasis on making use of cutting-edge technology, reconsidering traditional teaching strategies, and promoting interdisciplinary collaboration. Global virtual classrooms, gamification, immersive

DOI: 10.4018/979-8-3693-4058-5.ch015

learning environments, and real-world problem-solving projects are important fields. With competency-based testing and customized learning paths, students are given the tools they need to take control of their education. Diversity and inclusion widen perspectives and enhance the learning environment. Strategic partnerships with business and community stakeholders provide chances for practical learning and career readiness.

INTRODUCTION

Graduates with the ability to think critically, adapt, and be creative are needed in the rapidly evolving field of higher education. Good education requires innovative thinking, which is often associated with creativity. It means looking at problems from new perspectives, challenging norms, and developing original solutions. Fostering this style of thinking is not just a pedagogical choice, but also a strategic one to equip students for an unpredictable and changing future (Stek, 2023). Higher education is welcoming unorthodox thought in order to foster experimentation, discovery, and risk-taking as well as critical thinking and lifelong learning. The approach is driven by the rapid advancements in technology, including big data, virtual reality, and artificial intelligence, which are transforming organizations and professions and necessitating the acquisition of constantly changing skills to fully tap into their potential (Barth & Muehlfeld, 2022). Higher education institutions must adapt their curricula and teaching strategies to ensure that students are proficient with technology and capable of using it creatively to solve difficult challenges and bring about positive change.

Higher education institutions must adapt their curricula and teaching strategies to provide students with the skills they need to use technology to address challenging challenges and bring about positive change (Sidekerskienė & Damaševičius, 2023). Higher education must promote innovative thinking in order to successfully address complex societal issues including social inequality, climate change, and global health problems. By being inspired to be imaginative, tough, and flexible, children may transcend conventional disciplinary lines and go on to become future leaders and change makers.

"Out-of-the-box" thinking, which promotes critical thinking, inventive problem-solving, and active engagement, is becoming more and more popular in higher education. By moving away from passive learning and rote memory, this method helps students reach their full potential and gets them ready for a challenging situation. Because traditional curricula prioritize conformity over creativity, success depends on one's capacity for critical, creative, and inventive thought (Fu et al., 2021). Thinking beyond the box encourages active engagement, curiosity-driven research, and open-mindedness by forcing individuals to confront their preconceptions. Higher education institutions can empower students and prepare them to handle the complexity of the outside world by fostering an environment that welcomes experimentation, creativity, and risk-taking (Devine et al., 2021).

Because of the rapid advancements in technology, such as automation, blockchain, and artificial intelligence, higher education has to embrace creativity. Institutions must promote a culture of adaptability, multidisciplinary cooperation, and holistic problem-solving methods in order to keep up with the interconnection of the global economy (Bose et al., 2020). By encouraging educators and students to integrate several fields, such as STEMM, unconventional thinking helps them to solve complicated problems and promote creativity in their respective fields (van den Heerik et al., 2020).

In order to solve societal issues like social inequality, climate change, and global health problems in higher education, new thinking is crucial. It encourages creativity, resilience, empathy, and both personal and professional growth in students by pushing them to question assumptions, entertain different points of view, and embrace failure as a teaching opportunity. Students who think like this do better academically and develop the adaptability and resilience necessary to live in a complicated and uncertain environment (Huffman, 2020). In order to provide students the skills and viewpoints they need to thrive in higher education, it is imperative that they think creatively. Institutions that foster a culture of creativity, innovation, and flexibility can help students become lifelong learners, critical thinkers, and change agents who can solve current problems and influence the future.

Gap Analysis: Higher education must place a high priority on encouraging students to think creatively in order to prepare them for a world that is changing quickly. However, practical implementation plans are necessary. Plans and initiatives should be developed by educational institutions to successfully integrate creative thinking into their courses. To evaluate the effectiveness of these solutions, further research and data-driven techniques are needed. Reforming conventional educational models could also be necessary.

Objectives

- In an effort to improve readers' comprehension of creative thinking's importance and applicability in academic contexts, the chapter offers a thorough explanation of the concept in higher education.
- The chapter highlights the value of innovative thinking in higher education by outlining the drawbacks of conventional approaches and emphasizing the necessity of creativity, innovation, and critical thinking using tactics like immersive learning environments and multidisciplinary cooperation.

- In order to demonstrate the influence of new teaching approaches on student achievement, this chapter looks at case studies and best practices from higher education institutions. It also provides educators, administrators, and policymakers with practical advice.

EMBRACING INNOVATION IN HIGHER EDUCATION

Evolution of Traditional Education Paradigms

The shift in education from traditional approaches to those emphasizing critical thinking is being driven by the awareness that rote memorization and standardized testing are inadequate for preparing students for the complexity of the modern world. With this shift, the need of innovative teaching techniques, interdisciplinary perspectives, practical assessment, lifelong learning, and proactive social contributions is increased (Goh & Abdul-Wahab, 2020). Figure 1 shows the mental map for accepting innovation in higher education.

- **Recognition of the Limitations of Rote Memorization:** Students' ability to think critically and solve problems creatively was hampered by old educational systems' reliance on fact memorization and repetition. Instructors began to realize that memorization is not the same as comprehending and having the ability to apply information in real-world situations.
- **Emphasis on Inquiry-Based Learning:** Children are encouraged to ask questions, research subjects independently, and engage in hands-on activities using inquiry-based learning approaches that foster curiosity, critical thinking, and problem-solving abilities through information processing, conclusion drawing, and idea linkage.
- **Adoption of Active Learning Strategies:** More interactive and participatory teaching techniques that actively include students in the learning process have replaced traditional lectures. Students can use strategies including case studies, group discussions, problem-solving activities, and simulations to practice critical thinking in group settings.
- **Integration of Multidisciplinary Perspectives:** There has been an increasing focus on incorporating interdisciplinary methods into the curriculum due to the realization that real-world problems are frequently complex and call for a variety of viewpoints to be solved. Drawing upon several fields of study, including the humanities, social sciences, technology, and science, exposes students to diverse perspectives and improves their capacity to tackle intricate problems.

- **Focus on Metacognition and Reflection:** Teachers are realizing more and more how critical thinking abilities are developed through metacognition, or the capacity to examine one's own thought processes. Approaches like journaling, self-evaluation, and peer criticism motivate students to analyze their own logic, spot prejudices, and take into account different points of view.
- **Shift towards Authentic Assessment:** Higher-order thinking abilities like creativity, critical thinking, and problem-solving are frequently not measured by traditional standardized examinations. Teachers are looking into alternative assessment methods that let students show that they can think critically and apply their knowledge in real-world situations, such performance tasks, project-based exams, and portfolios.

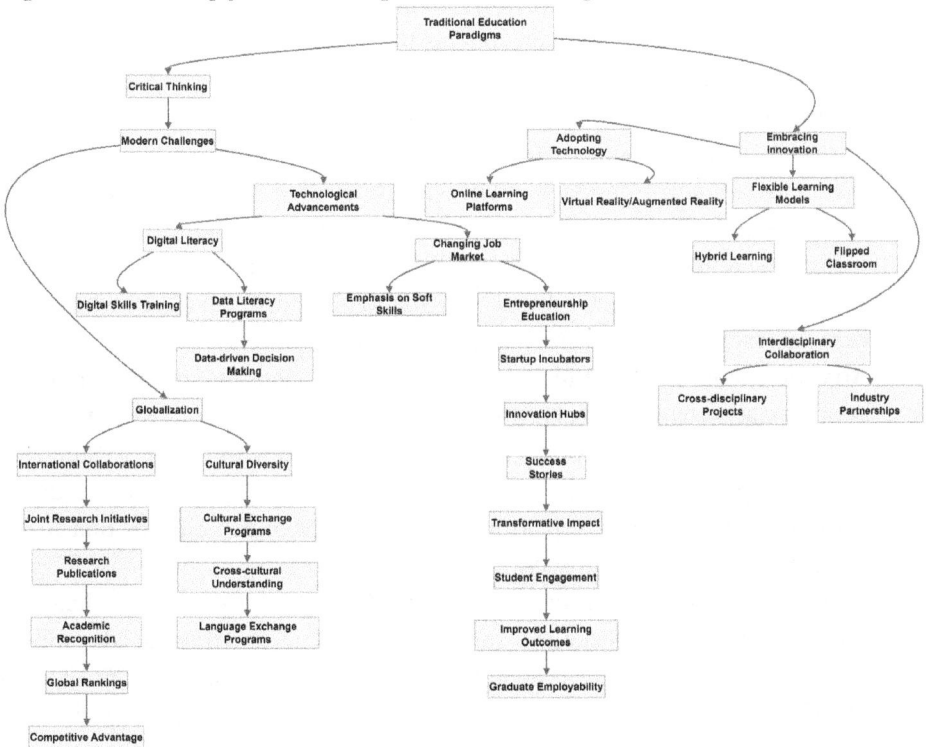

Figure 1. Mind map for embracing innovation in higher education

- **Integration of Technology:** The widespread use of technology in education has created new chances for the development of critical thinking abilities.

Students can connect dynamically with course material using educational technologies like virtual labs, interactive simulations, and online forums, which promote experimentation, discovery, and problem-solving.

Innovative Approaches in Modern Higher Education

It is obvious that innovative approaches are required in today's higher education as traditional techniques are no longer sufficient to educate students for demands. By embracing innovation, educational institutions may better equip students with the necessary skills, knowledge, and perspective (Tejedor et al., 2021).

- **Globalization:** The nature of work has changed as a result, and employers now want workers with a broad range of abilities, including critical thinking, problem-solving, creativity, and flexibility. It's possible that traditional teaching methods, which prioritized memory and information delivery above other abilities, did not provide students the tools they needed to thrive in the fast-paced labor market of today.
- **Complex Societal Challenges:** Numerous intricate issues confronting modern civilization include socioeconomic injustice, healthcare inequities, climate change, and technology upheaval. Innovative solutions that incorporate multidisciplinary viewpoints, original thought, and cooperation amongst many stakeholders are needed to address these problems. Conventional educational models frequently divide information into discrete fields, which hinders students' capacity to solve challenging real-world issues.
- **Advancements in Technology:** The availability, sharing, and consumption of information have all been transformed by the digital era. Resources for self-directed study, teamwork, and creativity are now available to students. Technology must be used by educational institutions to develop tailored learning paths, interactive platforms, and immersive experiences that foster critical thinking and creativity.
- **Changing Student Demographics and Expectations:** Diverse learning styles and backgrounds need for relevant, interesting, and flexible educational opportunities. To meet these demands, creative methods such as competency-based education, flipped classrooms, immersive learning, and project-based learning provide individualized, practical learning experiences.
- **Globalization and Interconnectedness:** The globe is becoming a more linked place, which offers possibilities and difficulties for higher education. As members of a global community, students must acquire cultural competency, effective communication techniques, and an international perspective in order to prosper in a multicultural environment. Students are prepared to

handle a variety of cultural and professional situations through innovative ways that combine global alliances, cross-cultural interactions, and international viewpoints.
- **Rapidly Changing Knowledge Landscape:** Knowledge is being created and disseminated at a faster rate, which is propelling ongoing breakthroughs across a range of sectors. To guarantee that students graduate with the most recent skills and knowledge pertinent to their chosen areas, higher education institutions must modify their curriculum and teaching strategies to keep up with these developments. Cutting-edge methods that prioritize problem-solving, critical thinking, and lifetime learning enable students to adjust to shifting conditions and maintain their competitiveness in the workplace.

Critical Thinking -Innovative Initiatives in Academia

Creative academic projects are growing in popularity as educators prepare pupils for success in a more complex world. Through allowing students to engage with the content, collaborate in groups, and apply their knowledge to real-world scenarios, these programs encourage critical thinking and provide them the skills necessary to think critically, creatively, and independently (Alenezi, 2021).

- **Problem-Based Learning (PBL):** PBL is an active learning strategy that involves group problem-solving to address real-world issues. Students approach challenging issues via inquiry, analysis, and synthesis rather than passively absorbing knowledge. By challenging students to apply their knowledge, assess the facts, and create solutions in a group environment, PBL promotes critical thinking.
- **Flipped Classroom Model:** By combining traditional lecture-based instruction with self-paced learning activities outside of the classroom, like watching video lectures or reading materials, the flipped classroom model enables students to interact with the material, exercise critical thinking, and get individualized help from their teachers.
- **Design Thinking:** Design thinking is an approach to problem-solving that emphasizes creativity, empathy, and iterative prototyping. In disciplines including engineering, business, and healthcare, it is frequently employed in academia to address challenging problems. By encouraging students to develop empathy for end users, it fosters creativity and critical thinking.
- **Interdisciplinary Collaboration:** Interdisciplinary collaboration unites academics from various backgrounds to handle complicated issues that call for different points of view, including students and professors. Students are exposed to many methods of thinking, learning, and problem-solving when

they collaborate across disciplines. Working across disciplines challenges students to synthesize information from different subjects, deal with ambiguity, and take into account different points of view, all of which foster critical thinking.
- **Undergraduate Research Opportunities:** Opportunities for undergraduate research provide students practical experience carrying out original research under the supervision of academic mentors. Students may hone their critical thinking abilities by conducting research and learning how to formulate research questions, create experiments, analyze data, and evaluate findings. Participating in research projects also develops curiosity, inventiveness, and intellectual independence.
- **Service-Learning Projects:** Through the integration of community service with academic coursework, service-learning projects enable students to apply classroom principles to real-world problems. Students that participate in service-learning initiatives gain critical thinking abilities via introspection, analysis, and problem-solving. Projects that involve service-learning also foster social responsibility, cultural competency, and empathy.
- **Peer-Led Learning Communities:** Peer-led learning communities provide students the chance to work in small groups with their peers to examine course materials, debate ideas, and complete projects. Peer-led learning communities support cooperative problem-solving, active engagement, and peer teaching as ways to develop critical thinking. Additionally, they provide a safe learning atmosphere where students are at ease taking chances and experimenting with new concepts.

TECHNOLOGICAL ADVANCEMENTS AND THEIR IMPACT ON LEARNING

Artificial intelligence (AI), virtual reality (VR), augmented reality (AR), and other technological innovations are transforming education by boosting student engagement, teaching and learning methodologies, and educational outcomes. Figure 2 illustrates the profound influence of technology progress on education (Bodolica & Spraggon, 2021; Penalva, 2022).

Exploration of Emerging Technologies

- **Artificial Intelligence (AI):** Artificial intelligence, or AI, is a technology that resembles a computer and mimics human intelligence. It allows for individualized learning in the classroom. It enhances learning experiences outside of

the classroom by analyzing student data, identifying strengths and shortcomings, and providing immediate feedback using adaptive learning algorithms (Das et al., 2024a; Durairaj et al., 2023a; Sharma et al., 2024a).
- **Virtual Reality (VR):** Users of virtual reality technology may engage in interactive experiences and realistic simulations within a computer-generated world. It provides chances for experiential learning in the classroom by letting students investigate virtual worlds, carry out experiments, and participate in simulations that would be unfeasible or impractical in the actual world (Boopathi et al., 2022).
- **Augmented Reality (AR):** Augmented Reality (AR) enhances learners' perception and interaction with their surroundings by superimposing digital information onto the real-world environment. Through the addition of multimedia content, interactive components, and contextual information to textbooks, learning materials, and physical objects, augmented reality (AR) applications in education enhance the learning process. For example, students studying anatomy can better comprehend complicated ideas by using augmented reality apps to view 3D representations of organs and bodily systems (Boopathi et al., 2023; Boopathi & Kumar, 2024a; Palaniappan et al., 2023; Senthil et al., 2023).

Integration of Technology into Teaching and Learning Practices

AI, VR, and AR are revolutionizing teaching and learning because they boost student engagement, tailor instruction, and enhance academic performance. Teachers may create immersive, dynamic, and flexible learning environments by integrating technology into their curriculum design (Prabhuswamy et al., 2024a; Sharma et al., 2024b; Venkatasubramanian et al., 2024a).

- **Personalized Learning:** Personalized learning experiences that are catered to the individual requirements, interests, and learning speed of each student are made possible by technology. Adaptive learning platforms driven by AI examine student data to create customized learning paths, suggest resources, and offer focused feedback. Technology encourages student engagement, motivation, and success by customizing lessons to each student's unique learning preferences and skill level.
- **Active Learning:** Active learning experiences that include students in practical tasks, group projects, and problem-solving exercises are made possible by technology. Experiential learning, experimentation, and discovery are made possible by interactive multimedia materials, simulation software, and virtual laboratories. Students that actively participate in the course material improve

their critical thinking abilities, expand their comprehension, and increase their retention of the material (Boopathi, 2023; Venkateswaran et al., 2023).

- **Blended Learning:** Using technology to improve the learning process, blended learning mixes traditional in-person instruction with online learning activities. In addition to traditional classroom education, virtual lectures, online conversations, and multimedia tools provide students flexibility, accessibility, and extra help. Students may study at their own pace and convenience thanks to blended learning models, which take into account a variety of learning preferences, styles, and schedules.
- **Collaborative Learning:** With the use of technology, teachers and students may collaborate on projects, share ideas, and work together no matter where they are in the world. The digital era demands collaboration and teamwork abilities, which are fostered via online collaboration tools, video conferencing platforms, and cloud-based productivity suites that provide real-time communication, file sharing, and co-authoring (Sangeetha et al., 2023; Ugandar et al., 2023).
- **Assessment and Feedback:** Technology helps students study more efficiently by streamlining the testing process and giving them quick feedback that helps them track their progress. Actionable insights into student performance, learning trends, and opportunities for development are produced via automated grading systems, learning analytics platforms, and online assessment tools. Through instantaneous feedback and practical insights, technology facilitates student learning, development, and success.

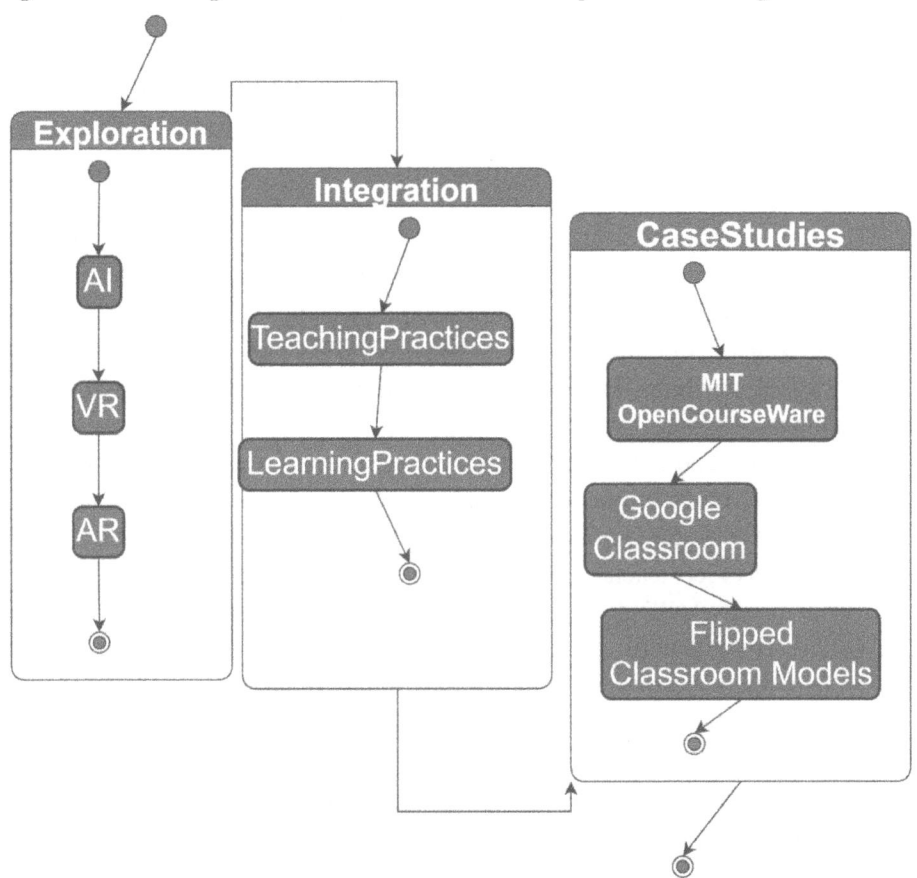

Figure 2. Technological advancements and their impact on learning

Case studies Illustrating the Transformative Potential of Technology in Education

Case studies demonstrate the transformative power of technology in education, emphasizing its ability to improve teaching outcomes, expand access, and empower learners. As technology evolves, educators must create inclusive, engaging, and effective learning environments (Boopathi, 2024; Boopathi & Kumar, 2024b).

- Khan Academy is an educational platform that is non-profit that provides free online materials and instructional videos in a variety of areas. It personalizes lessons using adaptive learning algorithms so that students may study at their

own speed and get the help they need. Research indicates that its users' confidence and academic performance regularly increase.
- MIT Open Courseware: The Massachusetts Institute of Technology (MIT) offers free online access to lecture notes, assignments, tests, and other materials from its esteemed faculty to students all over the world. This platform democratizes higher education and gives students the freedom to pursue their academic interests on their own.
- Duolingo: Duolingo is an interactive language-learning software that teaches foreign languages through games and quizzes that combine gamification and adaptive learning strategies. With its fun design, tailored feedback, and bite-sized courses, millions of users worldwide may learn languages easily and enjoyably, reaching skill levels that are on par with conventional classroom training.
- Google Classroom: Google Classroom is a learning management system that works with Google products to enable collaborative document editing, real-time feedback, and asynchronous communication between educators and students. It also lets teachers create, assign, and grade assignments.
- Academically brilliant students in grades 7 through 12 can attend Stanford Online High School, an independent, approved institution. It provides a college-readiness program that is taught fully online by Stanford University faculty members. Through interactive conversations, group projects, and live video lectures, students participate in a dynamic learning environment.
- Smart learning environments: To create immersive, interactive learning experiences, smart learning environments make use of cutting-edge technology like augmented reality, data analytics, and artificial intelligence. For instance, SMART Technologies has produced collaborative software and interactive whiteboards that let teachers design captivating multimedia classes and get immediate student input. With the use of these tools, teachers may better engage their students, promote active learning, and provide individualized education to meet the requirements of each student.
- Flipped Classroom Models: Inverted from typical teaching approaches, flipped classroom models use in-person class time for interactive discussions and activities and distribute educational content online after hours. Teachers may construct interactive video lessons, quizzes, and discussion prompts that student can participate with asynchronously using platforms like Flipgrid and Edpuzzle. Active learning, student-centered education, and a greater comprehension of the subject matter are all encouraged by flipped classroom methods.

PEDAGOGICAL TRANSFORMATION FOR CRITICAL THINKING

Rethinking Traditional Pedagogies to Foster Critical thinking Skills

Teachers should change their educational techniques to incorporate active learning, inquiry-based methodologies, and metacognitive tactics in order to enhance students' critical thinking abilities. This method, which incorporates critical thinking and rethinks established pedagogies, encourages self-directed lifelong learners. methods of training such as metacognitive techniques, problem-solving exercises, and reflection (Okolie et al., 2022).

- Emphasize Inquiry-Based Learning: Make the transition from a teacher-centered to a student-centered approach by encouraging students to explore, asking open-ended questions, and supporting them as they go through the inquiry process. Rather of just giving answers, lead conversations that compel students to exercise critical thinking, evaluate the evidence, and develop their own conceptual frameworks for difficult subjects.
- Encourage students to use their knowledge, evaluate data, and create solutions to real-world issues by including problem-solving exercises throughout the curriculum. As appropriate, provide scaffolding and assistance, but also push students to take charge of their education and think critically about issues.
- Promote Initiation of Active Participation: Engage students in critical thinking-provoking, active learning experiences instead of rote memorizing and lectures, which are forms of passive learning. Include group discussions, debates, case studies, and practical assignments that push students to think critically, assess the facts, and stand by their opinions.
- Create Metacognitive Strategies: Teach metacognitive techniques including goal-setting, self-reflection, and self-evaluation to help students become conscious of their own thought processes. Students should be encouraged to keep an eye on their own progress, pinpoint areas for development, and modify their tactics as necessary. Students become more autonomous and proficient learners as they strengthen their metacognitive abilities.
- Create Opportunities for Reflection: To assist students in consolidating their knowledge and drawing connections between ideas, schedule reflection time at different stages of the learning process. Urge your kids to think critically, express their ideas clearly, and weigh in on opposing perspectives. In-depth comprehension, critical thinking, and metacognitive awareness are all facilitated by reflection.

- Integrate Diverse views: To question students' presumptions, extend their worldview, and promote empathy, incorporate a variety of views and viewpoints into the curriculum. With books, guest speakers, multimedia materials, and hands-on learning opportunities, introduce kids to a range of voices, cultures, and life experiences. Urge pupils to analyze opposing viewpoints critically and to think about the effects of their own prejudices and preconceptions.
- Encourage a Growth Attitude Create a culture in the classroom where hard work, perseverance, and fortitude are valued more highly than natural talent. Motivate your kids to take on new challenges, develop from setbacks, and see errors as chances for improvement. Fostering a development mentality in pupils gives them the self-assurance and drive to take on challenging tasks and persevere in the face of setbacks.

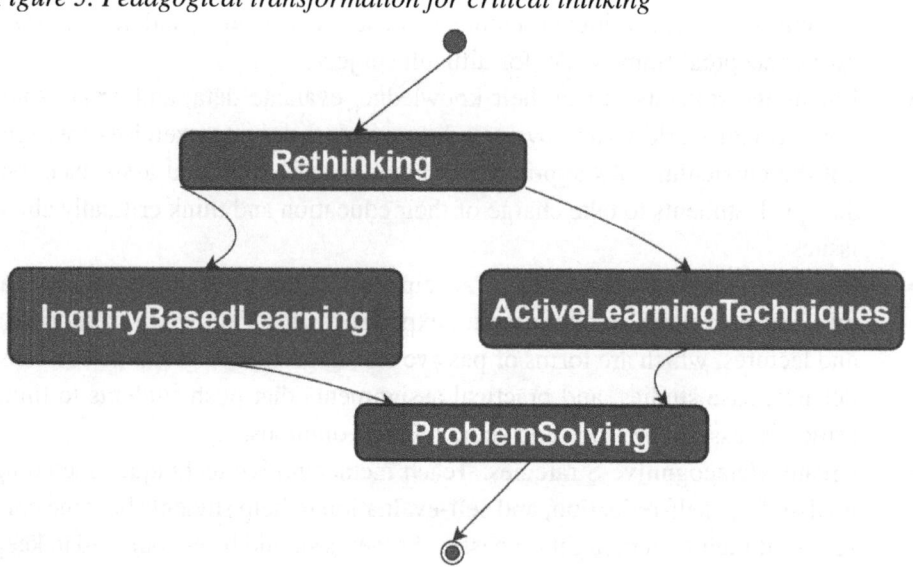

Figure 3. Pedagogical transformation for critical thinking

Strategies for Promoting Inquiry-Based Learning and Problem-Solving

Through genuine settings, collaborative activities, scaffolding, resource access, reflection, and a growth mentality, educators may build dynamic learning environments that support inquiry-based learning, problem-solving abilities, and a development mindset (Zhao, 2020).

- Ask Open-Ended Questions: Provide inquiries and opportunities for investigation in your open-ended questions to foster critical thinking and curiosity. Encourage pupils to conduct their own research, evaluate the available data, and come to their own conclusions rather than offering solutions. "What factors contributed to this historical event?" and "How might we solve this real-world problem?" are two examples of open-ended inquiries.
- Give Realistic Contexts: Place instruction in real-world settings that have relevance and significance for the lives of your pupils. Provide case studies, scenarios, and real-world situations that need students to use their knowledge and abilities to address real-world difficulties. By relating what they are learning to real-world situations, students are inspired to participate fully and use their critical thinking abilities.
- Promote Collaboration: Establish cooperative learning settings where students investigate challenging issues, exchange concepts, and together develop solutions. In addition to fostering empathy, cooperation, and communication skills, collaborative problem-solving exercises expose students to a range of viewpoints and methods. Encourage your pupils to synthesize different points of view, politely debate one another's views, and listen intently.
- Assist and scaffold when needed: To assist students in navigating the inquiry process and honing their problem-solving abilities, provide scaffolding and assistance. Divide difficult assignments into doable pieces, offer advice and criticism as needed, and then progressively hand over more authority to pupils as they demonstrate proficiency. Students that get scaffolding are more capable of overcoming obstacles, becoming independent, and gaining confidence.
- Apply Models of Inquiry-Based Learning: Use inquiry-based learning approaches like problem-based learning (PBL) or the 5E model (Engage, Explore, Explain, Elaborate, Evaluate). These models offer a well-organized framework for leading students through all stages of the inquiry process, from formulating queries and investigating ideas to creating justifications and assessing answers. Models of inquiry-based learning encourage critical thinking, metacognition, and active participation.

- Grant Resource Access: Give students access to a range of resources, including as internet databases, multimedia content, textbooks, and subject matter experts. To help them with their investigation and problem-solving, encourage students to obtain information through research, gather evidence, and consult a variety of sources. Instruct students in the critical assessment of information, the differentiation of trustworthy from untrustworthy sources, and the synthesis of knowledge from various viewpoints.
- Encourage Reflection: Schedule reflection time during the inquiry process to assist students in connecting the dots, solidifying their knowledge, and pinpointing areas in need of development. Students should be encouraged to explain their thought processes, reflect on their experiences, and explore other strategies. The act of reflecting strengthens comprehension, fosters metacognitive awareness, and improves problem-solving abilities.
- Encourage a Growth mentality: Encourage a growth mentality by highlighting the significance of work, tenacity, and persistence in the face of difficulties. Urge pupils to see errors as chances for development and learning rather than as failures. Honor effort and advancement rather than concentrating just on results. Fostering a development mentality in kids gives them the self-assurance and drive to take on challenging tasks and persevere in their educational endeavors.

Best Practices for Incorporating Active Learning Techniques in the Classroom

Using active learning strategies, teachers may increase student enthusiasm, engagement, and retention of the information by encouraging involvement, teamwork, critical thinking, and deep learning (Fields et al., 2021).

- Establish Specific Learning Objectives: Make sure your learning objectives are precise and in line with the lesson's objectives and content. Decide which particular information, abilities, and attitudes pupils should pick up via hands-on learning.
- Select the Right Activities: Choose interactive learning exercises that are appropriate for the course material, student body size, and classroom setting. Think about using a range of methods, including debates, role-playing, problem-solving activities, case studies, group discussions, and practical experiments.
- Make Sufficient Preparations: Make sure the students has the prior knowledge and abilities needed to participate in active learning activities. Give

pupils pre-reading tasks, background knowledge, or introductory lectures in order to get them ready for the activities that will come up.
- Encourage All Students to Take Part in the Learning Process: Ask questions, share ideas, and participate in class discussions to help all students take part in the learning process. Engage students and promote class involvement by using techniques like cold calling, think-pair-share, or polling.
- Establish a Helpful Learning Environment: Create a welcoming and inclusive learning environment in your classroom where kids are at ease taking chances, expressing their opinions, and working together with one another. Set guidelines for polite conversation and motivate kids to actively listen to others and weigh their points of view.
- Give clear directions: Clearly state instructions and expectations to ensure that students know what is expected of them during active learning activities. Provide students with the tools, models, and detailed instructions they need to study and achieve.
- Lead Work in Small Groups: Split up the class into smaller groups to encourage cooperation, dialogue, and peer education. To encourage responsibility and guarantee that everyone takes an active part in the group activity, assign duties or tasks to each group member.
- Provide prompt feedback: Give students prompt, helpful feedback about their performance, involvement, and contributions throughout interactive learning activities. Reward good conduct, clear up misunderstandings, and lead pupils to a deeper comprehension using feedback.
- Encourage Reflection: Schedule time for reflection following active learning exercises to assist students in connecting what they have learned, strengthening it, and pinpointing areas in which they still need to improve. Inquire of your students about their learnings, their contributions to the activity, and what they would do differently in the future.
- Evaluation of Learning Outcomes Use quizzes, group presentations, written reflections, and formative evaluations to gauge the learning objectives of your students. Evaluations must to be in line with the learning objectives and provide students a chance to show what they have learned, how to think critically, and how to apply what they have learned (Das et al., 2024b).

CREATING IMMERSIVE LEARNING ENVIRONMENTS

In the digital age, educators are utilizing innovative technologies like gamification, virtual reality, and AR to create immersive learning environments that engage students, foster collaboration, and improve learning outcomes, transforming traditional classrooms into dynamic spaces (Alfrey & O'Connor, 2020; Fields et al., 2021).

Utilizing Gamification Principles to Enhance Student Engagement:

Gamification is a tactic that incorporates elements of games into educational and other non-gaming situations to improve motivation, engagement, and learning. It encourages competitiveness, active engagement, teamwork, critical thinking, problem-solving, decision-making, autonomy, mastery, and purpose in students' learning journeys through the use of points, badges, leaderboards, and incentives (Beck et al., 2020).

Figure 4. Various creating immersive learning environments

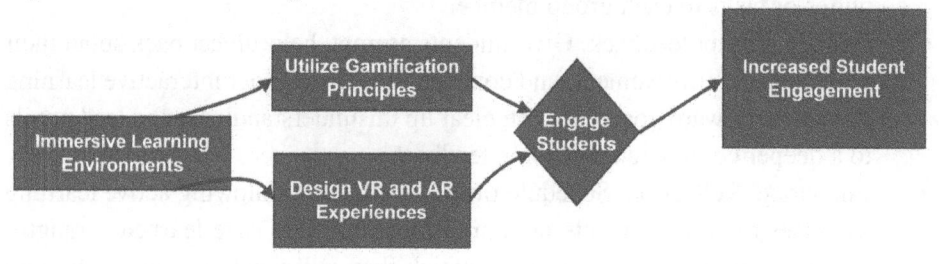

Designing Virtual Reality (VR) and Augmented Reality (AR) Experiences for Immersive Learning:

Through immersive learning environments, virtual reality (VR) and augmented reality (AR) technology improve students' comprehension of difficult ideas. While AR apps enrich conventional learning materials with interactive components, multimedia content, and contextual information, VR enables students to explore 3D models, interact with objects, and engage in realistic scenarios (Mulders et al., 2020).

Case Examples Demonstrating the Effectiveness of Immersive Learning Environments(Beck et al., 2023; De Back et al., 2023; Mulders et al., 2020)

- **ZapBox:** With the use of VR and AR technology, ZapBox is a reasonably priced mixed reality system that produces engaging educational experiences. Students utilize ZapBox headgear and controllers in the classroom to work together on projects, explore virtual worlds, and interact with digital items. Instructors can tailor lessons to meet the goals of the curriculum and give students chances for experiential learning that will improve their comprehension of abstract ideas.
- **Duolingo:** The language-learning app Duolingo uses gamification techniques to entice and keep users interested. As they advance through language classes, students receive points, badges, and awards through interactive exercises, quizzes, and challenges. When compared to conventional teaching techniques, Duolingo's immersive approach to language learning has been demonstrated to boost student engagement, retention, and competence levels.
- **Google Expeditions:** With Google Expeditions, students may experience virtual field trips to various locations throughout the globe in an immersive virtual reality environment. Students may tour historical locations, investigate ecosystems, and find cultural heritage sites in an immersive 360-degree world using a basic VR headset and smartphone. By giving students immersive experiences that spark their curiosity, creativity, and critical thinking, Google Expeditions makes learning come to life.

PROMOTING INTERDISCIPLINARY COLLABORATION

Interdisciplinary cooperation means bringing together experts from different academic disciplines to work on challenging issues and come up with creative solutions. It does this by bridging conventional disciplinary barriers using a range of viewpoints, skills, and approaches (Moirano et al., 2020). Figure 5 underscores the significance of fostering interdisciplinary collaboration.

Figure 5. Promoting interdisciplinary collaboration

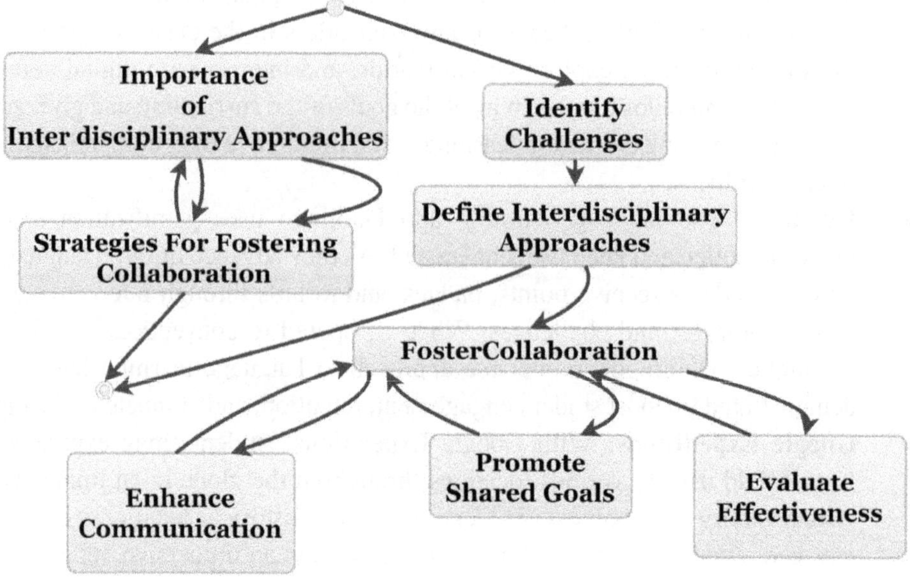

Importance of Interdisciplinary Approaches in Addressing Complex Challenges:

- **Holistic Understanding:** Interdisciplinary methods take into account a variety of viewpoints, elements, and aspects to provide a comprehensive understanding of difficult situations. Researchers can find hidden connections, patterns, and consequences by combining knowledge from other disciplines that would not be visible within a single disciplinary framework (Dillon et al., 2021).
- **Innovative Solutions:** Interdisciplinary cooperation promotes the cross-pollination of concepts and methods, which stimulates creativity, innovation, and unconventional thinking. Interdisciplinary teams may create unique solutions that solve challenging issues in more effective, efficient, and sustainable ways by utilizing a variety of skills and approaches (Mohanty et al., 2023; Rahamathunnisa et al., 2023).
- **Translational Impact:** Transforming academic knowledge into practical applications is one way that interdisciplinary research may have a translational influence. Interdisciplinary teams may integrate research results into practical solutions, policies, and interventions that meet social needs and encour-

age positive change by working with partners from business, government, and civil society..
- **Complex Systems Thinking:** The complexity, unpredictability, and interconnectivity of many real-world issues span several areas. Researchers may embrace systems thinking viewpoints that acknowledge the interdependencies and feedback loops present in complex systems by using interdisciplinary methodologies. Through comprehension of the intricate relationships among many components of a system, multidisciplinary groups may formulate more sophisticated and efficient approaches for addressing issues and resolving conflicts (Prabhuswamy et al., 2024b; Sharma et al., 2024c; Venkatasubramanian et al., 2024b).

Strategies for Fostering Collaboration Across Academic Disciplines

Interdisciplinary collaboration is vital for tackling complex challenges, fostering innovation, and advancing knowledge across academic disciplines by utilizing diverse perspectives, expertise, and methodologies (Van den Beemt et al., 2020). Interdisciplinary research centers and programs provide physical and intellectual spaces for collaboration across academic disciplines, fostering cross-disciplinary interactions and idea exchange. They also facilitate communication and networking through workshops, seminars, and networking events. Interdisciplinary curricula integrate interdisciplinary content and pedagogical approaches, preparing students for interdisciplinary collaboration. These programs offer courses, minors, or certificate programs that develop critical thinking, communication, and teamwork skills across disciplines. Emphasizing team science and collaborative research is emphasized in grant funding, promotion, and tenure criteria, providing incentives, funding opportunities, and recognition for interdisciplinary research projects.

Showcase of Successful Interdisciplinary Projects and Initiatives:

The Human Microbiome Project is an interdisciplinary research initiative involving researchers from various fields to study the interactions between the human microbiome and host physiology. It aims to characterize microbial communities in the human body and understand their role in health and disease. The Global Climate Change Initiative is a multi-disciplinary effort involving scientists from various fields to understand the drivers, impacts, and solutions to climate change. The Brain Initiative is a collaborative research initiative involving researchers from neuroscience, engineering, computer science, and medicine to map the brain, decipher its circuitry, and develop new therapies for brain disorders.

PERSONALIZED LEARNING AND COMPETENCY-BASED ASSESSMENT

Personalized learning is a teaching method that tailors education to individual student needs, focusing on differentiated support and self-directed learning. It uses competency-based assessment to measure proficiency, fostering deeper understanding and skill development (Van den Beemt et al., 2020; Wang et al., 2020).

Tailoring Learning Experiences to Individual Student Needs and Preferences:

Flexible learning pathways enable students to progress at their own pace and according to their individual needs, offering a variety of instructional resources, assignments, and assessment methods. Differentiated instruction caters to diverse needs and abilities, while personalized learning plans outline students' goals, strengths, growth areas, and strategies for success. Collaborative learning objectives are set, and instructional strategies are adjusted based on assessment data and feedback. Technology integration facilitates personalized learning experiences using adaptive learning software, online tutorials, interactive simulations, and virtual labs. Data analytics and learning algorithms track progress and recommend personalized interventions.

Implementing Competency-Based Assessment Methods to Measure Student Proficiency:

It emphasizes the importance of clear learning objectives, authentic assessments, rubrics, formative and summative assessment methods, and multiple measures of assessment in assessing student progress and proficiency. Clear learning objectives are essential for breaking down complex skills into measurable outcomes, while authentic assessments require students to apply their knowledge in real-world contexts. Rubrics outline specific criteria and performance expectations for each competency or learning outcome, providing clear guidelines for demonstrating mastery and success. Formative and summative assessments provide ongoing feedback and opportunities for improvement, while multiple measures, such as performance tasks, projects, presentations, portfolios, quizzes, and exams, provide a comprehensive picture of student learning and proficiency, accommodating diverse learning styles and preferences.

Case Studies Highlighting the Benefits of Personalized Learning and Competency-Based Assessment

Personalized learning and competency-based assessment are transformative methods that prioritize student-centered learning, mastery-based progression, and authentic assessment, creating engaging, effective, and equitable learning environments that prepare students for success in a constantly changing world (Fields et al., 2021). New Hampshire's PACE program, a competency-based education initiative, has improved student engagement, deeper learning, and higher achievement levels. Summit Public Schools, a network of charter schools in California, implements personalized learning models that prioritize student agency, mastery-based progression, and competency-based assessment. Students set personalized learning goals, work at their own pace, and receive targeted support from teachers. This approach has resulted in increased motivation, academic growth, and college readiness. Western Governors University (WGU), an online competency-based university, offers personalized, self-paced learning pathways for adult learners. Students progress through degree programs by demonstrating competency mastery through assessments like projects, papers, and exams. WGU's competency-based approach leads to high levels of student satisfaction and completion rates.

EMBRACING DIVERSITY, EQUITY, AND INCLUSION

Inclusive learning environments, promoting diversity and addressing access and success barriers in higher education, are crucial for fostering a culture of equity and inclusion, ensuring all students can thrive academically, socially, and emotionally(Agrawal et al., 2023; Das et al., 2024b; Durairaj et al., 2023b; Prabhuswamy et al., 2024b).

Creating Inclusive Learning Environments that Celebrate Diversity: It highlights how crucial it is to provide an inclusive, empathetic, and respectful learning environment in schools. Through diversity training and seminars, it promotes candid communication, understanding between cultures, and cross-cultural participation. To represent the diversity of human existence, the curriculum should include a range of voices, opinions, and experiences. To give underprivileged students a place to interact and speak up for their concerns, affinity groups and identity centers ought to be founded. Facilities on campus should be inclusive of and accessible to students from a variety of backgrounds, identities, and skill levels. It is important to offer students with disabilities, chronic diseases, or other accessibility problems with supportive services and assistive technology.

Addressing Barriers to Access and Success in Higher Education: By increasing the number of low-income, first-generation, and minority students who may apply for financial assistance, scholarships, and grants, the institution hopes to lower the financial obstacles to higher education. To assist students who are having financial difficulties, they are providing emergency money, merit scholarships, and need-based help. In addition, the institution actively seeks out students from underrepresented groups and provides focused outreach and support services. It also places a strong emphasis on diversity, equity, and inclusion in admissions and recruitment. Furthermore, the institution offers professional development opportunities to staff and faculty to improve inclusive teaching techniques and cultural competency (Babu et al., 2022; Ravisankar et al., 2023).

Examples of Initiatives Promoting Diversity, Equity, and Inclusion on Campus

It emphasizes the importance of promoting diversity, equity, and inclusion in higher education by addressing barriers to access, promoting cultural competence, and fostering a campus culture where all students feel valued, respected, and empowered to reach their full potential(Alfrey & O'Connor, 2020; Fields et al., 2021). To encourage diversity, equity, and inclusion in all facets of campus life, colleges and universities frequently establish offices dedicated to these topics. These offices offer programs, resources, and support services to help students from underrepresented backgrounds succeed in postsecondary education. Additionally, organizations provide grants, fellowships, and diversity scholarships to encourage individuals from underrepresented backgrounds to pursue higher education. In order to honor and appreciate the many identities, traditions, and accomplishments of students from marginalized populations, cultural heritage months and festivities are also organized. Task groups made up of educators, employees, students, and administrators evaluate the atmosphere on campus, pinpoint areas in need of development, and create tactical plans to advance inclusivity and diversity. These task forces evaluate policies and procedures, survey campus climates, and suggest courses of action to further DEI objectives.

BUILDING STRATEGIC PARTNERSHIPS FOR AUTHENTIC LEARNING

The section emphasizes the importance of forming strategic partnerships with industry, community, and global partners to enhance learning opportunities and bridge the gap between academia and the real world, preparing students with authentic experiences, practical skills, and valuable connections for academic and professional success (Beck et al., 2020; De Back et al., 2023; Mulders et al., 2020).

Figure 6. Building strategic partnerships for authentic learning

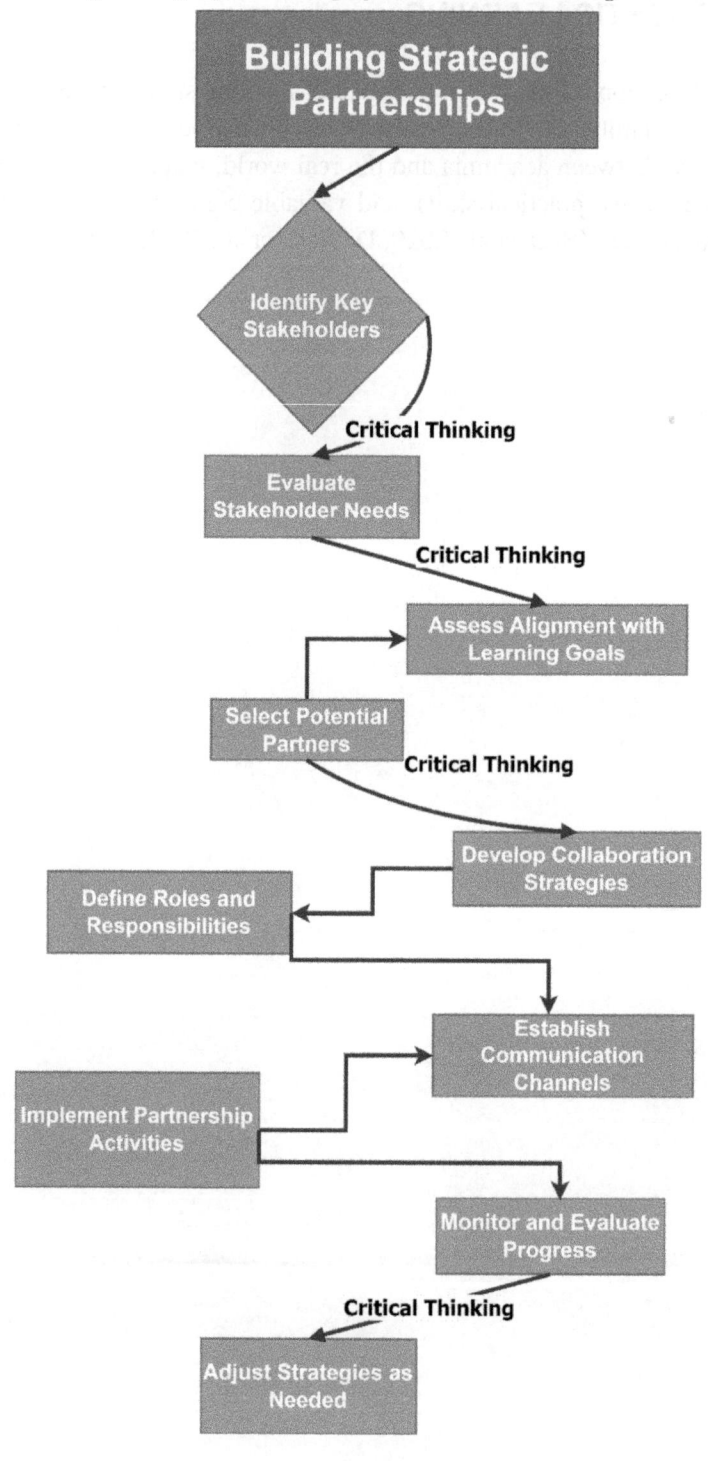

Collaborating with Industry, Community, and Global Partners: It highlights how crucial it is to establish industry relationships in order to provide students with practical learning opportunities, internships, and co-ops. In order to address community needs and encourage civic involvement, it also emphasizes the necessity of working in conjunction with local communities, nonprofits, and governmental institutions. In order to give students access to study abroad opportunities, cross-cultural interactions, and international learning experiences, It also emphasizes the necessity of global collaborations. These collaborations seek to improve students' intercultural competency and extend their horizons.

Establishing Meaningful Partnerships that Bridge the Gap

Forming strategic alliances with business, society, and international partners is crucial to provide students real-world experience, useful skills, and worthwhile connections. Through resource optimization, active student involvement, and cooperation with like-minded partners, schools and universities may effectively close the knowledge gap between the classroom and the real world (Alfrey & O'Connor, 2020). Clear objectives and criteria for long-term collaboration should be established, and the relationship should be in keeping with the institution's aims and values. Learning opportunities with additional value may be produced by combining partners' and academic institutions' shared resources and skills. Modern technology, real-world data, and industry experience may improve curricula and offer mentorship. Participation in partnership activities by students can give them exposure to real-world problems, networking opportunities, and practical experience. Enhancing the sustainability of the collaboration may be achieved by giving students the opportunity to assume leadership roles and use their expertise in real-world settings.

Showcase of Successful Partnerships and Their Impact

In order to develop new technologies, products, and solutions, universities and industry partners work together on research projects, community-based learning initiatives, and worldwide education collaborations. These collaborations support economic expansion while attending to industry demands. New technologies are created by engineering departments and IT businesses, and students gain real-world exposure through community-based learning initiatives. Global education partnerships provide the exposure of students to a wide range of cultures, languages, and viewpoints, therefore promoting intercultural competency and global citizenship.

CONCLUSIONS

This chapter inspects innovative methods to higher education, such as customized learning combined with strategic partnerships, competency-based assessment, diversity, equity, and inclusion. These aim to create a lively, friendly learning atmosphere that caters to students' diverse needs, prepares them for upcoming difficulties, and promotes lifelong learning. Institutions that implement these strategies can provide students with life-changing educational opportunities.

Globalization, technological advancements, and societal shifts will all affect higher education in the future. In order to meet the demands of companies, students, and society at large, educational institutions must employ cutting-edge technologies such as virtual reality, artificial intelligence, and online learning platforms. They also need to make education more accessible by offering opportunities for lifetime learning and flexible delivery strategies. A commitment to diversity, fairness, and inclusion is necessary for a more equitable society. Institutions should promote inclusion, dismantle structural obstacles, and cultivate a climate of respect, empathy, and belonging. Building meaningful partnerships, embracing change, and utilizing technology allow institutions to grow and adapt to meet the needs of students and society.

REFERENCES

Agrawal, A. V., Pitchai, R., Senthamaraikannan, C., Balaji, N. A., Sajithra, S., & Boopathi, S. (2023). Digital Education System During the COVID-19 Pandemic. In *Using Assistive Technology for Inclusive Learning in K-12 Classrooms* (pp. 104–126). IGI Global. DOI: 10.4018/978-1-6684-6424-3.ch005

Alenezi, M. (2021). Deep dive into digital transformation in higher education institutions. *Education Sciences*, 11(12), 770. DOI: 10.3390/educsci11120770

Alfrey, L., & O'Connor, J. (2020). Critical pedagogy and curriculum transformation in secondary health and physical education. *Physical Education and Sport Pedagogy*, 25(3), 288–302. DOI: 10.1080/17408989.2020.1741536

Babu, B. S., Kamalakannan, J., Meenatchi, N., Karthik, S., & Boopathi, S. (2022). Economic impacts and reliability evaluation of battery by adopting Electric Vehicle. *IEEE Explore*, 1–6.

Barth, J., & Muehlfeld, K. (2022). Thinking out of the box—By thinking in other boxes: A systematic review of interventions in early entrepreneurship vs. STEM education research. *Management Review Quarterly*, 72(2), 347–383. DOI: 10.1007/s11301-021-00248-3

Beck, D., Morgado, L., & O'Shea, P. (2020). Finding the gaps about uses of immersive learning environments: A survey of surveys. *Journal of Universal Computer Science*, 26(8), 1043–1073. DOI: 10.3897/jucs.2020.055

Beck, D., Morgado, L., & O'Shea, P. (2023). Educational Practices and Strategies with Immersive Learning Environments: Mapping of Reviews for using the Metaverse. *IEEE Transactions on Learning Technologies*.

Bodolica, V., & Spraggon, M. (2021). Incubating innovation in university settings: Building entrepreneurial mindsets in the future generation of innovative emerging market leaders. *Education + Training*, 63(4), 613–631. DOI: 10.1108/ET-06-2020-0145

Boopathi, S. (2023). Deep Learning Techniques Applied for Automatic Sentence Generation. In *Promoting Diversity, Equity, and Inclusion in Language Learning Environments* (pp. 255–273). IGI Global. DOI: 10.4018/978-1-6684-3632-5.ch016

Boopathi, S. (2024). Balancing Innovation and Security in the Cloud: Navigating the Risks and Rewards of the Digital Age. In *Improving Security, Privacy, and Trust in Cloud Computing* (pp. 164–193). IGI Global.

Boopathi, S., & Khare, R. KG, J. C., Muni, T. V., & Khare, S. (2023). Additive Manufacturing Developments in the Medical Engineering Field. In *Development, Properties, and Industrial Applications of 3D Printed Polymer Composites* (pp. 86–106). IGI Global.

Boopathi, S., & Kumar, P. (2024a). Advanced bioprinting processes using additive manufacturing technologies: Revolutionizing tissue engineering. *3D Printing Technologies: Digital Manufacturing, Artificial Intelligence, Industry 4.0*, 95.

Boopathi, S., & Kumar, P. (2024b). Advanced bioprinting processes using additive manufacturing technologies: Revolutionizing tissue engineering. *3D Printing Technologies: Digital Manufacturing, Artificial Intelligence, Industry 4.0*, 95.

Boopathi, S., Thillaivanan, A., Mohammed, A. A., Shanmugam, P., & VR, P. (2022). Experimental investigation on Abrasive Water Jet Machining of Neem Wood Plastic Composite. *IOP: Functional Composites and Structures, 4*, 025001.

Bose, N., Sarkar, P., Das, A., Samaddar, M., Roy, S., & Dutta, S. (2020). Thinking Out of the Box. *International Journal of English Learning & Teaching Skills*, 2(3), 1388–1411. DOI: 10.15864/ijelts.2309

Das, S., Lekhya, G., Shreya, K., Shekinah, K. L., Babu, K. K., & Boopathi, S. (2024a). Fostering Sustainability Education Through Cross-Disciplinary Collaborations and Research Partnerships: Interdisciplinary Synergy. In *Facilitating Global Collaboration and Knowledge Sharing in Higher Education With Generative AI* (pp. 60–88). IGI Global.

Das, S., Lekhya, G., Shreya, K., Shekinah, K. L., Babu, K. K., & Boopathi, S. (2024b). Fostering Sustainability Education Through Cross-Disciplinary Collaborations and Research Partnerships: Interdisciplinary Synergy. In *Facilitating Global Collaboration and Knowledge Sharing in Higher Education With Generative AI* (pp. 60–88). IGI Global.

De Back, T. T., Tinga, A. M., & Louwerse, M. M. (2023). Learning in immersed collaborative virtual environments: Design and implementation. *Interactive Learning Environments*, 31(8), 5364–5382. DOI: 10.1080/10494820.2021.2006238

Devine, H., Peralta-Alva, A., Selim, H., Eyraud, L., Sharma, P., & Wocken, L. (2021). *Private finance for development: Wishful thinking or thinking out of the box?* International Monetary Fund.

Dillon, S., Armstrong, E., Goudy, L., Reynolds, H., & Scurry, S. (2021). Improving special education service delivery through interdisciplinary collaboration. *Teaching Exceptional Children*, 54(1), 36–43. DOI: 10.1177/00400599211029671

Durairaj, M., Jayakumar, S., Karpagavalli, V., Maheswari, B. U., & Boopathi, S. (2023a). Utilization of Digital Tools in the Indian Higher Education System During Health Crises. In *Multidisciplinary Approaches to Organizational Governance During Health Crises* (pp. 1–21). IGI Global. DOI: 10.4018/978-1-7998-9213-7.ch001

Durairaj, M., Jayakumar, S., Karpagavalli, V., Maheswari, B. U., & Boopathi, S. (2023b). Utilization of Digital Tools in the Indian Higher Education System During Health Crises. In *Multidisciplinary Approaches to Organizational Governance During Health Crises* (pp. 1–21). IGI Global. DOI: 10.4018/978-1-7998-9213-7.ch001

Fields, L., Trostian, B., Moroney, T., & Dean, B. A. (2021). Active learning pedagogy transformation: A whole-of-school approach to person-centred teaching and nursing graduates. *Nurse Education in Practice*, 53, 103051. DOI: 10.1016/j.nepr.2021.103051 PMID: 33865084

Fu, S., Harman, R., & Zhang, M. Y. (2021). Critical creative out of the box thinking in COVID times. *School-University Partnerships*, 14(3), 238–259.

Goh, P. S.-C., & Abdul-Wahab, N. (2020). Paradigms to drive higher education 4.0. *International Journal of Learning. Teaching and Educational Research*, 19(1), 159–171.

Huffman, R. (2020). Thinking out of the box. *Journal of Public Child Welfare*, 14(1), 5–18. DOI: 10.1080/15548732.2020.1690186

Mohanty, A., Venkateswaran, N., Ranjit, P., Tripathi, M. A., & Boopathi, S. (2023). Innovative Strategy for Profitable Automobile Industries: Working Capital Management. In *Handbook of Research on Designing Sustainable Supply Chains to Achieve a Circular Economy* (pp. 412–428). IGI Global.

Moirano, R., Sánchez, M. A., & Štěpánek, L. (2020). Creative interdisciplinary collaboration: A systematic literature review. *Thinking Skills and Creativity*, 35, 100626. DOI: 10.1016/j.tsc.2019.100626

Mulders, M., Buchner, J., & Kerres, M. (2020). A framework for the use of immersive virtual reality in learning environments. [iJET]. *International Journal of Emerging Technologies in Learning*, 15(24), 208–224. DOI: 10.3991/ijet.v15i24.16615

Okolie, U. C., Igwe, P. A., Mong, I. K., Nwosu, H. E., Kanu, C., & Ojemuyide, C. C. (2022). Enhancing students' critical thinking skills through engagement with innovative pedagogical practices in Global South. *Higher Education Research & Development*, 41(4), 1184–1198. DOI: 10.1080/07294360.2021.1896482

Palaniappan, M., Tirlangi, S., Mohamed, M. J. S., Moorthy, R. S., Valeti, S. V., & Boopathi, S. (2023). Fused Deposition Modelling of Polylactic Acid (PLA)-Based Polymer Composites: A Case Study. In *Development, Properties, and Industrial Applications of 3D Printed Polymer Composites* (pp. 66–85). IGI Global.

Penalva, J. (2022). Innovation and leadership as design: A methodology to lead and exceed an ecological approach in higher education. *Journal of the Knowledge Economy*, 13(1), 430–446. DOI: 10.1007/s13132-021-00764-3

Prabhuswamy, M., Tripathi, R., Vijayakumar, M., Thulasimani, T., Sundharesalingam, P., & Sampath, B. (2024a). A Study on the Complex Nature of Higher Education Leadership: An Innovative Approach. In *Challenges of Globalization and Inclusivity in Academic Research* (pp. 202–223). IGI Global. DOI: 10.4018/979-8-3693-1371-8.ch013

Prabhuswamy, M., Tripathi, R., Vijayakumar, M., Thulasimani, T., Sundharesalingam, P., & Sampath, B. (2024b). A Study on the Complex Nature of Higher Education Leadership: An Innovative Approach. In *Challenges of Globalization and Inclusivity in Academic Research* (pp. 202–223). IGI Global. DOI: 10.4018/979-8-3693-1371-8.ch013

Rahamathunnisa, U., Subhashini, P., Aancy, H. M., Meenakshi, S., & Boopathi, S. (2023). Solutions for Software Requirement Risks Using Artificial Intelligence Techniques. In *Handbook of Research on Data Science and Cybersecurity Innovations in Industry 4.0 Technologies* (pp. 45–64). IGI Global.

Ravisankar, A., Sampath, B., & Asif, M. M. (2023). Economic Studies on Automobile Management: Working Capital and Investment Analysis. In *Multidisciplinary Approaches to Organizational Governance During Health Crises* (pp. 169–198). IGI Global.

Sangeetha, M., Kannan, S. R., Boopathi, S., Ramya, J., Ishrat, M., & Sabarinathan, G. (2023). Prediction of Fruit Texture Features Using Deep Learning Techniques. *2023 4th International Conference on Smart Electronics and Communication (ICOSEC)*, 762–768.

Senthil, T., Puviyarasan, M., Babu, S. R., Surakasi, R., Sampath, B., & Associates. (2023). Industrial Robot-Integrated Fused Deposition Modelling for the 3D Printing Process. In *Development, Properties, and Industrial Applications of 3D Printed Polymer Composites* (pp. 188–210). IGI Global.

Sharma, D. M., Ramana, K. V., Jothilakshmi, R., Verma, R., Maheswari, B. U., & Boopathi, S. (2024a). Integrating Generative AI Into K-12 Curriculums and Pedagogies in India: Opportunities and Challenges. *Facilitating Global Collaboration and Knowledge Sharing in Higher Education With Generative AI*, 133–161.

Sharma, D. M., Ramana, K. V., Jothilakshmi, R., Verma, R., Maheswari, B. U., & Boopathi, S. (2024b). Integrating Generative AI Into K-12 Curriculums and Pedagogies in India: Opportunities and Challenges. *Facilitating Global Collaboration and Knowledge Sharing in Higher Education With Generative AI*, 133–161.

Sharma, D. M., Ramana, K. V., Jothilakshmi, R., Verma, R., Maheswari, B. U., & Boopathi, S. (2024c). Integrating Generative AI Into K-12 Curriculums and Pedagogies in India: Opportunities and Challenges. *Facilitating Global Collaboration and Knowledge Sharing in Higher Education With Generative AI*, 133–161.

Sidekerskienė, T., & Damaševičius, R. (2023). Out-of-the-Box Learning: Digital Escape Rooms as a Metaphor for Breaking Down Barriers in STEM Education. *Sustainability (Basel)*, 15(9), 7393. DOI: 10.3390/su15097393

Stek, K. (2023). *A Challenge-Based Experiment Aiming to Develop Strategic Thinking an Inquiry into the Role of Stimulating Creativity for out-of-the-Box Thinking*. EasyChair.

Tejedor, S., Cervi, L., Pérez-Escoda, A., Tusa, F., & Parola, A. (2021). Higher education response in the time of coronavirus: Perceptions of teachers and students, and open innovation. *Journal of Open Innovation*, 7(1), 43. DOI: 10.3390/joitmc7010043

Ugandar, R., Rahamathunnisa, U., Sajithra, S., Christiana, M. B. V., Palai, B. K., & Boopathi, S. (2023). Hospital Waste Management Using Internet of Things and Deep Learning: Enhanced Efficiency and Sustainability. In *Applications of Synthetic Biology in Health, Energy, and Environment* (pp. 317–343). IGI Global.

Van den Beemt, A., MacLeod, M., Van der Veen, J., Van de Ven, A., Van Baalen, S., Klaassen, R., & Boon, M. (2020). Interdisciplinary engineering education: A review of vision, teaching, and support. *Journal of Engineering Education*, 109(3), 508–555. DOI: 10.1002/jee.20347

van den Heerik, R. A., Droog, E., Jong Tjien Fa, M., & Burgers, C. (2020). Thinking out of the box: Production of direct metaphor<? Br?> in a social media context. *Internet Pragmatics*, 3(1), 64–94. DOI: 10.1075/ip.00049.hee

Venkatasubramanian, V., Chitra, M., Sudha, R., Singh, V. P., Jefferson, K., & Boopathi, S. (2024a). Examining the Impacts of Course Outcome Analysis in Indian Higher Education: Enhancing Educational Quality. In *Challenges of Globalization and Inclusivity in Academic Research* (pp. 124–145). IGI Global.

Venkatasubramanian, V., Chitra, M., Sudha, R., Singh, V. P., Jefferson, K., & Boopathi, S. (2024b). Examining the Impacts of Course Outcome Analysis in Indian Higher Education: Enhancing Educational Quality. In *Challenges of Globalization and Inclusivity in Academic Research* (pp. 124–145). IGI Global.

Venkateswaran, N., Vidhya, R., Naik, D. A., Raj, T. M., Munjal, N., & Boopathi, S. (2023). Study on Sentence and Question Formation Using Deep Learning Techniques. In *Digital Natives as a Disruptive Force in Asian Businesses and Societies* (pp. 252–273). IGI Global. DOI: 10.4018/978-1-6684-6782-4.ch015

Wang, H.-H., Charoenmuang, M., Knobloch, N. A., & Tormoehlen, R. L. (2020). Defining interdisciplinary collaboration based on high school teachers' beliefs and practices of STEM integration using a complex designed system. *International Journal of STEM Education*, 7(1), 1–17. DOI: 10.1186/s40594-019-0201-4

Zhao, W. (2020). Epistemological flashpoint in China's classroom reform:(How) can a 'Confucian do-after-me pedagogy' cultivate critical thinking? *Journal of Curriculum Studies*, 52(1), 101–117. DOI: 10.1080/00220272.2019.1641844

KEY TERMS

AI: - Artificial Intelligence
AR: - Augmented Reality
DEI: - Diversity, Equity, and Inclusion
GPA: - Grade Point Average
LMS: - Learning Management System
MIT: - Massachusetts Institute of Technology
OHS: - Occupational Health and Safety
PACE: - Performance Assessment for Competency Education
PBL: - Problem-Based Learning
SMART: - Specific, Measurable, Achievable, Relevant, Time-bound
STEAM: - Science, Technology, Engineering, Arts, and Mathematics
VR: - Virtual Reality
WGU: - Western Governors University

Chapter 16
Critical Junctures in the Implementation of Inclusive Education in South Africa

Jabulani Ngcobo
Department of Basic Education, South Africa

ABSTRACT

The implementation of inclusive education in South Africa has undergone significant transformation since 2001. This chapter explores the critical junctures that have shaped the implementation of inclusive education in South Africa. In this regard, the chapter examines the key moments where policy changes, programmatic interventions, legal developments, and societal shifts may have influenced the country's approach to implementing inclusive education. The chapter argues that the critical junctures, evidenced by the country's history of education, policy and legislative changes, strategic programmatic interventions, court cases and legal challenges, have shaped the trajectory of implementing inclusive education in South Africa. Finally, the chapter argues that South Africa can advance inclusive practices and ensure equitable access to education for all learners by taking advantage of the strategic windows of opportunity created by critical junctures.

INTRODUCTION

The implementation of inclusive education in South Africa has undergone significant transformation since its introduction through Education White Paper 6 in 2001 (Department of Education, 2001). This chapter explores the critical junctures

DOI: 10.4018/979-8-3693-4058-5.ch016

that have shaped the course of implementing inclusive education in South Africa. In this regard, the chapter examines the critical instances where policy and legislative changes, strategic programmatic interventions, court cases and legal challenges, and societal shifts may have influenced the country's course of implementing inclusive education. For purposes of this chapter, critical junctures can be understood as moments of openness for radical institutional change, in which a range of conditions and options exist, are available and can plausibly be adopted (Capoccia & Daniel, 2007). This means that during critical junctures, a unique convergence of conditions, possibilities, alternatives and options creates windows of opportunity for adopting new policies, practices, interventions, or reforms that can lead to substantial shifts in the existing institutional arrangements (Acemoglu & Robinson, 2013).

The reference to 'openness' suggests that during critical junctures, there is a degree of receptiveness or flexibility within the system, allowing for the exploration and consideration of various options, alternatives, possibilities and approaches to addressing existing challenges and issues. This openness implies that stakeholders may be more willing or prone to embracing new ideas, directions, reforms, or strategies, which may not have been conceivable or politically viable during other times. Reference to 'radical institutional change' suggests the potential for significant transformative shifts in the institutions' underlying structures, norms, and processes. These changes may go beyond incremental adjustments and fundamentally alter how institutions evolve, operate, function, or are structured. Thus, critical junctures offer opportunities for initiating far-reaching institutional reforms that can (re)shape institutional arrangements in significant ways. This chapter, therefore, argues that in implementing inclusive education or any other policy intervention, it is essential to recognise and take advantage of critical junctures as strategic moments for effecting far-reaching and lasting institutional change. In this regard, it is crucial to recognise the instances, conditions, alternatives, and possibilities available to influence situations and advance innovative and transformative agendas.

HISTORICAL CONTEXT

History of Education in South Africa

The history of education in South Africa is intricately interweaved with the country's complex social, political, and economic realities, particularly the consequences of apartheid (Groener, 1999). In South Africa, it is almost impossible to talk about education without reference to the country's dark history of segregation and disenfranchisement. This is because apartheid, which emerged as a powerful political influence in 1948, established a system of institutionalised racial segregation and discrimination, shaping education in South Africa in profound ways (Seekings & Nattrass, 2005; Wills, 2011). Thus, the history of education in South Africa mirrors the country's history of exclusion. This legacy of apartheid continues to colour the realities and experiences of the people of South Africa, especially those who were relegated to the lowest rungs of the socio-economic ladder. This means that the legacy of apartheid continues to shape and influence the country's transformation trajectories.

Before the codification of apartheid into law, through the rise of the National Party to power in 1948, South Africa already had a racially divided education system, with separate schools for different racial groups (Pirie, 1992). However, with the formal weaving of the apartheid ideology into the country's legislative architecture, such as in the Bantu Education Act of 1953, the government strengthened its racial segregation efforts (Groener, 1999). For instance, the Bantu Education Act of 1953 led to the provision of separate and second-class education for black South Africans, preparing them for unskilled labour and subordinate roles in society (Seekings & Nattrass, 2005). This means that although there was access to education for black South Africans during this time, it was set as a trap to subordinate rather than empower them to participate in and contribute meaningfully to the lives of their families, communities and society. This means that education was a ball and chain around the necks of black South Africans, keeping them from enjoying the goods of their own country.

During apartheid, education provisioning was racially determined and inequitably resourced. For instance, schools for black communities were inadequately resourced compared to those attended by their white counterparts (Christie, 1985). The curriculum was engineered to reinforce racial stereotypes, promoting the superiority and dominance of white culture and history while suppressing and subordinating the cultural heritage and aspirations of black South Africans (Spaull, 2013). Consequently, the education system perpetuated inequality and provided minimal opportunities for black South Africans, projecting their education as a vehicle for achieving the objectives of the apartheid project. This means that apartheid education did not have good intentions for black South Africans; instead, it intended to exclude them from all aspects of social, political and economic life.

Specific programmatic initiatives propelled and nourished the apartheid ideology of government. For instance, access to quality education for black South Africans was severely restricted and undermined. Many black communities had to endure inadequate school infrastructure, overcrowded classrooms, shortages of qualified teachers, and inadequate access to educational materials (Spaull, 2013). In addition, raucous pass laws and racial segregation policies barred black families from accessing quality education in institutions of their choice, resulting in profound educational discrepancies and inequalities (Seekings & Nattrass, 2005). For instance, pass laws served as a substrate for the Group Areas Act, which restricted South Africans to designated racially zoned areas, often in underdeveloped regions. This led to all sorts of impediments and obstacles for black South Africans, making them unwanted foreigners in their own country.

However, it is incredible that, despite these challenges, education played a crucial role as a mechanism for resistance against apartheid. Schools and universities became centres of resistance, where students and teachers mobilised against discriminatory policies and laws, advocating for equality and social justice (Groener, 1999). The resilience of students to resist the subjugating influence of apartheid education led to significant institutional reforms, which served as a crucial institutional framework for laying the foundations of the democratic dispensation. For instance, the Soweto Uprising of 1976, triggered by the government's decision to impose Afrikaans as the medium of instruction in black schools, galvanised the determination of students to challenge the injustices of the education system and force the government to take a different institutional path.

The imposition of Afrikaans as a medium of instruction forced the apartheid government to reassess its strategies and make concessions in the face of growing opposition, eventually leading to the repeal of the policy and the gradual dismantling of apartheid-era educational structures. While the imposition of Afrikaans initially reinforced the apartheid government's control, it ultimately contributed to its eventual atrophy. For instance, the ignominious suppression of the 1976 protests, including the infamous shootings of unarmed students by security forces, bolstered the domestic and international denunciation of apartheid. This surge of resistance instigated domestic and international opposition forces to push back, hastening the demise of apartheid and paving the way for the democratic transition in South Africa.

Transition to Democracy and the Subsequent Policy Reforms

The end of apartheid in the early 1990s signalled a critical turning point in South Africa's history, promising democracy and equality for all citizens. Central to this commitment was the obligation to redress the entrenched educational disparities perpetuated by the apartheid regime (Groener, 1999). The democratic government recognised the criticality of this obligation and introduced wide-ranging reforms to promote equitable access to education. These reforms took various dimensions, including infrastructure development, teacher capacity building, curriculum reform, and the introduction of inclusive education policies (Seekings & Nattrass, 2005). The determined efforts post-apartheid to dismantle the apartheid educational architecture and foster inclusivity highlighted the government's recognition of education as a crucial instrument for redressing historical injustices and promoting social cohesion (Seekings & Nattrass, 2005).

However, despite significant strides in these and other domains, significant challenges persist in South Africa's education (Spaull, 2013). Enduring inequalities in educational opportunities and outcomes persist along racial and socio-economic lines, with marginalised groups, including persons with disabilities, facing significant barriers to accessing education (Adewumi et al., 2019; McKenzie et al., 2020; Ojo & Mathabathe, 2021; Spaull, 2013). Poverty, inadequate infrastructure, language disparities, societal beliefs and attitudes, limited curriculum choices, and inadequate resource provisioning have aggravated these enduring inequities (Donohue & Bornman, 2014; McKenzie et al., 2020; Trani et al., 2020). The interplay between historical consequences and current realities has accentuated the complexities of addressing educational inequality, with entrenched interests and bureaucratic inertia further impeding the effective implementation of transformative initiatives necessary for promoting equity and reversing historical injustices.

Addressing disparities in resource allocation among schools was a high priority in post-apartheid South Africa (African National Congress, 1994). For instance, policies were developed to improve school infrastructure, provide adequate teaching and learning support materials, and ensure equitable funding for historically disadvantaged schools. For example, the abolition of school fees in the poorest 40% of schools in 1998 sought to dismantle financial barriers and level the playing field for participation by all (Department of Education, 1998). Concurrently, investment in teacher development assumed critical importance, with the government prioritising teacher training and professional development programmes to enhance the quality of education delivery. Efforts were directed towards recruiting and retaining qualified teachers and improving their capacity to address learners' diverse learning needs. For instance, the South African Council for Educators (SACE) Act 31 of 2000 provided a minimum professional qualification for teachers, ensuring that teachers were adequately qualified (Republic of South Africa, 2001).

From the above, it can be discerned that the policy reform agenda pursued by the post-apartheid government played a critical role in transitioning the education system from one characterised by segregation and inequality to one that would promote inclusivity, equality, and social justice. As has been alluded to above, while significant progress has been achieved since 1994, persistent challenges remain, undermining the government's efforts towards achieving more equitable and inclusive education opportunities and outcomes for all South Africans. Thus, this chapter argues that the government must recognise and diligently capitalise on the strategic windows of opportunity that could lead to radical institutional change in implementing its policies.

BUILDING AN INCLUSIVE EDUCATION SYSTEM: POLICY AND LEGISLATIVE TRANSFORMATIONS

South Africa has undergone significant policy and legislative transformations in implementing inclusive education as part of the global education for all agenda. This chapter section examines the critical policy and legislative junctures that have influenced the implementation of inclusive education in South Africa. This section reflects on the implications of the critical legislative and policy junctures and how these may have taken the course of implementing inclusive education in specific directions.

Constitution of the Republic of South Africa Act 108 of 1996

The Constitution of the Republic of South Africa Act 108 of 1996 is a hallmark of progressive constitutionality globally. It safeguards the rights of all the country's citizens (Republic of South Africa, 1996a). The Constitution incorporates a Bill of Rights, which protects and upholds the rights of all, regardless of their race, gender, sex, pregnancy, marital status, ethnic or social origin, age, sexual orientation, disability, religion, conscience, belief, culture, language, and birth (Republic of South Africa, 1996a). This constitutional provision recognises 16 distinct identities and seeks to inclusively incorporate them as a bedrock of the fabric of South African society (Carrim, 2002). As an overarching law, the Constitution guarantees all South Africans the right to citizenship and equality before the law through Section 9(3), which enjoins "the state ... not [to] unfairly discriminate directly or indirectly against anyone on any grounds" mentioned above (Republic of South Africa, 1996, p. 7).

Emphasising equality as a substantive right alongside principles of human dignity and freedom, the Bill of Rights influences the interpretation of all other rights enshrined in the Constitution. The Constitution enshrines principles of equality and non-discrimination, explicitly prohibiting discrimination based on race, gender, ethnicity, religion, or any other grounds. This legal foundation ensures that all individuals, regardless of background and identity, must have equal access to quality education and training opportunities. Section 29 of the Constitution guarantees all citizens access to education and training, including those historically marginalised or excluded. In this regard, the Constitution encourages everyone to contribute to the nation's efforts to heal the divisions of the past and improve the quality of life of all citizens (Republic of South Africa, 1996). This call to equity is reflected in the suite of policies and legislation for addressing disparities in, for instance, access to education resources and opportunities nationally.

The Constitutional Court of the Republic of South Africa is the custodian of the Constitution and, in this regard, has made groundbreaking rulings regarding, for instance, access to education for all. In this regard, it can be argued that the Constitution has set the country on the path of transformation and presented opportunities for radical institutional change in many areas of education provisioning in South Africa. For instance, the Constitution has established accountability mechanisms in the education system, ensuring stakeholders, including parents, students, and communities, have a voice in decision-making processes and can hold the government accountable. This has strengthened transparency, responsiveness, and a service-oriented disposition in providing services, including education, leading to greater inclusivity and responsiveness to, for instance, the educational needs of all citizens.

White Paper on Education and Training, 1995

The White Paper on Education and Training emerged as the government's response to the demise of apartheid and to usher in a new education agenda that would promote inclusivity, equity, and quality (Department of Education, 1995). The promulgation of the White Paper was a byproduct of a critical juncture in South Africa's history: the transition from apartheid to democracy. This period gave the country strategic windows of opportunity to restructure the education system and address inequalities and injustices. The White Paper thus presented as a strategic document that guided the country's education transformation, steering it towards reconstruction and development and recovering it from the destructive debris of suppression and disenfranchisement.

The White Paper thus served as a foundational policy document mapping out the government's vision, objectives, and strategies for transforming and improving the country's education and training system (Department of Education, 1995). The primary purpose of the White Paper was to redress the historical imbalances in education by providing equitable opportunities for all learners, irrespective of their backgrounds and circumstances. This included addressing disparities regarding access to education, quality of education, and educational outcomes among different racial, socio-economic, and geographic groups. The White Paper thus mapped out and articulated a vision for inclusive and equitable education as a mechanism for overcoming and reversing the consequences of apartheid and ensuring that all learners have access to equitable education and training opportunities.

The White Paper emphasised the need to prioritise the education of historically disadvantaged communities and vulnerable groups, including persons with disabilities, to ensure equitable access to educational opportunities and resources (Department of Education, 1995). In this regard, the White Paper recognised the role of education in empowering individuals and communities and building a more prosperous and equitable society. By explicitly recognising the value of inclusive education, the White Paper signalled a departure from the exclusionary practices of the past and set the scene for crafting and introducing inclusive approaches to education in South Africa. Given its transformation focus as a foundational policy document, it was followed by a suite of policies and legislation crucial to the country's efforts to build an inclusive education system.

South African Schools Act 84 of 1996

The South African Schools Act (SASA) 84 of 1996 was enacted shortly after the quietus of apartheid and the ushering in of democracy, a period that represented a critical juncture in the dismantling of the discriminatory policies of the past, creating a new educational framework based on equality, non-discrimination, and inclusivity (Republic of South Africa, 1996b). The SASA thus represents a crucial critical juncture in South Africa's education history, symbolising post-apartheid South Africa's commitment to building a more socially just, peaceful and inclusive society through education. In this regard, the SASA places the country's education system on the path of breaking ties with its apartheid past. Since the promulgation of the SASA in 1996, crucial institutional reforms have been implemented in South Africa.

The SASA established the legal framework for the democratic governance and management of schools (Republic of South Africa, 1996b). In this regard, the SASA foregrounds equity, redress, and inclusivity and obligates schools to admit learners without discrimination and accommodate those with special needs to the extent possible. The SASA has replaced apartheid-era education laws and, in this regard, states that "a public school must admit learners and serve their educational requirements without unfairly discriminating in any way", which means that schools must provide quality education for all learners, irrespective of their differences (Republic of South Africa, 1996b, p. 2A-6). This is a radical departure from education access based on racial segregation, among other issues. It is a strategic position that humanises and enfranchises those relegated to second-class citizens in their own country, using education as an anchor.

The SASA recognises the right of learners with disabilities to access education on an equal basis with their non-disabled peers. It provides for establishing special schools and support services for learners with disabilities, as well as provisions for inclusive education in ordinary public schools. This is articulated in section 12(4) of the SASA, which states that the "... Member of the Executive Council must, where reasonably practicable, provide education for learners with special education needs at ordinary public schools and provide relevant educational support services for such learners" (Republic of South Africa, 1996b, p. 10). By codifying the principles of non-discrimination, equality, and inclusivity in education and laying the foundation for a more equitable and accessible education system, the SASA has ensured that inclusive education is not merely a policy recommendation but a legal obligation for educational institutions. In addition, as can be discerned from the above, the SASA opens the door for the education of learners with disabilities in ordinary public schools.

Education White Paper 6: Special Needs Education: Building an Inclusive Education and Training System

In South Africa, the country's framework for inclusive education is contained in Education White Paper 6 (Department of Education, 2001). Education White Paper 6 emerged as a response to historical injustices and systemic barriers faced by learners, including those with disabilities, marking a significant moment in South Africa's commitment to inclusivity and equity in education. Education White Paper 6 outlines the features of an inclusive education and training system and how the Education Ministry intends to build it (Department of Education, 2001). The White Paper outlines the necessity for creating supportive learning environments catering to the diverse learning needs of learners, including those with disabilities and other barriers. The White Paper emphasises the importance of eliminating educational disparities and equalising educational opportunities by attending to the specific learning needs of those denied equality and access by the education system. This means that the government must recognise and capitalise on strategic windows of opportunity for targeted reforms presented by the White Paper as a critical juncture to break down systemic barriers and set a foundation for cultivating a just and equitable education landscape.

The White Paper acknowledges the legacy of apartheid policies that marginalised learners with disabilities, especially those from socioeconomically depressed communities, highlighting the need for redressing historical injustices and ensuring their full participation in the education system. The White Paper represents a critical juncture in South Africa's quest for educational equity and social justice by recognising the need to address the systemic barriers historically excluding these learners. The White Paper establishes a legal foundation for inclusive education, enshrining the rights of learners experiencing barriers to learning and development, including those with disabilities, to access quality education and support services. This means that the White Paper provides a critical foundation for the enfranchising and humanising national efforts for the good of all citizens.

The White Paper sets out principles of non-discrimination, equal opportunities, and reasonable accommodation, providing a roadmap for transforming the education system to meet the diverse learning needs of learners. In this regard, the White Paper advocates for a shift from segregated to inclusive approaches that recognise and accommodate diversity within schools and classrooms nationwide. The White Paper promotes a continuum of support that emphasises early identification, inclusive classrooms, and individualised interventions to meet the diverse learning needs of learners. Essentially, the White Paper dismisses 'one size fits all' approaches to addressing the learning needs of learners. This shift represents a critical juncture in South Africa's educational philosophy, moving towards a more inclusive and responsive model of education that fosters belonging and celebrates and acknowledges differences.

Recognising the need to build the capacity of teachers, officials and other professionals, the White Paper emphasises the importance of continuous training and professional development in inclusive education practices. The White Paper acknowledges that children often fall behind in school for various reasons, which often have nothing to do with their inability to learn and everything to do with the strength of the support networks provided. Essentially, the White Paper argues that nothing matters more than teachers in these support networks; teachers matter because of their skills, knowledge, attitudes and values. In this regard, the White Paper calls for providing resources, support structures, and ongoing training opportunities to empower teachers to effectively meet the needs of learners with diverse learning needs. By investing in human capital and promoting a culture of inclusion within the education system, the White Paper lays the foundation for sustainable and transformative institutional change.

The White Paper also underlines the importance of partnerships and collaboration between government departments, civil society organisations, communities, and other stakeholders in advancing inclusive education. It calls for coordinated efforts to address systemic barriers, mobilise resources, and promote awareness and advocacy for inclusive education. By advocating for collaboration across sectors and stakeholders, the White Paper opens opportunities for collective action and shared responsibility in building an inclusive education and training system that values and leaves no learner behind. In this regard, the White Paper sets the education system on the path to recognising that all learners matter, all means all, and nothing less.

Education White Paper 5 on Early Childhood Education, 2005

Education White Paper 5 on Early Childhood Education represents a pivotal moment in recognising the importance of early childhood development and laying the foundation for an inclusive education system, starting from the earliest stages of life. The White Paper outlines the government's vision, principles, and strategies for developing and providing early childhood education in the country (Department of Education, 2005). The White Paper recognises the importance of early childhood development in shaping lifelong learning outcomes and addressing inequalities from the outset. By emphasising the significance of the early years in laying the foundation for future educational success, the White Paper represents a critical juncture in shifting the focus of education policies towards proactive interventions that promote inclusivity and equity from the earliest stages of life.

The White Paper articulates the government's framework for providing quality early childhood education and developing services that are accessible, affordable, inclusive, and high-quality. It elevates the importance of investing in the early years to ensure that all children, regardless of their socio-economic backgrounds or circumstances, can reach their full potential and participate fully in society. Recognising early identification, intervention and support as critical, the White Paper aims to address barriers to learning and development from an early age, laying a foundation for inclusive early childhood education for all children. Based on this vision, the government has relocated the early childhood development function from the Department of Social Development to the Department of Basic Education, presenting a suite of opportunities for strengthening inclusive early learning for all children from an early age (see, for example, Department of Basic Education, 2023).

Like its counterpart, Education White Paper 6, Education White Paper 5 on Early Childhood Education underlines the importance of partnerships and collaboration between government departments, communities, civil society organisations, non-governmental organisations and other stakeholders in advancing early childhood education goals (Department of Education, 2005). It calls for coordinated efforts to mobilise resources, share knowledge, and implement effective policies and programmes that support early childhood development. By encouraging collaboration across sectors and stakeholders, the White Paper creates opportunities for collective action and shared responsibility in building an inclusive early childhood development that supports the holistic development of children.

National Curriculum and Assessment Policy Statement, 2011

The National Curriculum and Assessment Policy Statement (CAPS) provides a national framework that guides curriculum development, implementation, and assessment in schools (Department of Basic Education, 2011). The CAPS serves as a blueprint for teachers, providing guidelines on what should be taught and assessed at each grade level across different subjects. The CAPS embodies the government's commitment to promoting inclusive education by ensuring that the curriculum is accessible, relevant, and responsive to the diverse learning needs of learners.

The primary purpose of the CAPS is to provide a clear and coherent curriculum framework that promotes quality education and prepares learners for further education, employment, and citizenship. It aims to foster the holistic development of learners, including their cognitive, emotional, social, and physical development, and to equip them with the knowledge, skills, attitudes and values required to succeed in a rapidly changing world. The transformation of the national curriculum has, for instance, resulted in the diversification of offerings for children and learners, for example, the learning programme for learners with profound intellectual disabilities, the first of its kind in the region (Department of Basic Education, 2023).

As can be discerned, these policy and legislative transformations have served as critical junctures and presented opportunities for the country to create an education system that is inclusive, equitable, and responsive to the diverse learning needs of learners. However, despite notable progress, challenges persist, particularly concerning resource allocation, teacher training, infrastructure, and support services provision. This means that efforts and collaboration by government agencies, teachers, parents, and civil society organisations to take advantage of critical junctures to push the education system forward are imperative to addressing challenges and advancing the objectives of inclusive education in South Africa.

Policy on Screening, Identification, Assessment and Support, 2014

The Policy on Screening, Identification, Assessment and Support (SIAS), promulgated in 2014, seeks to improve mechanisms, systems and processes for the early identification and support of learners experiencing barriers to learning, including disabilities, learning difficulties, and other learning needs (Department of Basic Education, 2014). The Policy outlines screening, assessment, and intervention procedures, emphasising early identification and targeted support for learners experiencing learning difficulties, including those with disabilities and other learning and support needs. The Policy thus goes beyond the technical aspects of referral and foregrounds the provision of targeted support to learners experiencing barriers to learning, as put forth in Education White Paper 6, that all children can learn and need support (Department of Education, 2001)

The Policy emphasises the importance of early screening and identification of learners who may require additional support. It encourages schools to implement regular screening processes to identify learners at risk of academic difficulties or experiencing barriers to learning and development. The Policy advocates for developing individualised support plans for learners who need additional support. These plans outline specific interventions and accommodations to address the unique learning needs of each learner and ensure their full participation in educational programmes. Since 2015, the Policy on SIAS has led to the training of 178 757 teachers, 10 786 officials, and since 2020, 8 337 ECD practitioners (Department of Basic Education, 2023). This progress includes the decision for the basic education sector to focus on the Foundation Phase (i.e., Grades R-3) in support of the early identification and intervention principle. The implementation of the Policy on SIAS suggests benefits for learners, with 42 603 out of 104 998 and 21 699 cases, against 6 577 referrals successfully resolved by district-based support teams (DBSTs) by retaining learners in their schools during 2023/24 (Department of Basic Education, 2024).

STRATEGIC PROGRAMMATIC INTERVENTIONS

Inclusive education initiatives in South Africa represent a pivotal step towards strengthening the education system and promoting the well-being of learners (Department of Education, 2001). These initiatives are designed to cultivate an educational environment that caters to the diverse learning needs of all learners, advocates for equity, and nurtures social inclusion (Donald et al., 1997). Through inclusive education, South Africa intends to dismantle barriers to learning and development, foster a sense of belonging, and prepare learners for active participation in their families, communities and society (Department of Education, 2001). In this chapter section, I reflect on the opportunities, possibilities and issues that specific strategic programmatic interventions have presented for implementing inclusive education in South Africa.

Birth of the Directorate: Inclusive Education

The birth of the Directorate: Inclusive Education from the Directorate: ELSEN, within the Department of Basic Education, in 2000 heralded a significant milestone in introducing inclusive education in South Africa. This transition symbolised the government's commitment to inclusivity and established a pivotal coordinating unit, which would present opportunities for advancing the government's efforts towards building an inclusive education and training system. However, while creating the Directorate: Inclusive Education represented a positive step forward, particularly in terms of organisational structure and strategic focus, it also introduced certain institutional dynamics that require critical examination.

From an institutional reform perspective, establishing the Directorate: Inclusive Education inadvertently strengthened a perception that the responsibility for inclusive education rested solely within the purview of this newly formed unit. This perception had the unintended consequence of potentially absolving other sections or units of their inherent responsibilities and contributions to ensuring inclusivity within the education system. By centralising the responsibility within a single directorate or unit, there emerged a risk of diffusing accountability and hindering the full utilisation of the sector's collective capacity to drive systemic change towards inclusivity. As argued by Ngcobo (2006), locating this responsibility within a single unit of the education system perpetuated the perception that the duty to remedy problems of exclusion lies solely on this unit's shoulders.

The inherent danger in this perception is its potential to undermine the holistic and collaborative nature of inclusive education reform. Inclusive education is not merely a single entity or section's responsibility but a multifaceted endeavour that necessitates concerted efforts across various sections or units and stakeholders within and across the education system. By relegating the responsibility primarily to the Directorate: Inclusive Education, there arises a risk of marginalising the contributions and expertise of other relevant units, thereby limiting the breadth and depth of the reform efforts. When this happens, collective obligation, effort and action are severely compromised, often leading to the selective implementation of inclusive education.

Furthermore, institutionalising inclusive education within a singular directorate or unit framework may inadvertently encourage complacency and stagnation within the broader basic education sector. By allocating exclusive responsibility to the Directorate: Inclusive Education, there exists a danger of diminishing the sense of collective ownership, obligation and commitment towards inclusive education goals among other sector components or units. This could impede the sector's ability to leverage its full potential for innovation, collaboration, and resource mobilisation towards the realisation of inclusive education objectives.

Inclusive education stands as a testament to the collective effort of diverse stakeholders rather than being solely reliant on individual endeavours. It necessitates a collaborative ethos grounded in a shared commitment to fostering inclusivity within educational settings. This collaborative approach accentuates and elevates the imperative for individuals, sections, units and organisations, each driven by their unique interests and expertise, to converge and contribute towards a common objective, project, and mission. This means inclusive education can only be achieved through inclusive means, mechanisms and actions.

The essence of inclusive education lies in cultivating a 'we are in this together' attitude, wherein individuals, units and stakeholders recognise that its success pivots on the interconnectedness of their efforts and the mutual benefits derived from collective action. In practical terms, this implies that various actors must find their respective places within the collaborative framework, learning to navigate and negotiate their roles in alignment with the overarching vision of inclusivity. Rather than operating in isolation or pursuing divergent agendas, stakeholders must synchronise their actions and movements, ensuring that they collectively generate outcomes that serve the common good.

Crucially, the effectiveness of inclusive education hinges upon the quality and value of collective efforts manifested in tangible improvements in the lives of learners at the school and classroom levels. Within these microcosms of educational practice, the impact of collaborative endeavours can be felt, as evidenced by equitable access, participation, and outcomes for all learners, including those with diverse learning needs and backgrounds. By measuring and determining the success of inclusive education through these tangible outcomes, stakeholders can gauge the efficacy of their collaborative efforts, identify areas for refinement and enhancement and capitalise on the strategic windows of opportunity, often provided by critical junctures, to advance their collective efforts towards an inclusive education and training system.

Mobilisation of Out-Of-School Learners with Disabilities

As defined by the Department of Education (2001), inclusive education represents a concerted effort to expand access to quality education for learners with disabilities. Central to this endeavour is identifying, acknowledging, and eliminating barriers hindering educational access, thereby ensuring equitable access to opportunities for all learners, irrespective of their abilities and identities (Republic of South Africa, 1996). By providing tailored accommodations, concessions, support services, and resources, inclusive education initiatives aim to empower learners, including those with disabilities, enabling them to actively participate in the educational process and unlock their academic potential (Department of Education, 2001).

A pivotal aspect of inclusive education in South Africa has been mobilising out-of-school children of school-going age with disabilities. According to data from the Department of Basic Education, the number of learners in public special schools increased from 64,000 in 2002 to 139,343 in 2022. Likewise, the number of learners with disabilities in ordinary public schools rose from 77,000 in 2002 to 121,461 in 2022. This enrolment surge not only signifies increased access to education for learners with disabilities but also enriches the diversity and inclusivity of classroom environments, particularly within ordinary schools. In other words, it shows that persons with disabilities matter and have a place in all schools, families, communities and society.

However, literature has raised concerns regarding the implications of the increase in the number of learners in special schools. While the rise in the number of learners in special schools may initially appear indicative of improved access to education for learners with disabilities, it also raises critical questions regarding its unintended contribution to educational segregation in South Africa, particularly between regular or ordinary and special schools. Directing a significant portion of resources into special schools to accommodate the increasing number of learners with disabilities may strain resources. For example, this may result in less or no funding for inclusive education initiatives, such as providing support services, teacher training, and accommodations within ordinary schools. When this happens, a perception may be created that the place of children with disabilities is in special schools and that ordinary schools are not for them.

Like many other countries globally, South Africa has committed to upholding the rights of persons with disabilities to inclusive education under international agreements, such as the United Nations Convention on the Rights of Persons with Disabilities (United Nations, 2006). Failing to provide inclusive educational opportunities in ordinary or regular schools may contravene these legal obligations and perpetuate discrimination against persons with disabilities. Exclusionary practices in education can contribute to the marginalisation of persons with disabilities, hindering their social and economic participation in society. Inclusive education engenders an environment where all learners can develop the skills and confidence required for leading fulfilling lives and contributing meaningfully to society. This means there is a need for a strategic understanding of the implications of enrolment trends within different educational contexts.

The rise in the number of learners with disabilities in special schools may be indicative of the impending crisis of a lack of spaces in these schools, given that the country only has 435 of them. As such, this increase may indicate the need to build capacity in ordinary public schools to teach more inclusively. South Africa has a window of opportunity to capitalise on the experiences and attitudes that already exist in some ordinary public schools, which already accommodate more than 50 per cent of learners with disabilities in public schools. The basic education sector must identify these islands of effectiveness and strategically replicate good practices from these schools to build an inclusive education system. The impending crisis of a lack of spaces in special schools also presents a strategic moment for the basic education sector to initiate fundamental institutional reforms in line with the imperatives of international conventions and treaties.

Building the capacity of ordinary public schools must be a key consideration as, despite the growing presence of learners with disabilities in regular or ordinary public schools, studies such as that conducted by the Equal Education Law Centre (2021) have highlighted significant concerns regarding the quality of education and support provided to these learners. Such findings suggest that ensuring access to education must entail more than mere enrolment (Pritchett, 2013); ensuring access to education must include adequate support mechanisms to facilitate meaningful participation and learning outcomes for all learners. This means that the following critical question must be addressed: How can the number of learners with disabilities who attend schools in their communities be increased and the quality of education to which they have access improved?

In essence, while the increase in the enrolment of learners with disabilities in special and ordinary schools reflects positive strides towards inclusive education, it also underscores the imperative of addressing systemic challenges to ensure equitable access and quality support services for all learners in all schools. This entails moving beyond numerical enrolment indicators to focus on the holistic enhancement of educational environments and practices, thereby realising the full potential of inclusive education.

Training of Teachers in Specialised Areas of Inclusion

Inclusive education initiatives facilitate the development of teacher capacities to respond to the diverse learning needs of learners (Department of Education, 2001). One of the priorities identified has been the improvement of teacher competences and qualifications in specialised areas of inclusion. The training of teachers in specialised areas has focused on training in Braille, South African Sign Language as Language of Learning and Teaching, Autism and other inclusive programmes (for instance, pre-literacy and pre-numeracy programmes). The intention has been to ensure that inclusive education principles are translated into classroom benefits for learners. Figure 1 below shows the number of teachers trained in specialised areas of inclusion per province since 2017.

Figure 1. Number of teachers trained in specialized areas of inclusion per province, 2017-2022 (Department of Basic Education, 2023)

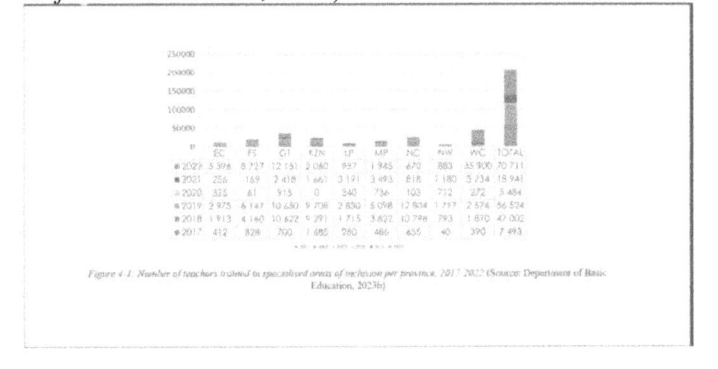

Figure 1 above reflects how the training of teachers in specialised areas of inclusion has pushed the basic education sector to enhance teacher capacities to address the diverse learning needs of learners. This reflects the importance of this programme on teachers' professional development and training to strengthen and contribute to developing a more inclusive education system. Learners with diverse learning needs, such as visual or hearing impairments, autism spectrum disorder, or other learning needs, may require specialised support and teaching strategies. Training teachers in specialised areas has thus equipped them with the knowledge and skills to effectively address the unique needs of these learners, ensuring that they receive appropriate accommodations and support to succeed academically.

By training teachers in specialised areas of inclusion, these initiatives have promoted inclusive practices that celebrate diversity and embrace each learner's unique strengths and challenges. Teachers have learned to develop inclusive, differentiated lesson plans, adapt instructional materials, and implement strategies that cater to the individual learning needs of learners, contributing to the deepening of the culture of inclusivity within schools. Training teachers in specialised areas of inclusion has ensured that learners who require additional support or accommodations are not left out of learning. The Department of Basic Education has reported that the number of learners identified and supported in their schools, rather than referred to other schools, has increased significantly. For instance, in 2023, 21,699 learners were identified and supported by retaining them in their schools, compared to 6,577 learners referred to other schools (Department of Basic Education, 2023). By equipping teachers with the knowledge and skills to effectively support learners, inclusive education initiatives help to ensure that all learners have equal opportunities to succeed academically and reach their full potential.

Teaching for All Initiative

The Teaching for All initiative, established through a collaborative partnership between the Department of Basic Education, the Department of Higher Education and Training, and the British Council in 2018, seeks to enhance inclusive education practices in schools and classrooms (British Council, 2018). This initiative intends to train teachers in the social model of inclusive education and equip them with pedagogies relevant to inclusive learning environments, aligning with the country's goal of building an inclusive education and training system.

The Teaching for All initiative contends that inclusive classrooms must provide optimal learning environments for all learners, fostering academic and social skills crucial for lifelong success. The initiative focuses on building the capacities of teachers through initial teacher education (ITE) and continuing professional teacher development (CPTD) activities, preparing teachers to implement inclusive education practices effectively. To this end, the Teaching for All initiative has facilitated the integration of inclusive education training modules, materials, workshops, and activities into universities and provincial education departments across the country, utilising blended or online learning modalities. The key deliverables of the Teaching for All initiative included a comprehensive research report on the state of inclusive education in South Africa (released in 2018), the development of NQF Level 6 modules for ITE programmes, and short courses for CPTD endorsed by the South African Council for Educators (SACE).

An impact evaluation of the Teaching for All initiative revealed positive outcomes, including the wide reach of the project in ITE, the adaptive and responsive implementation approach, shifts in the competences of student teachers for inclusive education, and support for in-service teachers through the development of CPTD materials (British Council, 2020). The evaluation highlighted the contextual relevance and effectiveness of the Teaching for All initiative materials and the significant shifts observed in student teachers' knowledge, skills, and dispositions towards inclusive education.

The Teaching for All initiative marks a critical juncture in the course of the implementation of inclusive education goals in South Africa. By adopting a comprehensive approach to teacher training and encouraging collaborative partnerships among key stakeholders, this initiative has catalysed transformative institutional change within the basic education sector. Integrating inclusive education principles into pre-service and in-service education sectors has been pivotal, signifying a shift towards more inclusive pedagogical practices and creating supportive learning environments for all learners. As such, the Teaching for All initiative has been crucial in the country's efforts to pursue inclusive education goals, as it offers a strategic vehicle towards building an education system with greater equity, access, and quality.

Audit of Full-Service Schools

Education White Paper 6 commits to "the designation and phased conversion of approximately 500 out of 20,000 primary schools to full-service schools, beginning with the 30 school districts that are part of the national district development programme" (Department of Education, 2001, p. 8). This initiative aimed to enhance the capacity of ordinary schools to cater to diverse learning needs and entrench inclusive education practices. By the end of 2018, provincial education departments had exceeded the sector target by designating 813 public ordinary schools as full-service schools, exceeding the intended 624 by 26.4%.

However, despite this apparent progress, a performance audit by the Auditor-General of South Africa (AGSA) into the functionality of full-service schools revealed significant inadequacies in, for instance, implementing the Policy on Screening, Identification, Assessment, and Support within these schools (Auditor-General of South Africa, 2019). According to the AGSA's findings, the failure of full-service schools to adequately support learners experiencing barriers to learning contributed to their continued underperformance (Auditor-General of South Africa, 2019). In other words, their being in full-service schools did not expose them to better support, as full-service schools did not have the required capacity to make things better for them. The performance audit pointed to the critical shortcomings in operationalising inclusive education principles within full-service schools, as envisaged in Education White Paper 6.

In response to the identified deficiencies, the Department of Basic Education issued Circular S4 of 2019, guiding provincial education departments in implementing the remedial measures recommended by the AGSA (Department of Basic Education, 2019c). For instance, Circular S4 of 2019 directed provincial education departments to consider suspending further designation of full-service schools for three years to implement the AGSA's recommendations. This resulted in provincial education departments terminating some schools as full-service schools as they could not operate as such, leaving the sector with 656 full-service schools. Moreover, a task team was established to develop standard operating procedures to guide the process of the designation, conversion, and resourcing of full-service schools in provincial education departments.

Subsequent to the issuing of Circular S4 of 2019, significant progress has been observed across several key areas: full-service schools were assessed for functionality, with 186 schools receiving support programmes and capacity-building initiatives to strengthen their capacity to address diverse learning needs of learners; 598 full-service schools were equipped with appropriate and proper sanitation facilities, addressing a critical aspect of infrastructure development necessary for creating conducive learning environments; and out of the 656 assessed full-service schools, 357 are implementing outreach programmes to support public ordinary schools (Department of Basic Education, 2024), thereby strengthening collaboration and knowledge-sharing within the broader education ecosystem, which is crucial for the expansion of inclusive education.

It can be concluded that the AGSA's findings and Circular S4 of 2019 provided a critical juncture for the turnaround of full-service schools, fundamentally recalibrating their designation as a mechanism for advancing inclusive education. Central to this transformative process was the decision to suspend the designation of full-service schools, a bold administrative manoeuvre fraught with inherent risks and challenges. For instance, suspending the designation of full-service schools carried a significant potential for backlash from various stakeholders, including communities, civil society organisations, teachers, and vested interests within the basic education sector. Such a decision could easily have been perceived as a system failure, inviting scrutiny and criticism of education officials responsible for implementing inclusive education. However, as can be concluded from the above evidence, this decision gave the sector windows of opportunity to advance its efforts towards effectively utilising full-service schools as an anchor for advancing inclusive education.

Implicit within the suspension of the designation of full-service schools was a candid acknowledgement of the deficiencies and challenges within the existing education system. By suspending further designations, the sector signalled a willingness to confront issues directly rather than perpetuate a flawed status quo. This courageous acknowledgement of shortcomings underscored a commitment to improvement and a departure from complacency towards proactive reform. Thus, the decision to suspend the designation of full-service schools implied a broader commitment to reform and progress within the education sector. It was a strategic shift towards prioritising long-term effectiveness over short-term expediency, even amid immediate challenges and uncertainties. This proactive approach to reform required courage and vision to navigate the complex political and administrative dynamics inherent within the education sector and to capitalise on the windows of opportunity provided by the AGSA's findings.

LANDMARK COURT CASES AND LEGAL CHALLENGES

Several landmark court cases have significantly shaped policy development and the implementation of inclusive education in South Africa. These cases have not only highlighted the importance of ensuring equal access to education for all learners but have also influenced the government's approach to addressing the learning needs of learners. These court cases have shaped and advanced the course of the implementation of inclusive education in South Africa. By highlighting the government's constitutional obligations to ensure equal access to education for all learners, including those with disabilities and other learning needs, these court cases and judgments have significantly influenced the implementation of inclusive education. They have underlined the need for measures to promote inclusive education, including providing adequate resources, support services, access, accommodations and concessions for learners, including those with disabilities. Moreover, they have bolstered the government's commitment to upholding the rights of all learners and addressing systemic barriers to education access and equity.

However, the purpose of this section is not to imply that the government must wait for the courts to rule against it to fulfil its constitutional mandates but that court orders, however ugly they may be when handed down, can present strategic windows of opportunity for radical institutional change. This means that court orders, however undesirable they may seem, can present strategic windows of opportunity during which radical institutional change can most effectively be effected. Given that such opportunities may be fleeting and time-bound, once they happen, the government must take strategic action to take advantage of them.

Western Cape Forum for Intellectual Disability v. Government of the Republic of South Africa

One of the groundbreaking court cases against the basic education sector is the *Western Cape Forum for Intellectual Disability v. Government of the Republic of South Africa* case, commonly referred to as the "Western Cape Forum Case". In this case, heard by the Western Cape High Court in 2010, the Court ruled that the government had failed to provide adequate educational opportunities for learners with severe to profound intellectual disabilities (High Court of South Africa, 2010). In this regard, the Court directed that the State take reasonable measures to give effect to the education rights of these children. In this case, the judgment elevated the government's obligation to provide inclusive education for all learners, regardless of their disabilities. The ruling prompted the government to review its practices regarding the education of children and learners with intellectual disabilities, developing new guidelines and initiatives to promote their access to basic education. From the perspective of the court order as a critical juncture, the court judgment affirmed the legal rights of learners with intellectual disabilities to access quality education on an equal basis with their peers. By acknowledging the rights of these learners to inclusive education, the government was compelled to prioritise the needs of learners with intellectual disabilities within the education system.

One of the key findings by the Court was that the government did not allocate adequate resources to give effect to the right to basic education for learners with severe to profound intellectual disabilities (High Court of South Africa, 2010). In response, in 2016, the National Treasury awarded the Department of Basic Education a Conditional Grant to implement the court order regarding access to basic education for learners with severe to profound intellectual disabilities (Department of Basic Education 2019). For the 2023/24 to 2025/26 Medium-Term Expenditure Framework (MTEF), the National Treasury has allocated approximately R817 million for transfers to provincial education departments (Department of Basic Education, 2023). The allocation of resources by the National Treasury to implement the court order represents a critical juncture in advancing inclusive education for learners with severe to profound intellectual disabilities. This allocation of resources has brought about several significant benefits for children with severe to profound intellectual disabilities, leveraging financial and other support to address longstanding deficiencies and catalyse positive change within the basic education system.

In response to the court order, the government was required to develop and implement policies and strategies to promote inclusive education for learners with severe to profound intellectual disabilities. This included measures to ensure these learners' access to learning. The Department of Basic Education has developed a learning programme for learners with profound intellectual disabilities using the existing national curriculum statement instead of developing a separate curriculum for this category of learners, the first of its kind in the country and region. It could be argued that the court order has enabled innovation regarding the differentiation of the national curriculum to ensure that learners with profound intellectual disability can access basic education. To support the implementation of the learning programme and provision of therapeutic support for learners in special care centres, the Department of Basic Education has facilitated the appointment of approximately 230 members of district-based transversal itinerant outreach teams. This means that these learners, especially those with profound intellectual disabilities, can now access some form of basic education and support, including assistive devices.

Moreover, before the court order, there was no data on learners enrolled in community-based special care centres, which means the Department of Basic Education could not account for them. However, in response to the court order, the Department of Basic Education has developed a database of 477 special care centres, 3,104 caregivers employed in special care centres and 9,325 learners in special care centres. It is essential to point out that although the court order applied to the Western Cape province, the Department of Basic Education, in its implementation, included all nine provincial education departments. This means that the implementation of the court order did not only benefit learners and children in the Western Cape but across the country.

Again, before the court order, the basic education sector did not plan to place learners with profound intellectual disabilities in schools. However, with the implementation of the court order, strides have been made to place learners with profound intellectual disabilities in community-based special care centres in schools. However, the pace of doing this has been sluggish and varied across provinces for various reasons. For instance, in 2024, the Department of Basic Education reported 7,712 learners in special care centres, of which 4,321 had profound intellectual disabilities and were accessing the learning programme (Department of Basic Education, 2024). However, data from the Department of Basic Education reveals that approximately 79 out of 8 764 learners were placed in schools during the second quarter of 2022/23. This signals a move to consider access to basic education for this category of children, but it is insufficient and requires urgent attention, as special care centres do not have qualified teachers who can teach using the learning programme. As a response, the Department of Basic Education has established a multidisciplinary task team to facilitate the placement of these learners in schools.

Flowing from the task team's work, the Department of Basic Education has issued Circular 28 of 2023, which directs provincial education departments to place all learners of school-going age, especially those in special care centres, in schools. The Circular refers Heads of Provincial Education Departments to section 3(3) of the South African Schools Act 84 of 1996, which states that every Member of the

Executive Council must ensure that there are enough school places so that every child who lives in their province can attend school as required by sections (1) and (2). In this regard, the Circular states that all learners who have mild to moderate intellectual disability, severe intellectual disability, and no intellectual disability, who are currently in community-based special care centres, must be enrolled in schools by the end of 2023/24, as they are not benefiting from the learning programme for learners with profound intellectual disability, offered in special care centres. The Circular also requests provincial education departments to clear all backlogs regarding the psycho-educational assessments of learners in special care centres to ensure that they can be placed in schools by the end of Term 1 of the 2024 academic year. (Department of Basic Education, 2023c).

The placement of learners in special care centres in schools will have significant benefits for the basic education sector, including the following: adhering to the constitutional, legal and policy imperatives, thus minimising costly litigations; the grant framework could be adapted, and the sector can then channel resources to schools, early childhood development centres and other appropriate institutions; children placed in schools can access quality education and a full basket of support that they are currently not receiving in special care centres; the support provided by transversal itinerant teams can then be channelled to ordinary public schools to support inclusive education programmes and initiatives; redirecting some of the resources and support to ordinary public schools will contribute to the sector's efforts to reduce referral of learners to special schools and strengthen the capacity of ordinary public schools to implement inclusive education. This means that this court order has and still presents strategic windows of opportunity for the basic education sector to adopt new ways of working to advance the implementation of inclusive education. This means the court order is a critical juncture that must be strategically taken advantage of before it loses its currency for various reasons.

Head of Department, Department of Education, Free State Province v Welkom High School and Another and Harmony High School and Another

In 2010, two teenage learners, one from Welkom High School and the other from Harmony High School, Free State province, faced exclusion from regular classes due to pregnancy, following the schools' pregnancy policies (Constitutional Court, 2013). Despite the learners' efforts to seek intervention from various authorities, including the Minister of Basic Education and the South African Human Rights Commission (SAHRC), their exclusion remained unchallenged initially.

In the case of the Welkom learner, despite the SAHRC's indication that such exclusion violates the learner's constitutional right to education, the school's governing body upheld its decision to enforce its pregnancy policy. Similarly, the Harmony High School learner's mother approached the Department of Education for assistance, resulting in departmental officials requesting the school to review the learner's case. However, the Harmony High School Governing Body did not reconsider its decision regarding the learner's exclusion, asserting the application of its pregnancy policy.

The matter culminated in a legal ruling that deemed the exclusion of pregnant learners from regular classes as discriminatory and a violation of their right to education. The Constitutional Court emphasised the importance of policies and supportive interventions to ensure pregnant learners are not unfairly deprived of their educational rights and opportunities. Consequently, the Constitutional Court ordered both schools to allow the affected learners to return to regular classes and receive the necessary support to continue their education without discrimination.

The ruling that held the exclusion of pregnant learners from regular classes to be discriminatory and a violation of their right to education heralded a significant achievement in addressing the systemic barriers faced by pregnant learners in accessing education. This ruling elevated the government's obligation to have policy mechanisms and supportive interventions in place to protect and uphold pregnant learners' educational rights and opportunities and mitigate the adverse consequences of discrimination. The Constitutional Court's emphasis on the importance of the policies reflects recognition of the multifaceted challenges pregnant learners face and the need for effective systemic interventions to address them effectively. By highlighting the discriminatory nature of excluding pregnant learners from regular classes, the Constitutional Court affirmed the fundamental principle that all learners have the right to education, irrespective of their differences, including pregnancy.

In response to the court order, the Department of Basic Education took proactive steps to develop the *Policy on the Prevention and Management of Learner Pregnancy in Schools*. This Policy, gazetted in December 2021, represents a significant stride towards promoting learners' constitutional right to basic education and ensuring their inclusion in the education system regardless of pregnancy or childbirth (Department of Basic Education, 2021). The primary objective of the Policy is to prevent the exclusion of pregnant learners from schools and to provide them with the necessary support to continue and complete their basic education. By explicitly prohibiting the discrimination and exclusion of pregnant learners and placing the obligation on schools to create supportive and inclusive learning environments, the Policy reinforces the principles of equality, non-discrimination, and inclusivity within the education system.

The legal ruling and the subsequent responses by the basic education sector represent critical junctures, providing strategic windows of opportunity for advancing the rights and inclusion of pregnant learners in education in South Africa. By affirming the illegality of discriminatory practices towards pregnant learners and placing an obligation on the government, including schools, to put in place proactive measures to support pregnant learners, the court order paves the way for a more inclusive and equitable education system that upholds the rights and dignity of all learners, including pregnant learners.

Governing Body of the Juma Masjid Primary School v. Ahmed Asruff Essay and Others

On 11 April 2011, the Constitutional Court delivered a judgment concerning the right to a basic education when a private property owner sought to evict a public school conducted on its premises. The applicants, the School Governing Body of the Juma Musjid Primary School (school) and the parents and guardians of the learners enrolled at the school appealed against an order granted by the KwaZulu-Natal High Court, Pietermaritzburg, which upheld the Juma Masjid Trust's application to evict the KwaZulu-Natal Member of the Executive Council for Education and, effectively, the learners and teachers of the school, from the private premises owned by the Trust.

In granting the eviction order, the High Court held that (a) the Trust was not performing a public function that required it to observe fair process towards the school; (b) the Trust owed no constitutional obligations to the Member of the Executive Council or the learners at the school; and (c) the Trust's right to property in terms of section 25 of the Constitution must be respected. The High Court further held that respecting, protecting and upholding the learners' right to basic education lies with the Member of the Executive Council, not the Trust. The School Governing Body unsuccessfully applied for leave to appeal to the Court of the High Court and the Supreme Court of Appeal.

In its application for leave to appeal to the Constitutional Court, the School Governing Body challenged the conduct of firstly, the Trust in enforcing its rights under section 25 of the Constitution as a private owner of the land; secondly, the High Court in its failure to exercise its constitutional obligation to develop the common law to protect the learners and thirdly, the High Court's failure to craft an appropriate order. Finally, the School Governing Body contended that, in making its decision, the High Court had failed to consider the paramountcy of children's best interests. The Centre for Child Law and the Socio-Economic Rights Institute (amici curiae) made useful submissions on this issue.

In hearing the application, the Constitutional Court stated that to understand the nature of the right to "a basic education" under section 29(1)(a), it was essential to reflect on it against other socio-economic rights. In this regard, the Court stated that unlike some of the other socio-economic rights, the right to a basic education is immediately realisable, and there is no internal limitation requiring that the right be "progressively realised" within "available resources" subject to "reasonable legislative measures". In this regard, the Court held that the right to a basic education in section 29(1)(a) may be limited only in terms of a law of general application, which is "reasonable and justifiable in an open and democratic society based on human dignity, equality and freedom". This right is, therefore, according to the Constitutional Court, distinct from the right to "further education" provided for in section 29(1)(b). The state is, in terms of that right, obliged, through reasonable measures, to make further education "progressively available and accessible."

The Court's interpretation of the right to a basic education as immediately realisable distinguishes it from other socio-economic rights, highlighting its foundational importance in ensuring the dignity and equality of all individuals. Unlike the rights subject to progressive realisation within available resources, the right to a basic education is deemed essential and non-derogable, emphasising the government's immediate obligation to provide quality education to all learners, including those with disabilities. This interpretation accentuates the paramountcy of inclusive education as a fundamental component of realising the right to a basic education. By affirming that this right must be fulfilled without delay and internal limitations, the Constitutional Court underlined the urgency of addressing barriers to access and ensuring that learners, including those with disabilities, are not left behind in South Africa's education system.

Furthermore, the Constitutional Court's delineation between the right to a basic education and the right to further education elevates the distinct obligations of the State in providing education at different levels. While the right to further education may be progressively realised, the right to a basic education demands immediate action to ensure that all learners, regardless of their abilities or backgrounds, receive a foundational education that equips them with essential knowledge, skills, attitudes and values. In this context, the court order can be regarded as a turning point in South Africa's journey towards inclusive education, clarifying the legal framework and obligations regarding providing basic education. By affirming the immediate realisability of the right to a basic education and emphasising the State's duty to provide inclusive education through reasonable and justifiable measures, the court order establishes a solid foundation for advancing inclusive education practices and policies in South Africa.

South African National Council for the Blind v. Minister of Basic Education

The *South African National Council for the Blind v. Minister of Basic Education* case, heard by the High Court of South Africa, Gauteng Provincial Division, in 2018, marked a significant milestone in implementing inclusive education in South Africa. The case addressed the critical issue of producing and delivering braille textbooks to all braille users at schools for the blind and full-service schools nationwide. The outcome of this case, as reflected in the settlement agreement between the South African National Council for the Blind and the Minister of Basic Education, elevated the fundamental rights of learners with visual impairments within the framework of constitutional provisions (High Court of South Africa, Gauteng Provincial Division, 2018).

The settlement agreement highlighted several key rights of learners with visual impairments, emphasising their right to receive all prescribed textbooks at the commencement of each academic year as an essential component of the right to a basic education guaranteed in the Constitution (High Court of South Africa, Gauteng Provincial Division, 2018). Furthermore, the settlement agreement affirmed the learners' right not to be discriminated against on the grounds of race and disability, including the right to equal access to all components of basic education, including learning and teaching support materials. The settlement agreement also elevated as a priority the learners' right to human dignity and to have their best interests kept paramount as guaranteed in the Constitution (High Court of South Africa, Gauteng Provincial Division, 2018).

To give effect to the settlement agreement, the Department of Basic Education and provincial education departments committed to undertaking various measures. These included conducting an audit of all the country's schools for the blind and full-service schools, printing and delivering braille textbooks for learners with visual impairment at these schools, producing master copies for use by provincial education departments, and engaging with each other through the Braille Advisory Committee established by the Department of Basic Education (High Court of South Africa, Gauteng Provincial Division, 2018). In 2021, significant progress had been made by procuring over 26 master copies of braille and large print language textbooks (Department of Basic Education, 2023). These were made available for download and reproduction by schools through the Department of Basic Education website (Department of Basic Education, 2023). This response ensured broader access to learning and teaching support materials for learners with visual impairments, facilitating their inclusion and participation in the educational process as guaranteed in the Constitution.

The implementation of the settlement agreement regarding providing braille textbooks for learners with visual impairments in South Africa has been led by the Directorate: Learning and Teaching Support Materials, representing a significant institutional shift away from the Directorate: Inclusive Education. This shift marks a fundamental change in the institutional approach to inclusive education in South Africa, as it broadens the scope of responsibility beyond the confines of the Directorate: Inclusive Education and integrates inclusive education responsibilities and practices into the mainstream education processes of the basic education sector.

This institutional shift recognises the reciprocity and interdependence between learning and teaching support materials and inclusive education. By placing the responsibility for implementing the settlement agreement under the Directorate: Learning and Teaching Support Materials, the Department of Basic Education acknowledges that access to appropriate learning and teaching support materials is essential for ensuring the inclusion and success of learners with visual impairments. This approach aligns with the principles of universal learning design, which advocate for creating flexible learning environments that accommodate the diverse needs of all learners, including those with disabilities.

Mainstreaming the implementation of inclusive education through the Directorate: Learning and Teaching Support Materials signifies a departure from a siloed approach to a more systemic inclusive education approach. Historically, the Directorate: Inclusive Education would have been perceived as bearing sole responsibility for addressing the learning needs of learners with disabilities, potentially leading to the marginalisation of inclusive education within the broader education system. The example of integrating inclusive education practices into the functions of the Directorate: Learning and Teaching Support Materials is signalling an undertaking to situate inclusivity across all aspects of education provision rather than treating it as a separate and isolated concern.

This institutional shift has several practical implications for delivering inclusive education services. The Directorate: Learning and Teaching Support Materials is likely, more than the Directorate: Inclusive Education, to have the mandate, infrastructure, resources, and expertise to develop, procure, and distribute learning and teaching support materials. Leveraging this capacity to implement inclusive education initiatives streamlines the process. It ensures more efficient and effective service delivery, which the Directorate: Inclusive Education would not have been able to do for, among others, the reasons above. Furthermore, by incorporating inclusive education considerations into the routine functions of the Directorate: Learning and Teaching Support Materials, the Department of Basic Education is encouraging a culture of inclusivity that permeates all levels of education administration rather than silo it within a singular unit.

The South African National Council for the Blind v. Minister of Basic Education case and the subsequent actions reflect how the Department of Basic Education took advantage of this strategic window of opportunity to advance the implementation of inclusive education. By affirming the rights of learners with visual impairments and implementing measures to address their needs, the initiatives implemented by the Department of Basic Education, in compliance with the settlement agreement, have contributed to enhancing the systemic capacity to build a more equitable and inclusive education system that upholds dignity, equality, and access to education for all learners. Therefore, this court case and settlement order have presented a strategic opportunity rather than a crisis for the basic education sector to advance its efforts of building an inclusive education and training system.

Recommendations for Future Directions, Policy Priorities, and Strategies

Looking ahead, South Africa has the opportunity to advance inclusive practices and ensure equitable access to education for all learners through various future directions, policy priorities, and strategies. Based on the work done so far, the country must recognise and capitalise on the strategic windows of opportunity to effect radical institutional change in key transformation areas. The government must use the opportunities created by various critical junctures to explore and consider multiple options, alternatives, possibilities, and approaches for addressing existing challenges and implementing its interventions, including inclusive education. This chapter section lifts some strategic focus areas the government may want to consider when implementing inclusive education when critical junctures emerge.

One crucial area of focus is increased investment in education, particularly in underprivileged communities. By prioritising funding and resources for education, South Africa can address resource constraints and provide adequate support for inclusive practices. This may include allocating resources for infrastructure development, teacher training, support services, and assistive technologies to meet the diverse needs of learners, especially those from marginalised backgrounds. This is important given that some court cases result from the consequences of constrained fiscal conditions, which undermine the capacity to pursue education for all imperatives adequately.

Policy development and implementation are critical in creating an enabling environment for inclusive practices. South Africa must review existing policies, identify gaps, and develop policies prioritising diversity, equity, and inclusion within the education system. For instance, the basic education sector must diligently utilise the strategic windows of opportunity provided by the review of Education White Paper 6, which is currently underway, to address shortcomings and advance the country's pursuance of the inclusive education agenda. This must include effective implementation at all levels and monitoring compliance and progress to ensure that inclusive practices are upheld and institutionalised.

Enhancing teacher training and professional development programmes is vital for equipping teachers with the necessary knowledge, skills, and competencies to implement inclusive practices effectively. This may include training on differentiating instruction, managing diverse classrooms, using assistive technologies, and creating inclusive learning environments. Ongoing support and mentoring for teachers are equally important to sustain inclusive practices over time. As argued above, the focus must be on building the capacity of ordinary public schools to accommodate learners' diverse learning needs and, where rational and reasonable, enable learners to attend schools in their neighbourhood.

Improving data collection systems and monitoring mechanisms is essential for tracking progress, identifying gaps, and informing evidence-based decision-making. This includes collecting disaggregated data on enrolments, retention, academic achievement, and participation rates of learners, especially those with disabilities and other learning needs. However, as indicated above, it will be essential to consider trends that are in line with the inclusive education and training system the government envisages. This means that the data generated must be utilised to steer the education system towards the imperatives of education for all agendas.

Lastly, promoting community engagement and raising awareness about the importance of inclusive education is essential for building support and mobilising action at the grassroots level. This may involve conducting awareness campaigns, community dialogues, and capacity-building initiatives to foster stakeholder understanding, acceptance, and collaboration. Furthermore, strengthening partnerships and collaboration among government agencies, civil society organisations, educational institutions, and other stakeholders is crucial for accelerating inclusive education initiatives. Collaborative efforts can leverage resources, expertise, and networks to scale up inclusive practices and maximise impact.

CONCLUSION

The journey towards implementing inclusive education in South Africa has been marked by significant transformation and evolution. This chapter reflected on the critical junctures that have shaped this journey, highlighting the strategic moments and windows of opportunity where policy changes, legal developments, and societal shifts have influenced the country's approach to inclusive education. From examining the historical context of education in South Africa to analysing policy and legislative transformations, strategic programmatic interventions, and court cases and legal challenges, it is evident that these critical junctures have played a crucial role in shaping the course of the implementation of inclusive education in the country.

Moving forward, South Africa stands at a juncture where it can further advance inclusive practices and ensure equitable access to education for all learners. By taking advantage of the strategic windows of opportunity created by a range of critical junctures, the government can build upon the foundations it has laid in the past to advance its efforts to build an inclusive education system that upholds the rights and dignity of all children. Embracing diversity, promoting collaboration, and fostering a culture of inclusivity will be essential in realising the vision of a truly inclusive education system in South Africa. Through ongoing dedication, innovation, strategic action and initiative, South Africa can advance towards ensuring every learner can thrive and succeed within an inclusive educational environment.

REFERENCES

Acemoglu, D., & Robinson, J. A. (2013). *Why nations fail. The origins of power, prosperity and poverty.* Profile Books.

Adewumi, T. M., Mosito, C., & Agosto, V. (2019). Experiences of teachers in implementing inclusion of learners with special education needs in selected Fort Beaufort District primary schools, South Africa. [01 March 2024]. *Cogent Education*, 6(1), 1–20. DOI: 10.1080/2331186X.2019.1703446

African National Congress. (1994). National election manifesto. Together we have won the right for all South Africans to vote. Available: https://www.anc1912.org.za/manifestos-1994-national-elections-manifesto/ [28 March 2024]

Auditor-General of South Africa. (2019). *Full-service schools. Presentation made at the DBE Interprovincial Meeting on Inclusive Education, 28 August 2019.* Auditor-General of South Africa.

British Council. (2018). *The state of inclusive education in South Africa and the implications for teacher training programmes. Research Report.* British Council.

British Council. (2020). *Embedding Inclusive Education in Teacher Professional Development in South Africa. Impact evaluation report on the Teaching for All project.* British Council.

Capoccia, G., & Daniel, R. K. (2007). The study of critical junctures. Theory, narrative and counterfactuals in institutional analysis. [27 March 2024]. *World Politics*, 59(3), 341–369. DOI: 10.1017/S0043887100020852

Christie, P. (1985). *The right to learn: The struggle for education in South Africa.* Ravan Press.

Constitutional Court. (2013). Head of Department, Department of Education, Free State Province v Welkom High School and Another; Head of Department, Department of Education, Free State Province v Harmony High School and Another (CCT 103/12) [2013] ZACC 25; 2013 (9) BCLR 989 (CC); 2014 (2) SA 228 (CC) (10 July 2013). Available: https://www.saflii.org/za/cases/ZACC/2013/25.html [26 March 2024].

Constitutional Court of South Africa. (2011). Governing Body of the Juma Musjid Primary School & Others v Ahmed Asruff Essay N.O. and Others (CCT 29/10) [2011] ZACC 13; 2011 (8) BCLR 761 (CC). Available: https://www.coursehero.com/file/138429113/MUSJID-CASEpdf/ [22 March 2024].

Department of Basic Education. (2019a). *National Strategy on Learner Attendance.*

Department of Basic Education. (2019b). *The state of inclusive education in South Africa. Every learner matters. Presentation to the Portfolio Committee on Basic Education.* Department of Basic Education.

Department of Basic Education. (2019c). *Circular S4 of 2019.* Department of Basic Education.

Department of Basic Education. (2021). *Policy on the Prevention and Management of Learner Pregnancy in Schools.* Government Printers.

Department of Basic Education. (2023a). *Presentation to the Council for Education Ministers: Providing Quality Inclusive Education to Learners with Special Education Needs.* Department of Basic Education.

Department of Basic Education. (2023b). *Progress on psycho-educational assessments and placement of out-of-school learners from special care centres in schools. Presentation to the Interprovincial Meeting on Inclusive Education held on 06 December 2023.* Department of Basic Education.

Department of Basic Education. (2024). *Presentation to the Special Heads of Departments Committee Meeting (HEDCOM): Inclusive Education.* Department of Basic Education.

Department of Education. (2001). *Education White Paper 6 on Inclusive Education: Special needs education: Building an inclusive education and training system.* Government Printers.

Donald, D., Lazarus, S., & Lolwana, P. (1997). *Educational psychology in social context: Challenges of development, social issues and special need in southern Africa.* Oxford University Press.

Donohue, D., & Bornman, J. (2014). The challenges of realising inclusive education in South Africa. *South African Journal of Education*, 34(2), 1–14. DOI: 10.15700/201412071114

Equal Education Law Centre. (2021). *Inclusive education: Learners with learning barriers. The right to an equal and quality education.* Equal Education Law Centre.

Groener, Z. (1999). Education policymaking in South Africa, education for liberation: Praxis challenges hegemony. In Groener, Z. (Ed.), *Comparative perspectives on language and literacy* (pp. 325–225). UNESCO.

High Court of South Africa Gauteng Provincial Division. (2018). *South African National Council for the Blind v. Minister of Basic Education*. High Court of South Africa Gauteng Provincial Division.

High Court of South Africa (Western Cape High Court, Cape Town). (2010). Western Cape Forum for Intellectual Disability v Government of the Republic of South Africa and Government of the Province of the Western Cape. High Court of South Africa (Western Cape High Court, Cape Town).

Human Rights Watch. (2015). *Barriers to inclusive education for children with disabilities in South Africa*. Human Rights Watch.

Human Rights Watch. (2019). *South Africa: Children with disabilities denied education*. Human Rights Watch.

McKenzie, J., Vergunst, R., Samuels, C., & Henkeman, T. (2020). The education of children with disabilities risks falling by the wayside. Available: https://www.news.uct.ac.za/campus/communications/updates/covid-19/sep-dec2020/-article/2020-05-28-the-education-of-children-with-disabilities-risks-falling-by-the-wayside[26 March 2024]

Ngcobo, E. J. (2006). *How do teachers position themselves within socially constructed discourses of disability and inclusion? A case study at a semi-rural township school in KwaZulu-Natal*. [A dissertation submitted in partial fulfilment of the requirements for the degree of Master of Education, University of KwaZulu-Natal]. University of KwaZulu-Natal Research Space. Available: https://researchspace.ukzn.ac.za/jspui/bitstream/10413/2094/1/Ngcobo_Edward_J_2006.pdf[27 March 2024].

Ojo, T. A., & Mathabathe, R. (2021). An investigation into the effectiveness of the Curriculum and Assessment Policy Statement (CAPS) in South African schools. *International Journal of Integrating Technology in Education*, 10(2), 23–38. DOI: 10.5121/ijite.2021.10203

Parliament of the Republic of South Africa. (2024). Media Statement: Basic Education Portfolio Committee notes progress in moving Early Childhood Development to Basic Education. Available: https://pmg.org.za/files/230606pcbasic_Media_Statement.docx[25 March 2024]

Pirie, G. H. (1992). Rolling segregation into apartheid: South African Railways, 1948-53. [26 March 2024]. *Journal of Contemporary History*, 27(4), 671–693. DOI: 10.1177/002200949202700407

Republic of South Africa. (1996a). *Constitution of the Republic of South Africa, 1996*. Government Printers.

Republic of South Africa. (1996b). *South African Schools Act 84 of 1996*. Government Printers.

Republic of South Africa. (2000). *South African Council for Educators Act 31 of 2000*. Government Printers.

Seekings, J., & Nattrass, N. (2005). *Class, race, and inequality in South Africa*. Yale University Press. DOI: 10.12987/yale/9780300108927.001.0001

Spaull, N. (2013). *South Africa's education crisis: The quality of education in South Africa 1994-2011*. Centre for Development and Enterprise.

Trani, J., Moodley, J., Anand, P., Graham, L., & Maw, M. T. T. (2020). Stigma of persons with disabilities in South Africa: Uncovering pathways from discrimination to depression and low self-esteem. *Social Science & Medicine*, 265, 1–12. DOI: 10.1016/j.socscimed.2020.113449 PMID: 33183862

UNESCO. (2016). *Global Education Monitoring Report 2016: Education for people and planet: Creating sustainable futures for all*. UNESCO.

UNESCO. (2017). *Inclusion and education: All means all*. UNESCO.

UNESCO. (2019). *Making every learner count: Inclusive education and accountability*. UNESCO.

Weber, E. (2008). *Educational change in South Africa: Reflections on local realities, practices, and reforms*. Sense Publishers. DOI: 10.1163/9789087906603

Wills, I. R. (2011). *The history of Bantu Education: 1948-1994*. [A thesis submitted to the Australian Catholic University in total fulfilment of the requirements for the Degree of Doctor of Philosophy]. Australian Catholic University Research Space. Available: https://acuresearchbank.acu.edu.au/download/f6bb666ae24a99a f27caf82f697d4328b132299cec03800214325a88e393c081/2003673/Wills_2011 _The_history_of_Bantu_education.pdf[15 March 2024].

KEY TERMS AND DEFINITIONS

Critical junctures: Moments of openness for radical institutional change in which a range of conditions and options exist and are available and can plausibly be adopted.

Implementation: Implementation refers to a range of actions carried out by public officials or street-level bureaucrats to ensure that the effects and benefits of government interventions are substantively experienced by target populations

Inclusive education: Inclusive education involves acknowledging and celebrating differences, awareness that all children need support and can learn, and creating enabling structures to respond to the diverse educational needs of learners.

Institution: Refers to a social structure or organisation established to fulfil specific functions, serve specific purposes, and regulate behaviours within a society and communities. Institutions can take various forms, including formal organisations, government agencies, and education systems. They are characterised by rules, norms, values, and practices that guide the behaviours of individuals and groups and shape interactions and relations within the society.

Institutional change: Refers to significant alterations or transformations in the rules, norms, structures, and practices that govern behaviours and interactions within organisations, institutions, or societies. These changes can occur at various levels, from individual organisations to societal systems, and may be driven by external or internal factors.

Institutional framework: Refers to the structure, system, and set of rules, regulations, and practices that govern the behaviours and interactions within organisations, institutions, and society in general. It provides the foundation for entities operating, making decisions, allocating resources, and enforcing norms and standards.

Strategic windows of opportunity: Refer to specific periods or instances, often created by critical junctures, during which favourable conditions exist to pursue agendas, approaches or strategies that can lead to significant institutional change but may not have been conceivable, available, viable or feasible at other times.

Chapter 17
Assessing Challenges and Opportunities for Females' Engagement in STEM:
Exploring the Integration of SDG-4 in Nigeria

Uchenna Kingsley Okeke
 https://orcid.org/0000-0002-8308-6676
University of Johannesburg, South Africa

Sam Ramaila
 https://orcid.org/0000-0002-7351-477X
University of Johannesburg, South Africa

ABSTRACT

This chapter explores the integration of Sustainable Development Goal 4 (SDG 4) in Nigeria, specifically focusing on the challenges and opportunities for females' involvement in Science, Technology, Engineering, and Mathematics (STEM). Recognizing the pivotal role of gender equality in achieving SDG 4's objectives of inclusive and equitable quality education, the chapter examines the barriers hindering females' participation in STEM and identifies potential avenues for enhancement. Through a comprehensive analysis of institutional, socio-cultural, and educational factors, the chapter elucidates the complexities surrounding females' engagement in STEM in the Nigerian context. Furthermore, it explores strategies to promote females' enrollment and retention in STEM education and careers. By shedding light on both challenges and opportunities, this chapter contributes to the

DOI: 10.4018/979-8-3693-4058-5.ch017

discourse on gender equality and educational development in Nigeria and offers insights for policymakers, educators, and stakeholders striving to advance females' participation in STEM fields in alignment with SDG 4

INTRODUCTION

Could women assume more substantial roles in the fields of Science, Technology, Engineering, and Mathematics (STEM) than they currently do, particularly in developing nations like Nigeria? It is questions of this nature that prompted the international community, as noted by Lawrence, Ihebuzor, and Lawrence (2020), to convene in 2015 at the World Education Forum in Incheon, Republic of Korea, where they embraced the 17 Sustainable Development Goals (SDGs) as the benchmark to guide societal development and serve as the yardstick for evaluating all future development endeavors. Notably, SDG 4 underscores the importance of inclusive, equitable quality education and the promotion of lifelong learning opportunities for all. This goal stands as a transformative force within the SDGs, emphasizing not only education as an end but as a vital conduit for global development through the active involvement of women in education, thus catalyzing progress across other SDGs.

According to the United Nations Educational, Scientific and Cultural Organization (UNESCO, 2016), there is a growing consensus on the pivotal role of sustainability education, as outlined in SDG 4 with its seven targets and three enablers, in fostering the sustainable development of nations. Sustainability education fosters reflective learning, imparts knowledge and skills, and empowers individuals to tackle complex sustainability challenges. However, despite these global efforts and consensus, evidence suggests that many developing countries, especially in Sub-Saharan Africa, are lagging in their pursuit of SDG 4 which focuses on gender inclusivity. A comprehensive assessment of the barriers hindering the achievement of SDG 4 and the interplay of these challenges could provide the groundwork for informed interventions capable of propelling a nation towards sustainable development (Lawrence et al., 2020).

In alignment with SDG 4 and the endeavor to bolster females' active participation in STEM, UNESCO's Medium-Term Strategy for 2014-2021 underscores the importance of gender equality across all its areas of expertise. UNESCO is committed to realizing this mandate through tangible programs and initiatives spanning its diverse competencies. This commitment is echoed in its 1996 Medium-Term Plan, which launched a six-year Special Project on Scientific, Technical, and Vocational Education of Girls in Africa, aimed at fostering girls' education and equipping them with competencies for self-reliance (UNESCO, 2006 as cited in Akinsowon and

Osisanwo, 2014). Despite the commendable nature of these strategies, their objectives have not been fully realized in developing countries such as Nigeria.

Studies indicate that women often face discouragement or lose interest in pursuing careers in STEM fields from a young age. Many girls in Nigeria, for instance, appear to lose interest in STEM subjects during adolescence (The Guardian Nigeria News, 2021). What factors contribute to this phenomenon? Data from the United Nations reveals that less than 30% of STEM professionals worldwide are women (Kent, 2021). Various explanations have been posited for women's apparent disinterest in STEM, including environmental and social barriers such as gender bias, stereotypes, and the perceived challenging nature of STEM disciplines. Despite the obstacles of gender discrimination and limited recognition within the scientific community, numerous women have made historic contributions to STEM, advancing our understanding of the world (Kent, 2021).

This chapter aims to assess the challenges and opportunities surrounding women's active participation in STEM in Nigeria, with a focus on female students' perceptions of STEM and the success stories of women professionals in STEM fields. Nigeria, being the most populous nation in Africa and the seventh most populous globally, accounting for 2.64% of the world's population, with a median age of 18.1 years, serves as an ideal case study (World Population Review, 2021). The study seeks to comprehend the factors that render STEM unappealing to female students through structured interviews. Additionally, it will analyze the challenges encountered by women professionals in STEM and how they surmounted these obstacles. Insights gleaned from the experiences of women professionals in STEM will offer potential solutions to address female students' lack of interest and provide them with role models to emulate on their journey toward successful STEM careers.

Chapter Objectives

The chapter endeavors to accomplish the following goals:

- Investigate the organizational frameworks that impede female involvement in STEM, encompassing gender stereotypes, wage disparities and opportunities, workplace harassment, and socio-cultural influences.
- Examine the factors that contribute to the lack of interest among female students in STEM.
- Propose models and instructional strategies to promote increased female engagement in STEM.

Background

The Global Transformative Agenda 2030, which includes 17 Sustainable Development Goals (SDGs), was embraced by Heads of State and Government at a dedicated UN summit held in Incheon, Republic of Korea in 2015. These SDGs are designed to extend and complete the work outlined in the Millennium Development Goals (MDGs), with the aim of guaranteeing human rights for all, fostering gender equality in every sphere, and harmonizing economic, social, and environmental aspects of development (United Nations International Children's Emergency Fund, UNICEF, 2020).

Education stands as the cornerstone of sustainable development and a critical catalyst for fostering future generations committed to sustainability (Zenelaj, 2013). The United Nations emphasized in 2012 that ensuring complete access to quality education is indispensable for sustainable development, poverty alleviation, gender equality, empowerment of women, and the active participation of both women and men, particularly the youth (Hanachor and Wordu, 2021). Okebukola (2013), referenced in Hanachor and Wordu (2021), highlights the importance of sustainable education in enhancing a nation's economy by cultivating skills and knowledge essential for fostering industrial growth, nurturing creativity, and fostering innovation.

SDG 4 of the 2030 Agenda, known as SDG 4, places significant emphasis on fostering inclusive and equitable quality education, alongside advocating for lifelong learning opportunities for all individuals. Sachs (2015) emphasizes the goal's commitment to ensuring global access to high-quality education, spanning from early childhood education to secondary education, and extending to advanced educational and training programs. This vision of inclusive quality education, as outlined by Hanachor and Wordu (2021), underscores the principle of education for all, with a particular focus on reaching vulnerable populations and promoting equal access to lifelong learning opportunities, encompassing both formal and informal educational pathways.

Preceding the adoption of the SDGs, Nigeria had established national goals as a participant in the Education for All (EFA) Goals. However, these goals remained unfulfilled, prompting the development of new objectives through the Education Sector Strategic Plan, which incorporates the objectives of SDG 4. Challenges such as the significant number of out-of-school children, estimated to be the highest globally at 12.7 million, and persistent gender disparities in basic education persist as pressing issues. The Education Sector Strategic Plan, organized around ten pillars, prioritizes STEM, which is particularly relevant to this discussion. The STEM objectives encompass a range of initiatives, including aligning curricula with global market demands, investing in STEM education, enhancing teaching, and learning environments, fostering innovation, promoting entrepreneurship and skill development, and improving female participation and quality in STEM fields, among other objectives (UNICEF, 2020).

STEM plays a crucial role in fostering national development by propelling economic, social, and environmental advancement and contributing to sustainable development. Peri et al. (2015) highlight the importance of this field in boosting national productivity and fostering economic growth. Both developed and developing countries increasingly prioritize STEM for human capital development to ensure long-term prosperity, recognizing its importance. Contemporary policymakers consider extensive STEM knowledge, especially specialized expertise in STEM fields, as essential aptitudes for a 21st-century economy. This recognition is evident in the substantial investments made by countries, particularly developed ones, to cultivate a skilled STEM workforce (Gonzalez and Kuenzi, 2012; Indiana Department of Education, IDOE, 2012).

Amidst global endeavors to promote inclusive and equitable quality education, concerns persist regarding the underrepresentation of females in STEM fields. The UNESCO Science Report 2021 highlights ongoing disparities, with only 22% of professionals in Artificial Intelligence (AI) worldwide being female. Marchant (2021) observes that although women represent one-third of researchers globally, achieving gender parity in life sciences in many countries, the projected period to bridge the global gender gap in STEM has significantly increased to 135.6 years. The low enrollment of females in STEM fields is viewed as a hindrance to the economic growth of European Union countries (Deming and Noray, 2019). The report emphasizes substantial gender disparities in Sub-Saharan Africa.

Gilbreath (2015) examines the impact of media, education, stereotypes, and work environments on women's diminished interest in STEM, highlighting how portrayals of women in the media as fragile and too aesthetically focused for challenging work negatively affect female perceptions of STEM professions. Stereotypes, such as the notion that women are not proficient in mathematics and that STEM fields belong to men, further deter female engagement in STEM. Onyekwelu (2019) observes a downward trend in female enrollment in STEM courses in Nigeria, particularly notable in Sub-Saharan Africa. Despite advancements in female enrollment in education overall, the gender disparity in STEM persists (Udeani and Ejikeme, 2011; Aderemi et al., 2013).

Recognizing the gender gap in STEM, the African Academy of Sciences (AAS) conducted a study to pinpoint factors hindering or facilitating women's careers in STEM in Africa (Mukhwana et al., 2020). This chapter identifies negative stereotyping as the primary obstacle to women's involvement in STEM. Sociocultural beliefs, gender stereotypes, and the absence of female role models all have an influence on the underrepresentation of females in STEM disciplines. This highlights the significance of addressing societal perceptions and providing role models to motivate and empower women to pursue STEM professions.

As a result, this chapter adopts a qualitative review of previous studies, extensively examining relevant literature on the participation of female professionals in STEM, with a specific emphasis on the Engineering sub-sector of STEM, particularly within the construction industry. Literature serves as a crucial source of evidence, integrating insights from published articles to guide the study.

Overview of Gender Imbalance in STEM

Global Perspective

Data on female employment and educational achievement have surged in the 21st century, with a growing number of women earning college and advanced degrees (Mandel and Semyonov, 2014). Fletcher's (2015) study revealed that women make up to 50 percent of the workforce in the United States of America (USA) and represent 57% of the country's college graduates, as supported by existing literature. Moreover, research suggests that, on average, women exhibit greater dedication and focus on their studies compared to men (DiPrete and Buchmann, 2013; Fletcher, 2015). However, according to United Nations data, less than 30% of STEM professionals worldwide are female (Kent, 2021). This raises the question: if these statistics hold true, why do women continue to be underrepresented in STEM careers?

There are indications that factors such as differences in the work patterns between males and females continue to influence the active participation of females in certain professions, such as STEM. STEM is recognized as a sector decisive to both national and global development in today's technologically propelled economy. There is a growing demand for STEM professionals propelled by economic and societal needs (Connors-Kellgren et al., 2016) and its strategic importance (Connors-Kellgren, et al., 2016). Professional endeavors within STEM have significantly fostered innovation and contributed to global competitiveness, economic advancement, and general quality of life (U.S. Economics and Statistics Administration, 2017).

Literature provides evidence confirming the perception of the engineering sub-sector of STEM as a field entrenched in male social constructs, emphasizing technical skills and physical abilities rather than the sociological attributes that females bring to the profession (Akinlolu and Haupt, 2019). Further studies suggest that females are excluded from this field because it is viewed as a male-dominated profession, and men fear diluting the traditional masculine image associated with it (Norberg and Johansson, 2021). Despite these challenges, some progress has been made globally towards gender inclusivity, educational advancement, and career opportunities for females. There has been a notable increase in the educational achievements of females worldwide over recent decades. However, there is a limited translation of these academic accomplishments into professional advancements for females in all areas of the engineering profession, particularly within the construction industry (Skarpenes and Nilsen, 2015; Navarro-Astor et al., 2017). This underscores the significant hurdles females encounter in translating their academic achievements into practical professional experience.

Females' participation in STEM studies, job searches, and professional roles remains notably low, leading to a significant underrepresentation of women in STEM fields. UNESCO (2017) reports that female students comprise only 35% of total enrollment in STEM-related fields in higher education globally. Kirsten (2019) found that women occupy a mere 11% of spots in STEM disciplines in the United Kingdom (UK). In the United States, females with advanced degrees make up 44.2% of the STEM workforce, while those with lower levels of academic certification constitute 25.8% (National Science Board, 2022). Similarly, the 2021 Statistical Yearbook of China Science and Technology indicates that females represent just 26.27% of personnel in research and development and 5.79% of the entire population of academics in the Chinese Academy of Sciences and Engineering (China Bureau of Statistics, 2022).

Numerous previous studies have indicated that females majoring in STEM disciplines are less likely than their male colleagues to secure employment in STEM professions or to continue in them (Sassler et al., 2011; Glass et al., 2013; Mann and DiPrete, 2013; Ma and Savas, 2014). Advocates for gender diversity in STEM have consistently argued that increasing the number of females in STEM-related courses and the STEM workforce could enhance female retention (Hill et al., 2010), consequently helping to reduce the overall gender wage gap in the labor force. Despite the extensive literature on the gender wage gap and its evolution over time (Mandel and Semyonov, 2014), these studies typically focus on the labor market as a whole or broad sectors thereof.

The Nigerian Context

Despite the global concerns of science educators regarding the need for greater female participation in STEM, the perception that STEM, particularly the physical sciences, is a male-dominated domain persists. Low female involvement in STEM is prevalent across all levels of education and professional ranks. STEM is crucial for societal development and should be inclusive of all individuals who desire to participate, regardless of their gender. Consequently, there is a need for Nigeria, along with other African nations, to address the challenge of gender equality in STEM professional practices (Ndirika and Agommuoh, 2017). Nigeria has made significant efforts to improve the quality of STEM education. According to Ndirika and Agommuoh (2017), the Nigerian government has recently focused on enhancing national capacity in STEM, aligning with the essential recommendation and objective of the government's Vision 20:2020 agenda for economic transformation. However, these efforts have not fully incorporated the importance of gender equity in STEM, and no national policies toward gender equality have been initiated. Despite the country's endeavors to enhance STEM education, there have been limited efforts to improve female participation in STEM (Ajani and Ojetunde, 2021). The gender gap in the enrollment of students in STEM courses is particularly pronounced in Nigeria, where traditional and societal standards places more emphasise male education and careers, discouraging female students from an early stage (Abdullahi et al., 2019; Jacob et al., 2021). This highlights the significant challenges faced by females in pursuing careers in STEM.

Factors Affecting Women's Active Participation in STEM in Nigeria

Despite increased efforts by government and stakeholders to promote STEM education among females, research indicates that significant barriers persist, discouraging women from pursuing careers in STEM (Akilu et al., 2023). Foley (2020) observed that although the challenges faced by females in STEM are less overt compared to 30 years ago, they still exist. Studies have identified various factors influencing women's active participation in the profession, including industry perception, gender stereotypes, cultural norms within the industry, gender hierarchy, restricted access to capitals and opportunities (Ajani and Ojetunde, 2021; Omenihu, 2021), societal expectations (Okorafor et al., 2015), and gender prejudice towards females in STEM (Fisher et al., 2021; Ndakogi, 2019; Ogundare and Abdullahi, 2021). Furthermore, female students encounter numerous societal and cultural challenges which could deter them from pursuing STEM careers, such as customary gender functions and expectations, lack of family backing, and social pressure to place emphasis on marriage and motherhood above educational and career aspirations. These challenges are elaborated upon below.

- ### *Masculine Perception of STEM*

Research by Cvencek et al. (2011) and Olmedo-Torre et al. (2018) has emphasized that the masculine narrative and perception surrounding STEM contribute significantly to the gender roles and stereotypes associated with STEM studies. Kirkland (2023) observed that individuals in STEM education and careers are commonly perceived by society as nerdy and masculine. There is a prevailing perception that certain STEM disciplines are predominantly male dominated, while fields such as social and health sciences are viewed as exclusively female domains. To explore public perceptions of STEM, Pantic et al. (2018) carried out two case studies involving the collection of drawings depicting a scientist as a means of assessing youths' perceptions of stereotypical characterizations of STEM. Participants were asked to draw their depiction of a scientist and to provide their opinions on questions such as "how would you describe a scientist?" and "what kind of work do scientists do?" The findings revealed that only 11.5% of participants depicted female scientists in their drawings. The study concluded that stereotypes persist, with the stereotypical image of a scientist being male, wearing glasses, and clad in a white lab coat.

In a similar vein, research conducted by Hand et al. (2017) indicated that teachers tend to link STEM professionals more strongly with masculine traits. The study further revealed that females were more closely associated with humanities disciplines. Both teachers and students involved in the study expressed the perception that boys excel more in STEM fields, whereas girls excel more in humanities disciplines (Hand et al., 2017). The stereotype of associating STEM professionals with masculine traits is a factor that discourages females from pursuing careers in STEM (Moss-Racusin et al., 2015; Wang and Degol, 2017).

• *Issues of Gender Stereotype, Wage Discrepancy and Advancement Opportunities*

In the construction industry in Nigeria, gender stereotypes pose another sociocultural challenge for females. Abdullahi et al. (2019) contend that there is a significant gender disparity in STEM disciplines in Nigeria, with women being severely underrepresented. According to Shapiro et al. (2017), females in STEM encounter numerous obstacles, including prejudice and a inadequacy of supportive work settings, which can hinder their professional advancement. Research by Sadler et al. (2012), Bian et al. (2017), and Luo et al. (2021) suggests that gender stereotypes regarding STEM are dominant in the social introduction of children into gender roles, and these prejudices have negative impact females' interest in STEM both academically and professionally. Studies conducted by Smith et al. (2013) and Dasgupta and Stout (2014) indicate that females have least likelihood than males to feel a sense of belonging and identity in STEM disciplines.

Gilbreath's (2015) study underscored the media's influential role in perpetuating gender stereotypes that affect female participation in STEM. It highlighted that numerous media portrayals convey the notion that females are not expected to excel in mathematics and science. These messages are pervasive, ranging from comic strips and news coverage to slogans on clothing and toy designs, all reinforcing the same narrative. Such narratives have detrimental effects on females' academic achievements and success in STEM-related fields, potentially hindering their participation. Many of these stereotypes may be inadvertent; for example, toys targeted at boys often emphasize vehicles and sports equipment, while those aimed at girls tend to feature dollhouses, dolls, and domestic items, thus subtly socializing them into traditional gender roles even at a young age.

Studies such as those by Sax et al. (2017) and Kong et al. (2020) underscore that gender bias is deeply ingrained in societal norms and discriminatory practices, contributing significantly to the low involvement of females in STEM. This bias dissuades female students from pursuing STEM fields due to their reluctance to align with the stereotypical masculine perceptions and social status associated with STEM. Yang and Shen's (2020) study highlighted the consensus among various research findings attributing the low involvement of females in STEM fields to sociocultural factors rather than biological ones. Gender stereotypes depicted in the media are easily assimilated and influence individuals' perception of reality. The media plays a crucial role in shaping adolescents' perceptions of scientists, thereby molding their image of scientists (Wang et al., 2023).

Nature of the Profession

This chapter does not aim to comprehensively investigate the reasons for female preferences in specific STEM disciplines. However, it draws on Cheryan et al.'s (2017) research into the philosophies of various STEM disciplines and why certain fields exhibit greater gender equality while others maintain significant gender differences. While STEM is often associated with a masculine culture perceived as unwelcoming to females, it's important to recognize that STEM disciplines vary in their cultures, which could significantly influence female preferences in certain fields. Cheryan et al. (2017) examined the six largest natural sciences and engineering fields at the college level, as provided by the National Science Foundation (2014). They found that the biological sciences, chemistry, mathematics, and statistics exhibit moderately balanced gender representation, whereas computer science, engineering, and physics are heavily dominated by males. This suggests that the nature of the engineering profession, particularly its physical aspects, may serve as a deterrent for female involvement.

The physically demanding nature of certain STEM fields, such as the construction industry, within a cultural context that views females as frail and unsuitable for such work, presents significant socio-cultural obstructions to female involvement in the industry in Nigeria (Adeniji et al., 2022). In addition to the physical challenges of the profession, there are other areas requiring essential skills that females inherently possess. Hence, the foundational principles of STEM fields, which are predominantly male dominated, are upheld and promoted by organizations. In other words, if these organizations implement policies that advocate for female values, it can gradually become the accepted norm over time.

The prevailing work culture in certain STEM fields, such as the construction sector, adheres strictly to rigid professional norms, including extended work hours, strict schedules, and high expectations for punctuality and availability, which are widely accepted as industry standards (Galea et al., 2018). The job demands can be exceedingly challenging, particularly for male workers, especially those engaged in on-site roles. When juxtaposed with the capabilities of the average woman, these demanding conditions serve as a basis for scrutinizing the underlying intentions behind the industry's regulations. Succeeding within such a work environment necessitates that females aspiring to build successful careers in the field adapt to its predominantly masculine nature, which has traditionally been tailored to accommodate men who historically assumed fewer responsibilities within family settings.

Socio-Cultural Impediments

Apart from the prevalence of male dominance, certain cultural presumptions regarding women's biological roles have been proposed as underlying factors contributing to gender inequality and hindering the professional progression of women, particularly within the deeply patriarchal context of Nigeria (Amusan, Saka, and Ahmed, 2017). These assumptions perpetuate the notion that women are primarily objects of beauty, expected to be provided for and maintained, and serve as the primary caregivers within the family structure. Traditionally, societal expectations dictate that women fulfill their roles as wives and mothers, often requiring them to adopt a submissive demeanor and channel their efforts into caring for their husbands and children (Aderemi and Olarinmoye, 2013). Echoing the findings of previous research, Durojaye et al. (2014) asserted that cultural norms in Nigeria have adverse implications for women's rights, resulting in gender discrimination and disparities.

The lives of married Nigerian women are largely centered around responsibilities such as childbearing, childcare, tending to their husbands, and managing household affairs (Bankole and Adeyeri, 2014). These duties often divert their attention from any previous professional aspirations they may have had prior to marriage. However, societal dynamics are evolving, and women are adapting to these changes. Consequently, female involvement in career advancement and business management is reshaping the traditional structure of Nigerian families (Kahkha et al., 2014). Despite various policies and laws implemented by the Nigerian government to address gender inequality issues, women in Nigeria continue to face instances of discrimination and inequity (Durojaye et al., 2014). Consequently, Durojaye et al. (2014) recommended strategies such as educational awareness campaigns, legal reforms, and the implementation of quota systems, among others, to combat discriminatory practices against women in Nigeria. Studies conducted by Ige (2013) and Okoroafor and Iheriohanma (2014) highlight that the socio-cultural reliance on women in many societies is a significant factor impeding their full participation across various sectors of public life.

Females encounter impediments to their complete liberation due to societal biases and regulations. Osimen et al. (2018) underscored the difficulty females face in realizing their full potential because of societal expectations dictating their behavior. Additionally, they are constrained by the dual roles they assume in both the productive and reproductive spheres of society. These roles encompass maternal and marital responsibilities, limiting their time and opportunities to engage in educational, economic, commercial, political, and leadership activities. Moreover, females' limited involvement in the construction industry may be influenced by societal and cultural norms that assign them the primary role of managing household and domestic affairs, often without recognition or reward. This poses a significant challenge to achieving a balance between work and family life. The challenge is exacerbated by the demanding nature of the construction industry's long working hours. Ahmed and Agboola (2020) observed that many construction professionals struggle with balancing work and family responsibilities, with females facing greater intensity of this conflict compared to males.

The Nigerian society exhibits strong patriarchal tendencies, which are widely recognized as a significant factor contributing to females' limited involvement in STEM fields, as documented in the literature. Patriarchal constraints are evident in various aspects, including the expectation for women to focus solely on household responsibilities, hindering their pursuit of professional development (Makama, 2013). Additionally, females are often identified and defined by their male relatives, further perpetuating patriarchal norms (Tijani-Adenle, 2016), and their autonomy and independence are restricted, requiring permission from husbands or fathers for certain activities or access to facilities (Adisa, Abdulraheem, and Isiaka, 2019). Anyangwe (2015) observed that the entrenched gender-based cultural practices in Nigerian society marginalize women, both within and beyond their professional pursuits, limiting their ability to make autonomous decisions, nurture ambitions, and pursue careers in male-dominated industries such as the construction sector.

To gain a thorough insight into the socio-cultural barriers hindering female engagement in the construction sector, this research investigated the cultural perceptions of women in Nigeria. This exploration is vital due to indications in existing literature suggesting that cultural values, beliefs, and perceptions exert considerable influence on the limited involvement of women in the construction industry (Jwasshaka and Amin, 2020). To substantiate these claims, particularly within the context of this study's demographics, an assessment of the cultural perspectives regarding women in Nigerian societies was conducted.

Cultural Perception, Status and Treatment of Women in Nigeria

Nigerian culture, like numerous African cultures, exhibits a preference for male offspring (Olarenwaju, Kona, and Dickson, 2015). Adebanjo (2020) elucidated in her research that this male privilege persists within Yoruba society, serving as a potent and defining factor perpetuating inequality across all aspects of society. Thus, patriarchy emerges as a socio-cultural norm within the cultural fabric of Nigeria. Allanana (2013) posits that patriarchy establishes socio-cultural norms that deprive women of equal rights with men, rendering them more susceptible to various forms of abuse—be it mental, emotional, physical, or sexual. Patriarchy further institutionalizes disparities in the access to resources, employment opportunities, societal status, and overall well-being, typically favoring males over females (Aluko, 2015). This standpoint is further supported by Attoh's (2014) study, which underscores that patriarchy engenders male dominance, wherein men predominantly hold positions of power and authority in both society and the family, being perceived as superior. However, contrasting perspectives emerge from various studies asserting that gender distinctions were not prominent in the pre-colonial culture of the Yoruba people. Case (2016) highlights in their study that the differentiation of sexes did not confer any form of hierarchy within pre-colonial Yoruba culture, suggesting that gender was not a defining organizing principle.

In certain Nigerian cultures, male offspring are favored in the inheritance allocation within families due to their perceived role as future heads of the family and clan, as well as the rarity of females assuming such leadership roles (Aluko, 2015). Additionally, studies indicate that females often do not experience better treatment within marriages in the patriarchal Yoruba culture. Kolawole, Abubakar, Owonibi, and Zaggi (2015) highlighted that instances of spousal abuse are often regarded as private matters between the husband and wife. Within the patriarchal traditions of Yoruba culture, wives are viewed as possessions of their husbands, granting the latter moral authority to discipline their wives as they see fit in response to perceived defiance or transgressions. This negative perception of wives within Yoruba culture significantly contributes to the mishandling of domestic violence cases by law enforcement agencies and fosters a culture of silence regarding abusive relationships.

In many Nigerian cultures, females are primarily engaged in agricultural work and food processing activities. However, despite their involvement, they typically do not have direct land ownership rights and are only able to cultivate land belonging to their husbands or families (Kolawole and Adeigbe, 2016). Moreover, females face significant restrictions in accessing farming resources, including land, agricultural tools, and financial support, as cultural norms often deny them the ability to own land. This lack of land ownership limits their access to loans and credit facilities, placing them at a disadvantage compared to males and hindering their active participation in commercial and economic endeavors (Okoroafor and Iheriohanma, 2014). These cultural norms confine female members of Nigerian society to predefined roles, making it challenging for them to pursue economic and professional advancement. However, through initiatives like this study and concerted efforts by government and non-governmental organizations, there is potential to enhance the active involvement of females in professional sectors such as the construction industry.

Despite enduring negative societal and cultural norms that hinder females' progress in fields like STEM, significant strides have been made in enhancing their legal status, particularly through initiatives like the Sustainable Development Goals (SDGs), which advocate for gender inclusivity. Additionally, both governmental and non-governmental organizations have implemented various women empowerment programs. These efforts have led to a notable increase in female enrollment in construction-related degree programs at Nigerian tertiary institutions (Saka, Adegbembo, and Anakor, 2022). This surge in enrollment is also driven by stakeholders' endeavors to attract a more skilled workforce, with a specific focus on encouraging greater female participation in the industry. The aim is to augment the presence of female professionals in construction and inspire young girls to consider careers in this field.

Drivers of Women's Participation in STEM

The critical question emerging from discussions surrounding low female participation in STEM is: "How can we enhance female engagement in the industry?" Addressing this query necessitates a thorough examination of the motivations driving the limited number of females involved in STEM professions. Despite the hurdles, research indicates that females who persevere in STEM disciplines often exhibit high stages of motivation and a robust commitment to making encouraging contributions within their domains (Akilu et al., 2023). For example, studies conducted by Okwelle and Alalibo (2017) and Richard et al. (2018) demonstrated that female students who continued their studies in STEM displayed elevated degrees of self-efficacy, intrinsic motivation, and a keen interest to make meaningful contributions to the society through their profession. Key contributing factors that could stimulate greater female participation in STEM include:

a. ***Role Models***: Cheryan et al. (2017) underscored that the lack of female representation in STEM fields significantly discourages female students aspiring to pursue careers in STEM. The study concludes that the absence of female role models across various STEM disciplines adversely affects female interest in these fields. This aligns with the findings of Weisgram and Bigler (2006), as cited in Cherney (2023), which suggest that interventions involving female role models can positively influence female interest in STEM. Factors such as the quality, quantity, and gender of role models play a significant role in shaping female career aspirations in STEM, with several studies indicating that female role models or mentors can effectively enhance women's interest and engagement in the field (Cheryan et al., 2017).

b. ***Sense of Belonging***: A critical aspect influencing young women's career choices is their sense of belonging, as highlighted by Cheryan et al. (2015). The extent of stereotypes associated with a field significantly affects women's willingness to pursue careers in that field. Fiske (2010), as cited in McNeill and Wei (2023), explains that a prevalent stereotype regarding STEM disciplines is the perception of masculinity associated with these fields, which is widely accepted by society within specific cultural contexts. According to Cheryan et al. (2017), stereotypes related to STEM disciplines encompass various aspects, including perceptions of the STEM workforce, value judgments, beliefs about work-life balance, and perceptions of the nature of work. The more pronounced these gender stereotypes within STEM disciplines, the lower the sense of belonging for women in STEM fields (Makarova et al., 2019), as these stereotypes predominantly emphasize the gender of STEM practitioners (Master et al., 2016; Ceci and Williams, 2015).

c. ***Self-belief in their Ability***: The correlation between self-efficacy and career aspirations is robust, suggesting that self-belief has a significant influence on females' interest in STEM disciplines. Bench et al. (2015) note that women tend to offer more realistic assessments of their abilities, while men may overestimate theirs, especially considering the higher proportion of male professionals in STEM compared to females. Various studies, including those by Domenech-Botoret et al. (2017), Pantic et al. (2018), and Charlesworth and Banaji (2019), identify self-efficacy as a significant factor contributing to the lower participation of female students in STEM disciplines. Smith et al. (2013) and Dasgupta and Stout (2014) argue that females often experience a diminished sense of belonging and identity in STEM disciplines compared to their male counterparts. Moreover, research by Nugent et al. (2015), Mohtar et al. (2019), Wang et al. (2020), and Lv et al. (2022) highlights the substantial impact of self-efficacy on the performance of students in STEM subjects as well as their interest in related professions. According to the PISA 2015 results, males tend to exhibit considerably higher self-efficacy than females in mathematics and science (OECD, 2015), particularly among females with strong gender stereotypes, who demonstrate notably lower levels of self-efficacy compared to males.

d. ***Influence of School Environment***: The role of school-related factors cannot be overstated in influencing female students' interest and academic performance in STEM fields. Within the school environment, teachers, instructional methods, curriculum, and educational materials all play significant roles. Teachers serve as crucial agents of socialization, shaping students' beliefs about STEM subjects. Research by Lee and Lee (2020) and Ekmekci and Serrano (2022) underscores the positive association between teacher quality and students' motivation and performance in STEM subjects. Female teachers serve as both role models and counterpoints to stereotypes suggesting innate male superiority in certain fields. Their presence can foster gender equity in classroom instruction and positively influence girls' engagement in STEM education. Moreover, employing effective instructional approaches in STEM subjects can create supportive learning environments that encourage greater female participation, as highlighted by research conducted by Kang and Keinonen (2017). Lastly, Benavot (2016) points out that the portrayal of gender roles in textbooks can impact students' perceptions of STEM competencies, potentially strengthening gender stereotypes and dissuading female students from pursuing STEM careers.

Models for Accelerating Females' Participation in the Construction Industry

According to Zhang et al. (2021), early career choice theories, influenced by Parson's (1905) tripartite model, view career decisions as logical and unbiased processes. This model posits that individuals' career choices hinge on three main factors: self-awareness, understanding of the occupation, and the relationship between these two factors. This notion of aligning individuals with suitable jobs is central to leading person-environment (P-E) professional development models, also known as trait-and-factor models (Moore, 2006). One such model, as explained by Ericksen and Schultheiss (2009), is Holland's theory of vocational personality and job environment, which suggests that persons prefer work environments that align with their personality types. Ericksen and Schultheiss (2009) also discuss other professional development models that integrate gender, cultural, and social considerations, such as the social cognitive career theory. This theory proposes that career decisions are influenced by cognitive-person variables (like self-efficacy, expected outcomes, and individual goals), personal factors (including gender and ethnicity), environmental influences (such as social, cultural, and economic factors), and learning experiences.

Other studies have proposed various measures to enhance female participation in STEM industries like the construction sector. Haruna et al. (2016) recommended increasing the involvement of female builders in government ministries overseeing the construction industry, supporting female practitioners as contractors or consultants, encouraging female participation as educators and researchers in universities, and offering postgraduate scholarships to female graduates in construction-related fields. Afolabi et al. (2019) suggested initiatives like well-funded mentorship programs for women, strengthened legislation and policies, the prosecution of sexual harassment cases, flexible work arrangements, and support from professional organizations and unions. The UN Women Report (2018) highlighted the importance of establishing high-level leadership for gender equality, ensuring fair treatment at work, prioritizing the health, safety, and well-being of female workers, and promoting education, training, and professional development opportunities for women. Holdsworth et al. (2020) emphasized the significance of psychological coping mechanisms, such as support from trusted networks of peers and family, alongside other resilience strategies outlined in existing literature.

The media holds significant potential for fostering greater female participation in STEM fields. By shaping students' perceptions of STEM careers, the media influences their expectations and interests in these fields (Tan et al., 2015). Gender stereotypes perpetuated in the media strongly impact girls' beliefs about their competence and interest in STEM careers, particularly during adolescence when they are forming their career identities (Steinke, 2017). Thus, rather than portraying females solely as objects of beauty suited only for humanities, the media can highlight their inherent strengths, as well as the valuable contributions and soft skills they bring to male-dominated STEM professions.

Carnemolla (2019) suggests that strategies aimed at enhancing female interest in STEM careers should focus on addressing the negative gender-influenced perceptions of the industry, its prevalent male-dominated culture, rigid work practices, and the lack of encouragement from educational institutions. Additionally, efforts to promote female participation in the profession should address employers' biased practices and choices, while ensuring the retention of female workers. This can be achieved through measures to report and penalize harassment of female employees, as well as enhancements in occupational health and safety standards (Francis, 2017; Work Place Gender Equality Agency, 2019; Galea, Powell, Loosemore, and Chappell, 2020).

Both educators and parents should carefully consider the language used in instruction. A recent study by Rhodes et al. (2019) demonstrated that employing action-oriented terms like "Let's do science" instead of identity-focused terms like "Let's be scientists" during science classes increased the persistence of female students. This change in linguistic cues was observed to be particularly effective in engaging more females in STEM, especially during their formative years, as evidenced by new science games that incorporated the scientific method. It is crucial to recognize that verbal cues play a significant role in shaping stereotypes, which can be internalized and negatively impact students' interest, motivation, and academic achievement. Cherney (2023) suggests that better utilization of positive linguistic cues may enhance the interest of females with higher self-efficacy in STEM fields, making STEM a more viable career option for them.

Strategies aimed at increasing female population in physics should prioritize generating interest in physics instead of focusing solely on academic accomplishment or competence. As noted earlier, adolescent females often lean towards careers in the humanities. Introducing females to the idea that careers in computer science, engineering, and physics can have significant societal impacts may inspire them to pursue these fields. Coding presents a promising avenue for encouraging females to explore STEM careers. Many companies are now developing robots and computer applications designed to teach coding skills to children from a young age. Additionally, more schools are integrating digital literacy and computer science into their curricula. These early interventions have the potential to yield positive outcomes in the future, potentially positioning coding as a subject as fundamental as reading, writing, and mathematics.

CONCLUSION

The challenge of low female participation in Science, Technology, Engineering, and Mathematics (STEM) education has been a persistent issue addressed, among other agendas, by the Sustainable Development Goals (SDGs) outlined by the United Nations. This study, in alignment with the SDGs' goal of gender inclusivity, delves into literature examining the factors hindering females' professional engagement in STEM. The review scrutinizes the status and impact of STEM on societal development, including an analysis of gender distribution in STEM professions globally and within Nigeria. A prevailing theme in the literature is the perception of STEM as a masculine domain, which contributes to the underrepresentation of females in the field.

Various perspectives on females' limited involvement in STEM, particularly in construction, were explored, shedding light on issues such as male dominance, female exclusion, and socio-cultural barriers. The literature identifies several key factors impeding females' active participation in the profession, including the masculine narrative surrounding the industry, gender stereotypes, wage disparities, advancement opportunities, and socio-cultural impediments. Within the socio-cultural context, patriarchal norms in Nigeria significantly restrict females, affecting their career aspirations and progress.

While acknowledging improvements in Nigeria's socio-economic and socio-political landscapes, this study underscores the persistence of certain cultural elements that continue to hinder females' professional growth, particularly in STEM industries. Gender equality is not only integral to the UN's 2030 Agenda for Sustainable Development but also crucial for accomplishing other sustainable development goals. Guaranteeing parallel opportunities for females in STEM education and expanding their participation in STEM disciplines are essential steps towards gender equality and sustainable development.

Drawing from previous research findings, this study highlights drivers of female participation in the construction industry, including opportunities for career advancement, job security, and equitable compensation. Strategies to enhance female participation in the industry, such as mentorship programs, changing the industry's masculine perception, and utilizing gender-appropriate linguistic cues, are proposed as potential avenues for promoting gender inclusivity and fostering a more diverse and equitable workforce.

REFERENCES

https://www.worldometers.info/world-population/Nigeria. (2021).

Abdullahi, N., Abubakar, A., Abubakar, M. J., & Aliyu, A. C. (2019). Gender Gap in Science and Technology Education in Nigeria. *International Journal of Education and Evaluation*, 5(3), 6–13. www.iiardpub.org

Aderemi, H. O., Hassan, O. M., Siyanbola, W. O., & Taiwo, K. (2013). Trends in Enrollment, Graduation and Staffing of Science and Technology Education in Nigeria Tertiary Institutions: A Gender Participation Perspective. *Educational Research Review*, 8(21), 2011–2020. http://www.academicjournals.org/ERR. DOI: 10.5897/ERR08.084

Ajani, M. O., & Ojetunde, S. M. (2021). Effects of Education Budget and Enrolment on Science, Technology, Engineering and Mathematics (STEM) Education in Nigeria. *International Journal of Educational Management*, 19(2), 30–41.

Akilu, I., Murtala, A., & Aminu, I. (2023). Enrollment Trends, Motivations, and Future Aspirations of Female Undergraduate Students in STEM Courses at Federal University Gusau – Nigeria. *Global Academic Journal of Humanities and Social Sciences*, 5(3), 142–150. DOI: 10.36348/gajhss.2023.v05i03.001

Akinsowon, O. A., & Osisanwo, F. Y. (2014). Enhancing Interest in Sciences, Technology and Mathematics (STEM) for the Nigerian Female Folk. *International Journal of Information Science*, 4(1), 8–12.

Benavot, A. (2016). Gender Bias is Rife in Textbooks. World Education Blog. https://world-education-blog.org/2016/03/08/gender-bias-is-rife-in-textbooks

Bench, S.W., Lench, H.C., Liew, J., Miner, K., & Flores, S.A. (2015). Gender Gaps in Overestimation of Mathematics Performance. *Sex Roles*, 72, 11, 11, 536-546

Ceci, S. J., & Williams, W. M. (2015). Women have Substantial Advantage in STEM Faculty Hiring, Except When Competing against More-Accomplished Men. *Frontiers in Psychology*, 6, 1532. DOI: 10.3389/fpsyg.2015.01532 PMID: 26539132

Charlesworth, T. E. S., & Banaji, M. R. (2019). Gender in Science, Technology, Engineering, and Mathematics: Issues, Causes, Solutions. *The Journal of Neuroscience : The Official Journal of the Society for Neuroscience*, 39(37), 7228–7243. DOI: 10.1523/JNEUROSCI.0475-18.2019 PMID: 31371423

Cherney, I. D. (2023). The STEM Paradox: Factors Affecting Diversity in STEM Fields. *Journal of Physics: Conference Series*, 2438(1), 012005. DOI: 10.1088/1742-6596/2438/1/012005

Cheryan, S., Master, A., & Meltzoff, A. N. (2015). Cultural Stereotypes as Gate-Keepers: Increasing Girls' Interest in Computer Science and Engineering by Diversifying Stereotypes. *Frontiers in Psychology*, 6, 49. DOI: 10.3389/fpsyg.2015.00049 PMID: 25717308

Cheryan, S., Ziegler, S. A., Montoya, A. K., & Jiang, L. (2017). Why are Some STEM Fields More Gender Balanced than Others? *Psychological Bulletin*, 143(1), 1–35. DOI: 10.1037/bul0000052 PMID: 27732018

Cheryan, S., Ziegler, S. A., Montoya, A. K., & Jiang, L. (2017). Why are Some STEM Fields More Gender Balanced than Others? *Psychological Bulletin*, 143(1), 1–35. DOI: 10.1037/bul0000052 PMID: 27732018

China Bureau of Statistics. (2022). China Statistical Yearbook on Science and Technology 2021. *China Statistics Press*. http://cnki.nbsti.net/CSYDMirror/Trade/yearbook/single/N2022010277?z=Z018

Connors-Kellgren, A., Parker, C. E., Blustein, D. L., & Barnett, M. (2016). Innovations and Challenges in Project-Based STEM Education: Lessons from ITEST. *Journal of Science Education and Technology*, 25(6), 825–832. DOI: 10.1007/s10956-016-9658-9

Cvencek, D., Meltzoff, A. N., & Greenwald, A. G. (2011). Math-gender Stereotypes in Elementary School Children. *Child Development*, 82(3), 766–779. DOI: 10.1111/j.1467-8624.2010.01529.x PMID: 21410915

Dasgupta, N., & Stout, J. G. (2014). Girls and Women in Science, Technology, Engineering, and Mathematics: Stemming the Tide and Broadening Participation in STEM Careers. *Policy Insights from the Behavioral and Brain Sciences*, 1(1), 21–29. DOI: 10.1177/2372732214549471

Deming, D. J., & Noray, K. L. (2019). STEM Careers and the Changing Skill Requirements of Work. *NBER Working Paper No.* 25065

Doménech-Betoret, F., Abellán-Roselló, L., & Gómez-Artiga, A. (2017). Self-efficacy, satisfaction, and academic achievement: The mediator role of students' Expectancy Value beliefs. *Frontiers in Psychology*, 8, 1–11. DOI: 10.3389/fpsyg.2017.01193 PMID: 28769839

Ekmekci, A., & Serrano, D. M. (2022). The Impact of Teacher Quality on Student Motivation, Achievement, and Persistence in Science and Mathematics. *Education Sciences*, 12(10), 649. DOI: 10.3390/educsci12100649

Ferriman, K., Lubinski, D., & Benbow, C. P. (2009). Work Preferences, Life Values, and Personal Views of Top Math/Science Graduate Students and the Profoundly Gifted: Developmental Changes and Gender Differences During Emerging Adulthood and Parenthood. *Journal of Personality and Social Psychology*, 97(3), 517–532. DOI: 10.1037/a0016030 PMID: 19686005

Fisher, C. R., Brookes, R. H., & Thompson, C. D. (2021). 'I don't Study Physics Anymore: A Cross-Institutional Australian Study on Factors Impacting the Persistence of Undergraduate Science Students. *Research in Science Education*. Advance online publication. DOI: 10.1007/s11165-021-09995-5

Fletcher, M. A. (2015). Women Continue to be underrepresented in STEM Industries. *Women of Color Magazine*, 14, 1, 22 – 24. https://www.jstor.org/stable/43769519

Gender Stereotype. (n.d.). Retrieved from https://guardian.ng/opinion/gender-stereotype-girls-and-science-education/

Gilbreath, L. C. (2015). Factors Impacting Women's Participation in STEM Fields. UVM Honors College Senior Theses. 65. https://scholarworks.uvm.edu/hcoltheses/65

Gilbreath, L. C. (2015). Factors Impacting Women's Participation in STEM Fields. UVM Honors College Senior Theses, 65. https://scholarworks.uvm.edu/hcoltheses/65

Glass, J. L., Sharon, S., Yael, L., & Katherine, M. M. (2013). What's So Special about STEM? A Comparison of Women's Retention in STEM and Professional Occupations. *Social Forces*, 92(2), 723–756. DOI: 10.1093/sf/sot092 PMID: 25554713

Gonzalez, H. B., & Kuenzi, J. J. (2012). *Science, Technology, Engineering and Mathematics (STEM) education: A Primer*. Congressional Research Service.

Hanachor, M. E., & Wordu, E. N. (2021). Achieving Sustainable Development Goal 4 in Nigeria: Problems and Prospects. *International Journal of Education, Learning and Development*, 9(2), 10–25.

Hand, S., Rice, L., & Greenlee, E. (2017). Exploring Teachers' and Students' Gender Role Bias and Students' Confidence in STEM Fields. *Social Psychology of Education*, 20(4), 929–945. DOI: 10.1007/s11218-017-9408-8

Hill, C., Corbett, C., & St. Rose, A. (2010). Why So Few? Women in Science, Technology, Engineering, and Mathematics. American Association of University Women. Retrieved from https://eric.ed.gov/?id=ED509653

Indiana Department of Education. (2012). Indiana's Science, Technology, Engineering and Mathematics (STEM) initiative plan. Available at www.doe.in.gov. Retrieved on 04/11/2021

Jacob, O. N., Lawan, A., & Yusuf, M. (2021).Perception of Female Students on the Challenges Facing the Woman Education at the University Level. *Electronic Research Journal of Behavioural Sciences*, 4, 24–36. https://doi.org/http://erjbehaviouralsciences.com/

Kang, J., & Keinonen, T. (2017). The Effect of Inquiry-Based Learning Experiences on Adolescents' Science Related Career Aspiration in the Finnish Context. *International Journal of Science Education*, 39(12), 1669–1689. DOI: 10.1080/09500693.2017.1350790

Kent, L. (2021). The Heroines STEM: Ten Women in Science You Should Know. Space+Science: A CNN Report. Available on https://edition.cnn.com/2020/01/27/world/women-in-science-you-should-know-scn/index.html

Kirkland, H. N. (2023). STEM Educators' Perceptions of Gender Bias and the Contributing Factors that Persist for Women in STEM Education. (Doctoral dissertation). Retrieved from https://scholarcommons.sc.edu/etd/7494

Kirsten, B. (2019) How Far have Women in STEM Come in the Last 100 Years. https://www.womeninstem.co.uk/engineering-maths/women-stem-come-last-years

Lawrence, A. W., Ihebuzor, N., & Lawrence, D. O. (2020). *Some Challenges Militating against Developing Countries Achieving SDG 4 on Targets: Nigeria as Case Study. Modern Economy, 11, 1307-1328.* Available on., DOI: 10.4236/me.2020.117093

Lee, S. W., & Lee, E. A. (2020). Teacher qualifcation matters: The Association between Cumulative Teacher Qualification and Students' Educational Attainment. *International Journal of Educational Development*, 77, 102218. DOI: 10.1016/j.ijedudev.2020.102218

Lv, B., Wang, J., Zheng, Y., Peng, X., & Ping, X. (2022). Gender Differences in High School Students' STEM Career Expectations: An Analysis Based on Multi-Group Structural Equation Model. *Journal of Research in Science Teaching*, 59(10), 1739–1764. Advance online publication. DOI: 10.1002/tea.21772

Ma, Y., & Savas, G. (2014). Which is more Consequential: Field of Study or Institutional Selectivity? *Review of Higher Education*, 37(2), 221–247. DOI: 10.1353/rhe.2014.0001

Makarova, E., Aeschlimann, B., & Herzog, W. (2019). The Gender Gap in STEM Fields: The Impact of the Gender Stereotype of Mathematics and Science on Secondary Students' Career Aspirations. *Frontiers in Education*, 4, 60. DOI: 10.3389/feduc.2019.00060

Mandel, H., & Semyonov, M. (2014). Gender Pay Gap and Employment Sector: Sources of Earnings Disparities in the United States, 1970 – 2010. *Demography*, 51(5), 1597–1618. DOI: 10.1007/s13524-014-0320-y PMID: 25149647

Mann, A., & DiPrete, T. A. (2013). Trends in Gender Segregation in the Choice of Science and Engineering Majors. *Social Science Research*, 42(6), 1519–1541. DOI: 10.1016/j.ssresearch.2013.07.002 PMID: 24090849

Marchant, N. (2021). The Gender Gap in Science and Technology, in Numbers. New Policies Needed to End Gender Disparity in STEM Sector/World Economic Forum.

Master, A., Cheryan, S., & Meltzoff, A. N. (2016). Computing Whether she Belongs: Stereotypes Undermine Girls' Interest and Sense of Belonging in Computer Science. *Journal of Educational Psychology*, 108(3), 424–437. DOI: 10.1037/edu0000061

McNeill, F., & Wei, L. (2023). Encouraging Young Women into STEM Careers: A Study Comparing Career Intention of Female STEM Students in China and Scotland. *Journal for STEM Education Research*. Advance online publication. DOI: 10.1007/s41979-023-00114-9

Mohtar, L. E., Halim, L., Rahman, N. A., Maat, S. M., & Osman, K. (2019). A Model of Interest in STEM Careers among Secondary School Students. *Journal of Baltic Science Education*, 18(3), 404–416. DOI: 10.33225/jbse/19.18.404

Moss-Racusin, C. A., Molenda, A. K., & Cramer, C. R. (2015). Can Evidence Impact Attitudes? Public Reactions to Evidence of Gender Bias in STEM Fields. *Psychology of Women Quarterly*, 39(2), 194–209. DOI: 10.1177/0361684314565777

Mukhwana, A. M., Abuya, T., Matanda, D., Omumbo, J., & Mabuka, J. (2020). Factors which Contribute to or Inhibit Women in Science, Technology, Engineering, and Mathematics in Africa. The African Academy of Science (AAS, Report). Nairobi. Available on https://uis.unesco.org/en/topic/women-science

National Science Board. (2022). Science and engineering indicators 2022. *National Science Foundation (NSB 2022-01)*. https://www.nsf.gov/nsb/sei/

National Science Foundation (2014). Table 2-17 Earned bachelor's degrees, by sex and field: 2000-2011

Ndirika, M. C., & Agommuoh, P. C. (2017). Investigating Factors Influencing Girls Participation in Science and Technology Education in Nigeria. *IOSR Journal of Research & Method in Education (IOSR-JRME)*, 7, 3, I, 50-54. www.iosrjournals.org

Nugent, G., Barker, B., Welch, G., Grandgenett, N., Wu, C., & Nelson, C. (2015). A Model of Factors Contributing to STEM Learning and Career Orientation. *International Journal of Science Education*, 37(7), 1067–1088. DOI: 10.1080/09500693.2015.1017863

Ogundare, S. A., & Abdullahi, A. Z. (2021). Assessment of Female Students' Enrollment in Sciences and Mathematics in Federal University Kashere, Gombe State. Zamfara. *International Journal of Education*, 1(1), 217–225. www.zijedufugusau.com

Okorafor, A. O., Woyengidubamo, K., & Okorafor, E. C. (2015). Women Participation in Science, Technology, Engineering and Mathematics in Nigeria: Challenges and Way Forward. *NAM Institute of the Empowerment of Women (NIEW). Journal*, 7, 99–112.

Okwelle, C. P., & Alalibo, J. T. (2017). Motivational Factors and Future Expectations that Influence the Choice of Engineering Programmes by Female Undergraduate Students in Nigeria. *Journal of Scientific and Engineering Research*, 4(11), 164–172. www.jsaer.com

Olmedo-Torre, N., Sanchez Carracedo, F., Salan Ballesteros, M. N., Lopez, D., Perez-Poch, A., & Lopez-Beltran, M. (2018). Do Female Motives for Enrolling Vary according to STEM Profile? *IEEE Transactions on Education*, 61(4), 289–297. DOI: 10.1109/TE.2018.2820643

Omenihu, I. (2021). Influence of Students' Factors on the Enrollment of Female Students in Science Oriented Courses in Nigeria Higher Institutions. *International Journal of Innovative Social & Science Education Research*, 9(2), 80–87.

Onyekwelu, B. A. (2019). Comparative Empirical Analysis of Female University Enrolment in STEM Courses in the Geopolitical Zones in Nigeria. *Modern Education and Computer Science*, 1, 24–32. DOI: 10.5815/ijmecs.2019.01.03

Organization for Economic Co-operation and Development. (OECD, 2015). The ABC of Gender Equality in Education: Aptitude, Behaviour, Confidence. *Paris, Organization for Economic Co-operation and Development.* https://www.oecd-ilibrary.org/education/the-abc-of-gender-equality-in-education_9789264229945-e

Pantic, K., Clarke-Midura, J., Poole, F., Roller, J., & Allan, V. (2018). Drawing a Computer Scientist: Stereotypical Representations or Lack of Awareness? *Computer Science Education*, 28(3), 232–254. DOI: 10.1080/08993408.2018.1533780

Pantic, K., Clarke-Midura, J., Poole, F., Roller, J., & Allan, V. (2018). Drawing a computer scientist: Stereotypical representations or lack of awareness? *Computer Science Education*, 28(3), 232–254. DOI: 10.1080/08993408.2018.1533780

Rhodes, M., Leslie, S. J., Yee, K. M., & Saunders, K. (2019). Subtle Linguistic Cues Increase Girls' Engagement in Science. *Psychological Science*, 30(3), 455–466. DOI: 10.1177/0956797618823670 PMID: 30721119

Richard, J., Luqman, O., & Amina, A. (2018). Overcoming the Barriers of Female Students Choice of Built Environment Courses. *Covenant Journal of Research in the Built Environment*, 6(2), 33–48.

Sassler, S., Glass, J. L., Levitte, Y., & Michelmore, K. M. (2011). The Missing Women in STEM? Accounting for Gender Differences in Entrance into Science, Technology, Engineering, and Math Occupations. *Presented at the 2012 Population Association of America annual meeting, Washington, D.C.*

Shapiro, C., Sax, L. J., & Rodgers, K. A. (2017). The Role of Stereotype Threats in Undermining Girls' and Women's Performance and Interest in STEM Fields. *Sex Roles*, 77(5&6), 363–375.

Smith, J. L., Lewis, K. L., Hawthorne, L., & Hodges, S. D. (2013). When Trying Hard isn't Natural: Women's Belonging with and Motivation for Male-Dominated STEM Fields as a Function of Effort Expenditure Concerns. *Personality and Social Psychology Bulletin*, 39(2), 131–143. DOI: 10.1177/0146167212468332 PMID: 23187722

Steinke, J. (2017). Adolescent girls' STEM identity formation and media images of STEM professionals: Considering the infuence of contextual cues. *Frontiers in Psychology*, 8, 716. DOI: 10.3389/fpsyg.2017.00716 PMID: 28603505

Tan, A. L., Jocz, J. A., & Zhai, J. (2015). Spiderman and Science: How Students' Perceptions of Scientists are Shaped by Popular Media. *Public Understanding of Science (Bristol, England)*, 26(5), 520–530. DOI: 10.1177/0963662515615086 PMID: 26582070

The Guardian Nigeria News. (2021). Gender Stereotype, Girls and Science Education. Nigeria and World News — Opinion. Available on https://guardian.ng/opinion/gender-stereotype-girls-and-science-education/

Udeani, U., & Ejikeme, C. (2011). A Decade into the 21st Century: Nigerian Women Scientists and Engineers Highly Under-Represented in Academia. The African Symposium, 11(2), 99-105 https://www.ncsu.edu/aern/TAS11.2/TAS11.2_10Udeani.pdf

UNESCO. (2017). Cracking the Code: Girls' and Women's Education in Science, Technology, Engineering And Mathematics (STEM). https://unesdoc.unesco.org/ark:/48223/pf0000253479

United Nations. (2012). The Future We Want, Outcome Document of the UN Conference on Sustainable Development. New York: United Nations.

United Nations International Children Emergency Fund (UNICEF). (2020). Independent Evaluation of the Effectiveness & Impact of the Sustainable Development Goal 4 Education in Nigeria. Inception Report.

Wang1, N., Tan, A. L., Zhou, X., Liu, K., Zeng, F. & Xiang, J. (2023). Gender Differences in High School Students' Interest in STEM Careers: A Multi-Group Comparison Based on Structural Equation Model. *International Journal of STEM Education*, 10(59), 1 -21. https://doi.org/DOI: 10.1186/s40594-023-00443-6

Wang, J. Y., Yang, M. Y., Lv, B. B., Zhang, F. X., Zheng, Y. H., & Sun, Y. H. (2020). Influencing Factors of 10th Grade Students' Science Career Expectations: A Structural Equation Model. *Journal of Baltic Science Education*, 19(4), 675–686. DOI: 10.33225/jbse/20.19.675

Wang, M. T., & Degol, J. L. (2017). Gender Gap in Science, Technology, Engineering, and Mathematics (STEM): Current Knowledge, Implications For Practice, Policy, and Future Directions. *Educational Psychology Review*, 29(1), 119–140. DOI: 10.1007/s10648-015-9355-x PMID: 28458499

Yang, J., & Shen, W. (2020). Master's Education in Stem Fields in China: Does Gender Matter? *Higher Education Policy*, 33(4), 667–688. DOI: 10.1057/s41307-020-00203-z

Zenelaj, E. (2013). Education for Sustainable Development. *European Journal of Sustainable Development*, 2(4), 227–232. DOI: 10.14207/ejsd.2013.v2n4p227

Compilation of References

Abdullahi, N., Abubakar, A., Abubakar, M. J., & Aliyu, A. C. (2019). Gender Gap in Science and Technology Education in Nigeria. *International Journal of Education and Evaluation*, 5(3), 6–13. www.iiardpub.org

Abulibdeh, A., Zaidan, E., & Abulibdeh, R. (2024). Navigating the confluence of artificial intelligence and education for sustainable development in the era of industry 4.0: Challenges, opportunities, and ethical dimensions. *Journal of Cleaner Production*, 437, 140527. Advance online publication. DOI: 10.1016/j.jclepro.2023.140527

Acemoglu, D., & Robinson, J. A. (2013). *Why nations fail. The origins of power, prosperity and poverty*. Profile Books.

Ackah-Jnr, F. R. (2016). *Implementation of inclusive early childhood education policy and change in Ghana: Four case sites of practice.* Unpublished Doctor of Philosophy Thesis. Griffith University, Australia.

Ackah-Jnr, F. R. (2018). System and school-level resources for transforming and optimising inclusive education in early childhood settings: What Ghana can learn. *European Journal of Education Studies*, 5(6), 203–220.

Ackah-Jnr, F. R. (2020a). Inclusive education, a best practice, policy and provision in education systems and schools: The rationale and critique. *European Journal of Education Studies*, 6(10), 171–183.

Ackah-Jnr, F. R. (2020b). The teacher should be learning: In-service professional development and learning of teachers implementing inclusive education in early childhood education settings. *International Journal of Whole Schooling*, 16(2), 93–121.

Ackah-Jnr, F. R. (2022). Enabling inclusive education: The leadership ecosystem in an early childhood-school-community context. *International Journal of Leadership in Education*, •••, 1–19. DOI: 10.1080/13603124.2022.2108508

Ackah-Jnr, F. R., Appiah, J., & Kwao, A. (2020). Inclusive language as a pedagogical and motivational tool in early childhood settings: Some observations. *Open Journal of Social Sciences*, 8(9), 176–184. DOI: 10.4236/jss.2020.89012

Ackah-Jnr, F. R., Appiah, J., Udah, H., Abedi, E., Yaro, K., Addo-Kissiedu, K., Agyei, I. K., & Opoku-Nkoom, I. (2022). COVID-19 pandemic experiences: Cross-border voices of international graduate students in Australia and America. *International Journal of Learning. Teaching and Educational Research*, 21(4), 97–113.

Ackah-Jnr, F. R., & Danso, J. B. (2019). Examining the physical environment of Ghanaian inclusive schools: How accessible, suitable and appropriate is such environment for inclusive education? *International Journal of Inclusive Education*, 23(2), 188–208. DOI: 10.1080/13603116.2018.1427808

Ackah-Jnr, F. R., & Udah, H. (2021). Implementing inclusive education in early childhood settings: The interplay and impact of exclusion, teacher qualities and professional development in Ghana. *Journal of Educational Research & Practice*, 11(1), 112–125. DOI: 10.5590/JERAP.2021.11.1.08

Adade Williams, P., Sikutshwa, L., & Shackleton, S. (2020). Acknowledging indigenous and local knowledge to facilitate collaboration in landscape approaches—Lessons from a systematic review. *Land (Basel)*, 9(9), 331. DOI: 10.3390/land9090331

Aderemi, H. O., Hassan, O. M., Siyanbola, W. O., & Taiwo, K. (2013). Trends in Enrollment, Graduation and Staffing of Science and Technology Education in Nigeria Tertiary Institutions: A Gender Participation Perspective. *Educational Research Review*, 8(21), 2011–2020. http://www.academicjournals.org/ERR. DOI: 10.5897/ERR08.084

Adewumi, T. M., Mosito, C., & Agosto, V. (2019). Experiences of teachers in implementing inclusion of learners with special education needs in selected Fort Beaufort District primary schools, South Africa. [01 March 2024]. *Cogent Education*, 6(1), 1–20. DOI: 10.1080/2331186X.2019.1703446

Aditi, G., Govindan, K., & Jha, P. C. (2024). Modelling of barriers in implementing sustainable manufacturer-supplier collaboration and coping strategies. *Journal of Cleaner Production*, 434, 139635. Advance online publication. DOI: 10.1016/j.jclepro.2023.139635

African National Congress. (1994). National election manifesto. Together we have won the right for all South Africans to vote. Available: https://www.anc1912.org.za/manifestos-1994-national-elections-manifesto/ [28 March 2024]

African Union. (2016). *Continental Education Strategy for Africa 2016-2025*. African Union.

Agrawal, A. V., Pitchai, R., Senthamaraikannan, C., Alangudi Balaji, N., Sajithra, S., & Boopathi, S. (2023). Digital Education System During the COVID-19 Pandemic. In Bell, J., & Gifford, T. (Eds.), (pp. 104–126). Advances in Educational Technologies and Instructional Design. IGI Global., DOI: 10.4018/978-1-6684-6424-3.ch005

Aidoo, B., Macdonald, M. A., Vesterinen, V.-M., Pétursdóttir, S., & Gísladóttir, B. (2022). Transforming teaching with ICT using the flipped classroom approach: Dealing with COVID-19 pandemic. *Education Sciences*, 12(6), 421. DOI: 10.3390/educsci12060421

Ainscow, M. (2020). Developing inclusive education systems: How can we move policies forward? *Journal of Educational Change*, 21(2), 145–165.

Ainscow, M. (2020). Inclusion and equity in education: Making sense of global challenges. *Prospects*, 49(3-4), 123–134. DOI: 10.1007/s11125-020-09506-w

Ainscow, M. (2022). *Inclusive education: Rethinking the task of creating equity in schools*. Routledge.

Ajani, M. O., & Ojetunde, S. M. (2021). Effects of Education Budget and Enrolment on Science, Technology, Engineering and Mathematics (STEM) Education in Nigeria. *International Journal of Educational Management*, 19(2), 30–41.

Akilu, I., Murtala, A., & Aminu, I. (2023). Enrollment Trends, Motivations, and Future Aspirations of Female Undergraduate Students in STEM Courses at Federal University Gusau – Nigeria. *Global Academic Journal of Humanities and Social Sciences*, 5(3), 142–150. DOI: 10.36348/gajhss.2023.v05i03.001

Akinsowon, O. A., & Osisanwo, F. Y. (2014). Enhancing Interest in Sciences, Technology and Mathematics (STEM) for the Nigerian Female Folk. *International Journal of Information Science*, 4(1), 8–12.

Akpan, J., & Beard, L. (2014). Assistive technology and mathematics education. *Universal Journal of Educational Research*, 2(3), 219–222. DOI: 10.13189/ujer.2014.020303

Alborno, N. (2017). The 'yes ... but' dilemma: Implementing inclusive education in emirati primary schools. *British Journal of Special Education*, 44(1), 26–45. DOI: 10.1111/1467-8578.12157

Alenezi, M. (2021). Deep dive into digital transformation in higher education institutions. *Education Sciences*, 11(12), 770. DOI: 10.3390/educsci11120770

Alfrey, L., & O'Connor, J. (2020). Critical pedagogy and curriculum transformation in secondary health and physical education. *Physical Education and Sport Pedagogy*, 25(3), 288–302. DOI: 10.1080/17408989.2020.1741536

Ali, M., & Abdel-Haq, M. K. (2021). Bibliographical analysis of artificial intelligence learning in Higher Education: Is the role of the human educator and educated a thing of the past? In *Fostering Communication and Learning With Underutilized Technologies in Higher Education* (pp. 36–52). IGI Global. DOI: 10.4018/978-1-7998-4846-2.ch003

Alkhateeb, H., Romanowski, M. H., Sellami, A., Abu-Tineh, A. M., & Chaaban, Y. (2022). Challenges facing teacher education in Qatar: Q methodology research. *Heliyon*, 8(7), e09845. DOI: 10.1016/j.heliyon.2022.e09845 PMID: 35847612

Allsopp, J. M. (2013). An enquiry into the factors that have contributed to the growth of the field of child and youth care work in South Africa [Unpublished master's thesis]. University of South Africa, Pretoria, South Africa.

Allsopp, J. M. (2020). Child and Youth Care Work in the South African Context: Towards a Model for Education and Practice [Unpublished doctoral dissertation]. Durban University of Technology, South Africa.

Alquraini, T. A., & Rao, S. M. (2020). Assessing teachers' knowledge, readiness, and needs to implement Universal Design for Learning in classrooms in Saudi Arabia. *International Journal of Inclusive Education*, 24(1), 103–114. DOI: 10.1080/13603116.2018.1452298

Alshboul, O., Al Mamlook, R. E., Shehadeh, A., & Munir, T. (2024). Empirical exploration of predictive maintenance in concrete manufacturing: Harnessing machine learning for enhanced equipment reliability in construction project management. *Computers & Industrial Engineering*, 190, 110046. Advance online publication. DOI: 10.1016/j.cie.2024.110046

Alves, F. (2021). Inclusive education in Brazil: Progress and challenges post-pandemic. *International Journal of Inclusive Education*, 26(3), 305–320.

Anamuah-Mensah, J., Adjei, A., & Agyemang, K. (2023). Inclusive education in Ghana: Progress and challenges. *Journal of African Education*, 10(1), 12–34.

Anderson, L. W., Krathwohl, D. R., Airasian, P. W., Cruikshank, K. A., Mayer, R. E., Pintrich, P. R., Raths, J., & Wittrock, M. C. (2001). *A taxonomy for learning, teaching, and assessing: A revision of Bloom's taxonomy of educational objectives, abridged edition*. Pearson.

Anjomshoaa, H., Ghazizadeh Hashemi, A. H., Jasim Alsadaji, A., Jasim Mohammed, Z., & Masoudi, S. (2022). The effect of flipped classroom on student learning outcomes; An overview. *Medical Education Bulletin*, 3(2), 431–440.

Ansari, W. (2023). Effective use of assistive technology for inclusive education in developing countries.. https://doi.org/DOI: 10.14293/PR2199.000268.v1

Appiah, J. K. (2022). *Enacting pedagogical leadership in early childhood education settings in Ghana. A cross case study of three schools*. Unpublished Doctoral Dissertation. Auburn University, Alabama.

ARC Centre of Excellence for Children and Families over the Life Course. (n.d.). *About Us*. https://www.lifecoursecentre.org.au/about-us

Archer, A., Cottingham, S., Grant, G., Lee, B., Mann, J., & Tinklin, T. (2014). Inclusive education in lifelong learning contexts. In *International Perspectives on Inclusive Education* (pp. 177–192). Routledge.

Aronson, J., Goodwin, N., Orlando, L., Eisenberg, C., & Cross, A. T. (2020). A world of possibilities: Six restoration strategies to support the United Nation's Decade on Ecosystem Restoration. *Restoration Ecology*, 28(4), 730–736. DOI: 10.1111/rec.13170

Artiles, A. J., & Kozleski, E. B. (2007). Beyond convictions: Interrogating culture, history, and power in inclusive education. *Language Arts*, 84(2), 173–181. DOI: 10.58680/la20075646

Atkins, E. R., & Cilliers, J. (2024). Education. ISS African Futures. https://futures.issafrica.org/thematic/06-education/#cite-this-research

Auditor-General of South Africa. (2019). *Full-service schools. Presentation made at the DBE Interprovincial Meeting on Inclusive Education, 28 August 2019*. Auditor-General of South Africa.

Australian Government. (n.d.). *Disability Standards for Education*. https://www.education.gov.au/disability-standards-education

Avramidis, E., & Kalyva, E. (2007). The influence of teaching experience and professional development on greek teachers' attitudes towards inclusion. *European Journal of Special Needs Education*, 22(4), 367–389. DOI: 10.1080/08856250701649989

Ayyildiz, E., & Erdogan, M. (2024). Addressing the challenges of using autonomous robots for last-mile delivery. *Computers & Industrial Engineering*, 190, 110096. Advance online publication. DOI: 10.1016/j.cie.2024.110096

Azizah, T., Fauzan, A., & Harisman, Y. (2022). "FLIPPED CLASSROOM TYPE PEER INSTRUCTION-BASED LEARNING" BASED ON A WEBSITE TO IMPROVE STUDENT'S PROBLEM SOLVING. *Infinity Journal*, 11(2), 325–348. DOI: 10.22460/infinity.v11i2.p325-348

Babu, B. S., Kamalakannan, J., Meenatchi, N., Karthik, S., & Boopathi, S. (2022). Economic impacts and reliability evaluation of battery by adopting Electric Vehicle. *IEEE Explore*, 1–6.

Bag, S., Sabbir Rahman, M., Ghai, S., Kumar Srivastava, S., Kumar Singh, R., & Mishra, R. (2024). Unveiling the impact of carbon-neutral policies on vital resources in Industry 4.0 driven smart manufacturing: A data-driven investigation. *Computers & Industrial Engineering*, 187, 109798. Advance online publication. DOI: 10.1016/j.cie.2023.109798

Ballantyne, J., & Retell, J. (2020). Teaching careers: Exploring links between well-being, burnout, self-efficacy and praxis shock. *Frontiers in Psychology*, 10, 2255. DOI: 10.3389/fpsyg.2019.02255 PMID: 32132940

Banks, J. A. (2008). Diversity, group identity, and citizenship education in a global age. *Educational Researcher*, 37(3), 129–139. DOI: 10.3102/0013189X08317501

Banks, J. A. (2015). *Cultural Diversity and Education: Foundations, Curriculum, and Teaching* (6th ed.). Routledge. DOI: 10.4324/9781315622255

Baratta, A., Cimino, A., Longo, F., & Nicoletti, L. (2024). Digital twin for human-robot collaboration enhancement in manufacturing systems: Literature review and direction for future developments. *Computers & Industrial Engineering*, 187, 109764. Advance online publication. DOI: 10.1016/j.cie.2023.109764

Barth, J., & Muehlfeld, K. (2022). Thinking out of the box—By thinking in other boxes: A systematic review of interventions in early entrepreneurship vs. STEM education research. *Management Review Quarterly*, 72(2), 347–383. DOI: 10.1007/s11301-021-00248-3

Baumfeld Andre, E., Reynolds, R., Caubel, P., Azoulay, L., & Dreyer, N. A. (2020). Trial designs using real-world data: The changing landscape of the regulatory approval process. *Pharmacoepidemiology and Drug Safety*, 29(10), 1201–1212. DOI: 10.1002/pds.4932 PMID: 31823482

Beck, D., Morgado, L., & O'Shea, P. (2020). Finding the gaps about uses of immersive learning environments: A survey of surveys. *Journal of Universal Computer Science*, 26(8), 1043–1073. DOI: 10.3897/jucs.2020.055

Beck, D., Morgado, L., & O'Shea, P. (2023). Educational Practices and Strategies with Immersive Learning Environments: Mapping of Reviews for using the Metaverse. *IEEE Transactions on Learning Technologies*.

Benavides, L. M. C., Tamayo Arias, J. A., Arango Serna, M. D., Branch Bedoya, J. W., & Burgos, D. (2020). Digital transformation in higher education institutions: A systematic literature review. *Sensors (Basel)*, 20(11), 3291. DOI: 10.3390/s20113291 PMID: 32526998

Benavot, A. (2016). Gender Bias is Rife in Textbooks. World Education Blog. https://world-education-blog.org/2016/03/08/gender-bias-is-rife-in-textbooks

Bench, S.W., Lench, H.C., Liew, J., Miner, K., & Flores, S.A. (2015). Gender Gaps in Overestimation of Mathematics Performance. *Sex Roles*, 72, 11, 11, 536-546

Bennett, S. V., Gunn, A. A., & Peterson, B. M. (2018). Preparing teachers for inclusive education: Key ingredients for success. *The Educational Forum*, 82(3), 301–314.

Berger, J.-L., & Lê Van, K. (2019). Teacher professional identity as multidimensional: Mapping its components and examining their associations with general pedagogical beliefs. *Educational Studies*, 45(2), 163–181. DOI: 10.1080/03055698.2018.1446324

Bergin, C., & Bergin, D. (2009). Attachment in the classroom. *Educational Psychology Review*, 21(2), 141–170. DOI: 10.1007/s10648-009-9104-0

Berkovich, I. (2020). Conceptualisations of empathy in K-12 teaching: A review of empirical research. *Educational Review*, 72(5), 547–566. DOI: 10.1080/00131911.2018.1530196

Bi, J., Chowdhry, S., Wu, S., Zhang, W., Masui, K., & Mischel, P. S. (2020). Altered cellular metabolism in gliomas—An emerging landscape of actionable co-dependency targets. *Nature Reviews. Cancer*, 20(1), 57–70. DOI: 10.1038/s41568-019-0226-5 PMID: 31806884

Bishnoi, M. M. (2020). Flipped classroom and digitization: An inductive study on the learning framework for 21st century skill acquisition. *JETT*, 11(1), 30–45.

Black, P., & Wiliam, D. (2009). Developing the theory of formative assessment. *Educational Assessment, Evaluation and Accountability*, 21(1), 5–31. DOI: 10.1007/s11092-008-9068-5

Bodolica, V., & Spraggon, M. (2021). Incubating innovation in university settings: Building entrepreneurial mindsets in the future generation of innovative emerging market leaders. *Education + Training*, 63(4), 613–631. DOI: 10.1108/ET-06-2020-0145

Bohns, V., & Flynn, F. (2021). Empathy and expectations of others' willingness to help. *Personality and Individual Differences*, 168, 110368. DOI: 10.1016/j.paid.2020.110368

Boopathi, S. (2024). Balancing Innovation and Security in the Cloud: Navigating the Risks and Rewards of the Digital Age. In *Improving Security, Privacy, and Trust in Cloud Computing* (pp. 164–193). IGI Global.

Boopathi, S., & Khare, R. KG, J. C., Muni, T. V., & Khare, S. (2023). Additive Manufacturing Developments in the Medical Engineering Field. In *Development, Properties, and Industrial Applications of 3D Printed Polymer Composites* (pp. 86–106). IGI Global.

Boopathi, S., & Kumar, P. (2024a). Advanced bioprinting processes using additive manufacturing technologies: Revolutionizing tissue engineering. *3D Printing Technologies: Digital Manufacturing, Artificial Intelligence, Industry 4.0*, 95.

Boopathi, S., & Kumar, P. (2024b). Advanced bioprinting processes using additive manufacturing technologies: Revolutionizing tissue engineering. *3D Printing Technologies: Digital Manufacturing, Artificial Intelligence, Industry 4.0*, 95.

Boopathi, S., Thillaivanan, A., Mohammed, A. A., Shanmugam, P., & VR, P. (2022). Experimental investigation on Abrasive Water Jet Machining of Neem Wood Plastic Composite. *IOP: Functional Composites and Structures*, 4, 025001.

Boopathi, S. (2023). Deep Learning Techniques Applied for Automatic Sentence Generation. In Becerra-Murillo, K., & Gámez, J. F. (Eds.), (pp. 255–273). Advances in Educational Technologies and Instructional Design. IGI Global., DOI: 10.4018/978-1-6684-3632-5.ch016

Booth, J., Coldwell, M., Müller, L.-M., Perry, E., & Zuccollo, J. (2021). Mid-career teachers: A mixed methods scoping study of professional development, career progression and retention. *Education Sciences*, 11(6), 299. DOI: 10.3390/educsci11060299

Booth, T., & Ainscow, M. (2016). *Guidebook for inclusive practices: Making it work*. Springer.

Bose, N., Sarkar, P., Das, A., Samaddar, M., Roy, S., & Dutta, S. (2020). Thinking Out of the Box. *International Journal of English Learning & Teaching Skills*, 2(3), 1388–1411. DOI: 10.15864/ijelts.2309

Boyle, C., Topping, K., Jindal-Snape, D., & Norwich, B. (2017). The effects of teachers' classroom management practices on pupils' academic and social outcomes. *Educational Psychology Review*, 29(2), 437–464.

Bozier, J., Chivers, E. K., Chapman, D. G., Larcombe, A. N., Bastian, N. A., Masso-Silva, J. A., Byun, M. K., McDonald, C. F., Alexander, L. E. C., & Ween, M. P. (2020). The evolving landscape of e-cigarettes: A systematic review of recent evidence. *Chest*, 157(5), 1362–1390. DOI: 10.1016/j.chest.2019.12.042 PMID: 32006591

Brackett, M. A., Rivers, S. E., & Salovey, P. (2011). Emotional intelligence: Implications for personal, social, academic, and workplace success. *Social and Personality Psychology Compass*, 5(1), 88–103. DOI: 10.1111/j.1751-9004.2010.00334.x

Bradshaw, D. G. (2020). Examining beliefs and practices of students with hidden disabilities and universal design for learning in institutions of higher education. *Journal of Higher Education Theory and Practice*, 20(15).

British Council. (2018). *The state of inclusive education in South Africa and the implications for teacher training programmes. Research Report*. British Council.

British Council. (2020). *Embedding Inclusive Education in Teacher Professional Development in South Africa. Impact evaluation report on the Teaching for All project*. British Council.

Brophy, J. (2006). Grade repetition. In R. Burns & D. Livingston (Eds.), *The Concise Encyclopedia of Education*. Pergamon.

Bruce, M., Podemski, R., & Anderson, C. (1991). Developing a global perspective: Strategies for teacher education programs. *Journal of Teacher Education*, 42(1), 21–27. DOI: 10.1177/002248719104200104

Buchanan, R., Mills, T., & Mooney, E. (2022). Working across time and space: Developing a framework for teacher leadership throughout a teaching career. In *Leadership for Professional Learning* (pp. 65–77). Routledge. DOI: 10.4324/9781003357384-5

Buckley, R. P., Arner, D., Veidt, R., & Zetzsche, D. (2020). Building FinTech ecosystems: Regulatory sandboxes, innovation hubs and beyond. *Wash. UJL & Pol'y*, 61, 55.

Budlender, D., & Wilson, T. (2019). Isibindi Ezikoleni: Reflections on the model. Unpublished manuscript, National Association of Child Care Workers (NACCW).

Budnyk, O., & Kotyk, M. (2020). Use of information and communication technologies in the inclusive process of educational institutions. *Journal of Vasyl Stefanyk Precarpathian National University*, 7(1), 15–23. DOI: 10.15330/jpnu.7.1.15-23

Burange, R., Agrawal, G., & Ingole, K. (2024). Design and implementation of low power D flip flop for embedded application. *AIP Conference Proceedings*, 2974(1), 020042. DOI: 10.1063/5.0182465

Calciolari, S., Cesarini, M., & Ruberti, M. (2024). Sustainability disclosure in the pharmaceutical and chemical industries: Results from bibliometric analysis and AI-based comparison of financial reports. *Journal of Cleaner Production*, 447, 141511. Advance online publication. DOI: 10.1016/j.jclepro.2024.141511

Caner, M., & Aydın, S. (2021). Self efficacy beliefs of pre-service teachers on technology integration. *Turkish Online Journal of Distance Education*, •••, 79–94. DOI: 10.17718/tojde.961820

Capoccia, G., & Daniel, R. K. (2007). The study of critical junctures. Theory, narrative and counterfactuals in institutional analysis. [27 March 2024]. *World Politics*, 59(3), 341–369. DOI: 10.1017/S0043887100020852

Carrington, B., Francis, P., Hutchings, M., Skelton, C., Read, B., Hall, I., & Mendick, H. (2008). Does the gender of the teacher really matter? Seven- to eight-year-olds' accounts of their interactions with their teachers. *Educational Studies*, 34(5), 449–464.

Carrington, B., Tymms, P., & Merrell, C. (2008). Role Models, School Improvement and the 'Net Generation'? New Evidence from Primary Schools in England. *British Educational Research Journal*, 34(3), 315–329. DOI: 10.1080/01411920701532202

Castro, J. V., & Carrillo Cruz, C. E. (2024). Dynamic efl teaching practices for students with visual impairment. *Revista Boletín Redipe*, 13(4), 109–121. DOI: 10.36260/rbr.v13i4.2114

Cavalieri, A., Reis, J., & Amorim, M. (2024). Socioenvironmental assessment and application process for IOT: A comprehensive approach. *Journal of Cleaner Production*, 436, 140348. Advance online publication. DOI: 10.1016/j.jclepro.2023.140348

Ceci, S. J., & Williams, W. M. (2015). Women have Substantial Advantage in STEM Faculty Hiring, Except When Competing against More-Accomplished Men. *Frontiers in Psychology*, 6, 1532. DOI: 10.3389/fpsyg.2015.01532 PMID: 26539132

Chakraborti, T., Sreedharan, S., & Kambhampati, S. (2020). The emerging landscape of explainable ai planning and decision making. *arXiv Preprint arXiv:2002.11697*.

Charlesworth, T. E. S., & Banaji, M. R. (2019). Gender in Science, Technology, Engineering, and Mathematics: Issues, Causes, Solutions. *The Journal of Neuroscience : The Official Journal of the Society for Neuroscience*, 39(37), 7228–7243. DOI: 10.1523/JNEUROSCI.0475-18.2019 PMID: 31371423

Cheng, M., Adekola, O., Albia, J., & Cai, S. (2022). Employability in higher education: A review of key stakeholders' perspectives. *Higher Education Evaluation and Development*, 16(1), 16–31. DOI: 10.1108/HEED-03-2021-0025

Cherney, I. D. (2023). The STEM Paradox: Factors Affecting Diversity in STEM Fields. *Journal of Physics: Conference Series*, 2438(1), 012005. DOI: 10.1088/1742-6596/2438/1/012005

Cheryan, S., Master, A., & Meltzoff, A. N. (2015). Cultural Stereotypes as Gate-Keepers: Increasing Girls' Interest in Computer Science and Engineering by Diversifying Stereotypes. *Frontiers in Psychology*, 6, 49. DOI: 10.3389/fpsyg.2015.00049 PMID: 25717308

Cheryan, S., Ziegler, S. A., Montoya, A. K., & Jiang, L. (2017). Why are Some STEM Fields More Gender Balanced than Others? *Psychological Bulletin*, 143(1), 1–35. DOI: 10.1037/bul0000052 PMID: 27732018

Child Hub Academy. (Undated). Practicing Supervision in Child Protection Settings. Online Training Course. Centre of Excellence for Looked After Children in Scotland (CELCIS), University of Strathclyde.

China Bureau of Statistics. (2022). China Statistical Yearbook on Science and Technology 2021. *China Statistics Press*. http://cnki.nbsti.net/CSYDMirror/Trade/yearbook/single/N2022010277?z=Z018

Choi, J., Cho, J., Choi, W. J., Lee, M., & Kim, B. (2022). A Layout Generator of Latch, Flip-Flop, and Shift Register for High-Speed Links. *2022 19th International SoC Design Conference (ISOCC)*, 19–20.

Christie, P. (1985). *The right to learn: The struggle for education in South Africa*. Ravan Press.

Chua, K., & Islam, M. (2021). The hybrid Project-Based Learning–Flipped Classroom: A design project module redesigned to foster learning and engagement. *International Journal of Mechanical Engineering Education*, 49(4), 289–315. DOI: 10.1177/0306419019838335

Coiro, J., Knobel, M., Lankshear, C., & Leu, D. J. (2014). *Handbook of research on new literacies*. Routledge. DOI: 10.4324/9781410618894

Collado-Valero, J., Rodríguez-Infante, G., Romero-González, M., Gamboa-Ternero, S., Navarro-Soria, I., & Lavigne-Cerván, R. (2021). Flipped classroom: Active methodology for sustainable learning in higher education during social distancing due to COVID-19. *Sustainability (Basel)*, 13(10), 5336. DOI: 10.3390/su13105336

Connors-Kellgren, A., Parker, C. E., Blustein, D. L., & Barnett, M. (2016). Innovations and Challenges in Project-Based STEM Education: Lessons from ITEST. *Journal of Science Education and Technology*, 25(6), 825–832. DOI: 10.1007/s10956-016-9658-9

Constitutional Court of South Africa. (2011). Governing Body of the Juma Musjid Primary School & Others v Ahmed Asruff Essay N.O. and Others (CCT 29/10) [2011] ZACC 13; 2011 (8) BCLR 761 (CC). Available: https://www.coursehero.com/file/138429113/MUSJID-CASEpdf/ [22 March 2024].

Constitutional Court. (2013). Head of Department, Department of Education, Free State Province v Welkom High School and Another; Head of Department, Department of Education, Free State Province v Harmony High School and Another (CCT 103/12) [2013] ZACC 25; 2013 (9) BCLR 989 (CC); 2014 (2) SA 228 (CC) (10 July 2013). Available: https://www.saflii.org/za/cases/ZACC/2013/25.html [26 March 2024].

Crompton, H., Bernacki, M., & Greene, J. A. (2020). Psychological foundations of emerging technologies for teaching and learning in higher education. *Current Opinion in Psychology*, 36, 101–105. DOI: 10.1016/j.copsyc.2020.04.011 PMID: 32604064

Cvencek, D., Meltzoff, A. N., & Greenwald, A. G. (2011). Math-gender Stereotypes in Elementary School Children. *Child Development*, 82(3), 766–779. DOI: 10.1111/j.1467-8624.2010.01529.x PMID: 21410915

D'Alessio, S. (2021). Inclusive education in Italy: A comprehensive approach to equity and participation. *European Journal of Special Education Research*, 9(1), 45–63.

Darling-Hammond, L. (2017). Teacher professional development: A review of the literature. *Journal of Teacher Education*, 68(4), 339–354.

Das, S., Lekhya, G., Shreya, K., Shekinah, K. L., Babu, K. K., & Boopathi, S. (2024). Fostering Sustainability Education Through Cross-Disciplinary Collaborations and Research Partnerships: Interdisciplinary Synergy. In *Facilitating Global Collaboration and Knowledge Sharing in Higher Education With Generative AI* (pp. 60–88). IGI Global.

Das, S., Lekhya, G., Shreya, K., Shekinah, K. L., Babu, K. K., & Boopathi, S. (2024a). Fostering Sustainability Education Through Cross-Disciplinary Collaborations and Research Partnerships: Interdisciplinary Synergy. In *Facilitating Global Collaboration and Knowledge Sharing in Higher Education With Generative AI* (pp. 60–88). IGI Global.

Das, S., Lekhya, G., Shreya, K., Shekinah, K. L., Babu, K. K., & Boopathi, S. (2024b). Fostering Sustainability Education Through Cross-Disciplinary Collaborations and Research Partnerships: Interdisciplinary Synergy. In *Facilitating Global Collaboration and Knowledge Sharing in Higher Education With Generative AI* (pp. 60–88). IGI Global.

Dasgupta, N., & Stout, J. G. (2014). Girls and Women in Science, Technology, Engineering, and Mathematics: Stemming the Tide and Broadening Participation in STEM Careers. *Policy Insights from the Behavioral and Brain Sciences*, 1(1), 21–29. DOI: 10.1177/2372732214549471

Das, S., Lekhya, G., Shreya, K., Lydia Shekinah, K., Babu, K. K., & Boopathi, S. (2024). Fostering Sustainability Education Through Cross-Disciplinary Collaborations and Research Partnerships: Interdisciplinary Synergy. In Yu, P., Mulli, J., Syed, Z. A. S., & Umme, L. (Eds.), (pp. 60–88). Advances in Higher Education and Professional Development. IGI Global., DOI: 10.4018/979-8-3693-0487-7.ch003

Davis, D., Davis, J., & Hunt, A. (2016). The Impact of Empathy on Leadership Effectiveness in Higher Education. *The International Journal of Educational Leadership Preparation*, 11(1), 1–14.

Davis, M. H. (2016). *Empathy: A social psychological approach*. Routledge.

Davis, M. H., Conklin, L., Smith, A., & Luce, C. (2016). Effect of perspective-taking on the cognitive representation of persons: A merging of self and other. *Journal of Personality and Social Psychology*, 70(4), 713–726. DOI: 10.1037/0022-3514.70.4.713 PMID: 8636894

Davis, M. H., & Hunt, J. (2016). Empathy in the context of philosophy. In Decety, J. (Ed.), *Empathy: From Bench to Bedside* (pp. 71–81). MIT Press.

De Back, T. T., Tinga, A. M., & Louwerse, M. M. (2023). Learning in immersed collaborative virtual environments: Design and implementation. *Interactive Learning Environments*, 31(8), 5364–5382. DOI: 10.1080/10494820.2021.2006238

De Nobrega, N., Shezi, N., Mlambo, N., Nkwane, E., Thabede, S., Nxumalo, G., Lunga, A., Buthelezi, S., Louw, I., Radebe, A., Mazibuko, J., Ntintili, K., & Thumbadoo, Z. (2023). The role of mentorship in relational child and youth care management: Stories from child and youth care mentors in South Africa. Relational Child & Youth Care Practice, 36(1), 60 – 78. ISSN 2410-2954.

De Waal, F. B. M. (2008). Putting the altruism back into altruism: The evolution of empathy. *Annual Review of Psychology*, 59(1), 279–300. DOI: 10.1146/annurev.psych.59.103006.093625 PMID: 17550343

Deci, E. L., Vallerand, R. J., Pelletier, L. G., & Ryan, R. M. (1991). Motivation and education: The self-determination perspective. *Educational Psychologist*, 26(3-4), 325–346. DOI: 10.1080/00461520.1991.9653137

Deming, D. J., & Noray, K. L. (2019). STEM Careers and the Changing Skill Requirements of Work. *NBER Working Paper No. 25065*

Denholm, C. (2005). Challenges and Questions facing the Development of Child and Youth Care work in Canadian Educational Settings. CYC-Net. https://cyc-net.org/CYC-Online/cycol-0805-denholm.html

Denholm, C. J. (1989). Child and youth care in school settings: Maximizing support and minimizing friction. *Journal of Child and Youth Care Work*, 5, 54–61.

DePalma, R., & Francis, D. A. (2014). Silence, nostalgia, violence, poverty...: What does 'culture' mean for South African sexuality educators? *Culture, Health & Sexuality*, 16(5), 547–561. DOI: 10.1080/13691058.2014.891050 PMID: 24654938

Department Basic Education Republic of South Africa. (2018). *Keynote address by the Minister of Basic Education Mrs.* Angie Motshekga. Department Basic Education Republic of South Africa.

Department of Basic Education (DBE) and MIET Africa. (2010). *The Action Step: National Model Conceptual Framework for Care and Support for Teaching and Learning. MIET Africa. Durban Department of Basic Education South Africa. (2014). A message to schools on identifying and supporting learners who are vulnerable.* Department of Basic Education South Africa.

Department of Basic Education, (2023). Presentation to the Portfolio Committee on Basic Education on Progress in the Implementation of Inclusive Education.

Department of Basic Education, South Africa. (2015). Policy on progression and promotion requirements. *Government Gazette*.

Department of Basic Education. (2011). *Curriculum Assessment Policy Statements*. CAPS.

Department of Basic Education. (2014). *National Policy on Screening, Identification, Assessment, and Support*. SIAS.

Department of Basic Education. (2014). *Policy framework on professional development for teachers in inclusive education.*

Department of Basic Education. (2019a). *National Strategy on Learner Attendance.*

Department of Basic Education. (2019b). *The state of inclusive education in South Africa. Every learner matters. Presentation to the Portfolio Committee on Basic Education.* Department of Basic Education.

Department of Basic Education. (2019c). *Circular S4 of 2019*. Department of Basic Education.

Department of Basic Education. (2021). *Policy on the Prevention and Management of Learner Pregnancy in Schools*. Government Printers.

Department of Basic Education. (2023a). *Presentation to the Council for Education Ministers: Providing Quality Inclusive Education to Learners with Special Education Needs*. Department of Basic Education.

Department of Basic Education. (2023b). *Progress on psycho-educational assessments and placement of out-of-school learners from special care centres in schools. Presentation to the Interprovincial Meeting on Inclusive Education held on 06 December 2023*. Department of Basic Education.

Department of Basic Education. (2024). *Presentation to the Special Heads of Departments Committee Meeting (HEDCOM): Inclusive Education*. Department of Basic Education.

Department of Education. (2001). *Education White Paper 6 on Inclusive Education: Special needs education: Building an inclusive education and training system*. Government Printers.

Department of Education. (2001). *Education White Paper 6: Special Needs Education: Building an Inclusive Education and Training System*. Pretoria: Government Printers.

Department of Health. (2012). *Integrated School Health Policy*.

Department of Social Development. (2014). Regulations for child and youth care workers, auxiliary child and youth care workers, and student child and youth care workers. Government Gazette, (No. R. 838), 31 October 2014.

Department of Social Development. Republic of South Africa. (2019). National child care and protection policy: Working together to advance the rights of all children to care and protection. Department of Social Development, Republic of South Africa. https://www.gov.za/sites/default/files/gcis_document/202102/national-child-care-and-protection-policy.pdf

Devaux, P. F. (1993). Lipid transmembrane asymmetry and flip-flop in biological membranes and in lipid bilayers: Current Opinion in Structural Biology 1993, 3: 489–494. *Current Opinion in Structural Biology*, 3(4), 489–494. DOI: 10.1016/0959-440X(93)90072-S

Devine, H., Peralta-Alva, A., Selim, H., Eyraud, L., Sharma, P., & Wocken, L. (2021). *Private finance for development: Wishful thinking or thinking out of the box?* International Monetary Fund.

DGMT. (2023). Escaping the inequality trap. Five year strategy: 2023 – 2027.

Dillon, S., Armstrong, E., Goudy, L., Reynolds, H., & Scurry, S. (2021). Improving special education service delivery through interdisciplinary collaboration. *Teaching Exceptional Children*, 54(1), 36–43. DOI: 10.1177/00400599211029671

Dinu, C. C., & Chian, M. M. (2023). Uncovering Principles for Curriculum Adaptation: A Practitioner and Researcher (Co) Reflexive Analysis. *Journal of Ethnographic and Qualitative Research*, 17(1).

Doğan, Y., Batdı, V., & Yaşar, M. D. (2023). Effectiveness of flipped classroom practices in teaching of science: A mixed research synthesis. *Research in Science & Technological Education*, 41(1), 393–421. DOI: 10.1080/02635143.2021.1909553

Doménech-Betoret, F., Abellán-Roselló, L., & Gómez-Artiga, A. (2017). Self-efficacy, satisfaction, and academic achievement: The mediator role of students' Expectancy Value beliefs. *Frontiers in Psychology*, 8, 1–11. DOI: 10.3389/fpsyg.2017.01193 PMID: 28769839

Donald, D., Lazarus, S., & Lolwana, P. (1997). *Educational psychology in social context: Challenges of development, social issues and special need in southern Africa*. Oxford University Press.

Donath, J. L., Lüke, T., Graf, E., Tran, U. S., & Götz, T. (2023). Does professional development effectively support the implementation of inclusive education? A Meta-Analysis. *Educational Psychology Review*, 35(30), 30. Advance online publication. DOI: 10.1007/s10648-023-09752-2

Donohue, D., & Bornman, J. (2014). The challenges of realising inclusive education in South Africa. *South African Journal of Education*, 34(2), 1–14. DOI: 10.15700/201412071114

Dumulescu, D., & Muţiu, A. I. (2021). Academic leadership in the time of COVID-19—Experiences and perspectives. *Frontiers in Psychology*, 12, 648344. DOI: 10.3389/fpsyg.2021.648344 PMID: 33959076

Durairaj, M., & Jayakumar, S. Monika, Karpagavalli, V. S., Maheswari, B. U., & Boopathi, S. (2023). Utilization of Digital Tools in the Indian Higher Education System During Health Crises: In C. S. V. Negrão, I. G. P. Maia, & J. A. F. Brito (Eds.), *Advances in Logistics, Operations, and Management Science* (pp. 1–21). IGI Global. DOI: 10.4018/978-1-7998-9213-7.ch001

Durlak, J. A., Weissberg, R. P., Dymnicki, A. B., Taylor, R. D., & Schellinger, K. B. (2011). The impact of enhancing students' social and emotional learning: A meta-analysis of school-based universal interventions. *Child Development*, 82(1), 405–432. DOI: 10.1111/j.1467-8624.2010.01564.x PMID: 21291449

Eisenberg, N., Spinrad, T. L., & Knafo-Noam, A. (2015). Prosocial development. In Lamb, M. E., & Lerner, R. M. (Eds.), *Handbook of child psychology and developmental science* (7th ed., Vol. 3, pp. 610–656). Wiley. DOI: 10.1002/9781118963418.childpsy315

Eisenberg, N., Spinrad, T. L., & Taylor, Z. E. (2014). *The handbook of virtue ethics*. Routledge.

Ekmekci, A., & Serrano, D. M. (2022). The Impact of Teacher Quality on Student Motivation, Achievement, and Persistence in Science and Mathematics. *Education Sciences*, 12(10), 649. DOI: 10.3390/educsci12100649

Engelhardt, C. F. (2023). *Building and sustaining trust during the COVID-19 pandemic: Lessons in P-12 educational leadership*. Unpublished Doctoral Thesis, State University of New York, Albany.

Equal Education Law Centre. (2021). *Inclusive education: Learners with learning barriers. The right to an equal and quality education*. Equal Education Law Centre.

Ericsson, N. R. (2021). Dynamic Econometrics in action: A biography of David F. Hendry. *International Finance Discussion Paper, 1311*.

Espelage, D. L., & Swearer, S. M. (2010). *Bullying in American Schools: A Social-Ecological Perspective on Prevention and Intervention*. Routledge. DOI: 10.4324/9780203842898

European Agency for Special Needs and Inclusive Education. (2015). *Key Principles for Promoting Quality in Inclusive Education: Recommendations for Policy Makers*. https://www.european-agency.org/sites/default/files/key-principles-for-promoting-quality-in-inclusive-education_EN.pdf

European Agency for Special Needs and Inclusive Education. (2021). *Inclusive education in action: Lessons from practice*. European Agency.

European Commission. (2021). *Union of Equality: Strategy for the Rights of Persons with Disabilities 2021-2030*. European Commission.

Eyler, J., & Giles, D. E. (1999). *Where's the Learning in Service-Learning?* Jossey-Bass.

Faruq, A. (2022). *A Phenomenological Examination of African American Men's Experiences in Community College* [PhD Thesis]. Walden University.

Fernandez, A. A., & Shaw, G. P. (2020). Academic leadership in a time of crisis: The Coronavirus and COVID-19. *Journal of Leadership Studies*, 14(1), 39–45. DOI: 10.1002/jls.21684

Ferriman, K., Lubinski, D., & Benbow, C. P. (2009). Work Preferences, Life Values, and Personal Views of Top Math/Science Graduate Students and the Profoundly Gifted: Developmental Changes and Gender Differences During Emerging Adulthood and Parenthood. *Journal of Personality and Social Psychology*, 97(3), 517–532. DOI: 10.1037/a0016030 PMID: 19686005

Fields, L., Trostian, B., Moroney, T., & Dean, B. A. (2021). Active learning pedagogy transformation: A whole-of-school approach to person-centred teaching and nursing graduates. *Nurse Education in Practice*, 53, 103051. DOI: 10.1016/j.nepr.2021.103051 PMID: 33865084

Finkelstein, S., Sharma, U., & Furlonger, B. (2021). The inclusive practices of classroom teachers: A scoping review and thematic analysis. *International Journal of Inclusive Education*, 25(6), 735–762. DOI: 10.1080/13603116.2019.1572232

Fisher, C. R., Brookes, R. H., & Thompson, C. D. (2021). 'I don't Study Physics Anymore: A Cross-Institutional Australian Study on Factors Impacting the Persistence of Undergraduate Science Students. *Research in Science Education*. Advance online publication. DOI: 10.1007/s11165-021-09995-5

Fletcher, M. A. (2015). Women Continue to be underrepresented in STEM Industries. *Women of Color Magazine*, 14, 1, 22 – 24. https://www.jstor.org/stable/43769519

Florian, L. (2014). Reimagining special education: Why new approaches are needed. *The SAGE Handbook of Special Education*, 9-23.

Florian, L., & Beaton, M. (2021). *Inclusive pedagogy in action: A framework for teaching and learning*. Cambridge University Press.

Florian, L., & Black-Hawkins, K. (2011). Exploring inclusive pedagogy. *British Educational Research Journal*, 37(5), 813–828. DOI: 10.1080/01411926.2010.501096

Florian, L., & Spratt, J. (2022). *The complexity of inclusion: Understanding and addressing inclusive education practices*. Cambridge University Press.

Fonsén, E., & Ukkonen-Mikkola, T. (2019). Early childhood education teachers' professional development towards pedagogical leadership. *Educational Research*, 61(2), 181–196. DOI: 10.1080/00131881.2019.1600377

Francis, D. A. (2012). Teacher positioning on the teaching of sexual diversity in South African schools. *Culture, Health & Sexuality*, 14(6), 597–611. DOI: 10.1080/13691058.2012.674558 PMID: 22574876

Francis, D. A. (2017). Homophobia and sexuality diversity in South African schools: A review. *Journal of LGBT Youth*, 14(4), 307–323. DOI: 10.1080/19361653.2017.1326868

Francis, D. A. (2019). "You know the homophobic stuff is not in me, like us, it comes from the community": The influence of broader social attitudes on South African teachers' attitudes toward homosexuality. *Sex Education*, 19(4), 413–427.

Francis, D. A., & Msibi, T. (2011). Teaching about heterosexism: Challenging homophobia in South Africa. *Journal of LGBT Youth*, 8(2), 157–173. DOI: 10.1080/19361653.2011.553713

Francis, D. A., & Reygan, F. (2016). *Sexuality, society & pedagogy*. Bloomsbury Publishing.

Freire, P. (1970). *Pedagogy of the Oppressed*. Continuum.

Fuchs, K. (2021a). Innovative teaching: A qualitative review of flipped classrooms. *International Journal of Learning. Teaching and Educational Research*, 20(3), 18–32.

Fu, S., Harman, R., & Zhang, M. Y. (2021). Critical creative out of the box thinking in COVID times. *School-University Partnerships*, 14(3), 238–259.

Galkiene, A., & Monkeviciene, O. (2021). *Improving inclusive education through Universal Design for Learning*. Springer Nature. DOI: 10.1007/978-3-030-80658-3

Gamble, J. (2008). *A Developmental Evaluation Primer*. The J.W. McConnell Family Foundation.

Garfat, T., Freeman, J., Gharabaghi, K., & Fulcher, L. (2018). Characteristics of a relational child and youth care approach revisited. *CYC-Online*, (10), 7–45.

Gates, E., & Curwood, J. E. (2023). A world beyond self: Empathy and pedagogy during times of global crisis. *Australian Journal of Language and Literacy*, 46(2), 195–209. DOI: 10.1007/s44020-023-00038-2

Gender Stereotype. (n.d.). Retrieved from https://guardian.ng/opinion/gender-stereotype-girls-and-science-education/

GenderDynamix.GenderIdentity&GenderExpressioninSouthAfrica: School'sManual.

Gharabaghi, K. (2018). Professionalization through doing. CYC-Net, (243), 32-35. https://cyc-net.org/cyc-online/may2019.pdf

Gharabaghi, K. (2019). Re-Launching Child and Youth Care Practice. CYC-Online, (September 2019), 9-15. https://www.cyc-net.org/cyc-online/sep2019.pdf

Giesenbauer, B., & Müller-Christ, G. (2020). University 4.0: Promoting the transformation of higher education institutions toward sustainable development. *Sustainability (Basel)*, 12(8), 3371. DOI: 10.3390/su12083371

Gilbreath, L. C. (2015). Factors Impacting Women's Participation in STEM Fields. UVM Honors College Senior Theses, 65. https://scholarworks.uvm.edu/hcoltheses/65

Gilbreath, L. C. (2015). Factors Impacting Women's Participation in STEM Fields. UVM Honors College Senior Theses. 65. https://scholarworks.uvm.edu/hcoltheses/65

Glass, J. L., Sharon, S., Yael, L., & Katherine, M. M. (2013). What's So Special about STEM? A Comparison of Women's Retention in STEM and Professional Occupations. *Social Forces*, 92(2), 723–756. DOI: 10.1093/sf/sot092 PMID: 25554713

Glutsch, N., & König, J. (2019). Pre-service teachers' motivations for choosing teaching as a career: Does subject interest matter? *Journal of Education for Teaching*, 45(5), 494–510. DOI: 10.1080/02607476.2019.1674560

Goh, P. S.-C., & Abdul-Wahab, N. (2020). Paradigms to drive higher education 4.0. *International Journal of Learning. Teaching and Educational Research*, 19(1), 159–171.

Goldhaber, A. B. (2021). Impact of ict integration on quality of education among secondary schools in usa. *Journal of Education*, 4(6), 53–61. DOI: 10.53819/81018102t5015

Gonzalez, H. B., & Kuenzi, J. J. (2012). *Science, Technology, Engineering and Mathematics (STEM) education: A Primer*. Congressional Research Service.

Gordon, D., & Rosenblum, L. P. (2019). *Accessible education for students with disabilities: Understanding Section 504 and the ADA*. Routledge.

Gorski, P. C. (2017). *Reaching and teaching students in poverty: Strategies for erasing the opportunity gap*. Teachers College Press.

Government of Canada. (1982). *Canadian Charter of Rights and Freedoms*. https://laws-lois.justice.gc.ca/eng/const/page-15.html

Government of India. (2009). *The Right of Children to Free and Compulsory Education Act*. https://www.india.gov.in/right-children-free-and-compulsory-education-act-2009-0

Government of South Africa. (1996). *South African Schools Act*. https://www.gov.za/documents/south-african-schools-act

Gray, M., & Lombard, A. (2022). Progress of the social service professions in South Africa's developmental social welfare system: Social work, and child and youth care work. International Journal of Social Welfare, 1–13. DOI: 10.1111/ijsw.12562

Greenberg, M. T., Weissberg, R. P., O'Brien, M. U., Zins, J. E., Fredericks, L., Resnik, H., & Elias, M. J. (2017). Enhancing school-based prevention and youth development through coordinated social, emotional, and academic learning. *The American Psychologist*, 58(6-7), 466–474. DOI: 10.1037/0003-066X.58.6-7.466 PMID: 12971193

Gregory, G. H., & Chapman, C. (2013). *Differentiated instructional strategies: One size doesn't fit all*. Corwin Press.

Groener, Z. (1999). Education policymaking in South Africa, education for liberation: Praxis challenges hegemony. In Groener, Z. (Ed.), *Comparative perspectives on language and literacy* (pp. 325–225). UNESCO.

Gu, J., Cavanagh, K., Baer, R., & Strauss, C. (2017). An empirical examination of the factor structure of compassion. *PLoS One*, 12(2), e0172471. DOI: 10.1371/journal.pone.0172471 PMID: 28212391

Gunderson, E. A., Ramirez, G., Levine, S. C., & Beilock, S. L. (2012). The role of parents and teachers in the development of gender-related math attitudes. *Sex Roles*, 66(3-4), 153–166. DOI: 10.1007/s11199-011-9996-2

Gyimah, E. K., Ackah-Jnr, F. R., & Yarquah, J. A. (2010). Determinants of differing teacher attitudes towards inclusive education practice. *Ghana Journal of Education: Issues and Practice*, 2(1), 84–97.

Hanachor, M. E., & Wordu, E. N. (2021). Achieving Sustainable Development Goal 4 in Nigeria: Problems and Prospects. *International Journal of Education, Learning and Development*, 9(2), 10–25.

Hand, S., Rice, L., & Greenlee, E. (2017). Exploring Teachers' and Students' Gender Role Bias and Students' Confidence in STEM Fields. *Social Psychology of Education*, 20(4), 929–945. DOI: 10.1007/s11218-017-9408-8

Hargreaves, A. (2000). Mixed Emotions: Teachers' Perceptions of Their Interactions with Students. *Teaching and Teacher Education*, 16(8), 811–826. DOI: 10.1016/S0742-051X(00)00028-7

Harris, S., Martin, M., & Diener, D. (2021). Circularity for circularity's sake? Scoping review of assessment methods for environmental performance in the circular economy. *Sustainable Production and Consumption*, 26, 172–186. DOI: 10.1016/j.spc.2020.09.018

Hartley, M., & Worsfold, K. (2018). *Education, disability and development: A comprehensive analysis*. Routledge.

Hartnack, A. (2019). Zero Dropout Schools Initiative – 2018 final qualitative evaluation report. Unpublished report.

Hattie, J. (2013). *Visible learning: A synthesis of over 800 meta-analyses relating to achievement*. Routledge.

Haug, S., Braveboy-Wagner, J., & Maihold, G. (2021). The 'Global South' in the study of world politics: Examining a meta category. *Third World Quarterly*, 42(9), 1923–1944. DOI: 10.1080/01436597.2021.1948831

Heacox, D. (2012). *Differentiating instruction in the regular classroom: How to reach and teach all learners*. Free Spirit Publishing.

Herek, G. (2012). Homosexuality and mental health. *Sexual Orientation: Science, Education, and Policy*. Retrieved from http://psychology.ucdavis.edu/rainbow/html/facts_mental_health.html#note1_text

Heritage, M. (2010). *Formative assessment: Making it happen in the classroom*. Corwin Press. DOI: 10.4135/9781452219493

Heyer, K. (2021). What is a human right to inclusive education? The promises and limitations of the CRPD's inclusion mandate. *Handbuch Inklusion International International Handbook of Inclusive Education*, 45. DOI: 10.2307/j.ctv1f70kvj.5

High Court of South Africa (Western Cape High Court, Cape Town). (2010). Western Cape Forum for Intellectual Disability v Government of the Republic of South Africa and Government of the Province of the Western Cape. High Court of South Africa (Western Cape High Court, Cape Town).

High Court of South Africa Gauteng Provincial Division. (2018). *South African National Council for the Blind v. Minister of Basic Education*. High Court of South Africa Gauteng Provincial Division.

Hill, C., Corbett, C., & St. Rose, A. (2010). Why So Few? Women in Science, Technology, Engineering, and Mathematics. American Association of University Women. Retrieved from https://eric.ed.gov/?id=ED509653

Hoffman, M. L. (2000). *Empathy and moral development: Implications for caring and justice*. Cambridge University Press. DOI: 10.1017/CBO9780511805851

Holmes, C. T. (2006). Low test scores + high retention rates = more dropouts. *Kappa Delta Pi Record*, 42(2), 56–58.

Hong, H., & Hamot, G. E. (2020). Differential effects of state testing policies and school characteristics on social studies educators' gate-keeping autonomy: A multilevel model. *Theory and Research in Social Education*, 48(1), 74–100. DOI: 10.1080/00933104.2019.1655508

Hosen, M., Ogbeibu, S., Giridharan, B., Cham, T.-H., Lim, W. M., & Paul, J. (2021). Individual motivation and social media influence on student knowledge sharing and learning performance: Evidence from an emerging economy. *Computers & Education*, 172, 104262. DOI: 10.1016/j.compedu.2021.104262

Howard, T. C. (2018). *Why Race and Culture Matter in Schools: Closing the Achievement Gap in America's Classrooms*. Teachers College Press.

https://www.worldometers.info/world-population/Nigeria. (2021).

Huang, R., Shen, Z., & Yao, X. (2024). How does industrial intelligence affect total-factor energy productivity? Evidence from China's manufacturing industry. *Computers & Industrial Engineering*, 188, 109901. Advance online publication. DOI: 10.1016/j.cie.2024.109901

Huffman, R. (2020). Thinking out of the box. *Journal of Public Child Welfare*, 14(1), 5–18. DOI: 10.1080/15548732.2020.1690186

Huijbregts, M., Spadafora, T., & Patel, L. (2023). Cash plus programmes for children and families in eastern and southern Africa: Examples from practice and lessons learnt. In *Handbook on Social Protection and Social Development in the Global South* (pp. 382–399). Edward Elgar Publishing. DOI: 10.4337/9781800378421.00038

Human Rights Watch. (2015). *Barriers to inclusive education for children with disabilities in South Africa*. Human Rights Watch.

Human Rights Watch. (2019). *South Africa: Children with disabilities denied education*. Human Rights Watch.

Husaini, D. C., Mphuthi, D. D., Chiroma, J. A., Abubakar, Y., & Adeleye, A. O. (2022). Nursing students' experiences of service-learning at community and hospital pharmacies in Belize: Pedagogical implications for nursing pharmacology. *PLoS One*, 17(11), e0276656. DOI: 10.1371/journal.pone.0276656 PMID: 36327317

Inclusive Education South Africa (IESA). (2022). *Annual Report 2022*. IESA.

Inclusive Education South Africa. (2019). *IESA EU Factsheet: What is inclusive education?* Inclusive Education South Africa.

Indiana Department of Education. (2012). Indiana's Science, Technology, Engineering and Mathematics (STEM) initiative plan. Available at www.doe.in.gov. Retrieved on 04/11/2021

Ishartono, N., Kholid, M. N., Arlinwibowo, J., & Afiyah, A. N. (2024). Integrating STEAM into flip flop model to improve students' understanding on composition of functions during online learning. *Infinity Journal*, 13(1), 45–60. DOI: 10.22460/infinity.v13i1.p45-60

Ismail, S. A. A., & Jarrah, A. M. (2019). Exploring Pre-Service Teachers' Perceptions of Their Pedagogical Preferences, Teaching Competence and Motivation. *International Journal of Instruction*, 12(1), 493–510. DOI: 10.29333/iji.2019.12132a

Itaborahy, L. (2012). State-sponsored homophobia: *A world survey of laws criminalising same-sex sexual acts between consenting adults.* Retrieved from http://www.irnweb.org/en/resources/chapters/view/state-sponsored-homophobia-aworld-survey-of-laws-criminalising-same-sex-sexual-acts-between-consentingadults

Jacob, O. N., Lawan, A., & Yusuf, M. (2021). Perception of Female Students on the Challenges Facing the Woman Education at the University Level. *Electronic Research Journal of Behavioural Sciences*, 4, 24–36. https://doi.org/http://erjbehaviouralsciences.com/

Jagadesh Kumar, M. (2020). National Education Policy: How does it Affect Higher Education in India? []. Taylor & Francis.]. *IETE Technical Review*, 37(4), 327–328. DOI: 10.1080/02564602.2020.1806491

Jamieson, L. (2013). *Child and youth care workers in South Africa: A technical brief.* AIDSTAR-Two Project, Management Sciences for Health.

Jennings, P. A., & Greenberg, M. T. (2009). The Prosocial Classroom: Teacher Social and Emotional Competence in Relation to Student and Classroom Outcomes. *Review of Educational Research*, 79(1), 491–525. DOI: 10.3102/0034654308325693

Jimerson, S. R., Pletcher, S. M. W., Graydon, K., Schnurr, B. L., Nickerson, A. B., & Kundert, D. K. (2006). Beyond grade retention and social promotion: Promoting the social and academic competence of students. *Psychology in the Schools*, 43(1), 85–97. DOI: 10.1002/pits.20132

Johnson, D. W., & Johnson, R. T. (2009). An educational psychology success story: Social interdependence theory and cooperative learning. *Educational Researcher*, 38(5), 365–379. DOI: 10.3102/0013189X09339057

Jones, S. M. (2013). Social and emotional learning: A critical appraisal. *Teachers College Record*, 115(8), 2114–2143.

Jurasaite-O'Keefe, E. (2021). *Individual, School, and National Factors Impacting Teachers' Workplace Learning: Discourses of Informal Learning in North America and Lithuania*. Routledge. DOI: 10.4324/9780367816605

Kalaiselvi, D., Ramaratnam, M. S., Kokila, S., Sarkar, R., Anandakumar, S., & Boopathi, S. (2024). Future Developments of Higher Education on Social Psychology: Innovation and Changes. In *Advances in Human and Social Aspects of Technology* (pp. 146–169). IGI Global. DOI: 10.4018/979-8-3693-2569-8.ch008

Kallio, T. J., Kallio, K.-M., Huusko, M., Pyykkö, R., & Kivistö, J. (2022). Balancing between accountability and autonomy: The impact and relevance of public steering mechanisms within higher education. *Journal of Public Budgeting, Accounting & Financial Management*, 34(6), 46–68. DOI: 10.1108/JPBAFM-10-2020-0177

Kalyan, B. S., Kaur, H., Pachori, K., & Singh, B. (2022). An efficient design of D flip flop in quantum-dot cellular automata (QCA) for sequential circuits. In *VLSI architecture for signal, speech, and image processing* (pp. 253–272). Apple Academic Press New York, USA.

Kamei-Hannan, C., Howe, J., Herrera, R., & Erin, J. (2012). Perceptions of teachers of students with visual impairments regarding assistive technology: A follow-up study to a university course. *Journal of Visual Impairment & Blindness*, 106(10), 666–678. DOI: 10.1177/0145482X1210601011

Kang, H. Y., & Kim, H. R. (2021). Impact of blended learning on learning outcomes in the public healthcare education course: A review of flipped classroom with team-based learning. *BMC Medical Education*, 21(1), 1–8. DOI: 10.1186/s12909-021-02508-y PMID: 33509176

Kang, J., & Keinonen, T. (2017). The Effect of Inquiry-Based Learning Experiences on Adolescents' Science Related Career Aspiration in the Finnish Context. *International Journal of Science Education*, 39(12), 1669–1689. DOI: 10.1080/09500693.2017.1350790

Kannan, V., Kuromiya, H., Gouripeddi, S. P., Majumdar, R., Madathil Warriem, J., & Ogata, H. (2020). Flip & Pair–a strategy to augment a blended course with active-learning components: Effects on engagement and learning. *Smart Learning Environments*, 7(1), 1–23. DOI: 10.1186/s40561-020-00138-3

Katz, D., Blumler, J. G., & Gurevitch, M. (2015). Uses and Gratifications Research. *Public Opinion Quarterly*, 38(4), 509–523. DOI: 10.1086/268109

Kefallinou, A., Symeonidou, S., & Meijer, C. J. W. (2020). Understanding the value of inclusive education and its implementation: A review of the literature. *Prospects*, 49(3-4), 135–152. DOI: 10.1007/s11125-020-09500-2

Kelly, O., Buckley, K., Lieberman, L. J., & Arndt, K. (2022). Universal Design for Learning-A framework for inclusion in Outdoor Learning. *Journal of Outdoor and Environmental Education*, 25(1), 75–89. DOI: 10.1007/s42322-022-00096-z

Kent, L. (2021). The Heroines STEM: Ten Women in Science You Should Know. Space+Science: A CNN Report. Available on https://edition.cnn.com/2020/01/27/world/women-in-science-you-should-know-scn/index.html

Kevser, H. (2021). The effects of the flipped classroom on deep learning strategies and engagement at the undergraduate level. *Participatory Educational Research*, 8(1), 379–394. DOI: 10.17275/per.21.22.8.1

Khumalo, S., & Hodgson, T. F. (2017). The right to basic education for learners with disabilities. In Basic Education Rights Handbook – Education Rights in South Africa (Chapter 5). https://section27.org.za/wp-content/uploads/2017/02/Chapter-5.pdf

Kirkland, H. N. (2023). STEM Educators' Perceptions of Gender Bias and the Contributing Factors that Persist for Women in STEM Education. (Doctoral dissertation). Retrieved from https://scholarcommons.sc.edu/etd/7494

Kirsten, B. (2019) How Far have Women in STEM Come in the Last 100 Years. https://www.womeninstem.co.uk/engineering-maths/women-stem-come-last-years

Koch, K. (2017). Stay in the box! embedded assistive technology improves access for students with disabilities. *Education Sciences*, 7(4), 82. DOI: 10.3390/educsci7040082

Krueger, M. (2019). Central themes in child and youth care. CYC-Net. https://www.cyc-net.org/cyc-online/cycol-0100-krueger.html

Kumar, D., Soni, G., Jabeen, F., Kumar Tiwari, N., Sariyer, G., & Ramtiyal, B. (2024). A hybrid Bayesian approach for assessment of industry 4.0 technologies towards achieving decarbonization in manufacturing industry. *Computers & Industrial Engineering*, 190, 110057. Advance online publication. DOI: 10.1016/j.cie.2024.110057

Lai, H.-M., Hsieh, P.-J., Uden, L., & Yang, C.-H. (2021). A multilevel investigation of factors influencing university students' behavioral engagement in flipped classrooms. *Computers & Education*, 175, 104318. DOI: 10.1016/j.compedu.2021.104318

Law, C. M., Jacko, J. A., Yi, J. S., & Choi, Y. S. (2020a). Developing new heuristics for evaluating universal design standards and guidelines. In *Contemporary Ergonomics 2006* (pp. 404–408). Taylor & Francis. DOI: 10.1201/9781003072072-96

Lawrence, A. W., Ihebuzor, N., & Lawrence, D. O. (2020). *Some Challenges Militating against Developing Countries Achieving SDG 4 on Targets: Nigeria as Case Study. Modern Economy, 11, 1307-1328*. Available on., DOI: 10.4236/me.2020.117093

Lee, J.-A., Kang, M. O., & Park, B. J. (2019). Factors influencing choosing teaching as a career: South Korean preservice teachers. *Asia Pacific Education Review*, 20(3), 467–488. DOI: 10.1007/s12564-019-09579-z

Lee, S. W. (2019). The impact of a pedagogy course on the teaching beliefs of inexperienced graduate teaching assistants. *CBE Life Sciences Education*, 18(1), ar5. DOI: 10.1187/cbe.18-07-0137 PMID: 30707641

Lee, S. W., & Lee, E. A. (2020). Teacher qualifcation matters: The Association between Cumulative Teacher Qualification and Students' Educational Attainment. *International Journal of Educational Development*, 77, 102218. DOI: 10.1016/j.ijedudev.2020.102218

Legislative Services Branch. (1982). *Constitution Acts, 1867 to 1982*. Justice.gc.ca. https://laws-lois.justice.gc.ca/eng/Const/page-15.html

Lennert Da Silva, A. L. (2022). Comparing teacher autonomy in different models of educational governance. *Nordic Journal of Studies in Educational Policy*, 8(2), 103–118. DOI: 10.1080/20020317.2021.1965372

Libby, P. (2021). The changing landscape of atherosclerosis. *Nature*, 592(7855), 524–533. DOI: 10.1038/s41586-021-03392-8 PMID: 33883728

Liu, B., Ash, J., Goel, S., Krishnamurthy, A., & Zhang, C. (2024a). Exposing attention glitches with flip-flop language modeling. *Advances in Neural Information Processing Systems*, •••, 36.

Li, Y., & Flowerdew, J. (2020). Teaching English for Research Publication Purposes (ERPP): A review of language teachers' pedagogical initiatives. *English for Specific Purposes*, 59, 29–41. DOI: 10.1016/j.esp.2020.03.002

Loreman, T. (2017). *Pedagogy for inclusive education*. Oxford Research Encyclopedia of Education., DOI: 10.1093/acrefore/9780190264093.013.148

Loreman, T. (2022). *Inclusive Education: Supporting Diversity in the Classroom* (3rd ed.). SAGE Publications.

Loughran, J. (2019). Pedagogical reasoning: The foundation of the professional knowledge of teaching. *Teachers and Teaching*, 25(5), 523–535. DOI: 10.1080/13540602.2019.1633294

Lv, B., Wang, J., Zheng, Y., Peng, X., & Ping, X. (2022). Gender Differences in High School Students' STEM Career Expectations: An Analysis Based on Multi-Group Structural Equation Model. *Journal of Research in Science Teaching*, 59(10), 1739–1764. Advance online publication. DOI: 10.1002/tea.21772

Mahwai, L. P., & Ross, E. (2023). Life orientation teachers' experiences of providing psychosocial support to high school learners in the Johannesburg West district. *South African Journal of Education*, 43(4), 2199. Advance online publication. DOI: 10.15700//saje.v43n4a2199

Makarova, E., Aeschlimann, B., & Herzog, W. (2019). The Gender Gap in STEM Fields: The Impact of the Gender Stereotype of Mathematics and Science on Secondary Students' Career Aspirations. *Frontiers in Education*, 4, 60. DOI: 10.3389/feduc.2019.00060

Makoelle, T. M. (2019). Teacher empathy: a prerequisite for an inclusive classroom. In Peters, M. A. (Ed.), *Encyclopedia of Teacher Education* (pp. 1–6). Springer Nature Singapore Pte Ltd. DOI: 10.1007/978-981-13-1179-6_43-1

Mandasari, B., & Wahyudin, A. Y. (2021). Flipped classroom learning model: Implementation and its impact on EFL learners' satisfaction on grammar class. *Ethical Lingua: Journal of Language Teaching and Literature*, 8(1), 150–158.

Mandel, H., & Semyonov, M. (2014). Gender Pay Gap and Employment Sector: Sources of Earnings Disparities in the United States, 1970 – 2010. *Demography*, 51(5), 1597–1618. DOI: 10.1007/s13524-014-0320-y PMID: 25149647

Mann, A., & DiPrete, T. A. (2013). Trends in Gender Segregation in the Choice of Science and Engineering Majors. *Social Science Research*, 42(6), 1519–1541. DOI: 10.1016/j.ssresearch.2013.07.002 PMID: 24090849

Maphanga, Canny. Transgender activistAreMphela foundmurdered,boyfriendquestioned, Mavhandu-Mudzusi, A. H. (2016). Experiences of lesbian, gay, bisexual, transgender and intersex students regarding sports participation in a South African rural-based university. *S.A. Journal for Research in Sport Physical Education and Recreation*, 38(2), 111–120.

Marchant, N. (2021). The Gender Gap in Science and Technology, in Numbers. New Policies Needed to End Gender Disparity in STEM Sector/World Economic Forum.

Martí, J., & Csajka, F. S. (2004). Transition path sampling study of flip-flop transitions in model lipid bilayer membranes. *Physical Review. E*, 69(6), 061918. DOI: 10.1103/PhysRevE.69.061918 PMID: 15244628

Master, A., Cheryan, S., & Meltzoff, A. N. (2016). Computing Whether she Belongs: Stereotypes Undermine Girls' Interest and Sense of Belonging in Computer Science. *Journal of Educational Psychology*, 108(3), 424–437. DOI: 10.1037/edu0000061

Masudin, I., Tsamarah, N., Restuputri, D. P., Trireksani, T., & Djajadikerta, H. G. (2024). The impact of safety climate on human-technology interaction and sustainable development: Evidence from Indonesian oil and gas industry. *Journal of Cleaner Production*, 434, 140211. Advance online publication. DOI: 10.1016/j.jclepro.2023.140211

Mavropoulou, S., Mann, G., & Carrington, S. (2021). The divide between inclusive education policy and practice in Australia and the way forward. *Journal of Policy and Practice in Intellectual Disabilities*, 18(1), 44–52. DOI: 10.1111/jppi.12373

Ma, Y., & Savas, G. (2014). Which is more Consequential: Field of Study or Institutional Selectivity? *Review of Higher Education*, 37(2), 221–247. DOI: 10.1353/rhe.2014.0001

McCully, C. (2001) Child and youth care work in the school environment. CYC-Net. https://cyc-net.org/cyc-online/cycol-0101-schools.html

McDonald, H. (2016). *Developmental evaluation: A tool to support innovation. 2016*. New Zealand Council for Educational Research., DOI: 10.18296/em.0012

McKenzie, J., Vergunst, R., Samuels, C., & Henkeman, T. (2020). The education of children with disabilities risks falling by the wayside. Available: https://www.news.uct.ac.za/campus/communications/updates/covid-19/sep-dec2020/-article/2020-05-28-the-education-of-children-with-disabilities-risks-falling-by-the-wayside[26 March 2024]

McKenzie, J. A., & Dalton, E. M. (2020). Universal design for learning in inclusive education policy in South Africa. *African Journal of Disability*, 9, 9. DOI: 10.4102/ajod.v9i0.776 PMID: 33392062

McLeskey, J., Rosenberg, M. S., & Westing, D. L. (2017). *Inclusion: Effective practices for all students* (3rd ed.). Pearson.

McNeill, F., & Wei, L. (2023). Encouraging Young Women into STEM Careers: A Study Comparing Career Intention of Female STEM Students in China and Scotland. *Journal for STEM Education Research*. Advance online publication. DOI: 10.1007/s41979-023-00114-9

McNutt, L., & Craddock, G. (2021a). Embracing universal design for transformative learning. *Universal Design 2021: From Special to Mainstream Solutions, 282*, 176.

McNutt, L., & Craddock, G. (2021b). Embracing universal design for transformative learning. *Universal Design 2021: From Special to Mainstream Solutions, 282*, 176.

Meyers, S., Rowell, K., Wells, M., & Smith, B. C. (2019). Teacher empathy: A model of empathy for teaching for student success. *College Teaching*, 67(3), 160–168. DOI: 10.1080/87567555.2019.1579699

Meyliana, Sablan, B., Surjandy, & Hidayanto, A. N. (2021). Flipped learning effect on classroom engagement and outcomes in university information systems class. *Education and Information Technologies*, ●●●, 1–19.

Michael, J. (2005). Life-space supervision in child and youth care practice. In Garfat, T., & Gannon, B. (Eds.), *Aspects of Child and youth care practice in the South African context*. Pretext.

Ministry of Education [MoE]. (2015). *Inclusive education policy.* Government of Ghana. https://www.sapghana.com/data/documents/Inclusive-Education-Policy-official-document.pdf

Ministry of Education. (2017). *National teachers' standards for Ghana guidelines*. MoE. https://ntc.gov.gh/wp-content/uploads/2021/12/NTS.pdf

Ministry of Education. (2018). *National pre-tertiary education curriculum framework (NPECF).* MoE. https://nacca.gov.gh/wp-content/uploads/2019/04/National-Pre-tertiary-Education-Curriculum-Framework -final.pdf

Ministry of Education. (2020). *Education sector performance report*. Ghana Ministry of Education.

Mitchell, D. (2017). *Diversities in education: Effective ways to reach all learners*. Routledge.

Mogale, M. L., & Modipane, M. C. (2021). The implementation of the progression policy in secondary schools of the Limpopo province in South Africa. *South African Journal of Education*, 41(1), 1853. DOI: 10.15700/saje.v41n1a1853

Mohamed Hashim, M. A., Tlemsani, I., & Matthews, R. (2021). Higher education strategy in digital transformation. *Education and Information Technologies*, ●●●, 1–25. PMID: 34539217

Mohammed, A. S., & Hlalele, D. (2023). Shaping teachers' enactment of inclusion through understanding in Ghana: A sense-making perspective. *Education 3-13*, 1–15. Doi:DOI: 10.1080/03004279.2023.2206838

Mohanty, A., Venkateswaran, N., Ranjit, P., Tripathi, M. A., & Boopathi, S. (2023). Innovative Strategy for Profitable Automobile Industries: Working Capital Management. In *Handbook of Research on Designing Sustainable Supply Chains to Achieve a Circular Economy* (pp. 412–428). IGI Global.

Mohtar, L. E., Halim, L., Rahman, N. A., Maat, S. M., & Osman, K. (2019). A Model of Interest in STEM Careers among Secondary School Students. *Journal of Baltic Science Education*, 18(3), 404–416. DOI: 10.33225/jbse/19.18.404

Moirano, R., Sánchez, M. A., & Štěpánek, L. (2020). Creative interdisciplinary collaboration: A systematic literature review. *Thinking Skills and Creativity*, 35, 100626. DOI: 10.1016/j.tsc.2019.100626

Morin, L., & Li, H. (1989). Design of synchronisers: A review. *IEE Proceedings. Part E. Computers and Digital Techniques*, 136(6), 557–564. DOI: 10.1049/ip-e.1989.0076

Morse, S. R. (2020). *A Phenomenological Study on Career Readiness among Graduates from College and Career Academy High Schools.*

Moss-Racusin, C. A., Molenda, A. K., & Cramer, C. R. (2015). Can Evidence Impact Attitudes? Public Reactions to Evidence of Gender Bias in STEM Fields. *Psychology of Women Quarterly*, 39(2), 194–209. DOI: 10.1177/0361684314565777

Mouza, C., Huí, Y., Pan, Y., Ozden, S., & Pollock, L. (2017). Resetting educational technology coursework for pre-service teachers: A computational thinking approach to the development of technological pedagogical content knowledge (tpack). *Australasian Journal of Educational Technology*, 33(3). Advance online publication. DOI: 10.14742/ajet.3521

Msibi, T. (2012). "I'm used to it now": Experiences of homophobia among queer youth in South African township schools. *Gender and Education*, 24(5), 515–533. DOI: 10.1080/09540253.2011.645021

Mukhwana, A. M., Abuya, T., Matanda, D., Omumbo, J., & Mabuka, J. (2020). Factors which Contribute to or Inhibit Women in Science, Technology, Engineering, and Mathematics in Africa. The African Academy of Science (AAS, Report). Nairobi. Available on https://uis.unesco.org/en/topic/women-science

Mulders, M., Buchner, J., & Kerres, M. (2020). A framework for the use of immersive virtual reality in learning environments. [iJET]. *International Journal of Emerging Technologies in Learning*, 15(24), 208–224. DOI: 10.3991/ijet.v15i24.16615

Mutisya, P. M., & Kanaga, M. (2022). Inclusive education in Kenya: Policy, practice, and progress. *East African Journal of Education Research*, 4(2), 78–92.

Narkhede, G., Pasi, B., Rajhans, N., & Kulkarni, A. (2023). Industry 5.0 and the future of sustainable manufacturing: A systematic literature review. In *Business Strategy and Development* (Vol. 6, Issue 4, pp. 704–723). John Wiley and Sons Inc. DOI: 10.1002/bsd2.272

Narkhede, G. B., Pasi, B. N., Rajhans, N., & Kulkarni, A. (2024). Industry 5.0 and sustainable manufacturing: A systematic literature review. *Benchmarking*. Advance online publication. DOI: 10.1108/BIJ-03-2023-0196

National Association of Child Care Workers. (2022). Output 1: Analysis of the programme and local needs and opportunities in the Lesedi and Letsatsi Solar Park Trust catchment areas. Unpublished research report, November 2022.

National Association of Child Care Workers. (2024). Experiences of learning barriers in education: Reflections of learners in Gauteng schools in the Isibindi Ezikoleni Programme. Unpublished research report, February 2024.

National Association of Child Care Workers. (2024). Isibindi Ezikoleni matric results: class of 2023

National Center on Universal Design for Learning. (n.d.). *About UDL*. http://www.udlcenter.org/aboutudl

National Centre for Promotion of Employment for Disabled People. (n.d.). *About NCPEDP*. https://www.ncpedp.org/about-ncpedp

National Science Board. (2022). Science and engineering indicators 2022. *National Science Foundation (NSB 2022-01)*. https://www.nsf.gov/nsb/sei/

National Science Foundation (2014). Table 2-17 Earned bachelor's degrees, by sex and field: 2000-2011

Navarro-Mateu, D., Franco-Ochoa, J., Valero-Moreno, S., & Prado-Gascó, V. (2019). To be or not to be an inclusive teacher: Are empathy and social dominance relevant factors to positive attitudes towards inclusive education? *PLoS One*, 14(12), e0225993. DOI: 10.1371/journal.pone.0225993 PMID: 31821354

Naveen, H. (2022). NEP, 2020: General Education Embedded with Skill and Vocational Education. *International Journal of Scientific Research in Science, Engineering and Technology*, 9(01), 65–75.

Ndirika, M. C., & Agommuoh, P. C. (2017). Investigating Factors Influencing Girls Participation in Science and Technology Education in Nigeria. *IOSR Journal of Research & Method in Education (IOSR-JRME)*, 7, 3, I, 50-54. www.iosrjournals.org

news24. 09 January 2020. Available: https://www.news24.com/news24/southafrica/news/transgender-activist-nare-mphelafound-murdered-boyfriend-questioned-20200109

Ngcobo, E. J. (2006). *How do teachers position themselves within socially constructed discourses of disability and inclusion? A case study at a semi-rural township school in KwaZulu-Natal*. [A dissertation submitted in partial fulfilment of the requirements for the degree of Master of Education, University of KwaZulu-Natal]. University of KwaZulu-Natal Research Space. Available: https://researchspace.ukzn.ac.za/jspui/bitstream/10413/2094/1/Ngcobo_Edward_J_2006.pdf[27 March 2024].

Niemi, H., Toom, A., & Kallioniemi, A. (Eds.). (2012). *The miracle of education: The principles and practices of teaching and learning in Finnish schools*. Sense Publishers. DOI: 10.1007/978-94-6091-811-7

Niesche, R., Eacott, S., Keddie, A., Gobby, B., MacDonald, K., Wilkinson, J., & Blackmore, J. (2023). Principals' perceptions of school autonomy and educational leadership. *Educational Management Administration & Leadership*, 51(6), 1260–1277. DOI: 10.1177/17411432211034174

Nixon, R. S., Smith, L. K., & Sudweeks, R. R. (2019). Elementary teachers' science subject matter knowledge across the teacher career cycle. *Journal of Research in Science Teaching*, 56(6), 707–731. DOI: 10.1002/tea.21524

Nugent, G., Barker, B., Welch, G., Grandgenett, N., Wu, C., & Nelson, C. (2015). A Model of Factors Contributing to STEM Learning and Career Orientation. *International Journal of Science Education*, 37(7), 1067–1088. DOI: 10.1080/09500693.2015.1017863

O'Neill, J. L. (2021). Accessibility for all abilities: How universal design, universal design for learning, and inclusive design combat inaccessibility and ableism. *Journal of Open Access to Law*, 9, 1.

Ödalen, J., Brommesson, D., Erlingsson, G. Ó., Schaffer, J. K., & Fogelgren, M. (2019). Teaching university teachers to become better teachers: The effects of pedagogical training courses at six Swedish universities. *Higher Education Research & Development*, 38(2), 339–353. DOI: 10.1080/07294360.2018.1512955

OECD. (2019). *Equity in education: Breaking down barriers to social mobility*. OECD Publishing. https://www.oecd.org/education/equity-in-education-9789264073234-en.htm

Ogata, B., Stelovsky, J., & Ogawa, M.-B. C. (2020). Flip-Flop Quizzes: A Case Study Analysis to Inform the Design of Augmented Cognition Applications. *Augmented Cognition. Human Cognition and Behavior: 14th International Conference, AC 2020, Held as Part of the 22nd HCI International Conference, HCII 2020, Copenhagen, Denmark, July 19–24, 2020. Proceedings*, 22(Part II), 106–117.

Ogundare, S. A., & Abdullahi, A. Z. (2021). Assessment of Female Students' Enrollment in Sciences and Mathematics in Federal University Kashere, Gombe State. Zamfara. *International Journal of Education*, 1(1), 217–225. www.zijedufugusau.com

Ojo, T. A., & Mathabathe, R. (2021). An investigation into the effectiveness of the Curriculum and Assessment Policy Statement (CAPS) in South African schools. *International Journal of Integrating Technology in Education*, 10(2), 23–38. DOI: 10.5121/ijite.2021.10203

Okolie, U. C., Igwe, P. A., Mong, I. K., Nwosu, H. E., Kanu, C., & Ojemuyide, C. C. (2022). Enhancing students' critical thinking skills through engagement with innovative pedagogical practices in Global South. *Higher Education Research & Development*, 41(4), 1184–1198. DOI: 10.1080/07294360.2021.1896482

Okorafor, A. O., Woyengidubamo, K., & Okorafor, E. C. (2015). Women Participation in Science, Technology, Engineering and Mathematics in Nigeria: Challenges and Way Forward. *NAM Institute of the Empowerment of Women (NIEW). Journal*, 7, 99–112.

Okwelle, C. P., & Alalibo, J. T. (2017). Motivational Factors and Future Expectations that Influence the Choice of Engineering Programmes by Female Undergraduate Students in Nigeria. *Journal of Scientific and Engineering Research*, 4(11), 164–172. www.jsaer.com

Olmedo-Torre, N., Sanchez Carracedo, F., Salan Ballesteros, M. N., Lopez, D., Perez-Poch, A., & Lopez-Beltran, M. (2018). Do Female Motives for Enrolling Vary according to STEM Profile? *IEEE Transactions on Education*, 61(4), 289–297. DOI: 10.1109/TE.2018.2820643

Olowe, M., & Olowe, N. E. (2024). Counselling approaches and educational support for business education in students with visual and hearing impairments: Enhancing accessibility and learning outcomes. *British Journal of Multidisciplinary and Advanced Studies*, 5(2), 24–38. DOI: 10.37745/bjmas.2022.0466

Omenihu, I. (2021). Influence of Students' Factors on the Enrollment of Female Students in Science Oriented Courses in Nigeria Higher Institutions. *International Journal of Innovative Social & Science Education Research*, 9(2), 80–87.

Onyekwelu, B. A. (2019). Comparative Empirical Analysis of Female University Enrolment in STEM Courses in the Geopolitical Zones in Nigeria. *Modern Education and Computer Science*, 1, 24–32. DOI: 10.5815/ijmecs.2019.01.03

Opoku, M. P., Rayner, C. S., Pedersen, S. J., & Cuskelly, M. (2021). Mapping the evidence-based research on Ghana's inclusive education to policy and practices: A scoping review. *International Journal of Inclusive Education*, 25(10), 1157–1173. DOI: 10.1080/13603116.2019.1600055

Organization for Economic Co-operation and Development. (OECD, 2015). The ABC of Gender Equality in Education: Aptitude, Behaviour, Confidence. *Paris, Organization for Economic Co-operation and Development.* https://www.oecd-ilibrary.org/education/the-abc-of-gender-equality-in-education_9789264229945-e

Özdemir, S. (2017). Basic technology competencies, attitude towards computer assisted education and usage of technologies in turkish lesson: A correlation. *International Education Studies*, 10(4), 160. DOI: 10.5539/ies.v10n4p160

Ozuna, E., & Steinhoff, L. (2024). "Look me in the eye, customer": How do face-to-face interactions in peer-to-peer sharing economy services affect customers' misbehavior concealment intentions? *Journal of Business Research*, 177, 114582. DOI: 10.1016/j.jbusres.2024.114582

Pacheco, D. A. de J., Rampasso, I. S., Michels, G. S., Ali, S. M., & Hunt, J. D. (2024). From linear to circular economy: The role of BS 8001:2017 for green transition in small business in developing economies. *Journal of Cleaner Production*, 439, 140787. Advance online publication. DOI: 10.1016/j.jclepro.2024.140787

Palaniappan, M., Tirlangi, S., Mohamed, M. J. S., Moorthy, R. S., Valeti, S. V., & Boopathi, S. (2023). Fused Deposition Modelling of Polylactic Acid (PLA)-Based Polymer Composites: A Case Study. In *Development, Properties, and Industrial Applications of 3D Printed Polymer Composites* (pp. 66–85). IGI Global.

Pantic, K., Clarke-Midura, J., Poole, F., Roller, J., & Allan, V. (2018). Drawing a Computer Scientist: Stereotypical Representations or Lack of Awareness? *Computer Science Education*, 28(3), 232–254. DOI: 10.1080/08993408.2018.1533780

Parliament of the Republic of South Africa. (2024). Media Statement: Basic Education Portfolio Committee notes progress in moving Early Childhood Development to Basic Education. Available: https://pmg.org.za/files/230606pcbasic_Media_Statement.docx [25 March 2024]

Parmaxi, A. (2023). Virtual reality in language learning: A systematic review and implications for research and practice. *Interactive Learning Environments*, 31(1), 172–184. DOI: 10.1080/10494820.2020.1765392

Pasi, B. N., Mahajan, S. K., & Rane, S. B. (2020a). Enabling Technologies and Current Research Scenario of Industry 4.0: A Systematic Review. *Lecture Notes in Mechanical Engineering*, 265–273. DOI: 10.1007/978-981-15-4485-9_28

Pasi, B. N., Mahajan, S. K., & Rane, S. B. (n.d.). REDESIGNING OF SMART MANUFACTURING SYSTEM BASED ON IoT: PERSPECTIVE OF DISRUPTIVE INNOVATIONS OF INDUSTRY 4.0 PARADIGM. In www.tjprc.org*SCOPUS Indexed Journal editor@tjprc.org*. www.tjprc.org

Pasi, B. N., Shinde, V. V., & Chavan, M. R. (2019). Teacher's perception towards their role in Course Level Project-Based Learning environment. In *Journal of Engineering Education Transformations, Special Issue* (Issue 1).

Pasi, B. N., Dongare, P. V., & Rawat, S. J. (2022). Prioritization of risks associated with the implementation of project-based learning concept in engineering institutions. *Higher Education. Skills and Work-Based Learning*, 12(6), 1070–1083. DOI: 10.1108/HESWBL-05-2022-0117

Pasi, B. N., Dongare, P. V., Rawat, S. J., Oza, A. D., Padheriya, H., Gupta, M., Kumar, S., & Kumar, M. (2023). Design and modeling to identify a defective workpiece in manufacturing process: An industry 4.0 perspective. *International Journal on Interactive Design and Manufacturing*. Advance online publication. DOI: 10.1007/s12008-023-01544-w

Pasi, B. N., Mahajan, S. K., & Rane, S. B. (2020b). The current sustainability scenario of Industry 4.0 enabling technologies in Indian manufacturing industries. *International Journal of Productivity and Performance Management*, 70(5), 1017–1048. DOI: 10.1108/IJPPM-04-2020-0196

Pasi, B. N., Mahajan, S. K., & Rane, S. B. (2022a). Development of innovation ecosystem framework for successful adoption of industry 4.0 enabling technologies in Indian manufacturing industries. *Journal of Science and Technology Policy Management*, 13(1), 154–185. DOI: 10.1108/JSTPM-10-2020-0148

Pasi, B. N., Mahajan, S. K., & Rane, S. B. (2023). Strategies for risk management in adopting Industry 4.0 concept in manufacturing industries. *Journal of Science and Technology Policy Management*, 14(3), 563–591. DOI: 10.1108/JSTPM-04-2021-0057

Paul, A., & Thilagham, K. KG, J.-, Reddy, P. R., Sathyamurthy, R., & Boopathi, S. (2024). Multi-criteria Optimization on Friction Stir Welding of Aluminum Composite (AA5052-H32/B4C) using Titanium Nitride Coated Tool. *Engineering Research Express*.

Penalva, J. (2022). Innovation and leadership as design: A methodology to lead and exceed an ecological approach in higher education. *Journal of the Knowledge Economy*, 13(1), 430–446. DOI: 10.1007/s13132-021-00764-3

Peters, S. J., Jordan, K., Adamek, M., Brown, M., Calhoun, C., Caldwell, J., & Wilcox, K. (2010). Engaging community partners to develop a comprehensive service learning program. *Journal of Community Practice*, 18(4), 434–450.

Phelan, P. (2015). *The Long and Short of it Child and Youth Care*. CYC-Net Press.

Pickett, K. E., Wilkinson, R. G., & Wilkinson, R. G. (2009). Income inequality and social dysfunction. *Annual Review of Sociology*, 35(1), 493–511. DOI: 10.1146/annurev-soc-070308-115926

Pinna, F., Garau, C., Maltinti, F., & Coni, M. (2020). Beyond architectural barriers: Building a bridge between disability and universal design. *International Conference on Computational Science and Its Applications*, 706–721. DOI: 10.1007/978-3-030-58820-5_51

Pirie, G. H. (1992). Rolling segregation into apartheid: South African Railways, 1948-53. [26 March 2024]. *Journal of Contemporary History*, 27(4), 671–693. DOI: 10.1177/002200949202700407

Pistolesi, F., Baldassini, M., & Lazzerini, B. (2024). A human-centric system combining smartwatch and LiDAR data to assess the risk of musculoskeletal disorders and improve ergonomics of Industry 5.0 manufacturing workers. *Computers in Industry*, 155, 104042. Advance online publication. DOI: 10.1016/j.compind.2023.104042

Plucker, J. A., Beghetto, R. A., & Dow, G. T. (2015). Why isn't creativity more important to educational psychologists? Potentials, pitfalls, and future directions in creativity research. *Educational Psychologist*, 50(3), 148–159.

Polity. (2020). South Africa's National LGBTI Strategy. Retrieved from Polity

Ponsamy, J. (2021). An exploration of the roles of child and youth care workers at schools within the Isibindi Ezikoleni programme [Master's thesis]. Durban University of Technology.

Pourdavood, R., & Song, X. (2021). Engaging pre-service and in-service teachers in online mathematics teaching and learning: Problems and possibilities. *International Journal of Learning Teaching and Educational Research*, 20(11), 96–114. DOI: 10.26803/ijlter.20.11.6

Prabhuswamy, M., Tripathi, R., Vijayakumar, M., Thulasimani, T., Sundharesalingam, P., & Sampath, B. (2024). A Study on the Complex Nature of Higher Education Leadership: An Innovative Approach. In *Challenges of Globalization and Inclusivity in Academic Research* (pp. 202–223). IGI Global. DOI: 10.4018/979-8-3693-1371-8.ch013

Professional Board for Child and Youth Care Work. (2021). *Concept note: The current crisis in the child and youth care work profession*. SACSSP.

Raduan, N. A., & Na, S.-I. (2020). An integrative review of the models for teacher expertise and career development. *European Journal of Teacher Education*, 43(3), 428–451. DOI: 10.1080/02619768.2020.1728740

Rahamathunnisa, U., Subhashini, P., Aancy, H. M., Meenakshi, S., & Boopathi, S. (2023). Solutions for Software Requirement Risks Using Artificial Intelligence Techniques. In *Handbook of Research on Data Science and Cybersecurity Innovations in Industry 4.0 Technologies* (pp. 45–64). IGI Global.

Rajabalee, Y. B., & Santally, M. I. (2021). Learner satisfaction, engagement and performances in an online module: Implications for institutional e-learning policy. *Education and Information Technologies*, 26(3), 2623–2656. DOI: 10.1007/s10639-020-10375-1 PMID: 33199971

Rastogi, S., Sharma, V., Bharti, P. S., Rani, K., Modi, G. P., Nikolajeff, F., & Kumar, S. (2021). The evolving landscape of exosomes in neurodegenerative diseases: Exosomes characteristics and a promising role in early diagnosis. *International Journal of Molecular Sciences*, 22(1), 440. DOI: 10.3390/ijms22010440 PMID: 33406804

Ravasz, R., Hudec, A., Maljar, D., Ondica, R., & Stopjakova, V. (2022). Introduction to Teaching the Digital Electronics Design using FPGA. *2022 20th International Conference on Emerging eLearning Technologies and Applications (ICETA)*, 549–554.

Ravisankar, A., Sampath, B., & Asif, M. M. (2023). Economic Studies on Automobile Management: Working Capital and Investment Analysis. In *Multidisciplinary Approaches to Organizational Governance During Health Crises* (pp. 169–198). IGI Global.

Reddy, P., Reddy, E., Chand, V., Paea, S., & Prasad, A. (2021). Assistive technologies: Saviour of mathematics in higher education. *Frontiers in Applied Mathematics and Statistics*, 6, 619725. Advance online publication. DOI: 10.3389/fams.2020.619725

Republic of South Africa. (1996a). *Constitution of the Republic of South Africa, 1996*. Government Printers.

Republic of South Africa. (1996b). *South African Schools Act 84 of 1996*. Government Printers.

Republic of South Africa. (2000). *South African Council for Educators Act 31 of 2000*. Government Printers.

Revathi, S., Babu, M., Rajkumar, N., Meti, V. K. V., Kandavalli, S. R., & Boopathi, S. (2024). Unleashing the Future Potential of 4D Printing: Exploring Applications in Wearable Technology, Robotics, Energy, Transportation, and Fashion. In *Human-Centered Approaches in Industry 5.0: Human-Machine Interaction, Virtual Reality Training, and Customer Sentiment Analysis* (pp. 131–153). IGI Global.

Reygan, F. (2019). Challenging homophobia and heteronormativity in South African schools. In *Research Handbook on Gender*. Sexuality and the Law.

Reyneke, R. (2023). Unveiling the significant contribution of child and youth care workers in South African township schools. University of the Free State. DOI: 10.2139/ssrn.4647035

Rhodes, M., Leslie, S. J., Yee, K. M., & Saunders, K. (2019). Subtle Linguistic Cues Increase Girls' Engagement in Science. *Psychological Science*, 30(3), 455–466. DOI: 10.1177/0956797618823670 PMID: 30721119

Richard, J., Luqman, O., & Amina, A. (2018). Overcoming the Barriers of Female Students Choice of Built Environment Courses. *Covenant Journal of Research in the Built Environment*, 6(2), 33–48.

Riddle, D. L. (2016). Equity in education: An international comparison of pupil perspectives. *Educational Research*, 58(4), 392–407.

Riess, H. (2017). The science of empathy. *Journal of Patient Experience*, 4(2), 74–77. DOI: 10.1177/2374373517699267 PMID: 28725865

Riggs, R., Felipe, C. M., Roldán, J. L., & Real, J. C. (2024). Information systems capabilities value creation through circular economy practices in uncertain environments: A conditional mediation model. *Journal of Business Research*, 175, 114526. Advance online publication. DOI: 10.1016/j.jbusres.2024.114526

Rimm-Kaufman, S. E., & Hulleman, C. S. (2020). *Social and emotional learning in the classroom: Promoting academic excellence and supporting social and emotional development*. Guilford Publications.

Rimm-Kaufman, S. E., & Hulleman, C. S. (2020). Social and emotional learning: A framework for promoting mental health and reducing risk behavior in children and youth. In Weist, M. D., Lever, N. A., Bradshaw, C. P., & Owens, J. S. (Eds.), *Handbook of School Mental Health* (2nd ed., pp. 19–34). Springer.

Roderick, M. (1994). Grade retention and school dropout: Investigating the association. *American Educational Research Journal*, 31(4), 729–759. DOI: 10.3102/00028312031004729

Romm, N., Nel, M., & Tlale, L. (2013). Inclusive education in South Africa: Progress and challenges. *International Journal of Inclusive Education*, 17(4), 435–452.

Romm, N., Nel, M., & Tlale, L. (2022). Challenges in implementing inclusive education in South Africa: A critical analysis. *International Journal of Inclusive Education*, 25(6), 543–560.

Rose, D. H., & Meyer, A. (2002). *Teaching every student in the digital age: Universal design for learning*. ASCD.

Rouse, M. (2017). Developing Critical Thinking Skills in the Digital Age. *Journal of Adolescent & Adult Literacy*, 61(1), 41–49. DOI: 10.1002/jaal.692

Rozeboom, S. A. (2021). From universal design for learning to universal design for communion with the living God. *Journal of Disability & Religion*, 25(3), 329–346. DOI: 10.1080/23312521.2021.1895024

Rural Health Research Gateway. (2022). *Improving Access to LGBTQIA+-Friendly Care in Rural Areas*. Retrieved from Rural Health Research Gateway.

Sahlberg, P. (2011). *Finnish lessons: What can the world learn from educational change in Finland?* Teachers College Press.

Sahlberg, P. (2022). *Finnish lessons 3.0: What can the world learn from educational change in Finland?* Teachers College Press.

Salifu, I., Agyekum, B., & Nketia, D. (2024). Teacher professional development (TPD) in Ghana: Constraints and solutions. *Professional Development in Education*, 1–18. Advance online publication. DOI: 10.1080/19415257.2024.2351947

Sangeetha, M., Kannan, S. R., Boopathi, S., Ramya, J., Ishrat, M., & Sabarinathan, G. (2023). Prediction of Fruit Texture Features Using Deep Learning Techniques. *2023 4th International Conference on Smart Electronics and Communication (ICOSEC)*, 762–768.

Sapire, I., Tshuma, L., & Herholdt, R. (2024). Spotlight on basic education completion and foundational learning: South Africa. Global Education Monitoring Report Team. Association for the Development of Education in Africa. https://unesdoc.unesco.org/ark:/48223/pf0000389034

Saravanan, S., Chandrasekar, J., Satheesh Kumar, S., Patel, P., Maria Shanthi, J., & Boopathi, S. (2024). The Impact of NBA Implementation Across Engineering Disciplines: Innovative Approaches. In *Advances in Higher Education and Professional Development* (pp. 229–252). IGI Global. DOI: 10.4018/979-8-3693-1666-5.ch010

Saravanan, A., Venkatasubramanian, R., Khare, R., Surakasi, R., Boopathi, S., Ray, S., & Sudhakar, M. (2022). POLICY TRENDS OF RENEWABLE ENERGY AND NON. *Renewable Energy*.

Sassler, S., Glass, J. L., Levitte, Y., & Michelmore, K. M. (2011). The Missing Women in STEM? Accounting for Gender Differences in Entrance into Science, Technology, Engineering, and Math Occupations. *Presented at the 2012 Population Association of America annual meeting, Washington, D.C.*

Sauntson, H. (2013). Sexual diversity and illocutionary silencing in the English National Curriculum. *Sex Education: Sexuality, Society and Learning*, 13, 395–408. Town. 22.

Saykili, A. (2019). Higher education in the digital age: The impact of digital connective technologies. *Journal of Educational Technology and Online Learning*, 2(1), 1–15. DOI: 10.31681/jetol.516971

Schaefer, L., & Clandinin, D. J. (2019). Sustaining teachers' stories to live by: Implications for teacher education. *Teachers and Teaching*, 25(1), 54–68. DOI: 10.1080/13540602.2018.1532407

Schirmer, S., & Visser, R. (2023). *One: Time to Fix South Africa's Failing Education System*. Centre for Development and Enterprise.

Seekings, J., & Nattrass, N. (2005). *Class, race, and inequality in South Africa*. Yale University Press. DOI: 10.12987/yale/9780300108927.001.0001

Senthil, T., Puviyarasan, M., Babu, S. R., Surakasi, R., Sampath, B., & Associates. (2023). Industrial Robot-Integrated Fused Deposition Modelling for the 3D Printing Process. In *Development, Properties, and Industrial Applications of 3D Printed Polymer Composites* (pp. 188–210). IGI Global.

Sevillano-Monje, V., Martín-Gutiérrez, Á., & Hervás-Gómez, C. (2022). The flipped classroom and the development of competences: A teaching innovation experience in higher education. *Education Sciences*, 12(4), 248. DOI: 10.3390/educsci12040248

Shapiro, C., Sax, L. J., & Rodgers, K. A. (2017). The Role of Stereotype Threats in Undermining Girls' and Women's Performance and Interest in STEM Fields. *Sex Roles*, 77(5&6), 363–375.

Sharma, D. M., Ramana, K. V., Jothilakshmi, R., Verma, R., Maheswari, B. U., & Boopathi, S. (2024). Integrating Generative AI Into K-12 Curriculums and Pedagogies in India: Opportunities and Challenges. *Facilitating Global Collaboration and Knowledge Sharing in Higher Education With Generative AI*, 133–161.

Sharma, D. M., Ramana, K. V., Jothilakshmi, R., Verma, R., Maheswari, B. U., & Boopathi, S. (2024a). Integrating Generative AI Into K-12 Curriculums and Pedagogies in India: Opportunities and Challenges. *Facilitating Global Collaboration and Knowledge Sharing in Higher Education With Generative AI*, 133–161.

Sharma, D. M., Ramana, K. V., Jothilakshmi, R., Verma, R., Maheswari, B. U., & Boopathi, S. (2024b). Integrating Generative AI Into K-12 Curriculums and Pedagogies in India: Opportunities and Challenges. *Facilitating Global Collaboration and Knowledge Sharing in Higher Education With Generative AI*, 133–161.

Sharma, D. M., Ramana, K. V., Jothilakshmi, R., Verma, R., Maheswari, B. U., & Boopathi, S. (2024c). Integrating Generative AI Into K-12 Curriculums and Pedagogies in India: Opportunities and Challenges. *Facilitating Global Collaboration and Knowledge Sharing in Higher Education With Generative AI*, 133–161.

Sharma, D. M., Venkata Ramana, K., Jothilakshmi, R., Verma, R., Uma Maheswari, B., & Boopathi, S. (2024). Integrating Generative AI Into K-12 Curriculums and Pedagogies in India: Opportunities and Challenges. In Yu, P., Mulli, J., Syed, Z. A. S., & Umme, L. (Eds.), (pp. 133–161). Advances in Higher Education and Professional Development. IGI Global., DOI: 10.4018/979-8-3693-0487-7.ch006

Shaw, R., & Patra, B. K. (2022). Classifying students based on cognitive state in flipped learning pedagogy. *Future Generation Computer Systems*, 126, 305–317. DOI: 10.1016/j.future.2021.08.018

Shukla, B., Soni, K., Sujatha, R., & Hasteer, N. (2023). Roadmap to inclusive curriculum: A step towards Multidisciplinary Engineering Education for holistic development. *Journal of Engineering Education Transformations*, 36(3), 134–145. DOI: 10.16920/jeet/2023/v36i3/23105

Shwartz, G., & Dori, Y. J. (2020). Transition into Teaching: Second career teachers' professional identity. *Eurasia Journal of Mathematics, Science and Technology Education*, 16(11), em1891. DOI: 10.29333/ejmste/8502

Sidekerskienė, T., & Damaševičius, R. (2023). Out-of-the-Box Learning: Digital Escape Rooms as a Metaphor for Breaking Down Barriers in STEM Education. *Sustainability (Basel)*, 15(9), 7393. DOI: 10.3390/su15097393

Silverajah, V. G., Wong, S. L., Govindaraj, A., Khambari, M. N. M., Rahmat, R. W. B. O., & Deni, A. R. M. (2022). A systematic review of self-regulated learning in flipped classrooms: Key findings, measurement methods, and potential directions. *IEEE Access : Practical Innovations, Open Solutions*, 10, 20270–20294. DOI: 10.1109/ACCESS.2022.3143857

Singh Madan, B., Najma, U., Pande Rana, D., & Kumar, P. K. J., S., S., & Boopathi, S. (2024). Empowering Leadership in Higher Education: Driving Student Performance, Faculty Development, and Institutional Progress. In *Advances in Educational Technologies and Instructional Design* (pp. 191–221). IGI Global. DOI: 10.4018/979-8-3693-0583-6.ch009

Singh, I. (2021). Role of Modern Technology in Education: An Overview of Indian National Education Policy 2020. *Multidisciplinary Issues in Social Science Research*, 101–120.

Siu, Y., & Morash, V. (2014). Teachers of students with visual impairments and their use of assistive technology: Measuring the proficiency of teachers and their identification with a community of practice. *Journal of Visual Impairment & Blindness*, 108(5), 384–398. DOI: 10.1177/0145482X1410800504

Slee, R. (2023). *Inclusive schooling: Reframing the discourse on exclusion and integration*. Routledge.

Smitha, S. (2020). National education policy (NEP) 2020-Opportunities and challenges in teacher education. [IJM]. *International Journal of Management*, 11(11).

Smith, D. D., & Tyler, N. C. (2010). *Introduction to special education: Making a difference*. Merrill/Pearson.

Smith, J. L., Lewis, K. L., Hawthorne, L., & Hodges, S. D. (2013). When Trying Hard isn't Natural: Women's Belonging with and Motivation for Male-Dominated STEM Fields as a Function of Effort Expenditure Concerns. *Personality and Social Psychology Bulletin*, 39(2), 131–143. DOI: 10.1177/0146167212468332 PMID: 23187722

Smith, S., & Jones, E. (1999). Technology infusion: Preparing teachers for transition services through web-based cases. *Career Development for Exceptional Individuals*, 22(2), 251–266. DOI: 10.1177/088572889902200207

Soon, V.Vestly Kong Liang Soon. (2023). A study of attitudes, skills, and barriers among the special education hearing impairment teachers in the use of assistive technology in teaching. *Journal of Advanced Research in Applied Sciences and Engineering Technology*, 35(1), 121–128. DOI: 10.37934/araset.34.3.121128

Sosa Díaz, M. J., Guerra Antequera, J., & Cerezo Pizarro, M. (2021a). Flipped classroom in the context of higher education: Learning, satisfaction and interaction. *Education Sciences*, 11(8), 416. DOI: 10.3390/educsci11080416

Sousa, D. A., & Tomlinson, C. A. (2018). *Differentiation and the brain: How neuroscience supports the learner-friendly classroom* (2nd ed.). Solution Tree Press., https://files.ascd.org/staticfiles/ascd/pdf/site ASCD/publications/books/Differentiation-and-the-Brain-2nd-ed-Sample-Chapters.pdf

South African Council for Educators (SACE). (2017). *Guidelines for teacher professional development in inclusive education.*

South African Council for Social Service Professions (SACSSP). (2014). Rules relating to conduct of child and youth care workers in practising their profession (Code of Ethics). Government Gazette, (38128), 31 October 2014.

South African Council for Social Service Professions (SACSSP). (2021). *Summit on the crisis in the child and youth care sector in South Africa and its impact on the welfare of children and youth: Summary of proceedings and resolutions.* SACSSP.

South African Disability Alliance. (n.d.). *About SADA.* http://www.sada.org.za/about-sada

South African Government. (2023). LGBTQIA+ Public Education Campaigns. Retrieved from gov.za

Spaltini, M., Terzi, S., & Taisch, M. (2024). Development and implementation of a roadmapping methodology to foster twin transition at manufacturing plant level. *Computers in Industry*, 154, 104025. Advance online publication. DOI: 10.1016/j.compind.2023.104025

Spaull, N. (2013). *South Africa's education crisis: The quality of education in South Africa 1994-2011*. Centre for Development and Enterprise.

Spaull, N. (2015). Schooling in South Africa: How low-quality education becomes a poverty trap. *South African Journal of Childhood Education*, 5(2), 111–131.

Specht, J., Howell, G., & Young, G. (2007). Students with special education needs in canada and their use off assistive technology during the transition to secondary school. *Childhood Education*, 83(6), 385–389. DOI: 10.1080/00094056.2007.10522956

Spencer, E., & Lucas, B. (2021). *Meta-Skills: Best practices in work-based learning A literature review*. University of Winchester.

Spigel, B., & Vinodrai, T. (2021). Meeting its Waterloo? Recycling in entrepreneurial ecosystems after anchor firm collapse. *Entrepreneurship and Regional Development*, 33(7–8), 599–620. DOI: 10.1080/08985626.2020.1734262

Sprecher, S., & Fehr, B. (2005). Compassionate love for close others and humanity. *Journal of Social and Personal Relationships*, 22(5), 629–651. DOI: 10.1177/0265407505056439

Spreitzenbarth, J. M., Bode, C., & Stuckenschmidt, H. (2024). Designing an AI purchasing requisition bundling generator. *Computers in Industry*, 155, 104043. Advance online publication. DOI: 10.1016/j.compind.2023.104043

Sravat, N., & Pathranarakul, P. (2022). Flipped learning pedagogy: Modelling the challenges for higher education in India. *International Journal of Learning and Change*, 14(2), 221–240. DOI: 10.1504/IJLC.2022.121137

Steinke, J. (2017). Adolescent girls' STEM identity formation and media images of STEM professionals: Considering the infuence of contextual cues. *Frontiers in Psychology*, 8, 716. DOI: 10.3389/fpsyg.2017.00716 PMID: 28603505

Stek, K. (2023). *A Challenge-Based Experiment Aiming to Develop Strategic Thinking an Inquiry into the Role of Stimulating Creativity for out-of-the-Box Thinking*. EasyChair.

Strauss, C., Taylor, B. L., Gu, J., Kuyken, W., Baer, R., Jones, F., & Cavanagh, K. (2016). What is compassion and how can we measure it? A review of definitions and measures. *Clinical Psychology Review*, 31(47), 15–27. DOI: 10.1016/j.cpr.2016.05.004 PMID: 27267346

Subban, P. (2006). Differentiated instruction: A research basis. *International Education Journal*, 7(7), 935–947.

Surajudeen, T., Ibironke, E. S., & Aladesusi, G. A. (2022). Special education teachers' readiness and self-efficacy in utilization of assistive technologies for instruction in secondary school. *Indonesian Journal of Community and Special Needs Education*, 3(1), 33–42. DOI: 10.17509/ijcsne.v3i1.44643

Tan, A. L., Jocz, J. A., & Zhai, J. (2015). Spiderman and Science: How Students' Perceptions of Scientists are Shaped by Popular Media. *Public Understanding of Science (Bristol, England)*, 26(5), 520–530. DOI: 10.1177/0963662515615086 PMID: 26582070

Tang, Y., Hare, R., & Ferguson, S. (2022). Classroom Evaluation of a Gamified Adaptive Tutoring System. *2022 IEEE Frontiers in Education Conference (FIE)*, 1–5.

Tejedor, S., Cervi, L., Pérez-Escoda, A., Tusa, F., & Parola, A. (2021). Higher education response in the time of coronavirus: Perceptions of teachers and students, and open innovation. *Journal of Open Innovation*, 7(1), 43. DOI: 10.3390/joitmc7010043

Telukdarie, A., Katsumbe, T., Mahure, H., & Murulane, K. (2024). Exploring the green economy – A systems thinking modelling approach. *Journal of Cleaner Production*, 436, 140611. Advance online publication. DOI: 10.1016/j.jclepro.2024.140611

The Alliance for Child Protection in Humanitarian Action. (2018). *Child Protection Case Management Supervision and Coaching Training*.

The Guardian Nigeria News. (2021). Gender Stereotype, Girls and Science Education. Nigeria and World News — Opinion. Available on https://guardian.ng/opinion/gender-stereotype-girls-and-science-education/

Thobejane, T. D. (2013). History of apartheid education and the problems of reconstruction in South Africa. *Sociolinguistic Studies*, 3(1), 1–12.

Thumbadoo, R. V. (2024). Children's mapping in Africa: Building on the Barbara Petchenik children's map competition. Cartouche, (100).

Thumbadoo, Z. (2013). Ways in Which Child and Youth Care Workers Support Child-Headed Households in Communities [Masters Thesis]. University of South Africa.

Thumbadoo, Z. (2021). The current crisis in the child and youth care work profession [PowerPoint presentation]. Professional Board for Child and Youth Care Work, South African Council for Social Service Professionals.

Thumbadoo, Z. S. (2020). Towards the development of a theoretical framework to guide child and youth care practice in South Africa [Doctoral dissertation]. Durban University of Technology.

Thumbadoo, Z., Ntintili, K., Taylor, D., & Thumbadoo, R. (2023). Children mapping their realities and aspirations: An innovative methodological tool with implications for practice, programme and policy. [ICA]. *Abstracts of the International Cartographic Association*, 6, 1–1. DOI: 10.5194/ica-abs-6-257-2023

Tierney, A. (2020). The scholarship of teaching and learning and pedagogic research within the disciplines: Should it be included in the research excellence framework? *Studies in Higher Education*, 45(1), 176–186. DOI: 10.1080/03075079.2019.1574732

Tohara, A. J. T. (2021). Exploring digital literacy strategies for students with special educational needs in the digital age. [TURCOMAT]. *Turkish Journal of Computer and Mathematics Education*, 12(9), 3345–3358.

Tomlinson, C. A. (2014). *The differentiated classroom: Responding to the needs of all learners* (2nd ed.). ASCD.

Tomlinson, C. A. (2017). *How to differentiate instruction in academically diverse classrooms?* ASCD.

Tomlinson, C. A., & Imbeau, M. B. (2010). *Leading and managing a differentiated classroom*. ASCD.

Tomlinson, C. A., & Moon, T. R. (2013). *Assessment and student success in a differentiated classroom*. ASCD.

Trani, J., Moodley, J., Anand, P., Graham, L., & Maw, M. T. T. (2020). Stigma of persons with disabilities in South Africa: Uncovering pathways from discrimination to depression and low self-esteem. *Social Science & Medicine*, 265, 1–12. DOI: 10.1016/j.socscimed.2020.113449 PMID: 33183862

Turnbull, H. R., Turnbull, A. P., Wehmeyer, M. L., & Shogren, K. A. (2022). Individuals with Disabilities Education Act (IDEA) and its impact on inclusive education in the United States. *The Journal of Special Education*, 56(4), 250–268.

Udeani, U., & Ejikeme, C. (2011). A Decade into the 21st Century: Nigerian Women Scientists and Engineers Highly Under-Represented in Academia. The African Symposium, 11(2), 99-105 https://www.ncsu.edu/aern/TAS11.2/TAS11.2_10Udeani.pdf

Ugandar, R., Rahamathunnisa, U., Sajithra, S., Christiana, M. B. V., Palai, B. K., & Boopathi, S. (2023). Hospital Waste Management Using Internet of Things and Deep Learning: Enhanced Efficiency and Sustainability. In *Applications of Synthetic Biology in Health, Energy, and Environment* (pp. 317–343). IGI Global.

UNESCO. (1994). *The Salamanca Statement and Framework for Action on Special Needs Education*. https://unesdoc.unesco.org/ark:/48223/pf0000097704

UNESCO. (1994). *The Salamanca Statement and Framework for Action on Special Needs Education.* UNESCO.

UNESCO. (2000). *Dakar Framework for Action: Education for All: Meeting our Collective Commitments.* UNESCO.

UNESCO. (2016). *Global Education Monitoring Report 2016: Education for people and planet: Creating sustainable futures for all.* UNESCO.

UNESCO. (2017). Cracking the Code: Girls' and Women's Education in Science, Technology, Engineering And Mathematics (STEM). https://unesdoc.unesco.org/ark:/48223/pf0000253479

UNESCO. (2017). *Education for people and planet: Creating sustainable futures for all.* UNESCO Publishing.

UNESCO. (2017). Education for sustainable development goals: Learning objectives. UNESCO. https://unesdoc.unesco.org/ark:/48223/pf0000247444

UNESCO. (2017). *Inclusion and education: All means all.* UNESCO.

UNESCO. (2019). *Education for all 2000-2015: Achievements and challenges.* UNESCO Publishing.

UNESCO. (2019). *Education for Sustainable Development Goals: Learning Objectives.* UNESCO.

UNESCO. (2019). *Making every learner count: Inclusive education and accountability.* UNESCO.

UNESCO. (2020). *Global Education Monitoring Report 2020: Inclusion and education: All means all.* UNESCO Publishing.

UNESCO. (2020). Global education monitoring report. Inclusion in education: All means all. United Nations Educational Cultural and Scientific Organisation, France. https://unesdoc.unesco.org/ark:/48223/pf0000373718

UNESCO. (2020). *Inclusion in education: Volume VI. Access to education for migrants, refugees, and internally displaced persons.* UNESCO Publishing.

UNESCO. (2022). Learning for empathy: A teacher exchange and support project. UNESCO. https://unesdoc.unesco.org/ark:/48223/pf0000384004

UNESCO. (2023). *Global Education Monitoring Report 2023: Technology and inclusion in education.* UNESCO Publishing.

UNESCO. (2023). What you need to know about education for sustainable development. UNESCO. https://www.unesco.org/en/education-sustainable-development/need-know

UNICEF. (2021). *Seen, counted, included: Using data to shed light on the well-being of children with disabilities*. UNICEF.

United Nations (UN). (1948). *Universal Declaration of Human Rights*. United Nations.

United Nations (UN). (1989). *Convention on the Rights of the Child*. United Nations.

United Nations (UN). (2006). *Convention on the Rights of Persons with Disabilities*. United Nations.

United Nations (UN). (2022). *Convention on the Rights of Persons with Disabilities and its Optional Protocol*. United Nations.

United Nations International Children Emergency Fund (UNICEF). (2020). Independent Evaluation of the Effectiveness & Impact of the Sustainable Development Goal 4 Education in Nigeria. Inception Report.

United Nations. (1948). *Universal Declaration of Human Rights*. https://www.un.org/en/about-us/universal-declaration-of-human-rights

United Nations. (1989). *Convention on the Rights of the Child (CRC)*. https://www.ohchr.org/en/professionalinterest/pages/crc.aspx

United Nations. (2006). *Convention on the Rights of Persons with Disabilities (CRPD)*. https://www.un.org/development/desa/disabilities/convention-on-the-rights-of-persons-with-disabilities.html

United Nations. (2012). The Future We Want, Outcome Document of the UN Conference on Sustainable Development. New York: United Nations.

United Nations. (n.d.). *Sustainable Development Goals (SDGs)*. https://sdgs.un.org/goals

United States Department of Education. (n.d.). *Individuals with Disabilities Education Act (IDEA)*. https://sites.ed.gov/idea/

Vaithianathan, V., Subbulakshmi, N., Boopathi, S., & Mohanraj, M. (2024). Integrating Project-Based and Skills-Based Learning for Enhanced Student Engagement and Success: Transforming Higher Education. In *Adaptive Learning Technologies for Higher Education* (pp. 345–372). IGI Global. DOI: 10.4018/979-8-3693-3641-0.ch015

Van den Beemt, A., MacLeod, M., Van der Veen, J., Van de Ven, A., Van Baalen, S., Klaassen, R., & Boon, M. (2020). Interdisciplinary engineering education: A review of vision, teaching, and support. *Journal of Engineering Education*, 109(3), 508–555. DOI: 10.1002/jee.20347

van den Heerik, R. A., Droog, E., Jong Tjien Fa, M., & Burgers, C. (2020). Thinking out of the box: Production of direct metaphor<? Br?> in a social media context. *Internet Pragmatics*, 3(1), 64–94. DOI: 10.1075/ip.00049.hee

Van Klinken, A. S., & Gunda, M. R. (2012). Taking up the cudgels against gay rights? Trends and trajectories in African Christian theologies on homosexuality. *Journal of Homosexuality*, 59(1), 114–138. DOI: 10.1080/00918369.2012.638549 PMID: 22269050

van Rooij, E. C. M., Fokkens-Bruinsma, M., & Goedhart, M. (2019). Preparing science undergraduates for a teaching career: Sources of their teacher self-efficacy. *Teacher Educator*, 54(3), 270–294. DOI: 10.1080/08878730.2019.1606374

Van Schie, K. (2012). Lesbian stands up to attackers. The Star. Retrieved from http://www.iol.co.za/the-star/lesbian-stands-up-to-attackers-1.1351609#.UJfE22c4Hbh

VanderVen, K., & Torre, C. A. (1999). A dynamical systems perspective on mediating violence in schools: Emergent roles of child and youth care workers. *Child and Youth Care Forum*, 28(6), 411–436. DOI: 10.1023/A:1022843525790

Varadharajan, M., Buchanan, J., & Schuck, S. (2020). Navigating and negotiating: Career changers in teacher education programmes. *Asia-Pacific Journal of Teacher Education*, 48(5), 477–490. DOI: 10.1080/1359866X.2019.1669136

Venkatasubramanian, V., Chitra, M., Sudha, R., Singh, V. P., Jefferson, K., & Boopathi, S. (2024). Examining the Impacts of Course Outcome Analysis in Indian Higher Education: Enhancing Educational Quality. In *Challenges of Globalization and Inclusivity in Academic Research* (pp. 124–145). IGI Global.

Venkatasubramanian, V., Chitra, M., Sudha, R., Singh, V. P., Jefferson, K., & Boopathi, S. (2024). Examining the Impacts of Course Outcome Analysis in Indian Higher Education: Enhancing Educational Quality. In *Challenges of Globalization and Inclusivity in Academic Research* (pp. 124–145). IGI Global. DOI: 10.4018/979-8-3693-1371-8.ch009

Venkatasubramanian, V., Chitra, M., Sudha, R., Singh, V. P., Jefferson, K., & Boopathi, S. (2024a). Examining the Impacts of Course Outcome Analysis in Indian Higher Education: Enhancing Educational Quality. In *Challenges of Globalization and Inclusivity in Academic Research* (pp. 124–145). IGI Global.

Venkatasubramanian, V., Chitra, M., Sudha, R., Singh, V. P., Jefferson, K., & Boopathi, S. (2024b). Examining the Impacts of Course Outcome Analysis in Indian Higher Education: Enhancing Educational Quality. In *Challenges of Globalization and Inclusivity in Academic Research* (pp. 124–145). IGI Global.

Venkateswaran, N., Vidhya, R., Naik, D. A., Raj, T. M., Munjal, N., & Boopathi, S. (2023). Study on Sentence and Question Formation Using Deep Learning Techniques. In *Digital Natives as a Disruptive Force in Asian Businesses and Societies* (pp. 252–273). IGI Global. DOI: 10.4018/978-1-6684-6782-4.ch015

Vergottini, M., & Weyers, M. (2020). The foundations and nature of South African school social work: An overview. Social Work/Maatskaplike Werk, 56(2).

Vilppu, H., Södervik, I., Postareff, L., & Murtonen, M. (2019). The effect of short online pedagogical training on university teachers' interpretations of teaching–learning situations. *Instructional Science*, 47(6), 679–709. DOI: 10.1007/s11251-019-09496-z

Wamsler, C., Wickenberg, B., Hanson, H., Olsson, J. A., Stålhammar, S., Björn, H., Falck, H., Gerell, D., Oskarsson, T., & Simonsson, E. (2020). Environmental and climate policy integration: Targeted strategies for overcoming barriers to nature-based solutions and climate change adaptation. *Journal of Cleaner Production*, 247, 119154. DOI: 10.1016/j.jclepro.2019.119154

Wang1, N., Tan, A. L., Zhou, X., Liu, K., Zeng, F. & Xiang, J. (2023). Gender Differences in High School Students' Interest in STEM Careers: A Multi-Group Comparison Based on Structural Equation Model. *International Journal of STEM Education*, 10(59), 1 -21. https://doi.org/DOI: 10.1186/s40594-023-00443-6

Wang, H.-H., Charoenmuang, M., Knobloch, N. A., & Tormoehlen, R. L. (2020). Defining interdisciplinary collaboration based on high school teachers' beliefs and practices of STEM integration using a complex designed system. *International Journal of STEM Education*, 7(1), 1–17. DOI: 10.1186/s40594-019-0201-4

Wang, J. Y., Yang, M. Y., Lv, B. B., Zhang, F. X., Zheng, Y. H., & Sun, Y. H. (2020). Influencing Factors of 10th Grade Students' Science Career Expectations: A Structural Equation Model. *Journal of Baltic Science Education*, 19(4), 675–686. DOI: 10.33225/jbse/20.19.675

Wang, L., O'Connor, D., Rinklebe, J., Ok, Y. S., Tsang, D. C., Shen, Z., & Hou, D. (2020). Biochar aging: Mechanisms, physicochemical changes, assessment, and implications for field applications. *Environmental Science & Technology*, 54(23), 14797–14814. DOI: 10.1021/acs.est.0c04033 PMID: 33138356

Wang, M. T., & Degol, J. L. (2017). Gender Gap in Science, Technology, Engineering, and Mathematics (STEM): Current Knowledge, Implications For Practice, Policy, and Future Directions. *Educational Psychology Review*, 29(1), 119–140. DOI: 10.1007/s10648-015-9355-x PMID: 28458499

Wang, Y., Shi, J., & Qu, G. (2024). Research on collaborative innovation cooperation strategies of manufacturing digital ecosystem from the perspective of multiple stakeholders. *Computers & Industrial Engineering*, 190, 110003. Advance online publication. DOI: 10.1016/j.cie.2024.110003

Wankhade, R. S. (2021). Higher Education and NEP-2020. *International Journal of Researches in Social Science and Information Studies*, 8(1), 51–56.

Watts-Taffe, S., Laster, B. P., Broach, L., Marinak, B., McDonald Connor, C., & Walker-Dalhouse, D. (2012). Differentiated instruction: Making informed teacher decisions. *The Reading Teacher*, 66(4), 303–314. DOI: 10.1002/TRTR.01126

Webb, A., & McQuaid, R. (2020). Recruitment and workforce development challenges in low-status sectors with high labour demand–childcare work. *CIPD Applied Research Conference 2020, The Shifting Landscape of Work and Working Lives*.

Weber, E. (2008). *Educational change in South Africa: Reflections on local realities, practices, and reforms*. Sense Publishers. DOI: 10.1163/9789087906603

Williams, J. C. (2012). Teachers as Facilitators. In O'Grady, G., Yew, E., Goh, K., & Schmidt, H. (Eds.), *One-Day, One-Problem*. Springer., DOI: 10.1007/978-981-4021-75-3_11

Wills, I. R. (2011). *The history of Bantu Education: 1948-1994*. [A thesis submitted to the Australian Catholic University in total fulfilment of the requirements for the Degree of Doctor of Philosophy]. Australian Catholic University Research Space. Available: https://acuresearchbank.acu.edu.au/download/f6bb666ae24a99af27caf82f697d4328b132299cec03800214325a88e393c081/2003673/Wills_2011_The_history_of_Bantu_education.pdf[15 March 2024].

Wilson, T. (2022). Report on the Baseline Research to Inform a 5-Year Strategy for NACCW's Work in Schools in the Lesedi and Letsatsi Solar Park Trust Catchment Areas.

Yadav, A., Israel, M., Bouck, E., Cobo, A., & Samuels, J. (2022). Achieving csforall: preparing special education pre-service teachers to bring computing to students with disabilities.. https://doi.org/DOI: 10.1145/3478431.3499333

Yamaguchi, Y. (2021). Inclusive education reforms in Japan: An analysis of policy changes and implementation challenges. *Asian Education Review*, 14(3), 123–145.

Yang, J., & Shen, W. (2020). Master's Education in Stem Fields in China: Does Gender Matter? *Higher Education Policy*, 33(4), 667–688. DOI: 10.1057/s41307-020-00203-z

Yildiz Durak, H. (2022a). Flipped classroom model applications in computing courses: Peer-assisted groups, collaborative group and individual learning. *Computer Applications in Engineering Education*, 30(3), 803–820. DOI: 10.1002/cae.22487

Zeldin, S., Christens, B. D., & Powers, J. L. (2015). *The psychology and practice of youth-adult partnership: Bridging generations for youth development and community change.* American Psychological Association.

Zenelaj, E. (2013). Education for Sustainable Development. *European Journal of Sustainable Development*, 2(4), 227–232. DOI: 10.14207/ejsd.2013.v2n4p227

Zero Dropout Campaign. (2021). School Dropout Gender Matters.

Zhai, X. (2022). ChatGPT user experience: Implications for education. *Available at SSRN* 4312418.

Zhang, L., Carter, R. A., & Hoekstra, N. J. (2024a). A critical analysis of universal design for learning in the US federal education law. *Policy Futures in Education*, 22(4), 469–474. DOI: 10.1177/14782103231179530

Zhang, Z. (2022). Toward the role of teacher empathy in students' engagement in English language classes. *Frontiers in Psychology*, 13, 880935. DOI: 10.3389/fpsyg.2022.880935 PMID: 35719575

Zhao, W. (2020). Epistemological flashpoint in China's classroom reform:(How) can a 'Confucian do-after-me pedagogy' cultivate critical thinking? *Journal of Curriculum Studies*, 52(1), 101–117. DOI: 10.1080/00220272.2019.1641844

Zhou, L., Parker, A., Smith, D., & Griffin-Shirley, N. (2011). Assistive technology for students with visual impairments: Challenges and needs in teachers' preparation programs and practice. *Journal of Visual Impairment & Blindness*, 105(4), 197–210. DOI: 10.1177/0145482X1110500402

Zou, D., Luo, S., Xie, H., & Hwang, G.-J. (2022). A systematic review of research on flipped language classrooms: Theoretical foundations, learning activities, tools, research topics and findings. *Computer Assisted Language Learning*, 35(8), 1811–1837. DOI: 10.1080/09588221.2020.1839502

About the Contributors

Medwin Dikwanyane Sepadi is a distinguished senior lecturer in the Department of Education Studies at the prestigious University of Limpopo in South Africa. Holding a PhD and a Master's degree in curriculum studies from the University of Limpopo, Dr. Sepadi has made significant contributions to the field of education through his extensive scholarly work. He has authored numerous journal articles published in both local and international journals, showcasing his expertise and impact in the field. Dr. Sepadi's presentations at various national and international conferences have further solidified his reputation as a thought leader in education. Additionally, his contributions to scholarly textbooks through insightful book chapters have provided valuable insights and perspectives to the academic community. Dr. Sepadi's research interests are focused on critical areas such as curriculum studies and policy, inclusive education, psychosocial issues in schools, teacher education, and continuous professional development. Currently, he is spearheading the editorial role for a groundbreaking book that delves into global practices in inclusive education curriculum and policy, underscoring his commitment to advancing educational research and practice on a global scale.

* * *

Francis R. AcKah-Jnr (PhD) teaches and researches at Griffith University. He is a keen educator with proven experience in higher education and has hands-on teaching, research and service in Inclusive Education, Leadership, Early Childhood, (Intercultural)Communication, Pedagogy and Applied Behaviour Analysis. He has research interests also in Parent-School-Community Partnership, International Education and Student Experience, Education Policy and Law. He believes everyone can learn and succeed within scaffolding and mentoring environments that ignite leadership and agency. Dr AcKah-Jnr has published high-quality articles and book chapters in inclusive education, leadership, early childhood, teacher education,

COVID-19, and more. He has collaborated with local and international researchers and scholars as an author, editor, external thesis examiner and project investigator. He is a lead reviewer for many reputable journals in education. His current research focuses on supporting teachers to develop new capacities, pedagogical leadership, and motivations to enhance inclusivity and sustainable education. He was a recipient of the Australia Council for Educational Leadership (ACEL) Award 2017.

John K. Appiah (Ph.D) is a lecturer in Numeracy, Pedagogy, Educational Leadership and Management in the Department of Basic Education at the University of Cape Coast. Prior to his appointment as a lecturer he served as the Research Project Manager of Quantitative Methods in Educational Research (QMER) at the College of Education, Auburn University, Alabama, USA where he obtained his doctorate degree. His research interest includes Pedagogical leadership in Early Childhood Education, Numeracy in Early Childhood Education, and Educational leadership.

Sampath Boopathi is an accomplished individual with a strong academic background and extensive research experience. He completed his undergraduate studies in Mechanical Engineering and pursued his postgraduate studies in the field of Computer-Aided Design. Dr. Boopathi obtained his Ph.D. from Anna University, focusing his research on Manufacturing and optimization. Throughout his career, Dr. Boopathi has made significant contributions to the field of engineering. He has authored and published over 225 research articles in internationally peer-reviewed journals, highlighting his expertise and dedication to advancing knowledge in his area of specialization. His research output demonstrates his commitment to conducting rigorous and impactful research. In addition to his research publications, Dr. Boopathi has also been granted one patent and has three published patents to his name. This indicates his innovative thinking and ability to develop practical solutions to real-world engineering challenges. With 17 years of academic and research experience, Dr. Boopathi has enriched the engineering community through his teaching and mentorship roles.

Ajay Chandel is working as an Associate Professor at Mittal School of Business, Lovely Professional University, Punjab. He has 14 years of teaching and research experience. He has published papers in SCOPUS, WOS, and UGC listed Journals in areas like Social Media Marketing, E-Commerce, and Consumer Behaviour. He has published cases on SMEs and Social Entrepreneurship in The Case Centre, UK. He also reviews The Case Journal, Emerald Group Publishing, and International Journal of Business and Globalisation, Inderscience. He has authored and developed MOOCs on Tourism and Hospitality Marketing under Epg-Pathshala- A gateway to all postgraduate courses (a UGC-MHRD project under its National Mission on Education Through ICT (NME-ICT).

Saurabh Chandra is an accomplished legal scholar and currently serves as an Associate Professor at the School of Law, Bennett University, India. With a robust academic foundation, he earned his Bachelor of Arts and Bachelor of Laws (B.A. LL.B.) from the prestigious Aligarh Muslim University (AMU). He further specialized in Business Laws, completing his Master of Laws (LL.M.) at the renowned National Law School of India University (NLSIU), Bangalore. Dr. Chandra's academic journey culminated in a Doctorate in Law (Ph.D.) from the esteemed National Law University. In addition to his impressive legal education from some of India's most prestigious institutions, Dr. Saurabh Chandra also holds a master's degree in Management with specialization in Human Resources in Management and another in Journalism and Mass Communication. With 16 years of teaching experience, he has established himself as an expert in Business and Corporate Laws, with numerous publications to his credit. Dr. Saurabh Chandra is a distinguished expert in Business and Corporate Laws, with a profound understanding of the intricate legal frameworks that govern the business world. His expertise is complemented by a robust portfolio of scholarly publications, which underscores his commitment to advancing knowledge in his field. Throughout his career, Dr. Chandra has consistently produced high-impact research that addresses critical issues in business and corporate law. His publications are widely recognized for their depth of analysis, innovative perspectives, and practical relevance. He has contributed extensively to leading journals, where his work has often set new standards for legal scholarship. His publications not only reflect his scholarly rigor but also his dedication to addressing contemporary challenges faced by businesses and policymakers. By bridging the gap between theoretical insights and real-world applications, Dr. Chandra's work serves as a valuable resource for academics, legal practitioners, and industry professionals alike. Dr. Chandra brings a wealth of experience in Academic Administration, having successfully held various key administrative positions. His diverse qualifications and extensive experience make him a distinguished figure in the academic and legal communities.

Nicia de Nobrega has been involved in research and monitoring and evaluation in the civil society sector for the past 15 years. Nicia holds a Masters degree in Research Psychology and currently oversees the monitoring and evaluation department at the National Association of Child Care Workers (NACCW), where she is exploring the application of routine monitoring and evaluation for measuring impact for and the organisation's research strategy and development. Nicia has supported the development of the data management systems of NACCW programmes, including the school-based Isibindi Ezikoleni child and youth care programme in South Africa. Nicia also secured the MTN Awards for Social Change in 2020 for good M&E practice in the non-profit sector. Nicia is also currently a doctoral candidate in research psychology conducting research on the characteristics and pathways of child survivors of abuse and neglect in the South African child protection system.

Shashank Mittal has done his FPM in Organizational behavior and Human Resource from Indian Institute of Management Raipur. He holds B. Tech from I.E.T. Lucknow. His post FPM work experience includes almost five years of industry and academics exposures in multiple roles. Prior to joining FPM, he has over two years of industrial experience and three years of teaching experience in various organizations. He has published multiple papers in ABDC ranked and SSCI indexed journals of international repute such as Journal of Knowledge Management, Journal of Behavioral and Experimental Finance, International Journal of Conflict Management, Journal of Management and Organization and Current Psychology. His current research interest includes Social identity, Knowledge exchanges, Status, Proactive helping, Employer branding, Organizational justice, and Humanitarian relief management. He enjoys badminton and cycling during leisure time.

Makobo Lydia Mogale is a lecturer in the Department of Curriculum Studies and Higher Education at the University of the Free State. She completed her PhD in 2022 at the Tshwane University of Technology, where she was awarded best Doctoral student of the year. Her research focuses on curriculum studies, with an interest in Education (progression) policy, learner support, and instructional practices. She has published several articles in her field in local and international accredited journals. Her current research focuses on supporting School Based Support Teams to develop inclusive intervention programmes for progressed learners.

Awudu Salaam Mohammed is a Lecturer at College of Distance Education, University of Cape Coast. His research interests include inclusive education, early childhood education, educational leadership, and qualitative research. He is also a part-time Lecturer at Ghana Muslim Mission College of Education, and works at Ghana Education Service, Mampong Municipal Education Directorate, as a SHS Coordinator.

Donald Nghonyama holds a Master's degree in international development and a B-Tech degree in Child and Youth Development and National Diploma in Education. He has worked in the children's sector of South Africa, in education and civil society sectors, for over 30 years. He heads up the membership division of the National Association of Child Care Workers (NACCW) and has been Deputy Director of the organisation for the past 10 years. He is responsible for the Youth

Development Programme ensuring youth involvement in NACCW activities, and has been involved in the development and expansion of the Isibindi Ezikoleni school-based child and youth care model in South Africa. He serves in civil society structures on children and youth matters; is the current Chairperson of the Professional Board for Child and Youth Care under the South African Council for Social Services Professions; Secretariat of FICE Africa under FICE International and a member of the coordinating body of FICE International.

Uchenna Kingsley Okeke is a Postdoctoral Research Fellow at the Department of Science and Technology Education, Faculty of Education, University of Johannesburg, South Africa. He holds a Bachelor of Education (B.Ed.) and a Master of Education (M.Ed.) in Teacher Education with focus on Physics/Mathematics instruction from the Department of Teacher Education, University of Ibadan, and a Doctor of Philosophy (Ph.D.) from the Department of Science and Technology Education, University of Ibadan. He was awarded the University of Ibadan Postgraduate College Teaching and Research Assistant and served in that capacity at the Department of Science and Technology Education, University of Ibadan, Nigeria. He is a Laurette of the prestigious CODESRIA Summer Research School, 2021 Cohort, on "African Studies and Area Studies in Africa". He has over 10 years teaching experience at both the primary, secondary and tertiary levels of education. He has published in both national and internal reputed peer reviewed journals. He enjoys reading, writing and watching sports.

Sam Ramaila is an Associate Professor in the Department of Science and Technology Education. He obtained PhD from the University of Johannesburg, MSc from the University of the Witwatersrand, BSc Hons, BSc and Higher Education Diploma from the University of the North. He currently serves as the Chairperson of Physics for Development, Education and Community Outreach Division of the South African Institute of Physics. He successfully coordinated the award winning Teacher Professional Development Project as well as the Review of Undergraduate Physics Education in Public Higher Education Institutions Project on behalf of the South African Institute of Physics. The Review of Undergraduate Physics Education in Public Higher Education Institutions Project culminated in the development of the Strategic Plan on the Enhancement of Physics Training in South Africa. In addition to teaching in both the undergraduate and postgraduate programmes in the UJ Faculty of Education, he supervises a number of postgraduate students at both Masters and PhD level. His research interests include nature of science, inquiry-based learning and teacher education.

C. Ravichandran is a Professor and Head of the Department of Chemistry at Easwari Engineering College.

Zeni Thumbadoo has worked in the South African children's sector for over 40 years – in service provision, contributing to children's policy, advocacy, and model development. Zeni holds a doctoral degree in child and youth care work and is a member of the Board of Directors of the International Child and Youth Care Network. She founded projects for improving children's services and has worked as Deputy Director of the National Association of Child Care Workers for nearly 30 years. Zeni was instrumental in developing the acclaimed Isibindi model and Safe Park model in South Africa and is presently involved in the scale-up of the Isibindi Ezikoleni model. She has contributed to the professionalization of the child and youth care field; served on qualifications-generating bodies; led the regulatory structure for child and youth care workers; and is on the Editorial Advisory Board of the Scottish Journal of Residential Child Care.

Theresa Wilson is a registered social worker with over 30 years of experience in the field of developmental social welfare. Areas of interest include community-based child protection, disability inclusion and sustainable development. Since 2000, she has served as a consultant in several African countries and the State of Palestine, collaborating with diverse donor agencies and governments. Her contributions include formative research such as situation analyses, needs assessments, and baseline studies to support policy development and programme design, evaluation research, and technical writing for policy briefs, concept notes, and training materials. Recently, she has provided technical assistance in the design of Isibindi Ezikoleni, a school-based child and youth care programme in South Africa. Theresa holds a MPhil in Sustainable Development from the University of Pretoria and an Honours degree in Social Work from the University of the Witwatersrand.

Index

A

academic autonomy 92, 93, 111, 112, 113
Accessibility 11, 65, 66, 67, 68, 69, 70, 71, 72, 75, 95, 98, 99, 100, 101, 114, 125, 202, 231, 233, 234, 235, 237, 239, 240, 241, 242, 243, 245, 247, 248, 249, 250, 253, 254, 255, 256, 258, 259, 260, 262, 263, 264, 265, 268, 269, 273, 332, 334, 336, 339, 374, 388
Accommodating 99, 125, 169, 260, 261, 297, 321, 335, 358, 387
active learning 42, 95, 282, 284, 285, 286, 287, 288, 291, 292, 293, 295, 306, 314, 315, 320, 321, 322, 323, 331, 332, 333, 336, 368, 371, 373, 376, 377, 380, 381, 395
apartheid 3, 9, 122, 127, 160, 220, 400, 401, 402, 403, 405, 406, 407, 433
assessment methodologies 98
Assistive Technology 53, 54, 55, 56, 57, 58, 59, 60, 61, 62, 63, 64, 65, 66, 67, 68, 69, 71, 72, 73, 74, 75, 76, 192, 197, 202, 213, 233, 236, 238, 240, 241, 242, 243, 245, 247, 248, 254, 257, 308, 388, 393
Atmosphere 77, 82, 83, 189, 202, 234, 297, 372, 388, 392

C

Child and Youth Care Work 121, 123, 126, 127, 128, 129, 130, 131, 132, 133, 134, 135, 146, 147, 154, 155, 156, 157, 158, 159, 160, 161
Child Protection 122, 131, 135, 136, 138, 140, 142, 144, 145, 148, 150, 151, 157, 160
Children and Youth 88, 123, 128, 131, 132, 160, 161, 162, 275
collaborative learning 6, 35, 43, 64, 70, 95, 171, 195, 202, 211, 233, 253, 270, 285, 287, 293, 297, 298, 299, 300, 301, 304, 317, 322, 323, 354, 358, 374, 386
Communication technologies 74, 165, 250
Community 12, 15, 16, 18, 20, 22, 27, 28, 32, 39, 40, 41, 44, 47, 57, 63, 64, 71, 75, 76, 77, 80, 82, 92, 94, 105, 109, 110, 117, 118, 122, 127, 128, 130, 131, 142, 144, 147, 150, 151, 153, 161, 196, 200, 204, 209, 216, 217, 218, 220, 221, 222, 223, 226, 227, 228, 233, 250, 254, 255, 262, 263, 264, 266, 268, 269, 270, 273, 275, 278, 279, 285, 302, 304, 306, 317, 320, 323, 326, 334, 336, 354, 358, 360, 366, 370, 372, 389, 391, 421, 422, 429, 438, 439
Competency-based assessment 386, 387, 392
conceptualization 1, 2, 7
Contexts 1, 2, 5, 10, 13, 17, 19, 21, 27, 29, 30, 31, 32, 45, 54, 56, 57, 62, 64, 71, 126, 141, 147, 152, 153, 155, 156, 162, 172, 179, 224, 255, 261, 262, 272, 273, 275, 276, 316, 317, 319, 321, 322, 325, 326, 327, 339, 348, 352, 354, 367, 379, 386, 414, 451
critical junctures 399, 400, 410, 413, 424, 428, 429, 430, 431, 434, 435
Critical thinking 95, 113, 167, 169, 170, 173, 189, 196, 197, 208, 210, 211, 212, 233, 261, 271, 278, 282, 283, 284, 290, 292, 293, 295, 297, 314, 315, 316, 319, 320, 322, 323, 324, 325, 326, 327, 333, 337, 339, 348, 365, 366, 367, 368, 369, 370, 371, 372, 374, 377, 379, 380, 382, 383, 385, 395, 398
Cultivating 38, 40, 84, 85, 86, 122, 179, 269, 270, 294, 407, 412, 440
Curriculum 16, 31, 39, 41, 43, 49, 55, 57, 58, 59, 72, 78, 79, 81, 82, 85, 86, 87, 92, 93, 94, 97, 98, 103, 113, 114, 117, 122, 125, 132, 135, 178, 189, 195, 198, 202, 205, 207, 217, 218, 219, 220, 221, 222, 223, 224, 225, 226, 227, 229, 235, 239, 247, 273, 274, 276, 282, 284, 287, 288, 289, 290, 291, 292, 306, 310, 330, 343, 345, 346,

347, 349, 351, 368, 371, 373, 377, 378, 383, 387, 393, 398, 401, 402, 403, 409, 410, 421, 433, 452

Curriculum Development 189, 205, 288, 409

curriculum reform 92, 402

D

Development 1, 2, 5, 6, 7, 8, 10, 11, 12, 14, 16, 17, 18, 19, 22, 26, 27, 28, 29, 30, 32, 33, 34, 38, 42, 43, 44, 45, 47, 48, 50, 51, 54, 56, 58, 59, 61, 62, 63, 64, 65, 67, 68, 70, 71, 72, 73, 74, 75, 76, 77, 78, 79, 82, 85, 86, 87, 88, 89, 93, 95, 97, 98, 102, 106, 107, 108, 113, 115, 117, 119, 122, 123, 124, 125, 126, 127, 128, 129, 130, 131, 132, 135, 137, 139, 141, 142, 143, 144, 146, 148, 150, 152, 153, 154, 156, 157, 158, 160, 162, 165, 166, 167, 168, 169, 170, 173, 177, 180, 182, 183, 184, 185, 188, 189, 190, 191, 196, 202, 203, 204, 205, 209, 210, 211, 212, 213, 214, 215, 216, 220, 225, 232, 234, 240, 241, 242, 243, 244, 245, 247, 248, 253, 254, 259, 261, 262, 263, 264, 265, 271, 272, 275, 277, 278, 279, 283, 286, 287, 288, 290, 291, 295, 299, 300, 301, 302, 304, 305, 306, 307, 310, 311, 314, 316, 317, 319, 324, 325, 327, 330, 331, 332, 333, 334, 335, 337, 338, 339, 341, 346, 348, 355, 356, 358, 360, 361, 369, 374, 377, 378, 379, 380, 386, 388, 394, 395, 396, 402, 403, 405, 407, 408, 409, 410, 411, 415, 416, 417, 418, 419, 422, 428, 429, 431, 432, 433, 434, 437, 438, 440, 441, 442, 443, 448, 450, 452, 453, 454, 455, 457, 458, 459, 461, 463

Differentiated instruction 5, 6, 14, 20, 84, 187, 189, 191, 192, 193, 197, 198, 199, 201, 235, 295, 343, 344, 347, 348, 349, 350, 351, 352, 353, 355, 356, 357, 358, 359, 360, 361, 363, 386

Disabilities 2, 3, 5, 7, 8, 9, 10, 11, 12, 13, 14, 15, 16, 17, 18, 19, 20, 23, 24, 28, 30, 31, 49, 51, 55, 66, 68, 70, 71, 75, 76, 79, 124, 125, 133, 155, 159, 192, 197, 200, 201, 202, 220, 232, 233, 234, 235, 238, 239, 241, 243, 247, 249, 250, 253, 257, 259, 260, 262, 263, 264, 266, 267, 268, 272, 274, 275, 277, 279, 315, 336, 388, 403, 405, 406, 407, 410, 413, 414, 419, 420, 421, 425, 427, 429, 433, 434

Diversity 2, 5, 6, 7, 8, 14, 15, 17, 21, 22, 23, 26, 32, 34, 36, 41, 45, 54, 77, 80, 82, 83, 85, 87, 95, 96, 98, 110, 114, 115, 125, 173, 188, 189, 198, 199, 200, 201, 217, 218, 219, 220, 222, 223, 224, 225, 226, 227, 228, 229, 239, 242, 253, 255, 256, 263, 264, 266, 267, 269, 270, 272, 273, 275, 276, 290, 291, 343, 344, 347, 352, 359, 361, 366, 387, 388, 392, 393, 398, 408, 413, 416, 428, 430, 443, 457

Diversity and inclusion 96, 114, 220, 222, 366

Dropout 122, 123, 125, 135, 136, 147, 158, 161, 162, 223, 343, 345, 363

E

Education 4.0 164, 165, 166, 167, 168, 169, 170, 171, 173, 174, 175, 177, 179, 180, 181, 395

Educational Technology 75, 187, 191, 192, 194, 195, 196, 310, 311

Education Policy 11, 30, 34, 47, 49, 56, 93, 98, 125, 135, 136, 191, 231, 247, 254, 255, 258, 281, 283, 286, 287, 288, 306, 309, 310, 311, 463

Emerging technologies 69, 72, 169, 210, 211, 249, 308, 372, 395

Empathic Practices 26, 29, 34, 35, 38, 39, 40, 42, 46

Empathy 25, 26, 27, 28, 29, 31, 34, 35, 36, 37, 38, 39, 40, 41, 42, 44, 45, 46, 48, 49, 50, 51, 52, 77, 78, 80, 81, 82, 83, 84, 85, 86, 87, 88, 222, 270, 275, 287, 367, 371, 372, 378, 379, 392

Empowerment 154, 222, 270, 440, 450, 461
Environments 2, 3, 6, 9, 10, 13, 15, 20, 22, 27, 30, 33, 34, 35, 36, 37, 39, 40, 41, 42, 44, 45, 46, 54, 69, 70, 72, 73, 77, 78, 79, 85, 86, 92, 93, 94, 95, 98, 99, 106, 108, 110, 112, 113, 114, 115, 119, 122, 128, 131, 150, 154, 156, 161, 164, 165, 168, 169, 174, 178, 180, 181, 185, 188, 189, 196, 200, 208, 209, 210, 211, 222, 224, 225, 231, 232, 233, 234, 235, 238, 239, 240, 241, 242, 243, 245, 246, 247, 248, 249, 250, 253, 260, 262, 263, 264, 265, 266, 267, 268, 269, 270, 271, 272, 273, 274, 275, 284, 285, 286, 288, 293, 295, 296, 297, 304, 307, 329, 338, 339, 341, 344, 347, 349, 360, 361, 366, 367, 373, 375, 376, 379, 382, 387, 393, 394, 395, 407, 413, 415, 416, 417, 418, 423, 427, 429, 440, 441, 452

Equitable 1, 2, 5, 6, 8, 9, 10, 12, 15, 16, 21, 27, 31, 32, 33, 39, 42, 51, 52, 55, 69, 72, 73, 83, 168, 180, 194, 196, 200, 218, 221, 227, 236, 240, 242, 251, 261, 265, 266, 267, 268, 269, 270, 273, 275, 290, 299, 329, 332, 343, 344, 347, 349, 357, 361, 387, 392, 399, 402, 403, 405, 406, 407, 410, 413, 414, 424, 428, 430, 437, 438, 440, 441, 455

evolution 1, 2, 6, 8, 9, 21, 48, 126, 152, 164, 168, 171, 206, 235, 283, 284, 368, 429, 443

F

Flexible Learning 165, 177, 179, 192, 234, 242, 245, 260, 269, 373, 386, 427
Flip-Flop Classroom Models 281, 282, 285, 306, 307
Fostering 5, 8, 15, 16, 17, 22, 40, 41, 42, 43, 45, 52, 56, 70, 77, 78, 81, 82, 83, 85, 86, 93, 96, 108, 110, 117, 126, 156, 165, 166, 169, 173, 204, 213, 217, 218, 219, 227, 245, 257, 261, 267, 269, 270, 271, 274, 275, 290, 294, 295, 308, 314, 315, 316, 320, 321, 322, 323, 325, 326, 331, 334, 335, 338, 339, 350, 358, 361, 366, 367, 378, 379, 380, 383, 385, 386, 387, 388, 394, 412, 416, 430, 438, 440, 441, 453, 455

funding structures 99, 100

G

Gender Inclusivity 438, 442, 450, 454, 455
Global South 25, 26, 27, 28, 29, 30, 31, 45, 46, 49, 51, 158, 395

H

Higher education 72, 75, 87, 91, 92, 93, 94, 95, 96, 97, 98, 99, 100, 101, 103, 104, 105, 106, 107, 109, 110, 111, 115, 116, 117, 118, 119, 128, 163, 165, 173, 178, 181, 183, 213, 214, 215, 216, 241, 257, 258, 259, 308, 309, 310, 313, 315, 316, 320, 328, 329, 330, 331, 332, 333, 334, 335, 337, 339, 340, 341, 342, 365, 366, 367, 368, 370, 371, 376, 387, 388, 392, 393, 394, 395, 396, 397, 398, 416, 443, 459, 463

I

Immersive learning 69, 169, 181, 250, 253, 296, 338, 365, 367, 370, 382, 393
implementation 1, 2, 3, 4, 5, 6, 7, 8, 9, 10, 11, 12, 13, 15, 17, 18, 20, 21, 22, 24, 28, 42, 47, 48, 49, 52, 54, 56, 57, 60, 61, 63, 64, 65, 66, 67, 68, 72, 73, 86, 94, 97, 102, 103, 114, 122, 124, 125, 128, 130, 132, 133, 136, 137, 139, 141, 142, 147, 148, 152, 153, 155, 157, 164, 183, 185, 189, 196, 199, 209, 210, 215, 233, 240, 243, 245, 248, 253, 259, 273, 274, 293, 298, 301, 304, 305, 306, 308, 329, 330, 333, 334, 335, 336, 337, 339, 341, 346, 349, 352, 358, 359, 360, 361, 363, 367, 394, 399, 403, 404, 409,

411, 412, 417, 419, 421, 422, 427, 428, 429, 430, 434, 447

Importance 6, 7, 8, 10, 12, 22, 26, 39, 46, 57, 68, 78, 79, 80, 86, 107, 124, 126, 135, 141, 151, 153, 173, 174, 191, 200, 201, 204, 218, 219, 220, 222, 225, 226, 231, 255, 261, 262, 263, 264, 265, 266, 267, 269, 275, 299, 327, 344, 367, 384, 386, 388, 389, 403, 407, 408, 409, 410, 415, 419, 423, 425, 429, 438, 440, 441, 442, 444, 453

Inclusive Education 1, 2, 3, 4, 5, 6, 7, 8, 9, 10, 11, 12, 13, 14, 15, 16, 17, 18, 19, 20, 21, 22, 23, 24, 25, 26, 27, 28, 29, 30, 31, 32, 33, 34, 35, 36, 38, 39, 42, 44, 45, 46, 47, 48, 49, 50, 51, 52, 53, 54, 55, 56, 60, 62, 63, 64, 65, 69, 72, 73, 74, 77, 78, 79, 80, 85, 86, 87, 89, 121, 123, 124, 125, 135, 157, 158, 188, 189, 191, 192, 193, 200, 201, 202, 223, 235, 239, 242, 243, 245, 246, 247, 248, 249, 250, 251, 254, 255, 256, 257, 258, 261, 262, 263, 264, 265, 266, 267, 268, 269, 272, 274, 275, 276, 277, 361, 362, 399, 400, 402, 403, 404, 406, 407, 408, 409, 410, 411, 412, 413, 414, 415, 416, 417, 418, 419, 420, 422, 425, 426, 427, 428, 429, 430, 431, 432, 433, 434, 435

inclusive practices 1, 9, 11, 12, 15, 16, 18, 21, 35, 39, 43, 48, 68, 69, 78, 79, 156, 245, 255, 265, 272, 276, 346, 360, 361, 399, 416, 428, 429, 430

Inclusivity 25, 26, 27, 28, 29, 30, 31, 32, 33, 34, 36, 39, 45, 46, 51, 71, 82, 84, 100, 110, 122, 123, 133, 135, 214, 216, 217, 218, 219, 220, 222, 225, 226, 243, 258, 259, 262, 267, 270, 272, 273, 310, 336, 339, 388, 396, 398, 402, 403, 405, 406, 407, 409, 411, 412, 413, 416, 424, 427, 430, 438, 442, 450, 454, 455

Industry 4.0 technologies 163, 164, 165, 168, 169, 170, 171, 172, 173, 174, 175, 176, 177, 178, 179, 180, 181, 183, 396

institutional change 400, 403, 405, 408, 417, 419, 428, 434, 435

institutional framework 402, 435

institutional transformation 104

Instructional Strategies 58, 63, 113, 167, 191, 193, 195, 199, 210, 211, 219, 234, 287, 337, 349, 350, 362, 386, 439

Interdisciplinary collaboration 365, 371, 383, 385, 394, 395, 398

Isibindi Ezikoleni Programme 121, 123, 124, 130, 132, 135, 137, 142, 144, 147, 149, 150, 155, 156, 159, 162

L

leadership 15, 28, 34, 39, 42, 47, 48, 87, 92, 93, 94, 104, 105, 106, 107, 115, 117, 118, 125, 146, 149, 150, 154, 166, 169, 189, 204, 205, 213, 214, 215, 255, 256, 258, 331, 391, 396, 448, 449, 453

Lgbtqia 217, 218, 220, 221, 222, 223, 224, 225, 226, 227, 229

Lifelong 32, 33, 52, 61, 95, 165, 167, 181, 189, 190, 203, 205, 208, 212, 234, 255, 261, 262, 263, 264, 265, 266, 267, 268, 269, 270, 271, 272, 273, 274, 275, 276, 282, 292, 298, 314, 317, 366, 367, 368, 377, 392, 408, 416, 438, 440

O

Outcomes 26, 29, 33, 39, 43, 45, 54, 58, 59, 69, 70, 75, 79, 80, 81, 83, 88, 92, 98, 99, 113, 122, 123, 124, 131, 136, 139, 143, 147, 148, 149, 150, 155, 156, 164, 166, 167, 169, 171, 172, 188, 190, 191, 192, 199, 201, 204, 206, 207, 208, 245, 261, 262, 263, 264, 270, 272, 274, 276, 283, 291, 292, 293, 306, 315, 316, 320, 321, 324, 325, 326, 327, 331, 334, 335, 336, 337, 338, 339, 340, 341, 348, 354, 356, 359, 372, 375, 381, 382, 386, 403, 405, 408, 412, 413, 414, 417, 452, 454

P

Pedagogical Content Knowledge (PCK) 208
Pedagogical transformation 377
peer interaction 210, 297, 298, 300, 307, 319, 320, 322, 323, 325
Policy 2, 3, 5, 6, 8, 9, 11, 12, 14, 17, 18, 19, 22, 23, 24, 25, 26, 27, 28, 30, 32, 33, 34, 43, 44, 45, 47, 49, 50, 51, 52, 54, 56, 64, 65, 66, 67, 68, 69, 72, 73, 78, 79, 87, 91, 92, 93, 94, 96, 97, 98, 99, 100, 101, 102, 103, 104, 105, 106, 107, 108, 109, 110, 111, 112, 113, 114, 115, 118, 119, 124, 125, 127, 130, 131, 135, 136, 153, 154, 158, 160, 184, 191, 217, 218, 220, 224, 228, 231, 232, 242, 243, 244, 245, 247, 253, 254, 255, 258, 259, 275, 277, 281, 283, 286, 287, 288, 305, 306, 309, 310, 311, 314, 343, 345, 346, 362, 363, 399, 400, 402, 403, 404, 405, 406, 407, 409, 410, 411, 417, 419, 422, 423, 424, 428, 429, 432, 433, 457, 463
Policy and Advocacy 54, 68, 69, 72, 242
policy directives 93, 94, 96, 97, 98, 99, 100, 112, 113, 115
Policy Implications 243
Principle 3, 166, 167, 218, 232, 265, 266, 268, 314, 411, 423, 440, 449
Professional Development 11, 12, 14, 18, 19, 34, 42, 43, 44, 47, 48, 50, 54, 56, 59, 61, 62, 63, 64, 65, 67, 72, 74, 77, 78, 79, 85, 86, 87, 89, 102, 107, 108, 117, 119, 153, 154, 188, 189, 196, 202, 203, 204, 205, 211, 212, 213, 215, 216, 220, 225, 234, 240, 245, 247, 248, 254, 259, 286, 288, 300, 301, 304, 305, 306, 307, 330, 331, 334, 338, 339, 346, 358, 360, 361, 388, 403, 408, 415, 429, 431, 448, 452, 453
Prosperous 261, 405
Psychosocial Support 123, 124, 134, 136, 138, 147, 149, 150, 159

Q

quality education 1, 2, 3, 4, 5, 6, 7, 10, 16, 21, 26, 27, 30, 32, 33, 38, 51, 52, 73, 122, 201, 221, 265, 286, 289, 316, 363, 401, 404, 406, 407, 409, 413, 420, 422, 425, 432, 437, 438, 440, 441

R

Rural 9, 17, 18, 21, 30, 63, 69, 127, 132, 196, 217, 218, 220, 221, 222, 223, 224, 226, 227, 228, 229, 233, 316, 329, 355, 433

S

School-based Child and Youth Care 123, 132, 133, 134, 152, 154, 155, 156
SDG 4 10, 16, 437, 438, 440, 459
Significance 77, 78, 93, 98, 124, 142, 166, 167, 173, 177, 178, 234, 325, 379, 380, 383, 409, 441, 453
social justice 1, 2, 5, 6, 7, 18, 21, 33, 41, 45, 129, 201, 217, 218, 219, 220, 221, 222, 224, 226, 227, 264, 267, 269, 402, 403, 407
Specialized Training 19, 156, 187, 188, 189, 190, 191, 192, 205, 211
STEM Education 393, 397, 398, 437, 440, 443, 444, 452, 454, 457, 459, 460, 463
Strategic partnerships 366, 389, 392
student-centered learning 169, 170, 282, 283, 285, 286, 287, 292, 305, 306, 307, 314, 339, 387
Support Systems 15, 18, 19, 53, 54, 60, 61, 62, 66, 72, 114, 196, 346
Sustainable Education 25, 26, 27, 29, 31, 32, 33, 45, 52, 440
Systematic literature review 116, 171, 172, 183, 395

T

Teacher Education 14, 18, 19, 31, 48, 49, 56, 57, 63, 67, 74, 88, 116, 190, 191, 192, 193, 210, 211, 214, 215, 245,

247, 310, 416
Teacher Roles 52
Teacher Training 8, 9, 10, 11, 12, 16, 17, 18, 19, 21, 22, 53, 54, 56, 57, 58, 59, 62, 72, 188, 191, 202, 209, 220, 225, 226, 240, 242, 247, 248, 275, 346, 403, 410, 413, 417, 428, 429, 431
technological integration 16, 22, 93, 100, 101, 304, 305, 306, 333, 334, 335, 339
Technological Solutions 231, 240
technology integration 19, 74, 91, 92, 93, 94, 95, 101, 103, 180, 193, 210, 241, 245, 282, 287, 291, 306, 307, 333, 386
transformative 1, 2, 21, 25, 31, 45, 56, 106, 127, 165, 166, 173, 240, 258, 339, 375, 387, 400, 403, 408, 417, 418, 438, 440

U

Universal Design 30, 68, 71, 72, 73, 231, 232, 233, 234, 235, 236, 237, 238, 239, 240, 243, 244, 246, 247, 248, 253, 255, 257, 258, 259, 260, 273, 274, 277, 278

Milton Keynes UK
Ingram Content Group UK Ltd.
UKHW031433151124
451150UK00007B/69